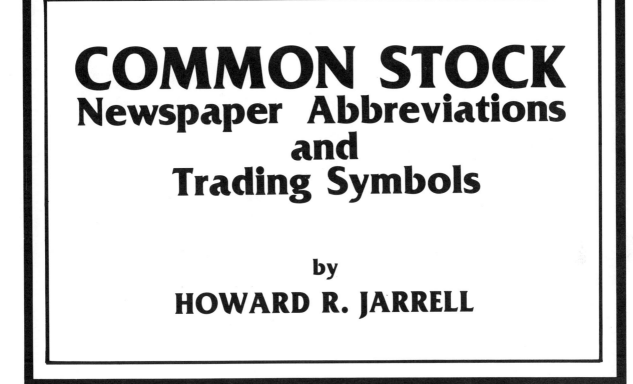

COMMON STOCK
Newspaper Abbreviations
and
Trading Symbols

by

HOWARD R. JARRELL

The Scarecrow Press, Inc.
Metuchen, N.J., & London
1989

Frontispiece: Clarence W. Barron, owner-editor of the Wall Street Journal, at the Royal Palm Hotel, Miami, 1927 (Romer Collection, Miami-Dade Public Library).

British Library Cataloguing-in-Publication data available

Library of Congress Cataloging-in-Publication Data

Jarrell, Howard R.
    Common stock newspaper abbreviations and trading symbols / by Howard R. Jarrell.
        p.   cm.
    ISBN 0-8108-2255-5 (alk. paper)
    1. Stock quotations--United States--Handbooks, manuals, etc.
2. Stock-exchange--United States--Abbreviations. I. Title.
HG4636.J37   1989
332.63'22'0973--dc20   89-10653

To Marilyn and Gene Wine
for their vintage friendship.

CONTENTS

FOREWORD

Mr. Jarrell took his undergraduate studies in business at the University of Dayton and studied librarianship at Case-Western Reserve University. He has held several positions as a business specialist and senior reference librarian with public and academic libraries in Florida and Ohio during the past twenty years. Recently retired, he is using his experience to compile reference works that are particularly useful to other librarians and their patrons.

This volume fills a void on our library shelves. Until the publication of his COMMON STOCK NEWSPAPER ABBREVIATIONS AND TRAD-ING SYMBOLS, it has been extremely difficult to decipher the newspaper abbreviations for stocks. Since I have learned of Mr. Jarrell's intentions to produce this book, I have eagerly awaited its publication. This work provides us with an all-in-one source for checking a newspaper abbreviation and determining the stock it represents or for checking a stock name to obtain its trading symbol.

I know that librarians and investors alike will be indebted to Mr. Jarrell for providing us with this comprehensive, easy-to-use source for information of this kind.

Phyllis Sue Alpert, Head
Business & Science Dept.
Miami-Dade Public Library
Miami, Florida

USER'S GUIDE

The purpose of this book is to provide the user with quick and ready references to the following information for companies with common stock.

1. The company name.
2. The Associated Press abbreviation for the company name as it appears in newspaper stock quotations.
3. The primary U.S. stock exchange or market where the company's stock is traded.
4. The trading or ticker symbol for the company.

The Associated Press (AP) and the United Press International (UPI) supply market quotations to newspapers. The Wall Street Journal uses AP quotations for New York Stock Exchange and American Stock Exchange listings. They use UPI quotations, which have longer and easier to understand abbreviations, for the NASDAQ over-the-counter listings. Barron's National Business and Financial Weekly and the New York Times use only AP quotations.

The information in this volume is given alphabetically in three separate parts. Part One is arranged by company names. Part Two is arranged by newspaper abbreviations for company names. Part Three is arranged by the market trading symbols. The user thereby has direct access to all of the information when any one component is known.

The scope of this work represents over sixty-three hundred stocks as they appear on the American Stock Exchange, the New York Stock Exchange, and the NASDAQ over-the-counter lists. NASDAQ is an acronym for the National Association of Security Dealers Automated Quotations.

Those lists are identified here in the following way.

1. American Stock Exchange as American.
2. New York Stock Exchange as New York.
3. NASDAQ National Market System as NAS NMS.
4. NASDAQ National List as NAS NL.
5. NASDAQ Supplemental List as NAS SL.

Abbreviations for preferred stocks, warrants and units are not included. They usually are just slight variations of the common stock abbreviations. Firms with only preferred stock and those with shares or units of beneficial interest are not listed.

State locations for many banking and financial institutions listed on the NASDAQ National Market System have been given to make their identification easier.

Companies are occasionally moved from one trading market to another. NASDAQ stocks are also sometimes moved within the three NASDAQ lists according to variations in their trading volume.

Some stocks are also listed on other exchanges. Standard & Poor's publications and the Moody's manuals can be used for identifying those regional stock exchanges, Canadian exchanges, and the overseas exchanges. Those sources are excellent for up-dating information presented in this book. Commerce Clearing House stock exchange loose-leaf services and the Wall Street Journal Index are also very useful sources of information.

PART ONE: ARRANGED BY COMPANY NAME

COMPANY NAME	MARKET LISTING	NEWSPAPER ABBREV.	TRADING SYMBOL
A&W Brands Inc	NAS NMS	A&W Bd	SODA
A.A. Importing Company Inc	NAS NL	AA Imp	ANTQ
AAR Corp	New York	AAR	AIR
Aaron Rents Inc	NAS NMS	AarnRt	ARON
Abbott Laboratories	New York	AbtLab	ABT
ABI American Businessphones Inc	American	ABI	AB
Abington Bancorp Inc (Massachusetts)	NAS NMS	AbingB	ABBK
ABIOMED Inc	American	Abimd	ABD
Abitibi-Price Inc	New York	Abitibi	ABY
ABM Gold Corp	American	ABM G	AGO
ABQ Corp	NAS NMS	ABQ	ABQC
Abraham Lincoln Federal Savings Bank (Pennsylvania)	NAS NMS	AbeLinc	ALFB
Abrams Industries Inc	NAS NMS	Abrams	ABRI
ABS Industries Inc	NAS NMS	ABS	ABSI
Academy Insurance Group Inc	NAS NMS	AcadIn	ACIG
ACC Corp	NAS NMS	ACC Cp	ACCC
Accel International Corp	NAS NMS	Accel	ACLE
Acceptance Insurance Holdings Inc	NAS NMS	AceptIn	ACPT
Acclaim Entertainment Inc	NAS NL	Acclaim	AKLM
Aceto Corp	NAS NMS	Aceto	ACET
ACM Government Income Fund Inc	New York	ACMIn	ACG
ACM Government Opportunity Fund	New York	ACM	AOF
ACM Government Securities Fund Inc	New York	ACMSc	GSF
ACM Government Spectrum Fund	New York	ACMSp	SI
ACMAT Corp	NAS NMS	ACMT	ACMT
Acme-Cleveland Corp	New York	AcmeC	AMT
Acme Electric Corp	New York	AcmeE	ACE
Acme Steel Co	NAS NMS	AcmeSt	ACME
Acme United Corp	American	AcmeU	ACU
Action Auto Rental Inc	NAS NMS	ActARt	AXXN
Action Auto Stores Inc	NAS NMS	ActAuSt	ACTA
Action Industries Inc	American	Action	ACX
Action Staffing Inc	NAS SL	ActnStf	ACTS
Actmedia Inc	NAS NMS	Actmd	ACTM
Acton Corp	American	Acton	ATN
Acuson Corp	NAS NMS	Acusn	ACSN
Acxiom Corp	NAS NMS	Acxiom	ACXM
ADAC Laboratories	NAS NMS	AdacLb	ADAC

COMPANY NAME	MARKET LISTING	NEWSPAPER ABBREV.	TRADING SYMBOL
The Adams Express Co	New York	AdaEx	ADX
Adams-Millis Corp	New York	AdamMl	ALL
Adams Resources & Energy Inc	American	AdmRs	AE
Adaptec Inc	NAS NMS	Adapt	ADPT
ADC Telecommunications Inc	NAS NMS	ADC	ADCT
Addington Resources Inc	NAS NMS	Adingtn	ADDR
Adelphia Communications Corp	NAS NL	Adelph	ADLAC
Adia Services Inc	NAS NMS	AdiaSv	ADIA
Admar Group Inc	NAS SL	Admar	ADMR
Adobe Resources Corp	New York	Adobe	ADB
Adobe Systems Inc	NAS NMS	AdobS	ADBE
Adtec Inc	NAS NMS	Adtec	JAIL
Advance Circuits Inc	NAS NMS	AdvCir	ADVC
Advance Display Technologies Inc	NAS SL	AdvDis	ADTI
Advance Ross Corp	NAS NMS	AdvRos	AROS
Advanced Computer Techniques Corp	NAS NMS	AdCpt	ACTP
Advanced Genetic Sciences Inc	NAS NMS	AdvGen	AGSI
Advanced Magnetics Inc	NAS NMS	AdvMag	ADMG
Advanced Marketing Services Inc	NAS NMS	AdMkSv	ADMS
Advanced Medical Products Inc	NAS SL	AdMdPd	ADVA
Advanced Micro Devices Inc	New York	AMD	AMD
Advanced NMR Systems Inc	NAS SL	AdNMR	ANMR
Advanced Polymer Systems Inc	NAS NMS	AdvPoly	APOS
Advanced Semiconductor Materials International N.V.	NAS NMS	AdvSem	ASMIF
Advanced Telecommunications Corp	NAS NMS	AdvTel	ATEL
ADVANTA Corp	NAS NMS	Advanta	ADVN
Advantage Companies Inc	NAS NMS	Advant	ADCO
Advatex Associates Inc	NAS NL	Advatex	ADTX
The Advest Group Inc	New York	Advest	ADV
Advo System Inc	NAS NMS	AdvoSy	ADVO
AEGON N.V.	NAS NMS	Aegon	AEGNY
AEL Industries Inc (Class A)	NAS NMS	AEL	AELNA
AEP Industries	NAS NMS	AEP	AEPI
Aequitron Medical Inc	NAS NMS	Aequtrn	AQTN
Aero Services International Inc	NAS NMS	AerSvc	AERO
Aerosonic Corp	NAS SL	Aerosn	ASON
Aetna Life & Casualty Co	New York	AetnLf	AET
Affiliated Banc Corp (Massachesetts)	NAS NMS	AflBcCp	ABCV
Affiliated Bankshares of Colorado Inc	NAS NMS	AflBsh	AFBK
Affiliated Publications Inc	New York	AfilPb	AFP
AFG Industries Inc	New York	AFG	AFG
AFN Inc	NAS SL	AFN	AMFN
AFP Imaging Corp	NAS SL	AFP	AFPC
Agency Rent-A-Car Inc	NAS NMS	AgncyR	AGNC
Agnico-Eagle Mines Ltd	NAS NMS	Agnico	AEAGF
Agouron Pharmaceuticals Inc	NAS SL	Agourn	AGPH
AGS Computers Inc	New York	AGS	AGS

COMPANY NAME	MARKET LISTING	NEWSPAPER ABBREV.	TRADING SYMBOL
H.F. Ahmanson & Co	New York	Ahmans	AHM
AIFS Inc	American	AIFS	AIF
Aileen Inc	New York	Aileen	AEE
AIM Telephones Inc	NAS NMS	AIM Tel	AIMT
Air Cargo Equipment Corp	NAS NMS	AirCrg	ARCE
Air Express International Corp	American	AirExp	AEX
Air Midwest Inc	NAS NMS	AirMd	AMWI
Air Products & Chemicals Inc	New York	AirPrd	APD
Air Sensors Inc	NAS SL	AirSen	ARSN
Air Wisconsin Services Inc	NAS NMS	AirWisc	ARWS
Airborne Freight Corp	New York	AirbFrt	ABF
AIRCOA Hospitality Services Inc	NAS NMS	AIRCOA	AIRC
AIRCOA Hotel Partners L.P.	American	Aircoa	AHT
Airgas Inc	New York	Airgas	AGA
Airlease Ltd	New York	Airlease	FLY
Airship Industries Ltd	NAS NMS	AirInd	AIRSY
Airship International Ltd	NAS SL	AirInt	BLMP
Airtran Corp	NAS NMS	Airtran	ATCC
Akorn Inc	NAS NL	Akorn	AKRN
A.L. Laboratories Inc	American	AL Lab	BMD
Alabama Federal S&L Assn	NAS NMS	AlaFdl	ALFD
Alamco Inc	American	Alamco	AXO
Alaska Air Group Inc	New York	AlskAir	ALK
Alaska Apollo Gold Mines Ltd	NAS SL	AlskAp	APLOF
AlaTenn Resources Inc	NAS NMS	Alaten	ATNG
Alba-Waldensian Inc	American	AlbaW	AWS
Albany International Corp (Class A)	NAS NMS	AlbnyIn	AAICA
Alberto-Culver Co	New York	Alberto	ACV
Alberto-Culver Co (Class A)	New York	AlbCulA	ACV.A
Albertson's Inc	New York	Albtsn	ABS
ALC Communications Corp	NAS NMS	ALC Cm	ALCC
Alcan Aluminium Ltd	New York	Alcan	AL
Alcide Corp	NAS SL	Alcide	ALCD
Alco Health Services Corp	NAS NMS	AlcoHlt	AAHS
Alco Standard Corp	New York	AlcoS	ASN
Alden Electronics Inc (Class A)	NAS NL	Alden	ADNEA
Aldus Corp	NAS NMS	Aldus	ALDC
Alex. Brown Inc	NAS NMS	AlexBr	ABSB
Alexander & Alexander Services Inc	New York	AlexAlx	AAL
Alexander & Baldwin Inc	NAS NMS	AlexBld	ALEX
Alexander Energy Corp	NAS NL	AlexEn	AEOK
Alexander's Inc	New York	Alexdr	ALX
Alfa Corp	NAS NMS	AlfaCp	ALFA
Alfa International Corp	NAS SL	AlfaInt	ALFE
Alfin Inc	American	Alfin	AFN
Algorex Corp	Nas NMS	Algorex	ALGO
Alico Inc	NAS NMS	Alico	ALCO
All American Semiconductor Inc	NAS SL	AllAm	SEMI

COMPANY NAME	MARKET LISTING	NEWSPAPER ABBREV.	TRADING SYMBOL
All American Television Inc	NAS NL	AllATV	ALLT
AllCity Insurance Co	NAS NMS	AllCity	ALCI
Alleghany Corp	New York	AllegCp	Y
Allegheny & Western Energy Corp	NAS NMS	AlegW	ALGH
Allegheny International Inc	New York	AlgInt	AG
Allegheny Ludlum Corp	New York	AlgLud	ALS
Allegheny Power System Inc	New York	AllgPw	AYP
The Allen Group Inc	New York	AllenG	ALN
Allen Organ Co (Class B)	NAS NMS	AlnOrg	AORGB
Alliance Bancorporation	American	AlliBc	ABK
Alliance Capital Management L.P.	New York	AlnCap	AC
Alliance Financial Corp	NAS NMS	AllFinl	ALFL
Alliance Imaging Inc	NAS NMS	AlnImg	AIMG
Alliance Tire & Rubber Company Ltd (Class A)	American	AlnTre	ATR.A
Alliant Computer Systems Corp	NAS NMS	Alliant	ALNT
Allied Bankshares Inc (Georgia)	NAS NMS	AlldBk	ABGA
Allied Capital Corp	NAS NMS	AlldCa	ALLC
ALLIED Group Inc	NAS NMS	AlldGp	ALGR
Allied Products Corp	New York	AlldPd	ADP
Allied Research Associates Inc	NAS NMS	AlldRsh	ARAI
Allied Security Inc	NAS SL	AlldSec	ASCY
Allied-Signal Inc	New York	AldSgnl	ALD
Allis-Chalmers Corp	New York	AllisC	AH
Alloy Computer Products Inc	NAS NMS	AloyCpt	ALOY
Allstar Inns L.P.	American	Allstr	SAI
Allstate Municipal Income Trust	New York	AlstMu	ALM
Allstate Municipal Income Trust II	New York	AlsMI	ALT
ALLTELL Corp	New York	ALLTL	AT
Allwaste Inc	NAS NMS	Allwast	ALWS
Aloette Cosmetics Inc	NAS NMS	Aloette	ALET
Alpha Industries Inc	American	AlphaIn	AHA
Alpha Microsystems	NAS NMS	AlphMic	ALMI
Alpha 1 Biomedicals Inc	NAS NMS	Alpha1	ALBM
Alpha Solarco Inc	NAS SL	AlphaSo	ASCO
Alpharel Inc	NAS NMS	Alpharl	AREL
The Alpine Group Inc	American	AlpinGr	AGI
Altai Inc	NAS NMS	Altai	ALTI
Altera Corp	NAS NMS	Altera	ALTR
Alternative Health Care Systems Inc	NAS SL	AltrHlt	AHCS
Altex Industries Inc	American	Altex	AII
Altos Computer Systems	NAS NMS	Altos	ALTO
Altron Inc	NAS NMS	Altron	ALRN
Altus Bank, A Federal Savings Bank (Alabama)	NAS NMS	Altus	ALTS
Aluminum Company of America	New York	Alcoa	AA
ALZA Corp	American	Alza	AZA
AM International Inc	New York	AM Intl	AM

COMPANY NAME	MARKET LISTING	NEWSPAPER ABBREV.	TRADING SYMBOL
Amax Gold Inc	New York	AmxG	AU
AMAX Inc	New York	Amax	AMX
Ambassador Financial Group Inc	NAS NMS	AmbFn	AFGI
AmBrit Inc	American	AmBrit	ABI
AMC Entertainment Inc	American	AMC	AEN
AMCA International Ltd	New York	AMCA	AIL
Amcast Industrial Corp	New York	Amcast	AIZ
Amcole Energy Corp	NAS NMS	Amcole	AMLE
AMCORE Financial Inc	NAS NMS	Amcor	AMFI
Amdahl Corp	American	Amdahl	AMH
A.M.E. Inc	NAS NMS	AME	AMEA
Amerada Hess Corp	New York	AmHes	AHC
AmerEco Environmental Services Inc	NAS SL	Amrco	AESC
Amerford International Corp	NAS SL	Amrfrd	AMRF
Ameriana Savings Bank, F.S.B. (Indiana)	NAS NMS	Amrian	ASBI
Ameribanc Inc (Missouri)	NAS NL	Amribc	ABNK
America First Guaranteed Income Fund	American	AmFGr	GF
America West Airlines Inc	NAS NMS	AWAirl	AWAL
American Aircraft Corp	NAS SL	AAcft	AARC
American Bank of Connecticut	American	ABkCT	BKC
American Bankers Insurance Group Inc	NAS NMS	ABnkr	ABIG
American Barrick Resources Corp	New York	ABrck	ABX
American Biltrite Inc	American	AmBilt	ABL
American Bionetics Inc	NAS SL	ABionet	AMBI
American Brands Inc	New York	AmBrnd	AMB
American Building Maintenance Industries	New York	ABldM	ABM
American Business Computers Corp	NAS SL	ABsCpt	ABCC
American Business Products Inc	New York	ABusPr	ABP
American Capacity Group Inc	NAS NMS	ACapac	ACGI
American Capital Bond Fund Inc	New York	ACapBd	ACB
American Capital Convertible Securities Inc	New York	ACapCv	ACS
American Capital Corp	American	AmCap	ACC
American Caiptal Income Trust	New York	ACapIn	ACD
American Capital Management & Research Inc	New York	ACMR	ACA
American Carriers Inc	NAS NMS	AmCarr	ACIX
American Century Corp	New York	ACentC	ACT
American City Business Journals Inc	NAS NMS	AmCity	AMBJ
American Claims Evaluation Inc	NAS SL	AClaim	AMCE
American Colloid Co	NAS NMS	AmColid	ACOL
American Communications & Television Inc	NAS SL	AmCom	ASTV
American Consolidated Gold Corp	NAS SL	ACGld	ACGC
American Consulting Corp	NAS NL	AmCnsl	ACCI
American Consumer Products Inc	NAS NMS	AConsu	ACPI
American Continental Corp	NAS NMS	AContl	AMCC
American Cruise Lines Inc	NAS SL	AmCrse	ACRL
American Cyanamid Co	New York	ACyan	ACY

COMPANY NAME	MARKET LISTING	NEWSPAPER ABBREV.	TRADING SYMBOL
American Ecology Corp	NAS NMS	AmEcol	ECOL
American Electric Power Company Inc	New York	AElPw	AEP
American Equine Products Inc	NAS SL	AEqune	WHOA
American Express Co	New York	AExp	AXP
American Family Corp	New York	AFaml	AFL
American Federal Saving Bank of Duval County (Florida)	NAS NMS	AFSvDu	AMJX
American Fiber Optics Corp	NAS SL	AFibOp	FIBR
American Filtrona Corp	NAS NMS	AFiltrn	AFIL
American First Corp	NAS NMS	AmFrst	AFCO
American Fructose Corp (Class A)	American	AFruc A	AFC.A
American Fructose Corp (Class B)	American	AFruc B	AFC.B
American General Corp	New York	AGnCp	AGC
American Government Income Fund	New York	AmGvI	AGF
American Greetings Corp (Class A)	NAS NMS	AGreet	AGREA
American Guaranty Financial Corp	NAS SL	AGtyF	AMGR
American Health Properties Inc	New York	AHltP	AHE
American Health Services Corp	NAS NMS	AHltSv	NMRC
American Healthcare Management Inc	American	AHlthM	AHI
American Heritage Life Investment Corp	New York	AHerit	AHL
American Hoist & Derrick Co	New York	AHoist	AHO
American Home Products Corp	New York	AHome	AHP
American Home Shield Corp	NAS NMS	AHSld	AHSC
American Income Life Insurance Co	NAS NMS	AminLf	AINC
American Income Properties L.P.	American	AmIPrp	IPS
American Indemnity Financial Corp	NAS NMS	AIndF	AIFC
American Information Technologies Corp	New York	Amrtc	AIT
American Integrity Corp	NAS NMS	AmIntg	AIIC
American International Group Inc	New York	AIntGr	AIG
American International Petroleum Corp	NAS SL	AmInPt	AIPN
American Israeli Paper Mills Ltd	American	AIsrael	AIP
American Land Cruisers Inc	American	AmLnd	RVR
American Learning Corp	NAS NL	AmLrn	READ
American List Corp	American	AmList	AMZ
American Locker Group Inc	NAS NMS	AmLck	ALGI
American Magnetics Corp	NAS NMS	AMagnt	AMMG
American Maize-Products Co (Class A)	American	AMzeA	AZE.A
American Maize-Products Co (Class B)	American	AMzeB	AZE.B
American Management Systems Inc	NAS NMS	AMS	AMSY
American Medical Alert Corp	NAS SL	AMdAlt	AMAC
American Medical Buildings Inc	American	AMBld	A
American Medical Electronics Inc	NAS SL	AMdE	AMEI
American Medical International Inc	New York	AMI	AMI
American Medical Technology Inc	NAS SL	AMdTc	AMMT
American Midland Corp	NAS NMS	AMidl	AMCO
American Mobile Systems Inc	NAS SL	AmMobl	AMSE
American National Insurance Co	NAS NMS	ANtIns	ANAT
American National Petroleum Co	NAS NL	ANtPt	ANPC

COMPANY NAME	MARKET LISTING	NEWSPAPER ABBREV.	TRADING SYMBOL
American Nuclear Corp	NAS NMS	ANuclC	ANUC
American Nursery Products Inc	NAS NMS	AmNurs	ANSY
American Oil & Gas Corp	American	AmOil	AOG
American Pacific Corp	NAS NMS	AmPac	APFC
American Passage Marketing Corp	NAS NMS	AmPsg	APAS
American Petrofina Inc (Class A)	American	AmPetf	API.A
American Physicians Service Group Inc	NAS NMS	APhyG	AMPH
American Pioneer Savings Bank (Florida)	NAS NMS	AmPion	APIO
American Power Conversion Corp	NAS NL	APwCnv	APCC
American Precision Industries Inc	American	APrec	APR
American President Companies Ltd	New York	APresd	APS
American Real Estate Partners L.P.	New York	AREst	ACP
American Realty Trust	New York	AmRlty	ARB
American Recreation Centers Inc	NAS NL	ARecr	AMRC
American Reliance Group Inc	NAS NMS	ARelian	ARIG
American Republic Bancorp	NAS NL	ARepBc	ARBC
American Restaurant Partners L.P.	American	ARestr	RMC
American Rice Inc	NAS NL	AmRice	RICE
American Safety Closure Corp	NAS SL	ASafty	ASCL
American S&L Assn of Florida	New York	ASLFla	AAA
American Savings Financial Corp (Washington)	NAS NMS	ASvWA	AMSB
American Science & Engineering Inc	American	ASciE	ASE
American Shared Hospital Services	American	AmShrd	AMS
The American Ship Building Co	New York	AShip	ABG
American Software Inc (Class A)	NAS NMS	ASoft	AMSWA
American Solar King Corp	NAS SL	ASolr	AMSKQ
American Southwest Mortgage Investments Corp	American	ASwM	ASR
American Stores Co	New York	AmStor	ASC
American Technical Ceramics Corp	American	ATechC	AMK
American Telecommunications Corp (British Columbia)	NAS SL	AmTlc	AMTTF
American Telemedia Network Inc	NAS NMS	AmTelmd	ATNN
American Telephone & Telegraph Co	New York	AT&T	T
American Television & Communications Corp (Class A)	NAS NMS	ATvCm	ATCMA
American Toxxic Control Inc	NAS SL	AToxxic	ATCX
American Travellers Corp	NAS NMS	AmTrav	ATVC
American Vision Centers Inc	NAS SL	AmVisn	AMVC
American Water Works Company Inc	New York	AmWtr	AWK
American Western Corp	NAS NMS	AWstCp	AWST
American Woodmark Corp	NAS NMS	AWood	AMWD
Americana Hotels & Realty Corp	New York	AmHotl	AHR
AmeriFirst Bank F.S.B. (Florida)	NAS NMS	AmFtBk	AMRI
AmeriHealth Inc	American	Amhlth	AHH
Amerihost Properties Inc	NAS SL	AmerPr	HOST
AmeriTrust Corp	NAS NMS	Amritr	AMTR

COMPANY NAME	MARKET LISTING	NEWSPAPER ABBREV.	TRADING SYMBOL
Ameriwest Financial Corp	NAS SL	Amnws	AMWS
Ameron Inc	New York	Ameron	AMN
Amertek Inc	NAS NMS	Amertk	ATEKF
Ames Department Stores Inc	New York	AmesDp	ADD
AMETEK Inc	New York	Ametk	AME
AMEV Securities Inc	New York	AmevSc	AMV
Amfac Inc	New York	Amfac	AMA
AmFed Financial Corp	NAS NMS	AmFedF	AFSL
Amgen Inc	NAS NMS	Amgen	AMGN
Amistar Corp	NAs NMS	Amistar	AMTA
Amity Bancorp Inc	NAS NMS	AmtyBc	AMTY
Amoco Corp	New York	Amoco	AN
Amoskeag Bank Shares Inc	NAS NMS	AmskBk	AMKG
Amoskeag Co	NAS NMS	Amosk	AMOS
AMP Inc	New York	AMP	AMP
Ampal-American Israel Corp (Class A)	American	Ampal	AIS.A
Ampco-Pittsburgh Corp	New York	Ampco	AP
Amplicon Inc	NAS NMS	Amplcn	AMPI
AMR Corp	New York	AMR	AMR
AMRE Inc	New York	Amre	AMM
AMREP Corp	New York	Amrep	AXR
Amserv Inc	NAS NMS	Amserv	AMSR
AmSouth Bancorporation	New York	AmSth	ASO
AmVestors Financial Corp	NAS NMS	Amvst	AVFC
Amwest Insurance Group Inc	American	Amwest	AMW
An-Con Genetics Inc	NAS SL	An-Con	ANCN
Anacomp Inc	New York	Anacmp	AAC
Anadarko Petroleum Corp	New York	Anadrk	APC
Analog Devices Inc	New York	Analog	ADI
Analogic Corp	NAS NMS	Anlogic	ALOG
Analysis & Technology Inc	NAS NMS	AnalyTc	AATI
Analysts International Corp	NAS NMS	AnalyI	ANLY
Analytical Surveys Inc	NAS SL	AnlySu	ANLT
Anaren Microwave Inc	NAS NMS	Anaren	ANEN
Anchor Glass Container Corp	New York	AnchGl	ANC
Anchor S&L Assn (New Jersey)	NAS NMS	AncrNJ	ANSL
Anchor Savings Bank F.S.B. (New York)	NAS NMS	AnchSv	ABKR
Andal Corp	American	Andal	ADL
Andersen Group Inc	NAS NMS	AndGr	ANDR
Andover Bancorp Inc	NAS NMS	AndvBc	ANDB
Andover Controls Corp	NAS NMS	Andovr	ANDO
Andover Togs Inc	NAS NMS	AndvTg	ATOG
Andrea Radio Corp	American	Andrea	AND
Andrew Corp	NAS NMS	Andrew	ANDW
Andrews Group Inc	NAS NL	AndwGp	AGRP
Andros Analyzers Inc	NAS NMS	Andros	ANDY
Angeles Corp	American	Angeles	ANG
Angeles Finance Partners	American	AnglFn	ANF

COMPANY NAME	MARKET LISTING	NEWSPAPER ABBREV.	TRADING SYMBOL
Angeles Mortgage Partners Ltd	American	AngMtg	ANM
Angelica Corp	New York	Angelic	AGL
Angell Real Estate Company Inc	New York	AnglRl	ACR
Anglo American Corp of South Africa Ltd	NAS NL	AngSA	ANGLY
Anglo American Gold Investment Company Ltd	NAS NL	AngAG	AAGIY
Anglo Energy Inc	American	AngE	AEL
Anheuser-Busch Companies Inc	New York	Anheus	BUD
Animed Inc	NAS NMS	Animed	VETS
Annandale Corp	NAS SL	Anndle	ANNA
Anthem Electronics Inc	New York	Anthm	ATM
Anthony Industries Inc	New York	Anthony	ANT
Antonovich Inc (Class A)	NAS NMS	Antonv	FURSA
AOI Coal Co	American	AOI	AOI
Aon Corp	New York	Aon Cp	AOC
APA Optics Inc	NAS SL	APAOp	APAT
Apache Corp	New York	Apache	APA
Apco Argentina Inc	NAS NL	Apco	APAGF
Apex Municipal Fund Inc	American	ApexM	new
API Enterprises Inc	NAS SL	API	APIE
Apogee Enterprises Inc	NAS NMS	ApogEn	APOG
Apogee Robotics Inc	NAS SL	ApogRb	APGE
Apollo Computer Inc	NAS NMS	ApoloC	APCI
Apple Bank for Savings (New York)	New York	ApplBk	ARK
Apple Computer Inc	NAS NMS	AppleC	AAPL
Applied Bioscience International Inc	NAS NMS	ABiosci	APBI
Applied Biosystems Inc	NAS NMS	ApldBio	ABIO
Applied Data Communications Inc	NAS NMS	ApldDt	ADCC
Applied DNA Systems Inc	NAS SL	Ap DNA	ADNA
Applied Magnetics Corp	New York	ApplM	APM
Applied Materials Inc	NAS NMS	ApldMt	AMAT
Applied Microbiology Inc	NAS SL	ApdMicr	APLY
Applied Power Inc (Class A)	NAS NMS	ApldPw	APWRA
Applied Solar Energy Corp	NAS NMS	ApldSlr	SOLR
Applied Spectrum Technologies Inc	NAS SL	ApldSpc	ASTI
Aquanautics Corp	NAS SL	Aquant	AQNT
AquaSciences International Inc	NAS SL	AquaSc	AQSI
Arabian Shield Development Co	NAS NMS	ArabSh	ARSD
Arbor Drugs Inc	NAS NMS	Arbor	ARBR
ARC International Corp	American	ARC	ATV
Archer-Daniels-Midland Co	New York	ArchDn	ADM
Archive Corp	NAS NMS	Archive	ACHV
ARCO Chemical Co	New York	ArcoCh	RCM
Arctic Alaska Fisheries Corp	American	AAlska	ICE
Arden Group Inc (Class A)	NAS NMS	Arden	ARDNA
Arden International Kitchens Inc	NAS SL	ArdenIn	AIKI
Argonaut Group Inc	NAS NMS	ArgoGp	AGII
Aridtech Inc	NAS NMS	Aritch	ARID

COMPANY NAME	MARKET LISTING	NEWSPAPER ABBREV.	TRADING SYMBOL
Aristech Chemical Corp	New York	Aristec	ARS
Arizona Commerce Bank	American	ArizCm	AZB
Arizona Instrument Corp	NAS NMS	ArizInst	QNTL
Arizona Land Income Corp (Class A)	American	ArzLd	AZL.A
Ark Restaurants Corp	American	ArkRst	RK
Arkansas Best Corp	New York	ArkBst	ABZ
Arkla Inc	New York	Arkla	ALG
Armada Corp	New York	Armada	ABW
Armatron International Inc	American	Armtrn	ART
Armco Inc	New York	Armco	AS
Armor All Products Corp	NAS NMS	Armor	ARMR
Armstrong World Industries Inc	New York	ArmWI	ACK
Armtek Corp	New York	Armtek	ARM
Arnold Industries Inc	NAS NMS	Arnold	AIND
Arnox Corp	NAS SL	Arnox	ARNX
Arrow Automotive Industries Inc	American	ArrowA	AI
Arrow Bank Corp	NAS NMS	ArowB	AROW
Arrow Electronics Inc	New York	ArowE	ARW
Artagraph Reproduction Technology Inc	NAS SL	Artagph	XARTF
Artech Recovery Systems Inc	NAS SL	Artech	ARTK
Artel Communications Corp	NAS NMS	Artel	AXXX
Artistic Greetings Inc	NAS NL	ArtistG	ARTG
ARTRA GROUP Inc	New York	Artra	ATA
Art's-Way Manufacturing Company Inc	NAS NMS	ArtWay	ARTW
Arvin Industries Inc	New York	Arvin	ARV
ARX Inc	New York	ARX	ARX
Aryt Optronics Industries Ltd	NAS NL	ArytOp	ARYTF
ASA International Ltd	NAS SL	ASA Int	ASAA
ASA Ltd	New York	ASA	ASA
Asamera Inc	American	Asmr	ASM
ASARCO Inc	New York	Asarco	AR
Asbestec Industries Inc	NAS NMS	Asbst	ASBS
ASDAR Corp	NAS SL	ASDR	ASDR
ASEA A.B.	NAS NL	ASEA	ASEAY
Asha Corp	NAS SL	Asha	ASHA
Ashland Coal Inc	New York	AshCoal	ACI
Ashland Oil Inc	New York	AshOil	ASH
Ashton-Tate	NAS NMS	Ashton	TATE
The Asia Pacific Fund Inc	New York	AsiaPc	APB
ASK Computer Systems Inc	NAS NMS	ASK	ASKI
Aspen Exploration Corp	NAS SL	AspenE	ASPN
Aspen Ribbons Inc	NAS NMS	AspenR	ARIB
Associated Banc-Corp	NAS NMS	AsdBnc	ASBC
Associated Communications Corp (Class A)	NAS NMS	AsCmA	ACCMA
Associated Communications Corp (Class B)	NAS NMS	AsCmB	ACCMB
Associated Companies Inc	NAS NMS	AssdCo	ASCI
Associated Hosts Inc	NAS NMS	AsdHst	AHST
Associated Materials Inc	NAS NL	AsdMat	ASML

COMPANY NAME	MARKET LISTING	NEWSPAPER ABBREV.	TRADING SYMBOL
AST Research Inc	NAS NMS	AST	ASTA
Astec Industries Inc	NAS NMS	Astec	ASTE
Astrex Inc	American	Astrex	ASI
Astro-Med Inc	NAS NMS	AstroM	ALOT
Astrocom Corp	NAS NMS	Astrcm	ACOM
Astronics Corp	NAS NMS	Astron	ATRO
Astrosystems Inc	NAS NMS	Astrosy	ASTR
A.T.&E. Corp	American	AT&E	ATW
AT&T Stock Fund (Also known as Equity Income Fund)	American	ATT Fd	ATF
Atalanta/Sosnoff Capital Corp	New York	AtalSos	ATL
Atari Corp	American	Atari	ATC
Atek Metals Center Inc	NAS NMS	Atek	ATKM
Athey Products Corp	NAS NMS	Athey	ATPC
Athlone Industries Inc	New York	Athlone	ATH
ATI Medical Inc	American	ATI	ATI
Atico Financial Corp	NAS NMS	AticoF	ATFC
Guy F. Atkinson Company of California	NAS NMS	Atkinsn	ATKN
Atlanta Gas Light Co	New York	AtlGas	ATG
Atlantic American Corp	NAS NMS	AtlAm	AAME
Atlantic Bancorporation (New Jersey)	NAS NMS	AtlnBc	ATBC
Atlantic Energy Inc	New York	AtlEnrg	ATE
Atlantic Federal Savings Bank (Maryland)	NAS NMS	AtlFSv	AFED
Atlantic Financial Federal	NAS NMS	AtlFin	ATLF
Atlantic Permanent Savings Bank F.S.B. (Virginia)	NAS NMS	AtlPrm	APER
Atlantic Richfield Co	New York	AtlRich	ARC
Atlantic Southeast Airlines Inc	NAS NMS	AtlSeAr	ASAI
Atlantis Group Inc	American	Atlants	AGH
Atlas Consolidated Mining & Development Corp (Class B)	American	AtlsCM	ACM.B
Atlas Corp	New York	AtlasCp	AZ
Attwood Oceanics Inc	NAS NMS	Attwood	ATWD
Audio/Video Affiliates Inc	New York	AudVd	AVA
Audiotronics Corp	American	Audiotr	ADO
Audiovox Corp	American	Audvx	VOX
Augat Inc	New York	Augat	AUG
Ault Inc	NAS SL	Ault	AULT
Ausimont Compo N.V.	New York	Ausimt	AUS
Auto-trol Technology Corp	NAS NMS	AutTrT	ATTC
Autoclave Engineers Inc	NAS NMS	Autoclv	ACLV
Autodesk Inc	NAS NMS	Autodk	ACAD
Autodie Corp	NAS NMS	Autodie	ADIE
AutoInfo Inc	NAS NMS	AutoInf	AUTO
Automated Language Processing Systems Inc	NAS NMS	AutLng	AILP
Automated Systems Inc	NAS NMS	AutoSy	ASII

COMPANY NAME	MARKET LISTING	NEWSPAPER ABBREV.	TRADING SYMBOL
Automatic Data Processing Inc	New York	AutoDt	AUD
Automatix Inc	NAS NMS	Autmtx	AITX
AutoMedix Sciences Inc	NAS SL	AutMed	AMED
AutoSpa AutoMalls Inc	NAS SL	AutoSpa	ATML
AutoSpa Corp	NAS NMS	Autospa	LUBE
Autotrol Corp	NAS NMS	AutoCp	AUTR
Avalon Corp	New York	Avalon	AVL
Avant-Garde Computing Inc	NAS NMS	AvntGr	AVGA
Avantek Inc	NAS NMS	Avntek	AVAK
Avatar Holdings Inc	NAS NMS	Avatar	AVTR
AVEMCO Corp	New York	AVMC	AVE
Avery Inc	NAS NMS	Avry	AVRY
Avery International Corp	New York	Avery	AVY
Avino Mines & Resources Ltd	NAS SL	Avino	AVMRF
Avnet Inc	New York	Avnet	AVT
Avon Products Inc	New York	Avon	AVP
Avondale Industries Inc	NAS NMS	Avndle	AVDL
AVX Corp	New York	AVX	AVX
AW Computer Systems Inc (Class A)	NAS NMS	AW A	AWCSA
Aydin Corp	New York	Aydin	AYD
Aztec Manufacturing Co	NAS NMS	AztcM	AZTC
B-B Real Estate Investment Corp	American	BB REI	BBR
B&H Bulk Carriers Ltd	NAS NL	BH Bulk	BULKF
B&H Ocean Carriers Ltd	American	B&H	BHO
Babbage's Inc	NAS NMS	Babage	BBGS
Badger Meter Inc	American	Badger	BMI
Badger Paper Mills Inc	NAS NMS	Badger	BPMI
Bailey Corp	NAS NL	Bailey	BAIB
Bairnco Corp	New York	Bairnco	BZ
J. Baker Inc	NAS NMS	BakrJ	JBAK
Michael Baker Corp	American	Baker	BKR
Baker Communications Inc	NAS SL	BakrCm	BAKR
Baker, Fentress & Co	NAS NMS	BakrFn	BKFR
Baker Hughes Inc	New York	BakrHu	BHI
Balchem Corp	NAS NMS	Balchm	BLCC
Baldor Electric Co	New York	Baldor	BEZ
Baldwin & Lyons Inc (Class A)	NAS NMS	BldLy	BWINA
Baldwin & Lyons Inc (Class B)	NAS NMS	BldLyB	BWINB
Baldwing Piano & Organ Co	NAS NMS	BaldPia	BPAO
Baldwin Securities Corp	American	BaldwS	BAL
Baldwin Technology Company Inc	American	Baldwin	BLD
Ball Corp	New York	Ball	BLL
Ballard Medical Products Inc	NAS NMS	Balard	BMED
Bally Manufacturing Corp	New York	BallyMf	BLY
Baltek Corp	NAS NMS	Baltek	BTEK
Baltimore Bancorp (Maryland)	New York	BaltBcp	BBB
Baltimore Gas & Electric Co	New York	BaltGE	BGE

COMPANY NAME	MARKET LISTING	NEWSPAPER ABBREV.	TRADING SYMBOL
Bamberger Polymers Inc	American	BambP	BPI
Banc One Corp	New York	BncOne	ONE
Banco Central S.A.	New York	BncCtr	BCM
Banco Popular de Puerto Rico	NAS NMS	BnPop	BPOP
Banco Santander	New York	BnSant	STD
BancOklahoma Corp	NAS NMS	Bancokl	BOKC
Bancorp Hawaii Inc	NAS NMS	BcpHw	BNHI
Bancorp. of Mississippi Inc	NAS NMS	BcMis	BOMS
Bancroft Convertible Fund Inc	American	BanFd	BCV
BancTec Inc	NAS NMS	Banctec	BTEC
BancTEXAS Group Inc	New York	BanTx	BTX
Bandag Inc	New York	Bandag	BDG
Bando McGlocklin Capital Corp	NAS NMS	BandoM	BMCC
Bangor Hydro-Electric Co	NAS NMS	BangH	BANG
Banister Continental Ltd	American	Banstr	BAN
Bank Building & Equipment Corporation of America	American	BnkBld	BB
Bank Leumi le-Israel B.M.	NAS NL	BkLeu	BKLMY
Bank Maryland Corp	NAS NL	BkMd	BKMD
Bank of Boston Corp	New York	BkBost	BKB
Bank of Delaware Corp	NAS NMS	BkDel	BDEL
Bank of East Tennessee	NAS SL	BkEtTn	EATN
Bank of Granite Corp (North Carolina)	NAS NMS	BkGrn	GRAIN
Bank of New England Corp	New York	BkNE	NEB
Bank of New Hampshire Corp	NAS NMS	BnkNH	BHNC
The Bank of New York Company Inc	New York	BkNY	BK
Bank of Redlands (California)	NAS NL	BkRedl	BOFR
Bank of San Francisco Holding Co	American	BkSFr	BOF
Bank of South Carolina	NAS SL	BkSC	BKSC
Bank of Stamford (California)	NAS NMS	BkStfd	BKST
Bank South Corp	NAS NMS	BkSou	BKSO
Bank Worcester Corp	NAS NMS	BkWorc	WCYS
BankAmerica Corp	New York	BnkAm	BAC
BankAtlantic A Federal Savings Bank	NAS NMS	BankAtl	ASAL
BankAtlantic Financial Corp	American	BkatlFn	BFC
BankEast Corp	NAS NMS	Bnkest	BENH
Bankers First Corp	NAS NMS	BnkFst	BNKF
Banker's Note Inc	NAS NMS	BkrNte	BKNT
Bankers Trust New York Corp	New York	BankTr	BT
Banknorth Group Inc	NAS NMS	Bnknth	BKNG
Banks of Iowa Inc	NAS NMS	BkIowa	BIOW
Banks of Mid-America Inc	NAS NMS	BkMAm	BOMA
BankVermont Corp	NAS NMS	Bankvt	BKVT
Banner Industries Inc	New York	Banner	BNR
BanPonce Corp	NAS NMS	BnPnc	BDEP
George Banta Company Inc	NAS NMS	Banta	BNTA
Barclays P.L.C.	New York	Barclay	BCS
C.R. Bard Inc	New York	Bard	BCR

COMPANY NAME	MARKET LISTING	NEWSPAPER ABBREV.	TRADING SYMBOL
Barden Corp	NAS NMS	Barden	BARD
Barnes Group Inc	New York	BarnGp	B
Barnett Banks of Florida Inc	New York	Barnet	BBF
Barnwell Industries Inc	American	Barnwl	BRN
Barr Laboratories Inc	American	BarrLb	BRL
Barrett Resources Corp	NAS NMS	BaretR	BARC
Barrier Science & Technology Inc	NAS SL	BarrSc	BUGX
Barris Industries Inc	NAS NMS	Barris	BRRS
Barrister Information Systems Corp	American	Baristr	BIS
R.G. Barry Corp	American	BaryRG	RGB
Barry Wright Corp	New York	BaryWr	BAR
Barry's Jewelers Inc	NAS NMS	BaryJw	BARY
Barton Industries Inc	NAS SL	Barton	BART
Baruch-Foster Corp	American	Baruch	BFO
Base Ten Systems Inc (Class A)	NAS NMS	BsTnA	BASEA
Base Ten Systems Inc (Class B)	NAS NL	BsTnB	BASEB
Basic American Medical Inc	NAS NMS	BasAm	BAMI
Basic Resources International Ltd	NAS NMS	BsRInt	BBAHF
BASIX Corporation	New York	BASIX	BAS
Bassett Funiture Industries Inc	NAS NMS	BsetF	BSET
B.A.T. Industries p.l.c.	American	BAT	BTI
Battle Mountain Gold Co	New York	BatlMt	BMG
Baukol-Noonan Inc	NAS NL	BaukNo	BAUK
Bausch & Lomb Inc	New York	Bausch	BOL
Baxter International Inc	New York	Baxter	BAX
Bay Financial Corp	New York	BayFin	BAY
Bay State Gas Co	New York	BayStG	BGC
Bay View Federal S&L Assn (California)	NAS NMS	BayVw	BVFS
BayBanks Inc	NAS NMS	BayBks	BBNK
Bayly Corp	NAS NMS	Bayly	BAYL
Bayou International Ltd	NAS NL	Bayou	BAYU
Bayou Steel Corp of La Place	American	Bayou	SYX
BB&T Financial Corp	NAS NMS	BB&T	BBIF
BCE Inc	New York	BCE	BCE
BDM International	American	BDM	BDM
Beaman Corp	NAS NL	Beaman	BECO
The Bear Stearns Companies Inc	New York	BearSt	BSC
The Beard Co	American	Beard	BEC
Bearings Inc	New York	Bearing	BER
BeautiControl Cosmetics Inc	NAS NMS	BeautiC	BUTI
Beauty Labs Inc	NAS NMS	BeautL	LABB
C.H. Beazer Holdings P.L.C.	NAS NMS	Beazer	BEZRY
Becton, Dickinson & Co	New York	BectDk	BDX
Beeba's Creations Inc	NAS NMS	Beebas	BEBA
Beecham Group p.l.c.	NAS NMS	Bechm	BHAMY
BEI Holdings Ltd	NAS NMS	BEI	BEIH
Beker Industries Corp	New York	Beker	BKI
Bel Fuse Inc	NAS NMS	BelFuse	BELF

COMPANY NAME	MARKET LISTING	NEWSPAPER ABBREV.	TRADING SYMBOL
Belden & Blake Energy Co.	American	BeldBlk	BBE
Belding Heminway Company Inc	New York	BeldnH	BHY
W. Bell & Company Inc	NAS NMS	BellW	BLLW
Bell Atlantic Corp	New York	BellAtl	BEL
Bell Industries Inc	New York	BelIn	BI
Bell Savings Bank PaSA (Pennsylvania)	NAS NMS	BellSv	BSBX
BellSouth Corp	New York	BellSo	BLS
Bellwether Exploration Co	NAS SL	Belwet	BELW
Belmac Corp	NAS SL	Belmac	BEMC
Belmoral Mines Ltd	NAS NL	Belmrl	BMEEF
A.H. Belo Corp	New York	BeloAH	BLC
Belvedere Corp	American	Belvdre	BLV
Bemis Company Inc	New York	Bemis	BMS
Ben & Jerry's Homemade Inc (Class A)	NAS NMS	BenJer	BJICA
Benafuels Inc	NAS SL	Benfuel	BENF
Benedict Nuclear Pharmaceuticals Inc	NAS SL	BenNuc	BENE
Beneficial Corp	New York	BenfCp	BNL
Benguet Corp (Class B)	New York	BengtB	BE
Benihana National Corp	NAS NMS	Benhan	BNHN
Benihana National Corp (Class A)	NAS NL	BenhnA	BNHNA
Benjamin Franklin S&L Assn (Oregon)	NAS NMS	BenjSv	BENJ
Bercor Inc	NAS NMS	Bercor	BECR
Beres Industries Inc	NAS SL	Beres	BERS
Bergen Brunswig Corp (Class A)	American	BergBr	BBC.A
Berkey Inc	New York	Berkey	BKY
W.R. Berkley Corp	NAS NMS	Berkley	BKLY
The Berkline Corp	NAS NMS	Berklne	BERK
The Berkshire Gas Co	NAS NMS	BerkGs	BGAS
Berkshire Hathaway Inc	NAS NMS	BerkHa	BKHT
Bermuda Star Lines Inc	American	BermSt	BSL
Berry Petroleum Co (Class A)	NAS NMS	BerryP	BRRYA
Best Buy Company Inc	New York	BestBy	BBY
Best Products Company Inc	New York	BestPd	BES
Bestway Rental Inc	NAS SL	Bestway	BEST
BET Public Limited Co	New York	BET	BEP
Bethel Bancorp (Maine)	NAS NMS	BethlBc	BTHL
The Bethlehem Corp	American	BethCp	BET
Bethlehem Steel Corp	New York	BethStl	BS
Betz Laboratories Inc	NAS NMS	BetzLb	BETZ
Beverly Enterprises Inc	New York	Bevrly	BEV
Beverly Investment Properties Inc	New York	BevIP	BIP
BF Enterprises Inc	NAS NL	BF Ent	BFEN
BGS Systems Inc	NAS NMS	BGS	BGSS
BHA Group Inc	NAS NMS	BHA	BHAG
BI Inc	NAS SL	BI Inc	BIAC
BIC Corp	American	BicCp	BIC
Big B Inc	NAS NMS	Big B	BIGB
Big Bear Inc	NAS NMS	BgBear	BGBR

COMPANY NAME	MARKET LISTING	NEWSPAPER ABBREV.	TRADING SYMBOL
Big O Tires Inc	NAS NL	BigOTr	BIGO
Bindley Western Industries Inc	NAS NMS	Bindly	BIND
Binghamton Savings Bank	NAS NMS	BingSv	BING
Bingo King Company Inc	NAS NMS	BingKg	BNGO
Binks Manufacturing Co	American	BinkMf	BIN
Bio-Logic Systems Corp	NAS NMS	BioLog	BLSC
Bio-Medicus Inc	NAS NMS	BiMedc	BMDS
Bio-Rad Laboratories Inc (Class A)	American	BioR A	BIO.A
Bio-Rad Laboratories Inc (Class B)	American	BioR B	BIO.B
Bio-Technology General Corp	NAS SL	BioTG	BTGC
Biocontrol Technology Inc	NAS SL	Bioctrl	BICO
Biocraft Laboratories Inc	New York	Biocft	BCL
Biogen N.V.	NAS NMS	Biogen	BGENF
Biomedical Dynamics Corp	NAS SL	BimdDy	BMDC
Biomerica Inc	NAS NMS	Biomer	BMRA
Biomet Inc	NAS NMS	Biomet	BMET
Biopharmaceuticals Inc	American	Biophm	BPH
Bioplasty Inc	NAS NMS	Bioplst	BIOP
Biosearch Medical Products Inc	NAS SL	BioMed	BMPI
Biosonics Inc	NAS NL	Bioson	BIOS
Biospherics Inc	NAS NMS	Biosph	BINC
Biotech Research Laboratories Inc	NAS NMS	BiotcR	BTRL
BioTechnica International Inc	NAS NMS	BioTInt	BIOT
Biotechnology Development Corp	NAS SL	BiotcDv	BIOD
Biotherapeutics Inc	American	Biother	BRX
Bird Inc	NAS NMS	BirdInc	BIRD
Birdfinder Corp	NAS SL	Birdfdr	BFTV
Birmingham Steel Corp	New York	BirmStl	BIR
The Birtcher Corp	NAS NMS	Birtchr	BIRT
Biscayne Holdings Inc	American	BiscH	BHA
Bishop Inc	NAS NMS	BishGr	BISH
BKLA Bancorp	NAS NL	BKLA	BKLA
The Black & Decker Corp	New York	BlackD	BDK
Black Hills Corp	New York	BlkHC	BKH
Black Industries Inc	NAS NMS	BlackI	BLAK
Blackstone Income Trust Inc	New York	Blkstn	BKT
Blasius Industries Inc	NAS NMS	Blasius	BLAS
Barry Blau & Partners Inc	NAS NMS	Blau	BBPI
Blessings Corp	American	Blessg	BCO
Blinder International Enterprises Inc	NAS NL	Blindr	BINL
H&R Block Inc	New York	BlkHR	HRB
Block Drug Co (Class A)	NAS NMS	BlckD	BLOCA
Blockbuster Entertainment Corp	NAS NMS	BlckEn	BBEC
Blount Inc (Class A)	American	BlountA	BLT.A
Blount Inc (Class B)	American	BlountB	BLT.B
Blue Arrow P.L.C.	New York	BlueAr	BAW
Blue Chip Value Fund Inc	New York	BluChp	BLU
Blyth Holdings Inc	NAS SL	Blyth	BLYH

COMPANY NAME	MARKET LISTING	NEWSPAPER ABBREV.	TRADING SYMBOL
Blyvooruitzicht Gold Mining Company Ltd	NAS NMS	Blyvoor	BLYVY
BMA Corp	NAS NMS	BMA	BMAC
BMC Industries Inc	New York	BMC	BMC
BMC Software Inc	NAS NL	BMC Sft	BMCS
BMJ Financial Corp	NAS NMS	BMJ	BMJF
BMR Financial Group Inc	NAS NMS	BMR Fin	BMRG
BNH Bancshares Inc	NAS NMS	BNH	BNHB
Boardroom Business Products Inc	NAS SL	BoardB	BDRM
Boatmen's Bancshares Inc	NAS NMS	BoatBn	BOAT
Bob Evans Farms Inc	NAS NMS	BobEvn	BOBE
Bobbie Brooks Inc	NAS NL	BobBrk	BBKS
Boddie-Noell Restaurant Properties Inc	American	Boddie	BNP
The Boeing Co	New York	Boeing	BA
Bogen Corp	NAS SL	Bogen	BOGN
Bogert Oil Co	NAS NMS	Bogert	BOGO
Bohemia Inc	NAS NMS	Bohema	BOHM
Boise Cascade Corp	New York	BoiseC	BCC
Bolar Pharmaceutical Company Inc	American	BlrPh	BLR
Bolt Beranek & Newman Inc	New York	BoltBr	BBN
Bolt Technology Corp	NAS NMS	BoltTc	BOLT
Bombay Palace Restaurants Inc	NAS NMS	Bombay	CURY
Bomed Medical Manufacturing Ltd	NAS SL	Bomed	BOMD
Bond International Gold Inc	New York	Bond	BIG
Bonneville Pacific Corp	NAS NMS	BonvlP	BPCO
Bonray Drilling Corp	NAS NL	Bonray	BNRY
Boole & Babbage Inc	NAS NMS	BooleB	BOOL
Boonton Electronics Corp	NAS NMS	BoonEl	BOON
Borden Chemicals & Plastics Limited Partnership	New York	BordC	BCP
Borden Inc	New York	Borden	BN
Borman's Inc	New York	Bormns	BRF
Boston Acoustics Inc	NAS NMS	BostAc	BOSA
Boston Bancorp	NAS NMS	BostBc	SBOS
Boston Celtics Limited Partnership	New York	BCelts	BOS
Boston Digital Corp	NAS NMS	BstnDig	BOST
Boston Edison Co	New York	BostEd	BSE
Boston Five Bancorp Inc	NAS NMS	BstnFB	BFCS
Boulevard Bancorp Inc	NAS NMS	Blvd Bc	BLVD
Bow Valley Industries Ltd	American	BowVal	BVI
Bowater Inc	New York	Bowatr	BOW
Bowater Industries p.l.c.	NAS NL	Bwater	BWTRY
Bowl America Inc (Class A)	American	BowlA	BWL.A
Bowmar Instrument Corp	American	Bowmr	BOM
Bowne & Company Inc	American	Bowne	BNE
W.H. Brady Co (Class A)	NAS NMS	BradyW	BRCOA
BRAE Corp	NAS NMS	BraeCp	BRAE
Brainerd International Inc	NAS SL	Branrd	BIRI
The Braintree Savings Bank	NAS NMS	Brantre	BTSB

COMPANY NAME	MARKET LISTING	NEWSPAPER ABBREV.	TRADING SYMBOL
Brajdas Corp	NAS NMS	Brajds	BRJS
Bralorne Resources Ltd	NAS NL	Bralrn	BRALF
Brand Companies Inc	NAS NMS	Brand	BRAN
Brandon Systems Corp	NAS NMS	Brandn	BRDN
Brandywine S&L Assn (Pennsylvania)	NAS NMS	BrndySv	BNDY
Branford Savings Bank (Connecticut)	NAS NMS	BrnfdSv	BSBC
Braniff Inc	NAS NL	Branif	BAIR
Brascan Ltd (Class A)	American	Brscn	BRS.A
Brazil Fund Inc	New York	Brazil	BZF
BRE Properties Inc	New York	BRE	BRE
Breakwater Resources Ltd	NAS NMS	Brkwt	BWRLF
Brenco Inc	NAS NMS	Brenco	BREN
Brendle's Inc	NAS NMS	Brendle	BRDL
Brenner Companies Inc	NAS NL	BrenerC	BNER
Brenton Banks Inc	NAS NL	BrentB	BRBK
Brentwood Instruments Inc	NAS SL	Brntwd	BRWD
Bridgford Foods Corp	NAS NMS	BrdgFd	BRID
Briggs & Stratton Corp	New York	BrigSt	BGG
Brilund Ltd	NAS SL	Brilund	BRILF
Brinkmann Instruments Inc	NAS NMS	Brnkmn	BRIK
BRIntec Corp	NAS NMS	BR Intec	BRIX
Bristol Gaming Corp	NAS SL	BristG	BRST
Bristol-Myers Co	New York	BristM	BMY
British Airways Plc	New York	BritAir	BAB
British Gas plc	New York	BritGas	BRG
British Land of America Inc	New York	BritLnd	BLA
The British Petroleum Company plc	New York	BritPt	BP
British Telecommunications plc	New York	BritTel	BTY
Britton Lee Inc	NAS NMS	BritLee	BLII
Broad National Bancorporation	NAS NL	BroadNt	BNBC
Broadview Savings Bank	NAS NL	BrdvwS	BDVFC
Broadway Financial Corp	NAS NMS	BdwyFn	BFCP
Broadway Holdings Inc	NAS SL	BwyHld	BWAY
Brock Hotel Corp	New York	Brock	BHC
The Broken Hill Proprietary Company Ltd	New York	BHP	BHP
Brokers Securities Inc	NAS SL	BrkrSc	BKRS
Brookfield Bancshares Corp (Illinois)	NAS NMS	Brkfld	BFBS
The Brooklyn Savings Bank (Connecticut)	NAS NMS	BklynSv	BRLN
The Brooklyn Union Gas Co	New York	BklyUG	BU
Brown & Sharpe Manufacturing Co	New York	BwnSh	BNS
Robert C. Brown & Company Inc	NAS NMS	BrwnRb	RCBI
Tom Brown Inc	NAS NMS	BrTom	TMBR
Brown-Forman Corp (Class A)	American	BrnFA	BFD.A
Brown-Forman Corp (Class B)	American	BrnFB	BFD.B
Brown Group Inc	New York	BrwnGp	BG
Brown Transport Company Inc	NAS NMS	BwnTrn	BTCI
Browning-Ferris Industries Inc	New York	BrwnF	BFI
BRT Realty Trust	New York	BRT	BRT

COMPANY NAME	MARKET LISTING	NEWSPAPER ABBREV.	TRADING SYMBOL
Bruno's Inc	NAS NMS	Brunos	BRNO
Brunswick Corp	New York	Brnwk	BC
Brush Wellman Inc	New York	BrshWl	BW
Bryn Mawr Bank Corp (Pennsylvania)	NAS NMS	BrynM	BMTCD
BSD Bancorp Inc	American	BSD	BSD
BSD Medical Corp	NAS SL	BSD	BSDM
BSN Corp	American	BSN	BSN
BT Financial Corp	NAS NMS	BT Fin	BTFC
BTR Realty Inc	NAS NMS	BTR	BTRI
Buckeye Financial Corp	NAS NMS	BckyFn	BCKY
Buckeye Partners L.P.	New York	Buckeye	BPL
Budget Rent a Car Corp	NAS NMS	Budget	BDGT
Buehler International Inc	NAS NMS	Buehlr	BULR
Buell Industries Inc	American	Buell	BUE
Buffelsfontein Gold Mining Company Ltd	NAS NL	Buffels	BFELY
Buffets Inc	NAS NMS	Buffet	BOCB
Buffton Corp	American	Buffton	BFX
Builders Design Inc	NAS NL	BldrDsg	BONI
Builders Transport Inc	NAS NMS	BuildT	TRUK
Bull & Bear Group Inc (Class A)	NAS NMS	BulBear	BNBGA
Bull Run Gold Mines Ltd	NAS NMS	BullRGd	BULL
Bundy Corp	New York	Bundy	BNY
Bunker Hill Income Securities Inc	New York	BunkrH	BHL
Burger King Investors Master L.P.	New York	BKInv	BKP
Burke Mills Inc	NAS SL	Burke	BMLS
Burlington Coat Factory Warehouse Corp	New York	BurlnCt	BCF
Burlington Northern Inc	New York	BrlNth	BNI
Burlington Resources Inc	New York	BrlRsc	BR
Burmah Oil Public Ltd Co	NAS NL	Burmh	BURMY
Burndy Corp	New York	Burndy	BDC
Burnham American Properties Inc	American	BurnAm	BMP
Burnham Pacific Properties Inc	American	BurnPP	BPP
Burnup & Sims Inc	NAS NMS	BurnpS	BSIM
Burr-Brown Corp	NAS NMS	BurrBr	BBRC
Burritt InterFinancial Bancorporation	NAS NMS	Burrit	BANQ
Bush Industries Inc	American	Bush	BSH
Business Cards of Tomorrow Inc	NAS SL	BusCrd	BUCS
Businessland Inc	New York	Businld	BLI
Butler Manufacturing Co	NAS NMS	ButlrMf	BTLR
Butler National Corp	NAS NMS	ButlrNt	BUTL
Byers Inc	NAS SL	Byers	BYRS
C&R Clothiers Inc	NAS SL	CR Clt	CLTH
C-COR Electronics Inc	NAS NMS	C COR	CCBL
C-TEC Corp	NAS NMS	CTEC	CTEX
C-TEC Corp (Class B)	NAS NL	CTEC B	CTEXB
CA Blockers Inc	NAS SL	CA Blk	LUNG
Cabarrus Savings Bank (North Carolina)	NAS NL	Cabarus	CASB

COMPANY NAME	MARKET LISTING	NEWSPAPER ABBREV.	TRADING SYMBOL
Cable Advertising Systems Inc	NAS SL	CblAdv	CABS
Cable Exchange Inc	NAS SL	CblExc	CBLX
Cable TV Industries	NAS NMS	CablTV	CATV
Cablevision Systems Corp	American	Cablvsn	CVC
Cabot Corp	New York	Cabot	CBT
Cabot Medical Corp	NAS NMS	CabotM	CBOT
Caché Inc	NAS NMS	Cache	CACH
CACI Inc (Class A)	NAS NMS	CACI	CACIA
Cadbury Schweppes PLC	NAS NMS	CbrySc	CADBY
Cade Industries Inc	NAS NMS	CadeIn	CADE
Cadema Corp	NAS SL	Cadema	CDMA
Cadence Design Systems Inc	NAS NMS	Cadence	CDNC
Cadmus Communications Corp	NAS NMS	Cadmu	CDMS
Cadnetix Corp	NAS NMS	Cadntx	CADX
Caesars New Jersey Inc	American	CaesNJ	CJN
Caesars World Inc	New York	Caesar	CAW
Cagle's Inc (Class A)	American	CagleA	CGL.A
Cal Fed Income Partners L.P.	New York	CalFIP	CFI
Cal Rep Bancorp Inc	NAS NMS	CalRep	CRBI
CalFed Inc	New York	CalFed	CAL
Calgene Inc	NAS NMS	Calgene	CGNE
Calgon Carbon Corp	NAS NMS	Calgon	CRBN
California Amplifier Inc	NAS NMS	CalAmp	CAMP
California Biotechnology Inc	NAS NMS	CalBio	CBIO
California Energy Co	American	CalEgy	NRG
California Financial Holding Co	NAS NMS	CalFncl	CFHC
California First Bank	NAS NMS	CalFst	CFBK
California Jockey Club	American	CalJky	CJ
California Micro Devices Corp	NAS NMS	CalMD	CAMD
California Microwave Inc	NAS NMS	CalMic	CMIC
California Real Estate Investment Trust	New York	CalRE	CT
California Water Service Co	NAS NMS	CalWtr	CWTR
Callahan Mining Corp	New York	Callhn	CMN
Callon Petroleum Co	NAS SL	Callon	CLNP
CalMat Co	New York	Calmat	CZM
Calprop Corp	American	Calprop	CPP
Calstar Inc	NAS NMS	Calstar	CSAR
Calton Inc	New York	Calton	CN
Calumet Industries Inc	NAS NMS	Calumt	CALI
CAM Data Systems Inc	NAS SL	CAM Dt	CADA
Cam-Net Communications Network Inc	NAS NL	CamNt	CWKTF
Cambrex Corp	NAS NMS	Cambrx	CBAM
Cambridge Analytical Associates Inc	NAS SL	CambAn	CAAN
Cambridge BioScience Corp	NAS NMS	CamBS	CBCX
The Cambridge Instrument Company plc	NAS NMS	CambIn	CAMBY
Cambridge Medical Technology Corp	NAS SL	CambM	CMTC
Camera Enterprises Inc	NAS SL	CamEnt	UCAM
Camera Platforms International Inc	NAS SL	CamPl	CMPL

COMPANY NAME	MARKET LISTING	NEWSPAPER ABBREV.	TRADING SYMBOL
Cameron Iron Works Inc	New York	CamrnI	CIW
Camille St. Moritz Inc	NAS SL	CamilSM	CMIL
Campbell Resources Inc	New York	CmpR	CCH
Campbell Soup Co	New York	CamSp	CPB
Campeau Corp	NAS NMS	Camp	CMAFC
Canadian Marconi Co	American	CMarc	CMW
Canadian Occidental Petroleum Ltd	American	CdnOc	CXY
Canadian Pacific Ltd	New York	CdnPac	CP
Canandaigua Wine Company Inc (Class A)	American	CWineA	CDG.A
Canandaigua Wine Company Inc (Class B)	American	CWineB	CDG.B
Candela Laser Corp	NAS SL	Candla	CLZR
Candlewood Bank & Trust Co	NAS SL	CndlBk	CDBK
Cannon Express Inc	NAS NL	CannEx	CANX
The Cannon Group Inc	New York	CanonG	CAN
Canon Inc	NAS NMS	CanonI	CANNY
Canonie Environmental Services Corp	NAS NMS	Canonie	CANO
Canrad Inc	NAS NMS	Canrad	CNRD
Canyon Resources Corp	NAS SL	CanyRs	CYNR
Cape Cod Bank & Trust Co	NAS NMS	CCBT	CCBT
Capital Associates Inc	NAS NMS	CapAsc	CAII
Capital Cities/ABC Inc	New York	CapCits	CCB
Capital Holding Corp	New York	CapHld	CPH
Capital Housing & Mortgage Partners	American	CapHo	CAP
Capital Southwest Corp	NAS NMS	CapSw	CSWC
Capitol Bancorporation	NAS NMS	CapBcp	CAPB
Capitol Transamerica Corp	NAS NMS	CapTr	CATA
Capt. Crab Inc	NAS NMS	CapCrb	CRAB
Card-Tel	NAS SL	CardTl	ACCT
Cardiac Control Systems Inc	NAS SL	Cardiac	CCSC
Cardinal Distribution Inc	NAS NMS	CrdnlD	CDIC
Cardinal Federal Savings Bank (Kentucky)	NAS NMS	CardFd	CAFS
Cardinal Industries Inc	NAS SL	CardIn	CDNI
Cardiopulmonary Technologies Inc	NAS SL	Cardpul	HART
Cardis Corp	American	Cardis	CDS
Care Enterprises Inc (Class A)	American	CareE A	CRE.A
Care Enterprises Inc (Class B)	American	CareE B	CRE.B
Care Plus Inc	NAS NMS	CarePl	CPLS
CareAmerica Inc	NAS SL	CareAm	CAMI
CareerCom Corp	New York	CareerC	CMO
Caribbean Select Inc	NAS SL	CaribSl	CSEL
Carlisle Companies Inc	New York	Carlisle	CSL
Carlton Communications PLC	NAS NMS	CarlCm	CCTVY
Carme Inc	NAS NMS	Carme	CAME
Carmel Container Systems Ltd	American	Carmel	KML
Carmike Cinemas Inc (Class A)	NAS NMS	Carmik	CMIKA
Carnival Cruise Lines Inc	American	CarnCr	CCL
Carolco Pictures Inc	New York	CarolP	CRC
Carolin Mines Ltd (Class A)	NAS NMS	Carolin	CRLNF

COMPANY NAME	MARKET LISTING	NEWSPAPER ABBREV.	TRADING SYMBOL
Carolina Bancorp Inc	NAS NMS	CaroBcp	FFCA
Carolina First Corp	NAS NL	CaroFst	CAFC
Carolina Freight Corp	New York	CaroFt	CAO
Carolina Mountain Holding Co	NAS SL	CaroMt	CMHC
Carolina Power & Light Co	New York	CarPw	CPL
Carolyn Bean Publishing Ltd	NAS SL	CarolB	CBEN
Carpenter Technology Corp	New York	CarTec	CRS
Carriage Industries Inc	New York	CargInd	CGE
Carrington Laboratories Inc	NAS NMS	Caringtn	CARN
Carson Pirie Scott & Co	New York	CarsP	CRN
Carter Hawley Hale Stores Inc	New York	CartH	CHH
Carter-Wallace Inc	New York	CartWl	CAR
Carteret Bancorp Inc	New York	CartBc	CBC
Carver Corp	NAS NMS	Carver	CAVR
CasaBlanca Industries Inc	American	Casblan	CAB
Cascade Corp	NAS NMS	Cascde	CASC
Cascade Natural Gas Corp	New York	CascNG	CGC
Casey's General Stores Inc	NAS NMS	Caseys	CASY
Cash America Investments Inc	American	CshAm	PWN
Caspen Oil Inc	American	Caspn	CNO
Castle & Cooke Inc	New York	CastlCk	CKE
A.M. Castle & Co	American	CastlA	CAS
Castle Convertible Fund Inc	American	CasFd	CVF
Castle Energy Corp	NAS NMS	CstlEn	CECX
The Casual Male Corp	NAS NMS	CaslMle	CMLE
Catalina Lighting Inc	American	CataLt	LTG
Catalyst Energy Corp	New York	Catlyst	CE
Catalyst Thermal Energy Corp	NAS NMS	CatlThr	CETH
Caterpillar Inc	New York	Caterp	CAT
Cato Corp (Class A)	NAS NMS	CatoCp	CACOA
Cavalier Homes Inc	American	CavalH	CXV
Cavco Industries Inc	NAS NL	Cavco	CVCO
Cayuga Savings Bank (New York)	NAS NMS	Cayuga	CAYB
CB&T Bancshares Inc	NAS NMS	CB T	CBTB
CB&T Financial Corp	NAS NMS	CB&T F	CBTF
CBI Industries Inc	New York	CBI In	CBH
CBS Inc	New York	CBS	CBS
CCA Industries Inc	NAS NMS	CCA	CCAM
CCB Financial Corp	NAS NMS	CCB	CCBF
CCNB Corp	NAS NMS	CCNB	CCNC
CCR Video Corp	NAS SL	CCR	CCCR
CCX Inc	New York	CCX	CCX
CDI Corp	American	CDI	CDI
Cedar Fair, L.P.	New York	CedrF	FUN
Cedar Income Federal 1 Ltd	NAS NL	CedarI	CEDR
Cel-Sci Corp	NAS NMS	CelSci	CELI
Celcor Inc	NAS SL	Celcor	CLCR
Celgene Corp	NAS NMS	Celgene	CELG

COMPANY NAME	MARKET LISTING	NEWSPAPER ABBREV.	TRADING SYMBOL
Cell Technology Inc	NAS NL	CellTch	CELL
Cellcom Corp	NAS SL	Cellcom	CLCM
Celltronics Inc	NAS SL	Celtr	CELT
Cellular America Inc	NAS SL	CellAm	CELM
Cellular Inc	NAS SL	CelrIn	CELS
Cellular Communications Inc	NAS NMS	CellCm	COMM
Cellular Products Inc	NAS SL	CelrPr	CELP
CEM Corp	NAS NMS	CEM	CEMX
CenCor Inc	NAS NMS	Cencor	CNCR
Centel Cable Television Co (Class A)	NAS NMS	CentelCb	CNCAA
Centel Corp	New York	Centel	CNT
The Centennial Group Inc	American	CentGp	CEQ
Centerbank (Connecticut)	NAS NMS	Centrbk	CTBX
Centercore Inc	NAS NL	Centcre	CCOR
Centerior Energy Corp	New York	CentEn	CX
Centerre Bancorporation	NAS NMS	CntrBc	CTBC
Centex Corp	New York	Centex	CTX
Centex Telemanagement Inc	NAS NMS	Centex	CNTX
Centocor Inc	NAS NMS	Centcor	CNTO
Central & South West Corp	New York	CenSoW	CSR
Central & Southern Holding Co	NAS NL	CtrlSou	CSBC
Central Bancorporation (Washington)	NAS NMS	CBcWa	CBWA
Central Bancshares of the South Inc	NAS NMS	CnBsh	CBSS
Central Banking System Inc	NAS NL	CnBSys	CSYS
Central Co-operative Bank (Massachusetts)	NAS NMS	CtrCOp	CEBK
Central Corp (Georgia)	NAS SL	CntrlCp	CTRL
Central Fidelity Banks Inc	NAS NMS	CFidBk	CFBS
Central Fund of Canada Ltd	American	CFCda	CEF
Central Holding Co	NAS NMS	CtrlHld	CHOL
Central Hudson Gas & Electric Corp	New York	CenHud	CNH
Central Illinois Public Service Co	New York	CnlIPS	CIP
Central Jersey Bancorp	NAS NMS	CJerB	CJER
Central Jersey Savings Bank S.L.A.	NAS NMS	CJerSv	CJSB
Central Louisiana Electric Company Inc	New York	CnLaEl	CNL
Central Maine Power Co	New York	CeMPw	CTP
Central Pacific Corp	American	CnPacC	CTA
Central Pacific Minerals N.L.	NAS NL	CPcMn	CPMNY
Central Pennsylvania Financial Corp	NAS NMS	CPaFin	CPSA
Central Reserve Life Corp	NAS NMS	CRsLf	CRLC
Central Securities Corp	American	CentSe	CET
Central Sprinkler Corp	NAS NMS	CnSprn	CNSP
Central Vermont Public Service Corp	New York	CVtPS	CV
Centronics Data Computer Corp	New York	CentrCp	CEN
CenTrust Savings Bank	American	Centrst	DLP
Centuri Inc	NAS NMS	Centuri	CENT
Century Bancorp Inc	NAS NMS	CntyBc	CNBK
Century Communications Corp (Class A)	American	CtyCom	CTY.A
Century Medicorp	NAS SL	CntyMd	CEMC

COMPANY NAME	MARKET LISTING	NEWSPAPER ABBREV.	TRADING SYMBOL
Century Papers Inc	NAS NMS	CntryP	CPAP
Century Park Pictures Corp	NAS SL	CntyPk	CPPC
Century Telephone Enterprises Inc	New York	CntryTl	CTL
Cenvest Inc	NAS NMS	Cenvst	CBCT
Cenvill Development Corp	American	CenvD	CVL
Cenvill Investors Inc	New York	Cenvill	CVI
Ceradyne Inc	NAS NMS	Cerdyn	CRDN
Ceramics Process Systems Corp	NAS NL	CeramPr	CPSX
CERBCO Inc	NAS NMS	Cerbco	CERB
Cermetek Microelectronics Inc	NAS NMS	Cermtk	CRMK
Cerner Corp	NAS NMS	Cerner	CERN
CerProbe Corp	NAS SL	Cerprb	CRPB
Certron Corp	NAS SL	Certron	CRTN
Cetec Corp	American	Cetec	CEC
Cetus Corp	NAS NMS	Cetus	CTUS
CF&I Steel Corp	NAS NMS	CFI St	CFIP
CFS Financial Corp	NAS NMS	CFS	CFSC
Challenger International Ltd	NAS NMS	ChalInt	CSTIF
Chalone Inc	NAS NMS	Chalone	CHLN
Chambers Development Co Inc (Class A)	American	ChDevA	CDV.A
Chambers Development Co Inc (Class B)	American	ChDevB	CDV.B
Champion Enterprises Inc	American	ChmpEn	CHB
Champion International Corp	New York	ChmpIn	CHA
Champion Parts Inc	NAS NMS	ChmpPr	CREB
Champion Products Inc	American	ChmpPd	CH
Champion Spark Plug Co	New York	ChmpSp	CHM
Chancellor Corp	NAS NMS	ChncCp	CHCR
Chandler Insurance Ltd	NAS NMS	ChanIns	CHANF
Chantal Pharmaceutical Corp	NAS SL	Chantl	CHTL
Chaparral Resources Inc	NAS NMS	Chapral	CHAR
Chaparral Steel Co	New York	ChpStl	CSM
Chapman Energy Inc	NAS NMS	ChapEn	CHPN
The Chariot Group Inc	American	Chariot	CGR
Charlotte Charles Inc	NAS NMS	CharCh	CAKE
Charming Shoppes Inc	NAS NMS	ChrmS	CHRS
The Charter Co	New York	ChartC	CHR
Charter-Crellin Inc	NAS NMS	ChtCrl	CRTR
Charter Federal S&L Assn (Virginia)	NAS NMS	ChrtFdl	CHFD
Charter Federal Savings Bank	NAS NMS	ChtFSB	CFED
Charter Medical Corp (Class A)	American	ChtMdA	CMD.A
Charter Medical Corp (Class B)	American	ChtMdB	CMD.B
Charter One Financial Inc	NAS NMS	ChtOne	COFI
Charter Power Systems Inc	American	ChtPwr	CHP
Chartwell Group Ltd	NAS NMS	Chrtwl	CTWL
The Chase Manhattan Corp	New York	Chase	CMB
Chase Medical Group Inc	American	ChsMed	CGO
Chattem Inc	NAS NMS	Chattm	CHTT

COMPANY NAME	MARKET LISTING	NEWSPAPER ABBREV.	TRADING SYMBOL
Bernard Chaus Inc	New York	Chaus	CHS
Check Robot Inc	NAS SL	ChkRobt	CKRB
Check Technology Corp	NAS NMS	ChkTch	CTCQ
Checkpoint Systems Inc	NAS NMS	ChkPt	CHEK
Chefs International Inc	NAS NL	ChefInt	CHEF
Chelsea Industries Inc	New York	Chelsea	CHD
ChemClear Inc	NAS NMS	Chmclr	CMCL
Chemed Corp	New York	Chemed	CHE
Chemex Pharmaceuticals Inc	NAS NMS	Chemex	CHMX
Chemfix Technologies Inc	NAS NMS	Chemfx	CFIX
Chemical Banking Corp	New York	ChmBk	CHL
Chemical Fabrics Corp	NAS NMS	ChFab	CMFB
Chemical Financial Corp	NAS NMS	ChmFin	CHFC
Chemical Leaman Corp	NAS NMS	ChLea	CLEA
Chemical Waste Management Inc	New York	ChWst	CHW
Cherne Enterprises Inc	NAS SL	Cherne	CHNE
The Cherokee Group	NAS NMS	Cheroke	CHKE
The Cherry Corp	NAS NMS	ChryCp	CHER
Chesapeake Corp	New York	Chspk	CSK
Chesapeake Industries Inc	NAS SL	ChesInd	CHES
Chesapeake Utilities Corp	NAS NMS	ChesUtl	CHPK
Cheshire Financial Corp	NAS NMS	Cheshre	CFNH
Chevron Corp	New York	Chevrn	CHV
Cheyenne Software Inc	NAS NMS	CheySf	CHEY
Chicago Milwaukee Corp	New York	ChiMlw	CHG
Chicago Pacific Corp	New York	ChiPac	CPA
Chicago Rivet & Machine Co	American	ChiRv	CVR
Chief Consolidated Mining Co	NAS SL	ChfCon	CFCM
Chieftain Development Company Ltd	American	ChfDv	CID
Child World Inc	NAS NMS	ChldWld	CWLD
Childrens Discovery Center of America Inc (Class A)	NAS NMS	ChldDis	CDCRA
Chili's Inc	NAS NMS	Chilis	CHLI
Chips & Technologies Inc	NAS NMS	ChipsTc	CHPS
Chipwich Inc (Class A)	NAS SL	Chpwch	CHIPA
Chiron Corp	NAS NMS	Chiron	CHIR
Chittenden Corp	NAS NMS	Chitnd	CNDN
Chock Full O'Nuts Corp	New York	ChkFull	CHF
Choice Drug Systems Inc	NAS SL	ChcDrg	DOSE
Chris-Craft Industries Inc	New York	ChrisCr	CCN
The Christiana Companies Inc	New York	Christn	CST
Chronar Corp	NAS NMS	Chronr	CRNR
Chrysler Corp	New York	Chryslr	C
The Chubb Corp	New York	Chubb	CB
Church & Dwight Company Inc	NAS NMS	ChrDwt	CRCH
Church's Fried Chicken Inc	New York	Churchs	CHU
Chyron Corp	New York	Chyron	CHY

COMPANY NAME	MARKET LISTING	NEWSPAPER ABBREV.	TRADING SYMBOL
CIGNA Corp	New York	CIGNA	CI
CILCORP Inc	New York	Cilcorp	CER
CIM High Yield Securities	American	CIM	CIM
CIMCO Inc	NAS NMS	Cimco	CIMC
Cincinnati Bell Inc	New York	CinBel	CSN
Cincinnati Financial Corp	NAS NMS	CinnFn	CINF
The Cincinnati Gas & Electric Co	New York	CinGE	CIN
Cincinnati Microwave Inc	NAS NMS	CinMic	CNMW
Cincinnati Milacron Inc	New York	CinMil	CMZ
Cineplex Odeon Corp	New York	CineOd	CPX
Cintas Corp	NAS NMS	Cintas	CTAS
Cipher Data Products Inc	NAS NMS	Cipher	CIFR
Ciprico Inc	NAS NMS	Ciprico	CPCI
Circadian Inc	NAS NMS	Circadn	CKDN
Circle Express Inc	NAS NMS	CirclEx	CEXX
Circle Fine Art Corp	NAS NMS	CirclFA	CFNE
Circle Income Shares Inc	NAS NL	CircInc	CINS
The Cirlce K Corp	New York	CircleK	CKP
Circon Corp	NAS NMS	Circon	CCON
Circuit City Stores Inc	New York	CirCty	CC
Circuit Systems Inc	NAS SL	CircSy	CSYI
Circus Circus Enterprises Inc	New York	Circus	CIR
Ciro Inc	NAS SL	Ciro	CIRI
C.I.S. Technologies Inc	NAS NMS	CIS Tch	CISIF
Citadel Gold Mines Inc	NAS SL	Citdl	CIGCF
Citadel Holding Corp	American	Citadel	CDL
Citicorp	New York	Citicrp	CCI
Citipostal Inc	NAS NMS	Citpst	CITI
Citizens & Southern Corp	NAS NMS	CtzSoCp	CSOU
Citizens Bank (North Carolina)	NAS NL	CitznBk	CIBA
Citizens Banking Corp (Michigan)	NAS NMS	CtzBkg	CBCF
Citizens Financial Group Inc	NAS NMS	CtzFG	CITN
Citizens First Bancorp	American	CitzFst	CFB
Citizens Insurance Company of America, Texas (Class A)	NAS NMS	CtzIns	CINNA
Citizens Savings Bank F.S.B. (Maryland)	NAS NMS	CtzSMd	CSBF
Citizens Savings Bank F.S.B. (New York)	NAS NMS	CtzSNY	CISA
Citizens Savings Financial Corp (Class A) (Florida)	NAS NMS	CitzSF	CSFCA
Citizens Security Group Inc	NAS NL	CtzSec	CSGI
Citizens Utilities Co (Class A)	NAS NMS	CtzU A	CITUA
Citizens Utilities Co (Class B)	NAS NMS	CtzU B	CITUB
City Holding Co	NAS NMS	CtyHld	CHCO
City National Corp	NAS NMS	CtyNC	CTYN
City Resources Ltd	NAS NMS	CityRs	CCIMF
City Savings Bank of Meriden (Connecticut)	NAS NMS	CitySv	CSBM
CityFed Financial Corp	NAS NMS	CityFed	CTYF

COMPANY NAME	MARKET LISTING	NEWSPAPER ABBREV.	TRADING SYMBOL
Citytrust Bancorp	New York	CityBcp	CYT
CK Federal Savings Bank (North Carolina)	NAS NMS	CK FSv	CKSB
Clabir Corp	New York	Clabir	CLG
Clabir Corp (Class B)	NAS SL	ClabrB	CLGBB
Claire's Stores Inc	New York	ClairSt	CLE
Clairson International Corp	NAS NMS	Clairsn	CLIC
Clarcor Inc	NAS NMS	Clarcor	CLRK
Claremont Capital Corp	American	Clarmt	CCM
Clark Consolidated Industries Inc	American	ClarkC	CLK
Clark Equipment Co	New York	ClarkE	CKL
Classic Corp	NAS NMS	ClasicC	WBED
Clayton Homes Inc	New York	ClayHm	CMH
Clayton Silver Mines Inc	NAS NL	ClaySlv	CLSM
CLC of America Inc	New York	CLC	CLC
Clean Harbors Inc	NAS NMS	CleanH	CLHB
Clear Channel Communications Inc	American	ClearCh	CCU
Clemente Global Growth Fund Inc	New York	ClmGlb	CLM
Cleopatra Kohlique Inc	NAS SL	CleKoh	CLEO
Cleveland-Cliffs Inc	New York	ClvClf	CLF
Cliff Engle Ltd	NAS SL	ClifEgl	CLIF
Cliffs Drilling Co	NAS NMS	ClifDr	CLDRV
Clini-Therm Corp	NAS SL	CliniTh	CLIN
Clinical Data Inc	NAS NMS	ClinDt	CLDA
Clinical Sciences Inc	NAS NMS	ClinSci	CLSC
Clinton Gas Systems Inc	NAS NMS	ClintGs	CGAS
The Clorox Co	New York	Clorox	CLX
The Clothestime Inc	NAS NMS	Cloth	CTME
Club Med Inc	New York	ClubMd	CMI
CMI Corp	American	CMI Cp	CMX
CML Group Inc	New York	CML	CML
CMS Advertising Inc	NAS SL	CMS Ad	CCMS
CMS Energy Corp	New York	CMS En	CMS
CMS Enhancements Inc	NAS NMS	CMS E	ACMS
CMX Corp	American	CMX Cp	CXC
CNA Financial Corp	New York	CNA Fn	CNA
CNA Income Shares Inc	New York	CNAI	CNN
CNB Bancshares Inc	NAS NMS	CNB	CNBE
CNL Financial Corp	NAS NMS	CNL Fn	CNLF
CNW Corp	New York	CNW	CNW
Co-Operative Bancorp (Massachusetts)	NAS NMS	CoOpBk	COBK
Coachman Inc	NAS SL	Cochmn	CINC
Coachmen Industries Inc	New York	Coachm	COA
Coast Federal S&L Assn (Florida)	NAS NMS	CoastF	CFSF
Coast R.V. Inc	American	CoastR	CRV
Coast S&L Assn (California)	New York	CoastSL	CSA
The Coastal Corp	New York	Coastal	CGP
CoastAmerica Corp	New York	Cstam	CAC
Coated Sales Inc	NAS NMS	CoatSl	RAGS

COMPANY NAME	MARKET LISTING	NEWSPAPER ABBREV.	TRADING SYMBOL
Cobb Resources Corp	NAS NMS	CobRsc	COBB
Cobe Laboratories Inc	NAS NMS	CobeLb	COBE
Coca-Cola Bottling Co. Consolidated	NAS NMS	CocaBtl	COKE
The Coca-Cola Company	New York	CocaCl	KO
Coca-Cola Enterprises Inc	New York	CocCE	CCE
CoCa Mines Inc	NAS NMS	CoCaM	COCA
Code-Alarm Inc	NAS NL	CodeAl	CODL
Codenoll Technology Corp	NAS NMS	Codenol	CODN
Codecard Inc	NAS SL	Codercd	CRCD
Coeur d'Alene Mines Corp	American	Coeur	CDE
Cognitive Systems Inc	NAS SL	CogntSy	CSAI
Cognitronics Corp	American	Cognitr	CGN
Cognos Inc	NAS NMS	Cognos	COGNF
Cohasset Savings Bank (Massachusetts)	NAS NMS	Cohaset	CHTB
Coherent Inc	NAS NMS	Cohernt	COHR
Cohu Inc	American	Cohu	COH
Coin Phones Inc	NAS SL	CoinPhn	OPER
Coleco Industries Inc	New York	Coleco	CLO
The Coleman Company Inc	New York	Colemn	CLN
Colgate-Palmolive Co	New York	ColgPal	CL
Collaborative Research Inc	NAS NMS	ColabR	CRIC
Collagen Corp	NAS NMS	Colagen	CGEN
Collective Federal Savings Bank (New Jersey)	NAS NMS	ColFdl	COFD
Collins Foods International Inc	New York	ColFds	CF
Collins Industries Inc	American	Collins	GO
Colonial American Bankshares Corp	NAS NMS	ColABn	CABK
Colonial BancGroup Inc (Class A)	NAS NMS	CBcgp A	CLBGA
Colonial BancGroup Inc (Class B)	NAS NMS	CBcgp B	CLBGB
Colonial Commercial Corp	NAS SL	ColCmc	CCOM
Colonial Gas Co	NAS NMS	ClnGas	CGES
The Colonial Group Inc (Class A)	NAS NMS	ColnGp	COGRA
Colonial Intermediate High Income Fund	New York	ColIHI	CIF
Colonial Life & Accident Insurance Co (Class B)	NAS NMS	ColLfAc	CACCB
Colonial Municipal Income Trust	New York	ColMu	CMU
Color Systems Technology Inc	American	ColorSy	CLR
Colorado Energy Corp	NAS NL	ColEngy	CRDO
Colorado National Bankshares Inc	NAS NMS	ColoNt	COLC
Colorado Prime Corp	American	ColPr	CPE
Colorocs Corp	NAS SL	Colorcs	CLRX
Columbia First Federal S&L Assn (Washington D.C.)	NAS NMS	ColFst	COAS
The Columbia Gas System Inc	New York	ColGas	CG
Columbia Pictures Entertainment Inc	New York	ColPict	KPE
Columbia Real Estate Investments Inc	American	ColREI	CIV
Columbia S&L Assn	New York	ColumS	CSV
COM Systems Inc	American	ComSy	CTM

COMPANY NAME	MARKET LISTING	NEWSPAPER ABBREV.	TRADING SYMBOL
Comair Inc	NAS NMS	Comair	COMR
COMARCO Inc	NAS NMS	Cmrco	CMRO
Combustion Engineering Inc	New York	CmbEn	CSP
Comcast Cablevision of Philadelphia Inc	NAS SL	ComcPh	CCPI
Comcast Corp (Class A)	NAS NMS	Comcst	CMCSA
Comcast Corp (special Class A)	NAS NMS	Cmcs sp	CMCSK
COMCOA Inc	NAS NMS	Comcoa	CCOA
Comdata Holdings Corp	NAS SL	CmdtHd	CMDT
Comdial Corp	NAS NMS	Cmdial	CMDL
Comdisco Inc	New York	Comdis	CDO
Comerica Inc	NAS NMS	Cmeric	CMCA
Comet Enterprises Inc	NAS SL	CometEn	STAM
Comfed Bancorp Inc	American	ComFd	CFK
Cominco Ltd	American	Cominc	CLT
Command Airways Inc	NAS NMS	CmdAir	COMD
Commerce Bancorp Inc (New Jersey)	NAS NMS	ComBc	COBA
Commerce Bancshares Inc (Missouri)	NAS NMS	CmBsh	CBSH
Commerce Clearing House Inc	NAS NMS	CmClr	CCLR
Commerce Group Corp	NAS SL	CmceG	CGCO
Commerce Total Return Fund Inc	American	CmceT	CTO
CommerceBancorp (California)	NAS NL	CmceBc	CBNB
Commercial Bancorp of Colorado (Class A)	NAS NMS	CmBCol	CBOCA
Commercial Credit Co	New York	CmcCrd	CCC
Commercial Federal Corp	NAS NMS	CmcFdl	CFCN
Commercial Intertech	NAS NMS	CmlTek	CTEK
Commercial Metals Co	New York	CmMtl	CMC
Commercial National Corp	NAS NMS	Cmcl Nt	CNCL
Commercial Programming Unlimited Inc	NAS NL	CmclPr	CPUI
Commodore Environmental Services Inc	NAS NMS	ComdE	COES
Commodore International Ltd	New York	Comdre	CBU
Commonwealth Bancshares Corp	NAS NMS	CwltBn	CBKS
Commonwealth Edison Co	New York	CmwE	CWE
Commonwealth Energy System	New York	ComES	CES
Commonwealth Mortgage Company Inc (Massachusetts)	NAS NMS	CmwMg	CCMC
Commonwealth S&L Assn F.A. (Florida)	NAS NMS	CmwSv	COMW
Commtron Corp	American	Comtrn	CMR
Communication Cable Inc (North Carolina)	NAS SL	CmCblNC	CABL
Communications & Cable Inc	NAS NMS	CmsCbl	CCAB
Communications Group Inc	NAS NL	ComGrp	CMGI
Communications Satellite Corp	New York	Comsat	CQ
Communications Systems Inc	NAS NMS	ComSy	CSII
Communications Transmission Inc	NAS NMS	ComTrn	CTIA
Community Bank System Inc (New York)	NAS NMS	CmtyBS	CBSI
Community Bankshares Inc (New Hampshire)	NAS NMS	CmtyBn	CBNH
Community National Bancorp Inc (New York)	NAS NMS	CNBNY	CNBT
Community Psychatric Centers	New York	CPsyc	CMY
COMNET Corp	NAS NMS	Comnet	CNET

COMPANY NAME	MARKET LISTING	NEWSPAPER ABBREV.	TRADING SYMBOL
Comp-U-Check Inc	NAS NMS	CmpU	CMUC
Compania Boliviana de Energia Electrica S.A.	NAS NL	CoBolv	BPWRF
COMPAQ Computer Corp	New York	Compaq	CPQ
Component Technology Corp	NAS NMS	CmpoT	CTEC
ComponentGuard Inc	NAS SL	Cmpgrd	PLUG
Comprehensive Care Corp	New York	CmpCre	CMP
Compression Labs Inc	NAS NMS	CmprsL	CLIX
Comptek Research Inc	American	Comptek	CTK
CompuChem Corp	NAS NMS	Cmpch	CCEM
Compucom Systems Inc	NAS NMS	Cmpcm	BYTE
CompuDyne Corp	American	CompD	CDC
CompuScan Inc	NAS NMS	Compus	CSCN
Computer & Communications Technology Corp	NAS NMS	CCTC	CCTC
Computer Associates International Inc	New York	CmpAs	CA
Computer Automation Inc	NAS NMS	CptAut	CAUT
Computer Communications Inc	NAS SL	CptCom	CCMM
Computer Components Corp	NAS SL	CptrCm	CPRC
Computer Consoles Inc	American	CmpCn	CCS
Computer Data Systems Inc	NAS NMS	CmpDt	CPTD
Computer Entry Systems Corp	NAS NMS	CES	CESC
The Computer Factory Inc	New York	CmFct	CFA
Computer Horizons Corp	NAS NMS	CmptH	CHRZ
Computer Identics Corp	NAS NMS	CmpIdn	CIDN
Computer Language Research Inc	NAS NMS	CmpLR	CLRI
Computer Memories Inc	NAS NMS	CmptM	CMIN
Computer Microfilm Corp	NAS NL	CmpMc	COMI
Computer Network Technology Corp	NAS SL	CptNwk	CMNT
Computer Power Inc	NAS NL	CptPwr	CPWR
Computer Products Inc	NAS NMS	CmpPr	CPRD
Computer Resources Inc	NAS SL	CmpRs	CRII
Computer Sciences Corp	New York	CompSc	CSC
Computer Task Group Inc	New York	CmpTsk	TSK
Computer Telephone Corp (Class 1)	NAS SL	CmpTel	CPTLA
ComputerCraft Inc	NAS SL	CptCft	CRFT
Computerland Corp	New York	Cptlnd	CLD
CompuTrac Inc	American	Cmptrc	LLB
COMSHARE Inc	NAS NMS	Comshr	CSRE
Comstock Group Inc	NAS NMS	Comstk	CSTK
Comstock Partners Strategy Fund Inc	New York	Comstk	CPF
Comstock Resources Inc	NAS SL	CmstkR	CMRE
Comtech Telecommunications Corp	NAS SL	Comtch	CMTL
Comtex Scientific Corp	NAS SL	Comtex	CMTX
Comtrex Systems Corp	NAS NMS	Comtrx	COMX
ConAgra Inc	New York	ConAg	CAG
Concept Inc	NAS NMS	CncptI	CCPT
Concept 90 Marketing Inc	NAS SL	Cnc 90	GYMS

COMPANY NAME	MARKET LISTING	NEWSPAPER ABBREV.	TRADING SYMBOL
Conchemco Inc	American	Cnchm	CKC
Concord Camera Corp	NAS NMS	CcdCam	LENS
Concord Career Colleges Inc	NAS NMS	ConcCC	CNCD
Concord Computing Corp	NAS NMS	ConcCm	CEFT
Concord Fabrics Inc	American	ConcdF	CIS
Concurrent Computer Corp	NAS NMS	ConcCpt	CCUR
Congress Steet Properties Inc	NAS NMS	ConStP	CSTP
CONMED Corp	NAS NMS	Conmed	CNMD
Connaught Biosciences Inc	NAS NMS	Connght	CSESF
Connecticut Bancorp Inc (Norwich)	NAS NL	CtBcp	NKBK
Connecticut Community Bank (Greenwich)	NAS SL	ConnCm	CCBK
Connecticut Energy Corp	New York	ConnE	CNE
Connecticut Natural Gas Corp	New York	ConnNG	CTG
Connecticut Water Service Inc	NAS NMS	ConnWt	CTWS
Connelly Containers Inc	American	Connly	CON
Conner Peripherals Inc	NAS NMS	ConrPr	CNNR
Conquest Exploration Co	American	Conqst	CQX
Conseco inc	New York	Consec	CNC
Conservative Savings Bank	NAS NL	ConsSv	CONS
Consolidated Edison Company of New York Inc	New York	ConsEd	ED
Consolidated Energy Partners L.P.	American	CnsEP	CPS
Consolidated Fibres Inc	NAS NMS	ConFbr	CFIB
Consolidated Freightways Inc	New York	CnsFrt	CNF
Consolidated Hydro Inc	NAS NL	CnsHyd	COHY
Consolidated Imaging Corp	NAS SL	ConsIm	CIMG
Consolidated Natural Gas Co	New York	ConsNG	CNG
Consolidated Oil & Gas Inc	American	ConsOG	CGS
Consolidated Papers Inc	NAS NMS	CnsPap	CPER
Consolidated Products Inc	NAS NMS	ConsPd	COPI
Consolidated Rail Corp	New York	Conrail	CRR
Consolidated Stores Corp	New York	CnStor	CNS
Consolidated-Tomoka Land Co	NAS NMS	CnsTom	CTLC
Constar International Inc	New York	Constr	CTR
Constellation Bancorp	NAS NMS	Cnst1Bc	CSTL
Constitution Bancorp of New England Inc	NAS NMS	CnBNE	CBNEV
Conston Corp	American	Constn	KCS
Consul Restaurant Corp	NAS NMS	Consul	CNSL
Consumers Financial Corp	NAS NMS	ConsFn	CFIN
Consumers Water Co	NAS NMS	ConWat	CONW
Contel Cellular Inc (Class A)	NAS NMS	Cont1Cl	CCXLA
Contel Corp	New York	Contel	CTC
Continental Circuits Corp	American	CtlCrc	CKT
The Continental Corp	New York	Cnt1Cp	CIC
Continental General Insurance Co	NAS NMS	Ct1Gn	CGIC
Continental Graphics Corp	American	ContGR	CIG
Continental Health Affiliates Inc	NAS NMS	Ct1H1th	CTHL
Continental Homes Holding Corp	NAS NMS	Ct1Hme	CONH

COMPANY NAME	MARKET LISTING	NEWSPAPER ABBREV.	TRADING SYMBOL
Continental Illinois Corp	New York	ContIll	CIL
Continental Illinois Holding Corp	New York	CtlIHld	CIH
Continental Information Systems Corp	New York	CntlInfo	CNY
Continental Materials Corp	American	ContMtl	CUO
Continental Medical Systems Inc	NAS NMS	CtlMed	CONT
Continental Ventures Inc	NAS SL	CtlVen	COVIV
The Continuum Company Inc	NAS NMS	Contin	CTUC
Control Data Corp	New York	CtData	CDA
Control Laser International Corp	NAS SL	CtLasr	CLSR
Control Resource Industries Inc	NAS NMS	CtrlRs	CRIX
Convenient Food Mart Inc	NAS NMS	CnvFd	CFMI
Convergent Inc	NAS NMS	Convgt	CVGT
Convergent Solutions Inc	NAS SL	CnvSol	CSOL
Conversion Industries Inc	NAS NMS	Convsn	CVSNF
Convertible Holdings Inc	New York	ConvHld	CNV
ConVest Energy Partners Ltd	American	Convst	CEP
Convex Computer Corp	NAS NMS	Convex	CNVX
The Cooper Companies Inc	New York	CoopCo	COO
Cooper Development Co	NAS NMS	CooprD	BUGS
Cooper Industries Inc	New York	Cooper	CBE
Cooper Life Sciences Inc	NAS NMS	CooprL	ZAPSV
Cooper Tire & Rubber Co	New York	CoprTr	CTB
Adolph Coors Co (Class B)	NAS NMS	Coors B	ACCOB
Copelco Financial Services Group Inc	American	Copelc	CFG
Copley Properties Inc	American	Copley	COP
Copperweld Corp	New York	Copwld	COS
Copytele Inc	NAS NMS	Copytle	COPY
Coradian Corp	NAS SL	Coradn	CDIN
Corcap Inc	American	Corcp	CCP
Corcom Inc	NAS NMS	Corcom	CORC
Cordis Corp	NAS NMS	Cordis	CORD
Core Industries Inc	New York	CoreIn	CRI
CoreStates Financial Corp	NAS NMS	CoreSt	CSFN
Corken International Corp	NAS SL	Corken	CORK
CornerStone Financial Corp	NAS NMS	CrnrFn	CSTN
Corning Glass Works	New York	CornGl	GLW
Corona Corp (Class A)	NAS NL	CoronaA	IRAFV
Corona Corp (Class B)	NAS NL	CoronaB	IRBFV
Corporate Capital Resources Inc	NAS SL	CpCapit	CCRS
Corporate Data Sciences Inc	NAS SL	CorpDt	CODS
Corporate Management Group Inc	NAS SL	CpMgt	KORP
Corporate Software Inc	NAS NMS	CorpSft	CSOF
Corrections Corporation of America	NAS NMS	CorctCp	CCAX
Corroon & Black Corp	New York	CorBlk	CBL
Cortonic Corp	NAS SL	Cortrnc	CTRN
Corvus Systems Inc	NAS NMS	Corvus	CRVS
Cosmetic & Fragrance Concepts Inc	NAS NMS	CosmFr	COSF
Cosmo Communications Corp	NAS NMS	Cosmo	CSMO

COMPANY NAME	MARKET LISTING	NEWSPAPER ABBREV.	TRADING SYMBOL
Cosmopolitan Care Corp	American	CosmCr	CCA
Costar Corp	NAS NMS	Costar	CSTR
Costco Wholesale Corp	NAS NMS	Costco	COST
Cottage Savings Association F.A. (Ohio)	NAS NMS	CotgSv	COTG
Cotton States Life & Health Insurance Co	NAS NMS	CtnSLf	CSLH
Counsellors Tandem Securities Fund Inc	New York	CTF	CTF
Country Lake Foods Inc	NAS NMS	CtryLk	CLFI
Country Wide Transport Services Inc	NAS NMS	CWTrns	CWTS
Countrywide Credit Industries Inc	New York	CntCrd	CCR
Countrywide Mortgage Investments Inc	New York	CntrMt	CWM
County Savings Bank (California)	NAS NMS	CountyS	CSBA
Courier Corp	NAS NMS	Courer	CRRC
Courier Dispatch Group Inc	NAS NMS	CourDis	CDGI
Courtaulds PLC	American	Courtld	COU
Cousins Home Furnishings Inc	NAS NL	CousH	CUZZ
Cousins Properties Inc	NAS NMS	CousP	COUS
Covington Development Group Inc	NAS NMS	Covngt	COVT
CP National Corp	New York	CP Nt	CPN
CPAC Inc	NAS NL	CPAC	CPAK
CPB Inc	NAS NMS	CPB	CPBI
CPC International Inc	New York	CPC	CPC
CPC Rexcel Inc	NAS NMS	CPC	CPST
CPI Corp	NAS NMS	CPI	CPIC
CPS Corporate Planning Services (Class A)	NAS SL	CPS Cp	CPSIA
CPT Corp	NAS NMS	CPT	CPTC
Cracker Barrel Old Country Store Inc	NAS NMS	CrkBrl	CBRL
Craft World International Inc	NAS SL	CrftWld	CWDI
Craftmatic/Contour Industries Inc	NAS NMS	Crftmtc	CRCC
Craig Corp	New York	Craig	CRA
Crane Co	New York	Crane	CR
Crawford & Co	NAS NMS	CrwfCo	CRAW
Cray Research Inc	New York	CrayRs	CYR
Crazy Eddie Inc	NAS NMS	CrzEd	CRZY
Creative Computer Applications Inc	NAS SL	CreatvC	CCAI
Creative Technologies Corp	NAS SL	CreatTc	CRTV
Credo Petroleum Corp	NAS SL	CredoPt	CRED
Crescott Inc	NAS NMS	Crescot	CRCTC
Crestar Financial Corp	NAS NMS	Crestar	CRFC
Crested Corp	NAS SL	CrstCp	CBAG
Crestmont Federal S&L Assn (New Jersey)	NAS NMS	CrstFdl	CRES
CRI Insured Mortgage Investments L.P.	New York	CRIIM	CRM
CRI Insured Mortgage Investments II Inc	New York	CRI II	CII
CRI Insured Mortgage Investments III L.P.	New York	CRI III	CTH
Criterion Group Inc (Class A)	NAS NMS	CritGp	CRITA
Critical Industries Inc	NAS NL	CritclIn	FYBR
Criticare Systems Inc	NAS NMS	Criticre	CXIM
Crompton & Knowles Corp	New York	CrmpK	CNK

COMPANY NAME	MARKET LISTING	NEWSPAPER ABBREV.	TRADING SYMBOL
Cronus Industries Inc	NAS NMS	Cronus	CRNS
Crop Genetics International Corp	NAS NMS	CropG	CROP
Philip Crosby Associates Inc	American	Crosby	ZDC
Cross & Trecker Corp	NAS NMS	CrosTr	CTCO
A.T. Cross Co (Class A)	American	Cross	ATX.A
Crossland Savings (New York)	New York	CrosldS	CRL
Crowley, Milner & Co	American	CrowlM	COM
Crown Anderson Inc	NAS NMS	CrwnAn	CRAN
Crown Books Corp	NAS NMS	CwnBk	CRWN
Crown Brands Inc	NAS SL	CrwnBd	CRON
Crown Central Petroleum Corp (Class A)	American	CrnCP	CNP.A
Crown Central Petroleum Corp (Class B)	American	CrCPB	CNP.B
Crown Cork & Seal Company Inc	New York	CrwnCk	CCK
Crown Crafts Inc	American	CwnCr	CRW
Crown Resource Corp	NAS SL	CwnRs	CRRS
CrownAmerica Inc	NAS NL	CrwnA	CRNA
CRS Sirrine Inc	New York	CRSS	DA
CryoDynamics Inc	NAS SL	CryoDy	CRYD
Crystal Brands Inc	New York	CrysBd	CBR
Crystal Oil Co	American	CrystO	COR
CSC Industries Inc	NAS NMS	CSC Ind	CPSL
CSK Corp	NAS NL	CSK	CSKKY
CSP Inc	NAS NMS	CSP	CSPI
CSS Industries Inc	American	CSS	CSS
CSX Corp	New York	CSX	CSX
C3 Inc	New York	C 3 Inc	CEE
CTS Corp	New York	CTS	CTS
Cubic Corp	American	Cubic	CUB
CUC International Inc	NAS NMS	CUC Int	CUCD
Cucos Inc	NAS SL	Cucos	CUCO
Culbro Corp	New York	Culbro	CUC
Cullen/Frost Bankers Inc	NAS NMS	CullnFr	CFBI
Cullinet Software Inc	New York	Culinet	CUL
Cullum Companies Inc	NAS NMS	Culum	CULL
Culp Inc	NAS NMS	Culp	CULP
The Cumberland Federal Savings Bank (Kentucky)	NAS NMS	CumbrFd	CMBK
Cumberland Gold Group Inc	NAS NL	CumbR	CRIG
Cummins Engine Company Inc	New York	CumEn	CUM
Cuplex Inc	American	Cuplex	CXI
Current Income Shares Inc	New York	CurInc	CUR
Curtice-Burns Foods Inc	American	Curtce	CBI
Curtiss-Wright Corp	New York	CurtW	CW
Cusac Industries Ltd	NAS SL	Cusac	CUSIF
Customedix Corp	American	Custmd	CUS
CutCo Industries Inc	NAS NL	Cutco	CUTC
CVB Financial Corp	NAS NMS	CVBFn	CVBF
CVN Companies Inc	NAS NMS	CVN	CMCO

COMPANY NAME	MARKET LISTING	NEWSPAPER ABBREV.	TRADING SYMBOL
CXR Telecom Corp	American	CXR	CXR
Cyanotech Corp	NAS SL	Cyntch	CYAN
Cybermedic Inc	NAS SL	Cybmed	CMED
CyberOptics Corp	NAS SL	CybrOpt	CYBE
CYBERTEK Corp	NAS NMS	Cybertk	CKCP
CyCare Systems Inc	New York	Cycare	CYS
Cypress Fund Inc	American	CyprFd	WJR
Cypress Semiconductor Corp	NAS NMS	CypSem	CYPR
Cyprus Minerals Co	NAS NMS	Cyprus	CYPM
Cytogen Corp	NAS NMS	Cytogn	CYTO
CytRx Corp	NAS NMS	CytRx	CYTR
D&N Financial Corp	NAS NMS	D&N Fn	DNFC
Dahlberg Inc	NAS NMS	Dahlbrg	DAHL
The Daiei Inc (Japan)	NAS NL	DaiEi	DAIEY
Daily Journal Co	NAS NMS	DlyJour	DJCO
Dairy Mart Convenience Stores Inc (Class A)	NAS NMS	DairyA	DMCVA
Dairy Mart Convenience Stores Inc (Class B)	NAS NMS	DairyB	DMCVB
Daisy Systems Corp	NAS NMS	DaisySy	DAZY
Dallas Corp	New York	Dallas	DLS
Dallas Semiconductor Corp	NAS NMS	DalSem	DSMI
Daltex Medical Sciences Inc	NAS SL	Daltex	DLTX
Dalton Communications Inc	NAS SL	Dalton	DALT
Damon Biotech Inc	NAS NMS	DmnBio	DBIO
Damon Corp	New York	DamnC	DMN
Damon Creations Inc	American	DamCr	DNI
Damson Energy Company L.P. (Class A)	American	DamEA	DEP.A
Damson Energy Company L.P. (Class B)	American	DamEB	DEP.B
Damson Oil Corp	American	Damson	DAM
Dana Corp	New York	DanaCp	DCN
Danaher Corp	New York	Danhr	DHR
Daniel Industries Inc	New York	Daniel	DAN
Dart Drug Stores Inc	NAS SL	DartDg	DDRG
Dart Group Corp (Class A)	NAS NMS	DartGp	DARTA
Dasa Corp	NAS SL	DasaCp	DASA
Dasibi Environmental Corp	NAS SL	Dasibi	DSBE
Data-Design Laboratories Inc	New York	DtaDsg	DDL
Data General Corp	New York	DataGn	DGN
Data I/O Corp	NAS NMS	Dta IO	DAIO
Data Measurement Corp	NAS NMS	DtMea	DMCB
Data Med Clinical Support Services Inc	NAS SL	DatMC	DMCS
Data Switch Corp	NAS NMS	DtSwtch	DASW
Data Translation Inc	NAS NMS	DtaTrn	DATX
Data Transmission Network	NAS SL	DtTrNw	DTLN
Dataflex Corp	NAS NMS	Datflx	DFLX
Datakey Inc	NAS NL	Datkey	DKEY

COMPANY NAME	MARKET LISTING	NEWSPAPER ABBREV.	TRADING SYMBOL
Datamag Inc	NAS SL	Dtamg	DMAG
Datamarine International Inc	NAS NMS	Datmar	DMAR
Datametrics Corp	American	Datamet	DC
DATAPHAZ Inc	NAS NMS	Datphz	DPHZ
Datapoint Corp	New York	Datapt	DPT
Dataproducts Corp	American	DataPd	DPC
Dataram Corp	American	Datarm	DTM
Datascope Corp	NAS NMS	Datscp	DSCP
Datasouth Computer Corp	NAS NMS	Dtasth	DSCC
Datavision Inc	NAS NMS	Datvsn	DVIS
Datron Systems Inc	NAS NMS	Datron	DTSI
Datum Inc	NAS NMS	Datum	DATM
Dauphin Deposit Corp	NAS NMS	Dauphn	DAPN
Davidson Tisdale Mines Ltd	NAS NL	DavTis	DDTTF
Davis Water & Waste Industries Inc	New York	DavWtr	DWW
Davox Corp	NAS NMS	Davox	DAVX
Dawson Geophysical Co	NAS NMS	Dawson	DWSN
Daxor Corp	American	Daxor	DXR
Dayton Hudson Corp	New York	DaytHd	DH
DBA Systems Inc	NAS NMS	DBA	DBAS
DCNY Corp	New York	DCNY	DCY
DDI Pharmaceuticals Inc	NAS NMS	DDI	DDIX
De Beers Consolidated Mines Ltd	NAS NL	DBeer	DBRSY
De Laurentiis Entertainment Group Inc	American	DeLau	DEG
De Laurentiis Film Partners L.P.	American	DLauF	DFP
De Rose Industries Inc	American	DeRose	DRI
De Tomaso Industries Inc	NAS NMS	DTomas	DTOM
Dean Foods Co	New York	DeanFd	DF
Dean Witter Government Income Trust	New York	DWGI	GVT
Deb Shops Inc	NAS NMS	DebSh	DEBS
Decision Systems Inc	NAS NL	DecisSy	DCSN
Decom Systems Inc	NAS NMS	Decom	DSII
Decor Corp	NAS NMS	Decor	DCOR
Decorator Industries Inc	American	Decorat	DII
Dee Corp PLC	New York	DeeCp	DEE
Deere & Co	New York	Deere	DE
Deerfield Federal S&L Assn (Illinois)	NAS NMS	DeerfSv	DEER
Defiance Precision Products Inc	NAS NMS	DefnPr	DEFI
DEKALB Corp (Class B)	NAS NMS	Dekalb	DKLBB
Del Electronic Corp	NAS SL	DelEl	DELE
Del Laboratories Inc	American	DelLab	DLI
Del Paint Corp	NAS SL	DlPaint	DELA
Del-Val Financial Corp	New York	DelVal	DVL
Delaware Otsego Corp	NAS NMS	DelaOts	DOCP
Delaware Savings Bank F.S.B.	NAS NMS	DelSvg	DESB
Delchamps Inc	NAS NMS	Delchm	DLCH
Dell Computer Corp	NAS NMS	DellCpt	DELL
Delmarva Power & Light Co	New York	DelmP	DEW

COMPANY NAME	MARKET LISTING	NEWSPAPER ABBREV.	TRADING SYMBOL
Delmed Inc	American	Delmed	DMD
Delphi Information System Inc	NAS NMS	DelpInf	DLPH
Delta Air Lines Inc	New York	DeltaAr	DAL
Delta Data Systems Corp	NAS SL	DeltaDt	DDSC
Delta Natural Gas Company Inc	NAS NMS	DeltNG	DGAS
Delta Woodside Industries Inc	NAS NMS	DltWod	DLWD
Deltak Corp	NAS NMS	Deltak	DLTK
DeltaUS Corp	NAS NMS	Deltaus	DLTA
The Deltona Corp	New York	Deltona	DLT
Deluxe Corp	New York	Deluxe	DLX
Denning Mobile Robotics Inc	NAS SL	Denning	GARD
Dennison Manufacturing Co	New York	DensMf	DSN
Denpac Corp	NAS SL	Denpac	DNPC
Dento-Med Industries Inc	NAS NMS	DentMd	DTMD
DEP Corp	NAS NMS	DEP	DEPC
Deposit Guaranty Corp	NAS NMS	DepGty	DEPS
Derma-Lock Medical Corp	NAS SL	DermaL	DERM
Designatronics Inc	American	Dsgntrn	DSG
Designcraft Industries Inc	American	DesgnI	DJI
Designhouse International Inc	NAS SL	Desgnh	DHIN
Designs Inc	NAS NL	DsgInc	DESI
DeSoto Inc	New York	DeSoto	DSO
DEST Corp	NAS NMS	Dest	DEST
Detection Systems Inc	NAS NMS	DetSy	DETC
Detrex Corp	NAS NMD	DetrxC	CTRX
Detroit & Canada Tunnel Corp	NAS NL	DetCan	DTUN
The Detroit Edison Co	New York	DetEd	DTE
Devcon International Corp	NAS NMS	Devcon	DEVC
Develcon Electronics Ltd	NAS NL	Develcn	DLCFF
Devon Group Inc	NAS NMS	Devon	DEVN
Dewey Electronic Corp	NAS NMS	Dewey	DEWY
Dexon Inc	NAS SL	Dexon	DEXO
The Dexter Corp	New York	Dexter	DEX
DH Technology Inc	NAS NMS	DH Tch	DHTK
Di Giorgio Corp	New York	DiGior	DIG
DI Industries Inc	American	DI Ind	DRL
Diagnostek Inc	NAS NMS	Diagnst	DXTK
Diagnostic Products Corp	New York	DiagPr	DP
Diagnostic/Retrieval Systems Inc (Class A)	American	Diag A	DRS.A
Diagnostic/Retrieval Systems Inc (Class B)	American	Diag B	DRS.B
Diagnostic Sciences Inc	NAS SL	DiagSc	DSIC
Diagonal Data Corp	NAS NL	DiagDt	DDAT
Dial REIT Inc	NAS NL	Dial Re	DEAL
Diamond Shamrock Offshore Partners L.P.	New York	DiaSO	DSP
Diamond Shamrock R&M Inc	New York	DShRM	DRM
The Diana Corp	New York	DianaCp	DNA

COMPANY NAME	MARKET LISTING	NEWSPAPER ABBREV.	TRADING SYMBOL
Diasonics Inc	American	Diasonc	DIA
Dibrell Brothers Inc	NAS NMS	Dibrel	DBRL
Diceon Electronics Inc	NAS NMS	Diceon	DICN
dick clark productions inc	NAS NMS	DClark	DCPI
Dickenson Mines Ltd (Class A)	American	DckMA	DML.A
Dickenson Mines Ltd	American	DckMB	DML.B
Diebold Inc	New York	Diebold	DBD
Digilog Inc	NAS NMS	Diglog	DILO
Digital Communications Associates Inc	New York	DigtlCm	DCA
Digital Equipment Corp	New York	Digital	DEC
Digital Microwave Corp	NAS NMS	DigMic	DMIC
Digital Optronics Corp	NAS SL	Digtl0p	DOCC
Digital Products Corp	NAS SL	DigPd	DIPC
Digital Solutions Inc	NAS SL	Digtl Sol	DGSI
Digital Transmission Inc (Class A)	NAS SL	DigTrA	DTINA
Digitech Inc	NAS NMS	Digtch	DGTC
Digitext Inc	NAS SL	Digitxt	DIGT
Dillard Department Stores Inc (Class A)	American	Dillard	DDS.A
Dime Savings Bank of New York FSB (Garden City)	New York	DimeNY	DME
The Dime Savings Bank of Wallingford (Connecticut)	NAS NMS	DimeCT	DIBK
Dimensional Medicine Inc	NAS SL	DimenMd	DMED
Diodes Inc	American	Diodes	DIO
Dionex Corp	NAS NMS	Dionex	DNEX
Dionics Inc	NAS NMS	Dionic	DION
Direct Action Marketing Inc	American	DirActn	DMK
Direct Pharmaceutical Corp	NAS SL	DctPhr	DPRX
Discovery Associates Inc	NAS SL	DisAsc	DIVY
Discus Corp	NAS SL	Discus	DISC
Disease Detection International Inc	NAS SL	DisDet	DIDII
The Walt Disney Co	New York	Disney	DIS
Distributed Logic Corp	NAS NMS	DistLog	DLOG
Diversco Inc	NAS NMS	Divrsc	DVRS
Diversified Energies Inc	New York	DEI	DEI
Diversified Foods Corp	NAS NMS	DvFood	DIFSD
Diversified Human Resources Group Inc	NAS SL	DivHum	HIRE
Diversified Industries Inc	New York	DivrsIn	DMC
Diversified Investment Group Inc	NAS NMS	DivInvt	DING
Diversified Technology Inc	NAS SL	DivTch	DVTI
Divi Hotels N.V.	American	DiviHtl	DVH
Dixie National Corp	NAS NL	DixieNt	DNLC
Dixie Yarns Inc	NAS NMS	DixieYr	DXYN
Dixieline Products Inc	American	Dixilne	DIX
Dixon Ticonderoga Co	American	DixnTi	DXT
Dixons Group plc	New York	DixnGp	DXN
DMI Furniture Inc	NAS NL	DMI	DMIF
DNA Plant Technology Corp	NAS NMS	DNA Pl	DNAP

COMPANY NAME	MARKET LISTING	NEWSPAPER ABBREV.	TRADING SYMBOL
D.O.C. Optics Corp	NAS NMS	DOC	COCO
Docugraphix Inc	NAS SL	Docgph	DOCX
Dollar General Corp	NAS NMS	DlrGnl	DOLR
Domain Technology Inc	NAS NMS	DomnT	DOMN
Dominguez Water Corp	NAS NMS	Domng	DOMZ
Dominion Bankshares Corp	NAS NMS	DomBk	DMBK
Dominion Federal S&L Assn (Virginia)	NAS NMS	DmnFdl	DFED
Dominion Resources Inc	New York	DomRs	D
Domtar Inc	New York	Domtr	DTC
Donaldson Company Inc	New York	Donald	DCI
Donegal Resources Ltd	NAS NMS	Donegal	DONEF
R.R. Donnelley & Sons Co	New York	Donley	DNY
Donnelly Corp	American	DonlyC	DON
Doskocil Companies Inc	NAS NMS	Doskcl	DOSK
Dotronix Inc	NAS NMS	Dotrnix	DOTX
Doughties's Foods Inc	NAS NL	Dghtie	DOBQ
Douglas & Lomason Co	NAS NMS	DglLom	DOUG
Dover Corp	New York	Dover	DOV
Dover Regional Financial Shares	NAS NL	DovrReg	DVRFS
The Dow Chemical Co	New York	DowCh	DOW
Dow Jones & Company Inc	New York	DowJns	DJ
Downey Designs International Inc	NAS NMS	DwnyDs	DDDI
Downey S&L Assn	New York	Downey	DSL
DPL Inc	New York	DPL	DPL
Dranetz Technologies Inc	NAS NMS	Drantz	DRAN
Dravo Corp	New York	Dravo	DRV
Dresdner Bank A.G.	NAS NL	DresBk	DRSDY
Dresher Inc	NAS NMS	Dreshr	DRES
The Dress Barn Inc	NAS NMS	DresB	DBRN
Dresser Industries Inc	New York	Dresr	DI
Drew Industries Inc	NAS NMS	DrewIn	DRWI
Drewry Photocolor Corp	NAS SL	Drewry	DREW
Drexel Bond-Debenture Trading Fund	New York	DrexB	DBF
Drexler Technology Corp	NAS NMS	Drexlr	DRXR
Dreyer's Grand Ice Cream Inc	NAS NMS	DreyGr	DRYR
The Dreyfus Corp	New York	Dreyfus	DRY
Dreyfus Strategic Government Income Fund	New York	DryStGn	DSI
Dreyfus Strategic Municipals Inc	New York	DryStr	LEO
Driefontein Consolidated Ltd	NAS NL	DriefC	DRFNY
Driver-Harris Co	American	DrivHar	DRH
Drug Emporium Inc	NAS NMS	DrgEm	DEMP
DRX Inc	NAS SL	DRX	DTRH
DS Bancor Inc (Connecticut)	NAS NMS	DS Bnc	DSBC
DSC Communications Corp	NAS NMS	DSC	DIGI
DST Systems Inc	NAS NMS	DST	DSTS
E.I. du Pont de Nemours & Co	New York	duPont	DD
Ducommun Inc	American	Ducom	DCO
Duff & Phelps Selected Utilities	New York	DuffPh	DNP

COMPANY NAME	MARKET LISTING	NEWSPAPER ABBREV.	TRADING SYMBOL
Duke Power Co	New York	DukeP	DUK
Duke Realty Investments Inc	New York	DukeRIn	DRE
Dumagami Mines Ltd	NAS NMS	Dumag	DMGIF
The Dun & Bradstreet Corp	New York	DunBd	DNB
Dunkin' Donuts Inc	NAS NMS	DunkDn	DUNK
Duplex Products Inc	American	Duplex	DPX
Duquesne Light Co	New York	DuqLt	DQU
Duquesne Systems Inc	NAS NMS	DuqSys	DUQN
Durakon Industries Inc	NAS NMS	Durkn	DRKN
Duramed Pharmaceuticals Inc	NAS NMS	Duramd	DRMD
Duratek Corp	NAS NMS	Duratek	DRTK
Durham Corp	NAS NMS	Durhm	DUCO
The Duriron Company Inc	NAS NMS	Duriron	DURI
Durr-Fillauer Medical Inc	NAS NMS	DurFil	DUFM
Dust Mac Mines Ltd	NAS SL	DustMc	DUSTF
Duty Free International Inc	American	DtyFr	DFI
DVI Financial Corp	NAS SL	DVIFn	DVIC
DWG Corp	American	DWG	DWG
DWI Corp	NAS SL	DWI	DWIC
Dyansen Corp	NAS NMS	Dyansn	DYAN
Dyatron Corp	NAS NMS	Dyatrn	DYTR
Dycom Industries Inc	NAS NMS	Dycom	DYCO
Dynamic Classics Ltd	NAS SL	DynCls	DYNC
Dynamic Sciences International Inc	NAS SL	DynmcSc	DYNS
Dynamics Corporation of America	New York	DynAm	DYA
Dynamics Research Corp	NAS NMS	DynRs	DRCO
Dynascan Corp	NAS NMS	Dynsc	DYNA
Dynatech Corp	NAS NMS	DytchC	DYTC
Dynatronics Laser Corp	NAS SL	DyntrL	DYNT
DynCorp	New York	Dyncrp	DYN
E&B Marine Inc	NAS NMS	EB Mar	EBMI
E-Systems Inc	New York	E Syst	ESY
E'town Corp	NAS NMS	ETown	EWAT
E-Z-Em Inc	NAS NMS	EZEM	EZEM
EA Engineering Science & Technology Inc	NAS NMS	EA Eng	EACO
EAC Industries Inc	American	EAC	EAC
Eagle Bancorp Inc	NAS NMS	EglBnc	EBCI
Eagle Bancshares Inc	NAS NMS	EaglBn	EBSI
Eagle Clothes Inc	American	EaglCl	EGL
Eagle Financial Corp	American	EaglFn	EAGL
Eagle-Picher Industries Inc	New York	EagleP	EPI
Eagle Telephonics Inc	NAS NMS	EagTl	EGLC
The Earth Technology Corp	NAS NMS	EarthT	ETCO
Easco Hand Tools Inc	NAS NMS	Easco	TOOL
East Texas S&L Assn of Tyler Texas	NAS NL	EastTx	ETSL
East Weymouth Savings Bank (Massachusetts)	NAS NMS	EastWy	EWSB

COMPANY NAME	MARKET LISTING	NEWSPAPER ABBREV.	TRADING SYMBOL
Eastco Industrial Safety Corp	NAS SL	Eastco	ESTO
Eastern Bancorp Inc	NAS NMS	EstnBc	VFBK
The Eastern Co	American	EstnCo	EML
Eastern Environmental Services Inc	NAS NMS	EstnEn	EESI
Eastern Gas & Fuel Associates	New York	EastGF	EFU
Eastern Utilities Associates	New York	EastUtl	EUA
Eastex Energy Inc	NAS NMS	Eastex	ETEX
EastGroup Properties	American	Estgp	EGP
Eastland Financial Corp	NAS NMS	EastFn	EAFC
Eastman Kodak Co	New York	EKodk	EK
Eastmaque Gold Mines Ltd	NAS NL	Estmaq	EMGVF
Eastover Bank for Savings (Mississippi)	NAS NL	EastBk	EOBK
Eaton Corp	New York	Eaton	ETN
Eaton Financial Corp	NAS NMS	EatnFn	EATO
Eaton Vance Corp	NAS NMS	EatVan	EAVN
ECC International Corp	New York	ECC	ECC
Echlin Inc	New York	Echlin	ECH
Echo Bay Mines Ltd	American	EchoB	ECO
ECI Telecom Ltd	NAS NMS	ECI Tel	ECILF
Ecogen Inc	American	Ecogn	ECN
Ecolab Inc	New York	Ecolab	ECL
Ecology & Environment Inc (Class A)	American	EcolEn	EEI.A
ECRM Inc	NAS NL	ECRM	new
Edac Technologies Corp	NAS NL	Edac	EDAC
Edgcomb Corp	NAS NMS	Edgcmb	EDGC
Edison Brothers Stores Inc	New York	EdisBr	EBS
Edison Control Corp	NAS NMS	EdisCtr	EDCO
Edison Sault Electric Co	NAS NMS	EdSault	EDSE
EDO Corp	New York	EDO	EDO
A.G. Edwards Inc	New York	Edward	AGE
EECO Inc	American	EECO	EEC
EFI Electronics Corp	NAS SL	EFIEle	EFIC
EG&G Inc	New York	EGG	EGG
Egghead Inc	NAS NL	Egghead	EGGS
Ehrlich Bober Financial Corp	American	EhrBbr	EB
E.I.L. Instruments Inc	NAS NMS	EIL Inst	EILI
EIP Microwave Inc	NAS NMS	EIP	EIPM
El Chico Corp	NAS NMS	ElChic	ELCH
El-De-Electro-Optic Development Ltd	NAS SL	ElDe El	ELOPF
El Pollo Asado Inc	NAS NMS	ElPollo	EPAI
El Paso Electric Co	NAS NMS	ElPas	ELPA
Elan Corporation plc	NAS NMS	Elan	ELANY
Elbit Computers Ltd	NAS NMS	Elbit	ELBTF
Elco Inudstries Inc	NAS NMS	Elco	ELCN
Elcor Corp	New York	Elcor	ELK
Elcotel Inc	NAS NMS	Elcotel	ECTL
Eldec Corp	NAS NMS	Eldec	ELDC

COMPANY NAME	MARKET LISTING	NEWSPAPER ABBREV.	TRADING SYMBOL
Eldon Industries Inc	New York	Eldon	ELD
Eldorado Bancorp	American	Eldorad	ELB
ElDorado Motor Corp	NAS SL	EldrM	EDMC
Electro-Catheter Corp	NAS NMS	ElCath	ECTH
Electro-Nucleonics Inc	NAS NMS	EleNucl	ENUC
Electro Rent Corp	NAS NMS	ElcRnt	ELRC
Electro Scientific Industries Inc	NAS NMS	ElcSci	ESIO
Electro-Sensors Inc	NAS NMS	ElcSens	ELSE
Electrolux AB (Class B)	NAS NMS	EluxAB	ELUXY
Electromagnetic Sciences Inc	NAS NMS	Elctmg	ELMG
Electromedics Inc	NAS SL	Elcmd	ELMD
Electronic Associates Inc	New York	ElecAs	EA
Electronic Control Systems Inc	NAS SL	ElctCtr	ELCS
Electronic Data Technologies	NAS NL	ElcDta	EDAT
Electronic Specialty Products Inc	NAS SL	ElctSpc	GEMS
Electronic Tele-Communications Inc (Class A)	NAS NMS	ElecTel	ETCIA
Electronics Missiles & Communications Inc	NAS SL	ElctMis	ECIN
ElectroSound Group Inc	American	ElecSd	ESD
Electrosource Inc	NAS SL	Elctsrc	ELSI
Elexis Corp	NAS NMS	Elexis	ELEX
Elgin National Industries Inc	New York	Elgin	ENW
Eli Scientific Inc	NAS SL	EliSci	ELIS
Eliot Savings Bank (Massachusetts)	NAS NMS	EliotSv	EBKC
Ellsworth Convertible Growth & Income Fund Inc	American	Elswth	ECF
Elmira Savings Bank FSB	NAS SL	ElmrSv	ESBK
Elmwood Federsl Savings Bank (Pennsylvania)	NAS NMS	ElmwdFd	EFSB
Elron Electronic Industries Ltd	NAS NMS	ElronEl	ELRNF
Elscint Ltd	New York	Elscint	ELT
Elsinore Corp	American	Elsinor	ELS
ELXSI Corp	NAS NMS	ELXSI	ELSX
EMC Corp	New York	EMC	EMC
EMC Insurance Group Inc	NAS NMS	EMC In	EMCI
EMCON Associates	NAS NMS	EMCON	MCON
Emerald Homes L.P.	New York	Emrld	EHP
Emerson Electric Co	New York	EmrsE	EMR
Emerson Radio Corp	New York	EmRad	EME
Emery Air Freight Corp	New York	EmryA	EAF
Emhart Corp	New York	Emhrt	EMH
EMPI Inc	NAS NMS	EMPI	EMPI
The Empire District Electric Co	New York	EmpDs	EDE
Empire Gas Corp	NAS SL	EmpGs	EGCSC
Empire of America Federal Savings Bank	American	EmpirA	EOA
Empire of Carolina Inc	American	EmCar	EMP

COMPANY NAME	MARKET LISTING	NEWSPAPER ABBREV.	TRADING SYMBOL
Empire-Orr Inc	NAS NMS	EmpOrr	EORR
Empire Savings Bank SLA (New Jersey)	NAS NMS	EmpSB	EMPR
Employers Casualty Co	NAS NL	EmpCas	ECRC
Empress Nacional de Electricidad sa	New York	EmpNa	ELE
EMS Systems Ltd	NAS SL	EMS Sy	EMSIF
Emulex Corp	NAS NMS	Emulex	EMLX
Encore Computer Corp	NAS NMS	Encore	ENCC
Encore Marketing International Inc	American	EncrM	EMI
Endevco Inc	American	Endvco	EI
Energas Co	NAS NMS	Enrgas	EGAS
Energen Corp	New York	Energen	EGN
Energy Assets International Corp	NAS SL	EnAset	EAIC
Energy Capital Development Corp	NAS SL	EnCap	ECDC
Energy Conversion Devices Inc	NAS NMS	EngCnv	ENER
Energy Development Partners Ltd	American	EnDvl	EDP
Energy Service Company Inc	American	ENSCO	ESV
EnergyNorth Inc	NAS NMS	Engnth	ENNI
ENEX Resources Corp	NAS NMS	EnexR	ENEX
Engelhard Corp	New York	EnglC	EC
Engex Inc	American	Engex	EGX
Engineered Support Systems Inc	NAS NMS	EngnSu	EAST
Engineered Systems & Development Corp	American	ESD	ESD
Engineering Measurements Co	NAS NMS	EngMea	EMCO
English China Clays Public Limited Co	NAS NMS	EngChn	ECLAY
English Greenhouse Products Corp	NAS SL	EngGrh	EGPC
Engraph Inc	NAS NMS	Engrph	ENGH
Ennis Business Forms Inc	New York	EnisBu	EBF
Enron Corp	New York	Enron	ENE
Enron Oil & Gas Co	New York	EnrOG	ENG
Enscor Inc	NAS NL	Enscor	ENCRF
Enseco Inc	NAS NMS	Enseco	NCCO
ENSERCH Corp	New York	Ensrch	ENS
Enserch Exploration Partners Ltd	New York	EnsExp	EP
Ensource Inc	New York	Ensrce	EEE
ENSR Corp	American	ENSR	ENX
Enterra Corp	New York	Entera	EN
Entertainment Marketing Inc	American	EntMkt	EM
Entertainment Publications Inc	NAS NMS	EntPub	EPUB
Entré Computer Centers Inc	NAS NMS	EntrCpt	ETRE
Entree Corp	NAS NMS	EntreCp	ETRC
Entronics Corp	NAS NMS	Entrnc	ENTC
Entwistle Co	NAS SL	Entwist	ENTW
Envirodyne Industries Inc	NAS NMS	Envrd	ENVR
Environmental Control Group Inc	NAS NMS	EnvCtl	ECGI
Environmental Diagnostics Inc	NAS SL	EnvDia	EDIT
Environmental Power Corp	NAS NMS	EnvPwr	POWR
Environmental Systems Co	New York	EnvSys	ESC
Environmental Tectonics Corp	NAS NMS	EnvrTc	ENVT

COMPANY NAME	MARKET LISTING	NEWSPAPER ABBREV.	TRADING SYMBOL
Environmental Treatment & Technologies Corp	New York	EnvTrt	ETT
Enviropact Inc	American	Envrpct	ENV
Envirosafe Services Inc	NAS NMS	Envirsf	ENVI
Envirosure Management Corp	NAS SL	Envrsur	ENVS
Enzo Biochem Inc	American	AnzoBi	ENZ
Enzon Inc	NAS NMS	Enzon	ENZN
Epic Health Group Inc	NAS SL	EpicHlt	EPIC
Epitope Inc	NAS SL	Epitope	EPTO
EPSCO Inc	NAS NMS	Epsco	EPSC
Epsilon Data Management Inc	NAS NMS	Epsiln	EPSI
EQK Green Acres L.P.	New York	EQK G	EGA
EQK Realty Investors I	New York	EQK Rt	EKR
Equifax Inc	New York	Equifax	EFX
Equimark Corp	New York	Equimk	EQK
The Equion Corp	NAS NMS	Equion	EQUI
Equipment Company of America	NAS SL	EqAm	ECOA
Equitable Bancorporation (Maryland)	NAS NMS	EqtBcp	EBNC
Equitable of Iowa Companies (Class A)	NAS NL	EqtIA	EQICA
Equitable of Iowa Companies (Class B)	NAS NMS	EqtIB	EQICB
Equitable Real Estate Shopping Centers L.P.	New York	EqtRl	EQM
Equitable Resources Inc	New York	EqtRes	EQT
Equitec Financial Group Inc	New York	Equitec	EFG
Equitex Inc	NAS NMS	Equitex	EQTX
Equity Bank (Connecticut)	NAS SL	EqtyBk	EQBK
Equity Oil Co	NAS NMS	EqtOil	EQTY
Erbamont N.V.	New York	Erbmnt	ERB
ERC International Inc	New York	ERC	ERC
LM Ericsson Telephone Co	NAS NMS	EricTl	ERICY
Erly Industries Inc	NAS NMS	ErlyInd	ERLY
Ero Industries Inc	American	Ero	ERO
Escagenitics Corp	American	Escagn	ESN
Escalade Inc	NAS NMS	Escalde	ESCA
ESI Industries Inc (Class A)	American	ESI	ESI.A
Espey Mfg & Electronics Corp	American	Espey	ESP
Esprit Systems Inc	American	Esprit	ETI
Esquire Radio & Electronics Inc	American	EsqRd	EE
ESSEF Corp	NAS NMS	ESSEF	ESSF
Esselte Business Systems Inc	New York	EssBus	ESB
Essex Chemical Corp	New York	EsexCh	ESX
Essex Corp	NAS NMS	Essex	ESEX
Essex County Gas Co	NAS NL	EsexCty	ECGC
Esterline Corp	New York	Estrlne	ESL
Ethyl Corp	New York	Ethyl	EY
Etz Lavud Ltd	American	EtzLav	ETZ
Eurocapital Corp	NAS SL	Eurocap	EURO
Evans & Sutherland Computer Corp	NAS NMS	EvnSut	ESCC

COMPANY NAME	MARKET LISTING	NEWSPAPER ABBREV.	TRADING SYMBOL
Evans Inc	NAS NMS	Evans	EVAN
Evansville Federal Savings Bank	NAS NMS	EvnsFS	EVSB
Everest & Jennings International Ltd (Class A)	American	EvrJ A	EJ.A
Everest & Jennings International Ltd (Class B)	American	EvrJ B	EJ.B
Everex Systems Inc	NAS NMS	Everex	EVRX
Evergood Products Inc	NAS NMS	Evrgd	EVFG
Evergreen Resources Inc	NAS NMS	Evrgrn	EVER
Exar Corp	NAS NMS	Exar	EXAR
Excel Bancorp Inc	NAS NMS	ExcelBc	XCEL
Excel Industries Inc	American	Excel	EXC
Excelan Inc	NAS NMS	Exceln	EXLN
Excelsior Income Shares Inc	New York	Excelsr	EIS
Exchange Bancorp Inc	NAS NMS	ExchBc	EXCG
Executive Telecommunications Inc	NAS SL	ExecTl	XTEL
Executone Information Systems Inc	NAS NMS	Exctne	XTON
Exovir Inc	NAS NMS	Exovir	XOVR
Expeditors International of Washington Inc	NAS NMS	ExpIn	EXPD
Exploration Co	NAS SL	Explor	TXCO
The Exploration Company of Louisiana Inc	NAS NMS	ExpLa	XCOL
Exposaic Industries Inc	NAS NMS	Exposc	EXPO
Exxon Corp	New York	Exxon	XON
F&M Financial Services Corp	NAS NMS	F&M	FMFS
F&M National Corp	NAS NMS	FM Nt	FMNT
Fab Industries Inc	American	FabInd	FIT
Fabri-Centers of America Inc	New York	FabCtr	FCA
Fabricland Inc	NAS NMS	Fabric	FBRC
Fair, Isaac & Company Inc	NAS NMS	FairIsc	FICI
Fairchild Industries Inc	New York	Fairchd	FEN
Fairfield Communities Inc	New York	Fairfd	FCI
Fairfield 1st Bank & Trust Co	NAS SL	FairFst	FRBK
Fairfield-Noble Corp	NAS NMS	FairNbl	FARF
Fairhaven International Ltd	NAS SL	Fairhvn	NIMSY
Falcon Cable Systems Company LP	American	FalCbl	FAL
Falcon Products Inc	NAS SL	FalcnPr	FLCP
Falconbridge Ltd	NAS NL	FalcLt	FALCF
FalcoOil & Gas Company Inc	NAS NMS	FalcoOil	FLOG
Fallstaff Brewing Corp	NAS NL	Falstaff	FALB
Famiglia Brands Inc	NAS SL	Famigl	FAMI
Family Bancorp	NAS NMS	FamBc	FMLY
Family Dollar Stores Inc	New York	FamDlr	FDO
Family Steak Houses of Florida Inc	NAS NMS	FamSt	RYFL
Famous Restaurants Inc	NAS NMS	FamRst	FAMS
Fansteel Inc	New York	Fanstel	FNL
Far West Financial Corp	New York	FarWst	FWF

COMPANY NAME	MARKET LISTING	NEWSPAPER ABBREV.	TRADING SYMBOL
Faradyne Electronics Corp	NAS NMS	FaradE	FARA
Farah Manufacturing Company Inc	New York	Farah	FRA
Farm & Home Savings Assn (Missouri)	NAS NMS	FrmHm	FAHS
Farm Fresh Inc	NAS NMS	FarmF	FFSH
Farm House Foods Corp	NAS NMS	FarHou	FHFC
Farmer Brothers Co	NAS NMS	FarmBr	FARM
Farmers Capital Bank Corp	NAS NL	FrmCB	FFKT
Farmers Group Inc	NAS NMS	FarGp	FGRP
Farmstead Telephone Group Inc	NAS SL	FarmTel	FONE
Farr Co	NAS NMS	Farr	FARC
Farragut Mortgage Co	NAS NMS	Fargut	FARR
Fastenal Co	NAS NMS	Fastenl	FAST
Fay's Drug Company Inc	New York	FayDrg	FAY
FB&T Corp	NAS NL	FB&T	FBTC
FBX Corp	NAS NMS	FBX	FBXC
FCS Labs Inc	NAS SL	FCS	FCSI
FDP Corp	NAS NMS	FDP	FDPC
Fedders Corp	New York	Feders	FJQ
Federal Express Corp	New York	FedExp	FDX
Federal-Mogul Corp	New York	FdMog	FMO
Federal National Mortgage Assn	New York	FedNM	FNM
Federal Paper Board Company Inc	New York	Fed1PB	FBO
Federal Realty Investment Trust	New York	FedRlty	FRT
Federal Resources Corp	NAS SL	Fd1Rsc	FDRC
The Federal Savings Bank (Connectucut)	NAS NMS	FdSvBk	TFSB
Federal Screw Works	NAS NMS	FdScrw	FSCR
Federal Signal Corp	New York	FdSgnl	FSS
Federated Financial S&L Assn (Wisconsin)	NAS NMS	FFnSL	FEDF
Federated Natural Resources Corp (Class B)	NAS NL	FedNtl	FNRCB
Ferro Corp	New York	Ferro	FOE
Ferrofluidics Corp	NAS NMS	Feroflu	FERO
Fertil-A-Chron Inc	NAS SL	Fertil	FRTL
Fertility & Genetics Research Inc	NAS SL	FertGn	BABY
FFB Corp	NAS NMS	FFB Cp	FFCT
FFP Partners L.P.	American	FFP	FFP
FGIC Corp	New York	FGIC	FGC
FHP International Corp	NAS NMS	FHP	FHPC
Fibreboard Corp	American	Fibrbd	FBD
Fibronics International Inc	NAS NMS	Fibronc	FBRX
Fidata Corp	American	Fidata	FID
Fidelity Federal S&L Assn of Tennessee	NAS NMS	FidFTn	FFTN
Fidelity Federal Savings Bank (Indiana)	NAS NMS	FFdIndi	FFMA
Fidelity Medical Inc	NAS SL	Fid1Md	FMSI
Fidelity National Financial Inc	American	Fid1Fn	FNF
Fidelity Savings Assn	NAS NL	FidSvA	FSVA
Fieldcrest Cannon Inc	New York	Fldcrst	FLD
Fifth Third Bancorp (Ohio)	NAS NMS	FifthT	FITB

COMPANY NAME	MARKET LISTING	NEWSPAPER ABBREV.	TRADING SYMBOL
Figgie International Holdings Inc (Class A)	NAS NMS	FiggieA	FIGIA
Fiddig International Holdings Inc (Class B)	NAS NMS	FiggieB	FIGIB
FileNet Corp	NAS NMS	FileNet	FILE
The Filtertek Companies	New York	Filtrk	FTK
Finalco Group Inc	NAS SL	Finalco	FLCO
Financial Benefit Group Inc (Class A)	NAS NL	FnBenA	FBGIA
Financial Corporation of America	New York	FinCpA	FIN
Financial Corporation of Santa Barbara	New York	FnSBar	FSB
Financial Industries Corp	NAS NL	FinlInd	FNIN
Financial News Composite Fund Inc	New York	FinNws	FIF
Financial News Network Inc	NAS NMS	FinNws	FNNI
Financial Trust Corp	NAS NMS	FnTrst	FITC
Find SVP Inc	NAS SL	Fnd SVP	FSVP
Finevest Foods Inc	New York	Finvst	FVF
Fingermatrix Inc	NAS NMS	Fingmx	FINX
Finnigan Corp	NAS NMS	Finigan	FNNG
Firecom Inc	NAS SL	Firecm	FRCM
Fireman's Fund Corp	New York	FireFd	FFC
First Alabama Bancshares Inc	NAS NMS	FAlaBk	FABC
First Albany Companies Inc	NAS NMS	FAlban	FACT
First Amarillo Bancorporation Inc	NAS NMS	FtAmar	FAMA
1st American Bancorp (Massachusetts)	NAS NMS	FtABcp	FAMB
First American Bank & Trust of Palm Beach County (Class A) (Florida)	NAS NMS	FABk A	FIAMA
First American Bank & Trust of Palm Beach County (Class B) (Florida)	NAS NL	FABk B	FIAMB
First American Cable Corp	NAS SL	FtAmCb	FATV
The First American Financial Corp	NAS NMS	FtAFn	FAMR
First American Corp (Tennessee)	NAS NMS	FtATn	FATN
First American Health Concepts Inc	NAS SL	FAmHlt	FAHC
First American Savings F.A. (Pennsylvania)	NAS NMS	FtAmSv	FSAM
First American Savings Bank FSB (Ohio)	NAS NMS	FACant	FASB
First AmFed Corp	NAS NMS	FtAFd	FAMF
The First Australia Fund Inc	American	FtAust	IAF
First Australia Prime Income Fund Inc	American	FAusPr	FAX
First Banc Securities Inc	NAS NMS	FtBnSc	FBSI
First Bancorp (North Carolina)	NAS NMS	FtBNC	FBNC
First Bancorporation of Ohio	NAS NMS	FBOh	FBOH
First Bank of Philadelphia	NAS SL	FBkPhl	FBKP
First Bank System Inc	New York	FtBkSy	FBS
First Boston Inc	New York	FBostn	FBC
First Boston Income Fund Inc	New York	FBosIF	FBF
First Boston Strategic Income Fund Inc	New York	FBosSt	FBI
First Capital Corp	NAS NMS	FtCapt	FCAP
First Capital Holdings Corp	New York	FCapHd	FCH

COMPANY NAME	MARKET LISTING	NEWSPAPER ABBREV.	TRADING SYMBOL
First Capitol Financial Corp (Colorado)	NAS NMS	FCapFn	FCFI
First Carolina Investors Inc	NAS NL	FtCarIn	FCAR
First Centennial Corp (Class A)	NAS SL	FCentn	FCLCA
First Central Financial Corp	American	FtCntrl	FCC
First Charter Corp	NAS NMS	FChart	FCTR
First Chicago Corp	New York	FstChic	FNB
First Citizens Bancshares Inc (Class A)	NAS NMS	FCtzBA	FCNCA
First Citizens Bancshares Inc (Class B)	NAS NMS	FCtzBB	FCNCB
First City Bankcorporation of Texas Inc	New York	FtBTex	FBT
First City Industries Inc	New York	FtCity	FCY
First Colonial Bankshares Corp (Class A) (Illinois)	NAS NMS	FColB	FCOLA
First Colorado Financial Corp	NAS NMS	FtColFn	FFCS
First Commerce Bancshares Inc (Nebraska)	NAS NL	FComrB	FCBI
First Commerce Corp (Louisiana)	NAS NMS	FComC	FCOM
First Commercial Bancorp (California)	NAS NMS	FComB	FCOB
First Commercial Bancshares (Alabama)	NAS NMS	FCmBc	FSCB
First Commercial Corp (Arkansas)	NAS NMS	FCmcl	FCLR
First Community Bancorp Inc (Illinois)	NAS NMS	FCmB	FRFD
The First Connecticut Small Business Investment Co	American	FtConn	FCO
First Eastern Corp (Pennsylvania)	NAS NMS	FtEstn	FEBC
First Empire State Corp	American	FEmp	FES
First Essex Bancorp Inc	NAS NMS	FtEsex	FESX
First Executive Corp	NAS NMS	FtExec	FEXC
First Family Group Inc	NAS NMS	FtFaml	FFAM
First Farwest Corp	NAS NMS	FFwst	FFWS
First Federal Bancorp Inc (Michigan)	American	FFBcp	FFS
First Federal of Alabama FSB	NAS NMS	FtFAla	FFAL
First Federal of Michigan	NAS NMS	FFMic	FFOM
First Federal of Western Pennsylvania	NAS NMS	FFWPa	FFWP
First Federal S&L Assn (Columbia, Tennessee)	NAS NL	FFColTn	FCTN
First Federal S&L Assn of Chattanooga	NAS NMS	FFdChat	FCHT
First Federal S&L Assn of Coeur D'Alene	NAS NMS	FFdCD	FCDA
First Federal S&L Assn of East Hartford	NAS NMS	FFdEH	FFES
First Federal S&L Assn of Fort Myers	NAS NMS	FFFtM	FFMY
First Federal S&L Assn of Georgetown	NAS NL	FFGtwn	FFGT
First Federal S&L Assn of Harrisburg	NAS NMS	FFdHar	FFHP
First Federal S&L Assn of LaGrange	NAS NMS	FFdLaG	FLAG
First Federal S&L Assn of Lenawee County	NAS NMS	FFdLen	LFSA
First Federal S&L Assn of South Carolina	NAS NMS	FtFdSC	FTSC
First Federal S&L Assn of Wooster (Ohio)	NAS NMS	FFWoos	FFSW
First Federal S&L of Kalamazoo	NAS NMS	FtFKal	FFKZ
First Federal Savings Bank (Alabama)	NAS NMS	FFdAla	FFSD
First Federal Savings Bank (Tennessee)	NAS NMS	FFDTn	FFOD

COMPANY NAME	MARKET LISTING	NEWSPAPER ABBREV.	TRADING SYMBOL
First Federal Savings Bank of Charlotte County (Florida)	NAS NMS	FFdChl	FSCC
First Federal Savings Bank of Elizabethtown (Kentucky)	NAS NMS	FFdElz	FFKY
First Federal Savings Bank of Georgia	NAS NMS	FFdGa	FSBG
First Federal Savings Bank of Montana	NAS NMS	FFMon	FFSM
First Federal Savings Bank of Perry	NAS NL	FtFdPry	FPRY
First Federal Savings Bank of Puerto Rico	NAS NMS	FFdPR	FFPR
First Federal Savings Bank of Tennessee	NAS NL	FtFdTn	FTSB
First Federal Savings of Arkansas F.A.	NAS NMS	FFArk	FARK
First Fidelity Bancorp Inc (West Virginia)	NAS NMS	FFidWV	FFWV
First Fidelity Bancorporation (New Jersey)	New York	FFB	FFB
First Financial Bancorp (Ohio)	NAS NMS	FFncl	FFBC
First Financial Corp (Wisconsin)	NAS NMS	FtFnCp	FFHC
First Financial Fund Inc	New York	FFinFd	FF
First Financial Holdings Inc (West Virginia)	NAS NMS	FtFnHd	FFCH
First Financial Management Corp	NAS NMS	FtFnMg	FFMC
First Financial Savings Assn F.A. (Ohio)	NAS NMS	FtFnSv	FFNS
First Financial Savings Assn (Pennsylvania)	NAS NMS	FFncPa	FIRF
First Fincorp Inc	NAS NL	FFncrp	FIFC
First Florida Banks Inc	NAS NMS	FtFlBk	FFBK
First Franklin Corp	NAS NMS	FtFrnk	FFHS
First Georgia Holding Corp	NAS NMS	FtGaHd	FGSV
First Golden Bancorporation	NAS NMS	FtGoldn	FGBC
First Hawaiian Inc	NAS NMS	FtHaw	FHWN
First Home Federal S&L Assn (Florida)	NAS NMS	FHomF	FSEB
First Home Savings Bank SLA (New Jersey)	NAS NMS	FtHmSv	FSPG
First Iberian Fund	American	FtIber	IBF
First Illinois Corp	NAS NMS	FtIllCp	FTIL
First Indiana Corp	NAS NMS	FtIndi	FISB
First Interstate Bancorp	New York	FIntste	I
First Interstate Corporation of Wisconsin	NAS NMS	FInsWi	FIWI
First Interstate of Iowa Inc	NAS NMS	FInIowa	FIIA
First Liberty Financial Corp	NAS NMS	FtLbty	FLFC
First Maryland Bancorp	NAS NMS	FMdB	FMDB
First Medical Devices Corp	NAS SL	FtMed	FMDC
First Michigan Bank Corp	NAS NMS	FtMich	FMBC
First Midwest Bancorp Inc	NAS NMS	FMidB	FMBI
First Mississippi Corp	New York	FtMiss	FRM
First Mutual Savings Bank (Washington)	NAS NMS	FMWA	FMSB
First National Bancorp (Georgia)	NAS NMS	FNtGa	FBAC
First National Cincinnati Corp	NAS NMS	FNCinn	FNAC

COMPANY NAME	MARKET LISTING	NEWSPSPER ABBREV.	TRADING SYMBOL
First National Corp (California)	American	FNtCal	FN
First National Corp (Ohio)	NAS NMS	FNDela	FTNC
First National Pennsylvania Corp	NAS NMS	FtNtlPa	FNPC
First NH Banks Inc	NAS NMS	FNHB	FINH
First Northern S&L Assn (Wisconsin)	NAS NMS	FNthSL	FNGB
First Oak Brook Bancshares Inc (Class A)	NAS NMS	FtOak	FOBBA
First of America Bank Corp (Michigan)	NAS NMS	FstAm	FABK
First of Long Island Corp	NAS NL	FstLI	FLIC
First Ohio Bancshares Inc	NAS NMS	FOhBn	FIRO
First Pennsylvania Corp	New York	FstPa	FPA
First Peoples Financial Corp	NAS NMS	FPeoFn	FPNJ
First Republic Bancorp Inc (California)	American	FtRpBc	FRC
First Savings Bank FSB (New Mexico)	NAS NMS	FSNM	FSBC
First Security Corp (Utah)	NAS NMS	FSecC	FSCO
First Security Corporation of KentuckY	NAS NMS	FtScKy	FSKY
First Security Financial Corp (North Carolina)	NAS NMS	FSecF	FSFC
First Service Bank for Savings (Massachusetts)	NAS NMS	FtSvBk	FSBK
1st Source Corp	NAS NMS	1stSrc	SRCE
First State Financial Services Inc	NAS NMS	FtStFin	FSFI
First Team Sports Inc	NAS SL	FtTeam	FTSP
First Tennessee National Corp	NAS NMS	FTenn	FTEN
First Union Corp	New York	FstUC	FTU
First Union Real Estate Equity & Mortgage Investments	New York	FUnRl	FUR
First United Bancshares Inc (Arkansas)	NAS NMS	FtUtd	UNTD
First Virginia Banks Inc	New York	FtVaBk	FVB
First Wachovia Corp	New York	FtWach	FW
First Western Financial Corp	NAS NMS	FtWFn	FWES
First Wisconsin Corp	New York	FtWisc	FWB
First Woburn Bancorp Inc	NAS NMS	FWobrn	WOBS
The First Women's Bank (New York)	NAS NMS	FtWomn	FWNY
First World Cheese Inc	NAS NL	FtWrld	FWCH
First Wyoming Bancorporation	American	FWymB	FWO
Firstbank of Illinois Co	NAS NMS	FstbkIll	FBIC
Firstcorp Inc (Class A)	American	Fstcrp	FCR.A
FirstFed America Inc	American	FstFd	FFA
FirstFed Financial Corp	New York	FstFed	FED
FirsTier Inc	NAS NMS	Firster	FRST
FirstMiss Gold Inc	NAS NMS	FtMiss	FRMG
Fischbach Corp	New York	Fischb	FIS
Fischer & Porter co	American	FischP	FP
FIserv Inc	NAS NMS	Fiserv	FISV
Fisher Business Systems Inc	NAS SL	FishBu	FBUS
Fisher Foods Inc	New York	FishFd	FHR
Fisher Scientific Group Inc	NAS NMS	FishSci	FSHG

COMPANY NAME	MARKET LISTING	NEWSPAPER ABBREV.	TRADING SYMBOL
Fisher Transportation Services Inc	NAS NMS	FishTrn	FTSI
Fisons plc	NAS NL	Fisons	FISNY
Fitchburg Gas & Electric Light Co	American	FitcGE	FGE
Flagler Bank Corp (Class A)	NAS NMS	Flagler	FLGLA
Flamemaster Corp	NAS NMS	Flamstr	FAME
Flanigan's Enterprises Inc	American	Flanign	QBDL
Flare Inc	NAS SL	Flare	FLAR
Fleet Norstar Financial Corp	New York	FltNors	FLT
Fleetwood Enterprises Inc	New York	FleetEn	FLE
Fleming Companies Inc	New York	Flemng	FLM
Flexsteel Industries Inc	NAS NMS	Flexstl	FLXS
Flextronics Inc	NAS NMS	Flextrn	FLEX
Flexwatt Corp	NAS SL	Flexwat	FWAT
Flight Dynamics Inc	NAS SL	FlgtDy	FLYT
The Flight International Group Inc	NAS NMS	FlghtIn	FLTI
FlightSafety International Inc	New York	FlghtSf	FSI
Floating Point Systems Inc	New York	FloatPt	FLP
Florafax International Inc	NAS SL	Florafx	FIIF
Florida East Coast Industries Inc	New York	FlaEC	FLA
Florida Employers Insurance Co	NAS NMS	FlaEIns	FLAEF
Florida Federal S&L Assn (St Petersburg)	NAS NMS	FlaFdl	FLFE
Florida First Federal Savings Bank (Panama City)	NAS NMS	FlaFst	FFPC
Florida National Banks of Florida Inc	NAS NMS	FlaNBF	FNBF
Florida Progress Corp	New York	FlaPrg	FPC
Florida Public Utilities Co	NAS NMS	FlaPU	FPUT
Florida Rock & Tank Lines Inc	NAS NMS	FlaRck	FRKT
Florida Rock Industries Inc	American	FlaRck	FRK
Florida Steel Corp	New York	FlaStl	FLS
Flow General Inc	New York	FlwGen	FGN
Flow Mole Corp	NAS NL	Flwmle	MOLE
Flow Systems Inc	NAS NMS	FlowSy	FLOW
Flowers Industries Inc	New York	Flower	FLO
John Fluke Mfg Co Inc	American	Fluke	FKM
Fluor Corp	New York	Fluor	FLR
The Fluorocarbon Co	NAS NMS	Flurocb	FCBN
FMC Corp	New York	FMC	FMC
FMC Gold Co	New York	FMC G	FGL
F.N.B. Corp	NAS NL	FNB Cp	FBAN
F N B Rochester Corp	NAS NMS	FNBRo	FNBR
FNW Bancorp Inc	NAS NMS	FNW	FNWB
FONAR Corp	NAS NMS	Fonar	FONR
Food Lion Inc (Class A)	NAS NMS	FLioA	FDLNA
Food Lion Inc	NAS NMS	FLioB	BDLNB
Foodarama Supermarkets Inc	American	Foodrm	FSM
Foodmaker Inc	New York	Foodmk	JIB
Foote, Cone & Belding Communications Inc	New York	FooteC	FCB
The Foothill Group Inc	New York	FthillG	FGI

COMPANY NAME	MARKET LISTING	NEWSPAPER ABBREV.	TRADING SYMBOL
For Better Living Inc	NAS NL	ForBetr	FBTR
Ford Motor Co	New York	FordM	F
Ford Motor Company of Canada Ltd	American	FordCn	FC
Foreland Corp	NAS SL	Forelnd	FORL
Foremost Corporation of America	NAS NMS	ForAm	FCOA
Forest City Enterprises Inc (Class A)	American	ForstC A	FCE.A
Forest City Enterprises Inc (Class B)	American	ForstC B	FCE.B
Forest Laboratories Inc	American	ForstL	FRX
Forest Oil Corp	NAS NMS	ForestO	FOIL
Formica Corp	New York	Formc	FOR
The Forschner Group Inc	NAS NMS	Forsch	FSNR
Forstmann & Company Inc	American	Frstm	FST
Fort Dearborn Income Securities Inc	New York	FtDear	FTD
Fort Howard Paper Co	New York	FtHowd	FHP
Fort Wayne National Corp	NAS NMS	FtWyne	FWNC
Fortune Financial Group Inc	NAS NMS	FortnF	FORF
Fortune 44 Co (Class A)	NAS SL	Frtne44	FORTA
Forum Group Inc	NAS NMS	Forum	FOUR
Forum Re Group Inc	NAS NL	FrmRe	FORM
L.B. Foster Co (Class A)	NAS NMS	Foster	FSTRA
Foster Wheeler Corp	New York	FostWh	FWC
Founders Bank (Connecticut)	NAS NL	FndrBk	FDBK
Fountain Powerboat Industries Inc	NAS NMS	FountPw	FPBT
Fourth Financial Corp	NAS NMS	FrthFn	FRTH
The Foxboro Co	New York	Foxbro	FOX
Foxmoor International Films Ltd	NAS SL	Foxmor	FOXI
FPA Corp	American	FPA	FPO
FPL Group Inc	New York	FPL Gp	FPL
Framingham Savings Bank (Massachusetts)	NAS NMS	FramSv	FSBX
The France Fund Inc	New York	Franc	FRN
The Frances Denney Companies Inc	NAS NMS	FranDn	DNNY
Franchiseit Corp	NAS SL	Franch	FICO
The Frankford Corp	NAS NMS	Frnkfd	FKFD
Franklin Computer Corp	NAS NMS	FrkCpt	FDOS
Franklin Consolidated Mining Company Inc	NAS SL	FrkCon	FKCM
The Franklin Corp	American	Frnkln	FKL
Franklin Electric Company Inc	NAS NMS	FrnkEl	FELE
Franklin First Financial Corp	NAS NMS	FrnkFst	FFFC
Franklin Resources Inc	New York	FrnkR	BEN
Franklin S&L Assn (Michigan)	NAS NMS	FrnkSL	FSLA
Franklin Savings Assn (Kansas)	NAS NL	FrnkSv	FSAK
Franklin Telecommunications Corp	NAS SL	FrnkTl	FTCO
Frederick's of Hollywood Inc	American	FrdHly	FHO
Free State Consolidated Gold Mines Ltd	NAS NL	FreSCn	FSCNY
Freeport-McMoRan Copper Co	New York	FMCC	FCX
Freeport-McMoRan Energy Partners Ltd	New York	FMEP	FMP
Freeport-McMoRan Gold Co	New York	FMGC	FAU
Freeport-McMoRan Inc	New York	FrptMc	FTX

COMPANY NAME	MARKET LISTING	NEWSPAPER ABBREV.	TRADING SYMBOL
Freeport-McMoRan Oil & Gas Roalty Trust	New York	FMOG	FMR
Freeport-McMoRan Resource Partners L.P.	New York	FMRP	FRP
Fremont General Corp	NAS NMS	Fremnt	FRMT
Frequency Electronics Inc	American	FreqEl	FEI
Fresh Juice Company Inc	NAS SL	FrJuce	FRSH
Fretter Inc	NAS NMS	Fretter	FTTR
Freymiller Trucking Inc	NAS NMS	Freym	FRML
Friedman Industries Inc	American	Friedm	FRD
Fries Entertainment Inc	American	FriesEn	FE
Frisch's Restaurants Inc	American	Frischs	FRS
Frontier Insurance Group Inc	NAS NMS	FrtrIns	FRTR
Frontier Texas Corp	NAS SL	FrntTx	FRTX
Fruehauf Corp (Class B)	New York	FruhfB	FTR.B
Fruit of the Loom Inc	American	FruitL	FTL
Fuddruckers Inc	NAS NMS	Fudrck	FUDD
Fuji Photo Film Company Ltd	NAS NL	FujiPh	FUJIY
H.B. Fuller Co	NAS NMS	FubrHB	FULL
Fulton Federal S&L Assn of Atlanta	NAS NMS	FultFS	FFSL
Fulton Financial Corp (Pennsylvania)	NAS NMS	Fulton	FULT
Fuqua Industries Inc	New York	Fuqua	FQA
The Fur Vault Inc	American	FurVlt	FRV
Furr's/Bishop's Cafeterias L.P.	New York	FurrsB	CAF
Futuresat Industries Inc	NAS SL	FutrSt	FSATE
G&K Services Inc (Class A)	NAS NMS	G&K Sv	GKSRA
The Gabelli Equity Trust Inc	New York	Gabeli	GAB
GAF Corp	New York	GAF	GAF
Gainsco Inc	American	Gainsco	GNA
Galactic Resources Ltd	NAS NMS	Galac	GALCF
Galagraph Ltd	NAS SL	Galgph	GALAF
Galaxy Cablevision L.P.	American	GalxCbl	GTV
Galaxy Carpet Mills Inc	American	GalaxC	GXY
Galaxy Cheese Co	NAS SL	GlxyCh	GALX
Galileo Electro-Optics Corp	NAS NMS	Galileo	GAEO
Arthur J. Gallagher & Co	New York	Gallagr	AJG
Lewis Galoob Toys Inc	New York	Galoob	GAL
Galveston-Houston Co	New York	GalHou	GHX
Galveston Resources Ltd (Class B)	NAS SL	GalvRs	GLVBF
Gambro AB	NAS NL	Gambro	GAMBY
Gaming & Technology Inc	NAS NMS	GamT	GATI
Gamma Biologicals Inc	NAS NMS	GamaB	GAMA
Gandalf Technologies Inc	NAS NMS	Gandlf	GANDF
Gander Mountain Inc	NAS NMS	Gander	GNDR
Gannett Company Inc	New York	Gannett	GCI
Gantos Inc	NAS NMS	Gantos	GTOS
The Gap Inc	New York	Gap	GPS
Garan Inc	American	Garan	GAN
Garden America Corp	NAS NMS	GardA	GACO

COMPANY NAME	MARKET LISTING	NEWSPAPER ABBREV.	TRADING SYMBOL
Garnet Resources Corp	NAS NL	Garnet	GARN
Gateway Bancorp Inc (New York)	NAS NMS	GtwBcp	GBAN
Gateway Bank (Connecticut)	NAS NMS	GatwB	GTWY
Gateway Communications Inc	NAS NMS	Gatway	GWAY
Gateway Federal S&L Assn (Ohio)	NAS NMS	GatwyFd	GATW
GATX Corp	New York	GATX	GMT
Gaylord Container Corp	American	GaylC	GCR
GBC Bancorp	NAS NMS	GBC Bc	GBCB
GBI International Industries Inc	NAS SL	GBI	GBII
GCA Corp	New York	GCA	GCA
Gearhart Industries Inc	New York	Gearht	GOI
GEICO Corp	New York	GEICO	GEC
Gelman Sciences Inc	American	GelmS	GSC
GEMCO NATIONAL INC	American	Gemco	GNL
Gemini Technology Inc	NAS SL	GemTc	GMTIF
Gen-Probe Inc	NAS NMS	GenPrb	GPRO
Gencor Industries Inc	NAS NMS	Gencor	GCOR
GenCorp Inc	New York	GnCrp	GY
GENDEX Corp	NAS NMS	GENDX	XRAY
Genentech Inc	New York	Genetch	GNE
General American Investors Company Inc	New York	GAInv	GAM
General Automation Inc	American	GnAuto	GA
General Binding Corp	NAS NMS	GnBnd	GBND
General Building Products Corp	NAS NMS	GBldPr	GBLD
General Ceramics Inc	NAS NMS	GenCer	GCER
General Cinema Corp	New York	GCinm	GCN
General Computer Corp	NAS NMS	GnCpt	GCCC
General DataComm Industries Inc	New York	GnData	GDC
General Development Corp	New York	GenDev	GDV
General Devices Inc	NAS SL	GnDvcs	GDIC
General Dynamics Corp	New York	GnDyn	GD
General Electric Co	New York	GenEl	GE
General Employment Enterprises Inc	American	GnEmp	JOB
General Energy Development Ltd	New York	GnEngy	GED
General Homes Corp	New York	GnHme	GHO
General Host Corp	New York	GnHost	GH
General Housewares Corp	New York	GnHous	GHW
General Instrument Corp	New York	GnInst	GRL
General Kinetics Inc	NAS NL	GnKinet	GKIE
General Magnaplate Corp	NAS NMS	GnMag	GMCC
General Microwave Corp	American	GnMicr	GMW
General Mills Inc	New York	GnMills	GIS
General Motors Corp	New York	GMot	GM
General Motors Class E Common Stock	New York	GM E	GME
General Motors Class H Common Stock	New York	GM H	GMH
General Nutrition Inc	New York	GNC	GNC
General Parametrics Corp	NAS NMS	GnPara	GPAR
General Public Utilities Corp	New York	GPU	GPU

COMPANY NAME	MARKET LISTING	NEWSPAPER ABBREV.	TRADING SYMBOL
General Re Corp	New York	GenRe	GRN
General Refractories Co	New York	GnRefr	GRX
General Sciences Corp	NAS NL	GnSci	GSCX
General Signal Corp	New York	GnSignl	GSX
Genesco Inc	New York	Gensco	GCO
Genesee Corp (Class B)	NAS NL	GenesCp	GENBB
Genetics Institute Inc	NAS NMS	GenetIn	GENI
Genex Corp	NAS NMS	Genex	GNEX
Genicom Corp	NAS NMS	Genicm	GECM
Genisco Technology Corp	American	Genisco	GES
Genlyte Group Inc	NAS NMS	Genlyte	GLYT
Genovese Drug Stores Inc	American	GenvD	GDX
GenRad Inc	New York	GnRad	GEN
Gentex Corp	NAS NMS	Gentex	GNTX
Genuine Parts Co	New York	GenuP	GPC
Genzyme Corp	NAS NMS	Genzym	GENZ
GEO International Corp	New York	GEO	GX
Geodome Resources Ltd	NAS NL	Geodme	GOEDF
Geodynamics Corp	NAS NMS	Geodyn	GDYN
Geodyne Resources Inc	NAS NMS	GeodRs	GEOD
Geonex Corp	NAS NMS	Geonex	GEOX
George Washington Corp	NAS NMS	GeoWsh	GWSH
Georgia Bonded Fibers Inc	NAS NMS	GaBnd	GBFH
Georgia Gulf Corp	New York	GaGulf	GGC
Georgia-Pacific Corp	New York	GaPac	GP
Geothermal Resources International Inc	American	GeoRes	GEO
Geraghty & Miller Inc	NAS NMS	Geraght	GMGW
Gerber Products Co	New York	GerbPd	GEB
Gerber Scientific Inc	New York	GerbSc	GRB
Geriatric & Medical Centers Inc	NAS NMS	GeriMd	GEMC
Germania Bank F.S.B (Illinois)	NAS NMS	GermF	GMFD
Germantown Savings Bank (Pennsylvania)	NAS NMS	GrmSv	GSBK
The Germany Fund Inc	New York	GerFd	GER
Getty Petroleum Corp	New York	Getty	GTY
GF Corp	New York	GF Cp	GFB
Giant Bay Resources Ltd	NAS NMS	GtBay	GPPXF
Giant Food Inc (Class A)	American	GiantF	GFS.A
GIANT GROUP LTD	New York	GIANT	GPO
Giant Yellowknife Mines Ltd	American	GntYl	GYK
Gibraltar Financial Corp	New York	GibrFn	GFC
C.R. Gibson Co	American	GibCR	GIBS
Gibson Greetings Inc	NAS NMS	GibsnG	GIBG
Giga-tronics Inc	NAS NMS	GigaTr	GIGA
Gilbert Associates Inc (Class A)	NAS NMS	GilbtA	GILBA
The Gillette Co	New York	Gillete	GS
Gish Biomedical Inc	NAS NMS	GishBi	GISH
Glamis Gold Ltd	NAS NMS	Glamis	GLGVF
P.H. Glatfelter Co	American	Glatflt	GLT

COMPANY NAME	MARKET LISTING	NEWSPAPER ABBREV.	TRADING SYMBOL
Glaxo Holdings p.l.c.	New York	Glaxo	GLX
Gleason Corp	New York	GleasC	GLE
Glenex Industries Inc	NAS NMS	Glenex	GLXIF
GLENFED Inc	New York	Glenfed	GLN
Glenmore Distilleries Co (Class B)	American	Glnmr	GDS.B
The Global Government Plus Fund Inc	New York	GlbGvt	GOV
Global Growth & Income Fund Inc	New York	GGInc	GGF
Global Income Plus Fund Inc	New York	GIncP1	GLI
Global Marine Inc	New York	GlbM	GLM
Global Natural Resources Inc	American	GlobNR	GNR
The Global Yield Fund Inc	New York	GlobYld	PGY
The GMI Group Inc	NAS NMS	GMI	GMED
Go Video Inc	NAS SL	GoVide	GOVO
Gold Coin Mining Inc	NAS SL	GldCoin	GLCN
Gold Express Corp	NAS SL	GoldEx	GDEX
Gold Fields of South Africa Ltd	NAS NL	GoldFd	GLDFY
Gold King Consolidated Inc	NAS SL	GoldK	GKCI
Gold Reserve Corp	NAS SL	GoldRs	GLDR
Gold Standard Inc	NAS SL	GldStd	GSTD
Golden Corral Realty Corp	NAS NMS	GldCorr	GCRA
Golden Cycle Gold Corp	NAS SL	GldCyc1	GCGC
Golden Enterprises Inc	NAS NMS	GoldEn	GLDC
Golden Knight Resources Inc	NAS NL	GldKngt	GKRVF
Golden North Resources Corp	NAS SL	GldNth	GNOXF
Golden Nugget Inc	New York	GldNug	GNG
Golden Poultry Company Inc	NAS NMS	GldPoul	CHIK
Golden Triangle Royalty & Oil Inc	NAS SL	GoldT	GTRO
Golden Valley Microwave Foods Inc	NAS NMS	GldnVly	GVMF
Golden West Financial Corp	New York	GldWF	GDW
Goldenbell Resources Inc	NAS SL	Gldnbel	GBLNF
The Goldfield Corp	American	GldFld	GV
Goldome	New York	Gldme	GDM
The Good Guys Inc	NAS NMS	GoodGy	GGUY
Goodheart Willcox Inc	NAS SL	Goodht	GWOX
GoodMark Foods Inc	NAS NMS	Goodmk	GDMK
The B.F. Goodrich Co	New York	Gdrich	GR
Goody Products Inc	NAS NMS	Goody	GOOD
The Goodyear Tire & Rubber Co	New York	Goodyr	GT
Gordex Minerals Ltd	NAS SL	Gordex	GXMNF
Gordon Jewelry Corp	New York	GordnJ	GOR
The Gorman-Rupp Co	American	GorRup	GRC
Gotaas-Larsen Shipping Corp	NAS NMS	Gotaas	GOTLF
Gottschalks Inc	New York	Gotchk	GOT
Gould Inc	New York	Gould	GLD
Gould Investors L.P.	American	GuldLP	GLP
Goulds Pumps Inc	NAS NMS	GouldP	GULD
W.R. Grace & Co	New York	Grace	GRA
Graco Inc	New York	Graco	GGG

COMPANY NAME	MARKET LISTING	NEWSPAPER ABBREV.	TRADING SYMBOL
Gradco Systems Inc	NAS NMS	Gradco	GRCO
Graham Corp	American	Graham	GHM
Graham Field Health Products Inc	American	GrhmFld	GFI
Graham-McCormick Oil & Gas Partnership	American	GrahMc	GOP
W.W. Grainger Inc	New York	Graingr	GWW
Grand Auto Inc	American	GrndAu	GAI
Granges Exploration Ltd	American	Grang	GXL
Granite Co-Operative Bank	NAS NMS	GranC	GNTE
Granite State Bankshares Inc	NAS NMS	GrantSt	GSBI
Graphic Industries Inc	NAS NMS	GrphI	GRPH
Graphic Packaging Corp	NAS NMS	GphPck	GPAK
Graphic Scanning Corp	NAS NMS	GrphSc	GSCC
Graphic Technology Inc	American	GrTch	GRT
Grease Monkey Holding Corp	NAS SL	GrMonk	GMHC
Great American Communications Co	NAS NMS	GAmCm	GACC
Great American Corp	NAS NMS	GtAmCp	GTAM
Great American First Savings Bank	New York	GtAFst	GTA
Great American Management & Investment Inc	NAS NL	GtAMg	GAMI
Great American Recreation Inc	NAS NMS	GtAmR	GRAR
The Great Atlantic & Pacific Tea Company Inc	New York	GtAtPc	GAP
Great Bay Bankshares Inc	NAS NMS	GrtBay	GBBS
Great Country Bank (Connecticut)	NAS NMS	GCtryB	GCBK
Great Falls Gas Co	NAS NMS	GtFalls	GRGC
Great Lakes Bancorp F.S.B.	NAS NMS	GtLkBc	GLBC
Great Lakes Chemical Corp	New York	GrtLkC	GLK
Great Northern Iron Ore Properties	New York	GNIrn	GNI
Great Northern Nekoosa Corp	New York	GtNNk	GNN
Great Southern Federal Savings Bank	NAS NMS	GtSoFd	GRBC
Great Western Financial Corp	New York	GtWFn	GWF
Great New York Savings Bank	NAS NMS	GtNYSv	GRTR
Great Washington Investors Inc	American	GtWash	GWI
A.P. Green Industries Inc	NAS NMS	Green	APGI
Green Mountain Power Corp	New York	GMP	GMP
Green Tree Acceptance Inc	New York	GrenTr	GNT
Greencastle Federal Savings Bank	NAS NL	GrncsSv	GRFS
Greenery Rehabilitation Group Inc	NAS NMS	GrnRhb	GRGI
Greenman Brothers Inc	American	Grenm	GMN
Greentree Software Inc	NAS SL	GrntrSft	GTSW
Greenwich Financial Corp	NAS NMS	GrnwcFn	GFCT
Greenwich Pharmaceuticals Inc	NAS NMS	GrnwPh	GRPI
Greiner Engineering Inc	American	Greiner	GII
Grenada Sunburst System Corp	NAS NMS	GrndSu	GSSC
Grey Advertising Inc	NAS NMS	GreyAd	GREY
The Greyhound Corp	New York	Greyh	G
G·R·I Corp	American	GRI	GRR
Griffin Technology Inc	NAS NMS	GrifTch	GRIF

COMPANY NAME	MARKET LISTING	NEWSPAPER ABBREV.	TRADING SYMBOL
Griffith Consumers Co	NAS NL	Grifith	FUEL
Grist Mill Co	NAS NMS	Grist	GRST
Groff Industries Inc	NAS NMS	Groff	GROF
Grossman's Inc	NAS NMS	Grosmn	GROS
Groundwater Technology Inc	NAS NMS	Grdwtr	GWTI
Group 1 Software Inc	NAS NMS	Group1	GSOF
GroveBank for Savings	NAS NMS	GroveB	GROV
Grow Group Inc	New York	GrowGp	GRO
Grow Ventures Corp	NAS SL	GrowVn	GPAX
Growth Stock Outlook Trust Inc	New York	GthStk	GSO
Grubb & Ellis Co	New York	GrubEl	GBE
Grub & Ellis Realty Income Trust	NAS NMS	GrubER	GRIT
Gruen Marketing Corp	American	Gruen	GMC
Grumman Corp	New York	Grumn	GQ
GTE Corp	New York	GTE	GTE
GTECH Corp	NAS NMS	Gtech	GTCH
GTI Corp	American	GTI	GTI
GTS Corp	NAS NMS	GTS	GTSC
Guaranty Bancshares Corp	NAS NL	GuarBn	GBNC
Guaranty National Corp	NAS NMS	GuarNt	GNIC
Guardian Bancorp	American	GrdnB	GB
Guardsman Products Inc	New York	GrdPrd	GPI
Guest Supply Inc	NAS NMS	GuestS	GEST
Guilford Mills Inc	New York	Gulfrd	GFD
Gulf + Western Inc	New York	GlfWst	GW
Gulf Applied Technologies Inc	NAS NMS	GlfApld	GATS
Gulf Canada Corp	American	GCda	GOC
Gulf Resources Resources & Chemical Corp	New York	GulfRs	GRE
Gulf States Utilities Co	New York	GlfStUt	GSU
Gull Laboratories Inc	NAS NL	GullLb	GULL
Gundle Environmental Systems Inc	American	Gundle	GUN
GV Medical Inc	NAS NMS	GV Med	GVMI
GW Utilities Ltd	American	GW Ut	GWT
GWC Corp	NAS NMS	GWC	GWCC
Gyrodyne Company of America Inc	NAS SL	Gyrody	GYRO
H&H Oil Tool Company Inc	NAS NMS	HHOilT	HHOT
H&Q Healthcare Investors	New York	HQ Hlt	HQH
Haber Inc	NAS NMS	Haber	HABE
Hach Co	NAS NMS	Hach	HACH
HADCO Corp	NAS NMS	Hadco	HDCO
Hadron Inc	NAS SL	Hadron	HDRN
Hadson Corp	New York	Hadson	HAD
Hako Minuteman Inc	NAS NMS	Hako	HAKO
HAL Inc	American	HAL	HA
Halifax Engineering Inc	American	Halifax	HX
Frank B. Hall & Company Inc	New York	HallFB	FBH
Hall Financial Group Inc	NAS NMS	HallFn	HALL

COMPANY NAME	MARKET LISTING	NEWSPAPER ABBREV.	TRADING SYMBOL
Halliburton Co	New York	Halbtn	HAL
The Hallwood Group Inc	New York	Halwod	HWG
Robert Halmi Inc	American	Halmi	RHI
Halsey Drug Co	NAS SL	Halsey	HADR
Hamilton Oil Corp	NAS NMS	HamOil	HAML
Hammond Co	NAS NMS	Hamnd	THCO
Hampton Healthcare Inc	American	HampH	HHI
Hampton Industries Inc	American	HamptI	HAI
Hampton Utilities Trust	American	HmpU	HU
Hamptons Bancshares Inc	NAS NMS	HampBn	HBSI
Hana Biologics Inc	NAS NMS	HanaBi	HANA
Hancock Fabrics Inc	New York	HanFb	HKF
John Hancock Income Securities Trust	New York	HanJS	JHS
John Hancock Investors Trust	New York	HanJI	JHI
Handleman Co	New York	Handlm	HDL
Handy & Harman	New York	HandH	HNH
M.A. Hanna Co	New York	Hanna	HNM
Hannaford Bros. Co	New York	Hanfrd	HRD
Hanson Trust PLC	New York	Hanson	HAN
HarCor Energy Co	NAS SL	Harcor	HARC
Harcourt Brace Jovanovich Inc	New York	HarBrJ	HBJ
Hard Rock Cafe plc	American	HrdRk	HRK
Harding Associates Inc	NAS NMS	HrdgAs	HRDG
Harken Oil & Gas Inc	NAS NMS	Harken	HOGI
The John H. Harland Co	New York	Harlnd	JH
Harley-Davidson Inc	New York	Harley	HDI
Harleysville Group Inc	NAS NMS	Harleys	HGIC
Harleysville National Corp	NAS NMS	HarlyNt	HNBC
Harleysville Savings Assn (Pennsylvania)	NAS NMS	HarlySv	HARL
Harlyn Products Inc	NAS NMS	Harlyn	HRLN
Harman International Industries Inc	New York	Harman	HAR
Harmon Industries Inc	NAS NMS	Harmon	HRMN
Harnischfeger Industries Inc	New York	Harnish	HPH
Harold's Stores Inc	NAS NMS	Harold	HRLD
The Harper Group Inc	NAS NMS	HarpG	HARG
Harris & Harris Group Inc	NAS NMS	HarisHa	HHGP
Harris Corp	New York	Harris	HRS
Harsco Corp	New York	Harsco	HSC
Hart Industries Inc	NAS SL	HartInd	HRTI
Hartford Steam Boiler Inspection & Insurance Co	NAS NMS	HrtfdS	HBOL
Hartmarx Corp	New York	Hartmx	HMX
Harvard Industries Inc	NAS NMS	HarvIn	HAVA
Harvard Knitwear Inc	NAS NMS	HarvKn	HVDK
Harvard Securities Group PLC	NAS NMS	HrvdSc	HARVY
The Harvey Group Inc	American	Harvey	HRA
Hasbro Inc	American	Hasbr	HAS
Hastings Manufacturing Co	American	Hasting	HMF

COMPANY NAME	MARKET LISTING	NEWSPAPER ABBREV.	TRADING SYMBOL
Hathaway Corp	NAS NMS	Hathw	HATH
Hatteras Income Securities Inc	New York	HattSe	HAT
Hauserman Inc	NAS NMS	Hauser	HASR
Haverty Furniture Companies Inc	NAS NMS	Havrty	HAVT
Haverty Funniture Companies Inc (Class A)	NAS NMS	HavFuA	HAVTA
Hawaiian Electric Industries Inc	New York	HawEl	HE
Hawkeye Bancorporation (Class B)	NAS NMS	HawkB	HWKB
Hawkeye Bancorporation (Class C)	NAS NMS	HawkC	HWKC
Hawkeye Entertainment Inc	NAS SL	HawkEn	SBIZ
Haywood S&L Assn	NAS NL	HaywdS	HWNC
HBO & Co	NAS NMS	HBO	HBOC
HCC Industries Inc	NAS NMS	HCC	HCCI
HDR Power Systems Inc	NAS NMS	HDR	HDRP
HE Ventures Inc	NAS SL	HE Ven	HEVN
Health & Rehabilitation Properties Trust	New York	HltRhb	HRP
Health Care Property Investors Inc	New York	HlthCP	HCP
Health Care REIT Inc	American	HlthCr	HCN
Health-Chem Corp	American	HlthCh	HCH
Health Images Inc	NAS NMS	HltImg	HIMG
Health Insurance of Vermont Inc	NAS NMS	HlthIns	HIVT
Health Management Associates Inc	American	HlthMn	HMA
Health-Mor Inc	American	HelthM	HMI
HealthCare COMPARE Corp	NAS NMS	HlthCo	HCCC
Healthcare International Inc (Class A)	American	HlI	HII.A
Healthcare Services Group Inc	NAS NMS	HlthCS	HCSG
Healthcare Services of America Inc	NAS NMS	HltcrS	HSAI
Healthco International Inc	NAS NMS	Hlthco	HLCO
Healthdyne Inc	NAS NMS	Hlthdyn	HDYN
HEALTHSOUTH Rehabilitation Corp	NAS NMS	HltsthR	HSRC
HealthVest	American	Hltvst	HVT
Healthwatch Inc	NAS SL	Hlthwc	HEAL
Heart Federal S&L Assn (California)	NAS NMS	HeartF	HFED
Heartland Express Inc	NAS NMS	Hrtlnd	HTLD
Hechinger Co (Class A)	NAS NMS	HchgA	HECHA
Hechinger Co (Class B)	NAS NMS	HchgB	HECHB
Heck's Inc	New York	Hecks	HEX
Hecla Mining Co	New York	HeclaM	HL
Heekin Can Inc	NAS NMS	Heekin	HEKN
HEI Corp (Texas)	NAS NMS	HEI Tx	HEIC
HEI Inc (Minnesota)	NAS NMS	HEI Mn	HEII
HEICO Corp	American	Heico	HEI
Heilig-Meyers Co	New York	Heilig	HMY
Hein-Werner Corp	American	HeinWr	HNW
H.J. Heinz Co	New York	Heinz	HNZ
C.H. Heist Corp	NAS NMS	HeistC	CHHC
Heldor Industries Inc	American	Heldor	HDR
Helen of Troy Corp	NAS NMS	HelenT	HELE
Helene Curtis Industries Inc	New York	HelneC	HC

COMPANY NAME	MARKET LISTING	NEWSPAPER ABBREV.	TRADING SYMBOL
Helix Technology Corp	NAS NMS	Helix	HELX
Helmerich & Payne Inc	New York	HelmP	HP
HelmResources Inc	American	HelmR	H
The Helvetia Fund Inc	New York	Helvet	SWZ
HemaCare Corp	NAS SL	HemaC	HEMA
Hemisphere Development Ltd	NAS SL	HemDv	HSDMF
Hemodynamics Inc	NAS SL	Hemody	HMDY
HemoTec Inc	NAS NMS	Hemtec	HEMO
The Henley Group Inc	NAS NMS	Henley	HENG
Henley Manufacturing Corp	NAS NMS	HenlMf	HNCO
Jack Henry & Associates Inc	NAS NMS	HnryJk	JKHY
Herbalife International Inc	NAS NL	Herblfe	HERB
Hercules Inc	New York	Herculs	HPC
Heritage Bancorp Inc (Massachusetts)	NAS NMS	HrtgBc	HNIS
Heritage Entertainment Inc	American	HeritEn	HHH
Heritage Financial Corp	NAS NL	HeritFn	HFHC
Heritage Financial Services Inc	NAS NMS	HrtFSv	HERS
Heritage Media Corp (Class A)	American	HtgMd	HTG.A
Herley Microwave Systems Inc	NAS NMS	Herley	HRLY
Hershey Foods Corp	New York	Hrshey	HSY
Hershey Oil Corp	American	HershO	HSO
Hewlett-Packard Co	New York	HewlPk	HWP
Hexcel Corp	New York	Hexcel	HXL
HHB Systems Inc	NAS NMS	HHB Sy	HHBX
Hi-Port Industries Inc	NAS NMS	Hi-Prt	HIPT
Hi-Shear Industries Inc	New York	HiShear	HSI
Hibernia Corp (Class A)	NAS NMS	Hiber	HIBCA
The Hibernia Savings Bank (Massachusetts)	NAS NMS	HiberSv	HSBK
Dow B. Hickam Inc	NAS NMS	Hickam	DBHI
J. Higby's Inc	NAS NMS	Higbys	HIGB
High Income Advantage Trust	New York	HiInco	YLD
High Plains Corp	NAS NL	HiPlain	HIPC
High Resolution Sciences Inc	NAS SL	HghRes	HIRS
The High Yield Income Fund Inc	New York	HiYld	HYI
High Yield Plus Fund Inc	New York	HiYldPl	HYP
Highland Superstores Inc	NAS NMS	HighlSu	HIGH
Highveld Steel & Vanadium Corp Ltd	NAS NL	Highvld	HSVLY
Highwood Resources Ltd	NAS NMS	Highwd	HIWDF
Hilb, Rogal & Hamilton Co	NAS NMS	HilbRg	HRHC
Hillenbrand Industries Inc	New York	Hillnbd	HB
Hills Department Stores Inc	New York	HillDp	HDS
Hilton Hotels Corp	New York	Hilton	HLT
HIMONT Inc	New York	Himont	HMT
Hinderliter Industries Inc	American	Hindrl	HND
Edward Hines Lumber Co	NAS NL	HneLu	HINE
Hipotronics Inc	American	Hiptron	HIP
Hitachi Ltd	New York	Hitachi	HIT
Hitech Engineering Co	NAS SL	HitchE	THEX

COMPANY NAME	MARKET LISTING	NEWSPAPER ABBREV.	TRADING SYMBOL
HITK Corp	NAS NMS	HITK	HITK
HMG Property Investors Inc	American	HMG	HMG
H.M.S.S. Inc	NAS NMS	HMSS	HMSS
HMO American Inc	NAS NMS	HMO	HMOA
Hodgson Houses Inc	NAS SL	Hodgsn	HDGH
Hofmann Industries Inc	American	Hofman	HOF
Hogan Systems Inc	NAS NMS	Hogan	HOGN
Holco Mortgage Acceptance Corp-1 (Class A)	American	Holco	HOL.A
Holiday Corp	New York	Holidy	HIA
Holiday RV Superstores Inc	NAS NL	HldyRV	RVEE
Holly Corp	American	HollyCp	HOC
Holly Farms Corp	New York	HollyFa	HFF
Hollywood Park Realty Enterprises Inc	NAS NL	HlwdPk	HTRFZ
D.H. Holmes Company Ltd	NAS NMS	HolmD	HLME
Home & City Savings Bank (New York)	NAS NMS	HmeCty	HCSB
Home Beneficial Corp (Class B)	NAS NMS	HmBen	HBENB
The Home Depot Inc	New York	HmeD	HD
Home Federal Corp (Maryland)	NAS NMS	HFMd	HFMD
Home Federal S&L Assn (California)	New York	HmFSD	HFD
Home Federal S&L Assn of San Francisco	NAS NMS	HmFSF	HFSF
Home Federal S&L Assn of the Rockies	NAS NMS	HmFRk	HROK
Home Federal S&L Assn of Upper East Tennessee	NAS NMS	HmFTn	HFET
Home Federal Savings Bank (Indiana)	NAS NMS	HFdInd	HOMF
Home Federal Savings Bank (N. Carolina)	NAS NL	HFdNC	HFSA
Home Federal Savings Bank (Ohio)	NAS NMS	HmFXn	HFOX
Home Federal Savings Bank (S. Carolina)	NAS NL	HmFChr	HFSB
Home Federal Savings Bank, Northern Ohio	NAS NMS	HmFNO	HFNO
Home Federal Savings Bank of Georgia	NAS NMS	HFdGa	HFGA
The Home Group Inc	New York	HmeGp	HME
Home Intensive Care, Inc	NAS NMS	HmInt	KDNY
Home National Corp	NAS NL	HmNtl	HNCP
Home Office Reference Laboratory Inc	NAS NMS	HORL	HORL
Home Port Bancorp Inc	NAS NMS	HmPrt	HPBC
Home S&L Assn Inc (North Carolina)	NAS NMS	HomeSL	HSLD
Home Savings Assn of Pennsylvania	NAS NMS	HmSvPa	HSPA
The Home Savings Bank (New York)	NAS NMS	HmeSav	HMSB
Home Shopping Network Inc	American	HomeSh	HSN
Home Unity S&L Assn (Pennsylvania)	NAS NMS	HUSB	HUSB
Homeowners Group Inc	NAS NL	HmowG	HOMG
Homestake Mining Co	New York	Hmstke	HM
Homestead Financial Corp	New York	HmstF	HFL
Homestead Financial Corp (Class B)	New York	HmFB	HFL.B
Homestead Savings Assn (Pennsylvania)	NAS NMS	HmstdS	HMSD
Hometown Bancorporation	NAS SL	HmtwBc	HTWN
HON INDUSTRIES Inc	NAS NMS	HonInd	HONI

COMPANY NAME	MARKET LISTING	NEWSPAPER ABBREV.	TRADING SYMBOL
Honda Motor Company Ltd	New York	Honda	HMC
Honeybee Inc	American	Honybe	HBE
Honeywell Inc	New York	Honwell	HON
Hooper Holmes Inc	American	HoopHl	HH
Hopper Soliday Corp	New York	HoprSol	HS
Horizon Bank A Savings Bank (Washington)	NAS NMS	HrzBk	HRZB
Horizon Corp	New York	Horizon	HZN
Horizon Financial Services Inc	NAS NMS	HrznFn	HFIN
Horizon Gold Shares Inc	NAS SL	HrzGld	HRIZ
Horizon Healthcare Corp	New York	HrzHlt	HHC
Horizon Industries Inc	NAS NMS	HorzInd	HRZN
George A Hormel & Co	American	Hormel	HRL
The Horn & Hardart Co	American	HrnHar	HOR
Hornbeck Offshore Services Inc	NAS SL	Hornbk	HOSS
Hospital Care Corporation of America	New York	HCA	HCA
Hospital Newspapers Group Inc	NAS NL	HospNw	HNGI
Hospital Staffing Services Inc	NAS NMS	HospSt	HSSI
Hosposable Products Inc	NAS NMS	Hospos	HOSP
Hotel Investors Trust/Corporation	New York	HotlInv	HOT
Houghton Mifflin Co	New York	HougM	HTN
House of Fabrics Inc	New York	HouFab	HF
Household International Inc	New York	HousInt	HI
Houston Industries Inc	New York	HouInd	HOU
Houston Oil Royalty Trust	New York	HouOR	RTH
Houston Oil Trust	American	HouOT	HO
Hovnanian Enterprises Inc	American	HovnE	HOV
Howard Bancorp	NAS NMS	HwrdB	HOBC
The Howard Savings Bank (New Jersey)	NAS NMS	HBNJ	HWRD
Howe Richardson Inc	American	HoweRh	HRI
Howell Corp	New York	HowlCp	HWL
Howell Industries Inc	American	HowlIn	HOW
Howtek Inc	American	Howtk	HTK
HPSC Inc	NAS NMS	HPSC	HPSC
HRE Properties	New York	HRE	HRE
HRI Group Inc	NAS NMS	HRI Gp	HRIGV
Hubbell Inc (Class A)	American	HubelA	HUB.A
Hubbell Inc (Class B)	American	HubelB	HUB.B
HUBCO Inc	American	HUBCO	HCO
Hudson Foods Inc	American	HudFd	HFI
Hudson General Corp	American	HudGn	HGC
Huffman Koos Inc	NAS NMS	HufKoo	HUFK
Huffy Corp	New York	Huffy	HUF
Hughes Homes Inc	NAS NMS	HghHm	HUHO
Hughes Supply Inc	New York	HughSp	HUG
Humana Inc	New York	Human	HUM
J.B. Hunt Transportation Services Inc	NAS NMS	HuntJB	JBNT
Hunt Manufacturing Co	New York	HuntM	HUN
Hunter Environmental Services Inc	NAS NL	HuntEn	HESI
Hunter-Melnor Inc	NAS NMS	HuntMl	HRMR

COMPANY NAME	MARKET LISTING	NEWSPAPER ABBREV.	TRADING SYMBOL
Huntingdon International Holdings plc	NAS NMS	HntgnIn	HRCLY
Huntington Bancshares Inc	NAS NMS	HuntgB	HBAN
Hurco Companies Inc	NAS NMS	Hurco	HURC
Hutchinson Technology Inc	NAS NMS	HutchT	HTCH
The E.F. Hutton Group Inc	New York	HuttEF	EFH
HWC Distribution Corp	NAS NMS	HWC	HWCD
Hycor Biomedical Inc	NAS SL	Hycor	HYBD
Hyde Athletic Industries Inc	NAS NMS	HydeAt	HYDE
The Hydraulic Co	New York	Hydral	THC
Hydro Flame Corp	NAS SL	HydFlm	HFLM
Hyponex Corp	NAS NMS	Hyponx	HYPX
Hytek Microsystems Inc	NAS NMS	HytekM	HTEK
IBI Security Service Inc (Class A)	NAS NMS	IBI	IBISA
IBP Inc	New York	IBP	IBP
IBS Technologies Ltd	NAS SL	IBS	IBSTF
IC Industries Inc	New York	IC Ind	ICX
ICEE-USA	American	ICEE	ICY
I.C.H. Corp	American	ICH	ICH
ICM Property Investors Inc	New York	ICM	ICM
ICN Biomedicals Inc	American	ICN Bio	BIM
ICN Pharmaceuticals Inc	New York	ICN Ph	ICN
ICOT Corp	NAS NMS	Icot	ICOT
Idaho Power Co	New York	IdahoP	IDA
IDB Bankholding Corporation Ltd	NAS NL	IDB	IDBBY
IDB Communications Group Inc	NAS NMS	IDB Cm	IDBX
Ideal Basic Industries Inc	New York	IdealB	IDL
Identix Inc	NAS SL	Identx	IDXX
IE Industries Inc	New York	IE Ind	IEL
IEC Electronics Corp	NAS NMS	IEC	IECE
IFR Systems Inc	NAS NMS	IFR	IFRS
IGENE Biotechnology Inc	NAS SL	IGENE	IGNE
IGI Inc	American	IGI	IG
II-VI Inc	NAS NMS	II-VI	IIVI
I.I.S. Intelligent Information Systems Ltd	NAS NMS	IIS	IISLF
ILC Technology Inc	NAS NMS	ILC	ILCT
Illinois Power Co	New York	IllPowr	IPC
Illinois Tool Works Inc	New York	ITW	ITW
Image Entertainment Inc	NAS SL	ImagEn	DISK
Image Retailing Group Inc	NAS SL	ImagRtl	IMAG
Imagine Films Entertainment Inc	NAS SL	ImgFlm	IFEI
Imark Industries Inc	NAS NL	Imark	IMAR
Imatron Inc	NAS NMS	Imatrn	IMAT
IMC Fertilizer Group Inc	New York	IMC F	IFL
Immucell Corp	NAS SL	Imucel	ICCC
Immucor Inc	NAS NMS	Imucor	BLUD
Immunex Corp	NAS NMS	Imunex	IMNX

COMPANY NAME	MARKET LISTING	NEWSPAPER ABBREV.	TRADING SYMBOL
Immunomedics Inc	NAS NMS	Imunmd	IMMU
Imo Delaval Inc	New York	ImoDv	IMD
Impact Systems Inc	NAS NMS	ImpctSy	MPAC
Imperial Bancopr	NAS NMS	ImprBc	IBAN
Imperial Chemical Industries PLC	New York	ImpCh	ICI
Imperial Corporation of America	New York	ICA	ICA
Imperial Holly Corp	NAS NMS	ImpHly	IHKSV
Imperial Oil Ltd (Class A)	American	ImpOil	IMO.A
Imre Corp	NAS SL	Imre	IMRE
Imreg Inc (Class A)	NAS NMS	Imreg	IMRGA
IMT Inc	NAS SL	IMT	IMIT
Imuno Therapeutic Inc	NAS SL	ImTher	IMNO
INA Investment Securities Inc	New York	INAIn	IIS
Inacomp Computer Centers Inc	NAS NMS	Inacmp	INAC
Inamed Corp	NAS SL	Inamed	IMDC
InBancshares	NAS NL	InBanc	INBA
Inca Resources Inc	NAS NMS	IncaRs	INCRF
Inco Ltd	New York	INCO	N
INCOMNET Inc	NAS SL	INCMNT	ICNT
Incstar Corp	American	Incstar	ISR
Independence Bancorp Inc (Pennsylvania)	NAS NMS	IndBc	INBC
Independence Federal Savings Bank (Washington D.C.)	NAS NMS	IndFdl	IFSB
Independence Square Income Securities Inc	NAS NL	IndSqS	ISIS
Independent Air Holdings Inc	NAS SL	IndepAir	IAIR
Independent Bancshares Inc (Texas)	NAS NMS	IndBnc	IBSI
Independent Bank Corp (Massachusetts)	NAS NMS	IndBC	INDB
Indepentent Bank Corp (Michigan)	NAS NMS	IndBkMi	IBCP
Independent BankGroup Inc	NAS NL	IndBkgp	IBGI
Independent Insurance Group Inc	NAS NMS	IndInsr	INDHK
Indepth Data Inc	NAS SL	Indepth	INDI
Index Technology Corp	NAS NMS	IndxTc	INDX
India Growth Fund	New York	India	IGF
Indian Head Banks Inc (New Hampshire)	NAS NMS	IndHBk	IHBI
Indiana Bancshares Inc	NAS NL	IndiBn	INBK
Indiana Energy Inc	New York	IndiEn	IEI
Indiana Federal S&L Assn (Indiana)	NAS NMS	IndiFdl	IFSL
Indiana Financial Investors Inc	NAS NMS	IndnaF	IFII
Indiana National Corp	NAS NMS	IndiNt	INAT
Indtech Corp	NAS SL	Indtch	INEC
Industrial Acoustics Company Inc	NAS NMS	InAcous	IACI
Industrial Electronic Hardware Corp	NAS NMS	IndEl	IEHC
Industrial Resources Inc	NAS NMS	IndRes	INDR
Industrial Training Corp	NAS NMS	IndTrn	ITCC
InFerGene Co	NAS SL	InFGne	IFGN
Infinite Graphics Inc	NAS NL	InfGrph	INFG
Infodata System Inc	NAS NMS	Infodat	INFD

COMPANY NAME	MARKET LISTING	NEWSPAPER ABBREV.	TRADING SYMBOL
Information International Inc	NAS NMS	InfoIntl	IINT
Information Resources Inc	NAS NMS	InfoRs	IRIC
Information Science Inc	NAS NMS	InfoSc	INSI
Informix Corp	NAS NMS	Infrmx	IFMX
Infotechnology Inc	NAS NMS	Infotch	ITCH
Infotron Systems Corp	NAS NMS	Inftrn	INFN
Infrasonics Inc	NAS SL	Infrsnc	IFRA
Ingersoll-Rand Co	New York	IngerR	IR
Ingles Markets Inc (Class A)	NAS NMS	InglMkt	IMKTA
Ingredient Technology Corp	New York	IngrTec	ITC
Initio Inc	NAS NMS	Initio	INTO
Inland Steel Industries Inc	New York	InldStl	IAD
Inmac Corp	NAS NMS	Inmac	INMC
Innovex Inc	NAS NMS	Innovex	INVX
INRAD Inc	NAS NMS	Inrad	INRD
Insilco Corp	New York	Insilco	INR
Insituform East Inc	NAS NMS	InsitE	INEI
Insituform Group Ltd	NAS NMS	Instgp	IGLSF
Insituform Gulf South Inc	NAS NMS	InsitGlf	IGSI
Insituform Mid-America Inc (Class A)	NAS NMS	InsitMd	INSMA
Insituform of North America Inc (Class A)	NAS NMS	Instfr	INSUA
Insituform Southeast Corp	NAS NMS	InstfrS	ISEC
InSpeech Inc	NAS NMS	Inspch	INSP
Inspiration Resources Corp	New York	InspRs	IRC
Insta Cool Inc of North America	NAS SL	InstaCl	KOOL
Insteel Industries Inc	American	Insteel	III
Instinet Corp	NAS NL	InstCp	INET
The Institute of Clinical Pharmacology PLC	NAS NMS	ICP	ICPYY
Instron Corp	American	Instron	ISN
Instructivision Inc	NAS SL	Instvsn	ISTC
Instrument Systems Corp	American	InstSy	ISY
Intech Inc	NAS NMS	Intech	INTE
Integon Corp	NAS NMS	Integon	ITGN
Integrated Circuits Inc	NAS NMS	ItgCirc	ICTM
Integrated Computer Graphic Inc	NAS NL	IntgCpt	ICGI
Integrated Device Technology Inc	NAS NMS	IntgDv	IDTI
Integrated Genetics Inc	NAS NMS	IntgGen	INGN
Integrated Resources Inc	New York	IntgRsc	IRE
Intek Diversified Corp	NAS SL	Intek	IDCC
Intel Corp	NAS NMS	Intel	INTC
Intellicall Inc	NAS NMS	Intelcal	INCL
Intellicorp	NAS NMS	Intelli	INAI
Intelligent Business Communications Corp	NAS SL	IntlBus	IBCC
Intelligent Electronics Inc	NAS NMS	IntelEl	INEL
Intelligent Systems Master L.P.	American	IntlgSy	INP
Inter-City Gas Corp	American	IntCty	ICG
Inter-Regional Financial Group Inc	New York	IntRFn	IFG

COMPANY NAME	MARKET LISTING	NEWSPAPER ABBREV.	TRADING SYMBOL
Inter-Tel Inc (Class A)	NAS NMS	IntrTel	INTLA
Interactive Technologies Inc	NAS NMS	InactTc	ITXI
InterCapital Income Securities Inc	New York	ItcpSe	ICB
Intercargo Corp	NAS NL	Intcar	ICAR
Interchange Financial Services Corp (New Jersey)	NAS NSL	IntrFn	ISBJ
Intercim Corp	NAS SL	Intrcim	ITCM
INTERCO INCORPORATED	New York	Interco	ISS
Intercontinental Life Corp	NAS NL	IntLfe	ILCO
Interface Inc (Class A)	NAS NMS	IntrfcI	IFSIA
Interface Systems Inc	NAS NMS	Interfc	INTF
InterFederal Savings Bank (Tennessee)	NAS NMS	IntrFd	IFED
Interferon Sciences Inc	NAS SL	Interfrn	IFSC
Interfund Corp	NAS SL	Intrfd	IFND
Intergraph Corp	NAS NMS	Intgph	INGR
Intergroup Corp	NAS NMS	Intgrp	INTG
Interhome Energy Inc	NAS NMS	Inthm	IHEIF
Interim Systems Corp	NAS NMS	IntrmSy	INSY
Interlake Corp	New York	Intrlke	IK
Interleaf Inc	NAS NMS	Intrleaf	LEAF
Interlogic Trace Inc	New York	Intlog	IT
Intermagnetics General Corp	NAS NMS	Intrmgn	INMA
Intermark Gaming International Inc	NAS SL	IntmkG	IGII
Intermark Inc	American	Intrmk	IMI
INTERMEC Corp	NAS NMS	Intmec	INTR
Intermedics Inc	New York	Intmed	ITM
Intermet Corp	NAS NMS	IntmetC	INMT
Intermetrics Inc	NAS NMS	Intrmtr	IMET
International Aluminum Corp	New York	IntAlu	IAL
International American Homes Inc	NAS NMS	IntAm	HOME
International Banknote Company Inc	American	IntBknt	IBK
International Broadcasting Corp	NAS NMS	InBcst	IBCA
International Business Machines Corp	New York	IBM	IBM
International Capital Equipment Ltd	NAS NMS	InCapE	ICEYF
International Congeneration Corp	NAS SL	IntCogn	ICGN
International Consumer Brands Inc	NAS SL	IntCon	ICBI
International Container Systems Inc	NAS NMS	IntCnt	ICSI
International Dairy Queen Inc (Class A)	NAS NMS	InDairA	INDQA
International Dairy Queen Inc (Class B)	NAS NMS	InDairB	INDQB
International Design Group Inc	NAS SL	IntDsg	IDGI
International Electronics Inc	NAS SL	IntlEl	IEIB
International Flavors & Fragrances Inc	New York	IntFlav	IFF
International Game Technology	NAS NMS	IGame	IGAM
International Genetic Engineering Inc	NAS NMS	IntGen	IGEI
International Holding Capital Corp	NAS NMS	IntHld	ISLH
International Income Property Inc	American	IIP	IIP
International Lease Finance Corp	NAS NMS	IntLse	ILFC
International Management & Research Corp	NAS SL	IntMgR	IMRC

COMPANY NAME	MARKET LISTING	NEWSPAPER ABBREV.	TRADING SYMBOL
International Microcomputer Software Inc	NAS SL	InMcSf	IMSF
International Microelectronics Products Inc	NAS NMS	IMP	IMPX
International Minerals & Chemical Corp	New York	IntMin	IGL
International Mobile Machines Corp	NAS NMS	InMobil	IMMC
International Multifoods Corp	New York	IntMult	IMC
International Nutrition & Genetics Corp	NAS SL	IntNtr	INGC
International Paper Co	New York	IntPap	IP
International Power Machines Corp	American	IntPwr	PWR
International Proteins Corp	American	IntProt	PRO
International Recovery Corp	American	IntRec	INT
International Rectifier Corp	New York	IntRect	IRF
International Remote Imaging Systems Inc	NAS NMS	IRIS	IRIS
International Research & Development Corp	NAS NMS	IntResh	IRDV
International Seaway Trading Corp	American	IntSeaw	INS
International Shipholding Corp	NAS NMS	IntShip	INSH
International Technology Corp	New York	IT Crp	ITX
International Telecharge Inc	American	IntTch	ITI
International Thoroughbred Breeders Inc	American	IntThr	ITB
International Totalizator Systems Inc	NAS NMS	IntTotlz	ITSI
International Yogurt Co	NAS SL	IntYog	YOCM
InterPharm Laboratories Ltd	NAS NL	Intphrm	IPLLF
Interphase Corp	NAS NMS	Intphse	INPH
The Interpublic Group of Companies Inc	New York	IntpbG	IPG
Interspec Inc	NAS NMS	Intspec	ISPC
Interstate Bakeries Corp	New York	IntBkr	IBC
Interstate Cellular Telecommunications Inc	NAS SL	IntrCel	ICTI
Interstate General Company L.P.	American	IGC	IGC
Interstate Power Co	New York	InstPw	IPW
Interstate Securities Inc	New York	IntSec	IS
Interstrat Resources Inc	NAS SL	Instat	ITERF
InterTAN Inc	NAS NMS	Inttan	ITAN
Intertrans Corp	NAS NMS	Intrtrn	ITRN
InterVoice Inc	NAS NL	Intvce	INTV
Intrex Financial Services Inc	NAS NMS	Intrex	TREX
Invacare Corp	NAS NMS	Invcr	IVCR
Invention, Design, Engineering Associates Inc	NAS NMS	InvtDsg	IDEA
Investment Technologies Inc	NAS SL	InvTech	IVES
Investors Heritage Life Insurance of Kentucky	NAS SL	InvLfKy	INLF
Investors Savings Bank (Virginia)	NAS NMS	InvstSL	ISLA
Investors Savings Corp (Minnesota)	NAS NMS	InvSav	INVS
Investors Title Co	NAS NMS	InvTitl	ITIC

COMPANY NAME	MARKET LISTING	NEWSPAPER ABBREV.	TRADING SYMBOL
Investors Trust Inc	NAS SL	InvTr	ITIN
INVG Mortgage Securities Corp	NAS NMS	INVG	INVG
Invitron Corp	NAS NMS	Invtrn	INVN
Iomega Corp	NAS NMS	Iomega	IOMG
Ionics Inc	American	Ionics	ION
Iowa-Illinois Gas & Electric Co	New York	IowIlG	IWG
Iowa National Bankshares Corp	NAS NMS	IowaNtl	INBS
Iowa Resources Inc	New York	IowaRs	IOR
Iowa Southern Utilities Co	NAS NMS	IowaSo	IUTL
IP Timberlands Ltd	New York	IPTim	IPT
IPALCO Enterprises Inc	New York	Ipalco	IPL
IPCO Corp	New York	IpcoCp	IHS
IPL Systems Inc (Class A)	NAS NMS	IPL Sy	IPLSA
IPM Technology Inc	American	IPM	IPM
Ironstone Group Inc	NAS SL	Ironstn	IRON
Iroquois Brands Ltd	American	IroqBrd	IBL
IRT Corp	American	IRT Cp	IX
IRT Property Co	New York	IRT	IRT
IRT Realty Services Inc	NAS SL	IRT Rlt	IRTR
Irvine Sensors Corp	NAS SL	Irvine	IRSN
Irving Bank Corp	New York	IrvBnk	V
Irwin Magnetic Systems Inc	NAS NMS	IrwnMg	IRWN
Irwin Union Corp	NAS SL	IrwnUn	IUCO
ISC Systems Corp	NAS NMS	ISC	ISCS
Isco Inc	NAS NMS	Isco	ISKO
ISI Systems Inc	American	ISI Sy	SYS
Isomedix Inc	NAS NMS	Isomdx	ISMX
Isomet Corp	NAS NL	Isomet	IOMT
Israel Investors Corp	NAS NL	IsrlInv	IICR
Isramco Inc	NAS SL	Isramc	ISRL
ISS-International Service System Inc	American	ISS	ISI
Istec Industry & Technology Ltd	NAS SL	IstecIn	ISTEF
The Italy Fund Inc	New York	Italy	ITA
Itel Corp	NAS NMS	Itel	ITELO
Ito-Yokado Company Ltd	NAS NMS	ItoYokd	IYCOY
ITT Corp	New York	ITT Cp	ITT
IU International Corp	New York	IU Int	IU
IVAX Corp	American	IvaxCp	IVX
Iverson Technology Corp (Class A)	American	Iverson	IVT.A
IWC Resources Corp	NAS NMS	IWC	IWCR
J&J Snack Foods Corp	NAS NMS	J&J Sn	JJSF
Jack Carl/312-Futures Inc	NAS SL	JckCarl	FUTR
Jackpot Enterprises Inc	New York	Jackpot	JACK
Jaclyn Inc	American	Jaclyn	JLN
Jaco Electronics Inc	NAS NMS	JacoEl	JACO
Jacobs Engineering Group Inc	American	Jacobs	JEC
Jacobson Stores Inc	NAS NMS	Jacbsn	JCBS

COMPANY NAME	MARKET LISTING	NEWSPAPER ABBREV.	TRADING SYMBOL
Jacor Communications Inc	NAS NMS	Jacor	JCOR
Jaguar plc	NAS NMS	Jaguar	JAGRY
JAMCO Ltd	NAS SL	JAM	MSST
James Madison Ltd	American	JMadsn	JML
James River Corporation of Virginia	New York	JRiver	JR
Jamesway Corp	New York	Jamsw	JMY
Jan Bell Marketing Inc	American	JanBel	JBM
Japan Air Lines Company Ltd	NAS SL	JapnAir	JAPNY
Jason Inc	NAS NMS	Jason	JASN
Jay Jacobs Inc	NAS NMS	JayJacb	JAYT
Jayark Corp	NAS SL	Jayark	JAYA
JB's Restaurants Inc	NAS NMS	JBRst	JBBB
Jefferies Group Inc	NAS NMS	JeffrGp	JEFG
Jefferson Bancorp Inc (Florida)	NAS NL	JeffBcp	JBNC
Jefferson Bank (Pennsylvania)	NAS NL	JeffBk	JFFN
Jefferson Bankshares Inc (Virginia)	NAS NMS	JefBsh	JBNK
Jefferson National Bank (New York)	NAS NMS	JeffNt	JNBK
Jefferson-Pilot Corp	New York	JeffPl	JP
Jefferson Smurfit Corp	NAS NMS	JefSmf	JJSC
Jennifer Convertibles Inc	NAS SL	JenfCv	JENN
Jepson Corp	New York	Jepson	JEP
Jerrico Inc	NAS NMS	Jerico	JERR
Jesup Group Inc	NAS NMS	Jesup	JGRP
Jet Capital Corp	American	JetCa	JTC
Jetborne International Inc	NAS NMS	Jetbrne	JETS
Jetronic Industries Inc	American	Jetron	JET
Jewelcor Inc	New York	Jwlcr	JC
Jewelmasters Inc	American	Jwlmst	JEM
JG Industries Inc	NAS NMS	JG Ind	JGIN
Jiffy Lube International Inc	NAS NMS	JifyLub	JLUB
JLG Industries Inc	NAS NMS	JLG	JLGI
John Adams Life Corp	NAS NMS	JAdams	JALC
John Hanson Savings Bank FSB	NAS NMS	JHansn	JHSL
Johnson & Johnson	New York	JohnJn	JNJ
Johnson Controls Inc	New York	JhnCn	JCI
Johnson Electronics Inc	NAS NMS	JhnsnE	JHSN
Johnson Products Company Inc	American	JohnPd	JPC
Johnson Worldwide Associates Inc (Class A)	NAS NMS	JWA	JWAIA
Johnston Industries Inc	New York	JohnInd	JII
Johnstown American Companies	American	JohnAm	JAC
Johnstown/Consolidated Realty Trust	New York	JhnCRt	JCT
Johnstown Savings Bank (Pennsylvania)	NAS NMS	JohnsSv	JSBK
Jones Intercable Inc	NAS NMS	JonIcbl	JOIN
Jones Intercable Inc (Class A)	NAS NMS	JoneI A	JOINA
Jones Medical Industries Inc	NAS NMS	JneMed	JMED
Jones Spacelink Ltd (Class A)	NAS NMS	JoneSpc	SPLKA
Earle M. Jorgensen Co	New York	Jorgen	JOR

COMPANY NAME	MARKET LISTING	NEWSPAPER ABBREV.	TRADING SYMBOL
Joslyn Corp	NAS NMS	Joslyn	JOSL
Jostens Inc	New York	Josten	JOS
Joulé Inc	American	Joule	JOL
J.P. Industries Inc	New York	JP Ind	JPI
JPM Industries Inc	NAS NL	JPM	JPMI
JRM Holdings Inc	NAS NMS	JRM	JRMX
J2 Communications	NAS SL	J2 Com	JTWO
Judicate Inc	NAS SL	Judicte	JUDGW
Judy's Inc	NAS NMS	Judys	JUDY
Jumping-Jack Shoes Inc	American	JumpJk	JJS
Juno Lighting Inc	NAS NMS	Juno	JUNO
Justin Industries Inc	NAS NMS	Justin	JSTN
JWP Inc	New York	JWP	JWP
K mart Corporation	New York	K mrt	KM
K-Tron International Inc	NAS NMS	KTron	KTII
Kahler Corp	NAS NMS	Kahler	KHLR
Kaisertech Ltd	New York	Kaisrtc	KLU
Kaman Corp (Class A)	NAS NMS	Kaman	KAMNA
M. Kamenstein Inc	NAS NMS	Kamnst	MKCO
Kaneb Energy Partners Ltd	New York	KanbEn	KEP
Kaneb Services Inc	New York	Kaneb	KAB
Kansas City Life Insurance Co	NAS NL	KnCtyL	KCLI
Kansas City Power & Light Co	New York	KCtyPL	KLT
Kansas City Southern Industries Inc	New York	KCSou	KSU
Kansas Gas & Electric Co	New York	KanGE	KGE
The Kansas Power & Light Co	New York	KanPL	KAN
Kaplan Industries Inc	NAS NL	Kaplan	KAPL
Kappa Networks Inc	American	Kappa	KPA
Carl Karcher Enterprises Inc	NAS NMS	Karchr	CARL
Kasler Corp	NAS NMS	Kasler	KASL
Katy Industries Inc	New York	KatyIn	KT
Kaufman & Broad Home Corp	New York	KaufBH	KBH
Kaufman & Broad Inc	New York	KaufB	KB
Kay Corp	American	KayCp	KAY
Kay Jewelers Inc	New York	KayJw	KJI
Kaydon Corp	NAS NMS	Kaydon	KDON
Kaypro Corp	NAS NMS	Kaypro	KPRO
KCR Technology Inc	NAS SL	KCR	KCRT
KCS Group Inc	NAS NMS	KCS Gp	KCSG
KDI Corp	New York	KDI	KDI
Keane Inc	NAS NMS	Keane	KEAN
Kearney-National Inc	American	KearNt	KNY
The Keith Group of Companies Inc	NAS SL	KeithGp	HKME
Keithly Instruments Inc	American	Keithly	KEI
Kelley Oil & Gas Partners Ltd	American	KlyOG	KLY
Kellogg Co	New York	Kellogg	K
Kellwood Co	New York	Kellwd	KWD

COMPANY NAME	MARKET LISTING	NEWSPAPER ABBREV.	TRADING SYMBOL
Kelly Services Inc (Class A)	NAS NMS	KlyS A	KELYA
Kelly Services Inc (Class B)	NAS NMS	KlyS B	KELYB
Kemper Corp	NAS NMS	Kemp	KEMC
Kemper High Income Trust	New York	KmpHi	KHI
Kenan Transport Co	NAS NMS	Kenan	KTCO
KenCope Energy Companies	NAS NMS	Kencop	KCOP
Kenilworth Systems Corp	NAS NMS	Kenlwt	KENS
Kennametal Inc	New York	Kenmt	KMT
Kenner Parker Toys Inc	New York	KPToy	KPT
Kent Electronics Corp	American	KentEl	KEC
Kentucky Central Life Insurance Co (Class A)	NAS NMS	KyCnL	KENCA
Kentucky Investors Inc	NAS NL	KyInvst	KINV
Kentucky Medical Insurance Co (Class A)	NAS SL	KyMd	KYMDA
Kentucky Utilities Co	New York	KyUtil	KU
Kenwin Shops Inc	American	Kenwin	KWN
Keptel Inc	NAS NMS	Keptel	KPTL
Kerkhoff Industries Inc	American	Kerkhf	KIX
Kerr Glass Manufacturing Corp	New York	KerrGl	KGM
Kerr-McGee Corp	New York	KerrMc	KMG
Kessler Products Ltd	American	Kesh	KSS
Ketchum & Company Inc	American	Ketchm	KCH
Kevlin Microwave Corp	NAS NMS	Kevlin	KVLM
Kewaunee Scientific Corp	NAS NMS	KewnSc	KEQU
Key Centurion Bancshares Inc	NAS NMS	KeyCen	KEYC
The Key Co (Class A)	American	KeyCoA	KC.A
The Key Co (Class B)	American	KeyCoB	KC.B
Key Tronic Corp	NAS NMS	KeyTrn	KTCC
KeyCorp	New York	Keycp	KEY
Keystone Camera Products Corp	American	KeyCa	KYC
Keystone Consolidated Industries Inc	New York	KeysCo	KES
Keystone Financial Inc	NAS NMS	KeyFnc	KSTN
Keystone Heritage Group Inc	NAS NMS	KeysHrt	KHGI
Keystone International Inc	New York	KeyInt	KII
Keystone Medical Corp	NAS SL	KeyMed	KMEC
Killearn Properties Inc	American	Kilern	KPI
Kimball International Inc (Class B)	NAS NMS	Kimbal	KBALB
Kimbark Oil & Gas Co	NAS NMS	Kimbrk	KIMB
Kimberly-Clark Corp	New York	KimbC	KMB
Kimmins Corp	NAS NMS	Kimin	KISC
Kimmins Environmental Service Corp	NAS NMS	KimEn	KEVIN
Kinark Corp	American	Kinark	KIN
Kinder-Care Learning Centers Inc	NAS NMS	Kinder	KIND
Kinetic Concepts Inc	NAS NMS	Kinetic	KNCI
King City Federal Saving Bank	NAS NL	KingCty	KCFB
King World Productions Inc	New York	KngWld	KWP
Kings Road Entertainment Inc	NAS NMS	KngsRd	KREN
Kingston Systems Inc	NAS SL	KingstS	PULP

COMPANY NAME	MARKET LISTING	NEWSPAPER ABBREV.	TRADING SYMBOL
Kirby Exploration Company Inc	American	Kirby	KEX
Kirin Brewery Ltd	NAS SL	KirinBr	KNBW
Kirschner Medical Corp	NAS NMS	Kirschn	KMDC
Kit Manufacturing Co	American	Kit Mfg	KIT
KLA Instruments Corp	NAS NMS	KLA	KLAC
Kleer-Vu Industries Inc	American	KleerV	KVU
Kleinert's Inc	NAS NL	Kleinrt	KLRT
Kleinwort Benson Australian Income Fund Inc	New York	KBAust	KBA
KLLM Transport Services Inc	NAS NMS	KLLM	KLLM
KLM Royal Dutch Airlines	New York	KLM	KLM
Kloof Gold Mining Company Ltd	NAS NL	KloofG	KLOFY
KMS Industries Inc	NAS NMS	KMS	KMSI
KMW Systems Corp	American	KMW	KMW
KN Energy Inc	New York	KN Eng	KNE
Knape & Vogt Manufacturing Co	NAS NMS	KnapeV	KNAP
Knight-Ridder Inc	New York	KnghtR	KRI
Knogo Corp	New York	Knogo	KNO
Knowledge Data Systems Inc	NAS SL	Knwldg	KDSI
Knutson Mortgage Corp	NAS NMS	Knutsn	KNMC
Koger Equity Inc	American	KogrEq	KE
Koger Properties Inc	New York	Koger	KOG
Kollmorgen Corp	New York	Kolmor	KOL
Komag Inc	NAS NMS	Komag	KMAG
Koppers Company Inc	New York	Kopers	KOP
The Korea Fund Inc	New York	Korea	KF
Koss Corp	NAS NMS	Koss	KOSS
Kraft Inc	New York	Kraft	KRA
Kreisler Manufacturing Corp	NAS NMS	Kreislr	KRSL
Krelitz Industries Inc	NAS NL	Krelitz	KRLZ
Krisch American Inns Inc	NAS SL	Krisch	INNS
K.R.M. Petroleum Corp	NAS SL	KRM	KRMC
The Kroger Co	New York	Kroger	KR
W.A. Krueger Co	NAS NMS	Kruger	KRUE
KRUG International Corp	NAS NMS	Krug	KRUG
Kubota Ltd	New York	Kubota	KUB
Kuhlman Corp	New York	Kuhlm	KUH
Kulicke & Soffa Industries Inc	NAS NMS	Kulcke	KLIC
Kurzweil Music Systems Inc	NAS NL	KurzM	KURM
Kustom Electronics Inc	NAS NMS	KustEl	KUST
KV Pharmaceutical Co	American	KV Ph	KV
Kyle Technology Corp	NAS SL	KyleTc	KYLE
Kyocera Corp	New York	Kyocer	KYO
Kysor Industrial Corp	New York	Kysor	KZ
L&N Housing Corp	New York	LN Ho	LHC
L Rex International Corp	NAS SL	L Rex	LREXF
L.A. Gear Inc	NAS NMS	LA Gear	LAGR

COMPANY NAME	MARKET LISTING	NEWSPAPER ABBREV.	TRADING SYMBOL
La Jolla Bancorp	American	Lajolla	LJC
La Petite Academy Inc	NAS NMS	LaPete	LPAI
La Pointe Industries Inc	American	LaPnt	LPI
La Quinta Motor Inns Inc	New York	LQuint	LQM
La Quinta Motor Inns L.P.	New York	LQuMt	LQP
La Teko Resources Ltd	NAS SL	LaTeko	LABORF
La-Z-Boy Chair Co	New York	LaZ By	LZB
LaBarge Inc	American	LaBarg	LB
LAC Minerals Ltd	New York	LAC	LAC
Laclede Gas Co	New York	LaclGs	LG
Laclede Steel Co	NAS NMS	LacldSt	LCLD
LADD Furniture Inc	NAS NMS	LaddFr	LADF
Lafarge Corp	New York	Lafarge	LAF
Laidlaw Transportation Ltd (Class A)	NAS NMS	LdlT A	LDMFA
Laidlaw Transportation Ltd (Class B)	NAS NMS	LdlT B	LDMFB
Lake Shore Bancorp Inc (Illinois)	NAS NMS	LkeShre	LSNB
Lake Sunapee Savings Bank FSB (New Hampshire)	NAS NMS	LkSun	LSSB
Lakeland Industries Inc	NAS NMS	Lakelnd	LAKE
Lakeland Savings Bank SLA (New Jersey)	NAS NMS	LakldS	LLSL
Lakewood Forest Products Ltd	NAS SL	LkwdFr	LSTIF
Lam Research Corp	NAS NMS	LamRs	LRCX
Tony Lama Company Inc	NAS NMS	LamaT	TLAM
Lamar Life Corp	NAS SL	Lamar	LLIC
The Lamson & Sessions Co	New York	LamSes	LMS
Lancaster Colony Corp	NAS NMS	Lancst	LANC
Lance Inc	NAS NMS	Lance	LNCE
Lancer Corp	American	Lancer	LAN
Land of Lincoln Savings & Loan	NAS NMS	LdLnSL	LOLS
Landbank Bancshares Corp	New York	LndBnc	LBC
Landmark American Corp	NAS NMS	LdkAm	LMAC
Landmark Bank for Savings (Massachusetts)	NAS NMS	LdmkB	LDMK
Landmark/Community Bancorp Inc	NAS NMS	LdmCB	LCBIV
Landmark Land Company Inc	American	Lndmk	LML
Landmark Savings Assn (Pennsylvania)	American	LdmkSv	LSA
Lands' End Inc	New York	LndEd	LE
Landsing Pacific Fund	American	LndPc	LPF
Langly Corp	NAS NMS	Langly	LCOR
Larizza Industries Inc	American	Larizz	LII
Larrys Ice Cream Inc	NAS SL	LaryIce	LARY
Laser Corp	NAS NMS	LaserCp	LSER
Laser Industries Ltd	American	Laser	LAS
Laser Master International Inc	NAS SL	LasrMst	LCII
Laser Photonics Inc	NAS SL	LaserP	LAZR
Laser Precision Corp	NAS NMS	LaserPr	LASR
Lasertechnics Inc	NAS SL	Lasrtch	LASX
Latshaw Enterprises Inc	American	Latshw	LAT

COMPANY NAME	MARKET LISTING	NEWSPAPER ABBREV.	TRADING SYMBOL
Laurel Entertainment Inc	NAS NMS	LaurelE	LAUR
Laurel Savings Assn	NAS NL	LaurlSv	LARL
Laurentian Capital Corp	American	Lauren	LQ
Lawrence Insurance Group Inc	American	LawrG	LWR
Lawsen Mardon Group Ltd (Class A)	American	Lawsn	LMG.A
Lawson Products Inc	NAS NMS	Lawsn	LAWS
Lawter International Inc	New York	LawtInt	LAW
Lazare Kaplan International Inc	American	LazKap	LKI
LCS Industries Inc	NAS NMS	LCS	LCSI
LDB Corp	NAS NMS	LDB	LDBCD
LDI Corp	NAS NMS	LDI Cp	LDIC
Le Peep Restaurants Inc	NAS SL	LePeep	LPEP
Leadville Corp	NAS SL	Leadvle	LEAD
Leadville Mining & Milling Corp	NAS SL	LeadMn	LDMM
Lear Petroleum Corp	New York	LearPt	LPT
Lear Petroleum Partners L.P.	American	LearPP	LPP
Learning Annex Inc	NAS SL	LrnAnx	ANNX
LeaRonal Inc	New York	Learnl	LRI
LecTec Corp	NAS NL	Lectec	LECT
Lee Data Corp	NAS NMS	LeeDta	LEDA
Lee Enterprises Inc	New York	LeeEnt	LEE
Lee Pharmaceuticals	American	LeePhr	LPH
Leeco Diagnostics Inc	NAS SL	Leeco	LECO
Legg Mason Inc	New York	LegMas	LM
Leggett & Platt Inc	New York	LegPlat	LEG
The Lehman Corp	New York	Lehmn	LEM
P. Leiner Nutritional Products Corp	American	Leiner	PLI
Leisure & Technology Inc	New York	LeisurT	LUX
Leisure Concepts Inc	NAS NMS	LeisCn	LCIC
Lennar Corp	New York	Lennar	LEN
LESCO Inc	NAS NMS	Lesco	LSCO
The Leslie Fay Companies Inc	New York	LeslFay	LES
Leucadia National Corp	New York	LeucNt	LUK
Levitt Corp	American	Levitt	LVT
Levon Resources Ltd	NAS SL	Levon	LVNVF
Lexicon Corp	NAS NMS	Lexicn	LEXI
Lexington Savings Bank (Massachusetts)	NAS NMS	LexingS	LEXB
Liberty All-Star Equity Fund	New York	LbtyAS	USA
The Liberty Corp	New York	LibtyCp	LC
Liberty Homes Inc (Class A)	NAS NMS	LbtyH A	LIBHA
Liberty Homes Inc (Class B)	NAS NMS	LbtyH B	LIBHB
Liberty National Bancorp Inc	NAS NMS	LibtNB	LNBC
Lieberman Enterprises Inc	NAS NMS	Liebr	LMAN
Life Care Communities Corp	NAS SL	LfeCare	LCCC
Life Technologies Inc	NAS NMS	LfeTch	LTEK
Lifecore Biomedical Inc	NAS NMS	Lfecore	CBM
Lifeline Systems Inc	NAS NMS	Lfelne	LIFE
Lifesurance Corp	NAS SL	Lifesur	LICO

COMPANY NAME	MARKET LISTING	NEWSPAPER ABBREV.	TRADING SYMBOL
Lifetime Corp	American	Lfetime	LFT
Liggett Group Inc	New York	Ligget	LIG
Lillian Vernon Corp	American	LilVer	LVC
Eli Lilly & Co	New York	Lilly	LLY
Lilly Industrial Coatings Inc (Class a)	NAS NMS	Lilly A	LICIA
The Limited Inc	New York	Limited	LTD
LIN Broadcasting Corp	NAS NMS	LinBrd	LINB
Lincoln Bancorp	NAS NMS	LincBc	LCNB
Lincoln Financial Corp	NAS NMS	LincFn	LFIN
Lincoln Foodservice Products Inc	NAS NMS	LincFd	LINN
Lincoln Logs Ltd	NAS NMS	LincLg	LLOG
Lincoln National Convertible Securities Fund Inc	New York	LncNtC	LNV
Lincoln National Corp	New York	LincNtl	LNC
Lincoln National Direct Placement Fund Inc	New York	LincPl	LND
Lincoln N.C. Realty Fund	American	LncNC	LRF
Lincoln Savings Bank (Pennsylvania)	NAS NMS	LincSB	LNSB
Lincoln Telecommunications Co	NAS NMS	LincTl	LTEC
Lindal Cedar Homes Inc	NAS NMS	LindH	LNDL
Lindberg Corp	NAS NMS	Lindbrg	LIND
Linear Instruments Corp	NAS SL	LinearI	LINR
Linear Technology Corp	NAS NMS	LinearT	LLTC
Linpro Specific Properties	American	LinPro	LPO
The Lionel Corp	American	Lionel	LIO
Liposome Company Inc	NAS NMS	Liposm	LIPO
Liposome Technology Inc	NAS NMS	LTI	LTIZ
Liqui-Box Corp	NAS NMS	LiqBox	LIQB
Littlefield, Adams & Co	American	Litfld	LFA
Litton Industries Inc	New York	Litton	LIT
Liz Claiborne Inc	NAS NMS	LizCla	LIZC
L.J. Simone Inc	NAS SL	LJ Sim	LJSI
LL&E Royalty Trust	New York	LLE Ry	LRT
Lo-Jack Corp	NAS SL	LoJack	LOJN
Loadmaster Systems Inc	NAS SL	Loadmst	LSMIF
Loan America Financial Corp	NAS NMS	LoanA	LAFC
Local Federal S&L Assn (Oklahoma)	NAS NMS	LocalF	LOCL
Lockheed Corp	New York	Lockhd	LK
Loctite Corp	New York	Loctite	LOC
Lodgistix Inc	NAS NMS	Lodgstx	LDGX
Loews Corp	New York	Loews	LTR
Logicon Inc	New York	Logicon	LGN
Logitek Inc	NAS SL	Logitek	LGTK
Lomas & Nettleton Financial Corp	New York	LomFn	LNF
Lomas & Nettleton Mortgage Investors	New York	LomMt	LOM
Lomas Mortgage Corp	New York	LomasM	LMC
London House Inc	NAS NMS	LondnH	LOND
Lone Star Industries Inc	New York	LnStar	LCE
Lone Star Technologies Inc	NAS NMS	LoneStr	LSST

COMPANY NAME	MARKET LISTING	NEWSPAPER ABBREV.	TRADING SYMBOL
The Long Island City Financial Corp	NAS NMS	LICFn	LICF
Long Island Lighting Co	New York	LILCo	LIL
Long Lake Energy Corp	NAS NMS	LongLke	LLEC
Longs Drug Stores Corp	New York	LongDr	LDG
Longview Fibre Co	NAS NMS	LongF	LFBR
Longwood Group Ltd	NAS SL	Longwd	LONG
Loral Corp	New York	Loral	LOR
The Lori Corp	American	LoriCp	LRC
Lorimar-Telepictures Corp	American	LorTel	LT
Lotus Development Corp	NAS NMS	Lotus	LOTS
Louisiana General Service Inc	New York	LaGenl	LGS
The Louisiana Land & Exploration Co	New York	LaLand	LLX
Louisiana-Pacific Corp	New York	LaPac	LPX
Louisville Gas & Electric Co	New York	LouvGs	LOU
Lowe's Companies Inc	New York	Lowes	LOW
Lowrance Electronics Inc	NAS NMS	Lowranc	LEIX
Loyola Capital Corp	NAS NMS	Loyola	LOYC
LPL Investment Group Inc (Class A)	NAS NMS	LPL	LPLIA
LSB Bancshares Inc (North Carolina)	NAS NMS	LSB NC	LXBX
LSB Bancshares Inc of South Carolina	NAS NL	LSB SC	LBSC
LSB Industries Inc	American	LSB Ind	LSB
LSI Lighting Systems Inc	NAS NMS	LSI Lt	LYTS
LSI Logic Corp	NAS NMS	LSI Lg	LLSI
The LTV Corp	New York	LTV	LTV
LTX Corp	NAS NMS	LTX	LTXX
The Lubrizol Corp	New York	Lubrzl	LZ
Luby's Cafeterias Inc	New York	Lubys	LUB
Lukens Inc	New York	Lukens	LUC
Lumex Inc	American	Lumex	LUM
Lund Enterprises Inc	NAS NMS	LundEnt	LUND
L. Luria & Son Inc	American	Luria	LUR
Luskin's Inc	NAS NMS	Luskin	LUSK
Luther Medical Products Inc	NAS SL	LuthMd	LUTH
Luxtec Corp	NAS SL	Luxtec	LUXT
The LVI Group Inc	New York	LVI Gp	LVI
LVMH Moet Hennessy Louis Vuitton	NAS NMS	LVMH	LVMH
Lydall Inc	American	Lydal	LDL
Lydenburg Platinum Ltd	NAS NL	Lydnbg	LYDPY
Lynch Corp	American	LynchC	LGL
LyphoMed Inc	NAS NMS	Lypho	LMED
M/A-Com Inc	New York	MACOM	MAI
MacDermid Inc	NAS NMS	MDmd	MACD
MacGregor Sporting Goods Inc	American	MacGrg	MGS
Machine Technology Inc	NAS NMS	MachTc	MTEC
Mack Trucks Inc	NAS NMS	MackTr	MACK
MacMillan Bloedel Ltd	MAS NMS	MB	MMBLF
Macmillan Inc	New York	Macmil	MLL

COMPANY NAME	MARKET LISTING	NEWSPAPER ABBREV.	TRADING SYMBOL
The MacNeal-Schwendler Corp	American	MacNSc	MNS
MacroChem Corp	NAS SL	MacrCh	MCHM
Madison Gas & Electric Co	NAS NMS	MadGE	MDSN
Magellan Petroleum Corp	NAS ML	MagelPt	MPC
Magma Copper Co	NAS NMS	MagmC	MGCP
Magma Power Co	NAS NMS	MagmP	MGMA
Magna Group Inc	NAS NMS	MagGp	MAGI
Magna International Inc	NAS NMS	MagnaI	MAGAF
MagnaCard Inc	NAS SL	MagnCd	HGCD
Magnetic Technologies Corp	NAS NL	MgtTc	MTCC
MAI Basic Four Inc	New York	MAIBF	MBF
Mail Boxes Coast To Coast Inc	NAS NL	MailBCs	MBCC
Mail Boxes, Etc	NAS NMS	MailBx	MAIL
Maine Public Service Co	American	MePS	MAP
Maione-Hirschberg Companies Inc	NAS NMS	Maione	MHCIV
Major Realty Corp	NAS NMS	MajRt	MAJR
Major Video Corp	NAS NMS	MajVid	MAJV
Makita Electric Works Ltd	NAS NMS	Makita	MKTAY
Malartic Hygrade Gold Mines (Canada) Ltd	American	Malart	MHG
The Malaysia Fund Inc	New York	Malaysa	MF
Mallard Coach Company Inc	NAS NMS	Mallard	MALC
Mallon Minerals Corp	NAS SL	Malon	MALN
Malrite Communications Group Inc	NAS NMS	Malrite	MALR
Malrite Communications Group Inc (Class A)	NAS NMS	MalritA	MALRA
Management Co Entertainment Group Inc	NAS SL	MgtCo	MCEG
Management Science America Inc	NAS NMS	MgtSci	MSAI
Manatron Inc	NAS NMS	Mantrn	MANA
Manhattan National Corp	New York	ManhNt	MLC
The Manitowoc Company Inc	NAS NMS	Manitw	MANT
Manor Care Inc	New York	ManrCr	MNR
Manufactured Homes Inc	American	ManfHo	MNH
Manufacturers Hanover Corp	New York	MfrHan	MHC
Manufacturers National Corp	NAS NMS	MfrsNt	MNTL
Manville Corp	New York	Manvl	MAN
MAPCO Inc	New York	MAPCO	MDA
Marathon Office Supply Inc	American	MrthOf	MAO
Marble Financial Corp	NAS NMS	MarbFn	MRBL
M/A/R/C Inc	NAS NMS	MARC	MARC
The Marcade Group Inc	New York	Marcde	MAR
Marci International Imports Inc	NAS NL	Marci	MRCI
MarCor Development Company Inc	NAS NL	Marcor	MAAR
The Marcus Corp	NAS NMS	Marcus	MRCS
Margaux Inc	NAS NMS	Margux	MRGX
Margo Nursery Farms Inc	NAS NMS	Margo	MRGO
Marietta Corp	NAS NMS	Mariet	MRTA
Marine Corp (Illinois)	NAS NMS	MarIll	MCOR
Marine Limited Partnership	NAS NAS	MarnL	MRNCZ

COMPANY NAME	MARKET LISTING	NEWSPAPER ABBREV.	TRADING SYMBOL
Marine Transport Lines Inc	NAS NMS	MarinT	MTLI
Marion Laboratories Inc	New York	Marion	MKC
Maritrans Partners L.P.	New York	Maritrn	TUG
Mark Controls Corp	NAS NMS	MarkCtl	MRCCV
Mark Twain Bancshares Inc	NAS NMS	MTwan	MTWN
Markel Corp	NAS NMS	Markel	MAKL
Market Facts Inc	NAS NMS	MktFct	MFAC
MarkitStar Inc	NAS SL	Markstr	MARK
Marlton Technologies Inc	American	Marlton	MTY
Marquest Medical Products Inc	NAS NMS	Marqst	MMPI
Marriott Corp	New York	Marriot	MHS
Mars Graphic Services Inc	American	MarsG	WMD
Mars Stores Inc	NAS NMS	MarsSt	MXXX
Marsam Pharmaceuticals Inc	NAS NMS	Marsm	MSAM
Marsh & McLennan Companies Inc	New York	MrshMc	MMC
Marsh Supermarkets Inc	NAS NMS	MrshSu	MARS
Marshall & Ilsley Corp	NAS NMS	Marshl	MRIS
Marshall Industries	New York	MrshIn	MI
Marten Transport Ltd	NAS NMS	Marten	MRTN
Martin Lawrence Limited Editions Inc	NAS NMS	MartnL	MLLE
Martin Marietta Corp	New York	MartM	ML
Maryland Federal S&L Assn	NAS NMS	MdFSL	MFSL
Masco Corp	New York	Masco	MAS
Masco Industries Inc	NAS NMS	MscoI	MASX
Massachusetts Computer Corp	NAS NMS	Mascmp	MSCP
MASSBANK Corp (Massachusetts)	NAS NMS	Massbk	MASB
MassMutual Corporate Investors	New York	MasCp	MCI
MassMutual Income Investors Inc	New York	MasInc	MIV
MASSTOR Systems Corp	NAS NMS	Masstor	MSCO
Mast Keystone Inc	NAS SL	Mast	MKEY
MATEC Corp	American	Matec	MXC
Material Sciences Corp	American	MatSci	MSC
Materials Research Corp	American	MatRsh	MTL
Matrix Corp	American	Matrix	MAX
Matrix Medica Inc	NAS SL	MtrxM	MMII
Matsushita Electric Industrial Company Ltd	New York	Matsu	MC
Mattel Inc	New York	Mattel	MAT
Matthews & Wright Group Inc	American	MattW	MW
Mauna Loa Macadamia Partners L.P.	New York	MauLoa	NUT
Maury Federal Savings Bank (Tennessee)	NAS NMS	Maury	MFED
Maverick Restaurant Corp	NAS NMS	Mavrck	MAVR
Max & Ermas Restaurants Inc	NAS NMS	MaxEr	MAXE
Maxco Inc	NAS NMS	Maxco	MAXC
Maxicare Health Plans Inc	NAS NMS	Maxcre	MAXI
Maxim Integrated Products Inc	NAS NMS	Maxim	MXIM
MaxPharma Inc	American	Maxphrm	MXP
Maxtor Corp	NAS NMS	Maxtor	MXTR

COMPANY NAME	MARKET LISTING	NEWSPAPER ABBREV.	TRADING SYMBOL
Maxus Energy Corp	New York	Maxus	MXS
Maxwell Laboratories Inc	NAS NMS	Maxwell	MXWL
MAXXAM Group Inc	New York	Maxam	MXM
The May Department Stores Co	New York	MayDS	MA
Mayfair Industries Inc	NAS NMS	MayfrIn	MAYF
Mayfair Super Markets Inc (Class A)	NAS NMS	MaySu	MYFRA
Mayflower Co-operative Bank (Massachusetts)	NAS NMS	MayflCo	MFLR
Mayflower Financial Corp	NAS NMS	MayflF	MFFC
Maynard Oil Co	NAS NMS	MaynOl	MOIL
J.W. Mays Inc	NAS NMS	MaysJ	MAYS
The Maytag Co	New York	Maytag	MYG
MBIA Inc	New York	MBIA	MBI
MBS Textbook Exchange Inc	NAS NMS	MBS	MBSX
MCA Inc	New York	MCA	MCA
McCaw Cellular Communications Inc (Class A)	NAS NMS	McCaw	MCAWA
McClain Industries Inc	NAS NMS	McClain	MCCL
McClatchy Newspapers Inc	American	McCla	MNI
McCormick & Company Inc	NAS NMS	McCrm	MCCRK
McCormick Capital Inc	NAS NL	McCrmC	MKOR
McDaniel Austin Corp	NAS SL	McDanl	ASTN
McDermott International Inc	New York	McDerI	MDR
McDonald & Company Investments Inc	New York	McDnl	MDD
McDonald's Corp	New York	McDld	MCD
McDonnell Douglas Corp	New York	McDnD	MD
McFaddin Ventures Inc	American	McFad	MV
McFarland Energy Inc	NAS NMS	McFarl	MCFE
McGill Manufacturing Company Inc	NAS NMS	McGill	MGLL
McGrath RentCorp	NAS NMS	McGrth	MGRC
McGraw-Hill Inc	New York	McGrH	MHP
MCI Communications Corp	NAS NMS	MCI	MCIC
McIntyre Mines Ltd	New York	McInt	MP
McKesson Corp	New York	McKes	MCK
McLean Industries Inc	New York	McLe	MII
McM Corp	NAS NL	MCM Cp	MCMC
MCO Holdings Inc	American	MCO Hd	MCO
MCO Resources Inc	American	MCO Rs	MCR
MCorp	New York	MCorp	M
McRae Industries Inc (Class A)	American	McRae A	MRI.A
McRae Industries Inc (Class b)	American	McRae B	MRI.B
M.D.C. Asset Investors Inc	New York	MDCA	MIR
M.D.C. Holdings Inc	New York	MDC	MDC
MDT Corp	NAS NMS	MDT Cp	MDTC
MDU Resources Group Inc	New York	MDU	MDU
The Mead Corp	New York	Mead	MEA
Measurex Corp	New York	Mesrx	MX
Mechanical Technology Inc	NAS NMS	MechTc	MTIX

COMPANY NAME	MARKET LISTING	NEWSPAPER ABBREV.	TRADING SYMBOL
Med Mobile Inc	NAS SL	MedMbl	MEDM
Medalist Industries Inc	NAS NMS	Medalst	MDIN
Medar Inc	NAS NMS	Medar	MDXR
MedChem Products Inc	American	Medch	MCH
Medco Containment Services Inc	NAS NMS	MedcC	MCCS
Medco Research Inc	NAS SL	MedcR	MEDR
Medex Inc	NAS NMS	Medex	MDEX
Media General Inc (Class A)	American	Media	MEG.A
Media Logistics Inc	NAS SL	MediLg	TSTM
Media Products Inc	NAS SL	MediaP	MDPI
MEDIAGENIC	NAS NMS	Medign	MGNC
Medical Action Industries Inc	NAS NMS	MedAct	MDCI
Medical Care International Inc	NAS NMS	MedCre	MEDC
Medical Devices Inc	NAS NL	MedDv	MDEV
Medical Graphics Corp	NAS NMS	MedGr	MGCC
Medical Imaging Centers of America Inc	NAS SL	MedImg	MIKA
Medical Management of America Inc	American	MdMgt	MMA
Medical Properties Inc	American	MedPr	MPP
Medical Sterilization Inc	NAS NMS	MedclSt	MSTI
Medicare-Glaser Corp	NAS NMS	MediGl	MGCO
Medicine Shoppe International Inc	NAS NMS	MedSh	MSII
Medicore Inc	American	Mdcore	MDK
MEDIQ Inc	American	Mediq	MED
Medmaster Systems Inc	NAS NMS	MedMst	MMST
Medphone Corp	NAS SL	Medphn	MPHO
Medstat Systems Inc	NAS NMS	Medstat	MDST
Medtronic Inc	New York	Medtrn	MDT
Megadata Corp	NAS NMS	Megdta	MSHK
MEI Diversified Inc	New York	MEI	MEI
Melamine Chemicals Inc	NAS NMS	Melami	MTWO
Mellon Bank Corp	New York	Mellon	MEL
Melville Corp	New York	Melvill	MES
MEM Company Inc	American	Mem	MEM
Memory Metals Inc	NAS SL	MemMtl	MRMT
Memory Sciences Corp	NAS SL	MemryS	MEMX
Memtek Inc	NAS SL	Memtek	METK
Mentor Corp	NAS NMS	Mentor	MNTR
Mentor Graphics Corp	NAS NMS	MentrG	MENT
Merchantile Bancorporation Inc (Missouri)	NAS NMS	MercBc	MTRC
Merchantile Bankshares Corp (Maryland)	NAS NMS	MercBk	MRBK
Mercantile Stores Company Inc	New York	MercSt	MST
The Merchants Bancorp Inc (Connecticut)	NAS NMS	MercBCt	NMBC
Merchants Bancshares Inc (Vermont)	NAS NMS	MrcBnc	MBVT
Merchants Bank of New York	NAS NMS	MerNY	MBNY
Merchants Capital Corp (Class A)	NAS NMS	MrCaA	MCBKA
Merchants Capital Corp (Class B)	NAS NMS	MrCaB	MCBKB
Merchants Group Inc	American	MrchGp	MGP
Merchants National Corp	NAS NMS	MrchNt	MCHN

COMPANY NAME	MARKET LISTING	NEWSPAPER ABBREV.	TRADING SYMBOL
Merck & Company Inc	New York	Merck	MRK
Mercury Entertainment Corp	NAS SL	MercEn	MCRY
Mercury General Corp	NAS NMS	MercGn	MRCY
Mercury S&L Assn	New York	MercSL	MSL
Meredith Corp	New York	Merdth	MDP
Meret Inc	NAS NMS	Meret	MRET
Meridian Bancorp Inc	NAS NMS	MrdnBc	MRDN
Meridian Diagnostic Inc	NAS NMS	MrdDia	KITS
Meridian Insurance Group Inc	NAS NMS	MerdIns	MIGI
Meridian National Corp	NAS SL	MrdnNt	MRCO
Meritor Savings Bank	NAS NMS	Meritr	MTOR
Merrill Corp	NAS NMS	MerilCp	MRLL
Merrill Lynch & Company Inc	New York	MerLyn	MER
Merrimac Industries Inc	American	Mermc	MRM
Merrimack Bancorp Inc	NAS NMS	Mermck	MRMK
Merry-Go-Round Enterprises Inc	NAS NMS	MeryG	MGRE
Merry Land & Investment Company Inc	NAS NMS	MeryLd	MERY
Mesa Airlines Inc	NAS NMS	MesaAr	MESL
Mesa Limited Partnership	New York	MesaLP	MLP
Mesa Offshore Trust	New York	MesaOf	MOS
Mesa Royalty Trust	New York	MesaR	MTR
Mesabi Trust	New York	Mesab	MSB
Mestek Inc	New York	Mestek	MCC
Met-Coil Systems Corp	NAS NMS	MetCoil	METS
Met-Pro Corp	American	MetPro	MPR
MetalBanc Corp	NAS SL	MtlBnc	MBAN
Metalclad Corp	NAS SL	Metlcld	MTLC
Metallurgical Industries Inc (Class A)	NAS SL	Metlrg	MTALA
Metex Corp	American	Metex	MTX
Methode Electronics Inc (Class A)	NAS NMS	MethdA	METHA
Methode Electronics Inc (Class B)	NAS NMS	MthdB	METHB
Metro Airlines Inc	NAS NMS	MetAir	MAIR
Metro Mobile CTS Inc	NAS NMS	MetrMbl	MMCT
Metro-Tel Corp	NAS NMS	MetrTl	MTRO
Metrobank N.A. (California)	American	Metrbk	MBN
Metropolitan Bancorp Inc	NAS NMS	MetBcp	METB
Metropolitan Consolidated Industries Inc	NAS NMS	MetrCn	MONY
Metropolitan Federal S&L Assn (Tennessee)	NAS NMS	MetrF	MFTN
Metropolitan Financial Corp (North Dakota)	New York	MetrFn	MFC
Metropolitan Financial S&L Assn (Texas)	NAS NMS	MetroSv	MSLA
Metropolitan Realty Corp	American	MetRlt	ECOW
The Mexico Fund Inc	New York	MexFd	MXF
Fred Meyer Inc	NAS NMS	MeyerF	MEYER
Meyers Parking System Inc	NAS NL	MeyrPk	MPSI
MFS Income & Opportunity Trust	New York	MFO	MFO
MFS Intermediate Income Trust	New York	MIN	MIN
MFS Multimarket Income Trust	New York	MMT	MMT

COMPANY NAME	MARKET LISTING	NEWSPAPER ABBREV.	TRADING SYMBOL
MFS Multimarket Total Return Trust	New York	MFT	MFT
MFS Municipal Income Trust	New York	MFM	MFM
MGI Properties	New York	MGI Prp	MGI
MGM Grand Inc	NAS NL	MGM Gr	MGMG
MGM/UA Communications Co	New York	MGMUA	MGM
MHI Group Inc	New York	MHI Gp	QMH
M/I Schottenstein Homes Inc	NAS NMS	MI Hom	MIHO
Michael Anthony Jewelers Inc	NAS NMS	MichAnt	MAJL
Michael Foods Inc	NAS NMS	MichlFd	MIKL
J. Michaels Inc	NAS NL	MichJ	MICH
Michaels Stores Inc	American	MichStr	MKE
Michigan Energy Resources Co	New York	MchER	MCG
Michigan National Corp	NAS NMS	MichNt	MNCO
Mickelberry Corp	New York	Micklby	MBC
Micom Systems Inc	NAS NMS	Micom	MICS
Micro Bio-Medics Inc	NAS SL	MicrBi	MBMI
Micro D Inc	NAS NMS	MicrD	MCRD
Micro Display Systems Inc	NAS NL	MicrDis	MDSI
Micro Imaging Systems Inc	NAS SL	MicImg	MISI
Micro Mask Inc	NAS NMS	MicrMk	MCRO
Micro Membranes Inc	NAS SL	MicMemb	MEMB
MicroAge Inc	NAS NMS	Micrage	MICA
Microbilt Corp	NAS NMS	MicBlt	BILT
Microbiological Sciences Inc	NAS NL	Micrbio	MBLS
Microcom Inc	NAS NMS	Micrcm	MNPI
Microdyne Corp	NAS NMS	Micrdy	MCDY
MicroEnergy Inc	NAS SL	MicrEn	MCRE
Micron Products Inc	American	Micron	PMR
Micron Technology Inc	NAS NMS	MicrTc	DRAM
Micropolis Corp	NAS NMS	Microp	MLIS
MicroPro International Corp	NAS NMS	Micrpro	MPRO
MICROS Systems Inc	NAS NMS	Micros	MCRS
Microsemi Corp	NAS NMS	MicSem	MSCC
Microsoft Corp	NAS NMS	Micsft	MSFT
Microwave Filter Company Inc	NAS NMS	MicrFlt	MFCO
Microwave Laboratories Inc	NAS NMS	MicrLb	MWAV
Mid-Am Inc	NAS NMS	MidAm	MIAM
Mid-America Bancorp (Kentucky)	NAS NMS	MidABc	MABC
Mid-America Industries Inc	American	MidAm	MAM
Mid-Hudson Savings Bank FSB (New York)	NAS NMS	MdHud	MHBK
Mid Maine Savings Bank F.S.B.	NAS NMS	MdMaine	MMSB
Mid-State Federal S&L Assn	NAS NMS	MdStFd	MSSL
MidConn Bank (Connecticut)	NAS NMS	MdConn	MIDC
Middle South Utilities Inc	New York	MidSUt	MSU
Middleby Corp	American	Midlby	MBY
Middlesex Water Co	NAS NMS	MdsxW	MSEX
MidFed Savings Bank	NAS NMS	MidFed	MFSB
The Midland Co	American	Midlnd	MLA

COMPANY NAME	MARKET LISTING	NEWSPAPER ABBREV.	TRADING SYMBOL
Midlantic Corp	NAS NMS	MidlCp	MIDL
MidSouth Corp	NAS NMS	MidSou	MSRR
Midway Airlines Inc	New York	MdwAir	MDW
Midwest Communications Corp	NAS NMS	MdwCm	MCOM
Midwest Energy Co	New York	MWE	MWE
Midwest Financial Group Inc	NAS NMS	MdwFn	MFGC
Migent Software Corp	NAS SL	Migent	MGNTF
Mikron Instrument Company Inc	NAS SL	Mikron	MIKR
Herman Miller Inc	NAS NMS	MillrHr	MLHR
Millicom Inc	NAS NMS	Millicm	MILL
Millipore Corp	New York	Millipre	MIL
Mills-Jennings Co	NAS SL	MillsJn	JKPT
Milton Roy Co	New York	MiltnR	MRC
Miltope Group Inc	NAS NMS	Miltope	MILT
Milwaukee Insurance Group Inc	NAS NMS	MilwIns	MILW
Mindscape Inc	NAS NMS	Mindscp	MIND
Mine Safety Appliances Co	NAS NMS	MineSf	MNES
Miners National Bancorp Inc	NAS NMS	MinrNtl	MNBC
MiniScribe Corp	NAS NMS	Miniscr	MINY
Minnesota Mining & Manufacturing Co	New York	MMM	MMM
Minnesota Power & Light Co	New York	MinnPL	MPL
Minnetonka Corp	NAS NMS	Minetk	MINL
Minntech Corp	NAS NMS	Minntc	MNTX
Monorco S.A.	NAS NL	Minorc	MNRCY
Minstar Inc	NAS NMS	Minstar	MNST
The Mischer Corp	NAS NMS	Mischer	MSHR
Mission Resource Partners LP	American	MsmRs	MRP
Mission West Properties	American	MissnW	MSW
Mr. Gasket Co	NAS NMS	MGask	MRGC
Mitchell Energy & Development Corp	American	MtchlE	MND
Mitek Systems Inc	NAS SL	MitekS	MITK
Mitel Corp	New York	Mitel	MLT
Mitsui & Company Ltd	NAS NMS	Mitsui	MITSY
MLX Corp	NAS NMS	MLX	MLXX
MMI Medical Inc	NAS NMS	MMI	MMIM
MMR Holding Corp	NAS NMS	MMR	MMRH
MNC Financial Inc	NAS NMS	MNC	MDNT
MNX Inc	NAS NMS	MNX	MNXI
Mobil Corp	New York	Mobil	MOB
Mobile America Corp	NAS NL	MblAm	NAME
Mobile Communications Corporation of America (Class A)	NAS NMS	MoblC A	MCCAA
Mobile Communications Corporation of America (Class B)	NAS NMS	MoblC B	MCCAB
Mobile Gas Service Corp	NAS NMS	MobGs	MBLE
Mobile National Corp	NAS SL	MoblNt	MBNC
Modern Controls Inc	NAS NMS	MOCON	MOCO
Modine Manufacturing Co	NAS NMS	Modine	MODI

COMPANY NAME	MARKET LISTING	NEWSPAPER ABBREV.	TRADING SYMBOL
Modular Technology Inc	NAS NMS	ModuTc	MTIK
Mohasco Corp	New York	Mohsc	MOH
Molecular Genetics Inc	NAS NMS	Moleclr	MOGN
Moleculon Inc	NAS SL	Moleculn	MBIO
Molex Inc	NAS NMS	Molex	MOLX
Molokai Ranch Ltd	NAS SL	Molokai	MKAI
Monarch Avalon Inc	NAS NMS	MonAvl	MAHI
Monarch Capital Corp	New York	MonCa	MON
The Monarch Machine Tool Co	New York	Monrch	MMO
Monitek Technologies Inc	NAS SL	Monitek	MTEK
Moniterm Corp	NAS NMS	Monitr	MTRM
Monitor Technologies Inc	NAS NMS	MoniTc	MLAB
Monoclonal Antibodies Inc	NAS NMS	MonAnt	MABS
Monsanto Co	New York	Monsan	MTC
The Montana Power Co	Mew York	MonPw	MTP
Montclair Savings Bank (New Jersey)	NAS NMS	MontSv	MSBI
Montedison SpA	New York	Monted	NMT
Montgomery Street Income Securities Inc	New York	MonSt	MTS
MONY Real Estate Investors	New York	MONY	MYM
Moodus Savings Bank	NAS SL	Moodus	MOOD
Moog Inc (Class A)	American	MoogA	MOG.A
Moog Inc (Class B)	American	MoogB	MOG.B
Moore Corporation Ltd	New York	Moore	MCL
Moore Financial Group Inc	NAS NMS	MoorF	MFGI
Moore-Handley Inc	NAS NMS	MoreHd	MHCO
Moore Medical Corp	American	MMed	MMD
Moore Products Co	NAS NMS	MooreP	MORP
Mor-Flo Industries Inc	NAS NMS	MorFlo	MORF
J.T. Moran Financial Corp	NAS SL	Moran	JTMC
J.P. Morgan & Company Inc	New York	Morgan	JPM
Morgan Grenfell SMALLCap Fund Inc	New York	MorgG	MGC
Morgan Keegan Inc	New York	MorKeg	MOR
Morgan, Olmstead, Kennedy & Gardner Capital Corp	NAS NMS	MOKG	MOKG
Morgan Products Ltd	New York	MorgnP	MGN
Morgan Stanley Group Inc	New York	MorgSt	MS
Morgan's Foods Inc	American	MorgnF	MR
Morino Associates Inc	NAS NMS	Morin	MOAI
Morrison Inc	NAS NMS	Morsn	MORR
Morrison Knudsen Corp	New York	MorKnd	MRN
Morsemere Financial Group Inc	NAS NMA	Mrsmr	MFGR
Mortgage & Realty Trust	New York	MtgRty	MRT
Mortgage Investment Plus Inc	American	MtgPl	MIP
Morton Thiokol Inc	New York	Morton	MTI
MOSCOM Corp	NAS NL	Moscom	MSCM
Mosinee Paper Corp	NAS NMS	Mosine	MOSI
Motel 6 L.P.	New York	Motel	SIX
Moto Photo Inc	NAS NL	MotoPh	MOTTO

COMPANY NAME	MARKET LISTING	NEWSPAPER ABBREV.	TRADING SYMBOL
Motor Club of America	NAS NMS	MotClb	MOTR
Motorola Inc	New York	Motorla	MOT
Mott's Super Markets Inc	American	Motts	MSM
Mountain Medical Equipment Inc	American	MtMed	MTN
Mountaineer Bankshares of West Virginia Inc	NAS NMS	MtnrBk	MTNR
MPSI System Inc	NAS NMS	MPSI	MPSG
M.S. Carriers Inc	NAS NMS	MSCar	MSCA
MSA Realty Corp	American	MSA	SSS
MSI Data Corp	American	MSI Dt	MSI
MSI Electronics Inc	NAS NL	MSI El	MSIE
MSR Exploration Ltd	American	MSR	MSR
MTS Systems Corp	NAS NMS	MTS	MTSC
Paul Mueller Co	NAS NMS	Mueller	MUEL
Multi-Color Corp	NAS NMS	MultClr	LABL
Multi-Local Media Corp	NAS NMS	MltLocl	MCMC
Multibank Financial Corp	NAS NMS	Multbk	MLTF
Multimedia Inc	NAS NMS	Multm	MMEDC
Multivest Corp	NAS SL	Multvst	MVST
Multnomah Kennel Club (Class A)	NAS NL	MultnA	MKNLA
Munford Inc	New York	Munfrd	MFD
Municipal Development Corp	NAS NMS	MuniDv	MUNI
MuniInsured Fund Inc	American	MunIn	MIF
Munivest Fund Inc	American	Munvst	MUF
Munsingwear Inc	New York	Munsng	MUN
Murgold Resources Inc	NAS SL	Murgold	MGDVF
Murphy Oil Corp	New York	MurpO	MUR
Murry Ohio Manufacturing Co	New York	MurryO	MYO
Muscocho Explorations Ltd	NAS NL	Muscoch	MUSMF
The Musicland Group Inc	New York	Muscld	TMG
Mustang Resources Corp	NAS NL	MustR	MUSE
Mutual Federal S&L Assn (North Carolina)	NAS NMS	MuFSL	MUTU
Mutual Federsl Savings Bank, A Stock Corp (Ohio)	NAS NL	MtlFdl	MFBZ
Mutual of Omaha Interest Shares Inc	New York	MutOm	MUO
Mycogen Corp	NAS NMS	Mycogn	MYCO
The L.E. Myers Company Group	New York	MyerL	MYR
Myers Industries Inc	American	MyerI	MYE
Mylan Laboratories Inc	New York	Mylan	MYL
Mylex Corp	NAS SL	Mylex	MYLX
N-W Group Inc	NAS NMS	NW Grp	NWGI
NAC Re Corp	NAS NMS	NAC RE	NREC
NACCO Industries Inc	New York	NACCO	NC
NAFCO Financial Group Inc	New York	NAFCO	NAF
Nahama & Weagant Energy Co	NAS SL	Naham	NAWE
Nalcap Holdings Inc	NAS NL	Nalcap	NPHIF
Nalco Chemical Co	New York	Nalco	NLC

COMPANY NAME	MARKET LISTING	NEWSPAPER ABBREV.	TRADING SYMBOL
Nanometrics Inc	NAS NMS	Nanomt	NANO
Nantucket Industries Inc	American	Nantck	NAN
Napa Valley Bancorp	NAS NMS	NapaVl	NVBC
Napco International Inc	NAS NMS	Napco	NPCO
Nash-Finch Co	NAS NMS	NashF	NAFC
Nashua Corp	New York	Nashua	NSH
Nasta International Inc	American	Nasta	NAS
National Australia Bank Ltd	New York	NtAust	NAB
National Banc of Commerce Co (West Virginia)	NAS NMS	NBkWV	NBCC
National Bancorp of Alaska Inc	NAS NMS	NB Alsk	NBAK
National Bancshares Corporation of Texas	NAS NMS	NBnTex	NBCT
National Business Systems Inc	NAS NMS	NBusSy	NBSIF
National City Bancorporation (Minnesota)	NAS NMS	NCtyB	NCBM
National City Corp	NAS NMS	NtlCity	NCTY
National Commerce Bancorporation	NAS NMS	NtCBc	NCBC
National Community Bank of New Jersey	NAS NMS	NCNJ	NCBR
National Computer Systems Inc	NAS NMS	NtCptr	NLCS
National Convenience Stores Inc	New York	NtlCnv	NCS
National Data Corp	NAS NMS	NData	NDTA
National Datacomputer Inc	NAS SL	NDtacpt	NDIC
National Education Corp	New York	NatEdu	NEC
National Enterprises Inc	New York	NtEnt	NEI
National Environmental Controls Inc	NAS SL	NEnvCt	NECT
National FSI Inc	NAS NL	Ntl FSI	NFSI
National Fuel Gas Co	New York	NatFG	NFG
National Gas & Oil Co	American	NtGsO	NLG
The National Guardian Corp	NAS NMS	NtGuard	NATG
National Health Enhancement Systems Inc	NAS SL	NtHlthE	NHES
National Health Laboratories Inc	NAS NMS	NHltLab	NHLI
National Healthcare Inc	NAS NMS	NtHltcr	NHCI
National Heritage Inc	New York	NtHert	NHR
National HMO Corp	NAS NMS	Nt HMO	NHMO
National Imaging Inc	NAS NL	NtImag	NIAM
National Industrial Bancorp Inc (Class A)	NAS SL	NtInBc	NIBCA
National Institute of Careers Inc	NAS SL	NtInst	NICE
National Insurance Group	NAS NMS	NtlIns	NAIG
National Intergroup Inc	New York	NlI	NII
National Lampoon Inc	NAS SL	NLamp	NLPI
National Loan Bank (Texas)	NAS NMS	NtLoan	NLBK
National Lumber & Supply Inc	NAS NMS	NtLumb	NTLB
National Media Corp	NAS SL	NtMedia	NMCOC
National Medical Enterprises Inc	New York	NMedE	NME
National Mercantile Bancorp	NAS NMS	NtMerc	MBLA
National Micronetics Inc	NAS NMS	NMicrn	NMIC
National Mine Service Co	New York	NMineS	NMS
National Patent Development Corp	American	NtPatnt	NPD
National Penn Bancshares Inc	NAS NMS	NtPenn	NPBC

COMPANY NAME	MARKET LISTING	NEWSPAPER ABBREV.	TRADING SYMBOL
National Pizza Co	NAS NMS	NtlPza	PIZA
National Presto Industries Inc	New York	NtPrest	NPK
National Properties Corp	NAS NMS	NtProp	NAPE
National Realty L.P.	American	NtRty	NLP
National Reference Publishing Inc	NAS NL	NtlRef	ZIPP
National Sanitary Supply Co	NAS NMS	NtSanit	NSSX
National Savings Bank of Albany	NAS NMS	NtlSav	NSBA
National Security Insurance Co	NAS NMS	NSecIns	NSIC
National Semiconductor Corp	New York	NtSemi	NSM
National Service Industries Inc	New York	NtSvIn	NSI
National-Standard Co	New York	NStand	NSD
National Technical Systems	NAS NMS	NTech	NTSC
National Transaction Network Inc	NAS SL	NtTran	NTNI
National Video Inc	NAS NMS	NVideo	NVIS
National Vision Services Inc	NAS SL	NVision	NVSI
National Western Life Insurance Co (Class A)	NAS NMS	NtWnLf	NWLIA
National Westminster Bank PLC	New York	NtWst	NW
Nationwide Legal Services Inc	NAS SL	NtwdLg	NLSI
Natural Alternatives Inc	NAS SL	NatAltr	NATA
Nature's Bounty Inc	NAS NMS	NatrBty	NBTY
Nature's Sunshine Products Inc	NAS NMS	NtrSun	AMTC
Navigators Group Inc	NAS NMS	NavgGp	NAVG
Navistar International Corp	New York	Navistr	NAV
NBD Bancorp Inc	New York	NBD	NBD
NBI Inc	New York	NBI	NBI
NBSC Corp	NAS NMS	NBSC	NSCB
NCF Financial Corp	American	NCF	NFC
NCH Corp	New York	NCH	NCH
NCNB Corp	New York	NCNB	NCB
NCR Corp	New York	NCR	NCR
ND Resources Inc	NAS SL	ND Rsc	NUDYE
NDL Products Inc	NAS SL	NDL	NDLP
NEC Corp	NAS NMS	NEC	NIPNY
NECO Enterprises Inc	American	NECO	NPT
NEECO Inc	NAS NMS	NEECO	NEEC
The Neiman-Marcus Group Inc	New York	NeimM	NMG
Nellcor Inc	NAS NMS	Nellcor	NELL
Nelson Holdings International Ltd	American	NelsnH	NHI
Nelson Thomas Inc	NAS NMS	NelsnT	TNEL
Nelson Thomas Inc (Class B)	NAS SL	NelsnB	TNELB
Neo-Lens Inc	NAS SL	Neolens	NEOL
NEOAX Inc	NAS NMS	NEOAX	NOAX
NeoRx Corp	NAS NMS	Neorx	NERX
NERCO Inc	New York	Nerco	NER
NESB Corp	NAS NMS	NESB	NESB
Nestor Inc	NAS NMS	Nestor	NEST
NetAir International Corp	NAS SL	NetAir	NTAR

COMPANY NAME	MARKET LISTING	NEWSPAPER ABBREV.	TRADING SYMBOL
NETI Technologies Inc	NAS SL	NETI	NETIF
Network Electronic Corp	NAS NMS	NtwkEl	NWRK
Network Equipment Technologies Inc	NAS NMS	NwkEq	NETX
Network Systems Corp	NAS NMS	NtwkSy	NSCO
Networked Picture Systems Inc	NAS SL	NetwkPc	NPSI
Neurotech Corp	NAS SL	Neurtch	NURO
Neutrogena Corp	NAS NMS	Neutrg	NGNA
Nevada Goldfields Corp	NAS NMS	NevGld	NGFCF
Nevada National Bancorporation	NAS NMS	NevNBc	NENB
Nevada Power Co	New York	NevPw	NVP
New American High Income Fund	New York	NwAm	NYB
New American Shoe Corp	New York	NwASh	AFS
New Bedford Institution for Savings	New York	NwBedf	NBB
New Brunswick Scientific Co	NAS NMS	NBrunS	NBSC
New England Bancorp Inc	NAS NL	NE Bcp	NBKC
New England Business Service Inc	NAS NMS	NE Bus	NEBS
New England Critical Care Inc	NAS NMS	NECrit	NECC
New England Electric System	New York	NEngEl	NES
New England Realty Assn	NAS NL	NEngRA	NEWRZ
New Hampshire Savings Bank Corp	NAS NMS	NHmB	NHSB
New Jersey Resources Corp	New York	NJRsc	NJR
New Jersey Savings Bank	NAS NMS	NJSvg	NJSB
New Jersey Steel Corp	NAS NMS	NJ Stl	NJST
New Line Cinema Corp	American	NewLine	NLN
New Mexico & Arizona Land Co	American	NMxAr	NZ
New Plan Realty Trust	New York	NPlnRl	NPR
New Process Co	American	NProc	NOZ
New Sky Communications Inc	NAS SL	NewSky	NSKY
New Visions Entertainment Corp	NAS NMS	NwVisn	NUCP
New World Entertainment Ltd	American	NWldE	NWE
New York Bancorp Inc	NAS NMS	NY Bcp	NYBC
New York Marine & General Insurance Co	NAS NMS	NY Mir	NYMG
New York State Electric & Gas Corp	New York	NYSEG	NGE
The New York Tax-Exempt Income Fund Inc	American	NYTEI	XTX
New York Testing Laboratories Inc	NAS SL	NYTst	NYTL
The New York Times Co (Class A)	American	NY Time	NYT.A
Newcor Inc	American	Newcor	NEW
Newell Co	New York	Newell	NWL
Newhall Investment Properties	New York	Nwhall	NIP
The Newhall Land & Farming Co	New York	Newhll	NHL
Newhall Resources	New York	NwhlRs	NR
Newman Federal S&L Assn (Georgia)	NAS NMS	NewSL	NFSL
Newmark & Lewis Co	American	NewLew	NLI
NewMil Bancorp Inc	NAS NMS	NMlBc	NMSB
Newmont Gold Co	New York	NwmtGd	NGC
Neworld Bancorp Inc (Massachusetts)	NAS NMS	NwldBk	NWOR
Newport Corp	NAS NMS	Newpt	NEWP
Newport Electronics Inc	NAS NMS	NewpEl	NEWE

COMPANY NAME	MARKET LISTING	NEWSPAPER ABBREV.	TRADING SYMBOL
Newport News Savings Bank (Virginia)	NAS NMS	NwprtN	NNSL
Newport Pharmaceuticals International Inc	NAS NMS	NwpPh	NWPH
The News Corporation Ltd	New York	NewsCp	NWS
NFS Financial Corp	NAS NMS	NFS	NFSF
NHD Stores Inc	NAS NMS	NHD Str	NHDI
Ni-Cal Developments Ltd	NAS NMS	NiCal	NICLF
Niagara Exhcange Corp	NAS NMS	NiagEx	NIEX
Niagara Mohawk Power Corp	New York	NiaMP	NMK
Niagara Share Corp	New York	NiagSh	NGS
Nicholas-Applegate Growth Equity Fund Inc	New York	NichApl	GEF
S.E. Nichols Inc	American	Nichols	NCL
Nichols-Homeshield Inc	NAS NMS	NichHm	NHIC
Nichols Institute	American	NichIn	LAB
Nichols Research Corp	NAS NMS	NichRs	NRES
Nicolet Intrument Corp	New York	Nicolet	NIC
NICOR Inc	New York	NICOR	GAS
NIKE Inc (Class B)	NAS NMS	NikeB	NIKE
NIPSCO Industries Inc	New York	NIPSCO	NI
Niravoice Inc (Class A)	NAS SL	Niravce	NIRAA
Nissan Motor Company Ltd	NAS NL	Nissan	NSANNY
NL Industries Inc	New York	NL Ind	NL
NMR of America Inc	NAS SL	NMR	NMRR
Nobel Insurance Ltd	NAS NMS	Nobel	NOBLF
Nobility Homes Inc	NAS SL	NobiltyH	NOBH
Noble Affiliates Inc	New York	NoblAf	NBL
Noble Drilling Corp	NAS NMS	NbleDr	NDCO
Noble Romans Inc	NAS SL	NobleR	NROM
Nodaway Valley Co	NAS NMS	Nodway	NVCO
Noel Indstries Inc	American	NoelInd	NOL
Noland Co	NAS NMS	Noland	NOLD
Nooney Realty Trust Inc	NAS NL	Nooney	NRTI
Nor-Quest Resources Ltd	NAS SL	NorQst	NQRLF
Nord Resources Corp	New York	NordRs	NRD
Nordson Corp	NAS NMS	Nordsn	NDSN
Nordstrom Inc	NAS NMS	Nordst	NOBE
Norfolk Southern Corp	New York	NflkSo	NSC
Normandy Oil & Gas Co	NAS NMS	NrmOG	NMDY
Norsk-Data A.S. (Class B)	NAS NMS	NorskB	NORKZ
Norsk Hydro a.s.	New York	Norsk	NHY
Norstan Inc	NAS NMS	Norstan	NRRD
Nortek Inc	New York	Nortek	NTK
North American Bancorporation Inc	NAS NL	NABcp	NOAB
North American Biologicals Inc	NAS NMS	NABio	NBIO
North American Holding Corp	NAS NMS	NAHld	NAHL
North American Holding Corp (Class A)	NAS NMS	NAHdA	NAHLA
North American Metals Corp	NAS SL	NAMtl	NAMVF

COMPANY NAME	MARKET LISTING	NEWSPAPER ABBREV.	TRADING SYMBOL
North American National Corp	NAS NMS	NoANat	NAMC
North American Savings Assn (Missouri)	NAS NL	NAmSv	NASA
North American Ventures Inc	NAS NMS	NAmV	NAVI
North Atlantic Industries Inc	NAS NMS	NAtIn	NATL
North Canadian Oils Ltd	American	NCdO	NCD
North Carolina Natural Gas Corp	NAS NMS	NCarG	NCNG
North East Insurance Co	NAS SL	NE Ins	NEIC
North European Oil Royalty Trust	New York	NEurO	NET
North Fork Bancorporation	NAS NMS	NoFkB	NFBC
North Hills Electronics Inc	NAS NMS	NthHill	NOHL
North Lily Mining Co	NAS NL	NthLily	NLMC
North Side Savings Bank (New York)	NAS NMS	NoSdeSv	NSBK
North Star Universal Inc	NAS NMS	NStarU	NSRU
North-West Telecommunicationa Inc	NAS NMS	NWstT	NOWT
Northeast Bancorp Inc	NAS NMS	NstBcp	NBIC
Northeast Savings F.A.	New York	NestSv	NSB
Northeast Utilities	New York	NoestUt	NU
NorthEastern Mortgage Company Inc	American	NeMtge	NM
Northern Air Freight Inc	NAS NMS	NoAir	NAFI
Northern States Power Co	New York	NoStPw	NSP
Northern Telecom Ltd	New York	NorTel	NT
Northern Trust Corp	NAS NMS	NorTrst	NTRS
Northgate Exploration Ltd	New York	Nthgat	NGX
Northland Cranberries Inc (Class A)	NAS NMS	NorldCr	CBRYA
Northland S&L Assn	NAS NL	NthldSv	NLSL
Northrop Corp	New York	Nortrp	NOC
Northwest Corp	New York	Norwst	NOB
Northwest Engineering Co	NAS NMS	NwEng	NWEN
Northwest Illinois Bancorp Inc	NAS NMS	NwstIll	NWIB
Northwest Natural Gas Co	NAS NMS	NwNG	NWNG
Northwest Teleproductions Inc	NAS NMS	NTelpd	NWTL
Northwestern National Life Insurance Co	NAS NMS	NwNLf	NWNL
Northwestern Public Service Co	NAS NMS	NWPS	NWPS
Northwestern States Portland Cement Co	NAS NL	NwPrC	NSTS
Northwestern Steel & Wire Co	New York	NwStW	NSW
Norton Co	New York	Norton	NRT
Norton Enterprises Inc	NAS NMS	NortnE	NRTN
Norwich Financial Corp (Connecticut)	NAS NMS	NorwFn	NSSB
Nostalgia Network Inc	NAS SL	NostN	NNET
Nova Corp	New York	Nova	NVA
Nova Pharmaceutical Corp	NAS NMS	NovaPh	NOVX
Novametrix Medical Systems Inc	NAS NMS	Novmtx	NMTX
Novar Electronics Corp	NAS NMS	Novar	NOVR
Novell Inc	NAS NMS	Novell	NOVL
Novellus Systems Inc	NAS NL	Novelus	NVLS
Novo Corp	NAS NMS	NovoCp	NOVO
Novo Industri A/S	New York	Novo	NVO
Nowsco Well Service Ltd	NAS NL	Nowsc	NWELF

COMPANY NAME	MARKET LISTING	NEWSPAPER ABBREV.	TRADING SYMBOL
Noxell Corp (Class B)	NAS NMS	Noxell	NOXLB
NRM Energy Company L.P.	American	NRM	NRM
NS Group Inc	American	NS Gp	NSS
Nu Horizons Electronics Corp	American	NuHrz	NUH
Nu-Med Inc	NAS NMS	NuMed	NUMS
Nuclear Data Inc	American	NuclDt	NDI
Nuclear Metals Inc	NAS NMS	NucMet	NUCM
Nuclear Support Services Inc	NAS NMS	NuclSpt	NSSI
Nucor Corp	New York	Nucor	NUE
Nucorp Energy Inc	NAS NMS	NucrpE	NUCO
NUI Corp	New York	NUI	NUI
Numac Oil & Gas Ltd	American	Numac	NMC
Numerex Corp	NAS NMS	Numerex	NUMR
Numerica Financial Corp	NAS NMS	Numrc	NUME
Nutmeg Industries Inc	NAS NMS	Nutmeg	NUTM
Nutri-Cheese Co	NAS SL	NutrCh	NCCI
Nuveen California Municipal Income Fund	New York	NvCMI	NCM
Nuveen California Municipal Value Fund Inc	New York	NuvCal	NCA
Nuveen Municipal Income Fund	New York	NvMuI	NMI
Nuveen Municipal Value Fund Inc	New York	NuvMu	NUV
Nuveen N.Y. Municipal Income Fund	American	NvNYM	NNM
Nuveen N.Y. Municipal Value Fund Inc	New York	NuvNY	NNY
Nuveen Premium Income Municipal Fund Inc	New York	NuvPI	NPI
NuVision Inc	NAS NMS	NuVisn	NUVI
NVRyan L.P.	American	NVRyn	NVR
NWA Inc	New York	NWA	NWA
NYCOR Inc	NAS NMS	NYCOR	NYCO
NYNEX Corp	New York	Nynex	NYN
Nytest Environmental Inc	NAS SL	Nytest	NYTS
Oak Hill Sportswear Corp	NAS NMS	OakHill	OHSC
Oak Industries Inc	New York	OakInd	OAK
Oakite Products Inc	New York	OakiteP	OKT
Oakwood Homes Corp	New York	Oakwd	OH
O'Brien Energy Systems Inc	American	OBrien	OBS
Occidental Petroleum Corp	New York	OcciPet	OXY
Occupational Medical Corporation of America Inc	NAS SL	OccuMd	OMCA
Occupational-Urgent Care Health Systems Inc	NAS NMS	OcuUrg	OUCH
Oce-Van Der Grinten N.V.	NAS NL	Oce-NY	OCENY
Ocean Drilling & Exploration Co	New York	ODECO	ODR
Oceaneering International Inc	NAS NMS	Oceaner	OCER
OCG Technology Inc	NAS NMS	OCG Tc	OCGT
Ocilla Industries Inc	NAS NMS	Ocilla	OCIL
Octel Communications Corp	NAS NMS	Octel	OCTL
Odetics Inc (Class A)	American	OdetA	O.A

COMPANY NAME	MARKET LISTING	NEWSPAPER ABBREV.	TRADING SYMBOL
Odetics Inc (Class B)	American	OdetB	O.B
Odyssey Entertainment Ltd	NAS SL	Odysey	ODYY
OEA Inc	American	OEA	OEA
Office Depot Inc	NAS NL	OfceDpt	ODEP
Officeland Inc	NAS NL	Oficeld	OFLDF
Offshore Logistics Inc	NAS NMS	OffsLog	OLOGP
The Ogilvy Group Inc	NAS NMS	Ogil Gp	OGIL
Ogden Corp	New York	Ogden	OG
Ogelbay Norton Co	NAS NMS	Oglbay	OGLE
The Ohio Art Co	American	OhArt	OAR
Ohio Bancorp	NAS NMS	OhioBc	OHBC
Ohio Casualty Corp	NAS NMS	OhioCas	OCAS
Ohio Edison Co	New York	OhioEd	OEC
The Ohio Mattress Co	New York	OhMatr	OMT
O.I. Corp	NAS SL	OICorp	OICO
Oil-Dri Corporation of America	NAS NMS	OilDri	OILC
Oilgear Co	NAS NMS	Oilgear	OLGR
Oklahoma Gas & Electric co	New York	OklaGE	OGE
Old Dominion Systems Inc	NAS NMS	OldDom	ODSI
Old Fashion Foods Inc	NAS NMS	OldFsh	OFFI
Old Kent Financial Corp	NAS NMS	OldKnt	OKEN
Old Republic International Corp	NAS NMS	OldRep	OLDR
Old Spagetti Warehouse Inc	NAS NMS	OldSpag	OSWI
Old Stone Corp	NAS NMS	OldStn	OSTN
Olin Corp	New York	Olin	OLN
Olson Industries Inc	NAS NMS	OlsonI	OLSN
The Olsten Corp	American	Olsten	OLS
Olympic Broadcasting Corp	NAS SL	OlyBdc	OBCCC
Olympic Savings Bank	NAS NL	OlymSv	OSBW
OMI Corp	NAS NMS	OMI Cp	OMIC
Omni Exploration Inc	NAS SL	OmniEx	OMNX
Omnicare Inc	New York	Omncre	OCR
Omnicom Group Inc	NAS NMS	Omnicm	OMCM
On-Line Software International Inc	New York	OnLne	OSI
Oncogene Science Inc	NAS NMS	Oncogn	ONCS
Oncor Inc	NAS SL	Oncor	ONCR
The One Bancorp	NAS NMS	OneBc	TONE
One Liberty Properties Inc	American	OneLibt	OLP
One Price Clothing Stores Inc	NAS NMS	OnePr	ONPR
One Valley Bancorp of West Virginia Inc	NAS NMS	OneVl	OVWV
Oneida Ltd	New York	Oneida	OCQ
Oneita Industries Inc	American	Oneita	ONA
ONEOK Inc	New York	ONEOK	OKE
O'okiep Copper Company Ltd	American	OOkiep	OKP
Oppenheimer Industries Inc	American	Oppenh	OPP
Oppenheimer Multi-Sector Income Trust	New York	OpnMl	OMS
Optek Technology Inc	NAS NMS	Optek	OPTX
Optelecom Inc	NAS SL	Optlcm	OPTC

COMPANY NAME	MARKET LISTING	NEWSPAPER ABBREV.	TRADING SYMBOL
Optical Coating Laboratory Inc	NAS NMS	OpticC	OCLI
Optical Radiation Corp	NAS NMS	OpticR	ORC
Optical Specialties Inc	NAS NMS	OpticlS	OSIX
Opto Mechanik Inc	NAS NMS	Opto	OPTO
Oracle Systems Corp	NAS NMS	Oracle	ORCL
Orange & Rockland Utilities Inc	New York	OranRk	ORU
Orange-co Inc	New York	OrngCo	OJ
Orange Free State Investments Ltd	NAS NL	OrangF	OFSLY
Orange Savings Bank	NAS SL	OrngSv	OSBK
Orbit Instrument Corp	NAS NMS	Orbit	ORBT
Oregon Metallurgical Corp	NAS NMS	OregMt	OREM
Oregon Steel Mills Inc	American	OregSt	OS
ORFA Corp of America	NAS NMS	Orfa	ORFA
Organogensis Inc	American	Orgngn	ORG
Orient Express Hotels Inc	New York	Orient	OEH
Orient Federal Savings Bank (Puerto Rico)	NAS NMS	OrntFd	OFSB
Original Italian Pasta Products Company Inc	NAS SL	OrigItl	ORIG
Oriole Homes Corp (Class A)	American	OriolH A	OHC.A
Oriole Homes Corp (Class B)	American	OriolH B	OHC.B
Orion Broadcast Group Inc	NAS SL	OrionBd	OBGI
Orion Capital Corp	New York	OrionC	OC
Orion Pictures Corp	New York	OrionP	OPC
Orion Research Inc	NAS NMS	OrionRs	ORIR
Ormand Industries Inc	American	Ormand	OMD
Orthomet Inc	NAS NMS	Orthmt	OMET
Osborn Communications Corp	NAS NL	Osborn	OSBN
Oshkosh B'Gosh Inc (Class A)	NAS NMS	OshA	GOSHA
Oshkosh B'Gosh Inc (Class B)	NAS NMS	OshB	GOSHB
Oshkosh Truck Corp (Class B)	NAS NMS	OshkT B	OTRKB
Oshman's Sporting Goods Inc	NAS NMS	Oshmn	OSHM
Osicom Technologies Inc	NAS NMS	Osicom	OSIC
Osmonics Inc	NAS NMS	Osmnc	OSMO
O'Sullivan Corp	American	OSulvn	OSL
Otisville BioPharm Inc	NAS SL	Otisvlle	OBPI
Otter Tail Power Co	NAS NMS	OttrTP	OTTR
Outback Oil & Mineral Exploration Corp	NAS SL	OutbOM	OUTB
Outboard Marine Corp	New York	OutbdM	OM
Outlet Communications Inc (Class A)	NAS NMS	OutletC	OCOMA
Overmyer Corp	NAS NL	Overmy	OMCO
Overseas Shipholding Group Inc	New York	OvShip	OSG
Ovex Fertility Corp	NAS SL	Ovex	OVEX
Ovonic Imaging Systems Inc	NAS NL	Ovonic	OVON
Owens & Minor Inc	New York	OwenM	OMI
Owens-Corning Fiberglas Corp	New York	OwenC	OCF
The Oxford Energy Co	American	OxfEgy	OEN
Oxford Industries Inc	New York	Oxford	OXM
The Oxidyne Group Inc	NAS NMS	Oxidyn	OXID

COMPANY NAME	MARKET LISTING	NEWSPAPER ABBREV.	TRADING SYMBOL
P&F Industries Inc (Class A)	NAS NMS	P F	PFINA
Pacad Inc	NAS SL	Pacad	BAGS
PACCAR Inc	NAS NMS	Pacar	PCAR
PACE Membership Warehouse Inc	NAS NMS	PACE	PMWI
Pacer Technology Inc	NAS NMS	PacTec	PTCH
Pacific American Income Shares Inc	New York	PacAS	PAI
Pacific Bancorporation	NAS NL	PacBcp	PABC
Pacific Dunlop Ltd	NAS NMS	PacDunl	PDLPY
Pacific Enterprises Ltd	New York	PacEnt	PET
Pacific First Financial Corp	NAS NMS	PacFst	PFFS
Pacific Gas & Electric Co	New York	PacGE	PCG
Pacific Inland Bancorp	NAS NL	PacInld	PIBC
Pacific International Services Corp	NAS NMS	PacIntl	PISC
Pacific Nuclear Systems Inc	NAS NMS	PacNuc	PACN
Pacific Resources Inc	New York	PacRes	PRI
Pacific Scientific Co	New York	PacSci	PSX
Pacific Silver Corp	NAS NMS	PacSlv	PASI
Pacific Telecom Inc	NAS NMS	PTelcm	PTCM
Pacific Telesis Group	New York	PacTel	PAC
Pacific Western Airlines Corp	NAS NMS	PacWst	PWA
PacifiCare Health Systems Inc	NAS NMS	PacifCr	PHSY
PacifiCorp	New York	Pacifcp	PPW
Pain Suppresion Labs Inc	NAS SL	PainSu	PAIN
PaineWebber Group Inc	New York	PainWb	PWJ
PALFED Inc	NAS NMS	Palfed	PALM
Pall Corp	American	PallCp	PLL
P.A.M. Transportation Services Inc	NAS NMS	PAM	PTSI
Pan Am Corp	New York	PanAm	PN
Pan Atlantic Re Inc	NAS NMS	PanAtl	PNRE
Pantech Research & Development Corp	NAS NMS	Pantch	PNTC
Pancho's Mexican Buffet Inc	NAS NMS	PancMx	PAMX
Pancretec Inc	NAS SL	Pancret	PNCR
Panhandle Eastern Corp	New York	PanEC	PEL
Pannill Knitting Company Inc	New York	Panill	PKC
Pansophic Systems Inc	New York	Pansph	PNS
Pantasote Inc	American	Pantast	PNT
Pantera's Corp	NAS NMS	Pantera	PANT
Par Pharmaceutical Inc	New York	ParPh	PRX
PAR Technology Corp	New York	ParTch	PTC
Paradyne Corp	New York	Pardyn	PDN
Paris Business Forms Inc	NAS NMS	ParisBu	PBFI
Park Communications Inc	NAS NMS	ParkCm	PARC
Park Electrochemical Corp	New York	ParkEl	PKE
Park-Ohio Industries Inc	NAS NMS	ParkOh	PKOH
Parker Drilling Co	New York	ParkDrl	PKD
Parker Hannifin Corp	New York	ParkHn	PH
Parkvale Savings Assn (Pennsylvania)	NAS NMS	PrkvlSv	PVSA

COMPANY NAME	MARKET LISTING	NEWSPAPER ABBREV.	TRADING SYMBOL
Parkway Co	NAS NMS	Parkwy	PKWY
Parlex Corp	NAS NMS	Parlex	PRLX
Pathe Computer Control Systems Corp	NAS SL	Pathe	QILT
Patient Technology Inc	American	PatTch	PTI
Patlex Corp	NAS NMS	Patlex	PTLX
Patrick Industries Inc	NAS NMS	PatrkI	PATK
Patrick Petroleum Co	New York	PatPtr	PPC
Patten Corp	New York	Patten	PAT
Pattern Processing Technologies Inc	NAS SL	ParnPr	PPRO
Paul Harris Stores Inc	NAS NMS	PaulH	PHRS
Pauley Petroleum Inc	American	PaulPt	PP
PAXAR Corp	American	Paxar	PXR
Frank Paxton Co (Class A)	NAS NMS	Paxton	PAXTA
Pay-Fone Systems Inc	American	PayFon	PYF
Paychex Inc	NAS NMS	Paychx	PAYX
Payco American Corp	NAS NMS	Payco	PAYC
Payless Cashways Inc	New York	PayCsh	PCI
Pay'n Save Inc	NAS NMS	PayNSv	PAYN
P C Quote Inc	NAS SL	PC Qut	PCQT
PCA International Inc	NAS NMS	PCA Int	PCAI
PCL Diversifund	American	PCL	DIV
PCS Inc	NAS NMS	PCS	PCSI
PDA Engineering	NAS NMS	PDA	PDAS
PEC Israel Economic Corp	American	PEC Isr	IEC
Peerless Manufacturing Co	NAS NMS	PeerMf	PMFG
Peerless Tube Co	American	PeerTu	PLS
Pegasus Gold Ltd	American	PegGld	PGU
Pelsart Resources N.J.	NAS SL	Pelsart	PELRY
Penguin Group Inc	NAS SL	Penguin	PNGR
The Penn Central Corp	New York	PenCn	PC
Penn Engineering & Manufacturing Corp	American	PenEM	PNN
Penn Pacific Corp	NAS SL	PennPc	PPAC
Penn Traffic Co	American	PenTr	PNF
Penn Treaty American Corp	NAS NMS	PenTrt	PTAC
Penn Virginia Corp	NAS NMS	PenV	PVIR
Pennbancorp	NAS NMS	Penbcp	PNBA
J.C. Penney Company Inc	New York	Penney	JCP
Pennsylvania Enterprises Inc	NAS NMS	PenaEn	PENT
Pennsylvania Power & Light Co	New York	PaPL	PPL
Pennsylvania Real Estate Investment Trust	American	PenRE	PEI
Pennview Savings Assn (Pennsylvania)	NAS NMS	Penvw	PSPA
Pennwalt Corp	New York	Penwlt	PSM
Pennzoil Co	New York	Pennzol	PZL
Penobscot Shoe Co	American	Penob	PSO
Penril Corp	American	Penril	PNL
Penta Systems International Inc	NAS SL	Penta	PSLI
Pentair Inc	NAS NMS	Pentair	PNTA

COMPANY NAME	MARKET LISTING	NEWSPAPER ABBREV.	TRADING SYMBOL
Pantech International Inc	NAS SL	Pentch	PNTK
Pentron Industries Inc	American	Pentron	PEN
PENWEST LTD	NAS NMS	Penwt	PENW
People Ridesharing Systems Inc	NAS SL	PeoRide	RIDE
Peoples Bancorp of Worcester Inc (Massachusetts)	NAS NMS	PBcWor	PEBW
Peoples Bancorporation (North Carolina)	NAS NMS	PeopBc	PBNC
People's Bank (Connecticut)	NAS NMS	PeoCT	PBCT
Peoples Energy Corp	New York	PeopEn	PGL
Peoples Federal Savings Bank of DeKalb County	NAS NL	PeoFdDe	PFDC
Peoples Heritage Financial Group Inc (Maine)	NAS NMS	PeopHrt	PIIBK
People's Savings Bank of Brockton (Massachusetts)	NAS NMS	PSBBrc	PBKB
The Peoples Savings Bank of New Britain (Connecticut)	NAS NMS	PeoSvCt	PBNB
Peoples Savings Bank FSB (Michigan)	NAS NMS	PeSvMch	PSBX
Peoples Westchester Savings Bank (New York)	NAS NMS	PeoWst	PWSB
The Pep Boys-Manny, Moe & Jack	New York	PepBy	PBY
PepsiCo Inc	New York	PepsiCo	PEP
Perception Technology Corp	NAS NMS	PercTc	PCEP
Perceptronics Inc	NAS NMS	Percpt	PERC
Peregrine Entertainment Ltd	NAS SL	Pergrn	MOVE
Perini Corp	American	PeriniC	PCR
Perini Investment Properties Inc	American	PeriniI	PNV
Peripheral Systems Inc	NAS SL	Periphl	PSIX
The Perkin-Elmer Corp	New York	PerkEl	PKN
Perkins Family Restaurants L.P.	New York	PerkF	PFR
Permian Basin Royalty Trust	New York	Prmian	PBT
Perpetual Savings Bank FSB (Virginia)	NAS NMS	PerpS	PASB
Perrigo Co	American	Perigo	PRR
Perry Drug Stores Inc	New York	PeryDr	PDS
Personal Computer Products INc	NAS SL	PerCpt	PCPI
Personal Diagnostics Inc	NAS SL	PerDia	PERS
J.M. Peters Company Inc	American	Peters	JMP
Petrie Stores Corp	New York	Petrie	PST
Petro Global Inc	NAS SL	Petro	PEAL
Petrol Industries Inc	NAS NMS	PetInd	PTRL
Petrolane Partners L.P.	New York	PtPar	LPG
Petroleum & Resources Corp	New York	PetRs	PEO
Petroleum Development Corp	NAS NMS	PetDv	PETD
Petroleum Equipment Tools Co	NAS NMS	PETCO	PTCO
Petroleum Heat & Power Company Inc (Class B)	American	PtHeat	PHP.B
Petroleum Helicopters Inc (voting)	NAS NL	PtHel	PHEL
Petroleum Helicopters Inc (non-voting)	NAS NL	PtHel	PHELK

COMPANY NAME	MARKET LISTING	NEWSPAPER ABBREV.	TRADING SYMBOL
Petroleum Investments Ltd	New York	PtrInv	PIL
Petrolite Corp	NAS NMS	Petrlte	PLIT
Petrominerals Corp	NAS NMS	Petrmn	PTRO
Pfizer Inc	New York	Pfizer	PFE
Pharmacia AB	NAS NMS	Phrmci	PHABY
PharmaControl Corp	NAS NMS	Phrmct	PHAR
PharmaKinetics Laboratories Inc	NAS NMS	Phrmk	PKLB
Pharmatec Inc	NAS SL	Phrmtc	PHTC
Phelps Dodge Corp	New York	PhelpD	PD
PHH Group Inc	New York	PHH	PHH
Philadelphia Electric Co	New York	PhilaEl	PE
Philadelphia Long Distance Telephone Co	American	PhlLD	PHI
Philadelphia Suburban Corp	New York	PhilSub	PSC
Philip Morris Companies Inc	New York	PhilMr	MO
Jean Philippe Fragrances Inc	NAS SL	PhilpJ	JEAN
Philips Industries Inc	New York	PhilpIn	PHL
Philips N.V.	New York	PhilGl	PHG
Phillips Petroleum Co	New York	PhilPet	P
Phillips-Van Heusen Corp	New York	PhlVH	PVH
PHLCORP Inc	New York	Phlcrp	PHX
PHM Corp	New York	PHM	PHM
Phoenix Advanced Technology Inc	NAS SL	PhnxAd	PATI
Phoenix American Inc	NAS NMS	PhnxAm	PHXA
Phoenix Medical Technology Inc	NAS NMS	PhnxMd	PHNX
Phoenix Re Corp	NAS NMS	PhnxRe	PXRE
Phoenix Realty Investors Inc	American	PhnxR	PHR
Phoenix Technologies Ltd	NAS NL	PhnxTc	PTEC
Phone-Mate Inc	NAS NMS	PhnMte	PHMT
Phonetel Technologies	NAS SL	Phonetl	PNTL
Photo Control Corp	NAS NMS	PhotoC	PHOC
Photo Marker Corp	NAS SL	PhotoMk	PMCP
Photographic Science Corp	NAS SL	PhotSci	PSCX
Photon Technology International Inc	NAS SL	Photon	PHON
Photronic Labs Inc	NAS NMS	PhtrLb	PLAB
PHP Healthcare Corp	NAS NMS	PHP	PHPH
Physicians Insurance Company of Ohio (Class A)	NAS NMS	PhysIn	PICOA
Physicians Pharmaceutical Services Inc	NAS SL	PhysPh	PHYP
Pic'N' Save Corp	NAS NMS	PicSav	PICN
Piccadilly Cafeterias Inc	NAS NMS	PicCafe	PICC
Pico Products Inc	American	PicoPd	PPI
PictureTel Corp	NAS SL	PicTel	PCTL
Piedmont Bankgroup Inc	NAS NMS	PiedB	PBGI
Piedmont Federal Savings Bank (Virginia)	NAS NMS	PiedSB	PFSB
Piedmont Mining Company Inc	NAS SL	PiedMn	PIED
Piedmont Management Company Inc	NAS NMS	PiedMg	PMAN
Piedmont Natural Gas Company Inc	New York	PiedNG	PNY
Piemonte Foods Inc	NAS NL	Piemnt	PIFI

COMPANY NAME	MARKET LISTING	NEWSPAPER ABBREV.	TRADING SYMBOL
Pier 1 Imports Inc	New York	Pier 1	PIR
Piezo Electric Products Inc	NAS NL	Piezo	PEPI
Pikeville National Corp	NAS NL	Pikevle	PKVL
Pilgrim Regional Bank Shares Inc	New York	PilgRg	PBS
Pilgrim's Pride Corp	New York	PilgPr	CHX
The Pillsbury Co	New York	Pilsbry	PSY
Pinnacle West Capital Corp	New York	PinWst	PNW
Pioneer American Holding Co	NAS NMS	PionAm	PAHC
Pioneer Electronic Corp	New York	PionrEl	PIO
Pioneer Financial Corp (Virginia)	NAS NMS	PionFn	PION
Pioneer Financial Services Inc (Illinois)	NAS NMS	PionF	PFSI
The Pioneer Group Inc	NAS NMS	PionGp	PIOG
Pioneer Hi-Bred International Inc	NAS NMS	PionHi	PHYB
Pioneer Savings Bank (Florida)	NAS NMS	PionSB	PSBF
Pioneer Savings Bank Inc (North Carolina)	NAS NMS	PionSv	PSBN
Pioneer-Standard Electronics Inc	NAS NMS	PionSt	PIOS
Pioneer Systems Inc	American	PionrSy	PAE
Piper Jaffray Inc	NAS NMS	PiprJaf	PIPR
Pitney Bowes Inc	New York	PitnyB	PBI
Pitt-DesMoines Inc	American	PitDsm	PDM
Pittsburgh & West Virginia Railroad	American	PitWVa	PW
The Pittston Co	New York	Pittstn	PCO
Pittway Corp	American	Pittway	PRY
Placer Dome Inc	New York	PlcrD	PDG
Plains Petroleum Co	New York	PlainsP	PLP
Plains Resources Inc	NAS NMS	PlainsR	PLNS
Plant Genetics Inc	NAS NMS	PlntGen	PGEN
The Planters Corp	NAS NMS	PlantCp	PNBT
Plantronics Inc	New York	Plantrn	PLX
Plasma-Therm Corp	NAS SL	PlasmT	PTIS
Plasti-Line Inc	NAS NMS	PlastLn	SIGN
Playboy Enterprises Inc	New York	Playboy	PLA
Plaza Commerce Bancorp	NAS NMS	PlzCBc	PLZA
Plenum Publishing Corp	NAS NMS	Plenum	PLEN
The Plessey Company plc	New York	Plesey	PLY
Plexus Corp	NAS NMS	PlexusC	PLXS
Plexus Resources Corp	NAS SL	PlexusR	PLUSF
Ply*Gem Industries Inc	American	PlyGem	PGI
Plymouth Five Cents Savings Bank (Massachusetts)	NAS NMS	PlyFve	THFI
Plymouth Rubber Company Inc (Class A)	American	PlyR A	PLR.A
Plymouth Rubber Company Inc (Class B)	American	PlyR B	PLR.B
PNC Financial Corp	New York	PNC	PNC
Pneumatic Scale Corp	American	PneuSc	PNU
Poe & Associates Inc	NAS NL	PoeAsc	POEA
Pogo Producing Co	New York	PogoPd	PPP
Polar Molecular Corp	NAS SL	PlrMol	PMCX
Polaris Industries Partners L.P.	American	PolrIn	SNO

COMPANY NAME	MARKET LISTING	NEWSPAPER ABBREV.	TRADING SYMBOL
Polaroid Corp	New York	Polard	PRD
Policy Management Systems Corp	NAS NMS	PlcyMg	PMSC
Polifly Financial Corp	NAS NMS	PolifyFn	PFLY
Polk Audio Inc	NAS NMS	PolkAu	POLK
Poly-Tech Inc	NAS NMS	PolyTch	POLY
Polydex Pharmaceuticals Ltd	NAS SL	Polydex	POLXF
Polymer International Corp	NAS NMS	Polymr	PICI
Ponce Federal Bank F.S.B. (Puerto Rico)	NAS NMS	PoncF	PFBS
Pop Radio Corp	NAS SL	PopRad	POPX
Pope & Talbot Inc	New York	PopTal	POP
Pope, Evans & Robbins Inc	American	PopeEv	Per
Porta Systems Corp	American	PortSys	PSI
Portage Industries Corp	American	Portage	PTG
Portec Inc	New York	Portec	POR
Portland General Corp	New York	PortGC	PGN
Ports of Call Inc	NAS NMS	PortsCl	POCI
Portsmouth Bank Shares Inc	NAS NMS	PortBk	POBS
Poseidon Pools of America Inc	NAS NMS	PosdnP	POOL
Possis Corp	NAS NMS	Possis	POSS
Postal Instant Press	American	PostlPr	PIP
Potlatch Corp	New York	Potltch	PCH
Potomec Electric Power Co	New York	PotmE	POM
Poughkeepsie Savings Bank F.S.B	NAS NMS	PoughSv	PKPS
Powell Industries Inc	NAS NMS	Powell	POWL
PPG Industries Inc	New York	PPG	PPG
Prab Robots Inc	NAS SL	PrabRbt	PRAB
Prairie Oil Royalties Company Ltd	American	PraireO	POY
Pratt & Lambert Inc	American	PratLm	PM
Pratt Hotel Corp	American	PratHt	PHC
Praxis Biologics Inc	NAS NMS	PraxBio	PRXS
Pre-Paid Legal Services Inc	American	PrpdLg	PPD
Precision Aerotech Inc	American	PrecsA	PAR
Precision Castparts Corp	NAS NMS	PrecCst	PCST
Precision Resources Inc	NAS SL	PrecRs	PRES
Precision Standard Inc	NAS NL	PrcStd	PCSN
Precision Target Marketing Inc	NAS NMS	PrecTrg	CSIT
Preferred Health Care Ltd	American	PfdHlt	PY
Preferred Risk Life Insurance Co	NAS NMS	PfdRsk	PFDR
Preferred Savings Bank Inc (North Carolina)	NAS NMS	PfdSav	PSLA
Premark International Inc	New York	Premrk	PMI
Premier Bancorp Inc (Lousiana)	NAS NMS	PrmrBc	PRBC
Premier Bancshares Corp (Virginia)	NAS NMS	PrmBnc	PBKC
Premier Financial Services Inc	NAS NL	PremFn	PREM
Premier Industrial Corp	New York	Premr	PRE
Presidential Airways Inc	NAS SL	PresAr	PAIR
Presidential Life Corp	NAS NMS	PresLf	PLFE
Presidential Realty Corp (Class A)	American	PresR A	PDL.A

COMPANY NAME	MARKET LISTING	NEWSPAPER ABBREV.	TRADING SYMBOL
Presidential Realty Corp (Class B)	American	PresR B	PDL.B
Presidio Oil Co (Class A)	American	Presd A	PRS.A
Presidio Oil Co (Class B)	American	Presd B	PRS.B
Presto-Tek Corp	NAS NL	PrestoT	PRTK
Preston Corp	NAS NMS	PrstnCp	PRTK
Priam Corp	NAS NMS	Priam	PRIA
T. Rowe Price Associates Inc	NAS NMS	PrceTR	TROW
Price Communications Corp	American	PrcCm	PR
The Price Co	NAS NMS	PriceCo	PCLB
Price/Stern/Sloan Publishers Inc	NAS NMS	PSS Pub	PSSP
Pricor Inc	NAS NL	Pricor	PRCO
Prima Energy Corp	NAS NL	Prima	PENG
Primages Inc	NAS SL	Primge	PRIM
Primark Corp	New York	Primrk	PMK
Prime Capital Corp	NAS NMS	PrmCap	PRME
Prime Computer Inc	New York	PrimeC	PRM
Prime Financial Partners L.P.	American	PrmFn	PFP
Prime Medical Services Inc	NAS NMS	PrmeMd	PMSI
Prime Motor Inns Inc	New York	PrimeM	PDQ
Prime Motor Inns L.P.	New York	PrMLt	PMP
PRIMEBANK FSB (Michigan)	NAS NMS	PrmeBk	PMBK
Primerica Corp	New York	Primca	PA
Princeton Diagnostic Laboratories of America	American	PrnDia	PDA
Princeville Corp	NAS NMS	Prinvl	PVDC
Printronix Inc	NAS NMS	Prtronx	PTNX
Prism Entertainment Corp	American	Prism	PRZ
Private Pay Phones Inc	NAS SL	PrivPay	PPPI
Pro-Dex Inc	NAS SL	ProDex	PDEX
Pro-Med Capital Inc	American	ProMed	PMC
ProCare Industries Inc	NAS SL	ProCre	PCRE
The Procter & Gamble Co	New York	ProctG	PG
Production Operators Corp	NAS NMS	ProdOp	PROP
Products Research & Chemical Corp	New York	PrdRs	PRC
Professional Care Inc	American	ProfCre	PCE
Professional Investors Insurance Group Inc	NAS NMS	ProfInv	PROF
Proffitt's Inc	NAS NMS	Proffitt	PRFT
Profit Systems Inc	NAS NMS	ProfitS	PFTS
Profit Technologies Inc	NAS NL	PrftTc	PRTE
Programming & Systems Inc	NAS NMS	ProgSys	PSYS
Progress Financial Corp	NAS NMS	ProgFn	PFNC
Progressive Bank Inc (New York)	NAS NMS	ProgBk	PSBK
The Progressive Corp (Ohio)	New York	ProgCp	PGR
Progressive Income Equity Fund Inc	New York	PrgInc	PYE
ProGroup Inc	NAS NMS	Progrp	PRGR
Proler International Corp	New York	Proler	PS
ProNet Inc	NAS NMS	Pronet	PNET

COMPANY NAME	MARKET LISTING	NEWSPAPER ABBREV.	TRADING SYMBOL
Property Capital Trust	American	PropCT	PCT
The Prospect Group Inc	NAS NMS	ProsGp	PROSZ
Prospect Park Financial Corp (New Jersey)	NAS NMS	PspctPk	PPSA
Protective Life Corp	NAS NMS	ProtLfe	PROT
Provena Foods Inc	NAS NMS	Prvena	PVNA
Providence & Worcest Railroad Co	NAS NL	PrvWor	PWRR
Providence Energy Corp	American	ProvEn	PVY
Provident American Corp	NAS NMS	ProvAm	PAMC
Provident Bancorp Inc	NAS NL	ProvBc	PRBK
Provident Bankshares Corp	NAS NMS	PrvBksh	PBKS
Provident Life & Accident Insurance Co	NAS NMS	PrvLfe	PACC
Prudential Financial Services Corp	NAS NMS	PrudFn	PFSL
Prudential Intermediate Income Fund Inc	New York	PruInt	PIF
Prudential Strategic Income Fund	New York	PruStr	PSF
PS Group Inc	New York	PS Grp	PSG
PSE Inc	American	PSE	POW
PSI Holdings Inc	New York	PSI	PIN
PSICOR Inc	NAS NMS	Psicor	PCOR
Psychemedics Corp	NAS SL	PsycCp	PCMC
Pubco Corp	NAS NMS	PubcoC	PUBO
Public Service Company of Colorado	New York	PSvCol	PSR
Public Service Company of New Hampshire	New York	PSNH	PNH
Public Service Company of New Mexico	New York	PSvNM	PNM
Public Service Company of North Carolina Inc	NAS NMS	PbSNC	PSNC
Public Service Enterprise Group Inc	New York	PSEG	PEG
Publicker Industries Inc	New York	Publick	PUL
Publishers Equipment Corp	NAS NMS	PublEq	PECN
Pueblo International Inc	New York	Pueblo	PII
Puerto Rican Cement Company Inc	New York	PR Cem	PRN
Puget Sound Bancorp	NAS NMS	PgSdBc	PSNB
Puget Sound Power & Light Co	New York	PugetP	PSD
Pulaski Furniture Corp	NAS NMS	PulaskF	PLFC
Pulaski S&L Assn (New Jersey)	NAS NMS	PulwS	PULS
Pulitzer Publishing Co	NAS NMS	PultzPb	PLTZC
Pullman Co	New York	Pullmn	PMN
Punta Gorda Isles Inc	American	PuntaG	PGA
Puritan-Bennett Corp	NAS NMS	PuritB	PBEN
Putnam High Income Convertible & Bond Fund	New York	PutnHi	PCF
Putnam Master Income Trust	New York	PutMas	PMT
Putnam Master Intermediate Income Trust	New York	PutMI	PIM
Putnam Premier Income Trust	New York	PutPr	PPT
Putnam Trust Co	NAS NL	PutnTr	PTNM
Pyramid Oil Co	NAS NL	PyrmO	PYOL
Pyramid Technology Corp	NAS NMS	PyrmT	PYRD
Pyro Energy Corp	New York	Pyro	BTU

COMPANY NAME	MARKET LISTING	NEWSPAPER ABBREV.	TRADING SYMBOL
Q-MED Inc	NAS NMS	QMED	QEKG
Qantel Corp	New York	Qantel	BQC
QED Exploration Inc	NAS NMS	QED	QEDX
QMax Technology Group Inc	NAS NMS	Qmax	QMAX
QMS Inc	New York	QMS	AQM
Quadrax Corp	NAS SL	Qdrax	QDRX
Quadrex Corp	NAS NMS	Quadrx	QUAD
Quaker Chemical Corp	NAS NMS	QuakCh	QCHM
Quaker Fabric Corp	American	QuakFb	CFQ
The Quaker Oats Co	New York	QuakO	OAT
Quaker State Corp	New York	QuakSC	KSF
Quality Food Centers Inc	NAS NMS	QuFood	QFCI
Quality Systems Inc	NAS NMS	QualSy	QSII
Quanex Corp	New York	Quanex	NX
Quantronix Corp	NAS NMS	Qntrnx	QUAN
Quantum Chemical Corp	New York	Quantm	CUE
Quantum Corp	NAS NMS	Quantm	QNTM
Quantum Diagnostics Ltd	NAS SL	QuanD	QTMCC
Quarex Industries Inc	NAS NMS	Quarex	QRXL
Quartz Inc	NAS SL	QuartzI	QURZ
Quartz Mountain Gold Corp	NAS NMS	QrtzMt	QZMGF
Qubix Graphic Systems Inc	NAS SL	Qubix	QBIX
Quebec Sturgeon River Mines Ltd	NAS NL	QuebcSt	QSRTF
Quebecor Inc	American	Quebc	PQB
Quest Biotechnology Inc	NAS SL	QuestBi	QBIO
Quest For Value Dual Purpose Fund Inc	New York	QstVl	KFV
Quest Medical Inc	NAS NMS	QuestM	QMED
Questar Corp	New York	Questar	STR
QuesTech Inc	NAS NMS	Questch	QTEC
The Quick & Reilly Group Inc	New York	QkReily	BQR
Quicksilver Inc	NAS NMS	Quikslv	QUIK
Quipp Inc	NAS NMS	Quipp	QUIP
Quixote Corp	NAS NMS	Quixte	QUIX
Qume Corp	NAS NMS	Qume	QUME
QVC Network Inc	NAS NMS	QVC	QVCN
Rabbit Software Corp	NAS NMS	RabbitS	RABT
RAC Mortgage Investment Corp	American	RAC	RMR
Rada Electronic Industries Ltd	NAS NL	RadaEl	RADIF
Radiation Disposal Systems Inc	NAS SL	RadtnDs	RDIS
Radiation Systems Inc	NAS NMS	RadSys	RADS
Radice Corp	New York	Radice	RI
Radionics Inc	NAS NMS	Radion	RADX
Radon Testing Corporation of America Inc	NAS SL	Radon	RDON
Radva Corp	NAS SL	Radva	RDVA
Brad Ragan Inc	American	Ragan	BRD
Ragen Corp	NAS NMS	Ragen	RAGN
RAI Research Corp	American	RAI	RAC

COMPANY NAME	MARKET LISTING	NEWSPAPER ABBREV.	TRADING SYMBOL
Railroad S&L Assn (Kansas)	NAS NL	RailSvg	RAIL
Rainbow Technologies Inc	NAS NL	RainbwTc	RNBO
Raleigh Federal Savings Bank (North Carolina)	NAS NMS	RalghFS	RFBK
Ralston Purina Co	New York	RalsPur	RAL
Ramada Inc	New York	Ramad	RAM
Ramapo Financial Corp	NAS NMS	RamFin	RMPO
Rand Capital Corp	NAS NL	RandCa	RAND
Rangaire Corp	NAS NMS	Rangar	RANG
Ranger Oil Ltd	New York	RangrO	RGO
The Rank Organization Plc	NAS NL	RankO	RANKY
Ransburg Corp	American	Ransbg	RBG
Rapitech Systems Inc	NAS SL	Rapitec	RPSY
Raritan Bancorp Inc	NAS NMS	RartnBc	RARB
Ratners Group plc	NAS NMS	Ratner	RATNY
Rauch Industries Inc	NAS NL	Rauch	RCHI
Raven Industries Inc	American	Raven	RAV
Ravenswood Financial Corp	NAS NL	Ravnwd	RAFI
Rax Restaurants Inc	NAS NMS	RZX	RAXR
Raychem Corp	New York	Raycm	RYC
Raycomm Transworld Industries Inc	NAS SL	Raycom	RACM
The Raymond Corp	NAS NMS	Raymd	RAYM
Raymond James Financial Inc	New York	RJamFn	RJF
Rayonier Timberlands L.P.	New York	Rayonr	LOG
Raytech Corp	New York	Raytch	RAY
Raytheon Co	New York	Raythn	RTN
RB Industries Inc	New York	RBInd	RBI
RB&W Corp	American	RBW	RBW
RCM Technologies Inc	NAS SL	RCM	RCMT
Re Capital Corp	American	ReCap	RCC
Rea Gold Corp	NAS SL	ReaGld	REOGF
Readicare Inc	NAS NMS	RediCr	REDI
Reading & Bates Corp	New York	ReadBt	RB
Reading Co	NAS NMS	Readg	RDGC
Real Estate Investment Trust of California	New York	REIT	RCT
Real Estate Securities Income Fund Inc	American	RESec	RIF
RealAmerica Co	NAS NL	RealAm	RACO
Realist Inc	NAS SL	Realist	RLST
Realty ReFund Trust	New York	RltRef	RRF
Realty South Investors Inc	American	RltSou	RSI
RECO International Inc	American	Reco	RNT
Recognition Equipment Inc	New York	RecnEq	REC
Recoton Corp	NAS NMS	Recotn	RCOT
Red Eagle Resources Cp	NAS SL	RedEagl	REDX
Red Lion Inns L.P.	American	RedLn	RED
Redken Laboratories Inc	NAS NMS	RedknL	RDKN
Redlaw Industries Inc	American	Redlw	RDL

COMPANY NAME	MARKET LISTING	NEWSPAPER ABBREV.	TRADING SYMBOL
Redman Industries Inc	New York	Redmn	RE
Reebok International Ltd	New York	Rebok	RBK
The Reece Corp	New York	Reece	RCE
Reeds Jewelers Inc	NAS NMS	ReedJwl	REED
Reeves Communications Corp	NAS NMS	Reeves	RVCC
REFAC Technology Development Corp	NAS NMS	Refac	REFC
Reflectone Inc	NAS NMS	Reflctn	RFTN
Regal-Beloit Corp	American	RegalB	RBC
Regal International Inc	New York	Regal	RGL
Regency Cruises Inc	NAS NMS	RgcyCr	SHIP
Regency Electronics Inc	NAS NMS	RgcyEl	RGCY
Regency Equities Corp	NAS NMS	RgcyEq	RGEQ
Regina Company Inc	NAS NMS	Regina	REGI
Regional Bancorp Inc	NAS NMS	ReglBc	REGB
Regional Federal Bancorp Inc	NAS NL	RegFdl	RFBI
Regional Financial Shares Investment Fund Inc	New York	ReglFn	BNC
Regis Corp	NAS NMS	Regis	RGIS
Reich & Tang L.P.	New York	ReichT	RTP
Reistertown Federal Savings Bank (Maryland)	NAS NMS	ReistFS	RFSB
Relational Technology Inc	NAS NMS	RelTch	RELY
Reliability Inc	NAS NMS	Reliab	REAL
Reliable Life Insurance Co	NAS NL	RelbLfe	RLIF
Reliance Group Holdings Inc	New York	RelGrp	REL
Renaissance GRX Inc	NAS SL	RenGRX	RENX
Repap Enterprises Corporation Inc	NAS NMS	Repap	RPAPF
Repco Inc	NAS NMS	Repco	RPCO
Repligen Corp	NAS NMS	Replgn	RGEN
Repro-Med Systems Inc	NAS SL	ReprMd	REPR
Republic American Corp	NAS NMS	RepAm	RAWC
Republic Automotive Parts Inc	NAS NMS	RpAuto	RAUT
Republic Bancorp Inc	NAS NL	RepBcp	RBNC
Republic Capital Group Inc	NAS NMS	RepCap	RSLA
Republic Gypsum Co	New York	RepGyp	RGC
Republic New York Corp	New York	RepNY	RNB
Republic Pictures Corp (Class A)	NAS NMS	RpPicA	RPICA
Republic Pictures Corp (Class B)	NAS NL	RpPicB	RPICB
Republic Resources Corp	NAS SL	RepRs	REPB
Republic Savings Financial Corp (Florida)	NAS NMS	RepSav	RSFC
Resdel Industries	NAS NMS	Resdel	RSDL
Research Frontiers Inc	NAS SL	RschFt	REFR
Research Inc	NAS NMS	ReshInc	RESR
Research Industries Corp	NAS NMS	RshInd	REIC
Residential Mortgage Investments Inc	American	RestMg	RMI
Residential Resources Mortgages Investments Corp	American	ResRs	RRR
Resorts International Inc (Class A)	American	ResrtA	RT.A

COMPANY NAME	MARKET LISTING	NEWSPAPER ABBREV.	TRADING SYMBOL
Resource Exploration Inc	NAS NMS	RscEx	REXI
Respironics Inc	NAS NMS	Respir	RESP
Restaurant Management Services Inc	NAS NMS	RestMg	RESM
Retailing Corporation of America	NAS NMS	Retail	RCOA
Reuter Inc	NAS NMS	ReuterI	REUT
Reuter Laboratories	NAS SL	ReutrLb	PEST
Reuters Holdings plc	NAS NMS	ReutrH	RTRSY
Revere Fund Inc	NAS NMS	ReverF	PREV
Rexcom Systems Corp	NAS SL	Rexcm	RXSC
Rexene Corp	New York	Rxene	RXN
Rexham Corp	New York	Rexhm	RXH
Rexon Inc	NAS NMS	Rexon	REXN
Rexworks Inc	NAS NMS	Rexwks	REXW
The Reynolds & Reynolds Co (Class A)	NAS NMS	ReyRy	REYNA
Reynolds Metals Co	New York	ReyMt	RLM
RF&P Corp-Non-voting Dividend Obligation Common Stock	NAS NL	RF&P	RFPCK
Rheometrics Inc	NAS NMS	Rheomt	RHEM
RHNB Corp	NAS NL	RHNB	RHNB
Rhodes Inc	New York	Rhodes	RHD
Rhone-Poulenc S.A.	NAS NMS	RhonPl	RHPOY
Ribi ImmunoChem Research Inc	NAS NMS	RibiIm	RIBI
Richardson Electronics Ltd	NAS NMS	RichEl	RELL
Richfood Holdings Inc (Class A)	NAS NMS	Richfd	RCHFA
Richmond Hills Savings Bank	NAS NMS	RchmHl	RICH
Richton International Corp	NAS NMS	Richton	RIHL
Ridgewood Properties Inc	NAS NMS	RdgwdP	RWPI
Riedel Environmental Technologies Inc	American	Riedel	RIE
Riggs National Corp	NAS NMS	RiggsNt	RIGS
Right Management Consultants Inc	NAS NMS	RghtMg	RMCI
Rio Algom Ltd	American	RioAl	ROM
Ripley Company Inc	NAS NL	Ripley	RIPY
Rise Technology Inc	NAS SL	RiseTc	RTEK
Riser Foods Inc (Class A)	American	Riser	RSR
Rite Aid Corp	New York	RiteAid	RAD
G.D. Ritzy's Inc	NAS NMS	Ritzys	RITZ
River Forest Bancorp	NAS NMS	RivFor	RFBC
River Oaks Industries Inc	New York	RvrOak	ROI
Riverbend International Corp	American	Rivbnd	RIV
Riverside Group Inc	NAS NMS	RvrsG	RSGI
Riverside National Bank (California)	NAS NMS	RivrNtl	RNRC
RJR Nabisco Inc	New York	RJR Nb	RJR
RLC Corp	New York	RLC	RLC
RLI Corp	New York	RLI Cp	RLI
RMS International Inc	American	RMS Int	RMS
Roadmaster Industries Inc	NAS SL	Roadmst	WHEL
Roadway Motor Plazas Inc	NAS NMS	RdwayM	RDWI
Roadway Services Inc	NAS NMS	RoadSv	ROAD

COMPANY NAME	MARKET LISTING	NEWSPAPER ABBREV.	TRADING SYMBOL
Roanoke Electric Steel Corp	NAS NMS	RoanEl	RESC
Robbins & Myers Inc	NAS NMS	RobMyr	ROBN
Robert Half Inc	NAS NMS	RbtHlf	RHII
Robert-Mark Inc (Class A)	American	RobMk	RMK.A
H.H. Robertson Co	New York	Robtsn	RHH
Robeson Industries Corp	NAS NMS	Robesn	RBSN
A.H. Robins Company Inc	New York	Robins	RAH
Robinson Nugent Inc	NAS NMS	RobNug	RNIC
Robotic Vision Systems Inc	NAS NMS	RobVsn	ROBV
Robotool Ltd	NAS SL	Robtool	ROBO
The Rochester Community Savings BAnk	NAS NMS	RochCS	RCSB
Rochester Gas & Electric Corp	New York	RochG	RGS
Rochester Telephone Corp	New York	RochTl	RTC
Rockaway Corp	New York	Rckwy	RKY
Rockefeller Center Properties Inc	New York	RckCtr	RCP
Rocking Horse Child Care Centers of America Inc	NAS SL	RockgH	RHCC
Rockingham Bancorp (New Hampshire)	NAS NMS	RckBcp	RBNH
Rockwell International Corp	New York	Rockwl	ROK
Rockwood Holding Co	NAS NMS	RckwdH	RKWD
Rockwood National Corp	NAS NL	RckwdN	RNC
Rocky Mount Undergarment Company Inc	NAS NMS	RMUnd	RMUC
Rocky Mountain Chocolate Factory Inc	NAS SL	RkMtCh	RMCF
Rodime PLC	NAS NL	Rodime	RODMY
Rodman & Renshaw Capital Group Inc	New York	RodRen	RR
Roebling Property Investors Inc	American	Roeblg	ROE
Rogers Corp	American	Rogers	ROG
Rohm & Haas Co	New York	RoHaas	ROH
Rohr Industries Inc	New York	Rohr	RHR
Rollins Environmental Services Inc	New York	RolinE	REN
Rollins Inc	New York	Rollins	ROL
Ronson Corp	NAS NMS	Ronson	RONC
Roosevelt Bank FSB (Missouri)	NAS NMS	RsvltFd	RFED
Ropak Corp	NAS NMS	Ropak	ROPK
Rorer Group Inc	New York	Rorer	ROR
Rose's Stores Inc	NAS NMS	RoseStr	RSTO
Rose's Stores Inc (Class B)	NAS NMS	RoseB	RSTOB
Rospatch Corp	NAS NMS	Rosptch	RPCH
Ross Cosmetics Distribution Centers Inc	NAS NMS	RossCs	RCDC
Ross Industries Inc	NAS SL	RossInd	ROSX
A.J. Ross Logistics Inc	NAS SL	RossLog	AJRL
Ross Stores Inc	NAS NMS	RossStr	ROST
RoTech Medical Corp	NAS NMS	RoTech	ROTC
L.F. Rothschild Unterberg, Towbin Holdings Inc	New York	Rothch	R
Roto-Rooter INc	NAS NMS	RotoRtr	ROTO
The Rouse Co	NAS NMS	Rouse	ROUS
Rowan Companies Inc	New York	Rowan	RDC

COMPANY NAME	MARKET LISTING	NEWSPAPER ABBREV.	TRADING SYMBOL
Rowe Furniture Corp	NAS NMS	RoweF	ROWE
Royal Bank of Pennsylvania (Class A)	NAS NL	RyBkPA	RBPAA
Royal Business Group Inc	NAS NMS	RoylBu	ROYG
Royal Dutch Petroleum Co	New York	RoylD	RD
Royal Gold Inc	NAS NMS	RoyGld	RGLD
Royal International Optical Corp	New York	RoyInt	RIO
Royal Palm Savings Assn (Florida)	NAS NMS	RoyPlm	RPAL
Royalpar Industries Inc	NAS NMS	Roylpr	ROYL
Royce Labs Inc	NAS SL	RoyceL	RLAB
Royce Value Trust Inc	New York	Royce	RVT
RPC Energy Services Inc	New York	RPC	RES
RPM Inc	NASDAQ	RPM	RPOW
RSI Corp	NAS NMS	RSI	RSIC
RTE Corp	New York	RTE	RTE
RTI Inc	NAS NMS	RTI	RTII
Rubbermaid Inc	New York	Rubmd	RBD
Ruddick Corp	American	Rudick	RDK
Rudy's Restaurant Group Inc	NAS NMS	Rudys	RUDY
Rule Industries Inc	NAS NMS	RuleInd	RULE
Russ Berrie & Company Inc	New York	RussBr	RUS
Russ Togs Inc	New York	RusTg	RTS
Russell Corp	New York	Russell	RML
Ryan, Beck & Co	NAS NMS	RyanBck	RBCO
Ryan's Family Steak Houses Inc	NAS NMS	RyanF	RYAN
Ryder System Inc	New York	Ryder	RDR
Rykoff-Sexton Inc	New York	Rykoff	RYK
The Ryland Group Inc	New York	Ryland	RYL
The Rymer Co	New York	Rymer	RYR
S&K Famous Brands Inc	NAS NMS	SK	SKFB
S-K-I Ltd	NAS NMS	SKI	SKII
Saatchi & Saatchi Company PLC	New York	Saatchi	SAA
Sabine Corp	New York	Sabine	SAB
Sabine Royalty Trust	New York	SabnR	SBR
SafeCard Services Inc	NAS NMS	Safecd	SFCD
SAFECO Corp	NAS NMS	Safeco	SAFC
Safeguard Health Enterprises Inc	NAS NMS	SafHlt	SFGD
Safeguard Scientifics Inc	New York	SfgdSc	SFE
Safety-Kleen Corp	New York	SaftKln	SK
Sag Harbour Savings Bank (New York)	NAS NMS	SagHbr	SGHB
Sage Analytics International Inc	NAS SL	SageAn	SAII
Sage Broadcasting Corp	NAS SL	SageBd	SAGB
Sage Energy Co	American	Sage	SAG
Sage Labs Inc	NAS SL	SageLb	SLAB
Sage Software Inc	NAS NMS	SageSft	SGSI
Sahara Casino Partners L.P.	New York	SahCas	SAH
Sahara Resorts Inc	NAS NMS	Sahara	SHRE
Sahlen & Associates Inc	NAS NMS	Sahlen	SALN

COMPANY NAME	MARKET LISTING	NEWSPAPER ABBREV.	TRADING SYMBOL
St. Helena Gold Mines Ltd	NAS NL	StHlGd	SGOLY
St. Ives Laboratories Corp	NAS NMS	StIves	SWIS
St. Joseph Light & Power Co	New York	StJoLP	SAJ
St. Jude Medical Inc	NAS NMS	StJude	STJM
St. Paul Bancorp Inc	NAS NMS	StPaulB	SPBC
The St. Paul Companies Inc	NAS NMS	StPaul	STPL
Salant Corp	New York	Salant	SLT
Salem Carpet Mills Inc	NAS NMS	SalCpt	SLCR
Salem Corp	American	Salem	SBS
Salick Health Care Inc	NAS NMS	Salick	SHCI
Salomon Inc	New York	Salomn	SB
Salvatori Opthalmics Inc	NAS SL	Sal Oph	EYES
Samna Corp	NAS NMS	Samna	SMNA
Samson Energy Company L.P.	American	Samson	SAM
San Carlos Milling Company Inc	American	SCarlo	SAN
San Diego Gas & Electric Co	New York	SDieGs	SDO
San Juan Basin Royalty Trust	New York	SJuanB	SJT
San Juan Fiberglass Pools Inc	NAS SL	SanJuan	SWIM
San Juan Racing Association Inc	New York	SJuanR	SJR
Sand Technology Systems Inc (Canada)	NAS SL	SandTc	SNDCF
Sandata Inc	NAS NL	Sandata	SAND
Sanderson Farms Inc	NAS NMS	SandFm	SAFM
The Sands Regent	NAS NMS	SandReg	SNDS
Sandwich Chef Inc	NAS NMS	SandChf	SHEF
The Sandwich Co-operative Bank (Massachusetts)	NAS NMS	SandCop	SWCB
Sandy Corp	American	Sandy	SDY
Sanford Corp	NAS NMS	Sanfrd	SANF
Sanmark-Stardust Inc	American	Sanmrk	SMK
Santa Anita Realty Enterprises Inc	New York	SAnitRt	SAR
Santa Fe Energy Partners L.P.	New York	SFeEP	SFP
Santa Fe Southern Pacific Corp	New York	SFeSP	SFX
Santa Monica Bank	NAS NL	StMonB	SANT
Santos Ltd	NAS NL	Santos	STOYD
Sanyo Electric Company Ltd	NAS NL	Sanyo	SANYY
Sara Lee Corp	New York	SaraLee	SLE
Saratoga Standardbreds Inc	NAS NMS	SaratSt	STGA
Sasol Ltd	NAS NL	Sasol	SASOY
Satellite Information Systems Co	NAS SL	SatlInf	SATI
Satellite Music Network Inc	NAS NMS	SatlMus	SMNI
B.F. Saul Real Estate Investment Trust	New York	SaulRE	BFS
Savannah Foods & Industries Inc	NAS NMS	SavnFd	SVAN
Savin Corp	New York	Savin	SVB
Saxon Oil Co	NAS NMS	SaxonO	SAXO
Saxon Oil Development Partners L.P.	American	SaxnO	SAX
S.A.Y. Industries Inc	NAS NMS	SAY Ind	SAYI
SAZTEC International Inc	NAS SL	Saztec	SAZZ
Sbarro Inc	American	Sbarro	SBA

COMPANY NAME	MARKET LISTING	NEWSPAPER ABBREV.	TRADING SYMBOL
SBE Inc	NAS SL	SBE	SBEI
SBT Corp	NAS NMS	SBT Cp	SBTC
Scan Graphics Inc	NAS SL	ScanGp	SCNG
Scan-Optics Inc	NAS NMS	ScanOp	SOCR
SCANA Corp	New York	SCANA	SCG
The Scandinavia Fund Inc	American	ScandF	SCF
Scanforms Inc	NAS NMS	Scnfrm	SCFM
Scat Hovercraft Inc	NAS SL	Scat	SCAT
Sceptre Resources Ltd	American	Sceptre	SRL
Schafer Value Trust Inc	New York	Schfr	SAT
Earl Scheib Inc	American	Scheib	ESH
R.P. Scherer Corp	NAS NMS	Scherer	SCHC
Scherer Healthcare Inc	NAS NL	SchrHlt	SCHR
Schering-Plough Corp	New York	SchrPlg	SGP
Schlumberger Ltd	New York	Schlmb	SLB
School Pictures Inc	American	SchoolP	PIX
A. Schulman Inc	NAS NMS	SchlmA	SHLM
Schult Homes Corp	NAS NMS	Schult	SHCO
The Charles Schwab Corp	New York	Schwb	SCH
Schwab Safe Company Inc	American	Schwab	SS
Schwartz Brothers Inc (Class A)	NAS NMS	SchwtzA	SWARA
Schwartz Brothers Inc (Class B)	NAS NL	SchwtzB	SWABV
SCI Systems Inc	NAS NMS	SCI Sy	SCIS
Scicom Data Services Ltd	NAS NMS	Scicom	SCIE
Science Dynamics Corp	NAS NMS	SciDyn	SIDX
Science Management Corp	American	SciMgt	SMG
Scientific-Atlanta Inc	New York	SciAtl	SFA
Scientific Leasing Inc	American	SciLsg	SG
Scientific Measurement Systems Inc	NAS SL	SciMeas	SCMS
Scientific Micro Systems Inc	NAS NMS	SciMic	SMSI
Scientific Software-Intercomp Inc	NAS NMS	SciSft	SSFT
Scientific Systems Services Inc	NAS SL	SciSyst	SSSV
SciMed Life Systems Inc	NAS NMS	Scimed	SMLS
Scitex Corporation Ltd	NAS NMS	Scitex	SCIXF
Scope Industries	American	Scope	SCP
SCOR U S Corp	New York	SCOR U	SUR
Score Board Inc	NAS SL	ScoreB	BSBL
Scorpion Technologies Inc (Class A)	NAS SL	Scorpn	SCPNA
Scott & Stringfellow Financial Inc	NAS NMS	ScotSt	SCOT
Scott Instruments Corp	NAS SL	ScotInst	SCTI
Scott Paper Co	New York	ScottP	SPP
Scotts Liquid Gold Inc	NAS SL	ScotLiq	SLIQ
Scotty's Inc	New York	Scottys	SHB
E.W. Scripps Co (Class A)	NAS NMS	Scripps	EWSCA
Scripps Howard Broadcasting Co	NAS NMS	ScripH	SCRP
Script Systems Inc	NAS SL	ScrptSy	SCPT
SCS/Compute Inc	NAS NMS	SCS	SCOM
Scudder New Asia Fund Inc	New York	ScdNA	SAF

COMPANY NAME	MARKET LISTING	NEWSPAPER ABBREV.	TRADING SYMBOL
Scurry-Rainbow Oil Ltd	American	ScurRn	SRB
SDNB Financial Corp	NAS NMS	SDNB	SDNB
Sea Containers Ltd	New York	SeaCnt	SCR
Sea Galley Stores Inc	NAS NMS	SeaGal	SEAG
Seaboard Corp	American	SbdCp	SEB
Seaboard S&L Assn (Virginia)	NAS NMS	SbdSav	SEAB
Seacoast Banking Corporation of Florida (Class A)	NAS NMS	SeaBnk	SBCFA
Seacoast Savings Bank (New Hampshire)	NAS NMS	SeacstS	SSBA
Seafood Inc	NAS SL	Seafood	SEFD
Seafoods From Alaska Inc	NAS SL	Seafds	SEAF
Seagate Technology	NAS NMS	Seagate	SGAT
The Seagram Company Ltd	New York	Seagrm	VO
Seagull Energy Corp	New York	Seagul	SGO
Seahawk Oil International Inc	NAS NL	Seahk	SEAK
Sealed Air Corp	New York	SealAir	SEE
Sealright Company Inc	NAS NMS	Sealrgt	SRCO
Seamen's Corp	American	Seamn	SMN
Seaport Corp	American	Seaport	SEO
Sears, Roebuck & Co	New York	Sears	S
Seaway Food Town Inc	NAS NMS	SeawFd	SEWY
Secom General Corp	NAS SL	Secom	SECM
Second National Federal Savings Bank (Maryland)	NAS NMS	ScNtFd	SNFS
Security American Financial Enterprises Inc	NAS NMS	SecAF	SAFE
Security Bancorp Inc	NAS NMS	SecBcp	SECB
Security Capital Corp	American	SecCap	SCC
Security Federal S&L Assn (Ohio)	NAS NL	SecFClv	SFSL
Security Federal Savings Bank (Montana)	NAS NMS	SecFdl	SFBM
Security Financial Group Inc	NAS NMS	SFGI	SFGI
Security Pacific Corp	New York	SecPac	SPC
Security Savings Bank S.L.A. (New Jersey)	NAS NMS	SecSLn	SSLN
Security Tag Systems Inc	NAS NMS	SecTag	STAG
Seeberg Corp	NAS SL	Seebrg	SBRG
Seeq Technology Inc	NAS NMS	SEEQ	SEEQ
SEI Corp	NAS NMS	SEI	SEIC
The Seibels Bruce Group Inc	NAS NMS	Seibel	SBIG
Seitel Inc	NAS SL	Seitel	SEIS
Selas Corporation of America	American	Selas	SLS
SelecTerm Inc	NAS NMS	Select	SLTM
Selective Insurance Group Inc	NAS NMS	SelctIns	SIGI
SelecTronics Inc	NAS SL	SelTrn	SELE
Seligman & Associates Inc	American	SeligAs	SLG
Selvac Corp	NAS SL	Selvac	SLVC
Semtech Corp	American	Semtch	SMH
Seneca Foods Corp	NAS NMS	Seneca	SENE
Senetek PLC	NAS SL	Senetek	SNTKY

COMPANY NAME	MARKET LISTING	NEWSPAPER ABBREV.	TRADING SYMBOL
Senior Service Corp	NAS SL	SenrSv	SENR
Sensor Control Corp	NAS NMS	SensrCtl	SNCO
Sensormatic Electronics Corp	NAS NMS	Sensor	SNSR
Sequa Corp (Class A)	New York	SequaA	SQA.A
Sequa Corp (Class B)	New York	SequaB	SQA.B
Sequel Corp	NAS SL	Sequel	SEQL
Sequent Computer Systems Inc	NAS NMS	Sequent	SQNT
Service Corporation International	New York	SvcCp	SRV
Service Fracturing Co	NAS NMS	SvcFrct	SERF
Service Merchandise Company Inc	NAS NMS	SvcMer	SMCH
Service Resources Corp	New York	SvcRes	SRC
ServiceMaster Limited Partnership	New York	Svcmst	SVM
Servico Inc	NAS NMS	Servico	SRVI
Servo Corporation of America	American	Servo	SCA
Servotronics Inc	American	Servotr	SVT
Seven Oaks International Inc	NAS NMS	SvOak	QPON
SFE Technologies	NAS NMS	SFE	SFEM
SFFed Corp	NAS NMS	SFFed	SFFD
SFM Corp	American	SFM	SFM
Shaer Shoe Corp	American	ShaerS	SHS
Shaklee Corp	New York	Shaklee	SHC
Shared Medical Systems Corp	NAS NMS	ShrMed	SMED
Sharper Image Corp	NAS NMS	ShrpIm	SHRP
Shaw Industries Inc	New York	ShawIn	SHX
Shawmut National Corp	NAS NMS	ShawNt	SHNA
Shearson Lehman Brothers Holdings Inc	New York	ShLeh	SHE
Shelby Federal Savings Bank (Indiana)	NAS NMS	ShelbyF	SHLB
Shelby Williams Industries Inc	New York	Shelby	SY
Sheldahl Inc	NAS NMS	Sheldl	SHEL
The Shell Transport & Trading Company p.l.c.	New York	ShellT	SC
Shelly Associates Inc	NAS SL	ShlyAsc	SHLY
Shelter Components Corp	American	ShltCm	SST
Shelton Savings Bank (Connecticut)	NAS NMS	Sheltn	SSAL
The Sherwin-Williams Co	New York	Shrwin	SHW
The Sherwood Group Inc	American	ShwdG	SHD
SHL Systemhouse Inc	NAS NMS	SHL Sy	SHKIF
Shoney's Inc	NAS NMS	Shoney	SHON
Shopco Laurel Centre L.P.	American	Shopco	LSC
Shopsmith Inc	NAS NMS	Shpsmt	SHOP
Shoreline Financial Corp	NAS NL	ShrlnFn	SLFC
Shorewood Packaging Corp	NAS NMS	Shrwd	SHOR
Showboat Inc	New York	Shwbt	SBO
Showscan Film Corp	NAS SL	Shwscn	SHOW
SI Handling Systems Inc	NAS SL	SI Hand	SIHS
Sidari Corp	NAS SL	Sidari	ZITI
Sierra Capital Realty Trust IV Co	NAS NMS	SierCa	SETD
Sierra Capital Realty Trust VI	American	SierCap	SZF

COMPANY NAME	MARKET LISTING	NEWSPAPER ABBREV.	TRADING SYMBOL
Sierra Capital Realty Trust VII	American	SierCa7	SZG
Sierra Health Services Inc	American	SierHS	SIE
Sierra Pacific Resources	New York	SierPac	SRP
Sierra Real Estate Equity Trust '84	NAS NMS	SierR 84	SETC
Sierra Spring Water Co	American	SierSpg	WTR
Sierracin Corp	American	Siercn	SER
SIFCO Industries Inc	American	Sifco	SIF
Sigma-Aldrich Corp	NAS NMS	SigmaAl	SIAL
Sigma Designs Inc	NAS NMS	SigmaD	SIGM
Sigmatron Nova Inc	NAS SL	Sigmtrn	SNIC
Signal Apparel Company Inc	New York	SgnlApl	SIA
Signet Banking Corp	New York	Signet	SBK
Sikes Corp (Class A)	American	SikesA	SK.A
Silicon General Inc	NAS NMS	Silicon	SILN
Silicon Graphics Inc	NAS NMS	SilcnGr	SGIC
Silicon Systems Inc	New York	SiliconS	SIL
Silicon Valley Bancshares (California)	NAS NMS	SilcVly	SIVB
Silicon Valley Group Inc	NAS NMS	SilicnVl	SVGI
Siliconix Inc	NAS NMS	Silicnx	SILI
Silk Greenhouse Inc	NAS NL	SlkGrn	SGHI
Silvar-Lisco	NAS NMS	SilvLis	SVRL
Silver King Mines Inc	NAS NMS	SlvKing	SILV
Silverado Mines Ltd	NAS SL	SlvMin	SLVRF
Silvercrest Corp	American	Silvrcst	SLV
Simmons First National Corp (Class A)	NAS NL	SimnFt	SFNCA
Simpson Industries Inc	NAS NMS	SimpIn	SMPS
Sir Speedy Printing Centres PLC	NAS SL	SirSpdy	SPEDY
Sirco International Corp	NAS NL	Sirco	SIRC
Sis Corp	NAS NMS	SisCp	SISB
Sizeler Property Investors Inc	New York	Sizeler	SIZ
Sizzler Restaurants International Inc	NAS NMS	Sizler	SIZZ
SJNB Financial Corp	NAS NL	SJNB	SJNB
SJW Corp	American	SJW	SJW
Skaneatels Savings Bank (New York)	NAS NMS	SkanSB	SKAN
SKF AB	NAS NMS	SKF AB	SKFRY
Skippers Inc	NAS NMS	Skipper	SKIP
Skolniks Inc	American	Skolnk	SKN
Skyline Chili Inc	NAS NL	SkyChili	SKCH
Skyline Corp	New York	Skyline	SKY
SkyWest	NAS NMS	SkyWst	SKYW
SL Industries Inc	New York	SL Ind	SL
Slater Development Corp	NAS SL	SlatrDv	SLAT
Slattery Group Inc	New York	Slattery	SGI
Smartcard International Inc	NAS SL	Smrtcd	SMRT
A.O. Smith Corp (Class A)	American	SmthA	SMC.A
A.O. Smith Corp (Class B)	American	SmthB	SMC.B
Smith International Inc	New York	SmithIn	SII
Smith Laboratories Inc	NAS NMS	SmithL	SMLB

COMPANY NAME	MARKET LISTING	NEWSPAPER ABBREV.	TRADING SYMBOL
The Smithfield Companies Inc	NAS NMS	Smthfld	HAMS
Smithfield Foods Inc	NAS NMS	SmthF	SFDS
SmithKline Beckman Corp	New York	SmkB	SKB
The J.M. Smucker Co	New York	Smuckr	SJM
Snap-on Tools Corp	New York	SnapOn	SNA
Snelling & Snelling Inc	NAS NMS	SnelSnl	SNEL
S.N.L. Financial Corp (Class A)	NAS NMS	SNL Fnc	SNLFA
Snyder Oil Partners L.P.	New York	Snyder	SOI
Society Corp	NAS NMS	Society	SOCI
The Society for Savings Bancorp Inc (Connecticut)	NAS NMS	SoctySv	SOCS
SofTech Inc	NAS NMS	Softech	SOFT
Software Publishing Corp	NAS NMS	SftwPb	SPCO
Software Services of America Inc	NAS NMS	SoftSv	SSOA
Solitec Inc	NAS NMS	Solitec	SOLI
Solitron Devices Inc	New York	Solitron	SOD
Solv-Ex Corp	NAS SL	SolvEx	SOLV
Somerset Bancorp Inc	NAS NMS	SomerB	SOMB
The Somerset Group Inc	NAS NMS	SomrG	SOMR
Somerset Savings Bank (Massachusetts)	NAS NMS	SomrSv	SOSA
Sonat Inc	New York	Sonat	SNT
Sonesta International Hotels Corp (Class A)	NAS NMS	Sonesta	SNSTA
Sonex Research Inc	NAS SL	Sonex	SONX
Sono Tek Corp	NAS SL	SonoTk	SOTK
Sonoco Products Co	NAS NMS	SonocP	SONO
Sonora Gold Corp	NAS NMS	Sonora	SONNF
Sony Corp	New York	SonyCp	SNE
Soo Line Corp	New York	SooLin	SOO
Sooner Defense of Florida Inc	NAS NMS	SoonDf	SOON
Sooner Federal S&L Assn	NAS NMS	SonrFd	SFOK
Sorg Inc	American	SorgInc	SRG
Sotheby's Holdings Inc (Class A)	American	Sothby	BID
Sound Advice Inc	NAS NMS	SoundA	SUND
Sound Warehouse Inc	NAS NMS	SoundW	SWHI
Source Capital Inc	New York	SourcC	SOR
South Carolina Federal Corp	NAS NMS	ScCarF	SCFB
South Carolina National Corp	NAS NMS	SCarNt	SCNC
South Jersey Industries Inc	New York	SJerIn	SJI
Southdown Inc	New York	Soudwn	SDW
Southeast Banking Corp	New York	SoestBk	STB
Southeastern Michigan Gas Enterprises Inc	NAS NMS	SMichG	SMGS
Southeastern S&L Co (North Carolina)	NAS NMS	SestSvL	SESL
Southern Bankshares Inc	NAS NMS	SthnBsh	SOBK
Southern California Edison Co	New York	SCalEd	SCE
Southern California Water Co	NAS NMS	SCalWt	SWTR
The Southern Co	New York	SouthCo	SO

COMPANY NAME	MARKET LISTING	NEWSPAPER ABBREV.	TRADING SYMBOL
Southern Educators Life Insurance Co	NAS NL	SouEdc	SOED
Southern Federal Savings Bank (Georgia)	NAS NL	SoFdGa	SFGA
Southern Indiana Gas & Electric Co	New York	SoIndGs	SIG
Southern Mineral Corp	NAS NMS	SoMinrl	SMIN
Southern National Corp	NAS NMS	SthnNt	SNAT
Southern New England Telecommunications Corp	New York	SNETI	SNG
Southern Pacific Petroleum N.L.	NAS NL	SoPcPt	SPPTY
Southern Starr Broadcasting Group Inc	NAS SL	SthStr	SSBG
Southern Union Co	New York	SoUnCo	SUG
SouthernNet Inc	NAS NMS	Sounet	SOUT
Southington Savings Bank (Connecticut)	NAS NMS	SthngS	SSBB
Southland Financial Corp	NAS NMS	SthdFn	SFIN
Southlife Holding Co	NAS NMS	Sthlfe	SLHC
Southmark Corp	New York	Soumrk	SM
SouthTrust Corp	NAS NMS	Soutrst	SOTR
Southwall Technologies Inc	NAS NMS	Souwal	SWTX
Southwest Airlines Co	New York	SwAirl	LUV
Southwest Bancorp (California)	American	SwBcp	SWB
Southwest Gas Corp	New York	SwtGas	SWX
Southwest National Corp	NAS NMS	SwstNt	SWPA
Southwest Realty Ltd	American	SwstRlt	SWL
Southwest Water Co	NAS NMS	SwWtr	SWWC
Southwestern Bell Corp	New York	SwBell	SBC
Southwestern Electric Service Co	NAS NMS	SwElSv	SWEL
Southwestern Energy Co	New York	SwEnr	SWN
Southwestern Public Service Co	New York	SwtPS	SPS
Sovereign Bancorp Inc	NAS NMS	SovBcp	SVRN
Sovran Financial Corp	New York	Sovran	SOV
Spain Fund Inc	New York	Spain	SNF
Span-America Medical Systems Inc	NAS NMS	SpanAm	SPAN
Spartan Motors Inc	NAS NMS	SprtMt	SPAR
Spartech Corp	American	Spartc	SH
Sparton Corp	New York	Sparton	SPA
Spear Financial Services Inc	NAS NMS	SpearF	SFNS
Spearhead Industries Inc	NAS NMS	Spear	SPRH
Specialized Systems Inc	NAS SL	SpecSys	SSII
Specialty Composites Corp	NAS NMS	SpecCm	SPCM
Specialty Equipment Companies Inc	New York	SpcEq	SPE
Spec's Music Inc	NAS NMS	Specs	SPEK
Spectra Pharmaceutical Services INc	NAS SL	SpcPhm	SPCT
SpecTran Corp	NAS NMS	Spctran	SPTR
Spectrum Cellular Corp	NAS SL	SpctrCl	SPCL
Spectrum Control Inc	NAS NMS	SpecCtl	SPEC
Speed-O-Print Business Machines Corp	American	SpedOP	SBM
Aaron Spelling Productions Inc	American	Spellng	SP
SPI Pharmaceuticals Inc	American	SPI Ph	SPI
S.P.I.-Suspension & Parts Industries Inc	NAS NMS	SPI Sus	SPILF

COMPANY NAME	MARKET LISTING	NEWSPAPER ABBREV.	TRADING SYMBOL
Spiegel Inc (Class A)	NAS NMS	Spiegel	SPGLA
Spire Corp	NAS NMS	Spire	SPIR
The Sporting Life Inc	NAS SL	SprtLfe	SPLF
Sportsmans Guide Inc	NAS SL	SprtGde	GIDE
Sprague Technologies Inc	New York	Sprage	SPG
Springboard Software Inc	NAS NMS	Sprngbd	SPBD
Springs Industries Inc	New York	Spring	SMI
Sprouse-Reitz Stores Inc	NAS NMS	Sprouse	STRS
SPS Technologies Inc	New York	SPSTec	ST
SPX Corp	New York	SPX Cp	SPW
Square D Co	New York	SquarD	SQD
Square Industries Inc	NAS NMS	SquareI	SQAI
Squibb Corp	New York	Squibb	SQB
SSMC Inc	New York	SSMC	SSM
STAAR Surgical Co	NAS NMS	StarSur	STAAR
Staff Builders Inc	NAS NMS	StafBld	STAF
Stage II Apparel Corp	American	Stage	SA
Stake Technology Ltd	NAS SL	StakeTc	STKLF
Stamford Capital Group Inc	NAS NMS	Stamfrd	CGPS
Stan West Mining Corp	NAS NMS	StanWst	SWMC
Standard Brands Paint Co	New York	StBPnt	SBP
Standard Commercial Corp	New York	StdCom	STW
Standard Federal Bank	New York	StFBk	SFB
Standard Havens Inc	American	StHavn	SHV
Standard Microsystems Corp	NAS NMS	StdMic	SMSC
Standard Motor Products Inc	New York	StMotr	SMP
Standard-Pacific Corp	New York	StdPac	SPF
The Standard Products Co	New York	StdPrd	SPD
The Standard Register Co	NAS NMS	StdReg	SREG
Standard Shares Inc	American	StdShr	SWD
Standex International Corp	New York	Standex	SXI
Stanford Telecommunications Inc	NAS NMS	StanfTl	STII
Stanhome Inc	New York	Stanhm	STH
Stanley Interiors Corp	NAS NMS	StnlyIn	STHF
The Stanley Works	New York	StanlWk	SWK
Stansbury Mining Corp	NAS NMS	Stansby	STBY
Staodynamics Inc	NAS NMS	Staodyn	SDYN
Star Classics Inc	NAS SL	StarCls	SCLS
Star Technologies Inc	NAS NMS	StarTc	STRR
Starpointe Savings Bank (New Jersey)	NAS NMS	StrptSv	STPT
The L.S. Starrett Co	New York	Starrett	SCX
Starrett Housing Corp	American	StarrtH	SHO
Stars To Go Inc	NAS NMS	Stars	STAR
Starstream Communications Group Inc	NAS SL	Starst	SCGI
State Mutual Securities Trust	New York	StaMSe	SMS
State-O-Maine Inc	NAS NMS	StMain	SOME
State Street Boston Corp	NAS NMS	StaStB	STBK
The Statesman Group Inc	NAS NMS	StateG	STTG

COMPANY NAME	MARKET LISTING	NEWSPAPER ABBREV.	TRADING SYMBOL
Stateswest Airlines Inc	NAS SL	StwAir	SWAL
Statewide Bancorp	NAS NMS	StwBc	STWB
Status Game Corp	NAS NMS	StatGm	STGM
Steego Corp	New York	Steego	STG
Steel of West Virginia Inc	NAS NMS	StlWVa	SWVA
Steel Technologies Inc	NAS NMS	SteelT	STTX
Stendig Industries Inc	NAS NMS	Stendig	CHZC
Step-Saver Data Systems Inc	NAS NMS	StepSvr	CODA
Stepan Co	American	Stepan	SCL
Sterling Bancorp	New York	StrlBcp	STL
Sterling Capital Corp	American	StrlCap	SPR
Sterling Electronics Corp	American	SterlEl	SEC
Sterling Medical Systems Inc	NAS SL	StrlMed	SSYS
Sterling Software Inc	American	SterlSft	SSW
Sterner Lighting Systems Inc	NAS NMS	SternL	SLTG
J.P. Stevens & Company Inc	New York	StevnJ	STN
Stevens Graphics Corp	American	StvGph	SVG
Steve's Homemade Ice Cream Inc (Class A)	NAS NL	SteveIC	STVEA
Stewart & Stevenson Services Inc	NAS NMS	StewStv	SSSS
Stewart Information Services Corp	NAS NMS	StwInf	SISC
Stewart Sandwiches Inc	NAS SL	StewSn	STEW
Stifel Financial Corp	New York	Stifel	SF
Stocker & Yale Inc	NAS NMS	StckYle	STKR
Stockholder Systems Inc (Class A)	NAS NMS	StockSy	SSIAA
Stokely USA Inc	NAS NMS	Stokely	STKY
Stolt Tankers & Terminals S.A.	NAS NMS	Stolt	STLTF
Stone & Webster Inc	New York	StoneW	SW
Stone Container Corp	New York	StoneC	STO
Stoneridge Resources Inc	New York	StonRs	SRE
Storage Equities Inc	New York	StorEq	SEQ
Storage Technology Corp	New York	StorTch	STK
Stotler Group Inc	NAS NMS	Stotler	STOT
Strategic Mortgage Investments Inc	New York	StratMt	STM
Strategic Planning Associates Inc (Cl.B)	NAS NMS	StratPl	SPAIB
Stratus Computer Inc	NAS NMS	Stratus	STRA
Strawbridge & Clothier (Class A)	NAS NMS	StrwbCl	STRWA
The Stride Rite Corp	New York	StridRt	SRR
Strober Organization Inc	NAS NMS	Strober	STRB
Structofab Inc	NAS NL	Structfb	STRU
Structural Dynamics Research Corp	NAS NMS	StrucDy	SDRC
Struthers Wells Corp	American	StrutW	SUW
Stryker Corp	NAS NMS	Strykr	STRY
Stuart Hall Company Inc	NAS NMS	StuartH	STUH
Stuarts Department Stores Inc	NAS NMS	StuDS	STUS
Student Loan Marketing Assn	New York	SallieM	SLM
Student Loan Marketing Assn (voting)	NAS NMS	StudL	SLMAJ
Sturm, Ruger & Company Inc	NAS NMS	StrmRg	STRM
STV Engineers Inc	NAS NMS	STV	STVI

COMPANY NAME	MARKET LISTING	NEWSPAPER ABBREV.	TRADING SYMBOL
Suave Shoe Corp	New York	SuavSh	SWV
Subaru of America Inc	NAS NMS	Subaru	SBRU
Suburban Bancorp Inc (Class A)	NAS NMS	SubBcp	SUBBA
Suburban Bankshares Inc (Class A)	NAS NL	SuburB	SBKSA
Sudbury Holdings Inc	NAS NMS	Sudbry	SUDS
Suffield Financial Corp	NAS NMS	SuffFin	SFCP
Suffolk Bancorp	NAS NMS	SuffBn	SUBK
Sumitomo Bank of California	NAS NMS	Sumito	SUMI
Summa Medical Corp	NAS NMS	Summa	SUMA
Summcorp	NAS NMS	Sumcrp	SMCR
The Summit Bancorporation	NAS NMS	SumitB	SUBN
Summit Health Ltd	NAS NMS	SumtHl	SUMH
Summit Holding Corp	NAS NMS	SumtH	SUHC
Summit Savings Assn (Washington)	NAS NMS	SumSav	SMMT
Summit Tax Exempt Bond Fund L.P.	American	SumtTx	SUA
Summit Technology Inc	NAS SL	SumitSc	BEAM
Sun City Industries Inc	American	SunCty	SNI
Sun Coast Plastics Inc	NAS NMS	SunCst	SUNI
Sun Company Inc	New York	SunCo	SUN
Sun Distributors L.P.	New York	SunDis	SDP
Sun Electric Corp	New York	SunEl	SE
Sun Energy Partners L.P.	New York	SunEng	SLP
Sun Microsystems Inc	NAS NMS	SunMic	SUNW
Sun State S&L Assn (Arizona)	NAS NMS	SunStSL	SSSL
Sunair Electronics Inc	NAS NMS	Sunair	SNRU
Sunbelt Nursery Group Inc	American	SunbNu	SBN
Sundstrand Corp	New York	Sundstr	SNS
SunGard Data Systems Inc	NAS NMS	SunGrd	SNDT
Sunlite Inc	NAS NMS	Sunlite	SNLT
Sunresorts Limited N.V. (Class A)	NAS NL	Sunrst	RSTAF
Sunrise Federal S&L Assn (Kentucky)	NAS NMS	SunrFd	SRSL
Sunrise Medical Inc	NAS NMS	SunMed	SNMD
Sunrise Preschool Inc	NAS SL	SunPre	SUNR
Sunshine-Jr. Stores Inc	American	SunJr	SJS
Sunshine Mining Holding Co	New York	SunMn	SSC
Sunstar Foods Inc	NAS NMS	SunstFd	SUNF
SunTrust Banks Inc	New York	SunTr	STI
Sunwest Financial Services Inc	NAS NMS	Sunwst	SFSI
Super Food Services Inc	American	SuprFd	SFS
Super Rite Foods Inc	NAS NMS	SupRte	SRFI
Super Value Stores Inc	New York	SupValu	SVU
The Superior Electric Co	NAS NMS	SupEl	SUPE
Superior Industries International Inc	American	SupInd	SUP
Superior Surgical Mfg Co Inc	American	SuprSr	SGC
Supertex Inc	NAS NMS	Suprtex	SUPX
Supradur Companies Inc	NAS SL	Suprad	SUPD
Supreme Equipment & Systems Corp	NAS NMS	SuprEq	SEQP
Surgical Care Affiliates Inc	NAS NMS	SurgAf	SCAF

COMPANY NAME	MARKET LISTING	NEWSPAPER ABBREV.	TRADING SYMBOL
Surgidyne Inc	NAS SL	Surgidy	SGDN
Survival Technology Inc	NAS NMS	SurvTc	SURV
Susquehanna Bancshares Inc	NAS NMS	SusqBn	SUSQ
Sutron Corp	NAS NMS	Sutron	STRN
Svenska Cellulosa AB	NAS NMS	SvenCel	SCAPY
Swank Inc	NAS NL	Swank	SNKIV
Swift Energy Co	American	SwftEng	SFY
Sybra Inc	NAS NMS	Sybra	SIBR
Sym-Tek Systems Inc	NAS NMS	SymTk	SYMK
Symbion Inc	NAS NMS	Symbin	SYMB
Symbol Technologies Inc	New York	SyblTc	SBL
Symbolics Inc	NAS NMS	Symblic	SMBX
Syms Corp	New York	SymsCp	SYM
Synalloy Corp	American	Synaloy	SYO
Synbiotics Corp	NAS NMS	Synbio	SBIO
Syncor International Corp	NAS NMS	Syncor	SCOR
Synercom Technology Inc	NAS NMS	Synrcm	SYNR
Synergen Inc	NAS NMS	Synergn	SYGN
Synergetics International Inc	NAS SL	Synget	SYNG
SynOptics Communications Inc	NAS NL	SynOpt	SNPX
Syntech International Inc	NAS NMS	Syntech	SYNEP
Syntex Corp	New York	Syntex	SYN
Synthetech Inc	NAS SL	Synthe	NZYM
Syntrex Inc	NAS NMS	Syntrex	STRX
Syntro Corp	NAS NMS	Syntro	SYNT
Syracuse Supply Co	NAS NMS	SyrSup	SYRA
Sysco Corp	New York	Sysco	SYY
System Industries Inc	NAS NMS	SystIn	SYSM
System Integrators Inc	New York	SystInt	SIN
Systematics Inc	NAS NMS	Systmt	SYST
Systems & Computer Technology Corp	NAS NMS	SystCpt	SCTC
Systems Engineering & Manufacturing Corp	American	SystEn	SEM
Systems Software Associates Inc	NAS NMS	SySoftw	SSAX
Tab Products Co	American	TabPrd	TBP
Taco Villa Inc	NAS NMS	TacVila	TVLA
Taco Viva Inc	NAS NMS	TacViv	TVIV
Tacoma Boatbuilding Co	New York	TacBt	TBO
The Taiwan Fund Inc	American	Taiwan	TWIN
Talley Industries Inc	New York	Talley	TAL
Talman Home Federal S&L Assn of Illinois	NAS NMS	Talman	TLMN
Tambrands Inc	New York	Tambd	TMB
Tandem Computers Inc	New York	Tandm	TDM
Tandon Corp	NAS NMS	Tandon	TCOR
Tandy Brands Inc	American	TandB	TAB
Tandy Corp	New York	Tandy	TAN
Tandycrafts Inc	New York	Tndycft	TAC
Taro Vit Industries Ltd	NAS NL	TaroVt	TAROF

COMPANY NAME	MARKET LISTING	NEWSPAPER ABBREV.	TRADING SYMBOL
Tasty Baking Co	American	Tasty	TBC
S. Taylor Companies Inc	NAS SL	TaylrS	TAYS
TBC Corp	NAS NMS	TBC	TBCC
TCA Cable TV Inc	NAS NMS	TCA	TCAT
TCBY Enterprises Inc	NAS NMS	TCBY	TCBY
TCF Financial Corp (Minnesota)	NAS NMS	TCF	TCFC
TCS Enterprises Inc	NAS NL	TCS Ent	TCSE
TCW Convertible Securities Fund Inc	New York	TCW	CVT
TDK Corp	New York	TDK	TDK
Team Inc	American	Team	TMI
TEC Inc	American	TEC	TCK
Tech Data Corp	NAS NMS	TchDta	TECD
Tech/Ops Landauer Inc	American	TchOpL	TOV
Tech-Ops Sevcon Inc	American	TchOpS	TOC
Tech-Sym Corp	New York	TchSym	TSY
Tech Time Inc	NAS SL	TchTme	TTME
Techdyne Inc	NAS NL	Tchdyn	TCDN
Technalysis Corp	NAS NMS	Tchnal	TECN
Technical Communications Corp	NAS NMS	TchCom	TCCO
Technical Tape Inc	American	TechTp	TTI
Technitrol Inc	American	Techtrl	TNL
Technodyne Inc	American	Technd	TND
Technogenetics Inc	NAS SL	Tchgen	TXNO
Technology Development Corp	NAS NL	TechDv	TDCX
Technology for Communications International Inc	NAS NMS	TcCom	TCII
TECO Energy Inc	New York	TECO	TE
Tecogen Inc	NAS NMS	Tecogen	TCGN
Tecumseh Products Co	NAS NMS	Tecum	TECU
Teeco Properties LP Co	NAS NL	Teeco	TPLPZ
Tejon Ranch Co	American	TejnR	TRC
Tekelec	NAS NMS	Tekelec	TKLC
Tekna Tool Inc	NAS SL	Tekna	TKNA
Teknowledge Inc	NAS NMS	Teknwd	TKAI
Tektronix Inc	New York	Tektrnx	TEK
TEL Electronics Inc	NAS SL	TEL El	TELS
Telco Systems Inc	NAS NMS	Telco	TELCO
Tele Art Inc	NAS SL	TeleArt	TLARF
Tele-Communications Inc (Class A)	NAS NMS	TlcmA	TCOMA
Tele-Communications Inc (Class B)	NAS NMS	TlcmB	TCOMB
Telecalc Inc	NAS SL	Telecalc	TLCC
Telecast Inc	NAS SL	Telecst	TCST
TeleCom Corp	New York	Telcom	TEL
Telecommunications Network Inc	NAS NMS	TelcN	TNII
TeleConcepts Corp	American	Telecon	TCC
Telecrafter Corp	NAS NMS	Telcrft	TLCR
Telecredit Inc	NAS NMS	Telcrd	TCRD
Teledyne Inc	New York	Teldyn	TDY

COMPANY NAME	MARKET LISTING	NEWSPAPER ABBREV.	TRADING SYMBOL
Teleflex Inc	American	Teleflex	TFX
Compania Telefonica Nacional de Espana S.A.	New York	Telef	TEF
Telefonosa de Mexico S.A.	NAS NL	TelMex	TFONY
Telemation Inc	NAS SL	Telmatn	TLMT
Telematrics International Inc	NAS NMS	Telmatc	TMAX
Telemundo Group Inc	NAS NMS	Telmdo	TLMD
Telemetics Corp	NAS SL	Telenet	TNET
Telephone & Data Systems Inc	American	TelDta	TDS
Telephone Specialists Inc	NAS SL	TelSpcl	TESP
TeleQuest Inc	NAS NMS	TelQst	TELQ
Telerate Inc	New York	Telrte	TLR
Telesphere International Inc	American	Telesph	TSP
Teletimer International Inc	NAS SL	Teletmr	TLTM
TeleVideo Systems Inc	NAS NMS	Telvid	TELV
Television Technology Corp	NAS SL	TelevTc	TVTK
The Telex Corp	New York	Telex	TC
Tellabs Inc	NAS NMS	Telabs	TLAB
Telos Corp	NAS NMS	Telos	TLOS
Telstar Corp	NAS SL	Telstar	TSTR
Telxon Corp	NAS NMS	Telxon	TLXN
Temco Home Health Care Products Inc	NAS NMS	Temco	TEMC
TEMPEST Technologies Inc	NAS NMS	TmpstTc	TTOI
Temple-Inland Inc	New York	Templ	TIN
Templeton Emerging Markets Fund Inc	American	TmplE	EMF
Templeton Global Income Fund	New York	TmpGl	TIM
TEMPO Enterprises Inc	American	Tempo	TPO
Temtex Industries Inc	NAS NMS	Temtex	TMTX
Tennant Co	NAS NMS	Tennant	TANT
Tenneco Inc	New York	Tennco	TGT
Tenney Engineering Inc	American	Tenney	TNY
Teradata Corp	NAS NMS	Teradta	TDAT
Teradyne Inc	New York	Terdyn	TER
Termiflex Corp	NAS NMS	Termflx	TFLX
Terminal Data Corp	NAS NMS	TermDt	TERM
Terra Mines Ltd	NAS NL	TeraM	TMEXF
Tesoro Petroleum Corp	New York	Tesoro	TSO
Teva Pharmaceutical Industries Ltd	NAS NMS	Teva	TEVIY
Texaco Canada Inc	American	TexCd	TXC
Texaco Inc	New York	Texaco	TX
Texas Air Corp	American	TexAir	TEX
Texas American Bancshares Inc	New York	TxABc	TXA
Texas American Energy Corp	NAS NL	TexAEn	COLD
Texas Eastern Corp	New York	TexEst	TET
Texas Industries Inc	New York	TexInd	TXI
Texas Instruments Inc	New York	TxInst	TXN
Texas Pacific Land Trust	New York	TxPac	TPL
Texas Utilities Co	New York	TexUtil	TXU

COMPANY NAME	MARKET LISTING	NEWSPAPER ABBREV.	TRADING SYMBOL
Texcel International Inc	NAS SL	Texcel	TXELC
Texfi Industries Inc	New York	Texfi	TXF
Texstyrene Corp	NAS SL	Texstyr	FOAM
Textron Inc	New York	Textrn	TXT
TGI Friday's Inc	New York	TGIF	TGI
TGX Corp	NAS NMS	TGX	XTGX
Thackey Corp	New York	Thack	THK
Thai Fund	New York	Thai	TTF
Theragenics Corp	NAS SL	Thrgen	THRX
Therapeutic Technologies Inc	NAS SL	TherTc	TTII
Thermal Industries Inc	NAS NL	ThrmIn	THMP
Thermal Profiles Inc	NAS NMS	TherPr	THPR
Thermedics Inc	American	Thrmd	TMD
Thermo Electron Corp	New York	ThrmEl	TMO
Thermo Environmental Corp	American	ThrmE	TEV
Thermo Instrument Systems Inc	American	ThrIns	THI
Thermo Process Systems Inc	American	ThrmP	TPI
Thermodynetics Inc	NAS SL	Thrmdy	TDYN
Thetford Corp	NAS NMS	Thetfd	THFR
Thomas & Betts Corp	New York	ThmBet	TNB
Thomas Edison Inns Inc	NAS SL	ThEdIn	TEIR
Thomas Industries Inc	New York	ThomIn	TII
Thomaston Mills Inc (Class A)	NAS NL	ThmMA	TMSTA
Thomaston Mills Inc (Class B)	NAS NL	ThmMB	TMSTB
Thompson Medical Company Inc	New York	ThmMed	TM
Thomson-CSF	NAS NMS	Thmsn	TCSFY
Thomson McKinnon Asset Management L.P.	New York	TMAM	TMA
Thor Energy Resources Inc	American	ThorEn	THR
Thor Industries Inc	New York	ThorInd	THO
Thorn Apple Valley Inc	NAS NMS	ThrnAV	TAVI
Thortec International Inc	New York	Thortec	THT
Thousand Trails Inc	NAS NMS	ThouTr	TRLS
3 CI Inc	NAS NMS	3CI	CCCI
Three D Departments Inc (Class A)	American	ThrD A	TDD.A
Three D Departments Inc (Class B)	American	ThrD B	TDD.B
3Com Corp	NAS NMS	3Com	COMS
Thrifty Rent-A-Car System Inc	NAS NMS	ThftyRt	TFTY
THT Lloyds Inc	NAS SL	THT Lyd	TXHI
TIC International Corp	NAS SL	TIC	TICI
Tidelands Royalty Trust "B"	NAS NL	TideR	TIRZC
Tidewater Inc	New York	Tidwtr	TDW
TIE/communications Inc	American	TIE	TIE
The Tierco Group Inc	NAS NMS	Tierco	TIER
Tiffany & Co	New York	Tiffny	TIF
Tiger International Inc	New York	TigerIn	TGR
Tigera Group Inc	NAS NMS	Tigera	TYGR
TII Industries Inc	American	TII	TI
Timberjack Corp	NAS NL	Tmbrjk	TJCK

COMPANY NAME	MARKET LISTING	NEWSPAPER ABBREV.	TRADING SYMBOL
The Timberland Co	American	TmbCo	TBL
Timberline Minerals Inc	NAS SL	TmbrM	TIMM
Timberline Software Corp	NAS NMS	TimbSf	TMBS
Time Inc	New York	Time	TL
Time Management Corp	NAS SL	TmeMgt	TMCO
The Times Mirror Co	New York	TmMir	TMC
The Timken Co	New York	Timken	TKR
Tinsley Laboratories Inc	NAS NL	Tinsly	TNSL
Tintoretto Inc	NAS SL	Tintoret	TNTO
TIS Mortgage Investment Co	New York	TIS	TIS
Titan Corp	New York	Titan	TTN
The TJX Companies Inc	New York	TJX	TJX
TM Communications Inc	NAS NMS	TM Com	TMCI
TNP Enterprises Inc	New York	TNP	TNP
TO FITNESS Inc	NAS SL	TOFIT	TFIT
Today Home Entertainment Inc	NAS SL	TdyHm	THEI
Todd-AO Corp	NAS NMS	ToddAO	TODD
Todd Shipyards Corp	New York	TodSh	TOD
Tofruzen Inc	NAS SL	Tofruz	YUMY
Tofutti Brands Inc	American	Tofutti	TOF
Tokheim Corp	New York	Tokhem	TOK
Tokio Marine & Fire Insurance Company Ltd	NAS NMS	TokioF	FKIOY
Toll Brothers Inc	New York	TollBr	TOL
Tolland Bank F.S.B. (Connecticut)	NAS NMS	Tolland	TOBK
Tompkins County Trust Co (New York)	NAS NMS	Tompkn	TCTC
Tonka Corp	New York	Tonka	TKA
Tons of Toys Inc	NAS SL	TonToy	TONS
Tootsie Roll Industries Inc	New York	TootR	TR
Topps Company Inc	NAS NMS	Topps	TOPP
Torchmark Corp	New York	Trchmk	TMK
Toreador Royalty Corp	NAS NMS	TorRoy	TRGL
The Toro Co	New York	Toro	TTC
Torotel Inc	American	Tortel	TTL
Tosco Corp	New York	Tosco	TOS
Total Assets Protection Inc	NAS SL	TotlAst	TAPP
Total Erickson Resources Ltd	NAS NL	TotlEr	TLEXF
Total Health Systems Inc	NAS NMS	TotlHlt	TLHT
Total Petroleum (North America) Ltd	America	TotlPt	TPN
Total Research Corp	NAS SL	Total Rs	TOTL
Total System Services Inc	NAS NMS	TotlSys	TSYS
Total Aluminum Corp	NAS NL	TothAl	TOTH
Tournigan Mining Explorations Ltd	NAS SL	TourM	TGNXF
Town & Country Jewelry Mfg Corp	American	TwCty	TNC
Towne-Paulsen Inc	NAS NL	TownPl	TOWN
Toyota Motor Corp	NAS NL	Toyota	TOYOY
Toys "R" Us Inc	New York	ToyRU	TOY
TPA of America Inc	American	TPA Am	TPS

COMPANY NAME	MARKET LISTING	NEWSPAPER ABBREV.	TRADING SYMBOL
TPI Enterprises Inc	NAS NMS	TPI En	TELE
Trace Products	NAS SL	TracePd	TRCE
Traditional Industries Inc	NAS NMS	TradInd	TRAD
Trak Auto Corp	NAS NMS	TrakAu	TRKA
Trammell Crow Real Estate Investors	New York	Tramel	TCR
Trans Financial Bancorp Inc	NAS NMS	TrnFnc	TRFI
Trans-Industries Inc	NAS NMS	TranIn	TRIN
Trans Leasing International INc	NAS NMS	TrnLsg	TLII
Trans-Lux Corp	American	TrnsLx	TLX
Trans-National Leasing Inc	NAS NMS	Trnsntl	TNLS
Trans World Airlines Inc	New York	TWA	TWA
Trans World Music Corp	NAS NMS	TrnMu	TWMC
Transact International INc	NAS SL	Trnsact	TACT
Transamerica Corp	New York	Transm	TA
Transamerica Income Shares Inc	New York	TranInc	TAI
TransCanada PipeLines Ltd	New York	TrnCda	TRP
TransCapital Financial Corp	New York	Trnscap	TFC
Transco Energy Co	New York	Transco	E
Transco Exploration Partners Ltd	New York	TranEx	EXP
Transcon Inc	New York	Transcn	TCL
Transducer Systems Inc	NAS NMS	Trnsdcr	TSIC
Transform Logic Corp	NAS SL	TrnfmL	TLOG
Transico Industries Inc (Class A)	American	TrnscoA	TNI.A
Transico Industries Inc (Class B)	American	TrnscoB	TNI.B
Transidyne General Corp	NAS NMS	Trnsdyn	TGCO
Transmation Inc	NAS NMS	Trnsmt	TRNS
Transmedia Network Inc	NAS SL	Trnmed	TMNI
TransNet Corp	NAS NMS	Trnsnt	TRNT
Transtech Industries Inc	NAS NMS	Trntch	TRTI
TransTechnology Corp	New York	TrnsTec	TT
Transtector Systems Inc	NAS NMS	Trnstct	TTOR
Transworld Bancorp	NAS NMS	TrwlBc	TWBC
The Tranzonic Companies	American	Trnzn	TNZ
The Travelers Corp	New York	Travler	TIC
TRC Companies Inc	American	TRC	TRR
Trenwick Group Inc	NAS NMS	Trnwck	TREN
Tri Coast Environmental Corp	NAS SL	TriCst	TOXY
Tri-Continental Corp	New York	TriCon	TY
Tri-State Motor Transit Company of Delaware	American	TriSM	TSM
Triad Systems Corp	NAS NMS	TriadSy	TRSC
The Triangle Corp	American	TriaCp	TRG
Triangle Home Products Inc	American	TriHme	THP
Triangle Industries Inc (Class A)	NAS NMS	TrianIn	TRIAA
Tribune Co	New York	Tribun	TRB
Tribune/Swab-Fox Companies Inc	NAS NL	TribSwb	TSFC
Tricentrol PLC	New York	Tricntr	TCT
Trico Products Corp	NAS NMS	TricoPd	TRCO

COMPANY NAME	MARKET LISTING	NEWSPAPER ABBREV.	TRADING SYMBOL
Tridex Corp	American	Tridex	TDX
Trimedyne Inc	NAS NMS	Trimed	TMED
Trinity Industries Inc	New York	Trinty	TRN
Trinova Corp	New York	Trinov	TNV
Trio-Tech International	NAS SL	TrioTch	TRTC
Trion Inc	NAS NMS	Trion	TRON
Triton Energy Corp	New York	TritEng	OIL
Triton Group Ltd	New York	TritnG	TGL
Tround International Inc	NAS SL	Tround	TROU
Trudy Corp	NAS SL	Trudy	TRDY
Trus Joist Corp	NAS NMS	TrusJo	TJCO
Trust America Service Corp	American	TstAm	TRS
Trustco Bank Corp NY (New York)	NAS NMS	TrNY	TRST
The Trustcompany Bancorporation (New Jersey)	NAS NMS	Trstco	TCBC
Trustcorp Inc	NAS NMS	Trstcp	TTCO
Truvel Corp	NAS SL	Truvel	TRVL
TRV Minerals Corp	NAS NMS	TRV	TRVMF
TRW Inc	New York	TRW	TRW
TS Industries Inc	NAS NMS	TS Ind	TNDS
Tseng Labs Inc	NAS SL	Tseng	TSNG
TSI Incorporated	NAS NMS	TSI	TSII
TSR Inc	NAS NMS	TSR	TSRI
T2 Medical Inc	American	T2 Md	TSQ
Tubos de Acero de Mexico S.A.	American	TubMex	TAM
Tucker Drilling Co	NAS NMS	TuckDr	TUCK
Tucker Holding Co	NAS NMS	TuckHd	TUHC
Tucson Electric Power Co	New York	TucsEP	TEP
Tudor Corporation Ltd	NAS NMS	Tudor	TDRLF
Tuesday Morning Inc	NAS NMS	TuesM	TUES
Tultex Corp	New York	Tultex	TTX
Tunex International Inc	NAS SL	Tunex	TUNX
Turf Paradise Inc	NAS NL	TurfPar	TURF
Turner Broadcasting System Inc (Class A)	American	TurnB A	TBS.A
Turner Broadcasting System Inc (Class B)	American	TurnB B	TBS.B
The Turner Corp	American	TurnrC	TUR
Turner Equity Investors Inc	American	TrnEq	TEQ
Tuscarora Plastic Inc	NAS NMS	TuscPl	TUSC
TVI Corp	NAS SL	TVI Cp	TVIE
TVX Broadcast Group Inc	NAS NMS	TVX	TVXG
TW Services Inc	New York	TW Svc	TW
20th Century Industries Inc	NAS NMS	20thCnIn	TWEN
Twin Disc Inc	New York	TwinDs	TDI
Twistee Treat Corp	NAS NMS	TwstTr	TWST
202 Data System Inc	NAS NMS	202 Dta	TOOT
Two Pesos Inc	American	TwPeso	TWP
Tyco Laboratories Inc	New York	TycoL	TYC
Tyco Toys Inc	NAS NMS	TycoTy	TTOY

COMPANY NAME	MARKET LISTING	NEWSPAPER ABBREV.	TRADING SYMBOL
Tylan Corp	NAS NMS	Tylan	TYLN
Tyler Corp	New York	Tyler	TYL
Tyrex Oil Co	NAS SL	Tyrex	TYRX
Tyson Foods Inc (Class A)	NAS NMS	Tyson	TYSNA
UAL Corp	New York	UAL Cp	UAL
UAS Automation Systems Inc	NAS SL	UAS	UASI
UDC-Universal Development L.P.	New York	UDC	UDC
UGI Corp	New York	UGI	UGI
ULTIMAP International Corp	NAS SL	Ultimap	UMAP
The Ultimate Corp	New York	Ultmte	ULT
Ultra Bancorporation	NAS NMS	UltrBc	ULTB
UNC Inc	New York	UNCInc	UNC
Uni-Marts Inc (Class A)	NAS NMS	UniMrt	UNMAA
Unibancorp Inc	NAS NMS	Unibcp	UBCP
UniCARE Financial Corp	American	UniCre	UFN
Unico American Corp	NAS NMS	UnicoA	UNAM
Unicorp American Corp	American	Unicorp	UAC
Unifast Industries Inc	NAS NMS	Unfast	UFST
Unifi Inc	NAS NMS	Unifi	UNFI
UniFirst Corp	New York	UniFrst	UNF
Uniforce Temporary Personnel Inc	NAS NMS	Unifrc	UNFR
Unigene Laboratories Inc	NAS NL	Unigene	UGNE
Unilever N.V.	New York	UnNV	UN
Unilever PLC	New York	Unilvr	UL
Unimar Co	American	Unimar	UMR
Unimed Inc	NAS NMS	Unimed	UMED
Union Camp Corp	New York	UCmp	UCC
Union Carbide Corp	New York	UCarb	UK
The Union Corp	New York	UnionC	UCO
Union Electric Co	New York	UnElec	UEP
Union Exploration Partners Ltd	New York	UnExp	UXP
Union National Corp	NAS NMS	UnNatl	UNBC
Union Pacific Corp	New York	UnPac	UNP
Union Planters Corp	NAS NMS	UnPlntr	UPCM
Union Texas Petroleum Holdings Inc	New York	UnTex	UTH
Union Valley Corp	American	UnValy	UVC
UnionFed Financial Corp	New York	UnfedF	UFF
Unisys Corp	New York	Unisys	UIS
Unit Corp	New York	Unit	UNT
United Artists Communications Inc (Class A)	NAS NMS	UACm	UACIA
United Asset Management Corp	New York	UAM	UAM
United Bankers Inc	NAS NMS	UnBkrs	UBKR
United Banks of Colorado Inc	NAS NMS	UBCol	UBKS
United Bankshares Inc (West Virginia)	NAS NMS	UBWV	UBSI
United Brands Co	New York	UnBrnd	UB

COMPANY NAME	MARKET LISTING	NEWSPAPER ABBREV.	TRADING SYMBOL
United Building Services Corporation of Delaware	NAS NMS	UnBldg	UBSC
United Cable Television Corp	New York	UCbTV	UCT
United Carolina Bancshares Corp	NAS NMS	UCaBk	UCAR
United Cities Gas Co	NAS NMS	UCtyGs	UCIT
United Coasts Corp	NAS NMS	UnCoast	UCOA
United Companies Financial Corp	NAS NMS	UnCosF	UNCF
United Counties Bancorporation	NAS NL	UCount	UCTC
United Dominion Realty Trust Inc	NAS NMS	UnDom	UDRT
United Education & Software	NAS NMS	UnEdS	UESS
United Federal S&L Assn (North Carolina)	NAS NL	UFedS	UFRM
United Financial Banking Co	NAS NL	UnFncl	UFBC
United Financial Corporation of South Carolina Inc	NAS NMS	UFinSC	UNSA
United Financial Group Inc	NAS NMS	UFnGrp	UFGI
United Fire & Casualty Co	NAS NMS	UFireC	UFCS
United Foods Inc (Class A)	American	UFoodA	UFD.A
United Foods Inc (Class B)	American	UFoodB	UFD.B
United-Guardian Inc	NAS NMS	UGrdn	UNIR
United HealthCare Corp	NAS NMS	UHltCr	UNIH
United Hearne Resources Ltd	NAS SL	UnHrn	UHRNF
United Home Life Insurance Co	NAS NMS	UtdHm	UHLI
The United Illuminating Co	New York	UIllum	UIL
United Industrial Corp	New York	UnitInd	UIC
United Inns Inc	New York	UnitInn	UI
United Insurance Companies Inc	NAS NMS	UtdIns	UICI
United Investors Management Co	NAS NMS	UtdInv	UTDMK
United Jersey Banks	New York	UJerBk	UJB
The United Kingdom Fund Inc	New York	UKing	UKM
United Medical Corp	American	UtMed	UM
United Merchants & Manufacturers Inc	New York	UtdMM	UMM
United Missouri Bancshares Inc	NAS NMS	UMoB	UMSB
United National Bank (New Jersey)	NAS NL	UBkNJ	UNBJ
United New Mexico Financial Corp	NAS NMS	UnNMx	BNKS
United Newspapers Public Limited Co	NAS NMS	UtdNwsp	UNEWY
United Park City Mines Co	New York	UPkMn	UPK
United Presidential Corp	NAS NMS	UPresd	UPCO
United Saver's Bancorp Inc	NAS NMS	UtdSvrs	USBI
United S&L Assn (Missouri)	NAS NMS	UnSvMo	UNSL
United Savings Assn (Class A) (Florida)	NAS NMS	UnSvFl	UNSVA
United Savings Bank (Oregon)	NAS NMS	USB Or	USBA
United Savings Bank (Virginia)	NAS NMS	USBkVa	USBK
United Savings Bank F.A. (Montana)	NAS NMS	USvBk	UBMT
United Service Source Inc	NAS NMS	UnSvSc	UNSI
United Shoppers of America Inc	NAS SL	UtdShp	USDA
United States Antimony Corp	NAS NMS	US Ant	USAC
United States Cellular Corp	American	US Cel	USM
Unites States Oil Co	NAS SL	US Oil	USOL

COMPANY NAME	MARKET LISTING	NEWSPAPER ABBREV.	TRADING SYMBOL
The United States Shoe Corp	New York	USShoe	USR
United States Surgical Corp	New York	Surg	USS
United Stationers Inc	NAS NMS	UStatn	USTR
United Stockyards Corp	New York	UnStck	COW
United Systems Technology Inc	NAS SL	UnSyTc	USTI
United Technologies Corp	New York	UnTech	UTX
United Telecommunications Inc	New York	UniTel	UT
United Television Inc	NAS NMS	UnTelev	UTVI
United Tote Inc	NAS NMS	UnTote	TOTE
United Vermont Bancorporation	NAS NMS	UnVtBn	UVTB
United Water Resources Inc	New York	UWR	UWR
Unitel Video Inc	American	UnitelV	UNV
UNITIL Corp	American	Unitil	UTL
Unitrode Corp	New York	Unitrde	UTR
Unitronix Corp	NAS NMS	Unitrnx	UTRX
Univar Corp	New York	Univar	UVX
Univation Inc	NAS SL	Univatn	UNIV
Universal Corp	New York	UnvlCp	UVV
Universal Foods Corp	New York	UnvFds	UFC
Universal Furniture Ltd	NAS NMS	UnvFr	UFURF
Universal Health Realty Income Trust	New York	UnvHR	UHT
Universal Health Services Inc (Class B)	NAS NMS	UnvHlt	UHSIB
Universal Holding Corp	NAS NMS	UnvHld	UHCO
Universal Matchbox Group Ltd	New York	UMatch	UMG
Universal Medical Buildings L.P.	New York	UnvMed	UMB
Universal Security Instruments Inc	NAS NMS	UnvSec	USEC
Universal Voltronics Corp	NAS NMS	UnVolt	UVOL
University Bank N.A.	American	UnvBk	UBN
University Genetics Co	NAS SL	UnvGen	UGEN
University National Bank & Trust Co (California)	NAS NMS	UnivBT	UNNB
University Patents Inc	American	UnvPat	UPT
University Savings Bank (Washington)	NAS NMS	UnvSvg	UFSB
University Science Partners Inc	NAS SL	UnvSci	USPI
UNO Restaurant Corp	American	UnoRt	UNO
Unocal Corp	New York	Unocal	UCL
UNR Industries Inc	NAS NL	UNR	UNRIQ
UNUM Corp	New York	UNUM	UNM
The Upjohn Co	New York	Upjohn	UPJ
Upper Peninsula Power Co	NAS NMS	UpenP	UPEN
U.S. Bancorp	NAS NMS	US Bcp	USBC
U.S. Energy Corp	NAS NMS	US Enr	USEG
US Facilities Corp	NAS NMS	US Facl	USRE
U.S. Gold Corp	NAS NMS	US Gold	USGL
U.S. Health Inc	NAS NMS	USHltI	USHI
U.S. Healthcare Inc	NAS NMS	US HltC	USHC
U.S. Home Corp	New York	USHom	UH
U.S. Intec Inc	NAS NMS	US Intc	INTX

COMPANY NAME	MARKET LISTING	NEWSPAPER ABBREV.	TRADING SYMBOL
US Minerals Exploration Co	NAS NMS	USMX	USMX
U.S. Precious Metals Inc	NAS NMS	US Prc	USPMF
US Realty Partners Ltd	NAS NL	USRlty	USRLZ
U.S. Shelter Corp	NAS NMS	US Shelt	USSS
U.S. Trust Corp	NAS NMS	US Trst	USTC
U S WEST Inc	New York	USWest	USW
U S WEST NewVector Group Inc (Class A)	NAS NMS	USWNV	USWNA
USA Bancorp Inc	NAS NMS	USA Bc	USAB
USACafes L.P.	New York	USACaf	USF
USAir Group Inc	New York	UsairG	U
USBANCORP Inc (Pennsylvania)	NAS NMS	USBPa	USBP
USENCO Inc	NAS SL	Usenco	USEN
USF&G Corp	New York	USFG	FG
USG Corp	New York	USG	USG
USLICO Corp	New York	USLICO	USC
USLIFE Corp	New York	USLIFE	USH
USLIFE Income Fund Inc	New York	UslfeF	UIF
USP Real Estate Investment Trust	American	USPRI	URT
USPCI Inc	New York	USPCI	UPC
UST Corp	NAS NMS	UST Cp	USTB
UST Inc	New York	UST	UST
USX Corp	New York	USX	X
Utah Medical Products Inc	NAS SL	UtahMd	UTMD
Utah Power & Light Co	New York	UtaPL	UTP
UtiliCorp United Inc	New York	UtiliCo	UCU
UTL Corp	NAS NMS	UTL	UTLC
V-Band Systems Inc	NAS NMS	V Band	VBAN
Vaal Reefs Exploration & Mining Company Ltd	NAS NL	VaalR	VAALY
Vacations To Go Inc	NAS SL	VacTGo	VTGO
Vacu-dry	NAS NL	VacDry	VDRY
Vader Group Inc	American	Vader	VDR
ValCom Inc	NAS NMS	Valcom	VLCM
Valdosta Federal S&L Assn	NAS NL	Valdost	VFSL
Valhi Inc	New York	Valhi	VHI
Valero Energy Corp	New York	Valero	VLO
Valero Natural Gas Partners L.P.	New York	ValNG	VLP
Valid Logic Systems Inc	NAS NMS	ValidLg	VLID
Vallen Corp	NAS NMS	Vallen	VALN
Valley Bancorporation (Wisconsin)	NAS NMS	ValyB	VYBN
Valley Bank (Vermont)	NAS SL	ValB VT	VBVT
Valley Capital Corp	NAS NMS	VlyCap	VCCN
Valley Federal S&L Assn	NAS NMS	ValFSL	VFED
Valley Federal Savings Bank (Alabama)	NAS SL	VlFdAla	VAFD
Valley Federal Savings Bank (Indiana)	NAS NL	VlyFed	VAFB
Valley Forge Corp	American	ValFrg	VF
Valley Industries Inc	New York	ValeyIn	VI

COMPANY NAME	MARKET LISTING	NEWSPAPER ABBREV.	TRADING SYMBOL
Valley National Bancorp (New Jersey)	NAS NMS	ValNBc	VNBP
Valley National Corp	NAS NMS	ValNtl	VNCP
Valley Resources Inc	American	ValyRs	VR
Valley West Bancorp	NAS NL	ValyWst	VWBN
Valmont Industries Inc	NAS NMS	Valmnt	VALM
The Valspar Corp	American	Valspr	VAL
Vaule Line Inc	NAS NMS	ValLn	VALU
Van Dorn Co	New York	VanDrn	VDC
Van Kampen Merritt Municipal Income Trust	New York	VKmp	VMT
Vanderbilt Gold Corp	NAS NMS	VanGld	VAGO
Vanguard Cellular-Systems Inc	NAS NMS	VgrdCl	VCEL
Vanzetti Systems Inc	NAS NMS	Vanzeti	VANZ
Varco International Inc	New York	Varco	VRC
Vari-Care Inc	NAS NMS	VariCre	VCRE
Varian Associates Inc	New York	Varian	VAR
Varitronic Systems Inc	NAS NMS	Varitrn	VRSY
Varity Corp	New York	Varity	VAT
Varlen Corp	NAS NMS	Varlen	VRLN
Varo Inc	New York	Varo	VRO
Vaughn's Inc	NAS SL	Vaughn	VGHN
Veeco Instruments Inc	New York	Veeco	VEE
Vega Biotechnologies Inc	NAS SL	VegaBio	VEGA
Velcro Industries N.V.	NAS NL	Velcro	VELCF
VeloBind Inc	NAS NMS	VeloBd	VBND
The Vendo Co	New York	Vendo	VEN
Ventrex Laboratories Inc	NAS NMS	Ventrex	VTRX
Venturian Corp	NAS NMS	Ventur	VENT
Verdix Corp	NAS SL	Verdix	VRDX
Verit Industries	American	Verit	VER
Vermont American Corp (Class A)	American	VtAmC	VAC.A
Vermont Financial Services Corp	NAS NMS	VtFin	VFSC
Vermont Research Corp	American	VtRsh	VRE
Veronex Resources Ltd	NAS NMS	Veronx	VEOXF
Versa Technologies Inc	NAS NMS	Versa	VRSA
Versar Inc	American	Versar	VSR
Vertex Communications Corp	NAS NMS	VertexC	VTEX
Vertipile Inc	American	Vertple	VRT
Vestar Inc	NAS NMS	Vestar	VSTR
Vestaur Securities Inc	New York	VestSe	VES
Vestro Foods Inc	NAS SL	Vestro	VEST
Vestron Inc	New York	Vestrn	VV
V.F. Corp	New York	VF Cp	VFC
VHC Ltd	NAS NL	VHC	VHCL
Viacom Inc	American	Viacm	VIA
Viatech Inc	American	Viatch	VTK
Vicon Fiber Optics Corp	NAS NMS	ViconF	VFOX
Vicon Industries Inc	American	Vicon	VII
VICORP Restaurants Inc	NAS NMS	Vicorp	VRES

COMPANY NAME	MARKET LISTING	NEWSPAPER ABBREV.	TRADING SYMBOL
Victoria Bankshares Inc	NAS NMS	VictBn	VICT
Victoria Creations Inc	NAS NMS	VictCr	VITC
Victoria Financial Corp	NAS SL	VictFn	VICF
Video Display Corp	NAS NMS	VidDsp	VIDE
Video Jukebox Network Inc	NAS SL	VidJuke	JUKE
Videoplex Inc	NAS SL	Videplx	VPLXE
Vie de France Corp	NAS NMS	Vie deFr	VDEF
View-Master Ideal Group Inc	NAS NMS	ViewMs	VMIG
Viking Freight Inc	NAS NMS	Viking	VIKG
Vikonics Inc	NAS NMS	Vikonic	VKSI
Village Super Market Inc	NAS NMS	VilSpM	LVGE
E.A. Viner Holdings Ltd	NAS NL	Viner	EAVK
Vintage Enterprises Inc	American	Vintge	VIN
Vintage Group Inc	NAS NL	Vintage	VINT
Vipont Laboratories Inc	NAS NMS	Vipont	VLAB
Viragen Inc	NAS SL	Viragen	VRGN
Viral Response Systems Inc	NAS SL	ViralRp	VRSI
Viratek Inc	NAS NMS	Viratek	VIRA
Virco Manufacturing Corp	American	Virco	VIR
Virgin Group plc	NAS NMS	VirgnG	VGINY
Virginia Beach Savings Bank	NAS NMS	VaBch	VABF
Virginia First Savings Bank FSB	NAS NMS	VaFst	VFSB
Viscount Resources Ltd	NAS SL	Viscnt	VISRF
Vishay Intertechnology Inc	New York	Vishay	VSH
Vision Sciences Inc	NAS SL	VsnSci	LENZ
Vision Technologies International Inc	NAS SL	VsnTch	IOLS
Vista Chemical Co	New York	VistaC	VC
Vista Organization Ltd	NAS NMS	VistaOr	VISA
Vista Resources Inc	NAS NL	VistaRs	VIST
Visual Graphics Corp (Class A)	American	VislGA	VGC.A
Visual Graphics Corp (Class B)	American	VislG B	VGC.B
Visual Industries Inc	NAS NMS	VisualI	VISC
Vitalink Communications Corp	NAS NMS	Vitalnk	VITA
Vitel Fiber Optics Corp	NAS SL	VitelFb	VTEL
Titronics Corp	NAS NMS	Vitronic	VITX
Vivigen Inc	NAS NMS	Vivigen	VIVI
VLSI Technology Inc	NAS NMS	VLSI	VLSI
VM Software Inc	NAS NMS	VM Sft	VMSI
VMS Hotel Investment Fund	American	VHT	VHT
VMX Inc	NAS NMS	VMX	VMXI
Voicemail International Inc	NAS SL	Voicml	VOIC
Volt Information Sciences Inc	NAS NMS	VoltInf	VOLT
Volunteer Bancshares Inc	NAS NL	VolunBc	VOLB
Volvo A.B.	NAS NMS	Volvo	VOLVY
The Vons Companies Inc	New York	Vons	VON
Voplex Corp	American	Voplex	VOT
Vornado Inc	New York	Vornad	VNO
Votrax Inc	NAS SL	Votrax	VOTX

COMPANY NAME	MARKET LISTING	NEWSPAPER ABBREV.	TRADING SYMBOL
VSE Corp	NAS NMS	VSE	VSEC
VTX Electronics Corp	American	VTX	VTX
Vulcan Corp	American	VulcCp	VUL
Vulcan Materials Co	New York	VulcM	VMC
Vulcan Packaging Inc	NAS NMS	VulcP	VIPLF
VWR Corp	NAS NMS	VWR	VWRX
Vyquest Inc	American	Vyqust	VY
The Wackenhut Corp	New York	Wackht	WAK
Wacoal Corp	NAS NL	Wacoal	WACLY
Wainoco Oil Corp	New York	Wainoc	WOL
Wal-Mart Stores Inc	New York	WalMt	WMT
Walbro Corp	NAS NMS	Walbro	WALB
Walgreen Co	New York	Walgrn	WAG
Walker Telecommunications Corp	NAS NMS	WlkrTel	WTEL
Wall to Wall Sound & Video Inc	NAS NMS	WallSnd	WTWS
Wallace Computer Services Inc	New York	WalCSv	WCS
Walshire Assurance Co	NAS NMS	Walshr	WALS
Waltham Corp	NAS NMS	WaltCp	WLBK
Wampler-Longacre-Rockingham Inc	NAS NL	Wamplr	WLRF
Wang Laboratories Inc (Class B)	American	WangB	WAN.B
Wang Laboratories Inc (Class C)	American	WangC	WAN.C
Ward White Group PLC	NAS NMS	WardWh	WWGPY
Warehouse Club Inc	NAS NMS	WrhseC	WCLB
Warner Communications Inc	New York	WarnC	WCI
Warner Computer Systems Inc	New York	WrnCpt	WCP
Warner-Lambert Co	New York	WarnrL	WLA
Warrantech Corp	NAS SL	Warntc	WTEC
Warren Five Cents Savings Bank (Massachusetts)	NAS NMS	Warren	WFCS
Warwick Insurance Managers Inc	NAS NMS	Warwk	WIMI
Washington Bancorp (New Jersey)	NAS NMS	WshBcp	WBNC
Washington Bancorporation (Washington, D.C.)	NAS NMS	WBcDC	WWBC
Washington Energy Co	NAS NMS	WashEn	WECO
Washington Federal S&L Assn of Seattle	NAS NMS	WFSL	WFSL
Washington Federal Savings Bank (Oregon)	NAS NMS	WshFOr	WFOR
Washington Federal Savings Bank (Washington, D.C.)	NAS NMS	WshFDC	WFSB
Washington Gas Gas Light Co	New York	WashGs	WGL
Washington Mutual Savings Bank	NAS NMS	WMSB	WAMU
Washington National Corp	New York	WshNat	WNT
The Washington Post Co (Class B)	American	WshPst	WPO.B
Washington Real Estate Investment Trust	American	WRIT	WRE
Washington Savings Bank	NAS NMS	WshSvg	WSBXV
Washington Scientific Industries Inc	NAS NMS	WshSci	WSCI
Washington Trust Bancorporation (Rhode Island)	NAS NL	WashTr	WASH

COMPANY NAME	MARKET LISTING	NEWSPAPER ABBREV.	TRADING SYMBOL
The Washington Water Power Co	New York	WshWt	WWP
Waste Management Inc	New York	Waste	WMX
Waste Recovery Inc	NAS SL	WasteRc	WRII
Waste Technology Corp	NAS SL	WasteTc	WTEK
Waterford Glass Group plc	NAS NMS	WatrfGl	WATFY
Waterhouse Investor Services Inc	NAS NMS	Watrhse	WHOO
Waters Instruments Inc	NAS NMS	WatrIn	WHRG
Watkins-Johnson Co	New York	WatkJn	WJ
Watsco Inc (Class A)	American	Watsc A	WSO.A
Watsco Inc (Class B)	American	Watsc B	WSO.B
Watts Industries Inc (Class A)	NAS NMS	WattsInd	WATTA
Wausau Paper Mills Co	NAS NMS	WausP	WSAU
Waverly Inc	NAS NMS	Waver	WAVR
Wavetech Inc	NAS SL	Wavetch	WAVE
Wavetek Corp	NAS NMS	Wavetk	WVTK
Waxman Industries Inc	NAS NMS	Waxmn	WAXM
The WCRS Group PLC	NAS NMS	WCRS	WCRSY
WD-40 Co	NAS NMS	WD 40	WDFC
Wean Inc	New York	WeanU	WID
Weatherford International Inc	American	Wthfrd	WII
Del E. Webb Corp	New York	WebbD	WBB
Del E. Webb Investment Properties Inc (Class A)	American	WebInv	DWP.A
Webster Clothes Inc	NAS NMS	WbstCl	WEBS
Webster Financial Corp	NAS NMS	WbstFn	WBST
Wedco Technology Inc	American	Wedco	WED
Wedgestone Financial Trust	New York	Wedgtn	WDG
Weigh-Tronix Inc	NAS NMS	WeigTr	WGHT
Weiman Company Inc	American	Weiman	WC
Weingarten Realty Inc	New York	WeingR	WRI
Weis Markets Inc	New York	WeisM	WMK
Weisfield's Inc	NAS NMS	Weisfld	WEIS
Weitek Corp	NAS NL	Weitek	WWTK
Welbilt Corp	NAS NMS	Weblt	WELB
Weldotron Corp	American	Weldtrn	WLD
Welkom Gold Holdings Ltd	NAS NL	WekG	WLKMY
Wellco Enterprises Inc	American	Wellco	WLC
Wellman Inc	New York	Wellmn	WLM
Wells American Corp	American	WellAm	WAC
Wells Fargo & Co	New York	WellsF	WFC
Wells Fargo Mortgage & Equity Trust	New York	WelFM	WFM
Wells-Gardner Electronics Corp	American	WelGrd	WGA
Wendt-Bristol Co	NAS NMS	Wendt	WNDT
Wendy's International Inc	New York	Wendys	WEN
Werner Enterprises Inc	NAS NMS	Werner	WERN
Wesbanco Inc	NAS NMS	Wesbnc	WSBC
Wesco Financial Corp	American	Wesco	WSC
Wespercorp	American	Wespcp	WP

COMPANY NAME	MARKET LISTING	NEWSPAPER ABBREV.	TRADING SYMBOL
Wessex Corp	NAS NMS	Wessex	WSSX
The West Company Inc	New York	West	WST
West Massachusetts Bankshares Inc	NAS NMS	WtMass	WMBS
West Newton Savings Bank (Massachusetts)	NAS NMS	WNewtn	WNSB
West Point-Pepperell Inc	New York	WtPtP	WPM
WESTAMERICA BANCORPORATION	American	WAmB	WAB
Westar Corp	NAS SL	Westar	WSTR
Westbridge Capital Corp	American	WstBrC	WBC
Westcoast Energy Inc	New York	WstctE	WE
Westcorp	American	Westcp	WCRP
Westerbeke Corp	NAS NMS	Wstrbke	WTBK
Western Acceptance Corp	NAS SL	WstAcp	WACP
Western Allenbee Oil & Gas Company Ltd	NAS NL	WtnAlen	WABEF
Western Auto Supply Co	NAS NMS	WstAut	WASC
Western Bank (Oregon)	NAS NMS	WtBank	WSBK
Western Bell Communications Inc	NAS SL	WstBell	WBEL
Western Capital Investment Corp	NAS NMS	WstCap	WECA
Western Carolina S&L Assn (North Carolina)	NAS NL	WtCaSv	WCAR
Western Commercial Inc	NAS NMS	WmCmc	WCCC
The Western Company of North America	New York	WCNA	WSN
Western Deep Levels Ltd	NAS NL	WDeep	WDEPY
Western Digital Corp	American	WDigitl	WDC
Western Federal S&L Assn (California)	NAS NMS	WstFSL	WFSA
Western Federal Savings Bank (Puerto Rico)	NAS NMS	WFdPR	WFPR
Western Financial Corp	NAS NMS	WnFncl	WSTF
Western Health Plans Inc	American	WstHlth	WHP
Western Investment Real Estate Trust	American	WIRET	WIR
Western Micro Technology Inc	NAS NMS	WMicTc	WSTM
Western Microwave Inc	NAS NMS	WMicr	WMIC
Western Publishing Group Inc	NAS NMS	WstnPb	WPGI
Western S&L Assn	New York	WstnSL	WSL
Western Union Corp	New York	WUnion	WU
Western Waste Industries	NAS NMS	WnWste	WWIN
Westinghouse Electric Corp	New York	WstgE	WX
WestMarc Communications Inc (Class A)	NAS NMS	WtMrcA	WSMCA
WestMarc Communications Inc (Class B)	NAS NL	WtMrcB	WSMCB
Westmark International Inc	NAS NMS	Wstmrk	WMRK
Westmoreland Coal Co	NAS NMS	WmorC	WMOR
Roy F. Weston Inc (Class A)	NAS NMS	Weston	WSTNA
Westport Bancorp Inc	NAS NMS	WstBc	WBAT
Westvaco Corp	New York	Wstvc	W
Westwood One Inc	NAS NMS	WstwO	WONE
Wetterau Inc	NAS NMS	Wettra	WETT
Wetterau Properties Inc	NAS NL	WetrPr	WTPR
Weyenberg Shoe Manufacturing Co	NAS NMS	Weynbg	WEYS
Weyerhaeuser Co	New York	Weyerh	WY

COMPANY NAME	MARKET LISTING	NEWSPAPER ABBREV.	TRADING SYMBOL
Wharf Resources Ltd	NAS NMS	Wharf	WFRAF
Wheelabrator Technologies Inc	NAS NMS	WhelTch	WHTI
The Wheeling & Lake Erie Railway Co	New York	WhelLE	WLE
Wheeling-Pittsburgh Steel Corp	New York	WhPit	WHX
Whirlpool Corp	New York	Whrlpl	WHR
Whitehall Corp	New York	Whitehl	WHT
Whiting Petroleum Corp	NAS SL	WhitPt	WPCO
Whitman Medical Corp	NAS SL	Whitmn	WHIT
Whittaker Corp	New York	Whittak	WKR
The Wholesale Club Inc	NAS NMS	Whlclub	WHLS
WICAT Systems Inc	NAS NMS	Wicat	WCAT
Wichita River Corp	American	WichRv	WRO
Wickes Companies Inc	New York	Wickes	WIX
WICOR Inc	New York	WICOR	WIC
Wiener Enterprises Inc	American	Wiener	WPB
Wiland Services Inc	NAS NMS	Wiland	WSVS
John Wiley & Sons Inc (Class A)	NAS NMS	WilyJ A	WILLA
John Wiley & Sons Inc (Class B)	NAS NL	WilyJ B	WILLB
Wilfred American Educational Corp	New York	Wilfred	WAE
Willamette Industries Inc	NAS NMS	Willamt	WMTT
Willcox & Gibbs Inc	New York	WillcG	WG
The A.L. Williams Corp	NAS NMS	WillAL	ALWC
W.W. Williams Co	NAS NMS	WillW	WWWM
The Williams Companies Inc	New York	William	WMB
Williams Industries Inc	NAS NMS	WillmI	WMSI
Williams-Sonoma Inc	NAS NMS	WmsSon	WSGC
Wilmington Savings Fund Society FSB	NAS NMS	WilSFS	WSFS
Wilmington Trust Co	NAS NMS	WilmT	WILM
Wilshire Oil Company of Texas	New York	WilshrO	WOC
Wilson Foods Corp	NAS NMS	WilsnF	WILF
Wilson Sporting Good Co	American	WlsnSp	WIL
Wiltek Inc	NAS SL	Wiltek	WLTK
Wilton Enterprises Inc	NAS NMS	Wilton	WLTN
Winchell's Donut Houses L.P.	New York	Winchl	WDH
Windmere Corp	NAS NMS	Windmr	WDMR
WINE Inc	NAS SL	WINE	VINO
Winjak Inc	New York	Winjak	WJI
Winn-Dixie Stores Inc	New York	WinDix	WIN
Winnebago Industries Inc	New York	Winnbg	WGO
Winners Corp	New York	Winner	WNR
Winston Furniture Company Inc	American	WinFur	WF
Winston Resources Inc	American	WinRs	WRS
Winthrop Insured Mortgage Investors II	American	WintIn	WMI
Wisconsin Energy Corp	New York	WisEn	WEC
Wisconsin Public Service Corp	New York	WisPS	WPS
Wisconsin Real Estate Investment Trust	NAS NL	WiscRE	WREI
Wisconsin Southern Gas Company Inc	NAS NMS	WisSGs	WISC
Wisconsin Toy Co	NAS NMS	WiscTy	WTOY

COMPANY NAME	MARKET LISTING	NEWSPAPER ABBREV.	TRADING SYMBOL
The Wiser Oil Co	NAS NMS	WiserO	WISE
Witco Corp	New York	Witco	WIT
WMS Industries Inc	New York	WMS	WMS
WNS Inc	NAS NMS	WNS	WNSI
Howard B. Wolf Inc	American	WolfHB	HBW
Wolf Financial Group Inc	NAS NL	WolfFn	WOFG
Wolohan Lumber Co	NAS NMS	Wolohn	WLHN
Wolverine Exploration Co	NAS NMS	WolvEx	WEXC
Wolverine Technologies Inc	New York	WolvTc	WOV
Wolverine World Wide Inc	New York	WolvrW	WWW
Woodhead Industries Inc	NAS NMS	Woodhd	WDHD
Woodstream Corp	American	Wdstrm	WOD
F.W. Woolworth Co	New York	Wlwth	Z
Workingmens Corp (Massachusetts)	NAS NMS	Wkmen	WCBK
Worlco Data Systems Inc	NAS SL	WorlcDt	WDSI
World Container Corp	NAS SL	WrldCn	WRLD
World Income Fund Inc	American	WldInc	WOI
World-Wide Technology Inc	NAS SL	WWYch	WOTK
WorldCorp Inc	New York	WrldCp	WOA
Worldwide Computer Services Inc	NAS NL	WldwdCpt	WCSI
Worldwide Value Fund Inc	New York	WrldVl	VLU
Worthen Banking Corp	American	Worthn	WOR
Worthington Industries Inc	NAS NMS	Worthg	WTHG
WPL Holdings Inc	New York	WPL Hld	WPL
WPP Group plc	NAS NMS	WPP Gp	WPPGY
William Wrigley Jr Co	New York	Wrigly	WWY
The Writer Corp	NAS NMS	Writer	WRTC
WSMP Inc	NAS NMS	WSMP	WSMP
WTD Industries Inc	NAS NMS	WTD	WTDI
WurlTech Industries Inc	New York	Wurltch	WUR
Wyle Laboratories	New York	WyleLb	WYL
Wyman-Gordon Co	NAS NMS	Wyman	WYMN
Wynn's International Inc	New York	Wynns	WN
Wyoming National Bancorporation	NAS NMS	WymngNt	WYNB
Wyse Technology	New York	Wyse	WYS
X-Rite Inc	NAS NMS	X-Rite	XRIT
Xebec	NAS NMS	Xebec	XEBC
Xerox Corp	New York	Xerox	XRX
Xeta Corp	NAS NL	Xeta	XETA
Xicor Inc	NAS NMS	Xicor	XICO
XL/Datacomp Inc	NAS NMS	XL Dt	XLDC
XOMA Corp	NAS NMS	XOMA	XOMA
Xplor Corp	NAS NMS	Xplor	XPLR
Xscribe Corp	NAS NMS	Xscribe	XSCR
Xsirus Scientific Inc	NAS SL	Xsirus	XSIR
XTRA Corp	New York	XTRA	XTR
Xylogics Inc	NAS NMS	Xylogic	XLGX

COMPANY NAME	MARKET LISTING	NEWSPAPER ABBREV.	TRADING SYMBOL
Xytronyx Inc	NAS SL	Xytrn	XYYX
Xyvision Inc	NAS NMS	Xyvsn	XYVI
The Yankee Companies Inc	American	YankCo	YNK
Yellow Freight System Inc of Delaware	NAS NMS	YlowF	YELL
York Financial Corp	NAS NMS	YrkFn	YFED
York International Corp	New York	YorkIn	YRK
York Research Corp	NAS NMS	YorkRs	YORK
Yorkridge-Calvert S&L Assn (Maryland)	NAS NMS	Yrkrdg	YCSL
Yuba Natural Resources Inc (Class A)	NAS SL	YUBAA	YUBAA
Yukon Energy Corp	NAS SL	YukonE	YUKN
Z-Seven Fund Inc	NAS NMS	Z Sevn	ZSEV
Zapata Corp	New York	Zapata	ZOS
Zayre Corp	New York	Zayre	ZY
Zemex Corp	New York	Zemex	ZMX
Zenith Electronics Corp	New York	ZenithE	ZE
Zenith Income Fund	New York	ZenIn	ZIF
Zenith Laboratories Inc	New York	ZenLab	ZEN
Zenith National Insurance Corp	New York	ZenNtl	ZNT
Zentec Corp	NAS NMS	Zentec	ZENT
Zero Corp	New York	Zero	ZRO
Zetek Inc	NAS SL	Zetek	ZETK
Zeus Components Inc	NAS NMS	Zeus	ZEUS
The Ziegler Company Inc	NAS NMS	Ziegler	ZEGL
Zimmer Corp	American	Zimer	ZIM
Zions Bancorporation (Utah)	NAS NMS	ZionUt	ZION
Zitel Corp	NAS NMS	Zitel	ZITL
The Zondervan Corp	NAS NMS	Zondvn	ZOND
Zurn Industries Inc	New York	ZurnIn	ZRN
The Zweig Fund Inc	New York	Zweig	ZF
Zycad Corp	NAS NMS	Zycad	ZCAD
Zygo Corp	NAS NMS	Zygo	ZIGO
ZyMOS Corp	NAS NMS	Zymos	ZMOS
Zytec Systems Inc	NAS SL	Zytec	ZSILF

NEWSPAPER ABBREV.	MARKET LISTING	TRADING SYMBOL	COMPANY NAME
A&W Bd	NAS NMS	SODA	A&W Brands Inc
AA Imp	NAS NL	ANTQ	A.A. Importing Company Inc
AAcft	NAS SL	AARC	American Aircraft Corp
AAlska	American	ICE	Arctic Alaska Fisheries Corp
AAR	New York	AIR	AAR Corp
AarnRt	NAS NMS	ARON	Aaron Rents Inc
AbeLinc	NAS NMS	ALFB	Abraham Lincoln Federal Savings Bank (Pennsylvania)
ABI	American	AB	ABI American Businessphones Inc
Abimd	American	ABD	ABIOMED Inc
AbingB	NAS NMS	ABBK	Abington Bancorp Inc (Massachusetts)
ABionet	NAS SL	AMBI	American Bionetics Inc
ABiosci	NAS NMS	APBI	Applied Bioscience International Inc
Abitibi	New York	ABY	Abitibi-Price Inc
ABkCT	American	BKC	American Bank of Connecticut
ABldM	New York	ABM	American Building Maintenance Industries
ABM G	American	AGO	ABM Gold Corp
ABnkr	NAS NMS	ABIG	American Bankers Insurance Group Inc
ABQ	NAS NMS	ABQC	ABQ Corp
Abrams	NAS NMS	ABRI	Abrams Industries Inc
ABrck	New York	ABX	American Barrick Resources Corp
ABS	NAS NMS	ABSI	ABS Industries Inc
ABsCpt	NAS SL	ABCC	American Business Computers Corp
AbtLab	New York	ABT	Abbott Laboratories
ABusPr	New York	ABP	American Business Products Inc
AcadIn	NAS NMS	ACIG	Academy Insurance Group Inc
ACapac	NAS NMS	ACGI	American Capacity Group Inc
ACapBd	New York	ACB	American Capital Bond Fund Inc
ACapCv	New York	ACS	American Capital Convertible Securities Inc
ACapIn	New York	ACD	American Capital Income Trust
ACC Cp	NAS NMS	ACCC	ACC Corp
Accel	NAS NMS	ACLE	Accel International Corp
Acclaim	NAS NL	AKLM	Acclaim Entertainment Inc
ACentC	New York	ACT	American Century Corp
AceptIn	NAS NMS	ACPT	Acceptance Insurance Holdings Inc
Aceto	NAS NMS	ACET	Aceto Corp
ACGld	NAS SL	ACGC	American Consolidated Gold Corp

NEWSPAPER ABBREV.	MARKET LISTING	TRADING SYMBOL	COMPANY NAME
AClaim	NAS SL	AMCE	American Claims Evaluation Inc
ACM	New York	AOF	ACM Government Opportunity Fund
AcmeC	New York	AMT	Acme-Cleveland Corp
AcmeE	New York	ACE	Acme Electric Corp
AcmeSt	NAS NMS	ACME	Acme Steel Co
AcmeU	American	ACU	Acme United Corp
ACMIn	New York	ACG	ACM Government Income Fund Inc
ACMR	New York	ACA	American Capital Management & Research Inc
ACMSc	New York	GSF	ACM Government Securities Fund Inc
ACMSp	New York	SI	ACM Government Spectrum Fund
ACMT	NAS NMS	ACMT	ACMAT Corp
AConsu	NAS NMS	ACPI	American Consumer Products Inc
AContl	NAS NMS	AMCC	American Continental Corp
ActARt	NAS NMS	AXXN	Action Auto Rental Inc
ActAuSt	NAS NMS	ACTA	Action Auto Stores Inc
Action	American	ACX	Action Industries Inc
Actmd	NAS NMS	ACTM	Actmedia Inc
ActnStf	NAS SL	ACTS	Action Staffing Inc
Acton	American	ATN	Acton Corp
Acusn	NAS NMS	ACSN	Acuson Corp
Acxiom	NAS NMS	ACXM	Acxiom Corp
ACyan	New York	ACY	American Cyanamid Co
AdacLb	NAS NMS	ADAC	ADAC Laboratories
AdaEx	New York	ADX	The Adams Express Co
AdamMl	New York	ALL	Adams-Millis Corp
Adapt	NAS NMS	ADPT	Adaptec Inc
ADC	NAS NMS	ADCT	ADC Telecommunications Inc
AdCpt	NAS NMS	ACTP	Advanced Computer Techniques Corp
Adelph	NAS NL	ADLAC	Adelphia Communications Corp
AdiaSv	NAS NMS	ADIA	Adia Services Inc
Adingtn	NAS NMS	ADDR	Addington Resources Inc
Admar	NAS SL	ADMR	Admar Group Inc
AdMdPd	NAS SL	ADVA	Advanced Medical Products Inc
AdMkSv	NAS NMS	ADMS	Advanced Marketing Services Inc
AdmRs	American	AE	Adams Resources & Energy Inc
AdNMR	NAS SL	ANMR	Advaned NMR Systems Inc
Adobe	New York	ADB	Adobe Resources Corp
AdobS	NAS NMS	ADBE	Adobe Systems Inc
Adtec	NAS NMS	JAIL	Adtec Inc
Advant	NAS NMS	ADCO	Advantage Companies Inc
Advanta	NAS NMS	ADVN	ADVANTA Corp
Advatex	NAS NL	ADTX	Advatex Associates Inc
AdvCir	NAS NMS	ADVC	Advance Circuits Inc
AdvDis	NAS SL	ADTI	Advance Display Technologies Inc
Advest	New York	ADV	The Advest Group Inc
AdvGen	NAS NMS	AGSI	Advanced Genetic Sciences Inc
AdvMag	NAS NMS	ADMG	Advanced Magnetics Inc

NEWSPAPER ABBREV.	MARKET LISTING	TRADING SYMBOL	COMPANY NAME
AdvoSy	NAS NMS	ADVO	Advo System Inc
AdvPoly	NAS NMS	APOS	Advanced Polymer Systems Inc
AdvRos	NAS NMS	AROS	Advance Ross Corp
AdvSem	NAS NMS	ASMIF	Advanced Semiconductor Materials International N.V.
AdvTel	NAS NMS	ATEL	Advanced Telecommunications Corp
Aegon	NAS NMS	AEGNY	AEGON N.V.
AEL	NAS NMS	AELNA	AEL Industries Inc (Class A)
AElPw	New York	AEP	American Electric Power Company Inc
AEP	NAS NMS	AEPI	AEP Industries Inc
AEqune	NAS SL	WHOA	American Equine Products Inc
Aequtrn	NAS NMS	AQTN	Aequitron Medical Inc
Aerosn	NAS SL	ASON	Aerosonic Corp
AerSvc	NAS NMS	AERO	Aero Services International Inc
AetnLf	New York	AET	Aetna Life & Casualty Co
AExp	New York	AXP	American Express Co
AFaml	New York	AFL	American Family Corp
AFG	New York	AFG	AFG Industries Inc
AFibOp	NAS SL	FIBR	American Fiber Optics Corp
AfilPb	New York	AFP	Affiliated Publications Inc
AFiltrn	NAS NMS	AFIL	American Filtrona Corp
AflBcCp	NAS NMS	ABCV	Affiliated Banc Corp (Massachusetts)
AflBsh	NAS NMS	AFBK	Affiliated Bankshares of Colorado Inc
AFN	NAS SL	AMFN	A F N Inc
AFP	NAS SL	AFPC	AFP Imaging Corp
AFruc A	American	AFC.A	American Fructose Corp
AFruc B	American	AFC.B	American Fructose Corp
AFSvDu	NAS NMS	AMJX	American Federal Savings Bank of Duval County (Florida)
AGnCp	New York	AGC	American General Corp
AgncyR	NAS NMS	AGNC	Agency Rent-A-Car Inc
Agnico	NAS NMS	AEAGF	Agnico-Eagle Mines Ltd
Agourn	NAS SL	AGPH	Agouron Pharmaceuticals Inc
AGreet	NAS NMS	AGREA	American Greetings Corp (Class A)
AGS	New York	AGS	AGS Computers Inc
AGtyF	NAS SL	AMGR	American Guaranty Financial Corp
AHerit	New York	AHL	American Heritage Life Investment Corp
AHlthM	American	AHI	American Healthcare Management Inc
AHltP	New York	AHE	American Health Properties Inc
AHltSv	NAS NMS	NMRC	American Health Services Corp
Ahmans	New York	AHM	H.F. Ahmanson & Co
AHoist	New York	AHO	American Hoist & Derrick Co
AHome	New York	AHP	American Home Products Corp
AHSld	NAS NMS	AHSC	American Home Shield Corp
AIFS	American	AIF	AIFS Inc
Aileen	New York	AEE	Aileen Inc
AIM Tel	NAS NMS	AIMT	AIM Telephones Inc
AIndF	NAS NMS	AIFC	American Indemnity Financial Corp

NEWSPAPER ABBREV.	MARKET LISTING	TRADING SYMBOL	COMPANY NAME
AIntGr	New York	AIG	American International Group Inc
AirbFrt	New York	ABF	Airborne Freight Corp
AIRCOA	NAS NMS	AIRC	AIRCOA Hospitality Services Inc
Aircoa	American	AHT	AIRCOA Hotel Partners L.P.
AirCrg	NAS NMS	ARCE	Air Cargo Equipment Corp
AirExp	American	AEX	Air Express International Corp
Airgas	New York	AGA	Airgas Inc
AirInd	NAS NMS	AIRSY	Airship Industries Ltd
AirInt	NAS SL	BLMP	Airship International Ltd
Airlease	New York	FLY	Airlease Ltd
AirMd	NAS NMS	AMWI	Air Midwest Inc
AirPrd	New York	APD	Air Products & Chemicals Inc
AirSen	NAS SL	ARSN	Air Sensors Inc
Airtran	NAS NMS	ATCC	Airtran Corp
AirWisc	NAS NMS	ARWS	Air Wisconsin Services Inc
AIsrael	American	AIP	American Israeli Paper Mills Ltd
Akorn	NAS NL	AKRN	Akorn Inc
AL Lab	American	BMD	A.L. Laboratories Inc
AlaFdl	NAS NMS	ALFD	Alabama Federal S&L Assn
Alamco	American	AXO	Alamco Inc
Alaten	NAS NMS	ATNG	AlaTenn Resources Inc
AlbaW	American	AWS	Alba-Waldensian Inc
Alberto	New York	ACV	Alberto-Culver Co
AlbCulA	New York	ACV.A	Alberto-Culver Co (Class A)
AlbnyIn	NAS NMS	AAICA	Albany International Corp (Class A)
Albtsn	New York	ABS	Albertson's Inc
ALC Cm	NAS NNS	ALCC	ALC Communications Corp
Alcan	New York	AL	Alcan Aluminium Ltd
Alcide	NAS SL	ALCD	Alcide Corp
Alcoa	New York	AA	Aluminum Company of America
AlcoHlt	NAS NMS	AAHS	Alco Health Services Corp
AlcoS	New York	ASN	Alco Standard Corp
Alden	NAS NL	ADNEA	Alden Electronics Inc (Class A)
AldSgnl	New York	ALD	Allied-Signal Inc
Aldus	NAS NMS	ALDC	Aldus Corp
AlegW	NAS NMS	ALGH	Allegheny & Western Energy Corp
AlexAlx	New York	AAL	Alexander & Alexander Services Inc
AlexBld	NAS NMS	ALEX	Alexander & Baldwin Inc
AlexBr	NAS NMS	ABSB	Alex. Brown Inc
Alexdr	New York	ALX	Alexander's Inc
AlexEn	NAS NL	AEOK	Alexander Energy Corp
AlfaCp	NAS NMS	ALFA	Alfa Corp
AlfaInt	NAS SL	ALFE	Alfa International Corp
Alfin	American	AFN	Alfin Inc
AlgInt	New York	AG	Allegheny International Inc
AlgLud	New York	ALS	Allegheny Ludlum Corp
Algorex	NAS NMS	ALGO	Algorex Corp
Alico	NAS NMS	ALCO	Alico Inc

NEWSPAPER ABBREV.	MARKET LISTING	TRADING SYMBOL	COMPANY NAME
AllAm	NAS SL	SEMI	All American Semiconductor Inc
AllATV	NAS NL	ALLT	All American Television Inc
AllCity	NAS NMS	ALCI	AllCity Insurance Co
AlldBk	NAS NMS	ABGA	Allied Bankshares Inc (Georgia)
AlldCa	NAS NMS	ALLC	Allied Capital Corp
AlldGp	NAS NMS	ALGR	ALLIED Group Inc
AlldPd	New York	ADP	Allied Products Corp
AlldRsh	NAS NMS	ARAI	Allied Research Associates Inc
AlldSec	NAS SL	ASCY	Allied Security Inc
AllegCp	New York	Y	Alleghany Corp
AllenG	New York	ALN	The Allen Group Inc
AllFinl	NAS NMS	ALFL	Alliance Financial Corp
AllgPw	New York	AYP	Allegheny Power System Inc
Alliant	NAS NMS	ALNT	Alliant Computer Systems Corp
AlliBc	American	ABK	Alliance Bancorporation
AllisC	New York	AH	Allis-Chalmers Corp
Allstr	American	SAI	Allstar Inns L.P.
ALLTL	New York	AT	ALLTEL Corp
Allwast	NAS NMS	ALWS	Allwaste Inc
AlnCap	New York	AC	Alliance Capital Management LP
AlnImg	NAS NMS	AIMG	Alliance Imaging Inc
AlnOrg	NAS NMS	AORGB	Allen Organ Co (Class B)
AlnTre	American	ATR.A	Alliance Tire & Rubber Company Ltd (Class A)
Aloette	NAS NMS	ALET	Aloette Cosmetics Inc
AloyCpt	NAS NMS	ALOY	Alloy Computer Products Inc
AlphaIn	American	AHA	Alpha Industries Inc
Alpha1	NAS NMS	ALBM	Alpha 1 Biomedicals Inc
Alpharl	NAS NMS	AREL	Alpharel Inc
AlphaSo	NAS SL	ASCO	Alpha Solarco Inc
AlpinGr	American	AGI	The Alpine Group Inc
AlpMic	NAS NMS	ALMI	Alpha Microsystems
AlskAir	New York	ALK	Alaska Air Group Inc
AlskAp	NAS SL	APLOF	Alaska Apollo Gold Mines Ltd
AlsMI	New York	ALT	Allstate Municipal Income Trust II
AlstMu	New York	ALM	Allstate Municipal Income Trust
Altai	NAS NMS	ALTI	Altai Inc
Altera	NAS NMS	ALTR	Altera Corp
Altex	American	AII	Altex Industries Inc
Altos	NAS NMS	ALTO	Altos Computer Systems
AltrHlt	NAS SL	AHCS	Alternative Health Care Systems Inc
Altron	NAS NMS	ALRN	Altron Inc
Altus	NAS NMS	ALTS	Altus Bank, A Federal Savings Bank (Alabama)
Alza	American	AZA	ALZA Corp
AM Intl	New York	AM	AM International Inc
AMagnt	NAS NMS	AMMG	American Magnetics Corp
Amax	New York	AMX	AMAX Inc

NEWSPAPER ABBREV.	MARKET LISTING	TRADING SYMBOL	COMPANY NAME
AmbFn	NAS NMS	AFGI	Ambassador Financial Group Inc
AmBilt	American	ABL	American Biltrite Inc
AMBld	American	A	American Medical Buildings Inc
AmBrit	American	ABI	AmBrit Inc
AmBrnd	New York	AMB	American Brands Inc
AMC	American	AEN	AMC Entertainment Inc
AMCA	New York	AIL	AMCA International Ltd
AmCap	American	ACC	American Capital Corp
AmCarr	NAS NMS	ACIX	American Carriers Inc
Amcast	New York	AIZ	Amcast Industrial Corp
AmCity	NAS NMS	AMBJ	American City Business Journals Inc
AmCnsl	NAS NL	ACCI	American Consulting Corp
Amcole	NAS NMS	AMLE	Amcole Energy Corp
AmColid	NAS NMS	ACOL	American Colloid Co
AmCom	NAS SL	ASTV	American Communications & Television Inc
Amcor	NAS NMS	AMFI	AMCORE Financial Inc
AmCrse	NAS SL	ACRL	American Cruise Lines Inc
AMD	New York	AMD	Advanced Micro Devices Inc
Amdahl	American	AMH	Amdahl Corp
AMdAlt	NAS SL	AMAC	American Medical Alert Corp
AMdE	NAS SL	AMEI	American Medical Electronics Inc
AMdTc	NAS SL	AMMT	American Medical Technology Inc
AME	NAS NMS	AMEA	A.M.E. Inc
AmEcol	NAS NMS	ECOL	American Ecology Corp
Ameron	New York	AMN	Ameron Inc
AmerPr	NAS SL	HOST	Amerihost Properties Inc
Amertk	NAS NMS	ATEKF	Amertek Inc
AmesDp	New York	ADD	Ames Department Stores Inc
Ametk	New York	AME	AMETEK Inc
AmevSc	New York	AMV	AMEV Securities Inc
Amfac	New York	AMA	Amfac Inc
AmFedF	NAS NMS	AFSL	AmFed Financial Corp
AmFGr	American	GF	America First Guaranteed Income Fund
AmFrst	NAS NMS	AFCO	American First Corp
AmFtBk	NAS NMS	AMRI	AmeriFirst Bank FSB (Florida)
Amgen	NAS NMS	AMGN	Amgen Inc
AmGvI	New York	AGF	American Government Income Fund
AmHes	New York	AHC	Amerada Hess Corp
Amhlth	American	AHH	AmeriHealth Inc
AmHotl	New York	AHR	Americana Hotels & Realty Corp
AMI	New York	AMI	American Medical International Inc
AMidl	NAS NMS	AMCO	American Midland Corp
AminLf	NAS NMS	AINC	American Income Life Insurance Co
AmInPt	NAS SL	AIPN	American International Petroleum Corp
AmIntg	NAS NMS	AIIC	American Integrity Corp
AmIPrp	American	IPS	American Income Properties L.P.
Amistar	NAS NMS	AMTA	Amistar Corp

NEWSPAPER ABBREV.	MARKET LISTING	TRADING SYMBOL	COMPANY NAME
AmLck	NAS NMS	ALGI	American Locker Group Inc
AmList	American	AMZ	American List Corp
AmLnd	American	RVR	American Land Cruisers Inc
AmLrn	NAS NL	READ	American Learning Corp
AmMobl	NAS SL	AMSE	American Mobile Systems Inc
AmNurs	NAS NMS	ANSY	American Nursery Products Inc
Amnws	NAS SL	AMWS	Ameriwest Financial Corp
Amoco	New York	AN	Amoco Corp
AmOil	American	AOG	American Oil & Gas Corp
Amosk	NAS NMS	AMOS	Amoskeag Co
AMP	New York	AMP	AMP Inc
AmPac	NAS NMS	APFC	American Pacific Corp
Ampal	American	AIS.A	Ampal-American Israel Corp (Class A)
Ampco	New York	AP	Ampco-Pittsburgh Corp
AmPetf	American	API.A	American Petrofina Inc (Class A)
AmPion	NAS NMS	APIO	American Pioneer Savings Bank (Florida)
Amplcn	NAS NMS	AMPI	Amplicon Inc
AmPsg	NAS NMS	APAS	American Passage Marketing Corp
AMR	New York	AMR	AMR Corp
Amrco	NAS SL	AESC	AmerEco Environmental Services Inc
Amre	New York	AMM	AMRE Inc
Amrep	New York	AXR	AMREP Corp
Amrfrd	NAS SL	AMRF	Amerford International Corp
Amrian	NAS NMS	ASBI	Ameriana Savings Bank FSB (Indiana)
Amribc	NAS NL	ABNK	Ameribanc Inc (Missouri)
AmRice	NAS NL	RICE	American Rice Inc
Amritr	NAS NMS	AMTR	AmeriTrust Corp
AmRlty	New York	ARB	American Realty Trust
Amrtc	New York	AIT	American Information Technologies Corp
AMS	NAS NMS	AMSY	American Management Systems Inc
Amserv	NAS NMS	AMSR	Amserv Inc
AmShrd	American	AMS	American Shared Hospital Services
AmskBk	NAS NMS	AMKG	Amoskeag Bank Shares Inc
AmSth	New York	ASO	AmSouth Bancorporation
AmStor	New York	ASC	American Stores Co
AmTelmd	NAS NMS	ATNN	American Telemedia Network Inc
AmTlc	NAS SL	AMTTF	American Telecommunications Corp (British Columbia)
AmTrav	NAS NMS	ATVC	American Travellers Corp
AmtyBc	NAS NMS	AMTY	Amity Bancorp Inc
AmVisn	NAS SL	AMVC	American Vision Centers Inc
Amvst	NAS NMS	AVFC	AmVestors Financial Corp
Amwest	American	AMW	Amwest Insurance Group Inc
AmWtr	New York	AWK	American Water Works Company Inc
AmxG	New York	AU	Amax Gold Inc
AMzeA	American	AZE.A	American Maize-Products Co (Class A)
AMzeB	American	AZE.B	American Maize-Producst Co (Class B)
An-Con	NAS SL	ANCN	An-Con Genetics Inc

NEWSPAPER ABBREV.	MARKET LISTING	TRADING SYMBOL	COMPANY NAME
Anacmp	New York	AAC	Anacomp Inc
Anadrk	New York	APC	Anadarko Petroleum Corp
Analog	New York	ADI	Analog Devices Inc
AnalyI	NAS NMS	ANLY	Analysts International Corp
AnalyTc	NAS NMS	AATI	Analysis & Technology Inc
Anaren	NAS NMS	ANEN	Anaren Microwave Inc
AnchGl	New York	ANC	Anchor Glass Container Corp
AnchSv	NAS NMS	ABKR	Anchor Savings Bank FSB (New York)
AncrNJ	NAS NMS	ANSL	Anchor S&L Assn (New Jersey)
Andal	American	ADL	Andal Corp
AndGr	NAS NMS	ANDR	Andersen Group Inc
Andovr	NAS NMS	ANDO	Andover Controls Corp
Andrea	American	AND	Andrea Radio Corp
Andrew	NAS NMS	ANDW	Andrew Corp
Andros	NAS NMS	ANDY	Andros Analyzers Inc
AndvBc	NAS NMS	ANDB	Andover Bancorp Inc (Massachusetts)
AndvTg	NAS NMS	ATOG	Andover Togs Inc
AndwGp	NAS NL	AGRP	Andrews Group Inc
AngAG	NAS NL	AAGIY	Anglo American Gold Investment Company Ltd
AngE	American	AEL	Anglo Energy Inc
Angeles	American	ANG	Angeles Corp
Angelic	New York	AGL	Angelica Corp
AnglFn	American	ANF	Angeles Finance Partners
AnglRl	New York	ACR	Angell Real Estate Company Inc
AngMtg	American	ANM	Angeles Mortgage Partners Ltd
AngSA	NAS NL	ANGLY	Anglo American Corporation of South Africa Ltd
Anheus	New York	BUD	Anheuser-Busch Companies Inc
Animed	NAS NMS	VETS	Animed Inc
Anlogic	NAS NMS	ALOG	Analogic Corp
AnlySu	NAS SL	ANLT	Analytical Surveys Inc
Anndle	NAS SL	ANNA	Annandale Corp
Anthm	New York	ATM	Anthem Electronics Inc
Anthony	New York	ANT	Anthony Industries Inc
ANtIns	NAS NMS	ANAT	American National Insurance Co
Antonv	NAS NMS	FURSA	Antonovich Inc (Class A)
ANtPt	NAS NL	ANPC	American National Petroleum Co
ANuclC	NAS NMS	ANUC	American Nuclear Corp
AOI	American	AOI	AOI Coal Co
Aon Cp	New York	AOC	Aon Corp
Ap DNA	NAS SL	ADNA	Applied DNA Systems Inc
Apache	New York	APA	Apache Corp
APAOp	NAS SL	APAT	APA Optics Inc
Apco	NAS NL	APAGF	Apco Argentina Inc
ApdMicr	NAS SL	APLY	Applied Microbiology Inc
ApexM	American	new	Apex Municipal Fund
APhyG	NAS NMS	AMPH	American Physicians Service Group Inc

NEWSPAPER ABBREV.	MARKET LISTING	TRADING SYMBOL	COMPANY NAME
API	NAS SL	APIE	API Enterprises Inc
ApldBio	NAS NMS	ABIO	Applied Biosystems Inc
ApldDt	NAS NMS	ADCC	Applied Data Communications Inc
ApldMt	NAS NMS	AMAT	Applied Materials Inc
ApldPw	NAS NMS	APWRA	Applied Power Inc (Class A)
ApldSlr	NAS NMS	SOLR	Applied Solar Energy Corp
Apld Spc	NAS SL	ASTI	Applied Spectrum Technologies Inc
ApogEn	NAS NMS	APOG	Apogee Enterprises Inc
ApogRb	NAS SL	APGE	Apogee Robotics Inc
ApoloC	NAS NMS	APCI	Apollo Computer Inc
ApplBk	New York	ARK	Apple Bank for Savings (New York)
AppleC	NAS NMS	AAPL	Apple Computer Inc
ApplM	New York	APM	Applied Magnetics Corp
APrec	American	APR	American Precision Industries Inc
APresd	New York	APS	American President Companies Ltd
APwCnv	NAS NL	APCC	American Power Conversion Corp
Aquant	NAS SL	AQNT	Aquanautics Corp
AquaSc	NAS SL	AQSI	AquaSciences International Inc
ArabSh	NAS NMS	ARSD	Arabian Shield Development Co
Arbor	NAS NMS	ARBR	Arbor Drugs Inc
ARC	American	ATV	ARC International Corp
ArchDn	New York	ADM	Archer-Daniels-Midland Co
Archive	NAS NMS	ACHV	Archive Corp
ArcoCh	New York	RCM	ARCO Chemical Co
Arden	NAS NMS	ARDNA	Arden Group Inc (Class A)
ArdenIn	NAS SL	AIKI	Arden International Kitchens Inc
ARecr	NAS NL	AMRC	American Recreation Centers Inc
ARelian	NAS NMS	ARIG	American Reliance Group Inc
ARepBc	NAS NL	ARBC	American Republic Bancorp
AREst	New York	ACP	American Real Estate Partners L.P.
ARestr	American	RMC	American Restaurant Partners L.P.
ArgoGp	NAS NMS	AGII	Argonaut Group Inc
Aristec	New York	ARS	Aristech Chemical Corp
Aritch	NAS NMS	ARID	Aridtech Inc
ArizCm	American	AZB	Arizona Commerce Bank
ArizInst	NAS NMS	QNTL	Arizona Instrument Corp
ArkBst	New York	ABZ	Arkansas Best Corp
Arkla	New York	ALG	Arkla Inc
ArkRst	American	RK	Ark Restaurants Corp
Armada	New York	ABW	Armada Corp
Armco	New York	AS	Armco Inc
Armor	NAS NMS	ARMR	Armor All Products Corp
Armtek	New York	ARM	Armtek Corp
Armtrn	American	ART	Armatron International Inc
ArmWI	New York	ACK	Armstrong World Industries Inc
Arnold	NAS NMS	AIND	Arnold Industries Inc
Arnox	NAS SL	ARNX	Arnox Corp
ArowB	NAS NMS	AROW	Arrow Bank Corp

NEWSPAPER ABBREV.	MARKET LISTING	TRADING SYMBOL	COMPANY NAME
ArowE	New York	ARW	Arrow Electronics Inc
ArrowA	American	AI	Arrow Automotive Industries Inc
Artagph	NAS SL	XARTF	Artagraph Reproduction Technology Inc
Artech	NAS SL	ARTK	Artech Recovery Systems Inc
Artel	NAS NMS	AXXX	Artel Communications Corp
ArtistG	NAS NL	ARTG	Artistic Greetings Inc
Artra	New York	ATA	ARTRA GROUP Inc
ArtWay	NAS NMS	ARTW	Art's-Way Manufacturing Company Inc
Arvin	New York	ARV	Arvin Industries Inc
ARX	New York	ARX	ARX Inc
ArytOp	NAS NL	ARYTF	Aryt Optronics Industries Ltd
ArzLd	American	AZL.A	Arizona Land Income Corp (Class A)
ASA	New York	ASA	ASA Ltd
ASA Int	NAS SL	ASAA	ASA International Ltd
ASafty	NAS SL	ASCL	American Safety Closure Corp
Asarco	New York	AR	ASARCO Inc
Asbst	NAS NMS	ASBS	Asbestec Industries Inc
ASciE	American	ASE	American Science & Engineering Inc
AsCmA	NAS NMS	ACCMA	Associated Communications Corp (Class A)
AsCmB	NAS NMS	ACCMB	Associated Communications Corp (Class B)
AsdBnc	NAS NMS	ASBC	Associated Banc-Corp
AsdHst	NAS NMS	AHST	Associated Hosts Inc
AsdMat	NAS NL	ASML	Associated Materials Inc
ASDR	NAS SL	ASDR	ASDAR Corp
ASEA	NAS NL	ASEAY	ASEA AB
Asha	NAS SL	ASHA	Asha Corp
AshCoal	New York	ACI	Ashland Coal Inc
AShip	New York	ABG	The American Ship Building Co
AshOil	New York	ASH	Ashland Oil Inc
Ashton	NAS NMS	TATE	Ashton-Tate
AsiaPc	New York	APB	The Asia, Pacific Fund Inc
ASK	NAS NMS	ASKI	ASK Computer Systems Inc
ASLFla	New York	AAA	American S&L Assn of Florida
Asmr	American	ASM	Asamera Inc
ASoft	NAS NMS	AMSWA	American Software Inc (Class A)
ASolr	NAS SL	AMSKQ	American Solar King Corp
AspenE	NAS SL	ASPN	Aspen Exploration Corp
AspenR	NAS NMS	ARIB	Aspen Ribbons Inc
AssdCo	NAS NMS	ASCI	Associated Companies Inc
AST	NAS NMS	ASTA	AST Research Inc
Astec	NAS NMS	ASTE	Astec Industries Inc
Astrcm	NAS NMS	ACOM	Astrocom Corp
Astrex	American	ASI	Astrex Inc
AstroM	NAS NMS	ALOT	Astro-Med Inc
Astron	NAS NMS	ATRO	Astronics Corp
Astrosy	NAS NMS	ASTR	Astrosystems Inc

NEWSPAPER ABBREV.	MARKET LISTING	TRADING SYMBOL	COMPANY NAME
ASvWA	NAS NMS	AMSB	American Savings Fincancial Corp (Washington)
ASwM	American	ASR	American Southwest Mortgage Investment Corp
AT&E	American	ATW	A.T.&E. Corp
AT&T	New York	T	American Telephone & Telegraph Co
AtalSos	New York	ATL	Atalanta/Sosnoff Capital Corp
Atari	American	ATC	Atari Corp
ATechC	American	AMK	American Technical Ceramics Corp
Atek	NAS NMS	ATKM	Atek Metals Center Inc
Athey	NAS NMS	ATPC	Athey Products Corp
Athlone	New York	ATH	Athlone Industries Inc
ATI	American	ATI	ATI Medical Inc
AticoF	NAS NMS	ATFC	Atico Financial Corp
Atkinsn	NAS NMS	ATKN	Guy F. Atkinson Company of California
AtlAm	NAS NMS	AAME	Atlantic American Corp
Atlants	American	AGH	Atlantis Group Inc
AtlasCp	New York	AZ	Atlas Corp
AtlEnrg	New York	ATE	Atlantic Energy Inc
AtlFin	NAS NMS	ATLF	Atlantic Financial Federal
AtlFSv	NAS NMS	AFED	Atlantic Federal Savings Bank (Maryland)
AtlGas	New York	ATG	Atlanta Gas Light Co
AtlnBc	NAS NMS	ATBC	Atlantic Bancorporation (New Jersey)
AtlPrm	NAS NMS	APER	Atlantic Permanent Savings Bank F.S.B. (Virginia)
AtlRich	New York	ARC	Atlantic Richfield Co
AtlsCM	American	ACM.B	Atlas Consolidated Mining & Development Corp (Class B)
AtlSeAr	NAS NMS	ASAI	Atlantic Southeast Airlines Inc
AToxxic	NAS SL	ATCX	American Toxxic Control Inc
ATT Fd	American	ATF	AT&T Stock Fund (also known as Equity Income Fund)
Attwood	NAS NMS	ATWD	Attwood Oceanics Inc
ATvCm	NAS NMS	ATCMA	American Television & Communications Corp (Class A)
Audiotr	American	ADO	Audiotronics Corp
AudVd	New York	AVA	Audio/Video Affiliates Inc
Audvx	American	VOX	Audiovox Corp
Augat	New York	AUG	Augat Inc
Ault	NAS SL	AULT	Ault Inc
Ausimt	New York	AUS	Ausimont Compo N.V.
AutLng	NAS NMS	AILP	Automated Language Processing Systems Inc
AutMed	NAS SL	AMED	AutoMedix Sciences Inc
Autmtx	NAS NMS	AITX	Automatix Inc
Autoclv	NAS NMS	ACLV	Autoclave Engineers Inc
AutoCp	NAS NMS	AUTR	Autotrol Corp

NEWSPAPER ABBREV.	MARKET LISTING	TRADING SYMBOL	COMPANY NAME
Autodie	NAS NMS	ADIE	Autodie Corp
Autodk	NAS NMS	ACAD	Autodesk Inc
AutoDt	New York	AUD	Automatic Data Processing Inc
AutoInf	NAS NMS	AUTO	AutoInfo Inc
AutoSpa	NAS SL	ATML	AutoSpa AutoMalls Inc
Autospa	NAS NMS	LUBE	AutoSpa Corp
AutoSy	NAS NMS	ASII	Automated Systems Inc
AutTrT	NAS NMS	ATTC	Auto-trol Technology Corp
Avalon	New York	AVL	Avalon Corp
Avatar	NAS NMS	AVTR	Avatar Holdings Inc
Avery	New York	AVY	Avery International Corp
Avino	NAS SL	AVMRF	Avino Mines & Resources Ltd
AVMC	New York	AVE	AVEMCO Corp
Avndle	NAS NMS	AVDL	Avondale Industries Inc
Avnet	New York	AVT	Avnet Inc
Avntek	NAS NMS	AVAK	Avantek Inc
AvntGr	NAS NMS	AVGA	Avant-Garde Computing Inc
Avon	New York	AVP	Avon Products Inc
Avry	NAS NMS	AVRY	Avery Inc
AVX	New York	AVX	AVX Corp
AW A	NAS NMS	AWCSA	AW Computer Systems Inc (Class A)
AWAirl	NAS NMS	AWAL	America West Airlines Inc
AWood	NAS NMS	AMWD	American Woodmark Corp
AWstCp	NAS NMS	AWST	American Western Corp
Aydin	New York	AYD	Aydin Corp
AztcM	NAS NMS	AZTC	Aztec Manufacturing Co
B&H	American	BHO	B&H Ocean Carriers Ltd
Babage	NAS NMS	BBGS	Babbage's Inc
Badger	American	BMI	Badger Meter Inc
Badger	NAS NMS	BPMI	Badger Paper Mills Inc
Bailey	NAS NL	BAIB	Bailey Corp
Bairnco	New York	BZ	Bairnco Corp
Baker	American	BKR	Michael Baker Corp
BakrCm	NAS SL	BAKR	Baker Communications Inc
BakrFn	NAS NMS	BKFR	Baker, Fentress & Co
BakrHu	New York	BHI	Baker Hughes Inc
BakrJ	NAS NMS	JBAK	J. Baker Inc
Balard	NAS NMS	BMED	Ballard Medical Products Inc
Balchm	NAS NMS	BLCC	Balchem Corp
Baldor	New York	BEZ	Baldor Electric Co
BaldPia	NAS NMS	BPAO	Baldwin Piano & Organ Co
Baldwin	American	BLD	Baldwin Technology Company Inc
BaldwS	American	BAL	Baldwin Securities Corp
Ball	New York	BLL	Ball Corp
BallyMf	New York	BLY	Bally Manufacturing Corp
BaltBcp	New York	BBB	Baltimore Bancorp (Maryland)
Baltek	NAS NMS	BTEK	Baltek Corp

NEWSPAPER ABBREV.	MARKET LISTING	TRADING SYMBOL	COMPANY NAME
BaltGE	New York	BGE	Baltimore Gas & Electric Co
BambP	American	BPI	Bamberger Polymers Inc
Bancokl	NAS NMS	BOKC	BancOklahoma Corp
Banctec	NAS NMS	BTEC	BancTec Inc
Bandag	New York	BDG	Bandag Inc
BandoM	NAS NMS	BMCC	Bando McGlocklin Capital Corp
BanFd	American	BCV	Bancroft Convertible Fund Inc
BangH	NAS NMS	BANG	Bangor Hydro-Electric Co
BankAtl	NAS NMS	ASAL	BankAtlantic A Federal Savings Bank
BankTr	New York	BT	Bankers Trust New York Corp
Bankvt	NAS NMS	BKVT	BankVermont Corp
Banner	New York	BNR	Banner Industries Inc
Banstr	American	BAN	Banister Continental Ltd
Banta	NAS NMS	BNTA	George Banta Company Inc
BanTx	New York	BTX	BancTEXAS Group Inc
Barclay	New York	BCS	Barclays PLC
Bard	New York	BCR	C.R. Bard Inc
Barden	NAS NMS	BARD	Barden Corp
BaretR	NAS NMS	BARC	Barrett Resources Corp
Baristr	American	BIS	Barrister Information Systems Corp
Barnet	New York	BBF	Barnett Banks of Florida Inc
BarnGp	New York	B	Barnes Group Inc
Barnwl	American	BRN	Barnwell Industries Inc
Barris	NAS NMS	BRRS	Barris Industries Inc
BarrLb	American	BRL	Barr Laboratories Inc
BarrSc	NAS SL	BUGX	Barrier Science & Technology Inc
Barton	NAS SL	BART	Barton Industries Inc
Baruch	American	BFO	Baruch-Foster Corp
BaryJw	NAS NMS	BARY	Barry's Jewelers Inc
BaryRG	American	RGB	R.G. Barry Corp
BaryWr	New York	BAR	Barry Wright Corp
BasAm	NAS NMS	BAMI	Basic American Medical Inc
BASIX	New York	BAS	BASIX Corp
BAT	American	BTI	B.A.T. Industries p.l.c.
BatlMt	New York	BMG	Battle Mountain Gold Co
BaukNo	NAS NL	BAUK	Baukol-Noonan Inc
Bausch	New York	BOL	Bausch & Lomb Inc
Baxter	New York	BAX	Baxter International Inc
BayBks	NAS NMS	BBNK	BayBanks Inc
BayFin	New York	BAY	Bay Financial Corp
Bayly	NAS NMS	BAYL	Bayly Corp
Bayou	NAS NL	BAYU	Bayou International Ltd
Bayou	American	SYX	Bayou Steel Corporation of La Place
BayStG	New York	BGC	Bay State Gas Co
BayVw	NAS NMS	BVFS	Bay View Federal S&L Assn (California)
BB&T	NAS NMS	BBIF	BB&T Financial Corp
BB REI	American	BBR	B-B Real Estate Investment Corp
BCE	New York	BCE	BCE Inc

NEWSPAPER ABBREV.	MARKET LISTING	TRADING SYMBOL	COMPANY NAME
BCelts	New York	BOS	Boston Celtics L.P.
BckyFn	NAS NMS	BCKY	Buckeye Financial Corp
BcMis	NAS NMS	BOMS	Bancorp of Mississippi Inc
BcpHw	NAS NMS	BNHI	Bancorp Hawaii Inc
BDM	American	BDM	BDM International Inc
BdwyFn	NAS NMS	BFCP	Broadway Financial Corp
Beaman	NAS NL	BECO	Beaman Corp
Beard	American	BEC	The Beard Co
Bearing	New York	BER	Bearings Inc
BearSt	New York	BSC	The Bear Stearns Companies Inc
BeautiC	NAS NMS	BUTI	BeautiControl Cosmetics Inc
BeautL	NAS NMS	LABB	Beauty Labs Inc
Beazer	NAS NMS	BEZRY	C.H. Beazer Holdings PLC
Bechm	NAS NMS	BHAMY	Beecham Group p.l.c.
BectDk	New York	BDX	Becton, Dickinson & Co
Beebas	NAS NMS	BEBA	Beeba's Creations Inc
BEI	NAS NMS	BEIH	BEI Holdings Ltd
Beker	New York	BKI	Beker Industries Corp
BeldBlk	American	BBE	Belden & Blake Energy Co
BeldnH	New York	BHY	Belding Heminway Company Inc
BelFuse	NAS NMS	BELF	Bel Fuse Inc
BelIn	New York	BI	Bell Industries Inc
BellAtl	New York	BEL	Bell Atlantic Corp
BellSo	New York	BLS	BellSouth Corp
BellSv	NAS NMS	BSBX	Bell Savings Bank PaSA (Pennsylvania)
BellW	NAS NMS	BLLW	W. Bell & Company Inc
Belmac	NAS SL	BEMC	Belmac Corp
Belmrl	NAS NL	BMEEF	Belmoral Mines Ltd
BeloAH	New York	BLC	A.H. Belo Corp
Belvdre	American	BLV	Belvedere Corp
Belwet	NAS SL	BELW	Bellwether Exploration Co
Bemis	New York	BMS	Bemis Company Inc
BenfCp	New York	BNL	Beneficial Corp
Benfuel	NAS SL	BENF	Benafuels Inc
BengtB	New York	BE	Benguet Corp (Class B)
Benhan	NAS NMS	BNHN	Benihana National Corp
BenhnA	NAS NL	BNHNA	Benihana National Corp (Class A)
BenJer	NAS NMS	BJICA	Ben & Jerry's Homemade Inc (Class A)
BenjSv	NAS NMS	BENJ	Benjamin Franklin S&L Assn (Oregon)
BenNuc	NAS SL	BENE	Benedict Nuclear Pharmaceuticals Inc
Bercor	NAS NMS	BECR	Bercor Inc
Beres	NAS SL	BERS	Beres Industries Inc
BergBr	American	BBC.A	Bergen Brunswig Corp (Class A)
Berkey	New York	BKY	Berkey Inc
BerkGs	NAS NMS	BGAS	The Berkshire Gas Co
BerkHa	NAS NMS	BKHT	Berkshire Hathaway Inc
Berkley	NAS NMS	BKLY	W.R. Berkley Corp
Berklne	NAS NMS	BERK	The Berkline Corp

NEWSPAPER ABBREV.	MARKET LISTING	TRADING SYMBOL	COMPANY NAME
BermSt	American	BSL	Bermuda Star Lines Inc
BerryP	NAS NMS	BRRYA	Berry Petroleum Co (Class A)
BestBy	New York	BBY	Best Buy Company Inc
BestPd	New York	BES	Best Products Company Inc
Bestway	NAS SL	BEST	Bestway Rental Inc
BET	New York	BEP	BET Public Limited Co
BethCo	American	BET	The Bethlehem Corp
Beth1Bc	NAS NMS	BTHL	Bethel Bancorp (Maine)
BethStl	New York	BS	Bethlehem Steel Corp
BetzLb	NAS NMS	BETZ	Betz Laboratories Inc
BevIP	New York	BIP	Beverly Investment Properties Inc
Bevrly	New York	BEV	Beverly Enterprises Inc
BF Ent	NAS NL	BFEN	BF Enterprises Inc
BgBear	NAS NMS	BGBR	Big Bear Inc
BGS	NAS NMS	BGSS	BGS Systems Inc
BH Bulk	NAS NL	BULKF	B&H Bulk Carriers Ltd
BHA	NAS NMS	BHAG	BHA Group Inc
BHP	New York	BHP	The Broken Hill Proprietary Company Ltd
BI Inc	NAS SL	BIAC	BI Inc
BicCp	American	BIC	BIC Corp
Big B	NAS NMS	BIGB	Big B Inc
BigOTr	NAS NL	BIGO	Big O Tires Inc
BimdDy	NAS SL	BMDC	Biomedical Dynamics Corp
BiMedc	NAS NMS	BMDS	Bio-Medicus Inc
Bindly	NAS NMS	BIND	Bindley Western Industries Inc
BingKg	NAS NMS	BNGO	Bingo King Company Inc
BingSv	NAS NMS	BING	Binghamton Savings Bank
BinkMf	American	BIN	Binks Manufacturing Co
Biocft	New York	Biocft	Biocraft Laboratories Inc
Bioctrl	NAS SL	BICO	Biocontrol Technology Inc
Biogen	NAS NMS	BGENF	Biogen N.V.
BioLog	NAS NMS	BLSC	Bio-Logic Systems Corp
BioMed	NAS SL	BMPI	Biosearch Medical Products Inc
Biomer	NAS NMS	BMRA	Biomerica Inc
Biomet	NAS NMS	BMET	Biomet Inc
Biophm	American	BPH	Biopharmaceuticals Inc
Bioplst	NAS NMS	BIOP	Bioplasty Inc
BioR A	American	BIO.A	Bio-Rad Laboratories Inc
BioR B	American	BIO.B	Bio-Rad Laboratories Inc
Bioson	NAS NL	BIOS	Biosonics Inc
Biosph	NAS NMS	BINC	Biospherics Inc
BiotcDv	NAS SL	BIOD	Biotechnology Development Corp
BiotcR	NAS NMS	BTRL	Biotech Research Laboratories Inc
BioTG	NAS SL	BTGC	Bio-Technology General Corp
Biother	American	BRX	Biotherapeutics Inc
BioTInt	NAS NMS	BIOT	BioTechnica International Inc
Birdfdr	NAS SL	BFTV	Birdfinder Corp
BirdInc	NAS NMS	BIRD	Bird Inc

NEWSPAPER ABBREV.	MARKET LISTING	TRADING SYMBOL	COMPANY NAME
BirmStl	New York	BIR	Birmingham Steel Corp
Birtchr	NAS NMS	BIRT	The Birtcher Corp
BiscH	American	BHA	Biscayne Holdings Inc
BishGr	NAS NMS	BISH	Bishop Inc
BkatlFn	American	BFC	BankAtlantic Financial Corp
BkBost	New York	BKB	Bank of Boston Corp
BkDel	NAS NMS	BDEL	Bank of Delaware Corp
BkEtTn	NAS SL	EATN	Bank of East Tennessee
BkGrn	NAS NMS	GRAIN	Bank of Granite Corp (North Carolina)
BKInv	New York	BKP	Burger King Investors Master L.P.
BkIowa	NAS NMS	BIOW	Banks of Iowa Inc
BKLA	NAS NL	BKLA	BKLA Bancorp
BkLeu	NAS NL	BKLMY	Bank Leumi le-Israel B.M.
BklynSv	NAS NMS	BRLN	The Brooklyn Savings Bank (Connecticut)
BklyUG	New York	BU	The Brooklyn Union Gas Co
BkMAm	NAS NMS	BOMA	Banks of Mid-America Inc
BkMd	NAS NL	BKMD	Bank Maryland Corp
BkNE	New York	NEB	Bank of New England Corp
BkNY	New York	BK	The Bank of New York Company Inc
BkRedl	NAS NL	BOFR	Bank of Redlands (California)
BkrNte	NAS NMS	BKNT	Banker's Note Inc
BkSC	NAS SL	BKSC	Bank of South Carolina
BkSFr	American	BOF	Bank of San Francisco Holding Co
BkSou	NAS NMS	BKSO	Bank South Corp
BkStfd	NAS NMS	BKST	Bank of Stamford (California)
BkWorc	NAS NMS	WCYS	Bank Worcester Corp
BlackD	New York	BDK	The Black & Decker Corp
BlackI	NAS NMS	BLAK	Black Industries Inc
Blasius	NAS NMS	BLAS	Blasius Industries Inc
Blau	NAS NMS	BBPI	Barry Blau & Partners Inc
BlckD	NAS NMS	BLOCA	Block Drug Co (Class A)
BlckEn	NAS NMS	BBEC	Blockbuster Entertainment Corp
BldLy	NAS NMS	BWINA	Baldwin & Lyons Inc (Class A)
BldLyB	NAS NMS	BWINB	Baldwin & Lyons Inc (Class B)
BldrDsg	NAS NL	BONI	Builders Design Inc
Blessg	American	BCO	Blessings Corp
Blindr	NAS NL	BINL	Blinder International Enterprises Inc
BlkHC	New York	BKH	Black Hills Corp
BlkHR	New York	HRB	H&R Block Inc
Blkstn	New York	BKT	Blackstone Income Trust Inc
BlountA	American	BLT.A	Blount Inc (Class A)
BlountB	American	BLT.B	Blount Inc (Class B)
BlrPh	American	BLR	Bolar Pharmaceutical Company Inc
BluChp	New York	BLU	Blue Chip Value Fund Inc
BlueAr	New York	BAW	Blue Arrow PLC
BlvdBc	NAS NMS	BLVD	Boulevard Bancorp Inc
Blyth	NAS SL	BLYH	Blyth Holdings Inc
Blyvoor	NAS NMS	BLYVY	Blyvooruitzicht Gold Mining Company Ltd

NEWSPAPER ABBREV.	MARKET LISTING	TRADING SYMBOL	COMPANY NAME
BMA	NAS NMS	BMAC	BMA Corp
BMC	New York	BMC	BMC Industries Inc
BMC Sft	NAS NL	BMCS	BMC Software Inc
BMJ	NAS NMS	BMJF	BMJ Financial Corp
BMR Fin	NAS NMS	BMRG	BMR Financial Group Inc
BncCtr	New York	BCM	Banco Central S.A.
BncOne	New York	ONE	Banc One Corp
BNH	NAS NMS	BNHB	BNH Bancshares Inc
BnkAm	New York	BAC	BankAmerica Corp
BnkBld	American	BB	Bank Building & Equipment Corporation of America
Bnkest	NAS NMS	BENH	BankEast Corp
BnkFst	NAS NMS	BNKF	Bankers First Corp
BnkNH	NAS NMS	BHNC	Bank of New Hampshire Corp
Bnknth	NAS NMS	BKNG	Banknorth Group Inc
BnPnc	NAS NMS	BDEP	BanPonce Corp
BnPop	NAS NMS	BPOP	Banco Popular de Puerto Rico
BnSant	New York	STD	Banco Santander
BoardB	NAS SL	BDRM	Boardroom Business Products Inc
BoatBn	NAS NMS	BOAT	Boatmen's Bancshares Inc
BobBrk	NAS NL	BBKS	Bobbie Brooks Inc
BobEvn	NAS NMS	BOBE	Bob Evans Farms Inc
Boddie	American	BNP	Boddie-Noell Restaurant Properties Inc
Boeing	New York	BA	The Boeing Co
Bogen	NAS SL	BOGN	Bogen Corp
Bogert	NAS NMS	BOGO	Bogert Oil Co
Bohema	NAS NMS	BOHM	Bohemia Inc
BoiseC	New York	BCC	Boise Cascade Corp
BoltBr	New York	BBN	Bolt Beranek & Newman Inc
BoltTc	NAS NMS	BOLT	Bolt Technology Corp
Bombay	NAS NMS	CURY	Bombay Palace Restaurants Inc
Bomed	NAS SL	BOMD	Bomed Medical Manufacturing Ltd
Bond	New York	BIG	Bond International Gold Inc
Bonray	NAS NL	BNRY	Bonray Drilling Corp
BonvlP	NAS NMS	BPCO	Bonneville Pacific Corp
BooleB	NAS NMS	BOOL	Boole & Babbage Inc
BoonEl	NAS NMS	BOON	Boonton Electronics Corp
BordC	New York	BCP	Borden Chemicals & Plastics L.P.
Borden	New York	BN	Borden Inc
Bormns	New York	BRF	Borman's Inc
BostAc	NAS NMS	BOSA	Boston Acoustics Inc
BostBc	NAS NMS	SBOS	Boston Bancorp
BostEd	New York	BSE	Boston Edison Co
Bowatr	New York	BOW	Bowater Inc
BowlA	American	BWL.A	Bowl America Inc (Class A)
Bowmr	American	BOM	Bowmar Instrument Corp
Bowne	American	BNE	Bowne & Company Inc
BowVal	American	BVI	Bow Valley Industries Ltd

NEWSPAPER ABBREV.	MARKET LISTING	TRADING SYMBOL	COMPANY NAME
BR Intec	NAS NMS	BRIX	BRIntec Corp
BradyW	NAS NMS	BRCOA	W.H. Brady Co (Class A)
BraeCp	NAS NMS	BRAE	BRAE Corp
Brajds	NAS NMS	BRJS	Brajdas Corp
Bralrn	NAS NL	BRALF	Bralorne Resources Ltd
Brand	NAS NMS	BRAN	Brand Companies Inc
Brandn	NAS NMS	BRDN	Brandon Systems Corp
Branif	NAS NL	BAIR	Braniff Inc
Branrd	NAS SL	BIRI	Brainerd International Inc
Brantre	NAS NMS	BTSB	The Braintree Savings Bank (Massachusetts)
Brazil	New York	BZF	Brazil Fund Inc
BrdgFd	NAS NMS	BRID	Bridgford Foods Corp
BrdvwS	NAS NL	BDVFC	Broadview Savings Bank
BRE	New York	BRE	BRE Properties Inc
Brenco	NAS NMS	BREN	Brenco Inc
Brendle	NAS NMS	BRDL	Brendle's Inc
BrenerC	NAS NL	BNER	Brenner Companies Inc
BrentB	NAS NL	BRBK	Brenton Banks Inc
BrigSt	New York	BGG	Briggs & Stratton Corp
Brilund	NAS SL	BRILF	Brilund Ltd
BristG	NAS SL	BRST	Bristol Gaming Corp
BristM	New York	BMY	Bristol-Myers Co
BritAir	New York	BAB	British Airways Plc
BritGas	New York	BRG	British Gas plc
BritLee	NAS NMS	BLII	Britton Lee Inc
BritLnd	New York	BLA	British Land of America Inc
BritPt	New York	BP	The British Petroleum Company p.l.c.
BritTel	New York	BTY	British Telecommunications plc
Brkfld	NAS NMS	BFBS	Brookfield Bancshares Corp
BrkrSc	NAS SL	BKRS	Brokers Securities Inc
Brkwt	NAS NMS	BWRLF	Breakwater Resources Ltd
BrlNth	New York	BNI	Burlington Northern Inc
BrlRsc	New York	BR	Burlington Resources Inc
BrndySv	NAS NMS	BNDY	Brandywine S&L Assn (Pennsylvania)
BrnFA	American	BFD.A	Brown-Forman Corp (Class A)
BrnFB	American	BFD.B	Brown-Forman Corp (Class B)
BrnfdSv	NAS NMS	BSBC	Branford Savings Bank (Connecticut)
Brnkmn	NAS NMS	BRIK	Brinkmann Instruments Inc
Brntwd	NAS SL	BRWD	Brentwood Instruments Inc
Brnwk	New York	BC	Brunswick Corp
BroadNt	NAS NL	BNBC	Broad National Bancorporation
Brock	New York	BHC	Brock Hotel Corp
Brscn	American	BRS.A	Brascan Ltd (Class A)
BrshWl	New York	BW	Brush Wellman Inc
BRT	New York	BRT	BRT Realty Trust
BrTom	NAS NMS	TMBR	Tom Brown Inc
Brunos	NAS NMS	BRNO	Bruno's Inc

NEWSPAPER ABBREV.	MARKET LISTING	TRADING SYMBOL	COMPANY NAME
BrwnF	New York	BFI	Browning-Ferris Industries Inc
BrwnGp	New York	BG	Brown Group Inc
BrwnRb	NAS NMS	RCBI	Robert C. Brown & Company Inc
BrynM	NAS NMS	BMTCD	Bryn Mawr Bank Corp (Pennsylvania)
BSD	American	BSD	BSD Bancorp Inc
BSD	NAS SL	BSDM	BSD Medical Corp
BsetF	NAS NMS	BSET	Bassett Furniture Industries Inc
BSN	American	BSN	BSN Corp
BsRInt	NAS NMS	BBAHF	Basic Resources International Ltd
BsTnA	NAS NMS	BASEA	Base Ten Systems Inc (Class A)
BsTnB	NAS NL	BASEB	Base Ten Systems Inc (Class B)
BstnDig	NAS NMS	BOST	Boston Digital Corp
BstnFB	NAS NMS	BFCS	Boston Five Bancorp Inc
BT Fin	NAS NMS	BTFC	BT Financial Corp
BTR	NAS NMS	BTRI	BTR Realty Inc
Buckeye	New York	BPL	Buckeye Partners L.P.
Budget	NAS NMS	BDGT	Budget Rent a Car Corp
Buehlr	NAS NMS	BULR	Buehler International Inc
Buell	American	BUE	Buell Industries Inc
Buffels	NAS NL	BFELY	Buffelsfontein Gold Mining Company Ltd
Buffet	NAS NMS	BOCB	Buffets Inc
Buffton	American	BFX	Buffton Corp
BuildT	NAS NMS	TRUK	Builders Transport Inc
BulBear	NAS NMS	BNBGA	Bull & Bear Group Inc (Class A)
BullRGd	NAS NMS	BULL	Bull Run Gold Mines Ltd
Bundy	New York	BNY	Bundy Corp
BunkrH	New York	BHL	Bunker Hill Income Securities Inc
Burke	NAS SL	BMLS	Burke Mills Inc
BurlnCt	New York	BCF	Burlington Coat Factory Warehouse Corp
Burmh	NAS NL	BURMY	Burmah Oil Public Limited Co
BurnAm	American	BMP	Burnham American Properties Inc
Burndy	New York	BDC	Burndy Corp
BurnPP	American	BPP	Burnham Pacific Properties Inc
BurnpS	NAS NMS	BSIM	Burnup & Sims Inc
BurrBr	NAS NMS	BBRC	Burr-Brown Corp
Burrit	NAS NMS	BANQ	Burritt InterFinancial Bancorporation
BusCrd	NAS SL	BUCS	Business Cards of Tomorrow Inc
Bush	American	BSH	Bush Industries Inc
Businld	New York	BLI	Businessland Inc
ButlrMf	NAS NMS	BTLR	Butler Manufacturing Co
ButlrNt	NAS NMS	BUTL	Butler National Corp
Bwater	NAS NL	BWTRY	Bowater Industries plc
BwnSh	New York	BNS	Brown & Sharpe Manufacturing Co
BwnTrn	NAS NMS	BTCI	Brown Transport Company Inc
BwyHld	NAS SL	BWAY	Broadway Holdings Inc
Byers	NAS SL	BYRS	Byers Inc
C COR	NAS NMS	CCBL	C-COR Electronics Inc

NEWSPAPER ABBREV.	MARKET LISTING	TRADING SYMBOL	COMPANY NAME
C 3 Inc	New York	CEE	C3 Inc
CA Blk	NAS SL	LUNG	CA Blockers Inc
Cabarus	NAS NL	CASB	Cabarrus Savings Bank (North Carolina)
CablTV	NAS NMS	CATV	Cable TV Industries
Cablvsn	American	CVC	Cablevision Systems Corp
Cabot	New York	CBT	Cabot Corp
CabotM	NAS NMS	CBOT	Cabot Medical Corp
Cache	NAS NMS	CACH	Caché Inc
CACI	NAS NMS	CACIA	CACI Inc (Class A)
CadeIn	NAS NMS	CADE	Cade Industries Inc
Cadema	NAS SL	CDMA	Cadema Corp
Cadence	NAS NMS	CDNC	Cadence Design Systems Inc
Cadmu	NAS NMS	CDMS	Cadmus Communications Corp
Cadntx	NAS NMS	CADX	Cadnetix Corp
Caesar	New York	CAW	Caesars World Inc
CaesNJ	American	CJN	Caesars New Jersey Inc
CagleA	American	CGL.A	Cagle's Inc (Class A)
CalAmp	NAS NMS	CAMP	California Amplifier Inc
CalBio	NAS NMS	CBIO	California Biotechnology Inc
CalEgy	American	NRG	California Energy Co
CalFed	New York	CAL	CalFed Inc
CalFIP	New York	CFI	Cal Fed Income Partners L.P.
CalFncl	NAS NMS	CFHC	California Financial Holding Co
CalFst	NAS NMS	CFBK	California First Bank
Calgene	NAS NMS	CGNE	Calgene Inc
Calgon	NAS NMS	CRBN	Calgon Carbon Corp
CalJky	American	CJ	California Jockey Club
Callhn	New York	CMN	Callahan Mining Corp
Callon	NAS SL	CLNP	Callon Petroleum Co
CalMD	NAS NMS	CAMD	California Micro Devices Corp
CalMic	NAS NMS	CMIC	California Microwave Inc
Calmat	New York	CZM	CalMat Co
Calprop	American	CPP	Calprop Corp
CalRE	New York	CT	California Real Estate Investment Trust
CalRep	NAS NMS	CRBI	Cal Rep Bancorp Inc
Calstar	NAS NMS	CSAR	Calstar Inc
Calton	New York	CN	Calton Inc
Calumt	NAS NMS	CALI	Calumet Industries Inc
CalWtr	NAS NMS	CWTR	California Water Service Co
CAM Dt	NAS SL	CADA	CAM Data Systems Inc
CambAn	NAS SL	CAAN	Cambridge Analytical Associates Inc
CambIn	NAS NMS	CAMBY	The Cambridge Instrument Company plc
CambM	NAS SL	CMTC	Cambridge Medical Technology Corp
Cambrx	NAS NMS	CBAM	Cambrex Corp
CamBS	NAS NMS	CBCX	Cambridge BioScience Corp
CamEnt	NAS SL	UCAM	Camera Enterprises Inc
CamilSM	NAS SL	CMIL	Camille St. Moritz Inc
CamNt	NAS NL	CWKTF	Cam-Net Communications Network Inc

NEWSPAPER ABBREV.	MARKET LISTING	TRADING SYMBOL	COMPANY NAME
Camp	NAS NMS	CMAFC	Campeau Corp
CamPl	NAS SL	CMPL	Camera Platforms International Inc
CamrnI	New York	CIW	Cameron Iron Works Inc
CamSp	New York	CPB	Campbell Soup Co
Candla	NAS SL	CLZR	Candela Laser Corp
CannEx	NAS NL	CANX	Cannon Express Inc
CanonG	New York	CAN	The Cannon Group Inc
CanonI	NAS NMS	CANNY	Canon Inc
Canonie	NAS NMS	CANO	Canonie Environmental Services Corp
Canrad	NAS NMS	CNRD	Canrad Inc
CanyRs	NAS SL	CYNR	Canyon Resources Corp
CapAsc	NAS NMS	CAII	Capital Associates Inc
CapBcp	NAS NMS	CAPB	Capitol Bancorporation
CapCits	New York	CCB	Capital Cities/ABC Inc
CapCrb	NAS NMS	CRAB	Capt. Crab Inc
CapHld	New York	CPH	Capital Holding Corp
CapHo	American	CAP	Capital Housing & Mortgage Partners
CapSw	NAS NMS	CSWC	Capital Southwest Corp
CapTr	NAS NMS	CATA	Capitol Transamerica Corp
CardFd	NAS NMS	CAFS	Cardinal Federal Savings Bank (Kentucky)
Cardiac	NAS SL	CCSC	Cardiac Control Systems Inc
CardIn	NAS SL	CDNI	Cardinal Industries Inc
Cardis	American	CDS	Cardis Corp
Cardpul	NAS SL	HART	Caridiopulmonary Technologies Inc
CardTl	NAS SL	ACCT	Card-Tel
CareAm	NAS SL	CAMI	CareAmerica Inc
CareE A	American	CRE.A	Care Enterprises Inc (Class A)
CareE B	American	CRE.B	Care Enterprises Inc (Class B)
CareerC	New York	CMO	CareerCom Corp
CarePl	NAS NMS	CPLS	Care Plus Inc
CargInd	New York	CGE	Carriage Industries Inc
CaribSl	NAS SL	CSEL	Caribbean Select Inc
Caringtn	NAS NMS	CARN	Carrington Laboratories Inc
CarlCm	NAS NMS	CCTVY	Carlton Communications PLC
Carlisle	New York	CSL	Carlisle Companies Inc
Carme	NAS NMS	CAME	Carme Inc
Carmel	American	KML	Carmel Container Systems Ltd
Carmik	NAS NMS	CMIKA	Carmike Cinemas Inc (Class A)
CarnCr	American	CCL	Carnival Cruise Lines Inc
CaroBcp	NAS NMS	FFCA	Carolina Bancorp Inc
CaroFst	NAS NL	CAFC	Carolina First Corp
CaroFt	New York	CAO	Carolina Freight Corp
CarolB	NAS SL	CBEN	Carolyn Bean Publishing Ltd
Carolin	NAS NMS	CRLNF	Carolin Mines Ltd (Class A)
CarolP	New York	CRC	Carolco Pictures Inc
CaroMt	NAS SL	CMHC	Carolina Mountain Holding Co
CarPw	New York	CPL	Carolina Power & Light Co

NEWSPAPER ABBREV.	MARKET LISTING	TRADING SYMBOL	COMPANY NAME
CarsP	New York	CRN	Carson Pirie Scott & Co
CartBc	New York	CBC	Carteret Bancorp Inc
CarTec	New York	CRS	Carpenter Technology Corp
CartH	New York	CHH	Carter Hawley Hale Stores Inc
CartWl	New York	CAR	Carter-Wallace Inc
Carver	NAS NMS	CAVR	Carver Corp
Casblan	American	CAB	CasaBlanca Industries Inc
Cascde	NAS NMS	CASC	Cascade Corp
CascNG	New York	CGC	Cascade Natural Gas Corp
Caseys	NAS NMS	CASY	Casey's General Stores Inc
CasFd	American	CVF	Castle Convertible Fund Inc
Caspn	American	CNO	Caspen Oil Inc
Castl A	American	CAS	A.M. Castle & Co
CastlCk	New York	CKE	Castle & Cooke Inc
CaslMle	NAS NMS	CMLE	The Casual Male Corp
CataLt	American	LTG	Catalina Lighting Inc
Caterp	New York	CAT	Caterpillar Inc
CatlThr	NAS NMS	CETH	Catalyst Thermal Energy Corp
Catlyst	New York	CE	Catalyst Energy Corp
CatoCp	NAS NMS	CACOA	Cato Corp (Class A)
CavalH	American	CXV	Cavalier Homes Inc
Cavco	NAS NL	CVCO	Cavco Industries Inc
Cayuga	NAS NMS	CAYB	Cayuga Savings Bank (New York)
CB T	NAS NMS	CBTB	CB&T Bancshares Inc
CB&T F	NAS NMS	CBTF	CB & T Financial Corp
CBI In	New York	CBH	CBI Industries Inc
CBcgp A	NAS NMS	CLBGA	Colonial BancGroup Inc (Class A)
CBcgp B	NAS NMS	CLBGB	Colonial BancGroup Inc (Class B)
CBcWa	NAS NMS	CBWA	Central Bancorporation (Washington)
CblAdv	NAS SL	CABS	Cable Advertising Systems Inc
CblExc	NAS SL	CBLX	Cable Exchange Inc
CbrySc	NAS NMS	CADBY	Cadbury Schweppes PLC
CBS	New York	CBS	CBS Inc
CCA	NAS NMS	CCAM	CCA Industries Inc
CCB	NAS NMS	CCBF	CCB Financial Corp
CCBT	NAS NMS	CCBT	Cape Cod Bank & Trust Co
CcdCam	NAS NMS	LENS	Concord Camera Corp
CCNB	NAS NMS	CCNC	CCNB Corp
CCR	NAS SL	CCCR	CCR Video Corp
CCTC	NAS NMS	CCTC	Computer & Communications Technology Inc
CCX	New York	CCX	CCX Inc
CDI	American	CDI	CDI Corp
CdnOc	American	CXY	Canadian Occidental Petroleum Ltd
CdnPac	New York	CP	Canadian Pacific Ltd
CedarI	NAS NL	CEDR	Cedar Income Federal 1 Ltd
CedrF	New York	FUN	Cedar Fair L.P.
Celcor	NAS SL	CLCR	Celcor Inc

NEWSPAPER ABBREV.	MARKET LISTING	TRADING SYMBOL	COMPANY NAME
Celgene	NAS NMS	CELG	Celgene Corp
CellAm	NAS SL	CELM	Cellular America Inc
CellCm	NAS NMS	COMM	Cellular Communications Inc
Cellcom	NAS SL	CLCM	Cellcom Corp
CellTch	NAS NL	CELL	Cell Technology Inc
CelrIn	NAS SL	CELS	Cellular Inc
CelrPr	NAS SL	CELP	Cellular Products Inc
CelSci	NAS NMS	CELI	Cel-Sci Corp
Celtr	NAS SL	CELT	Celltronics Inc
CEM	NAS NMS	CEMX	CEM Corp
CeMPw	New York	CTP	Central Maine Power Co
Cencor	NAS NMS	CNCR	CenCor Inc
CenHud	New York	CNH	Central Hudson Gas & Electric Corp
CenSoW	New York	CSR	Central & South West Corp
Centcor	NAS NMS	CNTO	Centocor Inc
Centcre	NAS NL	CCOR	Centercore Inc
Centel	New York	CNT	Centel Corp
CentelCb	NAS NMS	CNCAA	Centel Cable Television Co (Class A)
CentEn	New York	CX	Centerior Energy Corp
Centex	New York	CTX	Centex Corp
Centex	NAS NMS	CNTX	Centex Telemanagement Inc
CentGp	American	CEQ	The Centennial Group Inc
Centrbk	NAS NMS	CTBX	Centerbank (Connecticut)
CentrCp	New York	CEN	Centronics Data Computer Corp
Centrst	American	DLP	CenTrust Savings Bank
CentSe	American	CET	Central Securities Corp
Centuri	NAS NMS	CENT	Centuri Inc
CenvD	American	CVL	Cenvill Development Corp
Cenvill	New York	CVI	Cenvill Investors Inc
Cenvst	NAS NMS	CBCT	Cenvest Inc
CeramPr	NAS NL	CPSX	Ceramics Process Systems Corp
Cerbco	NAS NMS	CERB	CERBCO Inc
Cerdyn	NAS NMS	CRDN	Ceradyne Inc
Cermtk	NAS NMS	CRMK	Cermetek Microelectronics Inc
Cerner	NAS NMS	CERN	Cerner Corp
Cerprb	NAS SL	CRPB	CerProbe Corp
Certron	NAS SL	CRTN	Certron Corp
CES	NAS NMS	CESC	Computer Entry Systems Corp
Cetec	American	CEC	Cetec Corp
Cetus	NAS NMS	CTUS	Cetus Corp
CFCda	American	CEF	Central Fund of Canada Ltd
CFI St	NAS NMS	CFIP	CF & I Steel Corp
CFidBk	NAS NMS	CFBS	Central Fidelity Banks Inc
CFS	NAS NMS	CFSC	CFS Financial Corp
ChalInt	NAS NMS	CSTIF	Challenger International Ltd
Chalone	NAS NMS	CHLN	Chalone Inc
ChampSp	New York	CHM	Champion Spark Plug Co
ChanIns	NAS NMS	CHANF	Chandler Insurance Ltd

NEWSPAPER ABBREV.	MARKET LISTING	TRADING SYMBOL	COMPANY NAME
Chantl	NAS SL	CHTL	Chantal Pharmaceutical Corp
ChapEn	NAS NMS	CHPN	Chapman Energy Inc
Chapral	NAS NMS	CHAR	Chaparral Resources Inc
CharCh	NAS NMS	CAKE	Charlotte Charles Inc
Chariot	American	CGR	The Chariot Group Inc
ChartC	New York	CHR	The Charter Co
Chase	New York	CMB	The Chase Manhattan Corp
Chattm	NAS NMS	CHTT	Chattem Inc
Chaus	New York	CHS	Bernard Chaus Inc
ChcDrg	NAS SL	DOSE	Choice Drug Systems Inc
ChDevA	American	CDV.A	Chambers Development Company Inc (Class A)
ChDevB	American	CDV.B	Chambers Development Company Inc (Class B)
ChefInt	NAS NL	CHEF	Chefs International Inc
Chelsea	New York	CHD	Chelsea Industries Inc
Chemed	New York	CHE	Chemed Corp
Chemex	NAS NMS	CHMX	Chemex Pharmaceuticals Inc
Chemfx	NAS NMS	CFIX	Chemfix Technologies Inc
Cherne	NAS SL	CHNE	Cherne Enterprises Inc
Cheroke	NAS NMS	CHKE	The Cherokee Group
Cheshre	NAS NMS	CFNH	Cheshire Financial Corp
ChesInd	NAS SL	CHES	Chesapeake Industries Inc
ChesUtl	NAS NMS	CHPK	Chesapeake Utilities Corp
Chevrn	New York	CHV	Chevron Corp
CheySf	NAS NMS	CHEY	Cheyenne Software Inc
ChFab	NAS NMS	CMFB	Chemical Fabrics Corp
ChfCon	NAS SL	CFCM	Chief Consolidated Mining Co
ChfDv	American	CID	Chieftain Development Company Ltd
Chilis	NAS NMS	CHLI	Chili's Inc
ChiMlw	New York	CHG	Chicago Milwaukee Corp
ChiPac	New York	CPA	Chicago Pacific Corp
ChipsTc	NAS NMS	CHPS	Chips & Technologies Inc
Chiron	NAS NMS	CHIR	Chiron Corp
ChiRv	American	CVR	Chicago Rivet & Machine Co
Chitnd	NAS NMS	CNDN	Chittenden Corp
ChkFull	New York	CHF	Chock Full O'Nuts Corp
ChkPt	NAS NMS	CHEK	Checkpoint Systems Inc
ChkRobt	NAS SL	CKRB	Check Robot Inc
ChkTch	NAS NMS	CTCQ	Check Technology Corp
ChldDis	NAS NMS	CDCRA	Childrens Discovery Center of America Inc (Class A)
ChldWld	NAS NMS	CWLD	Child World Inc
ChLea	NAS NMS	CLEA	Chemical Leaman Corp
ChmBk	New York	CHL	Chemical Banking Corp
Chmclr	NAS NMS	CMCL	ChemClear Inc
ChmFin	NAS NMS	CHFC	Chemical Financial Corp
ChmpEn	American	CHB	Champion Enterprises Inc

NEWSPAPER ABBREV.	MARKET LISTING	TRADING SYMBOL	COMPANY NAME
ChmpIn	New York	CHA	Champion International Corp
ChmpPd	American	CH	Champion Products Inc
ChmpPr	NAS NMS	CREB	Champion Parts Inc
ChncCp	NAS NMS	CHCR	Chancellor Corp
ChpStl	New York	CSM	Chaparral Steel Co
Chpwch	NAS SL	CHIPA	Chipwich Inc (Class A)
ChrDwt	NAS NMS	CRCH	Church & Dwight Company Inc
ChrisCr	New York	CCN	Chris-Craft Industries Inc
Christn	New York	CST	The Christiana Companies Inc
ChrmS	NAS NMS	CHRS	Charming Shoppes Inc
Chronr	NAS NMS	CRNR	Chronar Corp
ChrtFdl	NAS NMS	CHFD	Charter Federal S&L Assn (Virginia)
Chrtwl	NAS NMS	CTWL	Chartwell Group Ltd
ChryCp	NAS NMS	CHER	The Cherry Corp
Chryslr	New York	C	Chrysler Corp
ChsMed	American	CGO	Chase Medical Group Inc
Chspk	New York	CSK	Chesapeake Corp
ChtCrl	NAS NMS	CRTR	Charter-Crellin Inc
ChtFSB	NAS NMS	CFED	Charter Federal Savings Bank
ChtMdA	American	CMD.A	Charter Medical Corp (Class A)
ChtMdB	American	CMD.B	Charter Medical Corp (Class B)
ChtOne	NAS NMS	COFI	Charter One Financial Inc
ChtPwr	American	CHP	Charter Power Systems Inc
Chubb	New York	CB	The Chubb Corp
Churchs	New York	CHU	Church's Fried Chicken Inc
ChWst	New York	CHW	Chemical Waste Management Inc
Chyron	New York	CHY	Chyron Corp
CIGNA	New York	CI	CIGNA Corp
Cilcorp	New York	CER	CILCORP Inc
CIM	American	CIM	CIM High Yield Securities
Cimco	NAS NMS	CIMC	CIMCO Inc
CinBel	New York	CSN	Cincinnati Bell Inc
CineOd	New York	CPX	Cineplex Odeon Corp
CinGE	New York	CIN	The Cincinnati Gas & Electric Co
CinMic	NAS NMS	CNMW	Cincinnati Microwave Inc
CinMil	New York	CMZ	Cincinnati Milacron Inc
CinnFn	NAS NMS	CINF	Cincinnati Financial Corp
Cintas	NAS NMS	CTAS	Cintas Corp
Cipher	NAS NMS	CIFR	Cipher Data Products Inc
Ciprico	NAS NMS	CPCI	Ciprico Inc
Circadn	NAS NMS	CKDN	Circadian Inc
CircInc	NAS NL	CINS	Circle Income Shares Inc
CircleK	New York	CKP	The Circle K Corp
CirclEx	NAS NMS	CEXX	Circle Express Inc
CirclFA	NAS NMS	CFNE	Circle Fine Art Corp
Circon	NAS NMS	CCON	Circon Corp
CircSy	NAS SL	CSYI	Circuit Systems Inc
CirCty	New York	CC	Circuit City Stores Inc

NEWSPAPER ABBREV.	MARKET LISTING	TRADING SYMBOL	COMPANY NAME
Circus	New York	CIR	Circus Circus Enterprises Inc
Ciro	NAS SL	CIRI	Ciro Inc
CIS Tch	NAS NMS	CISIF	C.I.S. Technologies Inc
Citadel	American	CDL	Citadel Holding Corp
Citdl	NAS SL	CIGCF	Citadel Gold Mines Inc
Citicrp	New York	CCI	Citicorp
Citpst	NAS NMS	CITI	Citipostal Inc
CityBcp	New York	CYT	Citytrust Bancorp
CityFed	NAS NMS	CTYF	CityFed Financial Corp
CityRs	NAS NMS	CCIMF	City Resources Ltd
CitySv	NAS NMS	CSBM	City Savings Bank of Meriden (Connecticut)
CitzFst	American	CFB	Citizens First Bancorp
CitznBk	NAS NL	CIBA	Citizens Bank (North Carolina)
CitzSF	NAS NMS	CSFCA	Citizens Savings Financial Corp (Class A) (Florida)
CJerB	NAS NMS	CJER	Central Jersey Bancorp
CJerSv	NAS NMS	CJSB	Central Jersey Savings Bank S.L.A.
CK FSv	NAS NMS	CKSB	CK Federal Savings Bank (North Carolina)
Clabir	New York	CLG	Clabir Corp
ClabrB	NAS SL	CLGBB	Clabir Corp (Class B)
Clairsn	NAS NMS	CLIC	Clairson International Corp
ClairSt	New York	CLE	Claire's Stores Inc
Clarcor	NAS NMS	CLRK	Clarcor Inc
ClarkC	American	CLK	Clark Consolidated Industries Inc
ClarkE	New York	CKL	Clark Equipment Co
Clarmt	American	CCM	Claremont Capital Corp
ClasicC	NAS NMS	WBED	Classic Corp
ClayHm	New York	CMH	Clayton Homes Inc
ClaySlv	NAS NL	CLSM	Clayton Silver Mines Inc
CLC	New York	CLC	CLC of America Inc
CleanH	NAS NMS	CLHB	Clean Harbors Inc
ClearCh	American	CCU	Clear Channel Communications Inc
CleKoh	NAS SL	CLEO	Cleopatra Kohlique Inc
ClifDr	NAS NMS	CLDRV	Cliffs Drilling Co
ClifEgl	NAS SL	CLIF	Cliff Engle Ltd
ClinDt	NAS NMS	CLDA	Clinical Data Inc
CliniTh	NAS SL	CLIN	Clini-Therm Corp
ClinSci	NAS NMS	CLSC	Clinical Sciences Inc
ClintGs	NAS NMS	CGAS	Clinton Gas Systems Inc
ClmGlb	New York	CLM	Clemente Global Growth Fund Inc
ClnGas	NAS NMS	CGES	Colonial Gas Co
Clorox	New York	CLX	The Clorox Co
Cloth	NAS NMS	CTME	The Clothestime Inc
ClubMd	New York	CMI	Club Med Inc
ClvClf	New York	CLF	Cleveland-Cliffs Inc
CMarc	American	CMW	Canadian Marconi Co

NEWSPAPER ABBREV.	MARKET LISTING	TRADING SYMBOL	COMPANY NAME
CmBCol	NAS NMS	CBOCA	Commercial Bancorp of Colorado (Class A)
CmbEn	New York	CSP	Combustion Engineering Inc
CmBsh	NAS NMS	CBSH	Commerce Bancshares Inc (Missouri)
CmCblNC	NAS SL	CABL	Communication Cable Inc
CmcCrd	New York	CCC	Commercial Credit Co
CmceBc	NAS NL	CBNB	CommerceBancorp (California)
CmceG	NAS SL	CGCO	Commerce Group Corp
CmceT	American	CTO	Commerce Total Return Fund Inc
CmcFdl	NAS NMS	CFCN	Commercial Federal Corp
Cmcl Nt	NAS NMS	CNCL	Commercial National Corp
CmclPr	NAS NL	CPUI	Commercial Programming Unlimited Inc
CmClr	NAS NMS	CCLR	Commerce Clearing House Inc
Cmcs sp	NAS NMS	CMCSK	Comcast Corp (special Class A)
CmdAir	NAS NMS	COMD	Command Airways Inc
Cmdial	NAS NMS	CMDL	Comdial Corp
CmdtHd	NAS SL	CMDT	Comdata Holdings Corp
Cmeric	NAS NMS	CMCA	Comerica Inc
CmFct	New York	CFA	The Computer Factory Inc
CMI Cp	American	CMX	CMI Corp
CML	New York	CML	CML Group Inc
CmlTek	NAS NMS	CTEK	Commercial Intertech
CmMtl	New York	CMC	Commercial Metals Co
CmpAs	New York	CA	Computer Associates International Inc
Cmpch	NAS NMS	CCEM	CompuChem Corp
Cmpcm	NAS NMS	BYTE	Compucom Systems Inc
CmpCn	American	CCS	Computer Consoles Inc
CmpCre	New York	CMP	Comprehensive Care Corp
CmpDt	NAS NMS	CPTD	Computer Data Systems Inc
Cmpgrd	NAS SL	PLUG	ComponentGuard Inc
CmpIdn	NAS NMS	CIDN	Computer Identics Corp
CmpLR	NAS NMS	CLRI	Computer Language Research Inc
CmpMc	NAS NL	COMI	Computer Microfilm Corp
CmpoT	NAS NMS	CTEC	Component Technology Corp
CmpPr	NAS NMS	CPRD	Computer Products Inc
CmpR	New York	CCH	Campbell Resources Inc
CmpRs	NAS SL	CRII	Computer Resources Inc
CmprsL	NAS NMS	CLIX	Compression Labs Inc
CmpTel	NAS SL	CPTLA	Computer Telephone Corp (Class 1)
CmptH	NAS NMS	CHRZ	Computer Horizons Corp
CmptM	NAS NMS	CMIN	Computer Memories Inc
Cmptrc	American	LLB	CompuTrac Inc
CmpTsk	New York	TSK	Computer Task Group Inc
CmpU	NAS NMS	CMUC	Comp-U-Check Inc
Cmrco	NAS NMS	CMRO	COMARCO Inc
CMS Ad	NAS SL	CCMS	CMS Advertising Inc
CMS E	NAS NMS	ACMS	CMS Enhancements Inc
CMS En	New York	CMS	CMS Energy Corp

NEWSPAPER ABBREV.	MARKET LISTING	TRADING SYMBOL	COMPANY NAME
CmsCbl	NAS NMS	CCAB	Communications & Cable Inc
CmstkR	NAS SL	CMRE	Comstock Resources Inc
CmtyBn	NAS NMS	CBNH	Community Bankshares Inc (New Hampshire)
CmtyBS	NAS NMS	CBSI	Community Bank System Inc (New York)
CmwE	New York	CWE	Commonwealth Edison Co
CmwMg	NAS NMS	CCMC	Commonwealth Mortgage Company Inc
CmwSv	NAS NMS	COMW	Commonwealth S&L Assn (Florida)
CMX Cp	American	CXC	CMX Corp
CNA Fn	New York	CNA	CNA Financial Corp
CNAI	New York	CNN	CNA Income Shares Inc
CNB	NAS NMS	CNBE	CNB Bancshares Inc
CnBNE	NAS NMS	CBNEV	Constitution Bancorp of New England Inc
CNBNY	NAS NMS	CNBT	Community National Bancorp Inc (New York)
CnBsh	NAS NMS	CBSS	Central Bancshares of the South Inc
CnBSys	NAS NL	CSYS	Central Banking System Inc
Cnc 90	NAS SL	GYMS	Concept 90 Marketing Inc
Cnchm	American	CKC	Conchemco Inc
CncptI	NAS NMS	CCPT	Concept Inc
CndlBk	NAS SL	CDBK	Candlewood Bank & Trust Co
CNL Fn	NAS NMS	CNLF	C N L Financial Corp
CnLaEl	New York	CNL	Central Louisiana Electric Company Inc
CnlIPS	New York	CIP	Central Illinois Public Service Co
CnPacC	American	CTA	Central Pacific Corp
CnsEP	American	CPS	Consolidated Energy Partners L.P.
CnsFrt	New York	CNF	Consolidated Freightways Inc
CnsHyd	NAS NL	COHY	Consolidated Hydro Inc
CnsPap	NAS NMS	CPER	Consolidated Papers Inc
CnSprn	NAS NMS	CNSP	Central Sprinkler Corp
CnstlBc	NAS NMS	CSTL	Constellation Bancorp
CnsTom	NAS NMS	CTLC	Consolidated-Tomoka Land Co
CnStor	New York	CNS	Consolidated Stores Corp
CntCrd	New York	CCR	Countrywide Credit Industries Inc
CntlCp	New York	CIC	The Continental Corp
CntlInfo	New York	CNY	Continental Information Systems Corp
CntrBc	NAS NMS	CTBC	Centerre Bancorporation
CntrlCp	NAS SL	CTRL	Central Corp (Georgia)
CntrMt	New York	CWM	Countrywide Mortgage Investments Inc
CntryP	NAS NMS	CPAP	Century Papers Inc
CntryTl	New York	CTL	Century Telephone Enterprises Inc
CntyBc	NAS NMS	CNBK	Century Bancorp Inc
CntyMd	NAS SL	CEMC	Century Medicorp
CntyPk	NAS SL	CPPC	Century Park Pictures Corp
CnvFd	NAS NMS	CFMI	Convenient Food Mart Inc
CnvSol	NAS SL	CSOL	Convergent Solutions Inc
CNW	New York	CNW	CNW Corp
Coachm	New York	COA	Coachmen Industries Inc

NEWSPAPER ABBREV.	MARKET LISTING	TRADING SYMBOL	COMPANY NAME
Coastal	New York	CGP	The Coastal Corp
CoastF	NAS NMS	CFSF	Coast Federal S&L Assn (Florida)
CoastR	American	CRV	Coast R.V. Inc
CoastSL	New York	CSA	Coast S&L Assn (California)
CoatSl	NAS NMS	RAGS	Coated Sales Inc
CobeLb	NAS NMS	COBE	Cobe Laboratories Inc
CoBolv	NAS NL	BPWRF	Compania Boliviana de Energia Electrica S.A.
CobRsc	NAS NMS	COBB	Cobb Resources Corp
CocaBtl	NAS NMS	COKE	Coca-Cola Bottling Company Consolidated
CocaCl	New York	KO	The Coca-Cola Co
CoCaM	NAS NMS	COCA	CoCa Mines Inc
CocCE	New York	CCE	Coca-Cola Enterprises Inc
Cochmn	NAS SL	CINC	Coachman Inc
CodeAl	NAS NL	CODL	Code-Alarm Inc
Codenol	NAS NMS	CODN	Codenoll Technology Corp
Codercd	NAS SL	CRCD	Codercard Inc
Coeur	American	CDE	Coeur d'Alene Mines Corp
Cognitr	American	CGN	Cognitronics Corp
Cognos	NAS NMS	COGNF	Cognos Inc
CogntSy	NAS SL	CSAI	Cognitive Systems Inc
Cohaset	NAS NMS	CHTB	Cohasset Savings Bank (Massachusetts)
Cohernt	NAS NMS	COHR	Coherent Inc
Cohu	American	COH	Cohu Inc
CoinPhn	NAS SL	OPER	Coin Phones Inc
ColABn	NAS NMS	CABK	Colonial American Bankshares Corp
ColabR	NAS NMS	CRIC	Collaborative Research Inc
Colagen	NAS NMS	CGEN	Collagen Corp
ColCmc	NAS SL	CCOM	Colonial Commercial Corp
Coleco	New York	CLO	Coleco Industries Inc
Colemn	New York	CLN	The Coleman Company Inc
ColEngy	NAS NL	CRDO	Colorado Energy Corp
ColLfAc	NAS NMS	CACCB	Colonial Life & Accident Insurance Co (Class B)
ColFdl	NAS NMS	COFD	Collective Federal Savings Bank (New Jersey)
ColFds	New York	CF	Collins Foods International Inc
ColFst	NAS NMS	COAS	Columbia First Federal S&L Assn (Washington D.C.)
ColGas	New York	CG	The Columbia Gas System Inc
ColgPal	New York	CL	Colgate-Palmolive Co
ColIHI	New York	CIF	Colonial Intermediate High Income Fund
Collins	American	GO	Collins Industries Inc
ColMu	New York	CMU	Colonial Municipal Income Trust
ColnGp	NAS NMS	COGRA	The Colonial Group Inc (Class A)
ColoNt	NAS NMS	COLC	Colorado National Bankshares Inc
Colorcs	NAS NMS	CLRX	Colorocs Corp
ColorSy	American	CLR	Color Systems Technology Inc

NEWSPAPER ABBREV.	MARKET LISTING	TRADING SYMBOL	COMPANY NAME
ColPict	New York	KPE	Columbia Pictures Entertainment Inc
ColPr	American	CPE	Colorado Prime Corp
ColREI	American	CIV	Columbia Real Estate Investments Inc
ColumS	New York	CSV	Columbia S&L Assn
Comair	NAS NMS	COMR	Comair Inc
ComBc	NAS NMS	COBA	Commerce Bankcorp Inc (New Jersey)
Comcoa	NAS NMS	CCOA	COMCOA Inc
ComcPh	NAS SL	CCPI	Comcast Cablevision of Philadelphia Inc
Comcst	NAS NMS	CMCSA	Comcast Corp (Class A)
ComdE	NAS NMS	COES	Commodore Environmental Services Inc
Comdis	New York	CDO	Comdisco Inc
Comdre	New York	CBU	Commodore International Ltd
ComES	New York	CES	Commonwealth Energy System
CometEn	NAS SL	STAM	Comet Enterprises Inc
ComFd	American	CFK	Comfed Bancorp Inc
ComGrp	NAS NL	CMGI	Communications Group Inc
Cominc	American	CLT	Cominco Ltd
Comnet	NAS NMS	CNET	COMNET Corp
Compaq	New York	CPQ	COMPAQ Computer Corp
CompD	American	CDC	CompuDyne Corp
CompSc	New York	CSC	Computer Sciences Corp
Comptek	American	CTK	Comptek Research Inc
Compus	NAS NMS	CSCN	CompuScan Inc
Comsat	New York	CQ	Communications Satellite Corp
Comshr	NAS NMS	CSRE	COMSHARE Inc
Comstk	NAS NMS	CSTK	Comstock Group Inc
Comstk	New York	CPF	Comstock Partners Strategy Fund Inc
ComSy	American	CTM	COM Systems Inc
ComSy	NAS NMS	CSII	Communications Systems Inc
Comtch	NAS SL	CMTL	Comtech Telecommunications Corp
Comtex	NAS SL	CMTX	Comtex Scientific Corp
Comtrn	American	CMR	Commtron Corp
ComTrn	NAS NMS	CTIA	Communications Transmission Inc
Comtrx	NAS NMS	COMX	Comtrex Systems Corp
ConAg	New York	CAG	ConAgra Inc
ConcCC	NAS NMS	CNCD	Concord Career Colleges Inc
ConcCm	NAS NMS	CEFT	Concord Computing Corp
ConcCpt	NAS NMS	CCUR	Concurrent Computer Corp
ConcdF	American	CIS	Concord Fabrics Inc
ConFbr	NAS NMS	CFIB	Consolidated Fibres Inc
Conmed	NAS NMS	CNMD	CONMED Corp
ConnCm	NAS SL	CCBK	Connecticut Community Bank
ConnE	New York	CNE	Connecticut Energy Corp
Connght	NAS NMS	CSESF	Connaught Biosciences Inc
Connly	American	CON	Connelly Containers Inc
ConnNG	New York	CTG	Connecticut Natural Gas Corp
ConnWt	NAS NMS	CTWS	Connecticut Water/Service Inc
Conqst	American	CQX	Conquest Exploration Co

NEWSPAPER ABBREV.	MARKET LISTING	TRADING SYMBOL	COMPANY NAME
Conrail	New York	CRR	Consolidated Rail Corp
ConrPr	NAS NMS	CNNR	Conner Peripherals Inc
Consec	New York	CNC	Conseco inc
ConsEd	New York	ED	Consolidated Edison Company of New York Inc
ConsFn	NAS NMS	CFIN	Consumers Financial Corp
ConsIm	NAS SL	CIMG	Consolidated Imaging Corp
ConsNG	New York	CNG	Consolidated Natural Gas Co
ConsOG	American	CGS	Consolidated Oil & Gas Inc
ConsPd	NAS NMS	COPI	Consolidated Products Inc
ConsSv	NAS NL	CONS	Conservative Savings Bank
Constn	American	KCS	Conston Corp
ConStP	NAS NMS	CSTP	Congress Street Properties Inc
Constr	New York	CTR	Constar International Inc
Consul	NAS NMS	CNSL	Consul Restaurant Corp
Contel	New York	CTC	Contel Corp
ContGr	American	CIG	Continental Graphics Corp
ContIll	New York	CIL	Continental Illinois Corp
Contin	NAS NMS	CTUC	The Continuum Company Inc
Cont1Cl	NAS NMS	CCXLA	Contel Cellular Inc (Class A)
ContMtl	American	CUO	Continental Materials Corp
Convex	NAS NMS	CNVX	Convex Computer Corp
Convgt	NAS NMS	CVGT	Convergent Inc
ConvHld	New York	CNV	Convertible Holdings Inc
Convsn	NAS NMS	CVSNF	Conversion Industries Inc
Convst	American	CEP	ConVest Energy Partners Ltd
ConWat	NAS NMS	CONW	Consumers Water Co
CoOpBk	NAS NMS	COBK	Co-Operative Bancorp (Massachusetts)
CoopCo	New York	COO	The Cooper Companies Inc
Cooper	New York	CBE	Cooper Industries Inc
CooprD	NAS NMS	BUGS	Cooper Development Co
CooprL	NAS NMS	ZAPSV	Cooper Life Sciences Inc
Coors B	NAS NMS	ACCOB	Adolph Coors Co (Class B)
Copelc	American	CFG	Copelco Financial Services Group Inc
Copley	American	COP	Copley Properties Inc
CoprTr	New York	CTB	Cooper Tire & Rubber Co
Copwld	New York	COS	Copperweld Corp
Copytle	NAS NMS	COPY	Copytele Inc
Coradn	NAS SL	CDIN	Coradian Corp
CorBlk	New York	CBL	Corroon & Black Corp
Corcom	NAS NMS	CORC	Corcom Inc
Corcp	American	CCP	Corcap Inc
CorctCp	NAS NMS	CCAX	Corrections Corporation of America
Cordis	NAS NMS	CORD	Cordis Corp
CoreIn	New York	CRI	Core Industries Inc
CoreSt	NAS NMS	CSFN	CoreStates Financial Corp
Corken	NAS SL	CORK	Corken International Corp
CornGl	New York	GLW	Corning Glass Works

NEWSPAPER ABBREV.	MARKET LISTING	TRADING SYMBOL	COMPANY NAME
CoronaA	NAS NL	IRAFV	Corona Corp (Class A)
CoronaB	NAS NL	IRBFV	Corona Corp (Class B)
CorpDt	NAS SL	CODS	Corporate Data Sciences Inc
CorpSft	NAS NMS	CSOF	Corporate Software Inc
Cortrnc	NAS SL	CTRN	Cortronic Corp
Corvus	NAS NMS	CRVS	Corvus Systems Inc
CosmCr	American	CCA	Cosmopolitan Care Corp
CosmFr	NAS NMS	COSF	Cosmetic & Fragrance Concepts Inc
Cosmo	NAS NMS	CSMO	Cosmo Communications Corp
Costar	NAS NMS	CSTR	Costar Corp
Costco	NAS NMS	COST	Costco Wholesale Corp
CotgSv	NAS NMS	COTG	Cottage Savings Assn F.A. (Ohio)
CountyS	NAS NMS	CSBA	County Savings Bank (California)
CourDis	NAS NMS	CDGI	Courier Dispatch Group Inc
Courer	NAS NMS	CRRC	Courier Corp
Courtld	American	COU	Courtaulds PLC
CousH	NAS NL	CUZZ	Cousins Home Furnishings Inc
CousP	NAS NMS	COUS	Cousins Properties Inc
Covngt	NAS NMS	COVT	Covington Development Group Inc
CP Ntl	New York	CPN	CP National Corp
CPAC	NAS NL	CPAK	CPAC Inc
CPaFin	NAS NMS	CPSA	Central Pennsylvania Financial Corp
CPB	NAS NMS	CPBI	CPB Inc
CPC	New York	CPC	CPC International Inc
CPC	NAS NMS	CPST	CPC Rexcel Inc
CpCapit	NAS SL	CCRS	Corporate Capital Resources Inc
CPcMn	NAS NL	CPMNY	Central Pacific Minerals N.L.
CPI	NAS NMS	CPIC	CPI Corp
CpMgt	NAS SL	KORP	Corporate Management Group Inc
CPS Co	NAS SL	CPSIA	CPS Corporate Planning Services (Class A)
CPsyc	New York	CMY	Community Psychiatric Centers
CPT	NAS NMS	CPTC	CPT Corp
CptAut	NAS NMS	CAUT	Computer Automation Inc
CptCft	NAS SL	CRFT	ComputerCraft Inc
CptCom	NAS SL	CCMM	Computer Communications Inc
Cptlnd	New York	CLD	Computerland Corp
CptNwk	NAS SL	CMNT	Computer Network Technology Corp
CptPwr	NAS NL	CPWR	Computer Power Inc
CptrCm	NAS SL	CPRC	Computer Components Corp
CR Clt	NAS SL	CLTH	C&R Clothiers Inc
Craig	New York	CRA	Craig Corp
Crane	New York	CR	Crane Co
CrayRs	New York	CYR	Cray Research Inc
CrCPB	American	CNP.B	Crown Central Petroleum Corp (Class B)
CrdnlD	NAS NMS	CDIC	Cardinal Distribution Inc
CreatTc	NAS SL	CRTV	Creative Technologies Corp
CreatvC	NAS SL	CCAI	Creative Computer Applications Inc

NEWSPAPER ABBREV.	MARKET LISTING	TRADING SYMBOL	COMPANY NAME
CredoPt	NAS SL	CRED	Credo Petroleum Corp
Crescot	NAS NMS	CRCTC	Crescott Inc
Crestar	NAS NMS	CRFC	Crestar Financial Corp
Crftmtc	NAS NMS	CRCC	Craftmatic/Contour Industries Inc
CrftWld	NAS SL	CWDI	Craft World International Inc
CRI II	New York	CII	CRI Insured Mortgage Investments II Inc
CRI III	New York	CTH	CRI Insured Mortgage Investments III LP
CRIIM	New York	CRM	CRI Insured Mortgage Investments L.P.
CritclIn	NAS NL	FYBR	Critical Industries Inc
CritGp	NAS NMS	CRITA	Criterion Group Inc (Class A)
Criticre	NAS NMS	CXIM	Criticare Systems Inc
CrkBrl	NAS NMS	CBRL	Cracker Barrel Old Country Store Inc
CrmpK	New York	CNK	Crompton & Knowles Corp
CrnCP	American	CNP.A	Crown Central Petroleum Corp (Class A)
CrnrFn	NAS NMS	CSTN	CornerStone Financial Corp
Cronus	NAS NMS	CRNS	Cronus Industries Inc
CropG	NAS NMS	CROP	Crop Genetics International Corp
Crosby	American	ZDC	Philip Crosby Associates Inc
CrosldS	New York	CRL	Crossland Savings (New York)
Cross	American	ATX.A	A.T. Cross Co (Class A)
CrosTr	NAS NMS	CTCO	Cross & Trecker Corp
CrowlM	American	COM	Crowley, Milner & Co
CRsLf	NAS NMS	CRLC	Central Reserve Life Corp
CRSS	New York	DA	CRS Sirrine Inc
CrstCp	NAS SL	CBAG	Crested Corp
CrstFdl	NAS NMS	CRES	Crestmont Federal S&L Assn (New Jersey)
CrwfCo	NAS NMS	CRAW	Crawford & Co
CrwnA	NAS NL	CRNA	CrownAmerica Inc
CrwnAn	NAS NMS	CRAN	Crown Anderson Inc
CrwnBd	NAS SL	CRON	Crown Brands Inc
CrwnCk	New York	CCK	Crown Cork & Seal Company Inc
CryoDy	NAS SL	CRTD	CryoDynamics Inc
CrysBd	New York	CBR	Crystal Brands Inc
CrystO	American	COR	Crystal Oil Co
CrzEd	NAS NMS	CRZY	Crazy Eddie Inc
CSC Ind	NAS NMS	CPSL	CSC Industries Inc
CshAm	American	PWN	Cash America Investments Inc
CSK	NAS NL	CSKKY	CSK Corp
CSP	NAS NMS	CSPI	CSP Inc
CSS	American	CSS	CSS Industries Inc
Cstam	New York	CAC	CoastAmerica Corp
CstlEn	NAS NMS	CECX	Castle Energy Corp
CSX	New York	CSX	CSX Corp
CtBcp	NAS NL	NKBK	Connecticut Bancorp Inc
CtData	New York	CDA	Control Data Corp
CTEC	NAS NMS	CTEX	C-TEC Corp
CTEC B	NAS NL	CTEXB	C-TEC Corp (Class B)
CTF	New York	CTF	Counsellors Tandem Securities Fund Inc

NEWSPAPER ABBREV.	MARKET LISTING	TRADING SYMBOL	COMPANY NAME
CtLasr	NAS SL	CLSR	Control Laser International Corp
CtlCrc	American	CKT	Continental Circuits Corp
CtlGn	NAS NMS	CGIC	Continental General Insurance Co
CtlHlth	NAS NMS	CTHL	Continental Health Affiliates Inc
CtlHme	NAS NMS	CONH	Continental Homes Holding Corp
CtlIHld	New York	CIH	Continental Illinois Holding Corp
CtlMed	NAS NMS	CONT	Continental Medical Systems Inc
CtlVen	NAS SL	COVIV	Continental Ventures Inc
CtnSLf	NAS NMS	CSLH	Cotton States Life & Health Insurance Co
CtrCOp	NAS NMS	CEBK	Central Co-operative Bank (Massachusetts)
CtrlHld	NAS NMS	CHOL	Central Holding Co
CtrlRs	NAS NMS	CRIX	Control Resources Industries Inc
CtrlSou	NAS NL	CSBC	Central & Southern Holding Co
CtryLk	NAS NMS	CLFI	Country Lake Foods Inc
CTS	New York	CTS	CTS Corp
CtyCom	American	CTY.A	Century Communications Corp (Class A)
CtyHld	NAS NMS	CHCO	City Holding Co
CtyNC	NAS NMS	CTYN	City National Corp
CtzBkg	NAS NMS	CBCF	Citizens Banking Corp (Michigan)
CtzFG	NAS NMS	CITN	Citizens Financial Group Inc
CtzIns	NAS NMS	CINNA	Citizens Insurance Company of America, Texas (Class A)
CtzSec	NAS NL	CSGI	Citizens Security Group Inc
CtzSMd	NAS NMS	CSBF	Citizens Savings Bank F.S.B. (Maryland)
CtzSNY	NAS NMS	CISA	Citizens Savings Bank F.S.B. (New York)
CtzSoCp	NAS NMS	CSOU	Citizens & Southern Corp
CtzU A	NAS NMS	CITUA	Citizens Utilities Co (Class A)
CtzU B	NAS NMS	CITUB	Citizens Utilities Co (Class B)
Cubic	American	CUB	Cubic Corp
CUC Int	NAS NMS	CUCD	CUC International Inc
Cucos	NAS SL	CUCO	Cucos Inc
Culbro	New York	CUC	Culbro Corp
Culinet	New York	CUL	Cullinet Software Inc
CullnFr	NAS NMS	CFBI	Cullen/Frost Bankers Inc
Culp	NAS NMS	CULP	Culp Inc
Culum	NAS NMS	CULL	Cullum Companies Inc
CumbR	NAS NL	CRIG	Cumberland Gold Group Inc
CumbrFd	NAS NMS	CMBK	The Cumberland Federal Savings Bank (Kentucky)
CumEn	New York	CUM	Cummins Engine Company Inc
Cuplex	American	CXI	Cuplex Inc
CurInc	New York	CUR	Current Income Shares Inc
Curtce	American	CBI	Curtice-Burns Foods Inc
CurtW	New York	CW	Curtiss-Wright Corp

NEWSPAPER ABBREV.	MARKET LISTING	TRADING SYMBOL	COMPANY NAME
Cusac	NAS SL	CUSIF	Cusac Industries Ltd
Custmd	American	CUS	Customedix Corp
Cutco	NAS NL	CUTC	CutCo Industries Inc
CVBFn	NAS NSM	CVBF	CVB Financial Corp
CVN	NAS NMS	CMCO	CVN Companies Inc
CVtPS	New York	CV	Central Vermont Public Service Corp
CWineA	American	CDG.A	Canandaigua Wine Company Inc
CWineB	American	CDG.B	Canandaigua Wine Company Inc
CwltBn	NAS NMS	CBKS	Commonwealth Bancshares Corp
CwnBk	NAS NMS	CRWN	Crown Books Corp
CwnCr	American	CRW	Crown Crafts Inc
CwnRs	NAS NMS	CRRS	Crown Resource Corp
CWTrns	NAS NMS	CWTS	Country Wide Transport Services Inc
CXR	American	CXR	CXR Telecom Corp
Cybertk	NAS NMS	CKCP	CYBERTEK Corp
Cybmed	NAS SL	CMED	Cybermedic Inc
CybrOpt	NAS SL	CYBE	CyberOptics Corp
Cycare	New York	CYS	CyCare Systems Inc
Cyntch	NAS SL	CYAN	Cyanotech Corp
CyprFd	American	WJR	Cypress Fund Inc
Cyprus	NAS NMS	CYPM	Cyprus Minerals Co
CypSem	NAS NMS	CYPR	Cypress Semiconductor Corp
Cytogn	NAS NMS	CYTO	Cytogen Corp
CytRx	NAS NMS	CYTR	CytRx Corp
D&N Fn	NAS NMS	DNFC	D&N Financial Corp
Dahlbrg	NAS NMS	DAHL	Dahlberg Inc
DaiEi	NAS NL	DAIEY	The Daiei Inc (Japan)
DairyA	NAS NMS	DMCVA	Dairy Mart Convenience Stores Inc (Class A)
DairyB	NAS NMS	DMCVB	Dairy Mart Convenience Stores Inc (Class B)
DaisySy	NAS NMS	DAZY	Daisy Systems Corp
Dallas	New York	DLS	Dallas Corp
DalSem	NAS NMS	DSMI	Dallas Semiconductor Corp
Daltex	NAS SL	DLTX	Daltex Medical Sciences Inc
Dalton	NAS SL	DALT	Dalton Communications Inc
DamCr	American	DNI	Damon Creations Inc
DamEA	American	DEP.A	Damson Energy Company LP (Class A)
DamEB	American	DEP.B	Damson Energy Company LP (Class B)
DamnC	New York	DMN	Damon Corp
Damson	American	DAM	Damson Oil Corp
DanaCp	New York	DCN	Dana Corp
Danhr	New York	DHR	Danaher Corp
Daniel	New York	DAN	Daniel Industries Inc
DartDg	NAS SL	DDRG	Dart Drug Stores Inc
DartGp	NAS NMS	DARTA	Dart Group Corp (Class A)
DasaCp	NAS SL	DASA	Dasa Corp

NEWSPAPER ABBREV.	MARKET LISTING	TRADING SYMBOL	COMPANY NAME
Dasibi	NAS SL	DSBE	Dasibi Environmental Corp
DataGn	New York	DGN	Data General Corp
Datamet	American	DC	Datametrics Corp
DataPd	American	DPC	Dataproducts Corp
Datapt	New York	DPT	Datapoint Corp
Datarm	American	DTM	Dataram Corp
Datflx	NAS NMS	DFLX	Dataflex Corp
Datkey	NAS NL	DKEY	Datakey Inc
Datmar	NAS NMS	DMAR	Datamarine International Inc
DatMC	NAS SL	DMCS	Data Med Clinical Support Services Inc
Datphz	NAS NMS	DPHZ	DATAPHAZ Inc
Datron	NAS NMS	DTSI	Datron Systems Inc
Datscp	NAS NMS	DSCP	Datascope Corp
Datum	NAS NMS	DATM	Datum Inc
Datvsn	NAS NMS	DVIS	Datavision Inc
Dauphn	NAS NMS	DAPN	Dauphin Deposit Corp
Davox	NAS NMS	DAVX	Davox Corp
DavTis	NAS NL	DDTTF	Davidson Tisdale Mines Ltd
DavWtr	New York	DWW	Davis Water & Waste Industries Inc
Dawson	NAS NMS	DWSN	Dawson Geophysical Co
Daxor	American	DXR	Daxor Corp
DaytHd	New York	DH	Dayton Hudson Corp
DBA	NAS NMS	DBAS	DBA Systems Inc
DBeer	NAS NL	DBRSY	De Beers Consolidated Mines Ltd
DckMA	American	DML.A	Dickenson Mines Ltd (Class A)
DckMB	American	DML.B	Dickenson Mines Ltd (Class B)
DClark	NAS NMS	DCPI	dick clark productions inc
DCNY	New York	DCY	DCNY Corp
DctPhr	NAS SL	DPRX	Direct Pharmaceutical Corp
DDI	NAS NMS	DDIX	DDI Pharmaceuticals Inc
DeanFd	New York	DF	Dean Foods Co
DebSh	NAS NMS	DEBS	Deb Shops Inc
DecisSy	NAS NL	DCSN	Decision Systems Inc
Decom	NAS NMS	DSII	Decom Systems Inc
Decor	NAS NMS	DCOR	Decor Corp
Decorat	American	DII	Decorator Industries Inc
DeeCp	New York	DEE	Dee Corporation PLC
Deere	New York	DE	Deere & Co
DeerfSv	NAS NMS	DEER	Deerfield Federal S&L Assn (Illinois)
DefnPr	NAS NMS	DEFI	Defiance Precision Products Inc
DEI	New York	DEI	Diversified Energies Inc
Dekalb	NAS NMS	DKLBB	DEKALB Corp (Class B)
DelaOts	NAS NMS	DOCP	Delaware Otsego Corp
DeLau	American	DEG	De Laurentiis Entertainment Group Inc
Delchm	NAS NMS	DLCH	Delchamps Inc
DelEl	NAS SL	DELE	Del Electronics Corp
DelLab	American	DLI	Del Laboratories Inc
DellCpt	NAS NMS	DELL	Dell Computer Corp

NEWSPAPER ABBREV.	MARKET LISTING	TRADING SYMBOL	COMPANY NAME
Delmed	American	DMD	Delmed Inc
DelmP	New York	DEW	Delmarva Power & Light Co
DelpInf	NAS NMS	DLPH	Delphi Information Systems Inc
DelSvg	NAS NMS	DESB	Delaware Savings Bank F.S.B.
DeltaAr	New York	DAL	Delta Air Lines Inc
DeltaDt	NAS SL	DDSC	Delta Data Systems Corp
Deltak	NAS NMS	DLTK	Deltak Corp
Deltaus	NAS NMS	DLTA	DeltaUS Corp
DeltNG	NAS NMS	DGAS	Delta Natural Gas Company Inc
Deltona	New York	DLT	The Deltona Corp
Deluxe	New York	DLX	Deluxe Corp
DelVal	New York	DVL	Del-Val Financial Corp
Denning	NAS SL	GARD	Denning Mobile Robotics Inc
Denpac	NAS SL	DNPC	Denpac Corp
DensMf	New York	DSN	Dennison Manufacturing Co
DentMd	NAS NMS	DTMD	Dento-Med Industries Inc
DEP	NAS NMS	DEPC	DEP Corp
DepGty	NAS NMS	DEPS	Deposit Guaranty Corp
DermaL	NAS SL	DERM	Derma-Lock Medical Corp
DeRose	American	DRI	De Rose Industries Inc
Desgnh	NAS SL	DHIN	Designhouse International Inc
DesgnI	American	DJI	Designcraft Industries Inc
DeSoto	New York	DSO	DeSoto Inc
Dest	NAS NMS	DEST	DEST Corp
DetCan	NAS NL	DTUN	Detroit & Canada Tunnel Corp
DetEd	New York	DTE	The Detroit Edison Co
DetrxC	NAS NMS	DTRX	Detrex Corp
DetSy	NAS NMS	DETC	Detection Systems Inc
Devcon	NAS NMS	DEVC	Devcon International Corp
Develcn	NAS NL	DLCFF	Develcon Electronics Ltd
Devon	NAS NMS	DEVN	Devon Group Inc
Dewey	NAS NMS	DEWY	Dewey Electronics Corp
Dexon	NAS SL	DEXO	Dexon Inc
Dexter	New York	DEX	The Dexter Corp
Dghtie	NAS NL	DOBQ	Doughtie's Foods Inc
DglLom	NAS NMS	DOUG	Douglas & Lomason Co
DH Tch	NAS NMS	DHTK	DH Technology Inc
DI Ind	American	DRL	DI Industries Inc
Diag A	American	DRS.A	Diagnostic/Retrieval Systems Inc (Class A)
Diag B	American	DRS.B	Diagnostic/Retrieval Systems Inc (Class B)
DiagDt	NAS NL	DDAT	Diagonal Data Corp
Diagnst	NAS NMS	DXTK	Diagnostek Inc
DiagPr	New York	DP	Diagnostic Products Corp
DiagSc	NAS SL	DSIC	Diagnostic Sciences Inc
Dial Re	NAS NMS	DEAL	Dial REIT Inc
DianaCp	New York	DNA	The Diana Corp

NEWSPAPER ABBREV.	MARKET LISTING	TRADING SYMBOL	COMPANY NAME
DiaSo	New York	DSP	Diamond Shamrock Offshore Partners L.P.
Diasonc	American	DIA	Diasonics Inc
Dibrel	NAS NMS	DBRL	Dibrell Brothers Inc
Diceon	NAS NMS	DICN	Diceon Electronics Inc
Diebold	New York	DBD	Diebold Inc
DiGior	New York	DIG	Di Giorgio Corp
Digital	New York	DEC	Digital Equipment Corp
Digitxt	NAS SL	DIGT	Digitext Inc
Diglog	NAS NMS	DILO	Digilog Inc
DigMic	NAS NMS	DMIC	Digital Microwave Corp
DigPd	NAS SL	DIPC	Digital Products Corp
Digtch	NAS NMS	DGTC	Digitech Inc
Digt1Cm	New York	DCA	Digital Communications Associates Inc
Digt1Op	NAS SL	DOCC	Digital Optronics Corp
Digt1Sol	NAS SL	DGSI	Digital Solutions Inc
DigTrA	NAS SL	DTINA	Digital Transmission Inc (Class A)
Dillard	American	DDS.A	Dillard Department Stores Inc (Class A)
DimeCT	NAS NMS	DIBK	The Dime Savings Bank of Wallingford (Connecticut)
DimenMd	NAS SL	DMED	Dimensional Medicine Inc
DimeNY	New York	DME	Dime Savings Bank of New York FSB
Diodes	American	DIO	Diodes Inc
Dionex	NAS NMS	DNEX	Dionex Corp
Dionic	NAS NMS	DION	Dionics Inc
DirActn	American	DMK	Direct Action Marketing Inc
DisAsc	NAS SL	DIVY	Discovery Associates Inc
Discus	NAS SL	DISC	Discus Corp
DisDet	NAS SL	DIDII	Disease Detection International Inc
Disney	New York	DIS	The Walt Disney Co
DistLog	NAS NMS	DLOG	Distributed Logic Corp
DivHum	NAS SL	HIRE	Diversified Human Resources Group Inc
DiviHtl	American	DVH	Divi Hotels N.V.
DivInvt	NAS NMS	DING	Diversified Investment Group Inc
Divrsc	NAS NMS	DVRS	Diversco Inc
DivrsIn	New York	DMC	Diversified Industries Inc
DivTch	NAS SL	DVTI	Diversified Technology Inc
DixieNt	NAS NL	DNLC	Dixie National Corp
DixieYr	NAS NMS	DXYN	Dixie Yarns Inc
Dixilne	American	DIX	Dixieline Products Inc
DixnGp	New York	DXN	Dixons Group plc
DixnTi	American	DXT	Dixon Ticonderoga Co
DLauF	American	DFP	De Laurentiis Film Partners L.P.
D1Paint	NAS SL	DELA	Del Paint Corp
D1rGn1	NAS NMS	DOLR	Dollar General Corp
D1tWod	NAS NMS	DLWD	Delta Woodside Industries Inc
DlyJour	NAS NMS	DJCO	Daily Journal Co
DMI	NAS NL	DMIF	DMI Furniture Inc
DmnBio	NAS NMS	DBIO	Damon Biotech Inc

NEWSPAPER ABBREV.	MARKET LISTING	TRADING SYMBOL	COMPANY NAME
DmnFdl	NAS NMS	DFED	Dominion Federal S&L Assn (Virginia)
DNA Pl	NAS NMS	DNAP	DNA Plant Technology Corp
DOC	NAS NMS	DOCO	D.O.C. Optics Corp
Docgph	NAS SL	DOCX	Docugraphix Inc
DomBk	NAS NMS	DMBK	Dominion Bankshares Corp
Domng	NAS NMS	DOMZ	Dominguez Water Corp
DomnT	NAS NMS	DOMN	Domain Technology Inc
DomRs	New York	D	Dominion Resources Inc
Domtr	New York	DTC	Domtar Inc
Donald	New York	DCI	Donaldson Company Inc
Donegal	NAS NMS	DONEF	Donegal Resources Ltd
Donley	New York	DNY	R.R. Donnelley & Sons Co
DonlyC	American	DON	Donnelly Corp
Doskcl	NAS NMS	DOSK	Doskocil Companies Inc
Dotrnix	NAS NMS	DOTX	Dotronix Inc
Dover	New York	DOV	Dover Corp
DovrReg	NAS NL	DVRFS	Dover Regional Financial Shares
DowCh	New York	DOW	The Dow Chemical Co
DowJns	New York	DJ	Dow Jones & Company Inc
Downey	New York	DSL	Downey S&L Assn
DPL	New York	DPL	DPL Inc
Drantz	NAS NMS	DRAN	Dranetz Technologies Inc
Dravo	New York	DRV	Dravo Corp
DresB	NAS NMS	DBRN	The Dress Barn Inc
DresBk	NAS NL	DRSDY	Dresdner Bank A.G.
Dreshr	NAS NMS	DRES	Dresher Inc
Dresr	New York	DI	Dresser Industries Inc
DrewIn	NAS NMS	DRWI	Drew Industries Inc
Drewry	NAS SL	DREW	Drewry Photocolor Corp
DrexB	New York	DBF	Drexel Bond-Debenture Trading Fund
Drexlr	NAS NMS	DRXR	Drexler Technology Corp
Dreyfus	New York	DRY	The Dreyfus Corp
DreyGr	NAS NMS	DRYR	Dreyer's Grand Ice Cream Inc
DrgEm	NAS NMS	DEMP	Drug Emporium Inc
DriefC	NAS NL	DRFNY	Driefontein Consolidated Ltd
DrivHar	American	DRH	Driver-Harris Co
DRX	NAS SL	DTRH	DRX Inc
DryStGn	New York	DSI	Dreyfus Strategic Government Income Fund
DryStr	New York	LEO	Dreyfus Strategic Municipals Inc
DS Bnc	NAS NMS	DSBC	DS Bancor Inc (Connecticut)
DSC	NAS NMS	DIGI	DSC Communications Corp
DsgInc	NAS NL	DESI	Designs Inc
Dsgntrn	American	DSG	Designatronics Inc
DShRM	New York	DRM	Diamond Shamrock R&M Inc
DST	NAS NMS	DSTS	DST Systems Inc
Dta IO	NAS NMS	DAIO	Data I/O Corp
DtaDsg	New York	DDL	Data-Design Laboratories Inc

NEWSPAPER ABBREV.	MARKET LISTING	TRADING SYMBOL	COMPANY NAME
Dtamg	NAS SL	DMAG	Datamag Inc
Dtasth	NAS NMS	DSCC	Datasouth Computer Corp
DtaTrn	NAS NMS	DATX	Data Translation Inc
DtMea	NAS NMS	DMCB	Data Measurement Corp
DTomas	NAS NMS	DTOM	De Tomaso Industries Inc
DtSwtch	NAS NMS	DASW	Data Switch Corp
DtTrNw	NAS SL	DTLN	Data Transmission Network
DtyFr	American	DFI	Duty Free International Inc
Ducom	American	DCO	Ducommun Inc
DuffPh	New York	DNP	Duff & Phelps Selected Utilities
DukeP	New York	DUK	Duke Power Co
DukeRIn	New York	DRE	Duke Realty Investments Inc
Dumag	NAS NMS	DMGIF	Dumagami Mines Ltd
DunBd	New York	DNB	The Dun & Bradstreet Corp
DunkDn	NAS NMS	DUNK	Dunkin' Donuts Inc
Duplex	American	DPX	Duplex Products Inc
duPont	New York	DD	E.I. du Pont de Nemours & Co
DuqLt	New York	DQU	Duquesne Light Co
DuqSys	NAS NMS	DUQN	Duquesne Systems Inc
Duramd	NAS NMS	DRMD	Duramed Pharmaceuticals Inc
Duratek	NAS NMS	DRTK	Duratek Corp
DurFil	NAS NMS	DUFM	Durr-Fillauer Medical Inc
Durhm	NAS NMS	DUCO	Durham Corp
Duriron	NAS NMS	DURI	The Duriron Company Inc
Durkn	NAS NMS	DRKN	Durakon Industries Inc
DustMc	NAS SL	DUSTF	Dusty Mac Mines Ltd
DvFood	NAS NMS	DIFSD	Diversified Foods Corp
DVIFn	NAS SL	DVIC	DVI Financial Corp
DWG	American	DWG	DWG Corp
DWGI	New York	GVT	Dean Witter Government Income Trust
DWI	NAS SL	DWIC	DWI Corp
DwnyDs	NAS NMS	DDDI	Downey Designs International Inc
Dyansn	NAS NMS	DYAN	Dyansen Corp
Dyatrn	NAS NMS	DYTR	Dyatron Corp
Dycom	NAS NMS	DYCO	Dycom Industries Inc
DynAm	New York	DYA	Dynamics Corporation of America
DynCls	NAS SL	DYNC	Dynamic Classics Ltd
Dyncrp	New York	DYN	DynCorp
DynmcSc	NAS SL	DYNS	Dynamic Sciences International Inc
DynRs	NAS NMS	DRCO	Dynamics Research Corp
Dynsc	NAS NMS	DYNA	Dynascan Corp
DyntrL	NAS SL	DYNT	Dynatronics Laser Corp
DytchC	NAS NMS	DYTC	Dynatech Corp
E Syst	New York	ESY	E-Systems Inc
EA Eng	NAS NMS	EACO	EA Engineering Science & Technology Inc
EAC	American	EAC	EAC Industries Inc
EaglBn	NAS NMS	EBSI	Eagle Bancshares Inc

NEWSPAPER ABBREV.	MARKET LISTING	TRADING SYMBOL	COMPANY NAME
EaglCl	American	EGL	Eagle Clothes Inc
EagleP	New York	EPI	Eagle-Picher Industries Inc
EaglFn	American	EAGL	Eagle Financial Corp
EagTl	NAS NMS	EGLC	Eagle Telephonics Inc
EarthT	NAS NMS	ETCO	The Earth Technology Corp
Easco	NAS NMS	TOOL	Easco Hand Tools Inc
EastBk	NAS NL	EOBK	Eastover Bank for Savings (Mississippi)
Eastco	NAS SL	ESTO	Eastco Industrial Safety Corp
Eastex	NAS NMS	ETEX	Eastex Energy Inc
EastFn	NAS NMS	EAFC	Eastland Financial Corp
EastGF	New York	EFU	Eastern Gas & Fuel Associates
EastTx	NAS NL	ETSL	East Texas S&L Assn of Tyler Texas
EastUtl	New York	EUA	Eastern Utilities Associates
EastWy	NAS NMS	EWSB	East Weymouth Savings Bank (Massachusetts)
EatnFn	NAS NMS	EATO	Eaton Financial Corp
Eaton	New York	ETN	Eaton Corp
EatVan	NAS NMS	EAVN	Eaton Vance Corp
EB Mar	NAS NMS	EBMI	E&B Marine Inc
ECC	New York	ECC	ECC International Corp
Echlin	New York	ECH	Echlin Inc
EchoB	American	ECO	Echo Bay Mines Ltd
ECI Tel	NAS NMS	ECILF	ECI Telecom Ltd
Ecogn	American	ECN	Ecogen Inc
Ecolab	New York	ECL	Ecolab Inc
EcolEn	American	EEI.A	Ecology & Environment Inc (Class A)
ECRM	NAS NL	new	ECRM Inc
Edac	NAS NL	EDAC	Edac Technologies Corp
Edgcmb	NAS NMS	EDGC	Edgcomb Corp
EdisBr	New York	EBS	Edison Brothers Stores Inc
EdisCtr	NAS NMS	EDCO	Edison Control Corp
EDO	New York	EDO	EDO Corp
EdSault	NAS NMS	EDSE	Edison Sault Electric Co
Edward	New York	AGE	A.G. Edwards Inc
EECO	American	EEC	EECO Inc
EFIEle	NAS SL	EFIC	EFI Electronics Corp
EGG	New York	EGG	EG&G Inc
Egghead	NAS NL	EGGS	Egghead Inc
EglBnc	NAS NMS	EBCI	Eagle Bancorp Inc
EhrBbr	American	EB	Ehrlich Bober Financial Corp
EIL Inst	NAS NMS	EILI	E.I.L. Instruments Inc
EIP	NAS NMS	EIPM	EIP Microwave Inc
EKodk	New York	EK	Eastman Kodak Co
Elan	NAS NMS	ELANY	Elan Corp plc
Elbit	NAS NMS	ELBTF	Elbit Computers Ltd
ElCath	NAS NMS	ECTH	Electro-Catheter Corp
ElcDta	NAS NL	EDAT	Electronic Data Technologies
ElChic	NAS NMS	ELCH	El Chico Corp

NEWSPAPER ABBREV.	MARKET LISTING	TRADING SYMBOL	COMPANY NAME
Elcmd	NAS SL	ELMD	Electromedics Inc
Elco	NAS NMS	ELCN	Elco Industries Inc
Elcor	New York	ELK	Elcor Corp
Elcotel	NAS NMS	ECTL	Elcotel Inc
ElcRnt	NAS NMS	ELRC	Electro Rent Corp
ElcSci	NAS NMS	ESIO	Electro Scientific Industries Inc
ElcSens	NAS NMS	ELSE	Electro-Sensors Inc
ElctCtr	NAS SL	ELCS	Electronic Control Systems Inc
Elctmg	NAS NMS	ELMG	Electromagnetic Sciences Inc
ElctMis	NAS SL	ECIN	Electronics Missiles & Communications Inc
ElctSpc	NAS SL	GEMS	Electronic Specialty Products Inc
Elctsrc	NAS SL	ELSI	Electrosource Inc
ElDe El	NAS SL	ELOPF	El-De-Electro-Optic Developments Ltd
Eldec	NAS NMS	ELDC	Eldec Corp
Eldon	New York	ELD	Eldon Industries Inc
Eldorad	American	ELB	Eldorado Bancorp
EldrM	NAS SL	EDMC	ElDorado Motor Corp
ElecAs	New York	EA	Electronic Associates Inc
ElecSd	American	ESG	ElectroSound Group Inc
ElecTel	NAS NMS	ETCIA	Electronic Tele-Communications Inc (Class A)
EleNucl	NAS NMS	ENUC	Electro-Nucleonics Inc
Elexis	NAS NMS	ELEX	Elexis Corp
Elgin	New York	ENW	Elgin National Industries Inc
EliotSv	NAS NMS	EBKC	Eliot Savings Bank (Massachusetts)
EliSci	NAS SL	ELIS	Eli Scientific Inc
ElmrSv	NAS SL	ESBK	Elmira Savings Bank FSB
ElmwdFd	NAS NMS	EFSB	Elmwood Federal Savings Bank (Pennsylvania)
ElPas	NAS NMS	ELPA	El Paso Electric Co
ElPollo	NAS NMS	EPAI	El Pollo Asado Inc
ElronEl	NAS NMS	ELRNF	Elron Electronic Industries Ltd
Elscint	New York	ELT	Elscint Ltd
Elsinor	American	ELS	Elsinore Corp
Elswth	American	ECF	Ellsworth Convertible Growth & Income Fund Inc
EluxAB	NAS NMS	ELUXY	Electrolux AB (Class B)
ELXSI	NAS NMS	ELSX	ELXSI Corp
EMC	New York	EMC	EMC Corp
EMC In	NAS NMS	EMCI	EMC Insurance Group Inc
EmCar	American	EMP	Empire of Carolina Inc
EMCON	NAS NMS	MCON	EMCON Associates
Emhrt	New York	EMH	Emhart Corp
EmpCas	NAS NL	ECRC	Employers Casualty Co
EmpDs	New York	EDE	The Empire District Electric Co
EmpGs	NAS SL	EGCSC	Empire Gas Corp
EMPI	NAS NMS	EMPI	EMPI Inc

NEWSPAPER ABBREV.	MARKET LISTING	TRADING SYMBOL	COMPANY NAME
EmpirA	American	EOA	Empire of America Federal Savings Bank
EmpNa	New York	ELE	Empress Nacional de Electricidad sa
EmpOrr	NAS NMS	EORR	Empire-Orr Inc
EmpSB	NAS NMS	EMPR	Empire Savings Bank SLA (New Jersey)
EmRad	New York	EME	Emerson Radio Corp
Emrld	New York	EHP	Emerald Homes L.P.
EmrsE	New York	EMR	Emerson Electric Co
EmryA	New York	EAF	Emery Air Freight Corp
EMS Sy	NAS SL	EMSIF	EMS Systems Ltd
Emulex	NAS NMS	EMLX	Emulex Corp
EnAset	NAS SL	EAIC	Energy Assets International Corp
EnCap	NAS SL	ECDC	Energy Capital Development Corp
Encore	NAS NMS	ENCC	Encore Computer Corp
EncrM	American	EMI	Encore Marketing International Inc
Endvco	American	EI	Endevco Inc
EnDvl	American	EDP	Energy Development Partners Ltd
Energen	New York	EGN	Energen Corp
EnexR	NAS NMS	ENEX	ENEX Resources Corp
EngChn	NAS NMS	ECLAY	English China Clays Public Limited Co
EngCnv	NAS NMS	ENER	Energy Conversion Devices Inc
Engex	American	EGX	Engex Inc
EngGrh	NAS SL	EGPC	English Greenhouse Products Corp
EnglC	New York	EC	Engelhard Corp
EngMea	NAS NMS	EMCO	Engineering Measurements Co
EngnSu	NAS NMS	EAST	Engineered Support Systems Inc
Engnth	NAS NMS	ENNI	EnergyNorth Inc
Engrph	NAS NMS	ENGH	Engraph Inc
EnisBu	New York	EBF	Ennis Business Forms Inc
Enrgas	NAS NMS	EGAS	Energas Co
EnrOG	New York	ENG	Enron Oil & Gas Co
Enron	New York	ENE	Enron Corp
ENSCO	American	ESV	Energy Service Company Inc
Enscor	NAS NL	ENCRF	Enscor Inc
Enseco	NAS NMS	NCCO	Enseco Inc
EnsExp	New York	EP	Enserch Exploration Partners Ltd
ENSR	American	ENX	ENSR Corp
Ensrce	New York	EEE	Ensource Inc
Ensrch	New York	ENS	ENSERCH Corp
Entera	New York	EN	Enterra Corp
EntMkt	American	EM	Entertainment Marketing Inc
EntPub	NAS NMS	EPUB	Entertainment Publications Inc
EntrCpt	NAS NMS	ETRE	Entré Computer Centers Inc
EntreCp	NAS NMS	ETRC	Entree Corp
Entrnc	NAS NMS	ENTC	Entronics Corp
Entwist	NAS SL	ENTW	Entwistle Co
EnvCtl	NAS NMS	ECGI	Environmental Control Group Inc
EnvDia	NAS SL	EDIT	Environmental Diagnostics Inc
Envirsf	NAS NMS	ENVI	Envirosafe Services Inc

NEWSPAPER ABBREV.	MARKET LISTING	TRADING SYMBOL	COMPANY NAME
EnvPwr	NAS NMS	POWR	Environmental Power Corp
Envrd	NAS NMS	ENVR	Envirodyne Industries Inc
Envrpct	American	ENV	Enviropact Inc
Envrsur	NAS SL	ENVS	Envirosure Management Corp
EnvrTc	NAS NMS	ENVT	Environmental Tectonics Corp
EnvSys	New York	ESC	Environmental Systems Co
EnvTrt	New York	ETT	Environmental Treatment & Technologies Corp
EnzoBi	American	ENZ	Enzo Biochem Inc
Enzon	NAS NMS	ENZN	Enzon Inc
EpicHlt	NAS SL	EPIC	Epic Health Group Inc
Epitope	NAS SL	EPTO	Epitope Inc
Epsco	NAS NMS	EPSC	EPSCO Inc
Epsiln	NAS NMS	EPSI	Epsilon Data Management Inc
EqAm	NAS SL	ECOA	Equipment Company of America
EQK G	New York	EGA	EQK Green Acres L.P.
EQK Rt	New York	EKR	EQK Realty Investors I
EqtBcp	NAS NMS	EBNC	Equitable Bancorporation (Maryland)
EqtyBk	NAS SL	EQBK	Equity Bank (Connecticut)
EqtIA	NAS NL	EQICA	Equitable of Iowa Companies (Class A)
EqtIB	NAS NMS	EQICB	Equitable of Iowa Companies (Class B)
EqtOil	NAS NMS	EQTY	Equity Oil Co
EqtRes	New York	EQT	Equitable Resources Inc
EqtRl	New York	EQM	Equitable Real Estate Shopping Centers L.P.
Equifax	New York	EFX	Equifax Inc
Equimk	New York	EQK	Equimark Corp
Equion	NAS NMS	EQUI	The Equion Corp
Equitec	New York	EFG	Equitec Financial Group Inc
Equitex	NAS NMS	EQTX	Equitex Inc
Erbmnt	New York	ERB	Erbamont N.V.
ERC	New York	ERC	ERC International Inc
EricTl	NAS NMS	ERICY	LM Ericsson Telephone Co
ErlyInd	NAS NMS	ERLY	Erly Industries Inc
Ero	American	ERO	Ero Industries Inc
Escagn	American	ESN	Escagenitics Corp
Escalde	NAS NMS	ESCA	Escalade Inc
ESD	American	ESD	Engineered Systems & Development Corp
EsexCh	New York	ESX	Essex Chemical Corp
EsexCty	NAS NL	ECGC	Essex County Gas Co
ESI	American	ESI.A	ESI Industries Inc (Class A)
Espey	American	ESP	Espey Manufacturing & Electronics Corp
Esprit	American	ETI	Esprit Systems Inc
EsqRd	American	EE	Esquire Radio & Electronics Inc
EssBus	New York	ESB	Esselte Business Systems Inc
ESSEF	NAS NMS	ESSF	ESSEF Corp
Essex	NAS NMS	ESEX	Essex Corp
Estgp	American	EGP	EastGroup Properties

NEWSPAPER ABBREV.	MARKET LISTING	TRADING SYMBOL	COMPANY NAME
Estmaq	NAS NL	EMGVF	Eastmaque Gold Mines Ltd
EstnBc	NAS NMS	VFBK	Eastern Bancorp Inc
EstnCo	American	EML	The Eastern Co
EstnEn	NAS NMS	EESI	Eastern Environmental Services Inc
Estrlne	New York	ESL	Esterline Corp
Ethyl	New York	EY	Ethyl Corp
ETown	NAS NMS	EWAT	E'town Corp
EtzLav	American	ETZ	Etz Lavud Ltd
Eurocap	NAS SL	EURO	Eurocapital Corp
Evans	NAS NMS	EVAN	Evans Inc
Everex	NAS NMS	EVRX	Everex Systems Inc
EvnsFS	NAS NMS	EVSB	Evansville Federal Savings Bank
EvnSut	NAS NMS	ESCC	Evans & Sutherland Computer Corp
Evrgd	NAS NMS	EVGD	Evergood Products Inc
Evrgrn	NAS NMS	EVER	Evergreen Resources Inc
EvrJ A	American	EJ.A	Everest & Jennings International Ltd (Class A)
EvrJ B	American	EJ.B	Everest & Jennings International Ltd (Class B)
Exar	NAS NMS	EXAR	Exar Corp
Excel	American	EXC	Excel Industries Inc
EscelBc	NAS NMS	XCEL	Excel Bancorp Inc
Exceln	NAS NMS	EXLN	Excelan Inc
Excelsr	New York	EIS	Excelsior Income Shares Inc
ExchBc	NAS NMS	EXCG	Exchange Bancorp Inc
Exctne	NAS NMS	XTON	Executone Information Systems Inc
ExecTl	NAS SL	XTEL	Executive Telecommunications Inc
Exovir	NAS NMS	XOVR	Exovir Inc
ExpIn	NAS NMS	EXPD	Expeditors International of Washington Inc
ExpLa	NAS NMS	XCOL	The Exploration Company of Louisiana Inc
Explor	NAS SL	TXCO	Exploration Co
Exposc	NAS NMS	EXPO	Exposaic Industries Inc
Exxon	New York	XON	Exxon Corp
EZEM	NAS NMS	EZEM	E-Z-Em Inc
1stSrc	NAS NMS	SRCE	1st Source Corp
F&M	NAS NMS	FMFS	F&M Financial Services Corp
FabCtr	New York	FCA	Fabri-Centers of America Inc
FabInd	American	FIT	Fab Industries Inc
FABk A	NAS NMS	FIAMA	First American Bank & Trust of Palm Beach County (Class A) (Florida)
FABk B	NAS NL	FIAMB	First American Bank & Trust of Palm Beach County (Class B) (Florida)
Fabric	NAS NMS	FBRC	Fabricland Inc
FACant	NAS NMS	FASB	First American Savings Bank FSB (Ohio)
Fairchd	New York	FEN	Fairchild Industries Inc

NEWSPAPER ABBREV.	MARKET LISTING	TRADING SYMBOL	COMPANY NAME
Fairfd	New York	FCI	Fairfield Communities Inc
FairFst	NAS SL	FRBK	Fairfield 1st Bank & Trust Co
Fairhvn	NAS SL	NIMSY	Fairhaven International Ltd
FairIsc	NAS NMS	FICI	Fair, Isaac & Company Inc
FairNbl	NAS NMS	FARF	Fairfield-Noble Corp
FAlaBk	NAS NMS	FABC	First Alabama Bancshares Inc
FAlban	NAS NMS	FACT	First Albany Companies Inc
FalCbl	American	FAL	Falcon Cable Systems Company LP
FalcLt	NAS NL	FALCF	Falconbridge Ltd
FalcnPr	NAS SL	FLCP	Falcon Products Inc
FalcoOil	NAS NMS	FLOG	FalcoOil & Gas Company Inc
Falstaff	NAS NL	FALB	Fallstaff Brewing Corp
FamBc	NAS NMS	FMLY	Family Bancorp
FamDlr	New York	FDO	Family Dollar Stores Inc
FAmHlt	NAS SL	FAHC	First American Health Concepts Inc
Famigl	NAS SL	FAMI	Famiglia Brands Inc
FamRst	NAS NMS	FAMS	Famous Restaurants Inc
FamSt	NAS NMS	RYFL	Family Steak Houses of Florida Inc
Fanstel	New York	FNL	Fansteel Inc
FaradE	NAS NMS	FARA	Faradyne Electronics Corp
Farah	New York	FRA	Farah Manufacturing Company Inc
FarGp	NAS NMS	FGRP	Farmers Group Inc
Fargut	NAS NMS	FARR	Farragut Mortgage Co
FarHou	NAS NMS	FHFC	Farm House Foods Corp
FarmBr	NAS NMS	FARM	Farmer Brothers Co
FarmF	NAS NMS	FFSH	Farm Fresh Inc
FarmTel	NAS SL	FONE	Farmstead Telephone Group Inc
Farr	NAS NMS	FARC	Farr Co
FarWst	New York	FWF	Far West Financial Corp
Fastenl	NAS NMS	FAST	Fastenal Co
FAusPr	American	FAX	First Australia Prime Income Fund Inc
FayDrg	New York	FAY	Fay's Drug Company Inc
FB&T	NAS NL	FBTC	FB&T Corp
FBkPhl	NAS SL	FBKP	First Bank of Philadelphia
FBOh	NAS NMS	FBOH	First Bancorporation of Ohio
FBosIF	New York	FBF	First Boston Income Fund Inc
FBosSt	New York	FBI	First Boston Strategic Income Fund Inc
FBostn	New York	FBC	First Boston Inc
FBX	NAS NMS	FBXC	FBX Corp
FCapFn	NAS NMS	FCFI	First Capitol Financial Corp (Colorado)
FCapHd	New York	FCH	First Capital Holdings Corp
FCentn	NAS SL	FCLCA	First Centennial Corp (Class A)
FChart	NAS NMS	FCTR	First Charter Corp
FCmB	NAS NMS	FRFD	First Community Bancorp Inc (Illinois)
FCmBc	NAS NMS	FSCB	First Commercial Bancshares (Alabama)
FCmcl	NAS NMS	FCLR	First Commercial Corp (Arkansas)
FColB	NAS NMS	FCOLA	First Colonial Bankshares Corp (Class A) (Illinois)

NEWSPAPER ABBREV.	MARKET LISTING	TRADING SYMBOL	COMPANY NAME
FComB	NAS NMS	FCOB	First Commercial Bancorp (California)
FComC	NAS NMS	FCOM	First Commerce Corp (Lousiana)
FComrB	NAS NL	FCBI	First Commerce Bancshares Inc (Nebraska)
FCS	NAS SL	FCSI	FCS Labs Inc
FCtzBA	NAS NMS	FCNCA	First Citizens Bancshares Inc (Class A)
FCtzBB	NAS NMS	FCNCB	First Citizens Bancshares Inc (Class B)
FdlRsc	NAS SL	FDRC	Federal Resources Corp
FdMog	New York	FMO	Federal-Mogul Corp
FDP	NAS NMS	FDPC	FDP Corp
FdScrw	NAS NMS	FSCR	Federal Screw Works
FdSgnl	New York	FSS	Federal Signal Corp
FdSvBk	NAS NMS	TFSB	The Federal Savings Bank (Connecticut)
Feders	New York	FJQ	Fedders Corp
FedExp	New York	FDX	Federal Express Corp
FedlPB	New York	FBO	Federal Paper Board Company Inc
FedNM	New York	FNM	Federal National Mortgage Assn
FedNtl	NAS NL	FNRCB	Federated Natural Resources Corp (Class B)
FedRlty	New York	FRT	Federal Realty Investment Trust
FEmp	American	FES	First Empire State Corp
Feroflu	NAS NMS	FERO	Ferrofluidics Corp
Ferro	New York	FOE	Ferro Corp
FertGn	NAS SL	BABY	Fertility & Genetics Research Inc
Fertil	NAS SL	FRTL	Fertil-A-Chron Inc
FFArk	NAS NMS	FARK	First Federal Savings of Arkansas F.A.
FFB	New York	FFB	First Fidelity Bancorporation (New Jersey)
FFB Cp	NAS NMS	FFCT	FFB Corp
FFBcp	American	FFS	First Federal Bancorp Inc (Michigan)
FFColTn	NAS NL	FCTN	First Federal S&L Assn (Tennessee)
FFdAla	NAS NMS	FFSD	First Federal Savings Bank (Alabama)
FFdCD	NAS NMS	FCDA	First Federal S&L Assn of Coeur D'Alene
FFdChat	NAS NMS	FCHT	First Federal S&L Assn of Chattanooga
FFdChl	NAS NMS	FSCC	First Federal Savings Bank of Charlotte County (Florida)
FFdEH	NAS NMS	FFES	First Federal S&L Assn of East Hartford
FFdElz	NAS NMS	FFKY	First Federal Savings Bank of Elizabethtown (Kentucky)
FFdGa	NAS NMS	FSBG	First Federal Savings Bank of Georgia
FFdHar	NAS NMS	FFHP	First Federal S&L Assn of Harrisburg
FFdIndi	NAS NMS	FFMA	Fidelity Federal Savings Bank (Indiana)
FFdLaG	NAS NMS	FLAG	First Federal S&L Assn of LaGrange
FFdLen	NAS NMS	LFSA	First Federal S&L Assn of Lenawee County
FFdPR	NAS NMS	FFPR	First Federal Savings Bank of Puerto Rico

NEWSPAPER ABBREV.	MARKET LISTING	TRADING SYMBOL	COMPANY NAME
FFdTn	NAS NMS	FFOD	First Federal Savings Bank (Tennessee)
FFFtM	NAS NMS	FFMY	First Federal S&L Assn of Fort Myers
FFGtwn	NAS NL	FFGT	First Federal S&L Assn of Georgetown
FFidWV	NAS NMS	FFWV	First Fidelity Bancorp Inc (West Virginia)
FFinFd	New York	FF	First Financial Fund Inc
FFMic	NAS NMS	FFOM	First Federal of Michigan
FFMon	NAS NMS	FFSM	First Federal Savings Bank of Montana
FFncl	NAS NMS	FFBC	First Financial Bancorp (Ohio)
FFncPa	NAS NMS	FIRF	First Financial Savings Assn (Pennsylvania)
FFncrp	NAS NL	FIFC	First Fincorp Inc
FFnSL	NAS NMS	FEDF	Federated Financial S&L Assn (Wisconsin)
FFP	American	FFP	FFP Partners L.P.
FFWoos	NAS NMS	FFSW	First Federal S&L Assn of Wooser (Ohio)
FFWPa	NAS NMS	FFWP	First Federal of Western Pennsylvania
FFwst	NAS NMS	FFWS	First Farwest Corp
FGIC	New York	FGC	FGIC Corp
FHomF	NAS NMS	FSEB	First Home Federal S&L Assn (Florida)
FHP	NAS NMS	FHPC	FHP International Corp
Fibrbd	American	FBD	Fibreboard Corp
Fibronc	NAS NMS	FBRX	Fibronics International Inc
Fidata	American	FID	Fidata Corp
FidFTn	NAS NMS	FFTN	Fidelity Federal S&L Assn of Tennessee
FidlFn	American	FNF	Fidelity National Financial Inc
FidlMd	NAS SL	FMSI	Fidelity Medical Inc
FidSvA	NAS NL	FSVA	Fidelity Savings Assn
FifthT	NAS NMS	FITB	Fifth Third Bancorp (Ohio)
FiggieA	NAS NMS	FIGIA	Figgie International Holdings Inc (Class A)
FiggieB	NAS NMS	FIGIB	Figgie International Holdings Inc (Class B)
FileNet	NAS NMS	FILE	FileNet Corp
Filtrk	New York	FTK	The Filtertek Companies
Finalco	NAS SL	FLCO	Finalco Group Inc
FinCpA	New York	FIN	Financial Corporation of America
Fingmx	NAS NMS	FINX	Fingermatrix Inc
Finigan	NAS NMS	FNNG	Finnigan Corp
FInIowa	NAS NMS	FIIA	First Interstate of Iowa Inc
FinlInd	NAS NL	FNIN	Financial Industries Corp
FinNws	New York	FIF	Financial News Composite Fund Inc
FinNws	NAS NMS	FNNI	Financial News Network Inc
FInsWi	NAS NMS	FIWI	First Interstate Corporation of Wisconsin
FIntste	New York	I	First Interstate Bancorp
Finvst	New York	FVF	Finevest Foods Inc
Firecm	NAS SL	FRCM	Firecom Inc

NEWSPAPER ABBREV.	MARKET LISTING	TRADING SYMBOL	COMPANY NAME
FireFd	New York	FFC	Fireman's Fund Corp
Firster	NAS NMS	FRST	FirsTier Inc
Fischb	New York	FIS	Fischbach Corp
FischP	American	FP	Fischer & Porter Co
Fiserv	NAS NMS	FISV	FIserv Inc
FishBu	NAS SL	FBUS	Fisher Business Systems Inc
FishFd	New York	FHR	Fisher Foods Inc
FishSci	NAS NMS	FSHG	Fisher Scientific Group Inc
FishTrn	NAS NMS	FTSI	Fisher Transportation Services Inc
Fisons	NAS NL	FISNY	Fisons plc
FitcGE	American	FGE	Fitchburg Gas & Electric Light Co
FlaEC	New York	FLA	Florida East Coast Industries Inc
FlaEIns	NAS NMS	FLAEF	Florida Employers Insurance Co
FlaFdl	NAS NMS	FLFE	Florida Federal S&L Assn
FlaFst	NAS NMS	FFPC	Florida First Federal Savings Bank
Flagler	NAS NMS	FLGLA	Flagler Bank Corp (Class A)
Flamstr	NAS NMS	FAME	Flamemaster Corp
FlaNBF	NAS NMS	FNBF	Florida National Banks of Florida Inc
Flanign	American	QBDL	Flanigan's Enterprises Inc
FlaPrg	New York	FPC	Florida Progress Corp
FlaPU	NAS NMS	FPUT	Florida Public Utilities Co
FlaRck	NAS NMS	FRKT	Florida Rock & Tank Lines Inc
FlaRck	American	RFK	Florida Rock Industries Inc
Flare	NAS SL	FLAR	Flare Inc
FlaStl	New York	FLS	Florida Steel Corp
Fldcrst	New York	FLD	Fieldcrest Cannon Inc
FleetEn	New York	FLE	Fleetwood Enterprises Inc
Flemng	New York	FLM	Fleming Companies Inc
Flexstl	NAS NMS	FLXS	Flexsteel Industries Inc
Flextrn	NAS NMS	FLEX	Flextronics Inc
Flexwat	NAS SL	FWAT	Flexwatt Corp
FlghtIn	NAS NMS	FLTI	The Flight International Group Inc
FlghtSf	New York	FSI	FlightSafety International Inc
FlgtDy	NAS SL	FLYT	Flight Dynamics Inc
FLioA	NAS NMS	FDLNA	Food Lion Inc (Class A)
FLioB	NAS NMS	FDLNB	Food Lion Inc (Class B)
FloatPt	New York	FLP	Floating Point Systems Inc
Florafx	NAS SL	FIIF	Florafax International Inc
Flower	New York	FLO	Flowers Industries Inc
FlowSy	NAS NMS	FLOW	Flow Systems Inc
FltNors	New York	FLT	Fleet Norstar Financial Corp
Fluke	American	FKM	John Fluke Manufacturing Company Inc
Fluor	New York	FLR	Fluor Corp
Flurocb	NAS NMS	FCBN	The Flurocarbon Co
FlwGen	New York	FGN	Flow General Inc
Flwmle	NAS NL	MOLE	Flow Mole Corp
FM Nt	NAS NMS	FMNT	F&M National Corp
FMC	New York	FMC	FMC Corp

NEWSPAPER ABBREV.	MARKET LISTING	TRADING SYMBOL	COMPANY NAME
FMC G	New York	FGL	FMC Gold Co
FMCC	New York	FCX	Freeport-McMoRan Copper Co
FMdB	NAS NMS	FMDB	First Maryland Bancorp
FMEP	New York	FMP	Freeport-McMoRan Energy Partners Ltd
FMGC	New York	FAU	Freeport-McMoRan Gold Co
FMidB	NAS NMS	FMBI	First Midwest Bancorp Inc
FMOG	New York	FMR	Freeport-McMoRan Oil & Gas Royalty Trust
FMRP	New York	FRP	Freeport-McMoRan Resource Partners L.P.
FMWA	NAS NMS	FMSB	First Mutual Savings Bank (Washington)
FNB Cp	NAS NL	FBAN	F.N.B. Corp
FnBenA	NAS NL	FBGIA	Financial Benefit Group Inc (Class A)
FNBRo	NAS NMS	FNBR	FNB Rochester Corp
FNCinn	NAS NMS	FNAC	First National Cincinnati Corp
Fnd SVP	NAS SL	FSVP	Find SVP Inc
FNDela	NAS NMS	FTNC	First National Corp (Ohio)
FndrBk	NAS NL	FDBK	Founders Bank (Connecticut)
FNHB	NAS NMS	FINH	First NH Banks Inc
FnSBar	New York	FSB	Financial Corporation of Santa Barbara
FNtCal	American	FN	First National Corp (California)
FNtGa	NAS NMS	FBAC	First National Bancorp (Georgia)
FNthSL	NAS NMS	FNGB	First Northern S&L Assn (Wisconsin)
FnTrst	NAS NMS	FITC	Financial Trust Corp
FNW	NAS NMS	FNWB	FNW Bancorp Inc
FOhBn	NAS NMS	FIRO	First Ohio Bancshares Inc
Fonar	NAS NMS	FONR	FONAR Corp
Foodmk	New York	JIB	Foodmaker Inc
Foodrm	American	FSM	Foodarama Supermarkets Inc
FooteC	New York	FCB	Foote, Cone & Belding Communications Inc
ForAm	NAS NMS	FCOA	Foremost Corporation of America
ForBetr	NAS NL	FBTR	For Better Living Inc
FordCn	American	FC	Ford Motor Company of Canada Ltd
FordM	New York	F	Ford Motor Co
Forelnd	NAS SL	FORL	Foreland Corp
ForestO	NAS NMS	FOIL	Forest Oil Corp
Formc	New York	FOR	Formica Corp
Forsch	NAS NMS	FSNR	The Forschner Group Inc
ForstC A	American	FCE.A	Forest City Enterprises Inc (Class A)
ForstC B	American	FCE.B	Forest City Enterprises Inc (Class B)
ForstL	American	FRX	Forest Laboratories Inc
FortnF	NAS NMS	FORF	Fortune Financial Group Inc
Forum	NAS NMS	FOUR	Forum Group Inc
Foster	NAS NMS	FSTRA	L.B. Foster Co (Class A)
FostWh	New York	FWC	Foster Wheeler Corp
FountPw	NAS NMS	FPBT	Fountain Powerboat Industries Inc
Foxbro	New York	FOX	The Foxboro Co
Foxmor	NAS SL	FOXI	Foxmoor International Films Ltd

NEWSPAPER ABBREV.	MARKET LISTING	TRADING SYMBOL	COMPANY NAME
FPA	American	FPO	FPA Corp
FPeoFn	NAS NMS	FPNJ	First Peoples Financial Corp
FPL Gp	New York	FPL	FPL Group Inc
FramSv	NAS NMS	FSBX	Framingham Savings Bank (Massachusetts)
Franc	New York	FRN	The France Fund Inc
Franch	NAS SL	FICO	Franchiseit Corp
FranDn	NAS NMS	DNNY	The Frances Denney Companies Inc
FrdHly	American	FHO	Frederick's of Hollywood Inc
Fremnt	NAS NMS	FRMT	Fremont General Corp
FreqEl	American	FEI	Frequency Electronics Inc
FreSCn	NAS NL	FSCNY	Free State Consolidated Gold Mines Ltd
Fretter	NAS NMS	FTTR	Fretter Inc
Freym	NAS NMS	FRML	Freymiller Trucking Inc
Friedm	American	FRD	Friedman Industries Inc
FriesEn	American	FE	Fries Entertainment Inc
Frischs	American	FRS	Frisch's Restaurants Inc
FrJuce	NAS SL	FRSH	Fresh Juice Company Inc
FrkCon	NAS SL	FKCM	Franklin Consolidated Mining Company Inc
FrkCpt	NAS NMS	FDOS	Franklin Computer Corp
FrmCB	NAS NL	FFKT	Farmers Capital Bank Corp
FrmHm	NAS NMS	FAHS	Farm & Home Savings Assn (Missouri)
FrmRe	NAS NL	FORM	Forum Re Group Inc
FrnkEl	NAS NMS	FELE	Franklin Electric Company Inc
Frnkfd	NAS NMS	FKFD	The Frankford Corp
FrnkFst	NAS NMS	FFFC	Franklin First Financial Corp
Frnkln	American	FKL	The Franklin Corp
FrnkR	New York	BEN	Franklin Resources Inc
FrnkSL	NAS NMS	FSLA	Frank S&L Assn (Michigan)
FrnkSv	NAS NL	FSAK	Franklin Savings Assn (Kansas)
FrnkTl	NAS SL	FTCO	Franklin Telecommunications Corp
FrntTx	NAS SL	FRTX	Frontier Texas Corp
FrptMc	New York	FTX	Freeport-McMoRan Inc
Frstm	American	FST	Forstmann & Company Inc
FrthFn	NAS NMS	FRTH	Fourth Financial Corp
Frtne44	NAS SL	FORTA	Fortune 44 Co (Class A)
FrtrInc	NAS NMS	FRTR	Frontier Insurance Group Inc
FruhfB	New York	FTR.B	Fruehauf Corp (Class B)
FruitL	American	FTL	Fruit of the Loom Inc
FSecC	NAS NMS	FSCO	First Security Corp (Utah)
FSecF	NAS NMS	FSFC	First Security Financial Corp (North Carolina)
FSNM	NAS NMS	FSBC	First Savings Bank FSB (New Mexico)
FstAm	NAS NMS	FABK	First of America Bank Corp (Michigan)
FstbkIll	NAS NMS	FBIC	Firstbank of Illinois Co
FstChic	New York	FNB	First Chicago Corp
Fstcrp	American	FCR.A	Firstcorp Inc (Class A)
FstFd	American	FFA	FirstFed America Inc

NEWSPAPER ABBREV.	MARKET LISTING	TRADING SYMBOL	COMPANY NAME
FstFed	New York	FED	FirstFed Financial Corp
FstLI	NAS NL	FLIC	First of Long Island Corp
FstPa	New York	FPA	First Pennsylvania Corp
FstUC	New York	FTU	First Union Corp
FtABcp	NAS NMS	FAMB	1st American Bancorp (Massachusetts)
FtAFd	NAS NMS	FAMF	First AmFed Corp
FtAFn	NAS NMS	FAMR	The First American Financial Corp
FtAmar	NAS NMS	FAMA	First Amarillo Bancorporation Inc
FtAmCb	NAS SL	FATV	First American Cable Corp
FtAmSv	NAS NMS	FSAM	First American Savings F.A. (Pennsylvania)
FtATn	NAS NMS	FATN	First American Corp (Tennessee)
FtAust	American	IAF	The First Australia Fund Inc
FtBkSy	New York	FBS	First Bank System Inc
FtBNC	NAS NMS	FBNC	First Bancorp (North Carolina)
FtBnSc	NAS NMS	FBSI	First Banc Securities Inc
FtBTex	New York	FBT	First City Bankcorporation of Texas Inc
FtCapt	NAS NMS	FCAP	First Capital Corp
FtCarIn	NAS NL	FCAR	First Carolina Investors Inc
FtCity	New York	FCY	First City Industries Inc
FtCntrl	American	FCC	First Central Financial Corp
FtColFn	NAS NMS	FFCS	First Colorado Financial Corp
FtConn	American	FCO	The First Connecticut Small Business Investment Co
FtDear	New York	FTD	Fort Dearborn Income Securities Inc
FTenn	NAS NMS	FTEN	First Tennessee National Corp
FtEsex	NAS NMS	FESX	First Essex Bancorp Inc
FtEstn	NAS NMS	FEBC	First Eastern Corp (Pennsylvania)
FtExec	NAS NMS	FEXC	First Executive Corp
FtFAla	NAS NMS	FFAL	First Federal of Alabama FSB
FtFaml	NAS NMS	FFAM	First Family Group Inc
FtFdPry	NAS NL	FPRY	First Federal Savings Bank of Perry
FtFdSC	NAS NMS	FTSC	First Federal S&L Assn of South Carolina
FtFdTn	NAS NL	FTSB	First Federal Savings Bank of Tennessee
FtFKal	NAS NMS	FFKZ	First Federal S&L of Kalamazoo
FtFlBk	NAS NMS	FFBK	First Florida Banks Inc
FtFnCp	NAS NMS	FFHC	First Financial Corp (Wisconsin)
FtFnHd	NAS NMS	FFCH	First Financial Holdings Inc (West Virginia)
FtFnMg	NAS NMS	FFMC	First Financial Management Corp
FtFnSv	NAS NMS	FFNS	First Financial Savings Assn FA (Ohio)
FtFrnk	NAS NMS	FFHS	First Franklin Corp
FtGaHd	NAS NMS	FGSV	First Georgia Holding Corp
FrGoldn	NAS NMS	FGBC	First Golden Bancorporation
FtHaw	NAS NMS	FHWN	First Hawaiian Inc
FthillG	New York	FGI	The Foothill Group Inc
FtHmSv	NAS NMS	FSPG	First Home Savings Bank S.L.A. (New Jersey)

NEWSPAPER ABBREV.	MARKET LISTING	TRADING SYMBOL	COMPANY NAME
FtHowd	New York	FHP	Fort Howard Paper Co
FtIber	American	IBF	First Iberian Fund
FtIllCp	NAS NMS	FTIL	First Illinois Corp
FtIndi	NAS NMS	FISB	First Indiana Corp
FtLbty	NAS NMS	FLFC	First Liberty Financial Corp
FtMed	NAS SL	FMDC	First Medical Devices Corp
FtMich	NAS NMS	FMBC	First Michigan Bank Corp
FtMiss	New York	FRM	First Mississippi Corp
FtMiss	NAS NMS	FRMG	FirstMiss Gold Inc
FtNtlPa	NAS NMS	FNPC	First National Pennsylvania Corp
FtOak	NAS NMS	FOBBA	First Oak Brook Bancshares Inc (Class A)
FtRpBc	American	FRC	First Republic Bancorp Inc (California)
FtScKy	NAS NMS	FSKY	First Security Corporation of Kentucky
FtStFin	NAS NMS	FSFI	First State Financial Services Inc
FtSvBk	NAS NMS	FSBK	First Service Bank for Savings (Massachusetts)
FtTeam	NAS SL	FTSP	First Team Sports Inc
FtUtd	NAS NMS	UNTD	First United Bancshares Inc (Arkansas)
FtVaBk	New York	FVB	First Virginia Banks Inc
FtWach	New York	FW	First Wachovia Corp
FtWFn	NAS NMS	FWES	First Western Financial Corp
FtWisc	New York	FWB	First Wisconsin Corp
FtWomn	NAS NMS	FWNY	The First Women's Bank (New York)
FtWrld	NAS NL	FWCH	First World Cheese Inc
FtWyne	NAS NMS	FWNC	Fort Wayne National Corp
Fudrck	NAS NMS	FUDD	Fuddruckers Inc
FujiPh	NAS NL	FUJIY	Fuji Photo Film Company Ltd
FulrHB	NAS NMS	FULL	H.B. Fuller Co
FultFS	NAS NMS	FFSL	Fulton Federal S&L Assn of Atlanta
Fulton	NAS NMS	FULT	Fulton Financial Corp (Pennsylvania)
FUnRl	New York	FUR	First Union Real Estate Equity & Mortgage Investments
Fuqua	New York	FQA	Fuqua Industries Inc
FurrsB	New York	CAF	Furr's/Bishop's Cafeterias L.P.
FurVlt	American	FRV	The Fur Vault Inc
FutrSt	NAS SL	FSATE	Futuresat Industries Inc
FWobrn	NAS NMS	WOBS	First Woburn Bancorp Inc
FWymB	American	FWO	First Wyoming Bancorporation
G&K Sv	NAS NMS	GKSRA	G&K Services Inc (Class A)
Gabeli	New York	GAB	The Gabelli Equity Trust Inc
GaBnd	NAS NMS	GBFH	Georgia Bonded Fibers Inc
GAF	New York	GAF	GAF Corp
GaGulf	New York	GGC	Georgia Gulf Corp
Gainsco	American	GNA	Gainsco Inc
GAInv	New York	GAM	General American Investors Company Inc
Galac	NAS NMS	GALCF	Galactic Resources Ltd

NEWSPAPER ABBREV.	MARKET LISTING	TRADING SYMBOL	COMPANY NAME
GalaxC	American	GXY	Galaxy Carpet Mills Inc
Galgph	NAS SL	GALAF	Galagraph Ltd
GalHou	New York	GHX	Galveston-Houston Co
Galileo	NAS NMS	GAEO	Galileo Electro-Optics Corp
Gallagr	New York	AJG	Arthur J. Gallagher & Co
Galoob	New York	GAL	Lewis Galoob Toys Inc
GalvRs	NAS SL	GLVBF	Galveston Resources Ltd (Class B)
GalxCbl	American	GTV	Galaxy Cablevision L.P.
GamaB	NAS NMS	GAMA	Gamma Biologicals Inc
Gambro	NAS NL	GAMBY	Gambro AB
GAmCm	NAS NMS	GACC	Great American Communications Co
GamT	NAS NMS	GATI	Gaming & Technology Inc
Gander	NAS NMS	GNDR	Gander Mountain Inc
Gandlf	NAS NMS	GANDF	Gandalf Technologies Inc
Gannett	New York	GCI	Gannett Company Inc
Gantos	NAS NMS	GTOS	Gantos Inc
Gap	New York	GPS	The Gap Inc
GaPac	New York	GP	Georgia-Pacific Corp
Garan	American	GAN	Garan Inc
GardA	NAS NMS	GACO	Garden America Corp
Garnet	NAS NL	GARN	Garnet Resources Corp
Gatway	NAS NMS	GWAY	Gateway Communications Inc
GatwB	NAS NMS	GTWY	Gateway Bank (Connecticut)
GatwyFd	NAS NMS	GATW	Gateway Federal S&L Assn (Ohio)
GATX	New York	GMT	GATX Corp
GaylC	American	GCR	Gaylord Container Corp
GBC Bc	NAS NMS	GBCB	GBC Bancorp
GBI	NAS SL	GBII	GBI International Industries Inc
GBldPr	NAS NMS	GBLD	General Building Products Corp
GCA	New York	GCA	GCA Corp
GCda	American	GOC	Gulf Canada Corp
GCinm	New York	GCN	General Cinema Corp
GCtryB	NAS NMS	GCBK	Great Country Bank (Connecticut)
Gdrich	New York	GR	The B.F. Goodrich Co
Gearht	New York	GOI	Gearhart Industries Inc
GEICO	New York	GEC	GEICO Corp
GelmS	American	GSC	Gelman Sciences Inc
Gemco	American	GNL	GEMCO NATIONAL INC
GemTc	NAS SL	GMTIF	Gemini Technology Inc
GenCer	NAS NMS	GCER	General Ceramics INc
Gencor	NAS NMS	GCOR	Gencor Industries Inc
GenDev	New York	GDV	General Development Corp
GENDX	NAS NMS	XRAY	GENDEX Corp
GenEl	New York	GE	General Electric Co
GenesCp	NAS NL	GENBB	Genesee Corp (Class B)
Genetch	New York	GNE	Genentech Inc
GenetIn	NAS NMS	GENI	Genetics Institute Inc
Genex	NAS NMS	GNEX	Genex Corp

NEWSPAPER ABBREV.	MARKET LISTING	TRADING SYMBOL	COMPANY NAME
Genicm	NAS NMS	GECM	Genicom Corp
Genisco	American	GES	Genisco Technology Corp
Genlyte	NAS NMS	GLYT	Genlyte Group Inc
GenPrb	NAS NMS	GPRO	Gen-Probe Inc
GenRe	New York	GRN	General Re Corp
Gensco	New York	GCO	Genesco Inc
Gentex	NAS NMS	GNTX	Gentex Corp
GenuP	New York	GPC	Genuine Parts Co
GenvD	American	GDX	Genovese Drug Stores Inc
Genzym	NAS NMS	GENZ	Genzyme Corp
GEO	New York	GX	GEO International Corp
Geodme	NAS NL	GOEDF	Geodome Resources Ltd
GeodRs	NAS NMS	GEOD	Geodyne Resources Inc
Geodyn	NAS NMS	GDYN	Geodynamics Corp
Geonex	NAS NMS	GEOX	Geonex Corp
GeoRes	American	GEO	Geothermal Resources International Inc
GeoWsh	NAS NMS	GWSH	George Washington Corp
Geraght	NAS NMS	GMGW	Geraghty & Miller Inc
GerbPd	New York	GEB	Gerber Products Co
GerbSc	New York	GRB	Gerber Scientific Inc
GerFd	New York	GER	The Germany Fund Inc
GeriMd	NAS NMS	GEMC	Geriatric & Medical Centers Inc
GermF	NAS NMS	GMFD	Germania Bank FSB (Illinois)
Getty	New York	GTY	Getty Petroleum Corp
GF Cp	New York	GFB	GF Corp
GGInc	New York	GGF	Global Growth & Income Fund Inc
GIANT	New York	GPO	GIANT GROUP LTD
GiantF	American	GFS.A	Giant Food Inc (Class A)
GibCR	American	GIBS	C.R. Gibson Co
GibrFn	New York	GFC	Gibraltar Financial Corp
GibsnG	NAS NMS	GIBG	Gibson Greetings Inc
GigaTr	NAS NMS	GIGA	Giga-tronics Inc
GilbtA	NAS NMS	GILBA	Gilbert Associates Inc (Class A)
Gillete	New York	GS	The Gillette Co
GIncPl	New York	GLI	Global Income Plus Fund Inc
GishBi	NAS NMS	GISH	Gish Biomedical Inc
Glamis	NAS NMS	GLGVF	Glamis Gold Ltd
Glatflt	American	GLT	P.H. Glatfelter Co
Glaxo	New York	GLX	Glaxo Holdings p.l.c.
GlbGvt	New York	GOV	The Global Government Plus Fund Inc
GlbM	New York	GLM	Global Marine Inc
GldCoin	NAS SL	GLCN	Gold Coin Mining Inc
GldCorr	NAS NMS	GCRA	Golden Corral Realty Corp
GldCycl	NAS SL	GCGC	Golden Cycle Gold Corp
GldFld	American	GV	The Goldfield Corp
GldKngt	NAS NL	GKRVF	Golden Knight Resources Inc
Gldme	New York	GDM	Goldome
Gldnbel	NAS SL	GBLNF	Goldenbell Resources Inc

NEWSPAPER ABBREV.	MARKET LISTING	TRADING SYMBOL	COMPANY NAME
GldNth	NAS SL	GNOXF	Golden North Resource Corp
GldNug	New York	GNG	Golden Nugget Inc
GldnVly	NAS NMS	GVMF	Golden Valley Microwave Foods Inc
GldPoul	NAS NMS	CHIK	Golden Poultry Company Inc
GldStd	NAS SL	GSTD	Gold Standard Inc
GldWF	New York	GDW	Golden West Financial Corp
GleasC	New York	GLE	Gleason Corp
Glenex	NAS NMS	GLXIF	Glenex Industries Inc
Glenfed	New York	GLN	GLENFED Inc
GlfApld	NAS NMS	GATS	Gulf Applied Technologies Inc
GlfStUt	New York	GSU	Gulf States Utilities Co
GlfWst	New York	GW	Gulf + Western Inc
Glnmr	American	GDS.B	Glenmore Distilleries Co (Class B)
GlobNR	American	GNR	Global Natural Resources Inc
GlobYld	New York	PGY	The Global Yield Fund Inc
GlxyCh	NAS SL	GALX	Galaxy Cheese Co
GM E	New York	GME	General Motors Class E Common Stock
GM H	New York	GMH	General Motors Class H Common Stock
GMI	NAS NMS	GMED	The GMI Group Inc
GMot	New York	GM	General Motors Corp
GMP	New York	GMP	Green Mountain Power Corp
GnAuto	American	GA	General Automation Inc
GnBnd	NAS NMS	GBND	General Binding Corp
GNC	New York	GNC	General Nutrition Inc
GnCpt	NAS NMS	GCCC	General Computer Corp
GnCrp	New York	GY	GenCorp Inc
GnData	New York	GDC	General DataComm Industries Inc
GnDvcs	NAS SL	GDIC	General Devices Inc
GnDyn	New York	GD	General Dynamics Corp
GnEmp	American	JOB	General Employment Enterprises Inc
GnEngy	New York	GED	General Energy Development Ltd
GnHme	New York	GHO	General Homes Corp
GnHost	New York	GH	General Host Corp
GnHous	New York	GHW	General Housewares Corp
GnInst	New York	GRL	General Instrument Corp
GNIrn	New York	GNI	Great Northern Iron Ore Properties
GnKinet	NAS NL	GKIE	General Kinetics Inc
GnMag	NAS NMS	GMCC	General Magnaplate Corp
GnMicr	American	GMW	General Microwave Corp
GnMills	New York	GIS	General Mills Inc
GnPara	NAS NMS	GPAR	General Parametrics Corp
GnRad	New York	GEN	GenRad Inc
GnRefr	New York	GRX	General Refractories Co
GnSci	NAS NL	GSCX	General Sciences Corp
GnSignl	New York	GSX	General Signal Corp
GntYl	American	GYK	Giant Yellowknife Mines Ltd
GoldEn	NAS NMS	GLDC	Golden Enterprises Inc
GoldEx	NAS SL	GDEX	Gold Express Corp

NEWSPAPER ABBREV.	MARKET LISTING	TRADING SYMBOL	COMPANY NAME
GoldFd	NAS NL	GLDFY	Gold Fields of South Africa Ltd
GoldK	NAS SL	GKCI	Gold King Consolidated Inc
GoldRs	NAS SL	GLDR	Gold Reserve Corp
GoldT	NAS SL	GTRO	Golden Triangle Royalty & Oil Inc
GoodGy	NAS NMS	GGUY	The Good Guys Inc
Goodht	NAS SL	GWOX	Goodheart Willcox Inc
Goodmk	NAS NMS	GDMK	GoodMark Foods Inc
Goody	NAS NMS	GOOD	Goody Products Inc
Goodyr	New York	GT	The Goodyear Tire & Rubber Co
Gordex	NAS SL	GXMNF	Gordex Minerals Ltd
GordnJ	New York	GOR	Gordon Jewelry Corp
GorRup	American	GRC	The Gorman-Rupp Co
Gotaas	NAS NMS	GOTLF	Gotaas-Larsen Shipping Corp
Gotchk	New York	GOT	Gottschalks Inc
Gould	New York	GLD	Gould Inc
GouldP	NAS NMS	GULD	Goulds Pumps Inc
GoVide	NAS SL	GOVO	Go Video Inc
GphPck	NAS NMS	GPAK	Graphic Packaging Corp
GPU	New York	GPU	General Public Utilities Corp
Grace	New York	GRA	W.R. Grace & Co
Graco	New York	GGG	Graco Inc
Gradco	NAS NMS	GRCO	Gradco Systems Inc
Graham	American	GHM	Graham Corp
GrahMc	American	GOP	Graham-McCormick Oil & Gas Partnership
Graingr	New York	GWW	W.W. Grainger Inc
GranC	NAS NMS	GNTE	Granite Co-Operative Bank
Grang	American	GXL	Granges Exploration Ltd
GrantSt	NAS NMS	GSBI	Granite State Bankshares Inc (New Hampshire)
GrdnB	American	GB	Guardian Bancorp
GrdPrd	New York	GPI	Guardsman Products Inc
Grdwtr	NAS NMS	GWTI	Groundwater Technology Inc
Green	NAS NMS	APGI	A.P. Green Industries Inc
Greiner	American	GII	Greiner Engineering Inc
GrenTr	New York	GNT	Green Tree Acceptance Inc
Grenm	American	GMN	Greenman Brothers Inc
GreyAd	NAS NMS	GREY	Grey Advertising Inc
Greyh	New York	G	The Greyhound Corp
GrhmFld	American	GFI	Graham Field Health Products Inc
GRI	American	GRR	G·R·I Corp
Grifith	NAS NL	FUEL	Griffith Consumers Co
GrifTch	NAS NMS	GRIF	Griffin Technology Inc
Grist	NAS NMS	GRST	Grist Mill Co
GrMonk	NAS SL	GMHC	Grease Monkey Holding Corp
GrmSv	NAS NMS	GSBK	Germantown Savings Bank (Pennsylvania)
GrncsSv	NAS NL	GRFS	Greencastle Federal Savings Bank
GrndAu	American	GAI	Grand Auto Inc
GrndSu	NAS NMS	GSSC	Grenada Sunburst System Corp

NEWSPAPER ABBREV.	MARKET LISTING	TRADING SYMBOL	COMPANY NAME
GrnRhb	NAS NMS	GRGI	Greenery Rehabilitation Group Inc
GrntrSft	NAS SL	GTSW	Greentree Software Inc
GrnwcFn	NAS NMS	GFCT	Greenwich Financial Corp
GrnwPh	NAS NMS	GRPI	Greenwich Pharmaceuticals Inc
Groff	NAS NMS	GROF	Groff Industries Inc
Grosmn	NAS NMS	GROS	Grossman's Inc
Group1	NAS NMS	GSOF	Group 1 Software Inc
GroveB	NAS NMS	GROV	GroveBank for Savings
GrowGp	New York	GRO	Grow Group Inc
GrowVn	NAS SL	GPAX	Grow Ventures Corp
GrphI	NAS NMS	GRPH	Graphic Industries Inc
GrphSc	NAS NMS	GSCC	Graphic Scanning Corp
GrtBay	NAS NMS	GBBS	Great Bay Bankshares Inc
GrTch	American	GRT	Graphic Technology Inc
GrtLkC	New York	GLK	Great Lakes Chemical Corp
GrubEl	New York	GBE	Grubb & Ellis Co
GrubER	NAS NMS	GRIT	Grubb & Ellis Realty Income Trust
Gruen	American	GMC	Gruen Marketing Corp
Grumn	New York	GQ	Grumman Corp
GtAFst	New York	GTA	Great American First Savings Bank
GtAmCp	NAS NMS	GTAM	Great American Corp
GtAMg	NAS NL	GAMI	Great American Management & Investment Inc
GtAmR	NAS NMS	GRAR	Great American Recreation Inc
GtAtPc	New York	GAP	The Great Atlantic & Pacific Tea Company Inc
GtBay	NAS NMS	GPPXF	Giant Bay Resources Ltd
GTE	New York	GTE	GTE Corp
Gtech	NAS NMS	GTCH	GTECH Corp
GtFalls	NAS NMS	GFGC	Great Falls Gas Co
GthStk	New York	GSO	Growth Stock Outlook Trust Inc
GTI	American	GTI	GTI Corp
GtLkBc	NAS NMS	GLBC	Great Lakes Bancorp FSB (Michigan)
GtNNk	New York	GNN	Great Northern Nekoosa Corp
GtNYSv	NAS NMS	GRTR	Greater New York Savings Bank
GTS	NAS NMS	GTSC	GTS Corp
GtSoFd	NAS NMS	GRBC	Great Southern Federal Savings Bank
GtWash	American	GWI	Greater Washington Investors Inc
GtwBcp	NAS NMS	GBAN	Gateway Bancorp Inc (New York)
GtWFn	New York	GWF	Great Western Financial Corp
GuarBn	NAS NL	GBNC	Guaranty Bancshares Corp
GuarNt	NAS NMS	GNIC	Guaranty National Corp
GuestS	NAS NMS	GEST	Guest Supply Inc
GuldLP	American	GLP	Gould Investors L.P.
Gulfrd	New York	GFD	Guilford Mills Inc
GulfRs	New York	GRE	Gulf Resources & Chemical Corp
GullLb	NAS NL	GULL	Gull Laboratories Inc
Gundle	American	GUN	Gundle Environmental Systems Inc

NEWSPAPER ABBREV.	MARKET LISTING	TRADING SYMBOL	COMPANY NAME
GV Med	NAS NMS	GVMI	GV Medical Inc
GW Ut	American	GWT	GW Utilities Ltd
GWC	NAS NMS	GWCC	GWC Corp
Gyrody	NAS SL	GYRO	Gyrodyne Company of America Inc
Haber	NAS NMS	HABE	Haber Inc
Hach	NAS NMS	HACH	Hach Co
Hadco	NAS NMS	HDCO	HADCO Corp
Hadron	NAS SL	HDRN	Hadron Inc
Hadson	New York	HAD	Hadson Corp
Hako	NAS NMS	HAKO	Hako Minuteman Inc
HAL	American	HA	HAL Inc
Halbtn	New York	HAL	Halliburton Co
Halifax	American	HX	Halifax Engineering Inc
HallFB	New York	FBH	Frank B. Hall & Company Inc
HallFn	NAS NMS	HALL	Hall Financial Group Inc
Halmi	American	RHI	Robert Halmi Inc
Halsey	NAS SL	HADR	Halsey Drug Co
Halwod	New York	HWG	The Hallwood Group Inc
Hamnd	NAS NMS	THCO	Hammond Co
HamOil	NAS NMS	HAML	Hamilton Oil Corp
HampBn	NAS NMS	HBSI	Hamptons Bancshares Inc
HampH	American	HHI	Hampton Healthcare Inc
HamptI	American	HAI	Hampton Industries Inc
HanaBi	NAS NMS	HANA	Hana Biologics Inc
Handlm	New York	HDL	Handleman Co
HanFb	New York	HKF	Hancock Fabrics Inc
Hanfrd	New York	HRD	Hannaford Brothers Co
HandH	New York	HNH	Handy & Harman
HanJI	New York	JHI	John Hancock Investors Trust
HanJS	New York	JHS	John Hancock Income Securities Trust
Hanna	New York	HNM	M.A. Hanna Co
Hanson	New York	HAN	Hanson Trust PLC
HarBrJ	New York	HBJ	Harcourt Brace Jovanovich Inc
Harcor	NAS SL	HARC	HarCor Energy Co
HarisHa	NAS NMS	HHGP	Harris & Harris Group Inc
Harken	NAS NMS	HOGI	Harken Oil & Gas Inc
Harley	New York	HDI	Harley-Davidson Inc
Harleys	NAS NMS	HGIC	Harleysville Group Inc
Harlnd	New York	JH	The John H. Harland Co
Harlyn	NAS NMS	HRJN	Harlyn Products Inc
HarlyNt	NAS NMS	HNBC	Harleysville National Corp
HarlySv	NAS NMS	HARL	Harleysville Savings Assn (Pennsylvania)
Harman	New York	HAR	Harman International Industries Inc
Harmon	NAS NMS	HRMN	Harmon Industries Inc
Harnish	New York	HPH	Harnischfeger Industries Inc
Harold	NAS NMS	HRLD	Harold's Stores Inc

NEWSPAPER ABBREV.	MARKET LISTING	TRADING SYMBOL	COMPANY NAME
HarpG	NAS NMS	HARG	The Harper Group Inc
Harris	New York	HRS	Harris Corp
Harsco	New York	HSC	Harsco Corp
HartInd	NAS SL	HRTI	Hart Industries Inc
Hartmx	New York	HMX	Hartmarx Corp
Harvey	American	HRA	The Harvey Group Inc
HarvIn	NAS NMS	HAVA	Harvard Industries Inc
HarvKn	NAS NMS	HVDK	Harvard Knitwear Inc
Hasbr	American	HAS	Hasbro Inc
Hasting	American	HMF	Hastings Manufacturing Co
Hathw	NAS NMS	HATH	Hathaway Corp
HattSe	New York	HAT	Hatteras Income Securities Inc
Hauser	NAS NMS	HASR	Hauserman Inc
HavFuA	NAS NMS	HAVTA	Haverty Furniture Companies Inc (Class A)
Havrty	NAS NMS	HAVT	Haverty Furniture Companies Inc
HawEl	New York	HE	Hawaiian Electric Industries Inc
HawkB	NAS NMS	HWKB	Hawkeye Bancorporation (Class B)
HawkC	NAS NMS	HWKC	Hawkeye Bancorporation (Class C)
HawkEn	NAS SL	SBIZ	Hawkeye Entertainment Inc
HaywdS	NAS NL	HWNC	Haywood S&L Assn
HBNJ	NAS NMS	HWRD	The Howard Savings Bank (New Jersey)
HBO	NAS NMS	HBOC	HBO & Co
HCA	New York	HCA	Hospital Care Corporation of America
HCC	NAS NMS	HCCI	HCC Industries Inc
HchgA	NAS NMS	HECHA	Hechinger Co (Class A)
HchgB	NAS NMS	HECHB	Hechinger Co (Class B)
HDR	NAS NMS	HDRP	HDR Power Systems Inc
HE Ven	NAS SL	HEVN	HE Ventures Inc
HeartF	NAS NMS	HFED	Heart Federal S&L Assn (California)
Hecks	New York	HEX	Heck's Inc
HeclaM	New York	HL	Hecla Mining Co
Heekin	NAS NMS	HEKN	Heekin Can Inc
HEI Mn	NAS NMS	HEII	HEI Inc (Minnesota)
HEI Tx	NAS NMS	HEIC	HEI Corp (Texas)
Heico	American	HEI	HEICO Corp
Heilig	New York	HMY	Heilig-Meyers Co
HeinWr	American	HNW	Hein-Werner Corp
Heinz	New York	HNZ	H.J. Heinz Co
HeistC	NAS NMS	CHHC	C.H. Heist Corp
Heldor	American	HDR	Heldor Industries Inc
HelenT	NAS NMS	HELE	Helen of Troy Corp
Helix	NAS NMS	HELX	Helix Technology Corp
HelmP	New York	HP	Helmerich & Payne Inc
HelmR	American	H	HelmResources Inc
HelneC	New York	HC	Helene Curtis Industries Inc
HelthM	American	HMI	Health-Mor Inc
Helvet	New York	SWZ	The Helvetia Fund Inc

NEWSPAPER ABBREV.	MARKET LISTING	TRADING SYMBOL	COMPANY NAME
HemaC	NAS SL	HEMA	HemaCare Corp
HemDv	NAS SL	HSDMF	Hemisphere Development Ltd
Hemody	NAS SL	HMDY	Hemodynamics Inc
Hemtec	NAS NMS	HEMO	HemoTec Inc
Henley	NAS NMS	HENG	The Henley Group Inc
HenlMf	NAS NMS	HNCO	Henley Manufacturing Corp
Herblfe	NAS NL	HERB	Herbalife International Inc
Herculs	New York	HPC	Hercules Inc
HeritEn	American	HHH	Heritage Entertainment Inc
HeritFn	NAS NL	HFHC	Heritage Financial Corp
Herley	NAS NMS	HRLY	Herley Microwave Systems Inc
HershO	American	HSO	Hershey Oil Corp
HewlPk	New York	HWP	Hewlett-Packard Co
Hexcel	New York	HXL	Hexcel Corp
HFdGa	NAS NMS	HFGA	Home Federal Savings Bank of Georgia
HFdInd	NAS NMS	HOMF	Home Federal Savings Bank (Indiana)
HFdNC	NAS NL	HFSA	Home Federal Savings Bank (North Carolina)
HFMd	NAS NMS	HFMD	Home Federal Corp (Maryland)
HghHm	NAS NMS	HUHO	Hughes Homes Inc
HghRes	NAS SL	HIRS	High Resolution Sciences Inc
HHB Sy	NAS NMS	HHBX	HHB Systems Inc
HHOilT	NAS NMS	HHOT	H&H Oil Tool Company Inc
Hi-Prt	NAS NMS	HIPT	Hi-Port Industries Inc
Hiber	NAS NMS	HIBCA	Hibernia Corp (Class A)
HiberSv	NAS NMS	HSBK	The Hibernia Savings Bank (Massachusetts)
Hickam	NAS NMS	DBHI	Dow B. Hickam Inc
Higbys	NAS NMS	HIGB	J. Higby's Inc
HighSu	NAS NMS	HIGH	Highland Superstores Inc
Highvld	NAS NL	HSVLY	Highveld Steel & Vanadium Corporation Ltd
Highwd	NAS NMS	HIWDF	Highwood Resources Ltd
HiInco	New York	YLD	High Income Advantage Trust
HilbRg	NAS NMS	HRHC	Hilb, Rogal & Hamilton Co
HillDp	New York	HDS	Hills Department Stores Inc
Hillnbd	New York	HB	Hillenbrand Industries Inc
Hilton	New York	HLT	Hilton Hotels Corp
Himont	New York	HMT	HIMONT Inc
Hindrl	American	HND	Hinderliter Industries Inc
HiPlain	NAS NL	HIPC	High Plains Corp
Hiptron	American	HIP	Hipotronics Inc
HiShear	New York	HSI	Hi-Shear Industries Inc
Hitachi	New York	HIT	Hitachi Ltd
HitchE	NAS SL	THEX	Hitech Engineering Co
HITK	NAS NMS	HITK	HITK Corp
HiYld	New York	HYI	The High Yield Income Fund Inc
HiYldPl	New York	HYP	High Yield Plus Fund Inc

NEWSPAPER ABBREV.	MARKET LISTING	TRADING SYMBOL	COMPANY NAME
HldyRV	NAS NL	RVEE	Holiday RV Superstores Inc
HlI	American	HII.A	Healthcare International Inc (Class A)
HltcrS	NAS NMS	HSAI	Healthcare Services of America Inc
HlthCh	American	HCH	Health-Chem Corp
HlthCo	NAS NMS	HCCC	HealthCare COMPARE Corp
Hlthco	NAS NMS	HLCO	Healthco International Inc
HlthCP	New York	HCP	Health Care Property Investors Inc
HlthCr	American	HCN	Health Care REIT Inc
HlthCS	NAS NMS	HCSG	Healthcare Services Group Inc
Hlthdyn	NAS NMS	HDYN	Healthdyne Inc
HlthIns	NAS NMS	HIVT	Health Insurance of Vermont Inc
HlthMn	American	HMA	Health Management Associates Inc
Hlthwc	NAS SL	HEAL	Healthwatch Inc
HltImg	NAS NMS	HIMG	Health Images Inc
HltRhb	New York	HRP	Health & Rehabilitation Properties Trust
HltsthR	NAS NMS	HSRC	HEALTHSOUTH Rehabilitation Corp
Hltvst	American	HVT	HealthVest
HlwdPk	NAS NL	HTRFZ	Hollywood Park Realty Enterprises Inc
HmBen	NAS NMS	HBENB	Home Beneficial Corp (Class B)
HmeCty	NAS NMS	HCSB	Home & City Savings Bank (New York)
HmeD	New York	HD	The Home Depot Inc
HmeGp	New York	HME	The Home Group Inc
HmeSav	NAS NMS	HMSB	The Home Savings Bank (New York)
HmFB	New York	HFL.B	Homestead Financial Corp (Class B)
HmFChr	NAS NL	HFSB	Home Federal Savings Bank (South Carolina)
HmFNO	NAS NMS	HFNO	Home Federal Savings Bank, Northern Ohio
HmFRk	NAS NMS	HROK	Home Federal S&L Assn of the Rockies
HmFSD	New York	HFD	Home Federal S&L Assn (California)
HmFSF	NAS NMS	HFSF	Home Federal S&L Assn of San Francisco
HmFTn	NAS NMS	HFET	Home Federal S&L Assn of Upper East Tennessee
HmFXn	NAS NMS	HFOX	Home Federal Savings Bank (Ohio)
HMG	American	HMG	HMG Property Investors Inc
HmInt	NAS NMS	KDNY	Home Intensive Care Inc
HmNtl	NAS NL	HNCP	Home National Corp
HMO	NAS NMS	HMOA	HMO American Inc
HmowG	NAS NL	HOMG	Homeowners Group Inc
HmPrt	NAS NMS	HPBC	Home Port Bancorp Inc
HmpU	American	HU	Hampton Utilities Trust
HMSS	NAS NMS	HMSS	H.M.S.S. Inc
HmstdS	NAS NMS	HMSD	Homestead Savings Assn (Pennsylvania)
HmstF	New York	HFL	Homestead Financial Corp
Hmstke	New York	HM	Homestake Mining Co
HmSvPa	NAS NMS	HSPA	Home Savings Association of Pennsylvania

NEWSPAPER ABBREV.	MARKET LISTING	TRADING SYMBOL	COMPANY NAME
HmtwBc	NAS SL	HTWN	Hometown Bancorporation
HneLu	NAS NL	HINE	Edward Hines Lumber Co
HnryJk	NAS NMS	JKHY	Jack Henry & Associates Inc
HntgnIn	NAS NMS	HRCLY	Huntingdon International Holdings pcl
Hodgsn	NAS SL	HDGH	Hodgson Houses Inc
Hofman	American	HOF	Hofmann Industries Inc
Hogan	NAS NMS	HOGN	Hogan Systems Inc
Holco	American	HOL.A	Holco Mortgage Acceptance Corp-1 (Class A)
Holidy	New York	HIA	Holiday Corp
HollyCp	American	HOC	Holly Corp
HollyFa	New York	HFF	Holly Farms Corp
HolmD	NAS NMS	HLME	D.H. Holmes Company Ltd
HomeSh	American	HSN	Home Shopping Network Inc
HomeSL	NAS NMS	HSLD	Home S&L Assn Inc (North Carolina)
Honda	New York	HMC	Honda Motor Company Ltd
HonInd	NAS NMS	HONI	HON INDUSTRIES Inc
Honwell	New York	HON	Honeywell Inc
Honybe	American	HBE	Honeybee Inc
HoopHl	American	HH	Hooper Holmes Inc
HoprSol	New York	HS	Hopper Soliday Corp
Horizon	New York	HZN	Horizon Corp
HORL	NAS NMS	HORL	Home Office Reference Laboratory Inc
Hormel	American	HRL	George A. Hormel & Co
Hornbk	NAS SL	HOSS	Hornbeck Offshore Services Inc
HorzInd	NAS NMS	HRZN	Horizon Industries Inc
HospNw	NAS NL	HNGI	Hospital Newspapers Group Inc
Hospos	NAS NMS	HOSP	Hosposable Products Inc
HospSt	NAS NMS	HSSI	Hospital Staffing Services Inc
HotlInv	New York	HOT	Hotel Investors Trust/Corporation
HouFab	New York	HF	House of Fabrics Inc
HougM	New York	HTN	Houghton Mifflin Co
HouInd	New York	HOU	Houston Industries Inc
HouOR	New York	RTH	Houston Oil Royalty Trust
HouOT	American	HO	Houston Oil Trust
HousInt	New York	HI	Household International Inc
HovnE	American	HOV	Hovnanian Enterprises Inc
HoweRh	American	HRI	Howe Richardson Inc
HowlCp	New York	HWL	Howell Corp
HowlIn	American	HOW	Howell Industries Inc
Howtk	American	HTK	Howtek Inc
HPSC	NAS NMS	HPSC	HPSC Inc
HQ Hlt	New York	HQH	H&Q Healthcare Investors
HrdgAs	NAS NMS	HRDG	Harding Associates Inc
HrdRk	American	HRK	Hard Rock Cafe plc
HRE	New York	HRE	HRE Properties
HRI Gp	NAS NMS	HRIGV	HRI Group Inc
HrnHar	American	HOR	The Horn & Hardart Co

NEWSPAPER ABBREV.	MARKET LISTING	TRADING SYMBOL	COMPANY NAME
Hrshey	New York	HSY	Hershey Foods Corp
HrtfdS	NAS NMS	HBOL	Hartford Steam Boiler Inspection & Insurance Co
HrtFSv	NAS NMS	HERS	Heritage Financial Services Inc
HrtgBc	NAS NMS	HNIS	Heritage Bancorp Inc (Massachusetts)
Hrtlnd	NAS NMS	HTLD	Heartland Express Inc
HrvdSc	NAS NMS	HARVY	Harvard Securities Group PLC
HrzBk	NAS NMS	HRZB	Horizon Bank, A Savings Bank (Washington)
HrzGld	NAS SL	HRIZ	Horizon Gold Shares Inc
HrzHlt	New York	HHC	Horizon Healthcare Corp
HrznFn	NAS NMS	HFIN	Horizon Financial Services Inc
HtgMd	American	HTG.A	Heritage Media Corp (Class A)
HUBCO	American	HCO	HUBCO Inc
HubelA	American	HUB.A	Hubbell Inc (Class A)
HubelB	American	HUB.B	Hubbell Inc (Class B)
HudFd	American	HFI	Hudson Foods Inc
HudGn	American	HGC	Hudson General Corp
Huffy	New York	HUF	Huffy Corp
HufKoo	NAS NMS	HUFK	Huffman Koos Inc
HughSp	New York	HUG	Hughes Supply Inc
Human	New York	HUM	Humana Inc
HuntEn	NAS NL	HESI	Hunter Environmental Services Inc
HuntgB	NAS NMS	HBAN	Huntington Bancshares Inc
HuntJB	NAS NMS	JBHT	J.B. Hunt Transportation Services Inc
HuntM	New York	HUN	Hunt Manufacturing Co
HuntMl	NAS NMS	HRMR	Hunter-Melnor Inc
Hurco	NAS NMS	HURC	Hurco Companies Inc
HUSB	NAS NMS	HUSB	Home Unity S&L Assn (Pennsylvania)
HutchT	NAS NMS	HTCH	Hutchinson Technology Inc
HuttEF	New York	EFH	The E.F. Hutton Group Inc
HWC	NAS NMS	HWCD	HWC Distribution Corp
HwrdB	NAS NMS	HOBC	Howard Bancorp
Hycor	NAS SL	HYBD	Hycor Biomedical Inc
HydeAt	NAS NMS	HYDE	Hyde Athletic Industries Inc
HydFlm	NAS SL	HFLM	Hydro Flame Corp
Hydral	New York	THC	The Hydraulic Co
Hyponx	NAS NMS	HYPX	Hyponex Corp
HytekM	NAS NMS	HTEK	Hytek Microsystems Inc
IBI	NAS NMS	IBISA	IBI Security Services Inc (Class A)
IBM	New York	IBM	International Business Machines Corp
IBP	New York	IBP	IBP Inc
IBS	NAS SL	IBSTF	IBS Technologies Ltd
IC Ind	New York	ICX	IC Industries Inc
ICA	New York	ICA	Imperial Corporation of America
ICEE	American	ICY	ICEE-USA
ICH	American	ICH	I.C.H. Corp

NEWSPAPER ABBREV.	MARKET LISTING	TRADING SYMBOL	COMPANY NAME
ICM	New York	ICM	ICM Property Investors Inc
ICN Bio	American	BIM	ICN Biomedicals Inc
ICN Ph	New York	ICN	ICN Pharmaceuticals Inc
Icot	NAS NMS	ICOT	ICOT Corp
ICP	NAS NMS	ICPYY	The Institute of Clinical Pharmacology PLC
IdahoP	New York	IDA	Idaho Power Co
IDB	NAS SL	IDBBY	IDB Bankholding Corporation Ltd
IDB Cm	NAS NMS	IDBX	IDB Communications Group Inc
IdealB	New York	IDL	Ideal Basic Industries Inc
Identx	NAS SL	IDXX	Identix Inc
IE Ind	New York	IEL	IE Industries Inc
IEC	NAS NMS	IECE	IEC Electronics Corp
IFR	NAS NMS	IFRS	IFR Systems Inc
IGame	NAS NMS	IGAM	International Game Technology
IGC	American	IGC	Interstate General Company LP
IGENE	NAS SL	IGNE	IGENE Biotechnology Inc
IGI	American	IG	IGI Inc
II-VI	NAS NMS	IIVI	II-VI Inc
IIP	American	IIP	International Income Property Inc
IIS	NAS NMS	IISLF	I.I.S. Intelligent Information Systems Ltd
ILC	NAS NMS	ILCT	ILC Technology Inc
IllPowr	New York	IPC	Illinois Power Co
ImagEn	NAS SL	DISK	Image Entertainment Inc
ImagRtl	NAS SL	IMAG	Image Retailing Group Inc
Imark	NAS NL	IMAR	Imark Industries Inc
Imatrn	NAS NMS	IMAT	Imatron Inc
IMC F	New York	IFL	IMC Fertilizer Group Inc
ImgFlm	NAS SL	IFEI	Imagine Films Entertainment Inc
ImoDv	New York	IMD	Imo Delaval Inc
IMP	NAS NMS	IMPX	International Microelectronics Products Inc
ImpCh	New York	ICI	Imperial Chemical Industries PLC
ImpctSy	NAS NMS	MPAC	Impact Systems Inc
ImpHly	NAS NMS	IHKSV	Imperial Holly Corp
ImpOil	American	IMO.A	Imperial Oil Ltd (Class A)
ImprBc	NAS NMS	IBAN	Imperial Bancorp
Imre	NAS SL	IMRE	Imre Corp
Imreg	NAS NMS	IMRGA	Imreg Inc (Class A)
IMT	NAS SL	IMIT	IMT Inc
ImTher	NAS SL	IMNO	Imuno Therapeutic Inc
Imucel	NAS SL	ICCC	Immucell Corp
Imucor	NAS NMS	BLUD	Immucor Inc
Imunex	NAS NMS	IMNX	Immunex Corp
Imunmd	NAS NMS	IMMU	Immunomedics Inc
Inacmp	NAS NMS	INAC	Inacomp Computer Centers Inc
InAcous	NAS NMS	IACI	Industrial Acoustics Company Inc

NEWSPAPER ABBREV.	MARKET LISTING	TRADING SYMBOL	COMPANY NAME
InactTc	NAS NMS	ITXI	Interactive Technologies Inc
INAIn	New York	IIS	INA Investment Securities Inc
Inamed	NAS SL	IMDC	Inamed Corp
InBanc	NAS NL	INBA	InBancshares
InBcst	NAS NMS	IBCA	International Broadcasting Corp
InCapE	NAS NMS	ICEYF	International Capital Equipment Ltd
IncaRs	NAS NMS	INCRF	Inca Resources Inc
INCMNT	NAS SL	ICNT	INCOMNET Inc
INCO	New York	N	Inco Ltd
Incstar	American	ISR	Incstar Corp
InDairA	NAS NMS	INDQA	International Dairy Queen Inc (Class A)
InDairB	NAS NMS	INDQB	International Dairy Queen Inc (Class B)
IndBc	NAS NMS	INBC	Independence Bancorp Inc (Pennsylvania)
IndBC	NAS NMS	INDB	Independent Bank Corp (Massachusetts)
IndBkgp	NAS NL	IBGI	Independent BankGroup Inc
IndBkMi	NAS NMS	IBCP	Independent Bank Corp (Michigan)
IndBnc	NAS NMS	IBSI	Independent Bancshares Inc (Texas)
IndEl	NAS NMS	IEHC	Industrial Electronic Hardware Corp
IndepAir	NAS SL	IAIR	Independent Air Holdings Inc
Indepth	NAS SL	INDI	Indepth Data Inc
IndFdl	NAS NMS	IFSB	Independence Federal Savings Bank (Washington D.C.)
IndHBk	NAS NMS	IHBI	Indian Head Banks Inc (New Hampshire)
India	New York	IGF	India Growth Fund
IndiBn	NAS NL	INBK	Indiana Bancshares Inc
IndiEn	New York	IEI	Indiana Energy Inc
IndiFdl	NAS NMS	IFSL	Indiana Federal S&L Assn
IndInsr	NAS NMS	INDHK	Independent Insurance Group Inc
IndiNt	NAS NMS	INAT	Indiana National Corp
IndnaF	NAS NMS	IFII	Indiana Financial Investors Inc
IndRes	NAS NMS	INDR	Industrial Resources Inc
IndSqS	NAS NL	ISIS	Independence Square Income Securities Inc
Indtch	NAS SL	INEC	Indtech Corp
IndTrn	NAS NMS	ITCC	Industrial Training Corp
IndxTc	NAS NMS	INDX	Index Technology Corp
InFGne	NAS SL	IFGN	InFerGene Co
InfGrph	NAS NL	INFG	Infinite Graphics Inc
Infodat	NAS NMS	INFD	Infodata System Inc
InfoIntl	NAS NMS	IINT	Information International Inc
InfoRs	NAS NMS	IRIC	Information Resources Inc
InfoSc	NAS NMS	INSI	Information Science Inc
Infotch	NAS NMS	ITCH	Infotechnology Inc
Infrmx	NAS NMS	IFMX	Informix Corp
Infrsnc	NAS SL	IFRA	Infrasonics Inc
Inftrn	NAS NMS	INFN	Infotron Systems Corp
IngerR	New York	IR	Ingersoll-Rand Co
InglMkt	NAS NMS	IMKTA	Ingles Markets Inc (Class A)

NEWSPAPER ABBREV.	MARKET LISTING	TRADING SYMBOL	COMPANY NAME
IngrTec	New York	ITC	Ingredient Technology Corp
Initio	NAS NMS	INTO	Initio Inc
InldStl	New York	IAD	Inland Steel Industries Inc
Inmac	NAS NMS	INMC	Inmac Corp
InMcSf	NAS SL	IMSF	International Microcomputer Software Inc
InMobil	NAS NMS	IMMC	International Mobile Machines Corp
Innovex	NAS NMS	INVX	Innovex Inc
Inrad	NAS NMS	INRD	INRAD Inc
Insilco	New York	INR	Insilco Corp
InsitE	NAS NMS	INEI	Insituform East Inc
InsitGlf	NAS NMS	IGSI	Insituform Gulf South Inc
InsitMd	NAS NMS	INSMA	Insituform Mid-America Inc (Class A)
Inspch	NAS NMS	INSP	InSpeech Inc
InspRs	New York	IRC	Inspiration Resources Corp
InstaCl	NAS SL	KOOL	Insta Cool Incorporated of North America
Instat	NAS SL	ITERF	Interstrat Resources Inc
InstCp	NAS NL	INET	Instinet Corp
Insteel	American	III	Insteel Industries Inc
Instfr	NAS NMS	INSUA	Insituform of North America Inc (Class A)
InstfrS	NAS NMS	ISEC	Insituform Southeast Corp
Instgp	NAS NMS	IGLSF	Insituform Group Ltd
InstPw	New York	IPW	Interstate Power Co
Instron	American	ISN	Instron Corp
InstSy	American	ISY	Instrument Systems Corp
Instvsn	NAS SL	ISTC	Instructivision Inc
IntAlu	New York	IAL	International Aluminum Corp
IntAm	NAS NMS	HOME	International American Homes Inc
IntBknt	American	IBK	International Banknote Company Inc
IntBkr	New York	IBC	Interstate Bakeries Corp
Intcar	NAS NL	ICAR	Intercargo Corp
IntCnt	NAS NMS	ICSI	International Container Systems Inc
IntCogn	NAS SL	ICGN	International Congeneration Corp
IntCon	NAS SL	ICBI	International Consumer Brands Inc
IntCty	American	ICG	Inter-City Gas Corp
IntDsg	NAS SL	IDGI	International Design Group Inc
Intech	NAS NMS	INTE	Intech Inc
Integon	NAS NMS	ITGN	Integon Corp
Intek	NAS NMS	IDCC	Intek Diversified Corp
Intel	NAS NMS	INTC	Intel Corp
Intelcal	NAS NMS	INCL	Intellicall Inc
IntelEl	NAS NMS	INEL	Intelligent Electronics Inc
Intelli	NAS NMS	INAI	Intellicorp
Interco	New York	ISS	INTERCO INCORPORATED
Interfc	NAS NMS	INTF	Interface Systems Inc
Interfrn	NAS SL	IFSC	Interferon Sciences Inc

NEWSPAPER ABBREV.	MARKET LISTING	TRADING SYMBOL	COMPANY NAME
IntFlav	New York	IFF	International Flavors & Fragrances Inc
IntgCpt	NAS NL	ICGI	Integrated Computer Graphics Inc
IntgDv	NAS NMS	IDTI	Integrated Device Technology Inc
IntGen	NAS NMS	IGEI	International Genetic Engineering Inc
IntgGen	NAS NMS	INGN	Integrated Genetics Inc
IntgRsc	New York	IRE	Integrated Resources Inc
Intgph	NAS NMS	INGR	Intergraph Corp
Intgrp	NAS NMS	INTG	Intergroup Corp
IntHld	NAS NMS	ISLH	International Holding Capital Corp
Inthm	NAS NMS	IHEIF	Interhome Energy Inc
IntlBus	NAS SL	IBCC	Intelligent Business Communications Corp
IntlEl	NAS SL	IEIB	International Electronics Inc
IntLfe	NAS NL	ILCO	Intercontinental Life Corp
IntlgSy	American	INP	Intelligent Systems Master L.P.
Intlog	New York	IT	Interlogic Trace Inc
IntLse	NAS NMS	ILFC	International Lease Finance Corp
Intmec	NAS NMS	INTR	INTERMEC Corp
Intmed	New York	ITM	Intermedics Inc
IntmetC	NAS NMS	INMT	Intermet Corp
IntMgR	NAS SL	IMRC	International Management & Research Corp
IntMin	New York	IGL	International Minerals & Chemical Corp
IntmkG	NAS SL	IGII	Intermark Gaming International Inc
IntMult	New York	IMC	International Multifoods Corp
IntNtr	NAS SL	INGC	International Nutrition & Genetics Corp
IntPap	New York	IP	International Paper Co
IntpbG	New York	IPG	The Interpublic Group of Companies Inc
Intphrm	NAS NL	IPLLF	InterPharm Laboratories Ltd
Intphse	NAS NMS	INPH	Interphase Corp
IntProt	American	PRO	International Proteins Corp
IntPwr	American	PWR	International Power Machines Corp
IntrCel	NAS SL	ICTI	Interstate Cellular Telecommunications Inc
Intrcim	NAS SL	ITCM	Intercim Corp
IntRec	American	INT	International Recovery Corp
IntRect	New York	IRF	International Rectifier Corp
IntResh	NAS NMS	IRDV	International Research & Development Corp
Intrex	NAS NMS	TREX	Intrex Financial Services Inc
IntrfcI	NAS NMS	IFSIA	Interface Inc (Class A)
IntrFd	NAS NMS	IFED	InterFederal Savings Bank (Tennessee)
Intrfd	NAS SL	IFND	Interfund Corp
IntRFn	New York	IFG	Inter-Regional Financial Group Inc
IntrFn	NAS NMS	ISBJ	Interchange Financial Services Corp (New Jersey)
Intrleaf	NAS NMS	LEAF	Interleaf Inc

NEWSPAPER ABBREV.	MARKET LISTING	TRADING SYMBOL	COMPANY NAME
Intrlke	New York	IK	Interlake Corp
Intrmgn	NAS NMS	INMA	Intermagnetics General Corp
Intrmk	American	IMI	Intermark Inc
IntrmSy	NAS NMS	INSY	Interim Systems Corp
Intrmtr	NAS NMS	IMET	Intermetrics Inc
IntrTel	NAS NMS	INTLA	Inter-Tel Inc (Class A)
Intrtrn	NAS NMS	ITRN	Intertrans Corp
IntSeaw	American	INS	International Seaway Trading Corp
IntSec	New York	IS	Interstate Securities Inc
IntShip	NAS NMS	INSH	International Shipholding Corp
Intspec	NAS NMS	ISPC	Interspec Inc
Inttan	NAS NMS	ITAN	InterTAN Inc
IntTch	American	ITI	International Telecharge Inc
IntThr	American	ITB	International Thoroughbred Breeders Inc
IntTotlz	NAS NMS	ITSI	International Totalizator Systems Inc
Intvce	NAS NL	INTV	InterVoice Inc
IntYog	NAS SL	YOCM	International Yogurt Co
Invcr	NAS NMS	IVCR	Invacare Corp
INVG	NAS NMS	INVG	INVG Mortgage Securities Corp
InvLfKy	NAS SL	INLF	Investors Heritage Life Insurance of Kentucky
InvSav	NAS NMS	INVS	Investors Savings Corp (Minnesota)
InvstSL	NAS NMS	ISLA	Investors Savings Bank (Virginia)
InvtDsg	NAS NMS	IDEA	Invention Design Engineering Associates Inc
InvTech	NAS SL	IVES	Investment Technologies Inc
InvTitl	NAS NMS	ITIC	Investors Title Co
InvTr	NAS SL	ITIN	Investors Trust Inc
Invtrn	NAS NMS	INVN	Invitron Corp
Iomega	NAS NMS	IOMG	Iomega Corp
Ionics	American	ION	Ionics Inc
IowaNtl	NAS NMS	INBS	Iowa National Bankshares Corp
IowaRs	New York	IOR	Iowa Resources Inc
IowaSo	NAS NMS	IUTL	Iowa Southern Utilities Co
IowIlG	New York	IWG	Iowa-Illinois Gas & Electric Co
Ipalco	New York	IPL	IPALCO Enterprises Inc
IpcoCp	New York	IHS	IPCO Corp
IPL Sy	NAS NMS	IPLSA	IPL Systems Inc (Class A)
IPM	American	IPM	IPM Technology Inc
IPTim	New York	IPT	IP Timberlands Ltd
IRIS	NAS NMS	IRIS	International Remote Imaging Systems Inc
Ironstn	NAS SL	IRON	Ironstone Group Inc
IroqBrd	American	IBL	Iroquois Brands Ltd
IRT	New York	IRT	IRT Property Co
IRT Cp	American	IX	IRT Corp
IRT Rlt	NAS SL	IRTR	IRT Realty Services Inc
IrvBnk	New York	V	Irving Bank Corp

NEWSPAPER ABBREV.	MARKET LISTING	TRADING SYMBOL	COMPANY NAME
Irvine	NAS SL	IRSN	Irvine Sensors Corp
IrwnMg	NAS NMS	IRWN	Irwin Magnetics Systems Inc
IrwnUn	NAS SL	IUCO	Irwin Union Corp
ISI Sy	American	SYS	ISI Systems Inc
ISC	NAS NMS	ISCS	ISC Systems Corp
Isco	NAS NMS	ISKO	Isco Inc
Isomdx	NAS NMS	ISMX	Isomedix Inc
Isomet	NAS NL	IOMT	Isomet Corp
Isramc	NAS SL	ISRL	Isramco Inc
IsrlInv	NAS NL	IICR	Israel Investors Corp
ISS	American	ISI	ISS-International Service System Inc
IstecIn	NAS SL	ISTEF	Istec Industry & Technology Ltd
IT Crp	New York	ITX	International Technology Corp
Italy	New York	ITA	The Italy Fund Inc
ItcpSe	New York	ICB	InterCapital Income Securities Inc
Itel	NAS NMS	ITELO	Itel Corp
ItgCirc	NAS NMS	ICTM	Integrated Circuits Inc
ItoYokd	NAS NMS	IYCOY	Ito-Yokado Company Ltd
ITT Cp	New York	ITT	ITT Corp
ITW	New York	ITW	Illinois Tool Works Inc
IU Int	New York	IU	IU International Corp
IvaxCp	American	IVX	IVAX Corp
Iverson	American	IVT.A	Iverson Technology Corp (Class A)
IWC	NAS NMS	IWCR	IWC Resources Corp
J&J Sn	NAS NMS	JJSF	J&J Snack Foods Corp
Jacbsn	NAS NMS	JCBS	Jacobson Stores Inc
Jackpot	New York	JACK	Jackpot Enterprises Inc
Jaclyn	American	JLN	Jaclyn Inc
Jacobs	American	JEC	Jacobs Engineering Group Inc
JacoEl	NAS NMS	JACO	Jaco Electronics Inc
Jacor	NAS NMS	JCOR	Jacor Communications Inc
JAdams	NAS NMS	JALC	John Adams Life Corp
Jaguar	NAS NMS	JAGRY	Jaguar plc
JAM	NAS SL	MSST	JAMCO Ltd
Jamsw	New York	JMY	Jamesway Corp
JanBel	American	JBM	Jan Bell Marketing Inc
JapnAir	NAS SL	JAPNY	Japan Air Lines Company Ltd
Jason	NAS NMS	JASN	Jason Inc
Jayark	NAS SL	JAYA	Jayark Corp
JayJacb	NAS NMS	JAYT	Jay Jacobs Inc
JBRst	NAS NMS	JBBB	JB's Restaurants Inc
JckCarl	NAS SL	FUTR	Jack Carl/312-Futures Inc
JefBsh	NAS NMS	JBNK	Jefferson Bankshares Inc (Virginia)
JeffBcp	NAS NL	JBNC	Jefferson Bancorp Inc (Florida)
JeffBk	NAS NL	JFFN	Jefferson Bank (Pennsylvania)
JeffNt	NAS NMS	JNBK	Jefferson National Bank (New York)
JeffPl	New York	JP	Jefferson-Pilot Corp

NEWSPAPER ABBREV.	MARKET LISTING	TRADING SYMBOL	COMPANY NAME
JeffrGp	NAS NMS	JEFG	Jefferies Group Inc
JefSmf	NAS NMS	JJSC	Jefferson Smurfit Corp
JenfCv	NAS SL	JENN	Jennifer Convertibles Inc
Jepson	New York	JEP	Jepson Corp
Jerico	NAS NMS	JERR	Jerrico Inc
Jesup	NAS NMS	JGRP	Jesup Group Inc
Jetbrne	NAS NMS	JETS	Jetborne International Inc
JetCa	American	JTC	Jet Capital Corp
Jetron	American	JET	Jetronic Industries Inc
JG Ind	NAS NMS	JGIN	JG Industries Inc
JHansn	NAS NMS	JHSL	John Hanson Savings Bank FSB
JhnCn	New York	JCI	Johnson Controls Inc
JhnCRt	New York	JCT	Johnstown/Consolidated Realty Trust
JhnsnE	NAS NMS	JHSN	Johnson Electronics Inc
JifyLub	NAS NMS	JLUB	Jiffy Lube International Inc
JLG	NAS NMS	JLGI	JLG Industries Inc
JMadsn	American	JML	James Madison Ltd
JneMed	NAS NMS	JMED	Jones Medical Industries Inc
JohnAm	American	JAC	Johnstown American Companies
JohnInd	New York	JII	Johnston Industries Inc
JohnJn	New York	JNJ	Johnson & Johnson
JohnPd	American	JPC	Johnson Products Company Inc
JohnsSv	NAS NMS	JSBK	Johnstown Savings Bank (Pennsylvania)
JoneI A	NAS NMS	JOINA	Jones Intercable Inc (Class A)
JoneSpc	NAS NMS	SPLKA	Jones Spacelinks Ltd (Class A)
JonIcbl	NAS NMS	JOIN	Jones Intercable Inc
Jorgen	New York	JOR	Earle M. Jorgensen Co
Joslyn	NAS NMS	JOSL	Joslyn Corp
Josten	New York	JOS	Jostens Inc
Joule	American	JOL	Joulé Inc
JP Ind	New York	JPI	J.P. Industries Inc
JPM	NAS NL	JPMI	JPM Industries Inc
JRiver	New York	JR	James River Corporation of Virginia
JRM	NAS NMS	JRMX	JRM Holdings Inc
J2 Com	NAS SL	JTWO	J2 Communications
Judicte	NAS SL	JUDGW	Judicate Inc
Judys	NAS NMS	JUDY	Judy's Inc
JumpJk	American	JJS	Jumping-Jack Shoes Inc
Juno	NAS NMS	JUNO	Juno Lighting Inc
Justin	NAS NMS	JSTN	Justin Industries Inc
JWA	NAS NMS	JWAIA	Johnson Worldwide Associates Inc (Class A)
Jwlcr	New York	JC	Jewelcor Inc
Jwlmst	American	JEM	Jewelmasters Inc
JWP	New York	JWP	JWP Inc
K mrt	New York	KM	K mart Corp
Kahler	NAS NMS	KHLR	Kahler Corp

NEWSPAPER ABBREV.	MARKET LISTING	TRADING SYMBOL	COMPANY NAME
Kaisrtc	New York	KLU	Kaisertech Ltd
Kaman	NAS NMS	KAMNA	Kaman Corp (Class A)
Kamnst	NAS NMS	MKCO	M. Kamenstein Inc
KambEn	New York	KEP	Kaneb Energy Partners Ltd
Kaneb	New York	KAB	Kaneb Services Inc
KanGE	New York	KGE	Kansas Gas & Electric Co
KanPL	New York	KAN	The Kansas Power & Light Co
Kaplan	NAS NL	KAPL	Kaplan Industries Inc
Kappa	American	KPA	Kappa Networks Inc
Karchr	NAS NMS	CARL	Carl Karcher Enterprises Inc
Kasler	NAS NMS	KASL	Kasler Corp
KatyIn	New York	KT	Katy Industries Inc
KaufB	New York	KB	Kaufman & Broad Inc
KaufBH	New York	KBH	Kaufman & Broad Home Corp
KayCp	American	KAY	Kay Corp
Kaydon	NAS NMS	KDON	Kaydon Corp
KayJw	New York	KJI	Kay Jewelers Inc
Kaypro	NAS NMS	KPRO	Kaypro Corp
KBAust	New York	KBA	Kleinwort Benson Australian Income Fund Inc
KCR	NAS SL	KCRT	KCR Technology Inc
KCS Gp	NAS NMS	KCSG	KCS Group Inc
KCSou	New York	KSU	Kansas City Southern Industries Inc
KCtyPL	New York	KLT	Kansas City Power & Light Co
KDI	New York	KDI	KDI Corp
Keane	NAS NMS	KEAN	Keane Inc
KearNt	American	KNY	Kearney-National Inc
KeithGp	NAS SL	HKME	The Keith Group of Companies Inc
Keithly	American	KEI	Keithly Instruments Inc
Kellogg	New York	K	Kellogg Co
Kellwd	New York	KWD	Kellwood Co
Kemp	NAS NMS	KEMC	Kemper Corp
Kenan	NAS NMS	KTCO	Kenan Transport Co
Kencop	NAS NMS	KCOP	KenCope Energy Companies
Kenlwt	NAS NMS	KENS	Kenilworth Systems Corp
Kenmt	New York	KMT	Kennametal Inc
KentEl	American	KEC	Kent Electronics Corp
Kenwin	American	KWN	Kenwin Shops Inc
Keptel	NAS NMS	KPTL	Keptel Inc
Kerkhf	American	KIX	Kerkhoff Industries Inc
KerrGl	New York	KGM	Kerr Glass Manufacturing Corp
KerrMc	New York	KMG	Kerr-McGee Corp
Keslr	American	KSS	Kessler Products Ltd
Ketchm	American	KCH	Ketchum & Company Inc
Kevlin	NAS NMS	KVLM	Kevlin Microwave Corp
KewnSc	NAS NMS	KEQU	Kewaunee Scientific Corp
KeyCa	American	KYC	Keystone Camera Products Corp
KeyCen	NAS NMS	KEYC	Key Centurion Bancshares Inc

NEWSPAPER ABBREV.	MARKET LISTING	TRADING SYMBOL	COMPANY NAME
KeyCoA	American	KC.A	The Key Co (Class A)
KeyCoB	American	KC.B	The Key Co (Class B)
Keycp	New York	KEY	KeyCorp
KeyFnc	NAS NMS	KSTN	Keystone Financial Inc
KeyInt	New York	KII	Keystone International Inc
KeyMed	NAS SL	KMEC	Keystone Medical Corp
KeysCo	New York	KES	Keystone Consolidated Industries Inc
KeysHrt	NAS NMS	KHGI	Keystone Heritage Group Inc
KeyTrn	NAS NMS	KTCC	Key Tronic Corp
Kilern	American	KPI	Killearn Properties Inc
Kimbal	NAS NMS	KBALB	Kimball International Inc (Class B)
KimbC	New York	KMB	Kimberly-Clark Corp
Kimbrk	NAS NMS	KIMB	Kimbark Oil & Gas Co
KimEn	NAS NMS	KEVIN	Kimmins Environmental Service Corp
Kimin	NAS NMS	KISC	Kimmins Corp
Kinark	American	KIN	Kinark Corp
Kinder	NAS NMS	KIND	Kinder-Care Learning Centers Inc
Kinetic	NAS NMS	KNCI	Kinetic Concepts Inc
KingCty	NAS NL	KCFB	King City Federal Savings Bank
KingstS	NAS SL	PULP	Kingston Systems Inc
Kirby	American	KEX	Kirby Exploration Company Inc
KirinBr	NAS SL	KNBW	Kirin Brewery Ltd
Kirschn	NAS NMS	KMDC	Kirschner Medical Corp
Kit Mfg	American	KIT	Kit Manufacturing Co
KLA	NAS NMS	KLAC	KLA Instruments Corp
KleerV	American	KVU	Kleer-Vu Industries Inc
Kleinrt	NAS NL	KLRT	Kleinert's Inc
KLLM	NAS NMS	KLLM	KLLM Transport Services Inc
KLM	New York	LKM	KLM Royal Dutch Airlines
KloofG	NAS NL	KLOFY	Kloof Gold Mining Company Ltd
KlyOG	American	KLY	Kelley Oil & Gas Partners Ltd
KlyS A	NAS NMS	KELYA	Kelly Services Inc (Class A)
KlyS B	NAS NMS	KELYB	Kelly Services Inc (Class B)
KmpHi	New York	KHI	Kemper High Income Trust
KMS	NAS NMS	KMSI	KMS Industries Inc
KMW	American	KMW	KMW Systems Corp
KN Eng	New York	KNE	KN Energy Inc
KnapeV	NAS NMS	KNAP	Knape & Vogt Manufacturing Co
KnCtyL	NAS NL	KCLI	Kansas City Life Insurance Cc
KnghtR	New York	KRI	Knight-Ridder Inc
KngsRd	NAS NMS	KREN	Kings Road Entertainment Inc
KngWld	New York	KWP	King World Productions Inc
Knogo	New York	KNO	Knogo Corp
Knutsn	NAS NMS	KNMC	Knutson Mortgage Corp
Knwldg	NAS SL	KDSI	Knowledge Data Systems Inc
Koger	New York	KOG	Koger Properties Inc
KogrEq	American	KE	Koger Equity Inc
Kolmor	New York	KOL	Kollmorgen Corp

NEWSPAPER ABBREV.	MARKET LISTING	TRADING SYMBOL	COMPANY NAME
Komag	NAS NMS	KMAG	Komag Inc
Kopers	New York	KOP	Koppers Company Inc
Korea	New York	KF	The Korea Fund Inc
Koss	NAS NMS	KOSS	Koss Corp
KPToy	New York	KPT	Kenner Parker Toys Inc
Kraft	New York	KRA	Kraft Inc
Kreislr	NAS NMS	KRSL	Kreisler Manufacturing Corp
Krelitz	NAS NL	KRLZ	Krelitz Industries Inc
Krisch	NAS SL	INNS	Krisch American Inns Inc
KRM	NAS SL	KRMC	K.R.M. Petroleum Corp
Kroger	New York	KR	The Kroger Co
Krug	NAS NMS	KRUG	KRUG International Corp
Kruger	NAS NMS	KRUE	W.A. Krueger Co
KTron	NAS NMS	KTII	K-Tron International Inc
Kubota	New York	KUB	Kubota Ltd
Kuhlm	New York	KUH	Kuhlman Corp
Kulcke	NAS NMS	KLIC	Kulicke & Soffa Industries Inc
KurzM	NAS NL	KURM	Kurzweil Music Systems Inc
KustEl	NAS NMS	KUST	Kustom Electronics Inc
KV Ph	American	KV	KV Pharmaceutical Co
KyCmL	NAS NMS	KENCA	Kentucky Central Life Insurance Co (Class A)
KyInvst	NAS NL	KINV	Kentucky Investors Inc
KyleTc	NAS SL	KYLE	Kyle Technology Corp
KyMd	NAS SL	KYMDA	Kentucky Medical Insurance Co (Class A)
Kyocer	New York	KYO	Kyocera Corp
Kysor	New York	KZ	Kysor Industrial Corp
KyUtil	New York	KU	Kentucky Utilities Co
L Rex	NAS SL	LREXF	L Rex International Corp
LA Gear	NAS NMS	LAGR	L.A. Gear Inc
LaBarg	American	LB	LaBarge Inc
LAC	New York	LAC	LAC Minerals Ltd
LacldSt	NAS NMS	LCLD	Laclede Steel Co
LaclGs	New York	LG	Laclede Gas Co
LaddFr	NAS NMS	LADF	LADD Furniture Inc
Lafarge	New York	LAF	Lafarge Corp
LaGenl	New York	LGS	Louisiana General Services Inc
Lajolla	American	LJC	La Jolla Bancorp
Lakelnd	NAS NMS	LAKE	Lakeland Industries Inc
LakldS	NAS NMS	LLSL	Lakeland Savings Bank SLA (New Jersey)
LaLand	New York	LLX	The Louisiana Land & Exploration Co
Lamar	NAS SL	LLIC	Lamar Life Corp
LamaT	NAS NMS	TLAM	Tony Lama Company Inc
LamRs	NAS NMS	LRCX	Lam Research Corp
LamSes	New York	LMS	The Lamson & Sessions Co
Lance	NAS NMS	LNCE	Lance Inc
Lancer	American	LAN	Lancer Corp

NEWSPAPER ABBREV.	MARKET LISTING	TRADING SYMBOL	COMPANY NAME
Lancst	NAS NMS	LANC	Lancaster Colony Corp
Langly	NAS NMS	LCOR	Langly Corp
LaPac	New York	LPX	Louisiana-Pacific Corp
LaPete	NAS NMS	LPAI	La Petite Academy Inc
LaPnt	American	LPI	La Pointe Industries Inc
Larizz	American	LII	Larizza Industries Inc
LaryIce	NAS SL	LARY	Larrys Ice Cream Inc
Laser	American	LAS	Laser Industries Ltd
LaserCo	NAS NMS	LSER	Laser Corp
LaserP	NAS SL	LAZR	Laser Photonics Inc
LaserPr	NAS NMS	LASR	Laser Precision Corp
LasrMst	NAS SL	LCII	Laser Master International Inc
Lasrtch	NAS SL	LASX	Lasertechnics Inc
LaTeko	NAS SL	LABORF	La Teko Resources Ltd
Latshw	American	LAT	Latshaw Enterprises Inc
LaurelE	NAS NMS	LAUR	Laurel Entertainment Inc
Lauren	American	LQ	Laurentian Capital Corp
LaurlSv	NAS NL	LARL	Laurel Savings Assn
LawrG	American	LWR	Lawrence Insurance Group Inc
Lawsn	American	LMG.A	Lawsen Mardon Group Ltd (Class A)
Lawsn	NAS NMS	LAWS	Lawson Products Inc
LawtInt	New York	LAW	Lawter International Inc
Laz By	New York	LZB	La-Z-Boy Chair Co
LazKap	American	LKI	Lazare Kaplan International Inc
LbtyAS	New York	USA	Liberty All-Star Equity Fund
LbtyH A	NAS NMS	LIBHA	Liberty Homes Inc (Class A)
LbtyH B	NAS NMS	LIBHB	Liberty Homes Inc (Class B)
LCS	NAS NMS	LCSI	LCS Industries Inc
LDB	NAS NMS	LDBCD	LDB Corp
LDI Cp	NAS NMS	LDIC	LDI Corp
LdkAm	NAS NMS	LMAC	Landmark American Corp
LdLnSL	NAS NMS	LOLS	Land of Lincoln Savings & Loan
LdlT A	NAS NMS	LDMFA	Laidlaw Transportation Ltd (Class A)
LdlT B	NAS NMS	LDMFB	Laidlaw Transportation Ltd (Class B)
LdmCB	NAS NMS	LCBIV	Landmark/Community Bancorp Inc
LdmkB	NAS NMS	LDMK	Landmark Bank for Savings (Massachusetts)
LdmkSv	American	LSA	Landmark Savings Assn (Pennsylvania)
LeadMn	NAS SL	LDMM	Leadville Mining & Milling Corp
Leadvle	NAS SL	LEAD	Leadville Corp
Learnl	New York	LRI	LeaRonal Inc
LearPP	American	LPP	Lear Petroleum Partners L.P.
LearPt	New York	LPT	Lear Petroleum Corp
Lectec	NAS NL	LECT	LecTec Corp
Leeco	NAS SL	LECO	Leeco Diagnostics Inc
LeeDta	NAS NMS	LEDA	Lee Data Corp
LeeEnt	New York	LEE	Lee Enterprises Inc
LeePhr	American	LPH	Lee Pharmaceuticals

NEWSPAPER ABBREV.	MARKET LISTING	TRADING SYMBOL	COMPANY NAME
LegMas	New York	LM	Legg Mason Inc
LegPlat	New York	LEG	Leggett & Platt Inc
Lehmn	New York	LEM	The Lehman Corp
Leiner	American	PLI	P. Leiner Nutritional Products Corp
LeisCn	NAS NMS	LCIC	Leisure Concepts Inc
LeisurT	New York	LUX	Leisure & Technology Inc
Lennar	New York	LEN	Lennar Corp
LePeep	NAS SL	LPEP	Le Peep Restaurants Inc
Lesco	NAS NMS	LSCO	LESCO Inc
LeslFay	New York	LES	The Leslie Fay Companies Inc
LeucNt	New York	LUK	Leucadia National Corp
Levitt	American	LVT	Levitt Corp
Levon	NAS SL	LNVF	Levon Resources Ltd
Lexicon	NAS NMS	LEXI	Lexicon Corp
LexingS	NAS NMS	LEXB	Lexington Savings Bank (Massachusetts)
LfeCare	NAS SL	LCCC	Life Care Communities Corp
Lfecore	NAS NMS	CBM	Lifecore Biomedical Inc
Lfelne	NAS NMS	LIFE	Lifeline Systems Inc
LfeTch	NAS NMS	LTEK	Life Technologies Inc
Lfetime	American	LFT	Lifetime Corp
LibtNB	NAS NMS	LNBC	Liberty National Bancorp Inc
LibtyCp	New York	LC	The Liberty Corp
LICFn	NAS NMS	LICF	The Long Island City Financial Corp
Liebr	NAS NMS	LMAN	Lieberman Enterprises Inc
Lifesur	NAS SL	LICO	Lifesurance Corp
Ligget	New York	LIG	Liggett Group Inc
LILCo	New York	LIL	Long Island Lighting Co
Lilly	New York	LLY	Eli Lilly & Co
Lilly A	NAS NMS	LICIA	Lilly Industrial Coatings Inc (Class A)
LilVer	American	LVC	Lillian Vernon Corp
Limited	New York	LTD	The Limited Inc
LinBrd	NAS NMS	LINB	LIN Broadcasting Corp
LincBc	NAS NMS	LCNB	Lincoln Bancorp
LincFd	NAS NMS	LINN	Lincoln Foodservice Products Inc
LincFn	NAS NMS	LFIN	Lincoln Financial Corp
LincLg	NAS NMS	LLOG	Lincoln Logs Ltd
LincNtl	New York	LNC	Lincoln National Corp
LincPl	New York	LND	Lincoln National Direct Placement Fund Inc
LincSB	NAS NMS	LNSB	Lincoln Savings Bank (Pennsylvania)
LincTl	NAS NMS	LTEC	Lincoln Telecommunications Co
Lindbrg	NAS NMS	LIND	Lindberg Corp
LindH	NAS NMS	LNDL	Lindal Cedar Homes Inc
LinearI	NAS SL	LINR	Linear Instruments Corp
LinearT	NAS NMS	LLTC	Linear Technology Corp
LinPro	American	LPO	Linpro Specific Properties
Lionel	American	LIO	The Lionel Corp
Liposm	NAS NMS	LIPO	Liposome Company Inc

NEWSPAPER ABBREV.	MARKET LISTING	TRADING SYMBOL	COMPANY NAME
LiqBox	NAS NMS	LIQB	Liqui-Box Corp
Litfld	American	LFA	Littlefield, Adams & Co
Litton	New York	LIT	Litton Industries Inc
LizCla	NAS NMS	LIZC	Liz Claiborne Inc
LJ Sim	NAS SL	LJSI	L.J. Simone Inc
LkeShre	NAS NMS	LSNB	Lake Shore Bancorp Inc (Illinois)
LkSun	NAS NMS	LSSB	Lake Sunapee Savings Bank FSB (New Hampshire)
LkwdFr	NAS SL	LSTIF	Lakewood Forest Products Ltd
LLE Ry	New York	LRT	LL&E Royalty Trust
LN Ho	New York	LHC	L&N Housing Corp
LncNC	American	LRF	Lincoln N.C. Realty Fund
LncNtC	New York	LNV	Lincoln National Convertible Securities Fund Inc
LndBnc	New York	LBC	Landbank Bancshares Corp
LndEd	New York	LE	Lands' End Inc
Lndmk	American	LML	Landmark Land Company Inc
LndPc	American	LPF	Landsing Pacific Fund
LnStar	New York	LCE	Lone Star Industries Inc
Loadmst	NAS SL	LSMIF	Loadmaster Systems Inc
LoanA	NAS NMS	LAFC	Loan America Financial Corp
LocalF	NAS NMS	LOCL	Local Federal S&L Assn (Oklahoma)
Lockhd	New York	LK	Lockheed Corp
Loctite	New York	LOC	Loctite Corp
Lodgstx	NAS NMS	LDGX	Lodgistix Inc
Loews	New York	LTR	Loews Corp
Logicon	New York	LGN	Logicon Inc
Logitek	NAS SL	LGTK	Logitek Inc
LoJack	NAS SL	LOJN	Lo-Jack Corp
LomasM	New York	LMC	Lomas Mortgage Corp
LomFn	New York	LNF	Lomas & Nettleton Financial Corp
LomMt	New York	LOM	Lomas & Nettleton Mortgage Investors
LondnH	NAS NMS	LOND	London House Inc
LoneStr	NAS NMS	LSST	Lone Star Technologies Inc
LongDr	New York	LDG	Longs Drug Stores Corp
LongF	NAS NMS	LFBR	Longview Fibre Co
LongLke	NAS NMS	LLEC	Long Lake Energy Corp
Longwd	NAS SL	LONG	Longwood Group Ltd
Loral	New York	LOR	Loral Corp
LoriCp	American	LRC	The Lori Corp
LorTel	American	LT	Lorimar-Telepictures Corp
Lotus	NAS NMS	LOTS	Lotus Development Corp
LouvGs	New York	LOU	Louisville Gas & Electric Co
Lowes	New York	LOW	Lowe's Companies Inc
Lowranc	NAS NMS	LEIX	Lowrance Electronics Inc
Loyola	NAS NMS	LOYC	Loyola Capital Corp
LPL	NAS NMS	LPLIA	LPL Investment Group Inc (Class A)
LQuint	New York	LQM	La Quinta Motor Inns Inc

NEWSPAPER ABBREV.	MARKET LISTING	TRADING SYMBOL	COMPANY NAME
LQuMt	New York	LQP	La Quinta Motor Inns L.P.
LrnAnx	NAS SL	ANNX	Learning Annex Inc
LSB Ind	American	LSB	LSB Industries Inc
LSB NC	NAS NMS	LXBK	LSB Bancshares Inc (North Carolina)
LSB SC	NAS NL	LBSC	LSB Bancshares Inc (South Carolina)
LSI Lg	NAS NMS	LLSI	LSI Logic Corp
LSI Lt	NAS NMS	LYTS	LSI Lighting Systems Inc
LTI	NAS NMS	LTIZ	Liposome Technology Inc
LTV	New York	LTV	The LTV Corp
LTX	NAS NMS	LTXX	LTX Corp
Lubrzl	New York	LZ	The Lubrizol Corp
Lubys	New York	LUB	Luby's Cafeterias Inc
Lukens	New York	LUC	Lukens Inc
Lumex	American	LUM	Lumex Inc
LundEnt	NAS NMS	LUND	Lund Enterprises Inc
Luria	American	LUR	L. Luria & Son Inc
Luskin	NAS NMS	LUSK	Luskin's Inc
LuthMd	NAS SL	LUTH	Luther Medical Products Inc
Luxtec	NAS SL	LUXT	Luxtec Corp
LVI Gp	New York	LVI	The LVI Group Inc
LVMH	NAS NMS	LVMH	LVMH Moet Hennessy Louis Vuitton
Lydal	American	LDL	Lydall Inc
Lydnbg	NAS NL	LYDPY	Lydenburg Platinum Ltd
LynchC	American	LGL	Lynch Corp
Lypho	NAS NMS	LMED	LyphoMed Inc
MacGrg	American	MGS	MacGregor Sporting Goods Inc
MachTc	NAS NMS	MTEC	Machine Technology Inc
MackTr	NAS NMS	MACK	Mack Trucks Inc
Macmil	New York	MLL	Macmillan Inc
MacNSc	American	MNS	The MacNeal-Schwendler Corp
MACOM	New York	MAI	M/A-Com Inc
MacrCh	NAS SL	MCHM	MacroChem Corp
MadGE	NAS NMS	MDSN	Madison Gas & Electric Co
MagelPt	NAS NL	MPC	Magellan Petroleum Corp
MagGp	NAS NMS	MAGI	Magna Group Inc
MagmC	NAS NMS	MGCP	Magma Copper Co
MagmP	NAS NMS	MGMA	Magma Power Co
MagnaI	NAS NMS	MAGAF	Magna International Inc
MagnCd	NAS SL	HGCP	MagnaCard Inc
MAIBF	New York	MBF	MAI Basic Four Inc
MailBCs	NAS NL	MBCC	Mail Boxes Coast To Coast Inc
MailBx	NAS NMS	MAIL	Mail Boxes Etc
Maione	NAS NMS	MHCIV	Maione-Hirschberg Companies Inc
MajRt	NAS NMS	MAJR	Major Realty Corp
MajVid	NAS NMS	MAJV	Major Video Corp
Makita	NAS NMS	MKTAY	Makita Electric Works Ltd
Malart	American	MHG	Malartic Hygrade Gold Mines Ltd

NEWSPAPER ABBREV.	MARKET LISTING	TRADING SYMBOL	COMPANY NAME
Malaysa	New York	MF	The Malaysia Fund Inc
Mallard	NAS NMS	MALC	Mallard Coach Company Inc
Malon	NAS SL	MALN	Mallon Minerals Corp
MalritA	NAS NMS	MALRA	Malrite Communications Group Inc (Class A)
Malrite	NAS NMS	MALR	Malrite Communications Group Inc
ManfHo	American	MNH	Manufactured Homes Inc
ManhNt	New York	MLC	Manhattan National Corp
Manitw	NAS NMS	MANT	The Manitowoc Company Inc
ManrCr	New York	MNR	Manor Care Inc
Mantrn	NAS NMS	MANA	Manatron Inc
Manvl	New York	MAN	Manville Corp
MAPCO	New York	MDA	MAPCO Inc
MarbFn	NAS NMS	MRBL	Marble Financial Corp
MARC	NAS NMS	MARC	M/A/R/C Inc
Marcde	New York	MAR	The Marcade Group Inc
Marci	NAS NL	MRCI	Marci International Imports Inc
Marcor	NAS NL	MAAR	MarCor Development Company Inc
Marcus	NAS NMS	MRCS	The Marcus Corp
Margo	NAS NMS	MRGO	Margo Nursery Farms Inc
Margux	NAS NMS	MRGX	Margaux Inc
Mariet	NAS NMS	MRTA	Marietta Corp
MarIll	NAS NMS	MCOR	Marine Corp (Illinois)
MarinT	NAS NMS	MTLI	Marine Transport Lines Inc
Marion	New York	MKC	Marion laboratories Inc
Maritrn	New York	TUG	Maritrans Partners L.P.
MarkCtl	NAS NMS	MRCCV	Mark Controls Corp
Markel	NAS NMS	MAKL	Markel Corp
Markstr	NAS SL	MARK	MarkitStar Inc
Marlton	American	MTY	Marlton Technologies Inc
MarnL	NAS NL	MRNCZ	Marine Ltd Partnership
Marqst	NAS NMS	MMPI	Marquest Medical Products Inc
Marriot	New York	MHS	Marriott Corp
MarsG	American	WMD	Mars Graphic Services Inc
Marshl	NAS NMS	MRIS	Marshall & Ilsley Corp
Marsm	NAS NMS	MSAM	Marsam Pharmaceuticals Inc
MarsSt	NAS NMS	MXXX	Mars Stores Inc
Marten	NAS NMS	MRTN	Marten Transport Ltd
MartM	New York	ML	Martin Marietta Corp
MartnL	NAS NMS	MLLE	Martin Lawrence Limited Editions Inc
Mascmp	NAS NMS	MSCP	Massachusetts Computer Corp
Masco	New York	MAS	Masco Corp
MasCp	New York	MCI	MassMutual Corporate Investors
MasInc	New York	MIV	MassMutual Income Investors Inc
Massbk	NAS NMS	MASB	MASSBANK Corp (Massachusetts)
Masstor	NAS NMS	MSCO	MASSTOR Systems Corp
Mast	NAS SL	MKEY	Mast Keystone Inc
Matec	American	MXC	MATEC Corp

NEWSPAPER ABBREV.	MARKET LISTING	TRADING SYMBOL	COMPANY NAME
Matrix	American	MAX	Matrix Corp
MatRsh	American	MTL	Materials Research Corp
MatSci	American	MSC	Material Sciences Corp
Matsu	New York	MC	Matsushita Electric Industrial Company Ltd
Mattel	New York	MAT	Mattel Inc
MattW	American	MW	Matthews & Wright Group Inc
MauLoa	New York	NUT	Mauna Loa Macadamia Partners L.P.
Maury	NAS NMS	MFED	Maury Federal Savings Bank (Tennessee)
Mavrck	NAS NMS	MAVR	Maverick Restaurant Corp
Maxam	New York	MXM	MAXXAM Group Inc
Maxco	NAS NMS	MAXC	Maxco Inc
Maxcre	NAS NMS	MAXI	Maxicare Health Plans Inc
MaxEr	NAS NMS	MAXE	Max & Ermas Restaurants Inc
Maxim	NAS NMS	MXIM	Maxim Integrated Products Inc
Maxphrm	American	MXP	MaxPharma Inc
Maxtor	NAS NMS	MXTR	Maxtor Corp
Maxus	New York	MXS	Maxus Energy Corp
Maxwell	NAS NMS	MXWL	Maxwell Laboratories Inc
MayDS	New York	MA	The May Department Stores Co
MayflCo	NAS NMS	MFLR	Mayflower Co-operative Bank (Massachusetts)
MayflF	NAS NMS	MFFC	Mayflower Financial Corp
MayfrIn	NAS NMS	MAYF	Mayfair Industries Inc
MaynOl	NAS NMS	MOIL	Maynard Oil Co
MaysJ	NAS NMS	MAYS	J.W. Mays Inc
MaySu	NAS NMS	MYFRA	Mayfair Super Markets Inc (Class A)
Maytag	New York	MYG	The Maytag Co
MB	NAS NMS	MMBLF	MacMillan Bloedel Ltd
MBIA	New York	MBI	MBIA Inc
MblAm	NAS NL	NAME	Mobile America Corp
MBS	NAS NMS	MBSX	MBS Textbook Exchange Inc
MCA	New York	MCA	MCA Inc
McCaw	NAS NMS	MCAWA	McCaw Cellular Communications Inc (Class A)
McCla	American	MNI	McClatchy Newspapers Inc
McClain	NAS NMS	MCCL	McClain Industries Inc
McCrm	NAS NMS	MCCRK	McCormick & Company Inc
McCrmC	NAS NL	MKOR	McCormick Capital Inc
McDanl	NAS SL	ASTN	McDaniel Austin Corp
McDerI	New York	MDR	McDermott International Inc
McDld	New York	MCD	McDonald's Corp
McDnD	New York	MD	McDonnell Douglas Corp
McDnl	New York	MDD	McDonald & Company Investments Inc
McFad	American	MV	McFaddin Ventures Inc
McFarl	NAS NMS	MCFE	McFarland Energy Inc
McGill	NAS NMS	MGLL	McGill Manufacturing Company Inc
McGrH	New York	MHP	McGraw-Hill Inc

NEWSPAPER ABBREV.	MARKET LISTING	TRADING SYMBOL	COMPANY NAME
McGrth	NAS NMS	MGRC	McGrath RentCorp
MchER	New York	MCG	Michigan Energy Resources Co
MCI	NAS NMS	MCIC	MCI Communications Corp
McInt	New York	MP	McIntyre Mines Ltd
McKes	New York	MCK	McKesson Corp
McLe	New York	MII	McLean Industries Inc
MCM Cp	NAS NL	MCMC	McM Corp
MCO Hd	American	MCO	MCO Holdings Inc
MCO Rs	American	MCR	MCO Resources Inc
MCorp	New York	M	MCorp
McRae A	American	MRI.A	McRae Industries Inc (Class A)
McRae B	American	MRI.B	McRae Industries Inc (Class B)
MDC	New York	MDC	M.D.C. Holdings Inc
MDCA	New York	MIR	M.D.C. Asset Investors Inc
MdConn	NAS NMS	MIDC	MidConn Bank (Connecticut)
Mdcore	American	MDK	Medicore Inc
MdFSL	NAS NMS	MFSL	Maryland Federal S&L Assn
MdHud	NAS NMS	MHBK	Mid-Hudson Savings Bank FSB (New York)
MdMaine	NAS NMS	MMSB	Mid Maine Savings Bank F.S.B.
MDmd	NAS NMS	MACD	MacDermid Inc
MdMgt	American	MMA	Medical Management of America Inc
MdStFd	NAS NMS	MSSL	Mid-State Federal S&L Assn
MdsxW	NAS NMS	MSEX	Middlesex Water Co
MDT Cp	NAS NMS	MDTC	MDT Corp
MDU	New York	MDU	MDU Resources Group Inc
MdwAir	New York	MDW	Midway Airlines Inc
MdwCm	NAS NMS	MCOM	Midwest Communications Corp
MdwFn	NAS NMS	MFGC	Midwest Financial Group Inc
Mead	New York	MEA	The Mead Corp
MechTc	NAS NMS	MTIX	Mechanical Technology Inc
MedAct	NAS NMS	MDCI	Medical Action Industries Inc
Medalst	NAS NMS	MDIN	Medalist Industries Inc
Medar	NAS NMS	MDXR	Medar Inc
MedcC	NAS NMS	MCCS	Medco Containment Services Inc
Medch	American	MCH	MedChem Products Inc
MedclSt	NAS NMS	MSTI	Medical Sterilization Inc
MedcR	NAS SL	MEDR	Medco Research Inc
MedCre	NAS NMS	MEDC	Medical Care International Inc
MedDv	NAS NL	MDEV	Medical Devices Inc
Medex	NAS NMS	MDEX	Medex Inc
MedGr	NAS NMS	MGCC	Medical Graphics Corp
Media	American	MEG.A	Media General Inc (Class A)
MediaP	NAS SL	MDPI	Media Products Inc
MediGl	NAS NMS	MGCO	Medicare-Glaser Corp
Medign	NAS NMS	MGNC	MEDIAGENIC
MediLg	NAS SL	TSTM	Media Logistics Inc
MedImg	NAS SL	MIKA	Medical Imaging Centers of America Inc
Mediq	American	MED	MEDIQ Inc

NEWSPAPER ABBREV.	MARKET LISTING	TRADING SYMBOL	COMPANY NAME
MedMbl	NAS SL	MEDM	Med Mobile Inc
MedMst	NAS NMS	MMST	Medmaster Systems Inc
Medphn	NAS SL	MPHO	Medphone Corp
MedPr	American	MPP	Medical Properties Inc
MedSh	NAS NMS	MSII	Medicine Shoppe International Inc
Medstat	NAS NMS	MDST	Medstat Systems Inc
Medtrn	New York	MDT	Medtronic Inc
Megdta	NAS NMS	MSHK	Megadata Corp
MEI	New York	MEI	MEI Diversified Inc
Melami	NAS NMS	MTWO	Melamine Chemicals Inc
Mellon	New York	MEL	Mellon Bank Corp
Melvill	New York	MES	Melville Corp
Mem	American	MEM	MEM Company Inc
MemMtl	NAS SL	MRMT	Memory Metals Inc
MemryS	NAS SL	MEMX	Memory Sciences Corp
Memtek	NAS SL	METK	Memtek Inc
Mentor	NAS NMS	MNTR	Mentor Corp
MentrG	NAS NMS	MENT	Mentor Graphics Corp
MePS	American	MAP	Maine Public Service Co
MercBc	NAS NMS	MTRC	Mercantile Bancorporation Inc (Missouri)
MercBCt	NAS NMS	NMBC	The Merchants Bancorp Inc (Connecticut)
MercBk	NAS NMS	MRBK	Mercantile Bankshares Corp (Maryland)
MercEn	NAS SL	MCRY	Mercury Entertainment Corp
MercGn	NAS NMS	MRCY	Mercury General Corp
Merck	New York	MRK	Merck & Company Inc
MercSL	New York	MSL	Mercury S&L Assn
MercSt	New York	MST	Mercantile Stores Company Inc
MerdIns	NAS NMS	MIGI	Meridian Insurance Group Inc
Merdth	New York	MDP	Meredith Corp
Meret	NAS NMS	MRET	Meret Inc
MerilCp	NAS NMS	MRLL	Merrill Corp
Meritr	NAS NMS	MTOR	Meritor Savings Bank
MerLyn	New York	MER	Merrill Lynch & Company Inc
Mermc	American	MRM	Merrimac Industries Inc
Mermck	NAS NMS	MRMK	Merrimack Bancorp Inc
MerNY	NAS NMS	MBNY	Merchants Bank of New York
MeryG	NAS NMS	MGRE	Merry-Go-Round Enterprises Inc
MeryLd	NAS NMS	MERY	Merry Land & Investment Company Inc
MesaAr	NAS NMS	MESL	Mesa Airlines Inc
Mesab	New York	MSB	Mesabi Trust
MesaLP	New York	MLP	Mesa Limited Partnership
MesaOf	New York	MOS	Mesa Offshore Trust
MesaR	New York	MTR	Mesa Royalty Trust
Mesrx	New York	MX	Measurex Corp
Mestek	New York	MCC	Mestek Inc
MetAir	NAS NMS	MAIR	Metro Airlines Inc
MetBcp	NAS NMS	METB	Metropolitan Bancorp Inc

NEWSPAPER ABBREV.	MARKET LISTING	TRADING SYMBOL	COMPANY NAME
MetCoil	NAS NMS	METS	Met-Coil Systems Corp
Metex	American	MTX	Metex Corp
MethdA	NAS NMS	METHA	Methode Electronics Inc (Class A)
MthdB	NAS NMS	METHB	Methode Electronics Inc (Class B)
Metlcld	NAS SL	MTLC	Metalclad Corp
Metlrg	NAS SL	MTALA	Metallurgical Industries Inc (Class A)
MetPro	American	MPR	Met-Pro Corp
Metrbk	American	MBN	Metrobank N.A. (California)
MetrCn	NAS NMS	MONY	Metropolitan Consolidated Industries Inc
MetrF	NAS NMS	MFTN	Metropolitan Federal S&L Assn (Tennessee)
MetrFn	New York	MFC	Metropolitan Financial Corp (North Dakota)
MetRlt	American	ECOW	Metropolitan Realty Corp
MetrMbl	NAS NMS	MMCT	Metro Mobile CTS Inc
MetroSv	NAS NMS	MSLA	Metropolitan Financial S&L Assn (Texas)
MetrTl	NAS NMS	MTRO	Metro-Tel Corp
MexFd	New York	MXF	The Mexico Fund Inc
MeyerF	NAS NMS	MEYER	Fred Meyer Inc
MeyrPk	NAS NL	MPSI	Meyers Parking System Inc
MFM	New York	MFM	MFS Municipal Income Trust
MFO	New York	MFO	MFS Income & Opportunity Trust
MfrHan	New York	MHC	Manufacturers Hanover Corp
MfrsNt	NAS NMS	MNTL	Manufacturers National Corp
MFT	New York	MFT	MFS Multimarket Total Return Trust
MGask	NAS NMS	MRGC	Mr. Gasket Co
MGI Prp	New York	MGI	MGI Properties
MGM Gr	NAS NL	MGMG	MGM Grand Inc
MGMUA	New York	MGM	MGM/UA Communications Co
MgtCo	NAS SL	MCEG	Management Company Entertainment Group Inc
MgtSci	NAS NMS	MSAI	Management Science America Inc
MgtTc	NAS NL	MTCC	Magnetic Technologies Corp
MHI Gp	New York	QMH	MHI Group Inc
MI Hom	NAS NMS	MIHO	M/I Schottenstein Homes Inc
MicBlt	NAS NMS	BILT	Microbilt Corp
MichAnt	NAS NMS	MAJL	Michael Anthony Jewelers Inc
MichJ	NAS NL	MICH	J. Michaels Inc
MichlFd	NAS NMS	MIKL	Michael Foods Inc
MichNt	NAS NMS	MNCO	Michigan National Corp
MichStr	American	MKE	Michaels Stores Inc
MicImg	NAS SL	MISI	Micro Imaging Systems Inc
Micklby	New York	MBC	Mickelberry Corp
MicMemb	NAS SL	MEMB	Micro Membranes Inc
Micom	NAS NMS	MICS	Micom Systems Inc
Micrage	NAS NMS	MICA	MicroAge Inc
MicrBi	NAS SL	MBMI	Micro Bio-Medics Inc

NEWSPAPER ABBREV.	MARKET LISTING	TRADING SYMBOL	COMPANY NAME
Micrbio	NAS NL	MBLS	Microbiological Sciences Inc
Micrcm	NAS NMS	MNPI	Microcom Inc
MicrD	NAS NMS	MCRD	Micro D Inc
MicrDis	NAS NL	MDSI	Micro Display Systems Inc
Micrdy	NAS NMS	MCDY	Microdyne Corp
MicrEn	NAS SL	MCRE	MicroEnergy Inc
MicrFlt	NAS NMS	MFCO	Microwave Filter Company Inc
MicrLb	NAS NMS	MWAV	Microwave Laboratories Inc
MicrMk	NAS NMS	MCRO	Micro Mask Inc
Micron	American	PMR	Micron Products Inc
Microp	NAS NMS	MLIS	Micropolis Corp
Micros	NAS NMS	MCRS	MICROS Systems Inc
Micrpro	NAS NMS	MPRO	MicroPro International Corp
MicrTc	NAS NMS	DRAM	Micron Technology Inc
MicSem	NAS NMS	MSCC	Microsemi Corp
Micsft	NAS NMS	MSFT	Microsoft Corp
MidABc	NAS NMS	MABC	Mid-America Bancorp (Kentucky)
MidAm	American	MAM	Mid-America Industries Inc
MidAm	NAS NMS	MIAM	Mid-Am Inc (Ohio)
MidFed	NAS NMS	MFSB	MidFed Savings Bank
Midlby	American	MBY	Middleby Corp
MidlCp	NAS NMS	MIDL	Midlantic Corp
Midlnd	American	MLA	The Midland Co
MidSou	NAS NMS	MSRR	MidSouth Corp
MidSUt	New York	MSU	Middle South Utilities Inc
Migent	NAS SL	MGNTF	Migent Software Corp
Mikron	NAS SL	MIKR	Mikron Instrument Company Inc
Millicm	NAS NMS	MILL	Millicom Inc
Millipre	New York	MIL	Millipore Corp
MillrHr	NAS NMS	MLHR	Herman Miller Inc
MillsJn	NAS SL	JKPT	Mills-Jennings Co
MiltnR	New York	MRC	Milton Roy Co
Miltope	NAS NMS	MILT	Miltope Group Inc
MilwIns	NAS NMS	MILW	Milwaukee Insurance Group Inc
MIN	New York	MIN	MFS Intermediate Income Trust
Mindscp	NAS NMS	MIND	Mindscape Inc
MineSf	NAS NMS	MNES	Mine Safety Appliances Co
Minetk	NAS NMS	MINL	Minnetonka Corp
Miniscr	NAS NMS	MINY	MiniScribe Corp
MinnPl	New York	MPL	Minnesota Power & Light Co
Minntc	NAS NMS	MNTX	Minntech Corp
Minorc	NAS NL	MNRCY	Minorco S.A.
MinrNtl	NAS NMS	MNBC	Miners National Bancorp Inc
Minstar	NAS NMS	MNST	Minstar Inc
Mischer	NAS NMS	MSHR	The Mischer Corp
MissnW	American	MSW	Mission West Properties
MitekS	NSL	MITK	Mitek Systems Inc
Mitel	New York	MLT	Mitel Corp

NEWSPAPER ABBREV.	MARKET LISTING	TRADING SYMBOL	COMPANY NAME
Mitsui	NAS NMS	MITSY	Mitsui & Company Ltd
MktFct	NAS NMS	MFAC	Market Facts Inc
MltLocl	NAS NMS	MLMC	Multi-Local Media Corp
MLX	NAS NMS	MLXX	MLX Corp
MMed	American	MMD	Moore Medical Corp
MMI	NAS NMS	MMIM	MMI Medical Inc
MMM	New York	MMM	Minnesota Mining & Manufacturing Co
MMR	NAS NMS	MMRH	MMR Holding Corp
MMT	New York	MMT	MFS Multimarket Income Trust
MNC	NAS NMS	MDNT	MNC Financial Inc
MNX	NAS NMS	MNXI	MNX Inc
MobGs	NAS NMS	MBLE	Mobile Gas Service Corp
Mobil	New York	MOB	Mobil Corp
MoblC A	NAS NMS	MCCAA	Mobile Communications Corporation of America (Class A)
MoblC B	NAS NMS	MCCAB	Mobile Communications Corporation of America (Class B)
MoblNt	NAS SL	MBNC	Mobile National Corp
MOCON	NAS NMS	MOCO	Modern Controls Inc
Modine	NAS NMS	MODI	Modine Manufacturing Co
ModuTc	NAS NMS	MTIK	Modular Technology Inc
Mohsc	New York	MOH	Mohasco Corp
MOKG	NAS NMS	MOKG	Morgan Olmstead Kennedy & Gardner Capital Corp
Moleclr	NAS NMS	MOGN	Molecular Genetics Inc
Moleculn	NAS SL	MBIO	Moleculon Inc
Molex	NAS NMS	MOLX	Molex Inc
Molokai	NAS SL	MKAI	Molokai Ranch Ltd
MonAnt	NAS NMS	MABS	Monoclonal Antibodies Inc
MonAvl	NAS NMS	MAHI	Monarch Avalon Inc
MonCa	New York	MON	Monarch Capital Corp
MoniTc	NAS NMS	MLAB	Monitor Technologies Inc
Monitek	NAS SL	MTEK	Monitek Technologies Inc
Monitr	NAS NMS	MTRM	Moniterm Corp
MonPw	New York	MTP	The Montana Power Co
Monrch	New York	MMO	The Monarch Machine Tool Co
Monsan	New York	MTC	Monsanto Co
MonSt	New York	MTS	Montgomery Street Income Securities Inc
Monted	New York	MNT	Montedison S.p.A.
MontSv	NAS NMS	MSBI	Montclair Savings Bank (New Jersey)
MONY	New York	MYM	MONY Real Estate Investors
Moodus	NAS SL	MOOD	Moodus Savings Bank
MoogA	American	MOG.A	Moog Inc (Class A)
MoogB	American	MOG.B	Moog Inc (Class B)
Moore	New York	MCL	Moore Corporation Ltd
MooreP	NAS NMS	MORP	Moore Products Co
MoorF	NAS NMS	MFGI	Moore Financial Group Inc
Moran	NAS SL	JTMC	JT Moran Financial Corp

NEWSPAPER ABBREV.	MARKET LISTING	TRADING SYMBOL	COMPANY NAME
MoreHd	NAS NMS	MHCO	Moore-Handley Inc
MorFlo	NAS NMS	MORF	Mor-Flo Industries Inc
Morgan	New York	JPM	J.P. Morgan & Company Inc
MorgG	New York	MGC	Morgan Grenfell SMALLCap Fund Inc
MorgnF	American	MR	Morgan's Foods Inc
MorgnP	New York	MGN	Morgan Products Ltd
MorgSt	New York	MS	Morgan Stanley Group Inc
Morin	NAS NMS	MOAI	Morino Associates Inc
MorKeg	New York	MOR	Morgan Keegan Inc
MorKnd	New York	MRN	Morrison Knudsen Corp
Morsn	NAS NMS	MORR	Morrison Inc
Morton	New York	MTI	Morton Thiokol Inc
Moscom	NAS NL	MSCM	MOSCOM Corp
Mosine	NAS NMS	MOSI	Mosinee Paper Corp
MotClb	NAS NMS	MOTR	Motor Club of America
Motel	New York	SIX	Motel 6 LP
MotoPh	NAS NL	MOTTO	Moto Photo Inc
Motorla	New York	MOT	Motorola Inc
Motts	American	MSM	Mott's Super Markets Inc
MPSI	NAS NMS	MPSG	MPSI System Inc
MrCaA	NAS NMS	MCBKA	Merchants Capital Corp (Class A)
MrCaB	NAS NMS	MCBKB	Merchants Capital Corp (Class B)
MrcBnc	NAS NMS	MBVT	Merchants Bancshares Inc (Vermont)
MrchGp	American	MGP	Merchants Group Inc
MrchNt	NAS NMS	MCHN	Merchants National Corp
MrdDia	NAS NMS	KITS	Meridian Diagnostic Inc
MrdnBc	NAS NMS	MRDN	Meridian Bancorp Inc
MrdnNt	NAS SL	MRCO	Meridian National Corp
MrshIn	New York	MI	Marshall Industries
MrshMc	New York	MMC	Marsh & McLennan Companies Inc
MrshSu	NAS NMS	MARS	Marsh Supermarkets Inc
Mrsmr	NAS NMS	MFGR	Morsemere Financial Group Inc
MrthOf	American	MAO	Marathon Office Supply Inc
MSA	American	SSS	MSA Realty Corp
MSCar	NAS NMS	MSCA	M.S. Carriers Inc
MscoI	NAS NMS	MASX	Masco Industries Inc
MSI Dt	American	MSI	MSI Data Corp
MSI El	NAS NL	MSIE	MSI Electronics Inc
MsmRs	American	MRP	Mission Resource Partners LP
MSR	American	MSR	MSR Exploration Ltd
MtchlE	American	MND	Mitchell Energy & Development Corp
MtgPl	American	MIP	Mortgage Investments Plus Inc
MtgRty	New York	MRT	Mortgage & Realty Trust
MtlBnc	NAS SL	MBAN	MetalBanc Corp
MtlFdl	NAS NL	MFBZ	Mutual Federal Savings Bank, A Stock Corp (Ohio)
MtMed	American	MTN	Mountain Medical Equipment Inc
MtnrBk	NAS NMS	MTNR	Mountaineer Bankshares of W. Va. Inc

NEWSPAPER ABBREV.	MARKET LISTING	TRADING SYMBOL	COMPANY NAME
MtrxM	NAS SL	MMII	Matrix Medica Inc
MTS	NAS NMS	MTSC	MTS Systems Corp
MTwan	NAS NMS	MTWN	Mark Twain Bancshares Inc
Mueller	NAS NMS	MUEL	Paul Mueller Co
MuFSL	NAS NMS	MUTU	Mutual Federal S&L Assn (North Carolina)
Multbk	NAS NMS	MLTF	Multibank Financial Corp
MultClr	NAS NMS	LABL	Multi-Color Corp
Multm	NAS NMS	MMEDC	Multimedia Inc
MultnA	NAS NL	MKNLA	Multnomah Kennel Club (Class A)
Multvst	NAS SL	MVST	Multivest Corp
Munfrd	New York	MFD	Munford Inc
MuniDv	NAS NMS	MUNI	Municipal Development Corp
MunIn	American	MIF	MuniInsured Fund Inc
Munsng	New York	MUN	Munsingwear Inc
Munvst	American	MUF	Munivest Fund Inc
Murgold	NAS SL	MGDVF	Murgold Resources Inc
MurpO	New York	MUR	Murphy Oil Corp
MurryO	New York	MYO	Murry Ohio Manufacturing Co
Muscld	New York	TMG	The Musicland Group Inc
Muscoch	NAS NL	MUSMF	Muscocho Explorations Ltd
MustR	NAS NL	MUSE	Mustang Resources Corp
MutOm	New York	MUO	Mutual of Omaha Interest Shares Inc
MWE	New York	MWE	Midwest Energy Co
Mycogn	NAS NMS	MYCO	Mycogen Corp
MyerI	American	MYE	Myers Industries Inc
MyerL	New York	MYR	The L.E. Myers Company Group
Mylan	New York	MYL	Mylan Laboratories Inc
Mylex	NAS SL	MYLX	Mylex Corp
NABcp	NAS NL	NOAB	North American Bancorporation Inc
NABio	NAS NMS	NBIO	North American Biologicals Inc
NAC RE	NAS NMS	NREC	NAC Re Corp
NACCO	New York	NC	NACCO Industries Inc
NAFCO	New York	NAF	NAFCO Financial Group Inc
Naham	NAS SL	NAWE	Nahama & Weagant Energy Co
NAHdA	NAS NMS	NAHLA	North American Holding Corp (Class A)
NAHld	NAS NMS	NAHL	North American Holding Corp
Nalcap	NAS NL	NPHIF	Nalcap Holdings Inc
Nalco	New York	NLC	Nalco Chemical Co
NAmSv	NAS NL	NASA	North American Savings Assn (Missouri)
NAMtl	NAS SL	NAMVF	North American Metals Corp
NAmV	NAS NMS	NAVI	North American Ventures Inc
Nanomt	NAS NMS	NANO	Nanometrics Inc
Nantck	American	NAN	Nantucket Industries Inc
NapaVl	NAS NMS	NVBC	Napa Valley Bancorp
Napco	NAS NMS	NPCO	Napco International Inc
NashF	NAS NMS	NAFC	Nash-Finch Co

NEWSPAPER ABBREV.	MARKET LISTING	TRADING SYMBOL	COMPANY NAME
Nashua	New York	NSH	Nashua Corp
Nasta	American	NAS	Nasta International Inc
NatAltr	NAS SL	NATA	Natural Alternatives Inc
NatEdu	New York	NEC	National Education Corp
NatFG	New York	NFG	National Fuel Gas Co
NAtIn	NAS NMS	NATL	North Atlantic Industries Inc
NatrBty	NAS NMS	NBTY	Nature's Bounty Inc
NavgGp	NAS NMS	NAVG	Navigators Group Inc
Navistr	New York	NAV	Navistar International Corp
NB Alsk	NAS NMS	NBAK	National Bancorp of Alaska Inc
NBD	New York	NBD	NBD Bancorp Inc
NBI	New York	NBI	NBI Inc
NBkWV	NAS NMS	NBCC	National Banc of Commerce Co (West Virginia)
NbleDr	NAS NMS	NDCO	Noble Drilling Corp
NBnTex	NAS NMS	NBCT	National Bancshares Corporation of Texas
NBrunS	NAS NMS	NBSC	New Brunswick Scientific Co
NBSC	NAS NMS	NSCB	NBSC Corp
NBusSy	NAS NMS	NBSIF	National Business Systems Inc
NCarG	NAS NMS	NCNG	North Carolina Natural Gas Corp
NCdO	American	NCD	North Canadian Oils Ltd
NCF	American	NFC	NCF Financial Corp
NCH	New York	NCH	NCH Corp
NCNB	New York	NCB	NCNB Corp
NCNJ	NAS NMS	NCBR	National Community Bank of New Jersey
NCR	New York	NCR	NCR Corp
NCtyB	NAS NMS	NCBM	National City Bancorporation (Minnesota)
ND Rsc	NAS SL	NUDYE	ND Resources Inc
NData	NAS NMS	NDTA	National Data Corp
NDL	NAS SL	NDLP	NDL Products Inc
NDtacpt	NAS SL	NDIC	National Datacomputer Inc
NE Bcp	NAS NL	NBKC	New England Bancorp Inc
NE Bus	NAS NMS	NEBS	New England Business Service Inc
NE Ins	NAS SL	NEIC	North East Insurance Co
NEC	NAS NMS	NIPNY	NEC Corp
NECO	American	NPT	NECO Enterprises Inc
NECrit	NAS NMS	NECC	New England Critical Care Inc
NEECO	NAS NMS	NEEC	NEECO Inc
NeimM	New York	NMG	The Neiman-Marcus Group Inc
Nellcor	NAS NMS	NELL	Nellcor Inc
NelsnB	NAS SL	TNELB	Nelson Thomas Inc (Class B)
NelsnH	American	NHI	Nelson Holdings International Ltd
NelsnT	NAS NMS	TNEL	Nelson Thomas Inc
NeMtge	American	NM	NorthEastern Mortgage Company Inc
NEngEl	New York	NES	New England Electric System
NEngRA	NAS NL	NEWRZ	New England Realty Assn

NEWSPAPER ABBREV.	MARKET LISTING	TRADING SYMBOL	COMPANY NAME
NEnvCt	NAS SL	NECT	National Environmental Controls Inc
NEOAX	NAS NMS	NOAX	NEOAX Inc
Neolens	NAS SL	NEOL	Neo-Lens Inc
Neorx	NAS NMS	NERX	NeoRx Corp
Nerco	New York	NER	NERCO Inc
NESB	NAS NMS	NESB	NESB Corp
Nestor	NAS NMS	NEST	Nestor Inc
NestSv	New York	NSB	Northeast Savings F.A.
NetAir	NAS SL	NTAR	NetAir International Corp
NETI	NAS SL	NETIF	NETI Technologies Inc
NetwkPc	NAS SL	NPSI	Networked Picture Systems Inc
NEurO	New York	NET	North European Oil Royalty Trust
Neurtch	NAS SL	NURO	Neurotech Corp
Neutrg	NAS NMS	NGNA	Neutrogena Corp
NevGld	NAS NMS	NGFCF	Nevada Goldfields Corp
NevNBc	NAS NMS	NENB	Nevada National Bancorporation
NevPw	New York	NVP	Nevada Power Co
Newcor	American	NEW	Newcor Inc
Newell	New York	NWL	Newell Co
Newhll	New York	NHL	The Newhall Land & Farming Co
NewLew	American	NLI	Newmark & Lewis Inc
NewLine	American	NLN	New Line Cinema Corp
NewpEl	NAS NMS	NEWE	Newport Electronics Inc
Newpt	NAS NMS	NEWP	Newport Corp
NewsCp	New York	NWS	The News Corporation Ltd
NewSky	NAS SL	NSKY	New Sky Communications Inc
NewSL	NAS NMS	NFSL	Newman Federal S&L Assn (Georgia)
NflkSo	New York	NSC	Norfolk Southern Corp
NFS	NAS NMS	NFSF	NFS Financial Corp
NHD Str	NAS NMS	NHDI	NHD Stores Inc
NHltLab	NAS NMS	NHLI	National Health Laboratories Inc
NHmB	NAS NMS	NHSB	New Hampshire Savings Bank Corp
NiagEx	NAS NMS	NIEX	Niagara Exchange Corp
NiagSh	New York	NGS	Niagara Share Corp
NiaMP	New York	NMK	Niagara Mohawk Power Corp
NiCal	NAS NMS	NICLF	Ni-Cal Developments Ltd
NichApl	New York	GEF	Nichols-Applegate Growth Equity Fund Inc
NichHm	NAS NMS	NHIC	Nichols-Homeshield Inc
NichIn	American	LAB	Nichols Institute
Nichols	American	NCL	S.E. Nichols Inc
NichRs	NAS NMS	NRES	Nichols Research Corp
Nicolet	New York	NIC	Nicolet Instrument Corp
NICOR	New York	GAS	NICOR Inc
NikeB	NAS NMS	NIKE	NIKE Inc (Class B)
NIPSCO	New York	NI	NIPSCO Industries Inc
Niravce	NAS SL	NIRAA	Niravoice Inc (Class A)
Nissan	NAS NL	NSANY	Nissan Motor Company Ltd

NEWSPAPER ABBREV.	MARKET LISTING	TRADING SYMBOL	COMPANY NAME
NJ Stl	NAS NMS	NJST	New Jersey Steel Corp
NJRsc	New York	NJR	New Jersey Resources Corp
NJSvg	NAS NMS	NJSB	New Jersey Savings Bank
NL Ind	New York	NL	NL Industries Inc
NLamp	NAS SL	NLPI	National Lampoon Inc
NlI	New York	NII	National Intergroup Inc
NMedE	New York	NME	National Medical Enterprises Inc
NMicrn	NAS NMS	NMIC	National Micronetics Inc
NMineS	New York	NMS	National Mine Service Co
NMlBc	NAS NMS	NMSB	NewMil Bancorp Inc
NMR	NAS SL	NMRR	NMR of America Inc
NMxAr	American	NZ	New Mexico & Arizona Land Co
NoAir	NAS NMS	NAFI	Northern Air Freight Inc
NoANat	NAS NMS	NAMC	North American National Corp
Nobel	NAS NMS	NOBLF	Nobel Insurance Ltd
NobiltyH	NAS SL	NOBH	Nobility Homes Inc
NoblAf	New York	NBL	Noble Affiliates Inc
NobleR	NAS SL	NROM	Noble Romans Inc
Nodway	NAS NMS	NVCO	Nodaway Valley Co
NoelInd	American	NOL	Noel Industries Inc
NoestUt	New York	NU	Northeast Utilities
NoFkB	NAS NMS	NFBC	North Fork Bancorporation
Noland	NAS NMS	NOLD	Noland Co
Nooney	NAS NL	NRTI	Nooney Realty Trust Inc
NordRs	New York	NRD	Nord Resources Corp
Nordsn	NAS NMS	NDSN	Nordson Corp
Nordst	NAS NMS	NOBE	Nordstrom Inc
NorldCr	NAS NMS	CBRYA	Northland Cranberries Inc (Class A)
NorQst	NAS SL	NQRLF	Nor-Quest Resources Ltd
Norsk	New York	NHY	Norsk Hydro a.s.
NorskB	NAS NMS	NORKZ	Norsk-Data A.S. (Class B)
Norstan	NAS NMS	NRRD	Norstan Inc
Nortek	New York	NTK	Nortek Inc
NorTel	New York	NT	Northern Telecom Ltd
NortnE	NAS NMS	NRTN	Norton Enterprises Inc
Norton	New York	NRT	Norton Co
Nortrp	New York	NOC	Northrop Corp
NorTrst	NAS NMS	NTRS	Northern Trust Corp
NorwFn	NAS NMS	NSSB	Norwich Financial Corp
Norwst	New York	NOB	Northwest Corp
NoSdeSv	NAS NMS	NSBK	North Side Savings Bank (New York)
NostN	NAS SL	NNET	Nostalgia Network Inc
NoStPw	New York	NSP	Northern States Power Co
Nova	New York	NVA	Nova Corp
NovaPh	NAS NMS	NOVX	Nova Pharmaceutical Corp
Novar	NAS NMS	NOVR	Novar Electronics Corp
Novell	NAS NMS	NOVL	Novell Inc
Novelus	NAS NL	NVLS	Novellus Systems Inc

NEWSPAPER ABBREV.	MARKET LISTING	TRADING SYMBOL	COMPANY NAME
Novmtx	NAS NMS	NMTX	Novametrix Medical Systems Inc
Novo	New York	NVO	Novo Industri A/S
NovoCp	NAS NMS	NOVO	Novo Corp
Nowsc	NAS NL	NWELF	Nowsco Well Service Ltd
Noxell	NAS NMS	NOXLB	Noxell Corp (Class B)
NPlnRl	New York	NPR	New Plan Realty Trust
NProc	American	NOZ	New Process Co
NRM	American	NRM	NRM Energy Company L.P.
NrmOG	NAS NMS	NMDY	Normandy Oil & Gas Co
NS Gp	American	NSS	NS Group Inc
NSecIns	NAS NMS	NSIC	National Security Insurance Co
NStand	New York	NSD	National-Standard Co
NStarU	NAS NMS	NSRU	North Star Universal Inc
NstBcp	NAS NMS	NBIC	Northeast Bancorp Inc
Nt HMO	NAS NMS	NHMO	National HMO Corp
NtAust	New York	NAB	National Australia Bank Ltd
NtCBc	NAS NMS	NCBC	National Commerce Bancorporation
NtCptr	NAS NMS	NLCS	National Computer Systems Inc
NTech	NAS NMS	NTSC	National Technical Systems
NTelpd	NAS NMS	NWTL	Northwest Teleproductions Inc
NtEnt	New York	NEI	National Enterprises Inc
NtGsO	American	NLG	National Gas & Oil Co
NtGuard	NAS NMS	NATG	The National Guardian Corp
NtHert	New York	NHR	National Heritage Inc
Nthgat	New York	NGX	Northgate Exploration Ltd
NthHill	NAS NMS	NOHL	North Hills Electronics Inc
NthldSv	NAS NL	NLSL	Northland S&L Assn
NthLily	NAS NL	NLMC	North Lily Mining Co
NtHltcr	NAS NMS	NHCI	National Healthcare Inc
NtHlthE	NAS SL	NHES	National Health Enhancement Systems Inc
NtImag	NAS NL	NIAM	National Imaging Inc
NtInBc	NAS SL	NIBCA	National Industrial Bancorp Inc (Class A)
NtInst	NAS SL	NICE	National Institute of Careers Inc
Ntl City	NAS NMS	NCTY	National City Corp
Ntl FSI	NAS NL	NFSI	National FSI Inc
NtlCnv	New York	NCS	National Convenience Stores Inc
NtlIns	NAS NMS	NAIG	National Insurance Group
NtLoan	NAS NMS	NLBK	National Loan Bank (Texas)
NtlPza	NAS NMS	PIZA	National Pizza Co
NtlRef	NAS NL	ZIPP	National Reference Publishing Inc
NtlSav	NAS NMS	NSBA	National Savings Bank of Albany
NtLumb	NAS NMS	NTLB	National Lumber & Supply Inc
NtMedia	NAS SL	NMCOC	National Media Corp
NtMerc	NAS NMS	MBLA	National Mercantile Bancorp
NtPatnt	American	NPD	National Patent Development Corp
NtPenn	NAS NMS	NPBC	National Penn Bancshares Inc
NtPrest	New York	NPK	National Presto Industries Inc

NEWSPAPER ABBREV.	MARKET LISTING	TRADING SYMBOL	COMPANY NAME
NtProp	NAS NMS	NAPE	National Properties Corp
NtrSun	NAS NMS	AMTC	Nature's Sunshine Products Inc
NtRty	American	NLP	National Realty L.P.
NtSanit	NAS NMS	NSSX	National Sanitary Supply Co
NtSemi	New York	NSM	National Semiconductor Corp
NtSvIn	New York	NSI	National Service Industries Inc
NtTran	NAS SL	NTNI	National Transaction Network Inc
NtwdLg	NAS SL	NLSI	Nationwide Legal Services Inc
NtwkEl	NAS NMS	NWRK	Network Electronic Corp
NtwkSy	NAS NMS	NSCO	Network Systems Corp
NtWnLf	NAS NMS	NWLIA	National Western Life Insurance Co (Class A)
NtWst	New York	NW	National Westminster Bank PLC
NuclDt	American	NDI	Nuclear Data Inc
NuclSpt	NAS NMS	NSSI	Nuclear Support Services Inc
NucMet	NAS NMS	NUCM	Nuclear Metals Inc
Nucor	New York	NUE	Nucor Corp
NucrpE	NAS NMS	NUCO	Nucorp Energy Inc
NuHrz	American	NUH	Nu Horizons Electronics Corp
NUI	New York	NUI	NUI Corp
Numac	American	NMC	Numac Oil & Gas Ltd
NuMed	NAS NMS	NUMS	Nu-Med Inc
Numerex	NAS NMS	NUMR	Numerex Corp
Numrc	NAS NMS	NUME	Numerica Financial Corp
Nutmeg	NAS NMS	NUTM	Nutmeg Industries Inc
NutrCh	NAS SL	NCCI	Nutri-Cheese Inc
NuvCal	New York	NCA	Nuveen California Municipal Value Fund Inc
NuVisn	NAS NMS	NUVI	NuVision Inc
NuvMu	New York	NUV	Nuveen Municipal Value Fund Inc
NuvNY	New York	NNY	Nuveen New York Municipal Value Fund Inc
NuvPI	New York	NPI	Nuveen Premium Income Municipal Fund Inc
NvCMI	New York	NCM	Nuveen California Municipal Income Fund
NVideo	NAS NMS	NVIS	National Video Inc
NVision	NAS SL	NVSI	National Vision Services Inc
NvMuI	New York	NMI	Nuveen Municipal Income Fund
NvNYM	American	NNM	Nuveen N.Y. Municipal Income Fund
NVRyn	American	NVR	NVRyan L.P.
NW Grp	NAS NMS	NWGI	N-W Group Inc
NWA	New York	NWA	NWA Inc
NwAm	New York	NYB	New American High Income Fund
NwASh	New York	AFS	New American Shoe Corp
NwBedf	New York	NBB	New Bedford Institution for Savings
NwEng	NAS NMS	NWEN	Northwest Engineering Co
Nwhall	New York	NIP	Newhall Investment Properties
NwhlRs	New York	NR	Newhall Resources

NEWSPAPER ABBREV.	MARKET LISTING	TRADING SYMBOL	COMPANY NAME
NwkEq	NAS NMS	NETX	Network Equipment Technologies Inc
NwldBk	NAS NMS	NWOR	Neworld Bancorp Inc (Massachusetts)
NWldE	American	NWE	New World Entertainment Ltd
NwmtGd	New York	NGC	Newmont Gold Co
NwNG	NAS NMS	NWNG	Northwest Natural Gas Co
NwNLf	NAS NMS	NWNL	Northwestern National Life Insurance Co
NwpPh	NAS NMS	NWPH	Newport Pharmaceuticals International Inc
NwPrC	NAS NL	NSTS	Northwestern States Portland Cement Co
NwprtN	NAS NMS	NNSL	Newport News Savings Bank (Virginia)
NWPS	NAS NMS	NWPS	Northwestern Public Service Co
NwstIll	NAS NMS	NWIB	Northwest Illinois Bancorp Inc
NWstT	NAS NMS	NOWT	North-West Telecommunications Inc
NwStW	New York	NSW	Northwestern Steel & Wire Co
NwtM	New York	NEM	Newmont Mining Corp
NwVisn	NAS NMS	NUCP	New Visions Entertainment Corp
NY Bcp	NAS NMS	NYBC	New York Bancorp Inc
NY Mir	NAS NMS	NYMG	New York Marine & General Insurance Co
NY Time	American	NYT.A	The New York Times Co (Class A)
NYCOR	NAS NMS	NYCO	NYCOR Inc
Nynex	New York	NYN	NYNEX Corp
NYSEG	New York	NGE	New York State Electric & Gas Corp
NYTEI	American	XTX	The New York Tax-Exempt Income Fund Inc
Nytest	NAS SL	NYTS	Nytest Environmental Inc
NYTst	NAS SL	NYTL	New York Testing Laboratories Inc
OakHill	NAS NMS	OHSC	Oak Hill Sportswear Corp
OakInd	New York	OAK	Oak Industries Inc
OakiteP	New York	OKT	Oakite Products Inc
Oakwd	New York	OH	Oakwood Homes Corp
OBrien	American	OBS	O'Brien Energy Systems Inc
OcciPet	New York	OXY	Occidental Petroleum Corp
OccuMd	NAS SL	OMCA	Occupational Medical Corporation of America Inc
Oce-NY	NAS NL	OCENY	Oce-Van Der Grinten N.V.
Oceaner	NAS NMS	OCER	Oceaneering International Inc
OCG Tc	NAS NMS	OCGT	OCG Technology Inc
Ocilla	NAS NMS	OCIL	Ocilla Industries Inc
Octel	NAS NMS	OCTL	Octel Communications Corp
OcuUrg	NAS NMS	OUCH	Occupational-Urgent Care Health Systems Inc
ODECO	New York	ODR	Ocean Drilling & Exploration Co
OdetA	American	O.A	Odetics Inc (Class A)
OdetB	American	O.B	Odetics Inc (Class B)
Odysey	NAS SL	ODYY	Odyssey Entertainment Ltd
OEA	American	OEA	OEA Inc
OfceDpt	NAS NL	ODEP	Office Depot Inc
OffsLog	NAS NMS	OLOGP	Offshore Logistics Inc

NEWSPAPER ABBREV.	MARKET LISTING	TRADING SYMBOL	COMPANY NAME
Oficeld	NAS NL	OFLDF	Officeland Inc
Ogden	New York	OG	Ogden Corp
OgilGp	NAS NMS	OGIL	The Ogilvy Group Inc
Oglbay	NAS NMS	OGLE	Oglebay Norton Co
OhArt	American	OAR	The Ohio Art Co
OhioBc	NAS NMS	OHBC	Ohio Bancorp
OhioCas	NAS NMS	OCAS	Ohio Casualty Corp
OhioEd	New York	OEC	Ohio Edison Co
OhMatr	New York	OMT	The Ohio Mattress Co
OICorp	NAS SL	OICO	O.I. Corp
OilDri	NAS NMS	OILC	Oil-Dri Corporation of America
Oilgear	NAS NMS	OLGR	Oilgear Co
OklaGE	New York	OGE	Oklahoma Gas & Electric Co
OldDom	NAS NMS	ODSI	Old Dominion Systems Inc
OldFsh	NAS NMS	OFFI	Old Fashion Foods Inc
OldKnt	NAS NMS	OKEN	Old Kent Financial Corp
OldRep	NAS NMS	OLDR	Old Republic International Corp
OldSpag	NAS NMS	OSWI	Old Spagetti Warehouse Inc
OldStn	NAS NMS	OSTN	Old Stone Corp
Olin	New York	OLN	Olin Corp
OlsonI	NAS NMS	OLSN	Olson Industries Inc
Olsten	American	OLS	The Olsten Corp
OlyBdc	NAS SL	OBCCC	Olympic Broadcasting Corp
OlymSv	NAS NL	OSBW	Olympic Savings Bank
OMI Cp	NAS NMS	OMIC	OMI Corp
Omncre	New York	OCR	Omnicare Inc
Omnicm	NAS NMS	OMCM	Omnicom Group Inc
OmniEx	NAS SL	OMNX	Omni Exploration Inc
Oncogn	NAS NMS	ONCS	Oncogene Science Inc
Oncor	NAS SL	ONCR	Oncor Inc
OneBc	NAS NMS	TONE	The One Bancorp
Oneida	New York	OCQ	Oneida Ltd
Oneita	American	ONA	Oneita Industries Inc
OneLibt	American	OLP	One Liberty Properties Inc
ONEOK	New York	OKE	ONEOK Inc
OnePr	NAS NMS	ONPR	One Price Clothing Stores Inc
OneVl	NAS NMS	OVWV	One Valley Bancorp of West Virginia Inc
OnLne	New York	OSI	On-Line Software International Inc
OOkiep	American	OKP	O'okiep Copper Company Ltd
OpnMl	New York	OMS	Oppenheimer Multi-Sector Income Trust
Oppenh	American	OPP	Oppenheimer Industries Inc
Optek	NAS NMS	OPTX	Optek Technology Inc
OpticC	NAS NMS	OCLI	Optical Coating Laboratory Inc
OpticlS	NAS NMS	OSIX	Optical Specialities Inc
OpticR	NAS NMS	ORCO	Optical Radiation Corp
Optlcm	NAS SL	OPTC	Optelecom Inc
Opto	NAS NMS	OPTO	Opto Mechanik Inc
Oracle	NAS NMS	ORCL	Oracle Systems Corp

NEWSPAPER ABBREV.	MARKET LISTING	TRADING SYMBOL	COMPANY NAME
OrangF	NAS NL	OFSLY	Orange Free State Investments Ltd
OranRk	New York	ORU	Orange & Rockland Utilities Inc
Orbit	NAS NMS	ORBT	Orbit Instrument Corp
OregMt	NAS NMS	OREM	Oregon Metallurgical Corp
OregSt	American	OS	Oregon Steel Mills Inc
Orfa	NAS NMS	ORFA	ORFA Corporation of America
Orgngn	American	ORG	Organogensis Inc
Orient	New York	OEH	Orient Express Hotels Inc
OrigItl	NAS SL	ORIG	Original Italian Pasta Products Company Inc
OriolH A	American	OHC.A	Oriole Homes Corp (Class A)
OriolH B	American	OHC.B	Oriole Homes Corp (Class B)
OrionBd	NAS SL	OBGI	Orion Broadcast Group Inc
OrionC	New York	OC	Orion Capital Corp
OrionP	New York	OPC	Orion Pictures Corp
OrionRs	NAS NMS	ORIR	Orion Research Inc
Ormand	American	OMD	Ormand Industries Inc
OrngCo	New York	OJ	Orange-co Inc
OrngSv	NAS SL	OSBK	Orange Savings Bank
OrntFd	NAS NMS	OFSB	Orient Federal Savings Bank (Puerto Rico)
Orthmt	NAS NMS	OMET	Orthomet Inc
Osborn	NAS NL	OSBN	Osborn Communications Corp
OshA	NAS NMS	GOSHA	Oshkosh B'Gosh Inc (Class A)
OshB	NAS NMS	GOSHB	Oshkosh B'Gosh Inc (Class B)
OshkT B	NAS NMS	OTRKB	Oshkosh Truck Corp (Class B)
Oshmn	NAS NMS	OSHM	Oshman's Sporting Goods Inc
Osicom	NAS NMS	OSIC	Osicom Technologies Inc
Osmnc	NAS NMS	OSMO	Osmonics Inc
OSulvn	American	OSL	O'Sullivan Corp
Otisvle	NAS SL	OBPI	Otisville BioPharm Inc
OttrTP	NAS NMS	OTTR	Otter Tail Power Co
OutbdM	New York	OM	Outboard Marine Corp
OutbOM	NAS SL	OUTB	Outback Oil & Mineral Exploration Corp
OutletC	NAS NMS	OCOMA	Outlet Communications Inc (Class A)
Overmy	NAS NL	OMCO	Overmyer Corp
Ovex	NAS SL	OVEX	Ovex Fertility Corp
Ovonic	NAS NL	OVON	Ovonic Imaging Systems Inc
OvShip	New York	OSB	Overseas Shipholding Group Inc
OwenC	New York	OCF	Owens-Corning Fiberglas Corp
OwenM	New York	OMI	Owens & Minor Inc
OxfEgy	American	OEN	The Oxford Energy Co
Oxford	New York	OXM	Oxford Industries Inc
Oxidyn	NAS NMS	OXID	The Oxidyne Group Inc
P F	NAS NMS	PFINA	P&F Industries Inc (Class A)
Pacad	NAS SL	BAGS	Pacad Inc
Pacar	NAS NMS	PCAR	PACCAR Inc

NEWSPAPER ABBREV.	MARKET LISTING	TRADING SYMBOL	COMPANY NAME
PacAS	New York	PAI	Pacific American Income Shares Inc
PacBcp	NAS SL	PABC	Pacific Bancorporation
PacDunl	NAS NMS	PDLPY	Pacific Dunlop Ltd
PACE	NAS NMS	PMWI	PACE Membership Warehouse Inc
PacEnt	New York	PET	Pacific Enterprises Ltd
PacFst	NAS NMS	PFFS	Pacific First Financial Corp
PacGE	New York	PCG	Pacific Gas & Electric Co
Pacifcp	New York	PPW	PacifiCorp
PacifCr	NAS NMS	PHSY	PacifiCare Health Systems Inc
PacInld	NAS NL	PIBC	Pacific Inland Bancorp
PacIntl	NAS NMS	PISC	Pacific International Services Corp
PacNuc	NAS NMS	PACN	Pacific Nuclear Systems Inc
PacRes	New York	PRI	Pacific Resources Inc
PacSci	New York	PSX	Pacific Scientific Co
PacSlv	NAS NMS	PASI	Pacific Silver Corp
PacTec	NAS SL	PTCH	Pacer Technology Inc
PacTel	New York	PAC	Pacific Telesis Group
PacWst	NAS NMS	PWA	Pacific Western Airlines Corp
PainSu	NAS SL	PAIN	Pain Suppresion Labs Inc
PainWb	New York	PWJ	PaineWebber Group Inc
Palfed	NAS NMS	PALM	PALFED Inc
PallCp	American	PLL	Pall Corp
PAM	NAS NMS	PTSI	P.A.M. Transportation Services Inc
PanAm	New York	PN	Pan Am Corp
PanAtl	NAS NMS	PNRE	Pan Atlantic Re Inc
PancMx	NAS NMS	PAMX	Pancho's Mexican Buffet Inc
Pancret	NAS SL	PNCR	Pancretec Inc
PanEC	New York	PEL	Panhandle Eastern Corp
Panill	New York	PKC	Pannill Knitting Company Inc
Pansph	New York	PNS	Pansophic Systems Inc
Pantast	American	PNT	Pantasote Inc
Pantch	NAS NMS	PNTC	Panatech Research & Development Corp
Pantera	NAS NMS	PANT	Pantera's Corp
PaPL	New York	PPL	Pensylvania Power & Light Co
Pardyn	New York	PDN	Paradyne Corp
ParisBu	NAS NMS	PBFI	Paris Business Forms Inc
ParkCm	NAS NMS	PARC	Park Communications Inc
ParkDrl	New York	PKD	Parker Drilling Co
ParkEl	New York	PKE	Park Electrochemical Corp
ParkHn	New York	PH	Parker Hannifin Corp
ParkOh	NAS NMS	PKOH	Park-Ohio Industries Inc
Parkwy	NAS NMS	PKWY	Parkway Co
Parlex	NAS NMS	PRLX	Parlex Corp
ParPh	New York	PRX	Par Pharmaceutical Inc
ParTch	New York	PTC	PAR Technology Corp
Pathe	NAS SL	QILT	Pathe Computer Control Systems Corp

NEWSPAPER ABBREV.	MARKET LISTING	TRADING SYMBOL	COMPANY NAME
Patlex	NAS NMS	PTLX	Patlex Corp
PatnPr	NAS SL	PPRO	Pattern Processing Technologies Inc
PatPtr	New York	PPC	Patrick Petroleum Co
PatrkI	NAS NMS	PATK	Patrick Industries Inc
PatTch	American	PTI	Patient Technology Inc
Patten	New York	PAT	Patten Corp
PaulH	NAS NMS	PHRS	Paul Harris Stores Inc
PaulPt	American	PP	Pauley Petroleum Inc
Paxar	American	PXR	PAXAR Corp
Paxton	NAS NMS	PAXTA	Frank Paxton Co (Class A)
Paychx	NAS NMS	PAYX	Paychex Inc
Payco	NAS NMS	PAYC	Payco American Corp
PayCsh	New York	PCI	Payless Cashways Inc
PayFon	American	PYF	Pay-Fone Systems Inc
PayNSv	NAS NMS	PAYN	Pay'n Save Inc
PBcWor	NAS NMS	PEBW	Peoples Bancorp of Worcester Inc (Massachusetts)
PbSNC	NAS NMS	PSNC	Public Service Company of North Carolina Inc
PC Qut	NAS SL	PCQT	P C Quote Inc
PCA Int	NAS NMS	PCAI	PCA International Inc
PCL	American	DIV	PCL Diversifund
PCS	NAS NMS	PCSI	PCS Inc
PDA	NAS NMS	PDAS	PDA Engineering
PEC Isr	American	IEC	PEC Israel Economic Corp
PeerMf	NAS NMS	PMFG	Peerless Manufacturing Co
PeerTu	American	PLS	Peerless Tube Co
PegGld	American	PGU	Pegasus Gold Ltd
Pelsart	NAS SL	PELRY	Pelsart Resources N.L.
PenaEn	NAS NMS	PENT	Pennsylvania Enterprises Inc
Penbcp	NAS NMS	PNBA	Pennbancorp
PenCn	New York	PC	The Penn Central Corp
PenEM	American	PNN	Penn Engineering & Manufacturing Corp
Penguin	NAS SL	PNGR	Penguin Group Inc
Penney	New York	JCP	J.C. Penney Company Inc
PennPc	NAS SL	PPAC	Penn Pacific Corp
Pennzol	New York	PZL	Pennzoil Co
Penob	American	PSO	Penobscot Shoe Co
PenRE	American	PEI	Pennsylvania Real Estate Investment Trust
Penril	American	PNL	Penril Corp
Penta	NAS SL	PSLI	Penta Systems International Inc
Pentair	NAS NMS	PNTA	Pentair Inc
Pentch	NAS SL	PNTK	Pentech International Inc
PenTr	American	PNF	Penn Traffic Co
Pentron	American	PEN	Pentron Industries Inc
PenTrt	NAS NMS	PTAC	Penn Treaty American Corp
PenV	NAS NMS	PVIR	Penn Virginia Corp

NEWSPAPER ABBREV.	MARKET LISTING	TRADING SYMBOL	COMPANY NAME
Penvw	NAS NMS	PSPA	Pennview Savings Assn (Pennsylvania)
Penwlt	New York	PSM	Pennwalt Corp
Penwt	NAS NMS	PENW	PENWEST LTD
PeoFdDe	NAS NL	PFDC	Peoples Federal Savings Bank of DeKalb County
PeopBc	NAS NMS	PBNC	Peoples Bancorporation (North Carolina)
PeopCT	NAS NMS	PBCT	People's Bank (Connecticut)
PeopEn	New York	PGL	Peoples Energy Corp
PeopHrt	NAS NMS	PIIBK	Peoples Heritage Financial Group Inc (Maine)
PeoRide	NAS SL	RIDE	People Ridesharing Systems Inc
PeoSvCt	NAS NMS	PBNB	The Peoples Savings Bank of New Britain (Connecticut)
PeoWst	NAS NMS	PWSB	Peoples Westchester Savings Bank (New York)
PepBy	New York	PBY	The Pep Boys-Manny Moe & Jack
PepsiCo	New York	PEP	PepsiCo Inc
Percpt	NAS NMS	PERC	Perceptronics Inc
PerCpt	NAS SL	PCPI	Personal Computer Products Inc
PercTc	NAS NMS	PCEP	Perception Technology Corp
PerDia	NAS SL	PERS	Personal Diagnostics Inc
Pergrn	NAS SL	MOVE	Peregrine Entertainment Ltd
Perigo	American	PRR	Perrigo Co
PeriniC	American	PCR	Perini Corp
PeriniI	American	PNV	Perini Investment Properties Inc
Periphl	NAS SL	PSIX	Peripheral Systems Inc
PerkEl	New York	PKN	The Perkin-Elmer Corp
PerkF	New York	PFR	Perkins Family Restaurants L.P.
PerpS	NAS NMS	PASB	Perpetual Savings Bank FSB (Virginia)
PeryDr	New York	PDS	Perry Drug Stores Inc
PeSvMch	NAS NMS	PSBX	Peoples Savings Bank FSB (Michigan)
PETCO	NAS NMS	PTCO	Petroleum Equipment Tools Co
PetDv	NAS NMS	PETD	Petroleum Development Corp
Peters	American	JMP	J.M. Peters Company Inc
PetInd	NAS NMS	PTRL	Petrol Industries Inc
Petrie	New York	PST	Petrie Stores Corp
Petrlte	NAS NMS	PLIT	Petrolite Corp
Petrmn	NAS NMS	PTRO	Petrominerals Corp
Petro	NAS SL	PEAL	Petro Global Inc
PetRs	New York	PEO	Petroleum & Resources Corp
PfdHlt	American	PY	Preferred Health Care Ltd
PfdRsk	NAS NMS	PFDR	Preferred Risk Life Insurance Co
PfdSav	NAS NMS	PSLA	Preferred Savings Bank Inc (North Carolina)
Pfizer	New York	PFE	Pfizer Inc
PgSdBc	NAS NMS	PSNB	Puget Sound Bancorp
PhelpD	New York	PD	Phelps Dodge Corp
PHH	New York	PHH	PHH Group Inc

NEWSPAPER ABBREV.	MARKET LISTING	TRADING SYMBOL	COMPANY NAME
PhilaEl	New York	PE	Philadelphia Electric Co
PhilGl	New York	PHG	Philips N.V.
PhilMr	New York	MO	Philip Morris Companies Inc
PhilPet	New York	P	Phillips Petroleum Co
PhilpIn	New York	PHL	Philips Industries Inc
PhilpJ	NAS SL	JEAN	Jean Philippe Frangrances Inc
PhilSub	New York	PSC	Philadelphia Suburban Corp
Phlcrp	New York	PHX	PHLCORP Inc
PhlLD	American	PHI	Philadelphia Long Distance Telephone Co
PhlVH	New York	PVH	Phillips-Van Heusen Corp
PHM	New York	PHM	PHM Corp
PhnMte	NAS NMS	PHMT	Phone-Mate Inc
PhnxAd	NAS SL	PATI	Phoenix Advanced Technology Inc
PhnxAm	NAS NMS	PHXA	Phoenix American Inc
PhnxMd	NAS NMS	PHNX	Phoenix Medical Technology Inc
PhnxR	American	PHR	Phoenix Realty Investors Inc
PhnxRe	NAS NMS	PXRE	Phoenix Re Corp
PhnxTc	NAS NL	PTEC	Phoenix Technologies Ltd
Phonetl	NAS SL	PNTL	Phonetel Technologies
PhotoC	NAS NMS	PHOC	Photo Control Corp
PhotoMk	NAS SL	PMCP	Photo Marker Corp
Photon	NAS SL	PHON	Photon Technology International Inc
PhotSci	NAS SL	PSCX	Photographic Science Corp
PHP	NAS NMS	PHPH	PHP Healthcare Corp
Phrmci	NAS NMS	PHABY	Pharmacia AB
Phrmct	NAS NMS	PHAR	PharmaControl Corp
Phrmk	NAS NMS	PKLB	PharmaKinetics Laboratories Inc
Phrmtc	NAS SL	PHTC	Pharmatec Inc
PhtrLb	NAS NMS	PLAB	Photronic Labs Inc
PhysIn	NAS NMS	PICOA	Physicians Insurance Company of Ohio (Class A)
PhysPh	NAS SL	PHYP	Physicians Pharmaceutical Services Inc
PicCafe	NAS NMS	PICC	Piccadilly Cafeterias Inc
PicoPd	American	PPI	Pico Products Inc
PicSav	NAS NMS	PICN	Pic'N' Save Corp
PicTel	NAS SL	PCTL	PictureTel Corp
PiedB	NAS NMS	PBGI	Piedmont Bankgroup Inc
PiedMg	NAS NMS	PMAN	Piedmont Management Company Inc
PiedMn	NAS SL	PIED	Piedmont Mining Company Inc
PiedNG	New York	PNY	Piedmont Natural Gas Company Inc
PiedSB	NAS NMS	PFSB	Piedmont Federal Savings Bank (Virginia)
Piemnt	NAS NL	PIFI	Piemonte Foods Inc
Pier 1	New York	PIR	Pier 1 Imports Inc
Piezo	NAS NL	PEPI	Piezo Electric Products Inc
Pikevle	NAS NL	PKVL	Pikeville National Corp
PilgPr	New York	CHX	Pilgrim's Pride Corp
PilgRg	New York	PBS	Pilgrim Regional Bank Shares Inc

NEWSPAPER ABBREV.	MARKET LISTING	TRADING SYMBOL	COMPANY NAME
Pilsbry	New York	PSY	The Pillsbury Co
PinWst	New York	PNW	Pinnacle West Capital Corp
PionAm	NAS NMS	PAHC	Pioneer American Holding Co
PionF	NAS NMS	PFSI	Pioneer Financial Services Inc (Illinois)
PionFn	NAS NMS	PION	Pioneer Financial Corp (Virginia)
PionGp	NAS NMS	PIOG	The Pioneer Group Inc
PionHi	NAS NMS	PHYB	Pioneer Hi-Bred International Inc
PionrEl	New York	PIO	Pioneer Electronic Corp
PionrSy	American	PAE	Pioneer Systems Inc
PionSB	NAS NMS	PSBF	Pioneer Savings Bank (Florida)
PionSt	NAS NMS	PIOS	Pioneer-Standard Electronics Inc
PionSv	NAS NMS	PSBN	Pioneer Savings Bank Inc (North Carolina)
PiprJaf	NAS NMS	PIPR	Piper Jaffray Inc
PitDsm	American	PDM	Pitt-DesMoines Inc
PitnyB	New York	PBI	Pitney Bowes Inc
Pittstn	New York	PCO	The Pittston Co
Pittway	American	PRY	Pittway Corp
PitWVa	American	PW	Pittsburgh & West Virginia Railroad
PlainsP	New York	PLP	Plains Petroleum Co
PlainsR	NAS NMS	PLNS	Plains Resources Inc
PlantCp	NAS NMS	PNBT	The Planters Corp
Plantrn	New York	PLX	Plantronics Inc
PlasmT	NAS SL	PTIS	Plasma-Therm Corp
PlastLn	NAS NMS	SIGN	Plasti-Line Inc
Playboy	New York	PLA	Playboy Enterprises Inc
PlcrD	New York	PDG	Placer Dome Inc
PlcyMg	NAS NMS	PMSC	Policy Management Systems Corp
Plenum	NAS NMS	PLEN	Plenum Publishing Corp
Plesey	New York	PLY	The Plessey Company plc
PlexusC	NAS NMS	PLXS	Plexus Corp
PlexusR	NAS SL	PLUSF	Plexus Resources Corp
PlntGen	NAS NMS	PGEN	Plant Genetics Inc
PlrMol	NAS SL	PMCX	Polar Molecular Corp
PlyFve	NAS NMS	THFI	Plymouth Five Cents Savings Bank (Massachusetts)
PlyGem	American	PGI	Ply*Gem Industries Inc
PlyR A	American	PLR.A	Plymouth Rubber Company Inc (Class A)
PlyR B	American	PLR.B	Plymouth Rubber Company Inc (Class B)
PlzCBc	NAS NMS	PLZA	Plaza Commerce Bancorp
PNC	New York	PNC	PNC Financial Corp
PneuSc	American	PNU	Pneumatic Scale Corp
PoeAsc	NAS NL	POEA	Poe & Associates Inc
PogoPd	New York	PPP	Pogo Producing Co
Polard	New York	PRD	Polaroid Corp
PolifyFn	NAS NMS	PFLY	Polifly Financial Corp
PolkAu	NAS NMS	POLK	Polk Audio Inc

NEWSPAPER ABBREV.	MARKET LISTING	TRADING SYMBOL	COMPANY NAME
PolrIn	American	SNO	Polaris Industries Partners L.P.
Polydex	NAS SL	POLXF	Polydex Pharmaceuticals Ltd
Polymr	NAS NMS	PICI	Polymer International Corp
PolyTch	NAS NMS	POLY	Poly-Tech Inc
PoncF	NAS NMS	PFBS	Ponce Federal Bank FSB (Puerto Rico)
PopeEv	American	PER	Pope, Evans & Robbins Inc
PopRad	NAS SL	POPX	Pop Radio Corp
PopTal	New York	POP	Pope & Talbot Inc
Portage	American	PTG	Portage Industries Corp
PortBk	NAS NMS	POBS	Portsmouth Bank Shares Inc
Portec	New York	POR	Portec Inc
PortGC	New York	PGN	Portland General Corp
PortsCl	NAS NMS	POCI	Ports of Call Inc
PortSys	American	PSI	Porta Systems Corp
PosdnP	NAS NMS	POOL	Poseidon Pools of America Inc
Possis	NAS NMS	POSS	Possis Corp
Postl Pr	American	PIP	Postal Instant Press
Potltch	New York	PCH	Potlatch Corp
PotmE	New York	POM	Potomec Electric Power Co
PoughSv	NAS NMS	PKPS	Poughkeepsie Savings Bank F.S.B.
Powell	NAS NMS	POWL	Powell Industries Inc
PPG	New York	PPG	PPG Industries Inc
PR Cem	New York	PRN	Puerto Rican Cement Company Inc
PrabRbt	NAS SL	PRAB	Prab Robots Inc
PraireO	American	POY	Prairie Oil Royalties Company Ltd
PratHt	American	PHC	Pratt Hotel Corp
PratLm	American	PM	Pratt & Lambert Inc
PraxBio	NAS NMS	PRXS	Praxis Biologics Inc
PrcCm	American	PR	Price Communications Corp
PrceTR	NAS NMS	TROW	T. Rowe Price Associates Inc
PrcStd	NAS NL	PCSN	Precision Standard Inc
PrdRs	New York	PRC	Products Research & Chemical Corp
PrecCst	NAS NMS	PCST	Precision Castparts Corp
PrecRs	NAS SL	PRES	Precision Resources Inc
PrecsA	American	PAR	Precision Aerotech Inc
PrecTrg	NAS NMS	CSIT	Precision Target Marketing Inc
PremFn	NAS NL	PREM	Premier Financial Services Inc
Premr	New York	PRE	Premier Industrial Corp
Premrk	New York	PMI	Premark International Inc
PresAr	NAS SL	PAIR	Presidential Airways Inc
Presd A	American	PRS.A	Presidio Oil Co (Class A)
Presd B	American	PRS.B	Presidio Oil Co (Class B)
PresLf	NAS NMS	PLFE	Presidential Life Corp
PresR A	American	PDL.A	Presidential Realty Corp (Class A)
PresR B	American	PDL.B	Presidential Realty Corp (Class B)
PrestoT	NAS NL	PRTK	Presto-Tek Corp
PrftTc	NAS NL	PRTE	Profit Technology Inc
PrgInc	New York	PYE	Progressive Income Equity Fund Inc

NEWSPAPER ABBREV.	MARKET LISTING	TRADING SYMBOL	COMPANY NAME
Priam	NAS NMS	PRIA	Priam Corp
PriceCo	NAS NMS	PCLB	The Price Co
Pricor	NAS NL	PRCO	Pricor Inc
Prima	NAS NL	PENG	Prima Energy Corp
Primca	New York	PA	Primerica Corp
PrimeC	New York	PRM	Prime Computer Inc
PrimeM	New York	PDQ	Prime Motor Inns Inc
Primge	NAS SL	PRIM	Primages Inc
Primrk	New York	PMK	Primark Corp
Prinvl	NAS NMS	PVDC	Princeville Corp
Prism	American	PRZ	Prism Entertainment Corp
PrivPay	NAS SL	PPPI	Private Pay Phones Inc
PrkvlSv	NAS NMS	PVSA	Parkvale Savings Assn (Pennsylvania)
PrmBnc	NAS NMS	PBKC	Premier Bancshares Corp
PrmCap	NAS NMS	PRME	Prime Capital Corp
PrmeBk	NAS NMS	PMBK	PRIMEBANK Federal Savings Bank (Michigan)
PrmeMd	NAS NMS	PMSI	Prime Medical Services Inc
PrmFn	American	PFP	Prime Financial Partners L.P.
Prmian	New York	PBT	Permian Basin Royalty Trust
PrMLt	New York	PMP	Prime Motor Inns L.P.
PrmrBc	NAS NMS	PRBC	Premier Bancorp Inc (Louisiana)
PrnDia	American	PDA	Princeton Diagnostic Laboratories of America
ProCre	NAS SL	PCRE	ProCare Industries Inc
ProctG	New York	PG	The Procter & Gamble Co
ProDex	NAS SL	PDEX	Pro-Dex Inc
ProdOp	NAS NMS	PROP	Production Operators Corp
ProfCre	American	PCE	Professional Care Inc
Proffitt	NAS NMS	PRFT	Proffitt's Inc
ProfInv	NAS NMS	PROF	Professional Investors Insurance Group Inc
ProfitS	NAS NMS	PFTS	Profit Systems Inc
ProgBk	NAS NMS	PSBK	Progressive Bank Inc (New York)
ProgCp	New York	PGR	The Progressive Corp (Ohio)
ProgFn	NAS NMS	PFNC	Progress Financial Corp
Progrp	NAS NMS	PRGR	ProGroup Inc
ProgSys	NAS NMS	PSYS	Programming & Systems Inc
Proler	New York	PS	Proler International Corp
ProMed	American	PMC	Pro-Med Capital Inc
Pronet	NAS NMS	PNET	ProNet Inc
PropCT	American	PCT	Property Capital Trust
ProsGp	NAS NMS	PROSZ	The Prospect Group Inc
ProtLfe	NAS NMS	PROT	Protective Life Corp
ProvAm	NAS NMS	PAMC	Provident American Corp
ProvBc	NAS NL	PRBK	Provident Bancorp Inc
ProvEn	American	PVY	Providence Energy Corp
PrpdLg	American	PPD	Pre-Paid Legal Services Inc

NEWSPAPER ABBREV.	MARKET LISTING	TRADING SYMBOL	COMPANY NAME
PrstnCp	NAS NMS	PTRK	Preston Corp
Prtronx	NAS NMS	PTNX	Printronix Inc
PrudFn	NAS NMS	PFSL	Prudential Financial Services Corp
PruInt	New York	PIF	Prudential Intermediate Income Fund Inc
PruStr	New York	PSF	Prudential Strategic Income Fund
PrvBksh	NAS NMS	PBKS	Provident Bankshares Corp
Prvena	NAS NMS	PVNA	Provena Foods Inc
PrvLfe	NAS NMS	PACC	Provident Life & Accident Insurance Co
PrvWor	NAS NL	PWRR	Providence & Worcester Railroad Co
PS Grp	New York	PSG	PS Group Inc
PSBBrc	NAS NMS	PBKB	People's Savings Bank of Brockton (Massachusetts)
PSE	American	POW	PSE Inc
PSEG	New York	PEG	Public Service Enterprise Group Inc
PSI	New York	PIN	PSI Holdings Inc
Psicor	NAS NMS	PCOR	PSICOR Inc
PSNH	New York	PNH	Public Service Company of New Hampshire
PspctPk	NAS NMS	PPSA	Prospect Park Financial Corp (New Jersey)
PSS Pub	NAS NMS	PSSP	Price/Stern/Sloan Publishers Inc
PSvCol	New York	PSR	Public Service Company of Colorado
PSvNM	New York	PNM	Public Service Company of New Mexico
PsycCp	NAS SL	PCMC	Psychemedics Corp
PTelcm	NAS NMS	PTCM	Pacific Telecom Inc
PtHeat	American	PHP.B	Petroleum Heat & Power Company Inc (Class B)
PtHel	NAS NL	PHEL	Petroleum Helicopters Inc (voting)
PtHel	NAS NL	PHELK	Petroleum Helicopters Inc (non-voting)
PtPar	New York	LPG	Petrolane Partners L.P.
PtrInv	New York	PIL	Petroleum Investments Ltd
PubcoC	NAS NMS	PUBO	Pubco Corp
PublEq	NAS NMS	PECN	Publishers Equipment Corp
Publick	New York	PUL	Publicker Industries Inc
Pueblo	New York	PII	Pueblo International Inc
PugetP	New York	PSD	Puget Sound Power & Light Co
PulaskF	NAS NMS	PLFC	Pulaski Furniture Corp
Pullmn	New York	PMN	The Pullman Co
PultzPb	NAS NMS	PLTZC	Pulitzer Publishing Co
PulwS	NAS NMS	PULS	Pulawski S&L Assn (New Jersey)
PuntaG	American	PGA	Punta Gorda Isles Inc
PuritB	NAS NMS	PBEN	Puritan-Bennett Corp
PutMas	New York	PMT	Putnam Master Income Trust
PutMI	New York	PIM	Putnam Master Intermediate Income Trust
PutnHi	New York	PCF	Putnam High Income Convertible & Bond Fund
PutnTr	NAS NL	PTNM	Putnam Trust Co
PutPr	New York	PPT	Putnam Premier Income Trust
PyrmO	NAS NL	PYOL	Pyramid Oil Co

NEWSPAPER ABBREV.	MARKET LISTING	TRADING SYMBOL	COMPANY NAME
PyrmT	NAS NMS	PYRD	Pyramid Technology Corp
Pyro	New York	BTU	Pyro Energy Corp
Qantel	New York	BQC	Qantel Corp
Qdrax	NAS SL	QDRX	Quadrax Corp
QED	NAS NMS	QEDX	QED Exploration Inc
QkReily	New York	BQR	The Quick & Reilly Group Inc
Qmax	NAS NMS	QMAX	QMax Technology Group Inc
QMed	NAS NMS	QEKG	Q-MED Inc
QMS	New York	AQM	QMS Inc
Qntrnx	NAS NMS	QUAN	Quantronix Corp
QrtzMt	NAS NMS	QZMGF	Quartz Mountain Gold Corp
QstVl	New York	KFV	Quest For Value Dual Purpose Fund Inc
Quadrx	NAS NMS	QUAD	Quadrex Corp
QuakCh	NAS NMS	QCHM	Quaker Chemical Corp
QuakFb	American	CFQ	Quaker Fabric Corp
QuakO	New York	OAT	The Quaker Oats Co
QuakSC	New York	KSF	Quaker State Corp
QualSy	NAS NMS	QSII	Quality Systems Inc
QuanD	NAS SL	QTMCC	Quantum Diagnostics Ltd
Quanex	New York	NX	Quanex Corp
Quantm	New York	CUE	Quantum Chemical Corp
Quantm	NAS NMS	QNTM	Quantum Corp
Quarex	NAS NMS	QRXL	Quarex Industries Inc
QuartzI	NAS SL	QURZ	Quartz Inc
Qubix	NAS SL	QBIX	Qubix Graphic Systems Inc
Quebc	American	PQB	Quebecor Inc
QuebcSt	NAS NL	QSRTF	Quebec Sturgeon River Mines Ltd
Questar	New York	STR	Questar Corp
QuestBi	NAS SL	QBIO	Quest Biotechnology Inc
Questch	NAS NMS	QTEC	QuesTech Inc
QuestM	NAS NMS	QMED	Quest Medical Inc
QuFood	NAS NMS	QFCI	Quality Food Centers Inc
Quikslv	NAS NMS	QUIK	Quicksilver Inc
Quipp	NAS NMS	QUIP	Quipp Inc
Quixte	NAS NMS	QUIX	Quixote Corp
Qume	NAS NMS	QUME	Qume Corp
QVC	NAS NMS	QVCN	QVC Network Inc
RabbitS	NAS NMS	RABT	Rabbit Software Corp
RAC	American	RMR	RAC Mortgage Investment Corp
RadaEl	NAS NL	RADIF	Rada Electronic Industries Ltd
Radice	New York	RI	Radice Corp
Radion	NAS NMS	RADX	Radionics Inc
Radon	NAS SL	RDON	Radon Testing Corporation of America Inc
RadSys	NAS NMS	RADS	Radiation Systems Inc
RadtnDs	NAS SL	RDIS	Radiation Disposal Systems Inc

NEWSPAPER ABBREV.	MARKET LISTING	TRADING SYMBOL	COMPANY NAME
Radva	NAS SL	RDVA	Radva Corp
Ragan	American	BRD	Brad Ragan Inc
Ragen	NAS NMS	RAGN	Ragen Corp
RAI	American	RAC	RAI Research Corp
RailSvg	NAS NL	RAIL	Railroad S&L Assn (Kansas)
RainbwTc	NAS NL	RNBO	Rainbow Technologies Inc
RalghFS	NAS NMS	RFBK	Raleigh Federal Savings Bank (North Carolina)
RalsPur	New York	RAL	Ralston Purina Co
Ramad	New York	RAM	Ramada Inc
RamFin	NAS NMS	RMPO	Rampo Financial Corp
RandCa	NAS NL	RAND	Rand Capital Corp
Rangar	NAS NMS	RANG	Rangaire Corp
RangrO	New York	RGO	Ranger Oil Ltd
RankO	NAS NL	RANKY	The Rank Organization Plc
Ransbg	American	RBG	Ransburg Corp
Rapitec	NAS SL	RPSY	Rapitech Systems Inc
RartnBc	NAS NMS	RARB	Raritan Bancorp Inc
Ratner	NAS NMS	RATNY	Ratners Group plc
Rauch	NAS NL	RCHI	Rauch Industries Inc
Raven	American	RAV	Raven Industries Inc
Ravnwd	NAS NL	RAFI	Ravenswood Financial Corp
RAX	NAS NMS	RAXR	Rax Restaurants Inc
Raycm	New York	RYC	Raychem Corp
Raycom	NAS SL	RACM	Raycomm Transworld Industries Inc
Raymd	NAS NMS	RAYM	The Raymond Corp
Rayonr	New York	LOG	Rayonier Timberlands L.P.
Raytch	New York	RAY	Raytech Corp
Raythn	New York	RTN	Raytheon Co
RBInd	New York	RBI	RB Industries Inc
RbtHlf	NAS NMS	RHII	Robert Half Inc
RBW	American	RBW	RB&W Corp
RchmHl	NAS NMS	RICH	Richmond Hills Savings Bank
RckBcp	NAS NMS	RBNH	Rockingham Bancorp (New Hampshire)
RckCtr	New York	RCP	Rockefeller Center Properties Inc
RckwdH	NAS NMS	RKWD	Rockwood Holding Co
RckwdN	NAS NL	RNC	Rockwood National Corp
Rckwy	New York	RKY	Rockaway Corp
RCM	NAS SL	RCMT	RCM Technologies Inc
RdgwdP	NAS NMS	RWPI	Ridgewood Properties Inc
RdwayM	NAS NMS	RDWI	Roadway Motor Plazas Inc
ReadBt	New York	RB	Reading & Bates Corp
Readg	NAS NMS	RDGC	Reading Co
ReaGld	NAS SL	REOGF	Rea Gold Corp
RealAm	NAS NL	RACO	RealAmerica Co
Realist	NAS SL	RLST	Realist Inc
Rebok	New York	RBK	Reebok International Ltd
ReCap	American	RCC	Re Capital Corp

NEWSPAPER ABBREV.	MARKET LISTING	TRADING SYMBOL	COMPANY NAME
RecnEq	New York	REC	Recognition Equipment Inc
Reco	American	RNT	RECO International Inc
Recotn	NAS NMS	RCOT	Recoton Corp
RedEagl	NAS SL	REDX	Red Eagle Resources Corp
RediCr	NAS NMS	REDI	Readicare Inc
RedknL	NAS NMS	RDKN	Redken Laboratories Inc
RedLn	American	RED	Red Lion Inns L.P.
Redlw	American	RDL	Redlaw Industries Inc
Redmn	New York	RE	Redman Industries Inc
Reece	New York	RCE	The Reece Corp
ReedJwl	NAS NMS	REED	Reeds Jewelers Inc
Reeves	NAS NMS	RVCC	Reeves Communications Corp
Refac	NAS NMS	REFC	REFAC Technology Development Corp
Reflctn	NAS NMS	RFTN	Reflectone Inc
Regal	New York	RGL	Regal International Inc
RegalB	American	RBC	Regal-Beloit Corp
RegFdl	NAS NL	RFBI	Regional Federal Bancorp Inc
Regina	NAS NMS	REGI	Regina Company Inc
Regis	NAS NMS	RGIS	Regis Corp
ReglBc	NAS NMS	REGB	Regional Bancorp Inc
ReglFn	New York	BNC	Regional Financial Shares Investment Fund Inc
ReichT	New York	RTP	Reich & Tang L.P.
ReistFS	NAS NMS	RFSB	Reistertown Federal Savings Bank (Maryland)
REIT	New York	RCT	Real Estate Investment Trust of California
RelbLfe	NAS NL	RLIF	Reliable Life Insurance Co
RelGrp	New York	REL	Reliance Group Holdings Inc
Reliab	NAS NMS	REAL	Reliability Inc
RelTch	NAS NMS	RELY	Relational Technology Inc
RenGRX	NAS SL	RENX	Renaissance GRX Inc
RepAm	NAS NMS	RAWC	Republic American Corp
Repap	NAS NMS	RPAPF	Repap Enterprises Corporation Inc
RepBcp	NAS NL	RBNC	Republic Bancorp Inc
RepCap	NAS NMS	RSLA	Republic Capital Group Inc
Repco	NAS NMS	RPCO	Repco Inc
RepGyp	New York	RGC	Republic Gypsum Co
Replgn	NAS NMS	RGEN	Repligen Corp
RepNY	New York	RNB	Republic New York Corp
ReprMd	NAS SL	REPR	Repro-Med Systems Inc
RepRs	NAS SL	REPB	Republic Resources Corp
RepSav	NAS NMS	RSFC	Republic Savings Financial Corp (Florida)
Resdel	NAS NMS	RSDL	Resdel Industries
RESec	American	RIF	Real Estate Securities Income Fund Inc
ReshInc	NAS NMS	RESR	Research Inc
Respir	NAS NMS	RESP	Respironics Inc

NEWSPAPER ABBREV.	MARKET LISTING	TRADING SYMBOL	COMPANY NAME
ResRs	American	RRR	Residential Resources Mortgages Investments Corp
Resrt A	American	RT.A	Resorts International Inc (Class A)
RestMg	American	RMI	Residential Mortgage Investments Inc
RestMg	NAS NMS	RESM	Restaurant Management Services Inc
Retail	NAS NMS	RCOA	Retailing Corporation of America
ReuterI	NAS NMS	REUT	Reuter Inc
ReutrH	NAS NMS	RTRSY	Reuters Holdings plc
ReutrLb	NAS SL	PEST	Reuter Laboratories Inc
ReverF	NAS NMS	PREV	Revere Fund Inc
Rexcm	NAS SL	RXSC	Rexcom Systems Corp
Reshm	New York	RXH	Rexham Corp
Rexon	NAS NMS	REXN	Rexon Inc
Rexwks	NAS NMS	REXW	Rexworks Inc
ReyMt	New York	RLM	Reynolds Metals Co
ReyRy	NAS NMS	REYNA	The Reynolds & Reynolds Co (Class A)
RF&P	NAS NL	RFPCK	RF&P Corp-Non-voting Dividend Obligation Common Stock
RgcyCr	NAS NMS	SHIP	Regency Cruises Inc
RgcyEl	NAS NMS	RGCY	Regency Electronics Inc
RgcyEq	NAS NMS	RGEQ	Regency Equities Corp
RghtMg	NAS NMS	RMCI	Right Management Consultants Inc
Rheomt	NAS NMS	RHEM	Rheometrics Inc
RHNB	NAS NL	RHNB	RHNB Corp
Rhodes	New York	RHD	Rhodes Inc
RhonPl	NAS NMS	RHPOY	Rhone-Poulenc S.A.
RibiIm	NAS NMS	BIBI	Ribi ImmunoChem Research Inc
RichEl	NAS NMS	RELL	Richardson Electronics Ltd
Richfd	NAS NMS	RCHFA	Richfood Holdings Inc (Class A)
Richton	NAS NMS	RIHL	Richton International Corp
Riedel	American	RIE	Riedel Envoronmental Technologies Inc
RiggsNt	NAS NMS	RIGS	Riggs National Corp
RioAl	American	ROM	Rio Algom Ltd
Ripley	NAS NL	RIPY	Ripley Company Inc
Riser	American	RSR	Riser Foods Inc (Class A)
RiseTc	NAS SL	RTEK	Rise Technology Inc
RiteAid	New York	RAD	Rite Aid Corp
Ritzys	NAS NMS	RITZ	G.D. Ritzy's Inc
Rivbnd	American	RIV	Riverbend International Corp
RivFor	NAS NMS	RFBC	River Forest Bancorp
RivrNtl	NAS NMS	RNRC	Riverside National Bank (California)
RJamFn	New York	RJF	Raymond James Financial Inc
RJR Nb	New York	RJR	RJR Nabisco Inc
RkMtCh	NAS SL	RMCF	Rocky Mountain Chocolate Factory Inc
RLC	New York	RLC	RLC Corp
RLI Cp	New York	RLI	RLI Corp
RltRef	New York	RRF	Realty ReFund Trust
RltSou	American	RSI	Realty South Investors Inc

NEWSPAPER ABBREV.	MARKET LISTING	TRADING SYMBOL	COMPANY NAME
RMS Int	American	RMS	RMS International Inc
RMUnd	NAS NMS	RMUC	Rock Mount Undergarment Company Inc
Roadmst	NAS SL	WHEL	Ròadmaster Industries Inc
RoadSv	NAS NMS	ROAD	Roadway Services Inc
RoanEl	NAS NMS	RESC	Roanoke Electric Steel Corp
Robesn	NAS NMS	RBSN	Robeson Industries Corp
Robins	New York	RAH	A.H. Robins Company Inc
RobMk	American	RMK.A	Robert-Mark Inc (Class A)
RobMyr	NAS NMS	ROBN	Robbins & Myers Inc
RobNug	NAS NMS	RNIC	Robinson Nugent Inc
Robtool	NAS SL	ROBO	Robotool Ltd
Robtsn	New York	RHH	H.H. Robertson Co
RobVsn	NAS NMS	ROBV	Robotic Vision Systems Inc
RochCS	NAS NMS	RCSB	The Rochester Community Savings Bank
RochG	New York	RGS	Rochester Gas & Electric Corp
RochTl	New York	RTC	Rochester Telephone Corp
RockgH	NAS SL	RHCC	Rocking Horse Child Care Centers of America Inc
Rockwl	New York	ROK	Rockwell International Corp
Rodime	NAS NL	RODMY	Rodime PLC
RodRen	New York	RR	Rodman & Renshaw Capital Group Inc
Roeblg	American	ROE	Roebling Property Investors Inc
Rogers	American	ROG	Rogers Corp
RoHaas	New York	ROH	Rohm & Haas Co
Rohr	New York	RHR	Rohr Industries Inc
RolinE	New York	REN	Rollins Environmental Services Inc
Rollins	New York	ROL	Rollins Inc
Ronson	NAS NMS	RONC	Ronson Corp
Ropak	NAS NMS	ROPK	Ropak Corp
Rorer	New York	ROR	Rorer Group Inc
RoseB	NAS NMS	RSTOB	Rose's Stores Inc (Class B)
RoseStr	NAS NMS	RSTO	Rose's Stores Inc
Rosptch	NAS NMS	RPCH	Rospatch Corp
RossCs	NAS NMS	RCDC	Ross Cosmetics Distribution Centers Inc
RossInd	NAS SL	ROSX	Ross Industries Inc
RossLog	NAS SL	AJRL	A.J. Ross Logistics Inc
RossStr	NAS NMS	ROST	Ross Stores Inc
RoTech	NAS NMS	ROTC	RoTech Medical Corp
Rothch	New York	R	L.F. Rothschild Unterberg Towbin Holdings Inc
RotoRtr	NAS NMS	ROTO	Roto-Rooter Inc
Rouse	NAS NMS	ROUS	The Rouse Co
Rowan	New York	RDC	Rowan Companies Inc
RoweF	NAS NMS	ROWE	Rowe Furniture Corp
Royce	New York	RVT	Royce Value Trust Inc
RoyceL	NAS SL	RLAB	Royce Labs Inc
RoyGld	NAS NMS	RGLD	Royal Gold Inc
RoyInt	New York	RIO	Royal International Optical Corp

NEWSPAPER ABBREV.	MARKET LISTING	TRADING SYMBOL	COMPANY NAME
RoylBu	NAS NMS	ROYG	Royal Business Group Inc
RoylD	New York	RD	Royal Dutch Petroleum Co
Roylpr	NAS NMS	ROYL	Royalpar Industries Inc
RoyPlm	NAS NMS	RPAL	Royal Palm Savings Assn (Florida)
RpAuto	NAS NMS	RAUT	Republic Automotive Parts Inc
RPC	New York	RES	RPC Energy Services Inc
RPM	NAS NMS	RPOW	RPM Inc
RpPicA	NAS NMS	RPICA	Republic Pictures Corp (Class A)
RpPicB	NAS NL	RPICB	Republic Pictures Corp (Class B)
RscEx	NAS NMS	REXI	Resource Exploration Inc
RschFt	NAS SL	REFR	Research Frontiers Inc
RshInd	NAS NMS	REIC	Research Industries Corp
RSI	NAS NMS	RSIC	RSI Corp
RsvltFd	NAS NMS	RFED	Roosevelt Bank FSB (Missouri)
RTE	New York	RTE	RTE Corp
RTI	NAS NMS	RTII	RTI Inc
Rubmd	New York	RBD	Rubbermaid Inc
Rudick	American	RDK	Ruddick Corp
Rudys	NAS NMS	RUDY	Rudy's Restaurant Group Inc
RuleInd	NAS NMS	RULE	Rule Industries Inc
RussBr	New York	RUS	Russ Berrie & Company Inc
Russell	New York	RML	Russell Corp
RusTg	New York	RTS	Russ Togs Inc
RvrOak	New York	ROI	River Oaks Industries Inc
RvrsG	NAS NMS	RSGI	Riverside Group Inc
Rxene	New York	RXN	Rexene Corp
RyanBck	NAS NMS	RBCO	Ryan Beck & Co
RyanF	NAS NMS	RYAN	Ryan's Family Steak Houses Inc
RyBkPA	NAS NL	RBPAA	Royal Bank of Pennsylvania (Class A)
Ryder	New York	RDR	Ryder System Inc
Rykoff	New York	RYK	Rykoff-Sexton Inc
Ryland	New York	RYL	The Ryland Group Inc
Rymer	New York	RYR	The Rymer Co
Saatchi	New York	SAA	Saatchi & Saatchi Company PLC
Sabine	New York	SAB	Sabine Corp
SabnR	New York	SBR	Sabine Royalty Trust
Safecd	NAS NMS	SFCD	SafeCard Services Inc
Safeco	NAS NMS	SAFC	SAFECO Corp
SafHlt	NAS NMS	SFGD	Safeguard Health Enterprises Inc
SaftKln	New York	SK	Safety-Kleen Corp
Sage	American	SAG	Sage Energy Co
SageAn	NAS SL	SAII	Sage Analytics International Inc
SageBd	NAS SL	SAGB	Sage Broadcasting Corp
SageLb	NAS SL	SLAB	Sage Labs Inc
SageSft	NAS NMS	SGSI	Sage Software Inc
SagHbr	NAS NMS	SGHB	Sag Harbour Savings Bank (New York)
Sahara	NAS NMS	SHRE	Sahara Resorts Inc

NEWSPAPER ABBREV.	MARKET LISTING	TRADING SYMBOL	COMPANY NAME
SahCas	New York	SAH	Sahara Casino Partners L.P.
Sahlen	NAS NMS	SALN	Sahlen & Associates Inc
Sal Oph	NAS SL	EYES	Salvatori Opthalmics Inc
Salant	New York	SLT	Salant Corp
SalCpt	NAS NMS	SLCR	Salem Carpet Mills Inc
Salem	American	SBS	Salem Corporation
Salick	NAS NMS	SHCI	Salick Health Care Inc
SallieM	New York	SLM	Student Loan Marketing Assn
Salomn	New York	SB	Salomon Inc
Samna	NAS NMS	SMNA	Samna Corp
Samson	American	SAM	Samson Energy Company L.P.
Sandata	NAS NL	SAND	Sandata Inc
SandChf	NAS NMS	SHEF	Sandwich Chef Inc
SandCop	NAS NMS	SWCB	The Sandwich Co-operative Bank (Massachusetts)
SandFm	NAS NMS	SAFM	Sanderson Farms Inc
SandReg	NAS NMS	SNDS	The Sands Regent
SandTc	NAS SL	SNDCF	Sand Technology Systems Inc (Canada) (Class A)
Sandy	American	SDY	Sandy Corp
Sanfrd	NAS NMS	SANF	Sanford Corp
SAnitRt	New York	SAR	Santa Anita Realty Enterprises Inc
SanJuan	NAS SL	SWIM	San Juan Fiberglass Pools Inc
Sanmrk	American	SMK	Sanmark-Stardust Inc
Santos	NAS NL	STOYD	Santos Ltd
Sanyo	NAS NL	SANYY	Sanyo Electric Company Ltd
SaraLee	New York	SLE	Sara Lee Corp
SaratSt	NAS NMS	STGA	Saratoga Standardbreds Inc
Sasol	NAS NL	SASOY	Sasol Ltd
SatlInf	NAS SL	SATI	Satellite Information Systems Co
SatlMus	NAS NMS	SMNI	Satellite Music Network Inc
SaulRE	New York	BFS	B.F. Saul Real Estate Investment Trust
Savin	New York	SVB	Savin Corp
SavnFd	NAS NMS	SVAN	Savannah Foods & Industries Inc
SaxnO	American	SAX	Saxon Oil Development Partners L.P.
SaxonO	NAS NMS	SAXO	Saxon Oil Co
SAY Ind	NAS NMS	SAYI	S.A.Y. Industries Inc
Saztec	NAS SL	SAZZ	SAZTEC International Inc
Sbarro	American	SBA	Sbarro Inc
SbdCp	American	SEB	Seaboard Corp
SbdSav	NAS NMS	SEAB	Seaboard S&L Assn (Virginia)
SBE	NAS SL	SBEI	SBE Inc
SBT Cp	NAS NMS	SBTC	SBT Corp
SCalEd	New York	SCE	Southern California Edison Co
SCalWt	NAS NMS	SWTR	Southern California Water Co
SCANA	New York	SCG	SCANA Corp
ScandF	American	SCF	The Scandinavia Fund Inc
ScanGp	NAS SL	SCNG	Scan Graphics Inc

NEWSPAPER ABBREV.	MARKET LISTING	TRADING SYMBOL	COMPANY NAME
ScanOp	NAS NMS	SOCR	Scan-Optics Inc
SCarlo	American	SAN	San Carlos Milling Company Inc
SCarNt	NAS NMS	SCNC	South Carolina National Corp
Scat	NAS SL	SCAT	Scat Hovercraft Inc
ScdNA	New York	SAF	Scudder New Asia Fund Inc
Sceptre	American	SRL	Sceptre Resources Ltd
Scheib	American	ESH	Earl Scheib Inc
Scherer	NAS NMS	SCHC	R.P. Scherer Corp
Schfr	New York	SAT	Schafer Value Trust Inc
SchlmA	NAS NMS	SHLM	A. Schulman Inc
Schlmb	New York	SLB	Schlumberger Ltd
SchoolP	American	PIX	School Pictures Inc
SchrHlt	NAS NL	SCHR	Scherer Healthcare Inc
SchrPlg	New York	SGP	Schering-Plough Corp
Schult	NAS NMS	SHCO	Schult Homes Corp
Schwab	American	SS	Schwab Safe Company Inc
Schwb	New York	SCH	The Charles Schwab Corp
SchwtzA	NAS NMS	SWARA	Schwartz Brothers Inc (Class A)
SchwtzB	NAS NL	SWABV	Schwartz Brothers Inc (Class B)
SCI Sy	NAS NMS	SCIS	SCI Systems Inc
SciAtl	New York	SFA	Scientific-Atlanta Inc
Scicom	NAS NMS	SCIE	Scicom Data Services Ltd
SciDyn	NAS NMS	SIDX	Science Dynamics Corp
SciLsg	American	SG	Scientific Leasing Inc
SciMeas	NAS SL	SCMS	Scientific Measurement Systems Inc
Scimed	NAS NMS	SMLS	SciMed Life Systems Inc
SciMgt	American	SMG	Science Management Corp
SciMic	NAS NMS	SMSI	Scientific Micro Systems Inc
SciSft	NAS NMS	SSFT	Scientific Software-Intercomp Inc
SciSyst	NAS SL	SSSV	Scientific Systems Services Inc
Scitex	NAS NMS	SCIXF	Scitex Corporation Ltd
Scnfrm	NAS NMS	SCFM	Scanforms Inc
ScNtFd	NAS NMS	SNFS	Second National Federal Savings Bank (Maryland)
Scope	American	SCP	Scope Industries
SCOR U	New York	SUR	SCOR U.S. Corp
ScoreB	NAS SL	BSBL	Score Board Inc
Scorpn	NAS SL	SCPNA	Scorpion Technologies Inc (Class A)
ScotInst	NAS SL	SCTI	Scott Instruments Corp
ScotLiq	NAS SL	SLIQ	Scotts Liquid Gold Inc
ScotSt	NAS NMS	SCOT	Scott & Stringfellow Financial Inc
ScottP	New York	SPP	Scott Paper Co
Scottys	New York	SHB	Scotty's Inc
ScripH	NAS NMS	SCRP	Scripps Howard Broadcasting Co
Scripps	NAS NMS	EWSCA	E.W. Scripps Co (Class A)
ScrptSy	NAS SL	SCPT	Script Systems Inc
SCS	NAS NMS	SCOM	SCS/Compute Inc
ScurRn	American	SRB	Scurry-Rainbow Oil Ltd

NEWSPAPER ABBREV.	MARKET LISTING	TRADING SYMBOL	COMPANY NAME
SDieGs	New York	SDO	San Diego Gas & Electric Co
SDNB	NAS NMS	SDNB	SDNB Financial Corp
SeaBnk	NAS NMS	SBCFA	Seacoast Banking Corporation of Florida (Class A)
SeaCnt	New York	SCR	Sea Containers Ltd
SeacstS	NAS NMS	SSBA	Seacoast Savings Bank (New Hampshire)
Seafds	NAS SL	SEAF	Seafoods From Alaska Inc
Seafood	NAS SL	SEFD	Seafood Inc
SeaGal	NAS NMS	SEAG	Sea Galley Stores Inc
Seagate	NAS NMS	SGAT	Seagate Technology
Seagrm	New York	VO	The Seagram Company Ltd
Seagul	New York	SGO	Seagull Energy Corp
Seahk	NAS NL	SEAK	Seahawk Oil International Inc
SealAir	New York	SEE	Sealed Air Corp
Sealrgt	NAS NMS	SRCO	Sealright Company Inc
Seamn	American	SMN	Seamen's Corp
Seaport	American	SEO	Seaport Corp
Sears	New York	S	Sears Roebuck & Co
SeawFd	NAS NMS	SEWY	Seaway Food Town Inc
SecAF	NAS NMS	SAFE	Security American Financial Enterprises Inc
SecBcp	NAS NMS	SECB	Security Bancorp Inc
SecCap	American	SCC	Security Capital Corp
SecFClv	NAS NL	SFSL	Security Federal S&L Assn (Ohio)
SecFdl	NAS NMS	SFBM	Security Federal Savings Bank (Montana)
Secom	NAS SL	SECM	Secom General Corp
SecPac	New York	SPC	Security Pacific Corp
SecSLn	NAS NMS	SSLN	Security Savings Bank SLA (New Jersey)
SecTag	NAS NMS	STAG	Security Tag Systems Inc
Seebrg	NAS SL	SBRG	Seeberg Corp
SEEQ	NAS NMS	SEEQ	Seeq Technology Inc
SEI	NAS NMS	SEIC	SEI Corp
Seibel	NAS NMS	SBIG	The Seibels Bruce Group Inc
Seitel	NAS SL	SEIS	Seitel Inc
Selas	American	SLS	Selas Corporation of America
SelctIns	NAS NMS	SIGI	Selective Insurance Group Inc
Select	NAS NMS	SLTM	SelecTerm Inc
SeligAs	American	SLG	Seligman & Associates Inc
SelTrn	NAS SL	SELE	SelecTronics Inc
Selvac	NAS SL	SLVC	Selvac Corp
Semtch	American	SMH	Semtech Corp
Seneca	NAS NMS	SENE	Seneca Foods Corp
Senetek	NAS SL	SNTKY	Senetek PLC
SenrSv	NAS SL	SENR	Senior Service Corp
Sensor	NAS NMS	SNSR	Sensormatic Electronics Corp
SensrCtl	NAS NMS	SNCO	Sensor Control Corp
SequaA	New York	SQA.A	Sequa Corp (Class A)
SequaB	New York	SQA.B	Sequa Corp (Class B)

NEWSPAPER ABBREV.	MARKET LISTING	TRADING SYMBOL	COMPANY NAME
Sequel	NAS SL	SEQL	Sequel Corp
Sequent	NAS NMS	SQNT	Sequent Computer Systems Inc
Servico	NAS NMS	SRVI	Servico Inc
Servo	American	SCA	Servo Corporation of America
Servotr	American	SVT	Servotronics Inc
SestSvL	NAS NMS	SESL	Southeastern S&L Co (North Carolina)
SFE	NAS NMS	SFEM	SFE Technologies
SFeEP	New York	SFP	Santa Fe Energy Partners L.P.
SFeSP	New York	SFX	Santa Fe Southern Pacific Corp
SFFed	NAS NMS	SFFD	SFFed Corp (California)
SfgdSc	New York	SFE	Safeguard Scientifics Inc
SFGI	NAS NMS	SFGI	Security Financial Group Inc (Minnesota)
SFM	American	SFM	SFM Corp
SftwPb	NAS NMS	SPCO	Software Publishing Corp
SgnlApl	New York	SIA	Signal Apparel Company Inc
ShaerS	American	SHS	Shaer Shoe Corp
Shaklee	New York	SHC	Shaklee Corp
ShawIn	New York	SHX	Shaw Industries Inc
ShawNt	NAS NMS	SHNA	Shawmut National Corp
Shelby	New York	SY	Shelby Williams Industries Inc
ShelbyF	NAS NMS	SHLB	Shelby Federal Savings Bank (Indiana)
Sheldl	NAS NMS	SHEL	Sheldahl Inc
ShellT	New York	SC	The Shell Transport & Trading Company p.l.c.
Sheltn	NAS NMS	SSAL	Shelton Savings Bank (Connecticut)
SHL Sy	NAS NMS	SHKIF	SHL Systemhouse Inc
ShLeh	New York	SHE	Shearson Lehman Brothers Holdings Inc
ShltCm	American	SST	Shelter Components Corp
ShlyAsc	NAS SL	SHLY	Shelly Associates Inc
Shoney	NAS NMS	SHON	Shoney's Inc
Shopco	American	LSC	Shopco Laurel Centre L.P.
Shpsmt	NAS NMS	SHOP	Shopsmith Inc
ShrlnFn	NAS NL	SLFC	Shoreline Financial Corp
ShrMed	NAS NMS	SMED	Shared Medical Systems Corp
ShrpIm	NAS NMS	SHRP	Sharper Image Corp
Shrwd	NAS NMS	SHOR	Shorewood Packaging Corp
Shrwin	New York	SHW	The Sherwin-Williams Co
Shwbt	New York	SBO	Showboat Inc
ShwdG	American	SHD	The Sherwood Group Inc
Shwscn	NAS SL	SHOW	Showscan Film Corp
SI Hand	NAS SL	SIHS	SI Handling Systems Inc
Sidari	NAS SL	ZITI	Sidari Corp
SierCa	NAS NMS	SETD	Sierra Capital Realty Trust IV Co
SierCap	American	SZF	Sierra Capital Realty Trust VI
SierCa7	American	SZG	Sierra Capital Realty Trust VII
Siercn	American	SER	Sierracin Corp
SierHS	American	SIE	Sierra Health Services Inc

NEWSPAPER ABBREV.	MARKET LISTING	TRADING SYMBOL	COMPANY NAME
SierPac	New York	SRP	Sierra Pacific Resources
SierR 84	NAS NMS	SETC	Sierra Real Estate Equity Trust '84
SierSpg	American	WTR	Sierra Spring Water Co
Sifco	American	SIF	SIFCO Industries Inc
SigmaAl	NAS NMS	SIAL	Sigma-Aldrich Corp
SigmaD	NAS NMS	SIGM	Sigma Designs Inc
Sigmtrn	NAS SL	SNIC	Sigmatron Nova Inc
Signet	New York	SBK	Signet Banking Corp
SikesA	American	SK.A	Sikes Corp (Class A)
SilcnGr	NAS NMS	SGIC	Silicon Graphics Inc
SilcVly	NAS NMS	SIVB	Silicon Valley Bancshares (California)
SilicnVl	NAS NMS	SVGI	Silicon Valley Group Inc
Silicnx	NAS NMS	SILI	Siliconix Inc
Silicon	NAS NMS	SILN	Silicon General Inc
SiliconS	New York	SIL	Silicon Systems Inc
SilvLis	NAS NMS	SVRL	Silvar-Lisco
Silvrcst	American	SLV	Silvercrest Corp
SimnFt	NAS NL	SFNCA	Simmons First National Corp (Class A)
SimpIn	NAS NMS	SMPS	Simpson Industries Inc
Sirco	NAS NL	SIRC	Sirco International Corp
SirSpdy	NAS SL	SPEDY	Sir Speedy Printing Centres PLC
SisCp	NAS NMS	SISB	Sis Corp
Sizeler	New York	SIZ	Sizeler Property Investors Inc
Sizler	NAS NMS	SIZZ	Sizzler Restaurants International Inc
SJerIn	New York	SJI	South Jersey Industries Inc
SJNB	NAS NL	SJNB	SJNB Financial Corp
SJuanB	New York	SJT	San Juan Basin Royalty Trust
SJuanR	New York	SJR	San Juan Racing Association Inc
SJW	American	SJW	SJW Corp
SK	NAS NMS	SKFB	S&K Famous Brands Inc
SkanSB	NAS NMS	SKAN	Skaneateles Savings Bank (New York)
SKF AB	NAS NMS	SKFRY	SKF AB
SKI	NAS NMS	SKII	S-K-I Ltd
Skipper	NAS NMS	SKIP	Skippers Inc
Skolnk	American	SKN	Skolniks Inc
SkyChili	NAS NL	SKCH	Skyline Chili Inc
Skyline	New York	SKY	Skyline Corp
SkyWst	NAS NMS	SKYW	SkyWest Inc
SL Ind	New York	SL	SL Industries Inc
SlatrDv	NAS SL	SLAT	Slater Development Corp
Slattery	New York	SGI	Slattery Group Inc
SlkGrn	NAS NL	SGHI	Silk Greenhouse Inc
SlvKing	NAS NMS	SILV	Silver King Mines Inc
SlvMin	NAS SL	SLVRF	Silverado Mines Ltd
SMichG	NAS NMS	SMGS	Southeastern Michigan Gas Enterprises Inc
SmithIn	New York	SII	Smith International Inc
SmithL	NAS NMS	SMLB	Smith Laboratories Inc

NEWSPAPER ABBREV.	MARKET LISTING	TRADING SYMBOL	COMPANY NAME
SmkB	New York	SKB	SmithKline Beckman Corp
Smrtcd	NAS SL	SMRT	Smartcard International Inc
SmthA	American	SMC.A	A.O. Smith Corp (Class A)
SmthB	American	SMC.B	A.O. Smith Corp (Class B)
SmthF	NAS NMS	SFDS	Smithfield Foods Inc
Smthfld	NAS NMS	HAMS	The Smithfield Companies Inc
Smuckr	New York	SJM	The J.M. Smucker Co
SnapOn	New York	SNA	Snap-on Tools Corp
SnelSnl	NAS NMS	SNEL	Snelling & Snelling Inc
SNETI	New York	SNG	Southern New England Telecommunications Corp
SNL Fnc	NAS NMS	SNLFA	S.N.L. Financial Corp (Class A)
Snyder	New York	SOI	Snyder Oil Partners L.P.
SoCarF	NAS NMS	SCFB	South Carolina Federal Corp
Society	NAS NMS	SOCI	Society Corp
SoctySv	NAS NMS	SOCS	The Society for Savings Bancorp Inc (Connecticut)
SoestBk	New York	STB	Southeast Banking Corp
SoFdGa	NAS NL	SFGA	Southern Federal Savings Bank (Georgia)
Softech	NAS NMS	SOFT	SofTech Inc
SoftSv	NAS NMS	SSOA	Software Services of America Inc
SoIndGs	New York	SIG	Southern Indiana Gas & Electric Co
Solitec	NAS NMS	SOLI	Solitec Inc
Solitron	New York	SOD	Solitron Devices Inc
SolvEx	NAS SL	SOLV	Solv-Ex Corp
SoMinrl	NAS NMS	SMIN	Southern Mineral Corp
SomerB	NAS NMS	SOMB	Somerset Bancorp Inc
SomrG	NAS NMS	SOMR	The Somerset Group Inc
SomrSv	NAS NMS	SOSA	Somerset Savings Bank (Massachusetts)
Sonat	New York	SNT	Sonat Inc
Sonesta	NAS NMS	SNSTA	Sonesta International Hotels Corp (Class A)
Sonex	NAS SL	SONX	Sonex Research Inc
SonocP	NAS NMS	SONO	Sonoco Products Co
Sonora	NAS NMS	SONNF	Sonora Gold Corp
SonoTk	NAS SL	SOTK	Sono Tek Corp
SonrFd	NAS NMS	SFOK	Sooner Federal S&L Assn
SonyCp	New York	SNE	Sony Corp
SooLin	New York	SOO	Soo Line Corp
SoonDf	NAS NMS	SOON	Sooner Defense of Florida Inc
SoPcPt	NAS NL	SPPTY	Southern Pacific Petroleum N.L.
SorgInc	American	SRG	Sorg Inc
Sothby	American	BID	Sotheby's Holdings Inc (Class A)
Soudwn	New York	SDW	Southdown Inc
SouEdc	NAS NL	SOED	Southern Educators Life Insurance Co
Soumrk	New York	SM	Southmark Corp
SoUnCo	New York	SUG	Southern Union Co
SoundA	NAS NMS	SUND	Sound Advice Inc

NEWSPAPER ABBREV.	MARKET LISTING	TRADING SYMBOL	COMPANY NAME
SoundW	NAS NMS	SWHI	Sound Warehouse Inc
Sounet	NAS NMS	SOUT	SouthernNet Inc
SourcC	New York	SOR	Source Capital Inc
SouthCo	New York	SO	The Southern Co
Soutrst	NAS NMS	SOTR	SouthTrust Corp
Souwal	NAS NMS	SWTX	Southwall Technologies Inc
SovBcp	NAS NMS	SVRN	Sovereign Bancorp Inc
Sovran	New York	SOV	Sovran Financial Corp
Spain	New York	SNF	Spain Fund Inc
SpanAm	NAS NMS	SPAN	Span-America Medical Systems Inc
Spartc	American	SH	Spartech Corp
Sparton	New York	SPA	Sparton Corp
SpcEq	New York	SPE	Specialty Equipment Companies Inc
SpcPhm	NAS SL	SPCT	Spectra Pharmaceutical Services Inc
Spctran	NAS NMS	SPTR	SpecTran Corp
SpctrCl	NAS SL	SPCL	Spectrum Cellular Corp
Spear	NAS NMS	SPRH	Spearhead Industries Inc
SpearF	NAS NMS	SFNS	Spear Financial Services Inc
SpecCm	NAS NMS	SPCM	Specialty Composites Corp
SpecCtl	NAS NMS	SPEC	Spectrum Control Inc
Specs	NAS NMS	SPEK	Spec's Music Inc
SpecSys	NAS SL	SSII	Specialized Systems Inc
SpedOP	American	SBM	Speed-O-Print Business Machines Corp
Spellng	American	SP	Aaron Spelling Productions Inc
SPI Ph	American	SPI	SPI Pharmaceuticals Inc
SPI Sus	NAS NMS	SPILF	S.P.I.-Suspension & Parts Industries Ltd
Spiegel	NAS NMS	SPGLA	Spiegel Inc (Class A)
Spire	NAS NMS	SPIR	Spire Corp
Sprage	New York	SPG	Sprague Technologies Inc
Spring	New York	SMI	Springs Industries Inc
Sprngbd	NAS NMS	SPBD	Springboard Software Inc
Sprouse	NAS NMS	STRS	Sprouse-Reitz Stores Inc
SprtGde	NAS SL	GIDE	Sportsmans Guide Inc
SprtLfe	NAS SL	SPLF	The Sporting Life Inc
SprtMt	NAS NMS	SPAR	Spartan Motors Inc
SPSTec	New York	ST	SPS Technologies Inc
SPX Cp	New York	SPW	SPX Corp
SquarD	New York	SQD	Square D Co
SquareI	NAS NMS	SQAI	Square Industries Inc
Squibb	New York	SQB	Squibb Corp
SSMC	New York	SSM	SSMC Inc
StafBld	NAS NMS	STAF	Staff Builders Inc
Stage	American	SA	Stage II Apparel Corp
StakeTc	NAS SL	STLKF	Stake Technology Ltd
Stamfrd	NAS NMS	CGPS	Stamford Capital Group Inc
StaMSe	New York	SMS	State Mutual Securities Trust
Standex	New York	SXI	Standex International Corp

NEWSPAPER ABBREV.	MARKET LISTING	TRADING SYMBOL	COMPANY NAME
StanfTl	NAS NMS	STII	Stanford Telecommunications Inc
Stanhm	New York	STH	Stanhome Inc
StanlWk	New York	SWK	The Stanley Works
Stansby	NAS NMS	STBY	Stansbury Mining Corp
StanWst	NAS NMS	SWMC	Stan West Mining Corp
Staodyn	NAS NMS	SDYN	Staodynamics Inc
StarCls	NAS SL	SCLS	Star Classics Inc
Starrett	New York	SCX	The L.S. Starrett Co
StarrtH	American	SHO	Starrett Housing Corp
Stars	NAS NMS	STAR	Stars To Go Inc
Starst	NAS SL	SCGI	Starstream Communications Group Inc
StarSur	NAS NMS	STAAR	STAAR Surgical Co
StarTc	NAS NMS	STRR	Star Technologies Inc
StaStB	NAS NMS	STBK	State Street Boston Corp
StateG	NAS NMS	STTG	The Statesman Group Inc
StatGm	NAS NMS	STGM	Status Game Corp
StBPnt	New York	SBP	Standard Brands Paint Co
StckYle	NAS NMS	STKR	Stocker & Yale Inc
StdCom	New York	STW	Standard Commercial Corp
StdMic	NAS NMS	SMSC	Standard Microsystems Corp
StdPac	New York	SPF	Standard-Pacific Corp
StdPrd	New York	SPD	The Standard Products Co
StdReg	NAS NMS	SREG	The Standard Register Co
StdShr	American	SWD	Standard Shares Inc
Steego	New York	STG	Steego Corp
SteelT	NAS NMS	STTX	Steel Technologies Inc
Stendig	NAS NMS	CHZC	Stendig Industries Inc
Stepan	American	SCL	Stepan Co
StepSvr	NAS NMS	CODA	Step-Saver Data Systems Inc
SterlEl	American	SEC	Sterling Electronics Corp
SterlSft	American	SSW	Sterling Software Inc
SternL	NAS NMS	SLTG	Sterner Lighting Systems Inc
SteveIC	NAS NL	STVEA	Steve's Homemade Ice Cream Inc (Class A)
StevnJ	New York	STN	J.P. Stevens & Company Inc
StewSn	NAS SL	STEW	Stewart Sandwiches Inc
StewStv	NAS NMS	SSSS	Stewart & Stevenson Services Inc
StFBk	New York	SFB	Standard Federal Bank
StHavn	American	SHV	Standard Havens Inc
SthdFn	NAS NMS	SFIN	Southland Financial Corp
Sthlfe	NAS NMS	SLHC	Southlife Holding Co
StHlGd	NAS NL	SGOLY	St. Helena Gold Mines Ltd
SthnBsh	NAS NMS	SOBK	Southern Bankshares Inc
SthngS	NAS NMS	SSBB	Southington Savings Bank (Connecticut)
SthnNt	NAS NMS	SNAT	Southern National Corp
SthStr	NAS SL	SSBG	Southern Starr Broadcasting Group Inc
Stifel	New York	SF	Stifel Financial Corp
StIves	NAS NMS	SWIS	St. Ives Laboratories Corp
StJoLP	New York	SAJ	St. Joseph Light & Power Co

NEWSPAPER ABBREV.	MARKET LISTING	TRADING SYMBOL	COMPANY NAME
StJude	NAS NMS	STJM	St. Jude Medical Inc
StlWVa	NAS NMS	SWVA	Steel of West Virginia Inc
StMain	NAS NMS	SOME	State-O-Maine Inc
StMonB	NAS NL	SANT	Santa Monica Bank
StMotr	New York	SMP	Standard Motor Products Inc
StnlyIn	NAS NMS	STHF	Stanley Interiors Corp
StockSy	NAS NMS	SSIAA	Stockholder Systems Inc (Class A)
Stokely	NAS NMS	STKY	Stokely USA Inc
Stolt	NAS NMS	STLTF	Stolt Tankers & Terminals S.A.
StoneC	New York	STO	Stone Container Corp
StoneW	New York	SW	Stone & Webster Inc
StonRs	New York	SRE	Stoneridge Resources Inc
StorEq	New York	SEQ	Storage Equities Inc
StorTch	New York	STK	Storage Technology Corp
Stotler	NAS NMS	STOT	Stotler Group Inc
StPaul	NAS NMS	STPL	The St. Paul Companies Inc
StPaulB	NAS NMS	SPBC	St. Paul Bancorp Inc
StratMt	New York	STM	Strategic Mortgage Investments Inc
StratPl	NAS NMS	SPAIB	Strategic Planning Associates Inc (Class B)
Stratus	NAS NMS	STRA	Stratus Computer Inc
StridRt	New York	SRR	The Stride Rite Corp
StrlBcp	New York	STL	Sterling Bancorp
StrlCap	American	SPR	Sterling Capital Corp
StrlMed	NAS SL	SSYS	Sterling Medical Systems Inc
StrmRg	NAS NMS	STRM	Sturm Ruger & Company Inc
Strober	NAS NMS	STRB	Strober Organization Inc
StrptSv	NAS NMS	STPT	Starpointe Savings Bank (New Jersey)
StrucDy	NAS NMS	SDRC	Structural Dynamics Research Corp
Structfb	NAS NL	STRU	Structofab Inc
StrutW	American	SUW	Struthers Wells Corp
StrwbCl	NAS NMS	STRWA	Strawbridge & Clothier (Class A)
Strykr	NAS NMS	STRY	Stryker Corp
StuartH	NAS NMS	STUH	Stuart Hall Company Inc
StudL	NAS NMS	SLMAJ	Student Loan Marketing Assn (voting)
StuDS	NAS NMS	STUS	Stuarts Department Stores Inc
STV	NAS NMS	STVI	STV Engineers Inc
StvGph	American	SVG	Stevens Graphics Corp
StwAir	NAS SL	SWAL	Stateswest Airlines Inc
StwBc	NAS NMS	STWB	Statewide Bancorp
StwInf	NAS NMS	SISC	Stewart Information Services Corp
SuavSh	New York	SWV	Suave Shoe Corp
Subaru	NAS NMS	SBRU	Subaru of America Inc
SubBcp	NAS NMS	SUBBA	Suburban Bancorp Inc (Class A)
SuburB	NAS NL	SBKSA	Suburban Bankshares Inc (Class A)
Sudbry	NAS NMS	SUDS	Sudbury Holdings Inc
SuffBn	NAS NMS	SUBK	Suffolk Bancorp
SuffFin	NAS NMS	SFCP	Suffield Financial Corp

NEWSPAPER ABBREV.	MARKET LISTING	TRADING SYMBOL	COMPANY NAME
Sumcrp	NAS NMS	SMCR	Summcorp
SumitB	NAS NMS	SUBN	The Summit Bancorporation
Sumito	NAS NMS	SUMI	Sumitomo Bank of California
SumitTc	NAS SL	BEAM	Summit Technology Inc
Summa	NAS NMS	SUMA	Summa Medical Corp
SumSav	NAS NMS	SMMT	Summit Savings Assn (Washington)
SumtH	NAS NMS	SUHC	Summit Holding Corp
SumtHl	NAS NMS	SUMH	Summit Health Ltd
SumtTx	American	SUA	Summit Tax Exempt Bond Fund L.P.
Sunair	NAS NMS	SNRU	Sunair Electronics Inc
SunbNu	American	SBN	Sunbelt Nursery Group Inc
SunCo	New York	SUN	Sun Company Inc
SunCst	NAS NMS	SUNI	Sun Coast Plastics Inc
SunCty	American	SNI	Sun City Industries Inc
SunDis	New York	SDP	Sun Distributors L.P.
Sundstr	New York	SNS	Sundstrand Corp
SunEl	New York	SE	Sun Electric Corp
SunEng	New York	SLP	Sun Energy Partners L.P.
SunGrd	NAS NMS	SNDT	SunGard Data Systems Inc
SunJr	American	SJS	Sunshine-Jr. Stores Inc
Sunlite	NAS NMS	SNLT	Sunlite Inc
SunMed	NAS NMS	SNMD	Sunrise Medical Inc
SunMic	NAS NMS	SUNW	Sun Microsystems Inc
SunMn	New York	SSC	Sunshine Mining Holding Co
SunPre	NAS SL	SUNR	Sunrise Preschool Inc
SunrFd	NAS NMS	SRSL	Sunrise Federal S&L Assn (Kentucky)
Sunrst	NAS NL	RSTAF	Sunresorts Ltd N.V. (Class A)
SunstFd	NAS NMS	SUNF	Sunstar Foods Inc
SunStSL	NAS NMS	SSSL	Sun State S&L Assn (Arizona)
SunTr	New York	STI	SunTrust Banks Inc
Sunwst	NAS NMS	SFSI	Sunwest Financial Services Inc
SupEl	NAS NMS	SUPE	The Superior Electric Co
SupInd	American	SUP	Superior Industries International Inc
Suprad	NAS SL	SUPD	Supradur Companies Inc
SuprEq	NAS NMS	SEQP	Supreme Equipment & Systems Corp
SuprFd	American	SFS	Super Food Services Inc
SuprSr	American	SGC	Superior Surgical Mfg Co Inc
SupRte	NAS NMS	SRFI	Super Rite Foods Inc
Suprtex	NAS NMS	SUPX	Supertex Inc
SupValu	New York	SVU	Super Value Stores Inc
SurgAf	NAS NMS	SCAF	Surgical Care Affiliates Inc
Surgidy	NAS SL	SGDN	Surgidyne Inc
SurvTc	NAS NMS	SURV	Survival Technology Inc
SusqBn	NAS NMS	SUSQ	Susquehanna Bancshares Inc
Sutron	NAS NMS	STRN	Sutron Corp
SvcCp	New York	SRV	Service Corporation International
SvcFrct	NAS NMS	SERF	Service Fracturing Co
SvcMer	NAS NMS	SMCH	Service Merchandise Company Inc

NEWSPAPER ABBREV.	MARKET LISTING	TRADING SYMBOL	COMPANY NAME
Svcmst	New York	SVM	ServiceMaster L.P.
SvcRes	New York	SRC	Service Resources Corp
SvenCel	NAS NMS	SCAPY	Svenska Cellulosa AB
SvOak	NAS NMS	QPON	Seven Oaks International Inc
SwAirl	New York	LUV	Southwest Airlines Co
Swank	NAS NL	SNKIV	Swank Inc
SwBcp	American	SWB	Southwest Bancorp (California)
SwBell	New York	SBC	Southwestern Bell Corp
SwElSv	NAS NMS	SWEL	Southwestern Electric Service Co
SwEnr	New York	SWN	Southwestern Energy Co
SwftEng	American	SFY	Swift Energy Co
SwstNt	NAS NMS	SWPA	Southwest National Corp
SwstRlt	American	SWL	Southwest Realty Ltd
SwtGas	New York	SWX	Southwest Gas Corp
SwtPS	New York	SPS	Southwestern Public Service Co
SwWtr	NAS NMS	SWWC	Southwest Water Co
SyblTc	New York	SBL	Symbol Technologies Inc
Sybra	NAS NMS	SIBR	Sybra Inc
Symbin	NAS NMS	SYMB	Symbion Inc
Symblic	NAS NMS	SMBX	Symbolics Inc
SymsCp	New York	SYM	Syms Corp
SymTk	NAS NMS	SYMK	Sym-Tek Systems Inc
Synaloy	American	SYO	Synalloy Corp
Synbio	NAS NMS	SBIO	Synbiotics Corp
Syncor	NAS NMS	SCOR	Syncor International Corp
Synergn	NAS NMS	SYGN	Synergen Inc
Synget	NAS SL	SYNG	Synergetics International Inc
SynOpt	NAS NL	SNPX	SynOptics Communications Inc
Synrcm	NAS NMS	SYNR	Synercom Technology Inc
Syntech	NAS NMS	SYNEP	Syntech International Inc
Syntex	New York	SYN	Syntex Corp
Synthe	NAS SL	NZYM	Synthetech Inc
Syntrex	NAS NMS	STRX	Syntrex Inc
Syntro	NAS NMS	SYNT	Syntro Corp
SyrSup	NAS NMS	SYRA	Syracuse Supply Co
Sysco	New York	SYY	Sysco Corp
SySoftw	NAS NMS	SSAX	Systems Software Associates Inc
SystCpt	NAS NMS	SCTC	Systems & Computer Technology Corp
SystEn	American	SEM	Systems Engineering & Manufacturing Corp
SystIn	NAS NMS	SYSM	System Industries Inc
SystInt	New York	SIN	System Integrators Inc
Systmt	NAS NMS	SYST	Systematics Inc
TabPrd	American	TBP	Tab Products Co
TacBt	New York	TBO	Tacoma Boatbuilding Co
TacVila	NAS NMS	TVLA	Taco Villa Inc
TacViv	NAS NMS	TVIV	Taco Viva Inc

NEWSPAPER ABBREV.	MARKET LISTING	TRADING SYMBOL	COMPANY NAME
Taiwan	American	TWN	The Taiwan Fund Inc
Talley	New York	TAL	Talley Industries Inc
Talman	NAS NMS	TLMN	Talman Home Federal S&L Assn of Illinois
Tambd	New York	TMB	Tambrands Inc
TandB	American	TAB	Tandy Brands Inc
Tandm	New York	TDM	Tandem Computers INc
Tandon	NAS NMS	TCOR	Tandon Corp
Tandy	New York	TAN	Tandy Corp
TaroVt	NAS NL	TAROF	Taro Vit Industries Ltd
Tasty	American	TBC	Tasty Baking Co
TaylrS	NAS SL	TAYS	S. Taylor Companies Inc
TBC	NAS NMS	TBCC	TBC Corp
TCA	NAS NMS	TCAT	TCA Cable TV Inc
TCBY	NAS NMS	TCBY	TCBY Enterprises Inc
TcCom	NAS NMS	TCII	Technology for Communications International Inc
TCF	NAS NMS	TCFC	TCF Financial Corp (Minnesota)
TchCom	NAS NMS	TCCO	Technical Communications Corp
TchDta	NAS NMS	TECD	Tech Data Corp
Tchdyn	NAS NL	TCDN	Techdyne Inc
Tchgen	NAS NMS	TXNO	Technogenetics Inc
Tchnal	NAS NMS	TECN	Technalysis Corp
TchOpL	American	TOV	Tech/Ops Landauer Inc
TchOpS	American	TOC	Tech-Ops Sevcon Inc
TchSym	New York	TSY	Tech-Sym Corp
TchTme	NAS SL	TTME	Tech Time Inc
TCS Ent	NAS NL	TCSE	TCS Enterprises Inc
TCW	New York	CVT	TCW Convertible Securities Fund Inc
TDK	New York	TDK	TDK Corp
TdyHm	NAS SL	THEI	Today Home Entertainment Inc
Team	American	TMI	Team Inc
TEC	American	TCK	TEC Inc
TechDv	NAS NL	TDCX	Technology Development Corp
Technd	American	TND	Technodyne Inc
TechTp	American	TTI	Technical Tape Inc
Techtrl	American	TNL	Technitrol Inc
TECO	New York	TE	TECO Energy Inc
Tecogen	NAS NMS	TCGN	Tecogen Inc
Tecum	NAS NMS	TECU	Tecumseh Products Co
Teeco	NAS NL	TPLPZ	Teeco Properties L.P. Co
TejnR	American	TRC	Tejon Ranch Co
Tekelec	NAS NMS	TKLC	Tekelec
Tekna	NAS SL	TKNA	Tekna Tool Inc
Teknwd	NAS NMS	TKAI	Teknowledge Inc
Tektrnx	New York	TEK	Tektronix Inc
TEL El	NAS SL	TELS	TEL Electronics Inc
Telabs	NAS NMS	TLAB	Tellabs Inc
TelcN	NAS NMS	TNII	Telecommunications Network Inc

NEWSPAPER ABBREV.	MARKET LISTING	TRADING SYMBOL	COMPANY NAME
Telco	NAS NMS	TELC	Telco Systems Inc
Telcom	New York	TEL	TeleCom Corp
Telcrd	NAS NMS	TCRD	Telecredit Inc
Telcrft	NAS NMS	TLCR	Telecrafter Corp
TelDta	American	TDS	Telephone & Data Systems Inc
Teldyn	New York	TDY	Teledyne Inc
TeleArt	NAS SL	TLARF	Tele Art Inc
Telecalc	NAS SL	TLCC	Telecalc Inc
Telecon	American	TCC	TeleConcepts Corp
Telecst	NAS SL	TCST	Telecast Inc
Telef	New York	TEF	Companie Telefonica Nacional de Espana S.A.
Teleflex	American	TFX	Teleflex Inc
Telenet	NAS SL	TNET	Telenetics Corp
Telesph	American	TSP	Telesphere International Inc
Teletmr	NAS SL	TLTM	Teletimer International Inc
TelevTc	NAS SL	TVTK	Television Technology Corp
Telex	New York	TC	The Telex Corp
Telmatc	NAS NMS	TMAX	Telematrics International Inc
Telmatn	NAS SL	TLMT	Telemation Inc
Telmdo	NAS NMS	TLMD	Telemundo Group Inc
TelMex	NAS NL	TFONY	Telefonosa de Mexico SA
Telos	NAS NMS	TLOS	Telos Corp
TelQst	NAS NMS	TELQ	TeleQuest Inc
Telrte	New York	TLR	Telerate Inc
TelSpcl	NAS SL	TESP	Telephone Specialists Inc
Telstar	NAS SL	TSTR	Telstar Corp
Telvid	NAS NMS	TELV	TeleVideo Systems Inc
Telxon	NAS NMS	TLXN	Telxon Corp
Temco	NAS NMS	TEMC	Temco Home Health Care Products Inc
Templ	New York	TIN	Temple-Inland Inc
TEMPO	American	TPO	TEMPO Enterprises Inc
Temtex	NAS NMS	TMTX	Temtex Industries INc
Tennant	NAS NMS	TANT	Tennant Co
Tennco	New York	TGT	Tenneco Inc
Tenney	American	TNY	Tenney Engineering Inc
Teradta	NAS NMS	TDAT	Teradata Corp
TeraM	NAS NL	TMEXF	Terra Mines Ltd
Terdyn	New York	TER	Teradyne Inc
TermDt	NAS NMS	TERM	Terminal Data Corp
Termflx	NAS NMS	TFLX	Termiflex Corp
Tesoro	New York	TSO	Tesoro Petroleum Corp
Teva	NAS NMS	TEVIY	Teva Pharmaceutical Industries Ltd
Texaco	New York	TX	Texaco Inc
TexAEn	NAS NL	COLD	Texas American Energy Corp
TexAir	American	TEX	Texas Air Corp
TexCd	American	TXC	Texaco Canada Inc
Texcel	NAS SL	TXELC	Texcel International Inc

NEWSPAPER ABBREV.	MARKET LISTING	TRADING SYMBOL	COMPANY NAME
TexEst	New York	TET	Texas Eastern Corp
Texfi	New York	TXF	Texfi Industries Inc
TexInd	New York	TXI	Texas Industries Inc
Texstyr	NAS SL	FOAM	Texstyrene Corp
Textrn	New York	TXT	Textron Inc
TexUtil	New York	TXU	Texas Utilities Co
TGIF	New York	TGI	TGI Friday's Inc
TGX	NAS NMS	XTGX	TGX Corp
Thack	New York	THK	Thackey Corp
Thai	New York	TTF	Thai Fund
ThEdIn	NAS SL	TEIR	Thomas Edison Inns Inc
TherPr	NAS NMS	THPR	Thermal Profiles Inc
TherTc	NAS SL	TTII	Therapeutic Technologies Inc
Thetfd	NAS NMS	THFR	Thetford Corp
ThftyRt	NAS NMS	TFTY	Thrifty Rent-A-Car System Inc
ThmBet	New York	TNB	Thomas & Betts Corp
ThmMA	NAS NL	TMSTA	Thomaston Mills Inc (Class A)
ThmMB	NAS NL	TMSTB	Thomaston Mills Inc (Class B)
ThmMed	New York	TM	Thompson Medical Company Inc
Thmsn	NAS NMS	TCSFY	Thomson-CSF
ThomIn	New York	TII	Thomas Industries Inc
ThorEn	American	THR	Thor Energy Resources Inc
ThorInd	New York	THO	Thor Industries Inc
Thortec	New York	THT	Thortec International Inc
ThouTr	NAS NMS	TRLS	Thousand Trails Inc
ThrD A	American	TDD.A	Three D Departments Inc (Class A)
ThrD B	American	TDD.B	Three D Departments Inc (Class B)
3CI	NAS NMS	CCCI	3 CI Inc
3Com	NAS NMS	COMS	3Com Corp
Thrgen	NAS SL	THRX	Theragenics Corp
ThrIns	American	THI	Thermo Instrument Systems Inc
Thrmd	American	TMD	Thermedics Inc
Thrmdy	NAS SL	TDYN	Thermodynetics Inc
ThrmE	American	TEV	Thermo Environmental Corp
ThrmEl	New York	TMO	Thermo Electron Corp
ThrmIn	NAS NL	THMP	Thermal Industries Inc
ThrmP	American	TPI	Thermo Process Systems Inc
ThrnAV	NAS NMS	TAVI	Thorn Apple Valley Inc
THT Lyd	NAS SL	TXHI	THT Lloyds Inc
TIC	NAS SL	TICI	TIC International Corp
TideR	NAS NL	TIRZC	Tidelands Royalty Trust "B"
Tidwtr	New York	TDW	Tidewater Inc
TIE	American	TIE	TIE/communications Inc
Tierco	NAS NMS	TIER	The Tierco Group Inc
Tiffny	New York	TIF	Tiffany & Co
Tigera	NAS NMS	TYGR	Tigera Group Inc
TigerIn	New York	TGR	Tiger International Inc
TII	American	TI	TII Industries Inc

NEWSPAPER ABBREV.	MARKET LISTING	TRADING SYMBOL	COMPANY NAME
TimbSf	NAS NMS	TMBS	Timberline Software Corp
Time	New York	TL	Time Inc
Timken	New York	TKR	The Timken Co
Tinsly	NAS NL	TNSL	Tinsley Laboratories Inc
Tintoret	NAS SL	TNTO	Tintoretto Inc
TIS	New York	TIS	TIS Mortgage Investment Co
Titan	New York	TTN	Titan Corp
TJX	New York	TJX	The TJX Companies Inc
TlcmA	NAS NMS	TCOMA	Tele-Communications Inc (Class A)
TlcmB	NAS NMS	TCOMB	Tele-Communications Inc (Class B)
TM Com	NAS NMS	TMCI	TM Communications Inc
TMAM	New York	TMA	Thomson McKinnon Asset Management L.P.
TmbCo	American	TBL	The Timberland Co
Tmbrjk	NAS NL	TJCK	Timberjack Corp
TmbrM	NAS SL	TIMM	Timerline Minerals Inc
TmeMgt	NAS SL	TMCO	Time Management Corp
TmMir	New York	TMC	The Times Mirror Co
TmpGl	New York	TIM	Templeton Global Income Fund
TmplE	American	EMF	Templeton Emerging Markets Fund Inc
TmpstTc	NAS NMS	TTOI	TEMPEST Technologies Inc
Tndycft	New York	TAC	Tandycrafts Inc
TNP	New York	TNP	TNP Enterprises Inc
ToddAO	NAS NMS	TODD	Todd-AO Corp
TodSh	New York	TOD	Todd Shipyards Corp
TOFIT	NAS SL	TFIT	TO FITNESS Inc
Tofruz	NAS SL	YUMY	Tofruzen Inc
Tofutti	American	TOF	Tofutti Brands Inc
Tokhem	New York	TOK	Tokheim Corp
TokioF	NAS NMS	TKIOY	Tokio Marine & Fire Insurance Company Ltd
Tolland	NAS NMS	TOBK	Tolland Bank F.S.B. (Connecticut)
TollBr	New York	TOL	Toll Brothers Inc
Tompkn	NAS NMS	TCTC	Tompkins County Trust Co (New York)
Tonka	New York	TKA	Tonka Corp
TonToy	NAS SL	TONS	Tons of Toys Inc
TootRl	New York	TR	Tootsie Roll Industries Inc
Topps	NAS NMS	TOPP	Topps Company Inc
Toro	New York	TTC	The Toro Co
TorRoy	NAS NMS	TRGL	Toreador Royalty Corp
Tortel	American	TTL	Torotel Inc
Tosco	New York	TOS	Tosco Corp
TotalRs	NAS SL	TOTL	Total Research Corp
TothAl	NAS NL	TOTH	Toth Aluminum Corp
TotlAst	NAS SL	TAPP	Total Assets Protection Inc
TotlEr	NAS NL	TLEXF	Total Erickson Resources Ltd
TotlHlt	NAS NMS	TLHT	Total Health Systems Inc
TotlPt	American	TPN	Total Petroleum (North America) Ltd
TotlSys	NAS NMS	TSYS	Total System Services Inc

NEWSPAPER ABBREV.	MARKET LISTING	TRADING SYMBOL	COMPANY NAME
TourM	NAS SL	TGNXF	Tournigan Mining Explorations Ltd
TownPl	NAS NL	TOWN	Towne-Paulsen Inc
Toyota	NAS NL	TOYOY	Toyota Motor Corp
ToyRU	New York	TOY	Toys "R" Us Inc
TPA Am	American	TPS	TPA of America Inc
TPI En	NAS NMS	TELE	TPI Enterprises Inc
TracePd	NAS SL	TRCE	Trace Products
TradInd	NAS NMS	TRAD	Traditional Industries Inc
TrakAu	NAS NMS	TRKA	Trak Auto Corp
Tramel	New York	TCR	Trammell Crow Real Estate Investors
TranEx	New York	EXP	Transco Exploration Partners Ltd
TranIn	NAS NMS	TRIN	Trans-Industries Inc
TranInc	New York	TAI	Transamerica Income Shares Inc
Transcn	New York	TCL	Transcon Inc
Transco	New York	E	Transco Energy Co
Transm	New York	TA	Transamerica Corp
Travler	New York	TIC	The Travelers Corp
TRC	American	TRR	TRC Companies Inc
Trchmk	New York	TMK	Torchmark Corp
TriaCp	American	TRG	The Triangle Corp
TriadSy	NAS NMS	TRSC	Triad Systems Corp
TrianIn	NAS NMS	TRIAA	Triangle Industries Inc (Class A)
TribSwb	NAS NL	TSFC	Tribune/Swab-Fox Companies Inc
Tribun	New York	TRB	Tribune Co
Tricntr	New York	TCT	Tricentrol PLC
TriCom	New York	TY	Tri-Continental Corp
TricoPd	NAS NMS	TRCO	Trico Products Corp
TriCst	NAS SL	TOXY	Tri Coast Environmental Corp
Tridex	American	TDX	Tridex Corp
TriHme	American	THP	Triangle Home Products Inc
Trimed	NAS NMS	TMED	Trimedyne Inc
Trinov	New York	TNV	Trinova Corp
Trinty	New York	TRN	Trinity Industries Inc
Trion	NAS NMS	TRON	Trion Inc
TrioTch	NAS SL	TRTC	Trio-Tech International
TriSM	American	TSM	Tri-State Motor Transit Company of Delaware
TritEng	New York	OIL	Triton Energy Corp
TritnG	New York	TGL	Triton Group Ltd
TrnCda	New York	TRP	TransCanada PipeLines Ltd
TrnEq	American	TEQ	Turner Equity Investors Inc
TrnfmL	NAS SL	TLOG	Transform Logic Corp
TrnFnc	NAS NMS	TRFI	Trans Financial Bancorp Inc
TrnLsg	NAS NMS	TLII	Trans Leasing International Inc
Trnmed	NAS SL	TMNI	Transmedia Network Inc
TrnMu	NAS NMS	TWMC	Trans World Music Corp
Trnsact	NAS SL	TACT	Transact International Inc
Trnscap	New York	TFC	TransCapital Financial Corp

NEWSPAPER ABBREV.	MARKET LISTING	TRADING SYMBOL	COMPANY NAME
TrnscoA	American	TNI.A	Transico Industries Inc
TrnscoB	American	TNI.B	Transico Industries Inc
Trnsdcr	NAS NMS	TSIC	Transducer Systems Inc
Trnsdyn	NAS NMS	TGCO	Transidyne General Corp
TrnsLx	American	TLX	Trans-Lux Corp
Trnsmt	NAS NMS	TRNS	Transmation Inc
Trnsnt	NAS NMS	TRNT	TransNet Corp
Trnsntl	NAS NMS	TNLS	Trans-National Leasing Inc
Trnstct	NAS NMS	TTOR	Transtector Systems Inc
TrnsTec	New York	TT	TransTechnology Corp
Trntch	NAS NMS	TRTI	Transtech Industries Inc
Trnwck	NAS NMS	TREN	Trenwick Group Inc
TrNY	NAS NMS	TRST	Trustco Bank Corp (New York)
Trnzn	American	TNZ	The Tranzonic Companies
Tround	NAS SL	TROU	Tround International Inc
Trstco	NAS NMS	TCBC	The Trustcompany Bancorporation (New Jersey)
Trstcp	NAS NMS	TTCO	Trustcorp Inc
Trudy	NAS SL	TRDY	Trudy Corp
TrusJo	NAS NMS	TJCO	Trus Joist Corp
Truvel	NAS SL	TRVL	Truvel Corp
TRV	NAS NMS	TRVMF	TRV Minerals Corp
TRW	New York	TRW	TRW Inc
TrwlBc	NAS NMS	TWBC	Transworld Bancorp
TS Ind	NAS NMS	TNDS	TS Industries Inc
Tseng	NAS SL	TSNG	Tseng Labs Inc
TSI	NAS NMS	TSII	TSI Inc
TSR	NAS NMS	TSRI	TSR Inc
TstAm	American	TRS	Trust America Service Corp
T2 Md	American	TSQ	T2 Medical Inc
TubMex	American	TAM	Tubos de Acero de Mexico S.A.
TuckDr	NAS NMS	TUCK	Tucker Drilling Co
TuckHd	NAS NMS	TUHC	Tucker Holding Co
TucsEP	New York	TEP	Tucson Electric Power Co
Tudor	NAS NMS	TDRLF	Tudor Corporation Ltd
TuesM	NAS NMS	TUES	Tuesday Morning Inc
Tultex	New York	TTX	Tultex Corp
Tunex	NAS SL	TUNX	Tunex International Inc
TurfPar	NAS NL	TURF	Turf Paradise Inc
TurnB A	American	TBS.A	Turner Broadcasting System Inc
TurnB B	American	TBS.B	Turner Broadcasting System Inc
TurnrC	American	TUR	The Turner Corp
TuscPl	NAS NMS	TUSC	Tuscarora Plastics Inc
TVI Cp	NAS SL	TVIE	TVI Corp
TVX	NAS NMS	TVXG	TVX Broadcast Group Inc
TW Svc	New York	TW	TW Services Inc
TWA	New York	TWA	Trans World Airlines Inc
TwCty	American	TNC	Town & Country Jewelry Mfg Corp

NEWSPAPER ABBREV.	MARKET LISTING	TRADING SYMBOL	COMPANY NAME
20thCnIn	NAS NMS	TWEN	20th Century Industries Inc
TwinDs	New York	TDI	Twin Disc Inc
202 Dta	NAS NMS	TOOT	202 Data System Inc
TwPeso	American	TWP	Two Pesos Inc
TwstTr	NAS NMS	TWST	Twistee Treat Corp
TxABc	New York	TXA	Texas American Bancshares Inc
TxInst	New York	TXN	Texas Instruments Inc
TxPac	New York	TPL	Texas Pacific Land Trust
TycoL	New York	TYC	Tyco Laboratories Inc
TycoTy	NAS NMS	TTOY	Tyco Toys Inc
Tylan	NAS NMS	TYLN	Tylan Corp
Tyler	New York	TLY	Tyler Corp
Tyrex	NAS SL	TYRX	Tyrex Oil Co
Tyson	NAS NMS	TYSNA	Tyson Foods Inc (Class A)
UACm	NAS NMS	UACIA	United Artists Communications Inc (Class A)
UAL Cp	New York	UAL	UAL Corp
UAM	New York	UAM	United Asset Management Corp
UAS	NAS SL	UASI	UAS Automation Systems Inc
UBCol	NAS NMS	UBKS	United Banks of Colorado Inc
UBkNJ	NAS NL	UNBJ	United National Bank (New Jersey)
UBWV	NAS NMS	UBSI	United Bankshares Inc (West Virginia)
UCaBk	NAS NMS	UCAR	United Carolina Bancshares Corp
UCarb	New York	UK	Union Carbide Corp
UCbTV	New York	UCT	United Cable Television Corp
UCmp	New York	UCC	Union Camp Corp
UCount	NAS NL	UCTC	United Counties Bancorporation
UCtyGs	NAS NMS	UCIT	United Cities Gas Co
UDC	New York	UDC	UDC-Universal Development L.P.
UFedS	NAS NL	UFRM	United Federal S&L Assn (North Carolina)
UFinSC	NAS NMS	UNSA	United Financial Corporation of South Carolina Inc
UFireC	NAS NMS	UFCS	United Fire & Casualty Co
UFnGrp	NAS NMS	UFGI	United Financial Group Inc
UFoodA	American	UFD.A	United Foods Inc (Class A)
UFoodB	American	UFD.B	United Foods Inc (Class B)
UGI	New York	UGI	UGI Corp
UGrdn	NAS NMS	UNIR	United-Guardian Inc
UHltCr	NAS NMS	UNIH	United HealthCare Corp
UIllum	New York	UIL	The United Illuminating Co
UJerBk	New York	UJB	United Jersey Banks
UKing	New York	UKM	The United Kingdom Fund Inc
Ultimap	NAS SL	UMAP	ULTIMAP International Corp
Ultmte	New York	ULT	The Ultimate Corp
UltrBc	NAS NMS	ULTB	Ultra Bancorporation
UMatch	New York	UMG	Universal Matchbox Group Ltd

NEWSPAPER ABBREV.	MARKET LISTING	TRADING SYMBOL	COMPANY NAME
UMoB	NAS NMS	UMSB	United Missouri Bancshares Inc
UnBkrs	NAS NMS	UBKR	United Bankers Inc
UnBldg	NAS NMS	UBSC	United Building Services Corporation of Delaware
UnBrnd	New York	UB	United Brands Co
UNCInc	New York	UNC	UNC Inc
UnCoast	NAS NMS	UCOA	United Coasts Corp
UnCosF	NAS NMS	UNCF	United Companies Financial Corp
UnDom	NAS NMS	UDRT	United Dominion Realty Trust Inc
UnEdS	NAS NMS	UESS	United Education & Software
UnElec	New York	UEP	Union Electric Co
UnExp	New York	UXP	Union Exploration Partners Ltd
Unfast	NAS NMS	UFST	Unifast Industries Inc
UnfedF	New York	UFF	UnionFed Financial Corp
UnFncl	NAS NL	UFBC	United Financial Banking Co
UnHrn	NAS SL	UHRNF	United Hearne Resources Ltd
Unibcp	NAS NMS	UBCP	Unibancorp Inc
UnicoA	NAS NMS	UNAM	Unico American Corp
Unicorp	American	UAC	Unicorp American Corp
UniCre	American	UFN	UniCARE Financial Corp
Unifi	NAS NMS	UNFI	Unifi Inc
Unifrc	NAS NMS	UNFR	Uniforce Temporary Personnel Inc
UniFrst	New York	UNF	UniFirst Corp
Unigene	NAS NL	UGNE	Unigene Laboratories Inc
Unilvr	New York	UL	Unilever PLC
Unimar	American	UMR	Unimar Co
Unimed	NAS NMS	UMED	Unimed Inc
UniMrt	NAS NMS	UNMAA	Uni-Marts Inc (Class A)
UnionC	New York	UCO	The Union Corp
Unisys	New York	UIS	Unisys Corp
Unit	New York	UNT	Unit Corp
UniTel	New York	UT	United Telecommunications Inc
UnitelV	American	UNV	Unitel Video Inc
Unitil	American	UTL	UNITIL Corp
UnitInd	New York	UIC	United Industrial Corp
UnitInn	New York	UI	United Inns Inc
Unitrde	New York	UTR	Unitrode Corp
Unitrnx	NAS NMS	UTRX	Unitronix Corp
Univar	New York	UVX	Univar Corp
Univatn	NAS SL	UNIV	Univation Inc
UnivBT	NAS NMS	UNNB	University National Bank & Trust Co (California)
UnNatl	NAS NMS	UNBC	Union National Corp
UnNMx	NAS NMS	BNKS	United New Mexico Financial Corp
UnNV	New York	UN	Unilever N.V.
Unocal	New York	UCL	Unocal Corp
UnoRt	American	UNO	UNO Restaurant Corp
UnPac	New York	UNP	Union Pacific Corp

NEWSPAPER ABBREV.	MARKET LISTING	TRADING SYMBOL	COMPANY NAME
UnPlntr	NAS NMS	UPCM	Union Planters Corp
UNR	NAS NL	UNRIQ	UNR Industries Inc
UnStck	New York	COW	United Stockyards Corp
UnSvFl	NAS NMS	UNSVA	United Savings Assn (Florida) (Class A)
UnSvMo	NAS NMS	UNSL	United S&L Assn (Missouri)
UnSvSc	NAS NMS	UNSI	United Service Source Inc
UnSyTc	NAS SL	USTI	United Systems Technology Inc
UnTech	New York	UTX	United Technologies Corp
UnTelev	NAS NMS	UTVI	United Television Inc
UnTex	New York	UTH	Union Texas Petroleum Holdings Inc
UnTote	NAS NMS	TOTE	United Tote Inc
UNUM	New York	UNM	UNUM Corp
UnValy	American	UVC	Union Valley Corp
UnvBk	American	UBN	University Bank N.A.
UnvFds	New York	UFC	Universal Foods Corp
UnvFr	NAS NMS	UFURF	Universal Furniture Ltd
UnvGen	NAS SL	UGEN	University Genetics Co
UnvHld	NAS NMS	UHCO	Universal Holding Corp
UnvHlt	NAS NMS	UHSIB	Universal Health Services Inc (Class B)
UnvHR	New York	UHT	Universal Health Realty Income Trust
UnvlCp	New York	UVV	Universal Corp
UnvMed	New York	UMB	Universal Medical Buildings L.P.
UnVolt	NAS NMS	UVOL	Universal Voltronics Corp
UnvPat	American	UPT	University Patents Inc
UnvSci	NAS SL	USPI	University Science Partners Inc
UnvSec	NAS NMS	USEC	Universal Security Instruments Inc
UnvSvg	NAS NMS	UFSB	University Savings Bank (Washington)
UnVtBn	NAS NMS	UVTB	United Vermont Bancorporation
UPenP	NAS NMS	UPEN	Upper Peninsula Power Co
UPkMn	New York	UPK	United Park City Mines Co
Upjohn	New York	UPJ	The Upjohn Co
UPresd	NAS NMS	UPCO	United Presidential Corp
US Ant	NAS NMS	USAC	United States Antimony Corp
US Bcp	NAS NMS	USBC	U.S. Bancorp
US Cel	American	USM	United States Cellular Corp
US Enr	NAS NMS	USEG	U.S. Energy Corp
US Facl	NAS NMS	USRE	US Facilities Corp
US Gold	NAS NMS	USGL	U.S. Gold Corp
US HltC	NAS NMS	USHC	U.S. Healthcare Inc
US Intc	NAS NMS	INTX	U.S. Intec Inc
US Oil	NAS SL	USOL	United States Oil Co
US Prc	NAS NMS	USPMF	U.S. Precious Metals Inc
US Shelt	NAS NMS	USSS	U.S. Shelter Corp
US Surg	New York	USS	United States Surgical Corp
US Trst	NAS NMS	USTC	U.S. Trust Corp
USA Bc	NAS NMS	USAB	USA Bancorp Inc
USACaf	New York	USF	USACafes L.P.
UsairG	New York	U	USAir Group Inc

NEWSPAPER ABBREV.	MARKET LISTING	TRADING SYMBOL	COMPANY NAME
USB Or	NAS NMS	USBA	United Savings Bank (Oregon)
USBkVa	NAS NMS	USBK	United Savings Bank (Virginia)
USBPa	NAS NMS	USBP	USBANCORP Inc (Pennsylvania)
Usenco	NAS SL	USEN	USENCO Inc
USFG	New York	FG	USF&G Corp
USG	New York	USG	USG Corp
USHltI	NAS NMS	USHI	U.S. Health Inc
USHom	New York	UH	U.S. Home Corp
UslfeF	New York	UIF	USLIFE Income Fund Inc
USLICO	New York	USC	USLICO Corp
USLIFE	New York	USH	USLIFE Corp
USMX	NAS NMS	USMX	US Minerals Exploration Co
USPCI	New York	UPC	USPCI Inc
USPRI	American	URT	USP Real Estate Investment Trust
USRlty	NAS NL	USRLZ	US Realty Partners Ltd
USShoe	New York	USR	The United States Shoe Corp
UST	New York	UST	UST Inc
UST Cp	NAS NMS	USTB	UST Corp
UStatn	NAS NMS	USTR	United Stationers Inc
USvBk	NAS NMS	UBMT	United Savings Bank F.A. (Montana)
USWest	New York	USW	U S WEST Inc
USWNV	NAS NMS	USWNA	U S WEST NewVector Group Inc (Class A)
USX	New York	X	USX Corp
UtahMd	NAS SL	UTMD	Utah Medical Products Inc
UtaPL	New York	UTP	Utah Power & Light Co
UtdHm	NAS NMS	UHLI	United Home Life Insurance Co
UtdIns	NAS NMS	UICI	United Insurance Companies Inc
UtdInv	NAS NMS	UTDMK	United Investors Management Co
UtdMM	New York	UMM	United Merchants & Manufacturers Inc
UtdNwsp	NAS NMS	UNEWY	United Newspapers Public Limited Co
UtdShp	NAS SL	USDA	United Shoppers of America Inc
UtdSvrs	NAS NMS	USBI	United Saver's Bancorp Inc
UtiliCo	New York	UCU	UtiliCorp United Inc
UTL	NAS NMS	UTLC	UTL Corp
UtMed	American	UM	United Medical Corp
UWR	New York	UWR	United Water Resources Inc
V Band	NAS NMS	VBAN	V-Band Systems Inc
VaalR	NAS NL	VAALY	Vaal Reefs Exploration & Mining Company Ltd
VaBch	NAS NMS	VABF	Virginia Beach Savings Bank
VacDry	NAS NL	VDRY	Vacu-dry Co
VacTGo	NAS SL	VTGO	Vacations To Go Inc
Vader	American	VDR	Vader Group Inc
VaFst	NAS NMS	VFSB	Virginia First Savings Bank FSB
ValB VT	NAS SL	VBVT	Valley Bank (Vermont)
Valcom	NAS NMS	VLCM	ValCom Inc
Valdost	NAS NL	VFSL	Valdosta Federal S&L Assn

NEWSPAPER ABBREV.	MARKET LISTING	TRADING SYMBOL	COMPANY NAME
Valero	New York	VLO	Valero Energy Corp
ValeyIn	New York	VI	Valley Industries Inc
ValFrg	American	VF	Valley Forge Corp
ValFSL	NAS NMS	VFED	Valley Federal S&L Assn
Valhi	New York	VHI	Valhi Inc
Valid Lg	NAS NMS	VLID	Valid Logic Systems Inc
Vallen	NAS NMS	VALN	Vallen Corp
ValLn	NAS NMS	VALU	Value Line Inc
Valmnt	NAS NMS	VALM	Valmont Industries Inc
ValNBc	NAS NMS	VNBP	Valley National Bancorp (New Jersey)
ValNG	New York	VLP	Velero Natural Gas Partners L.P.
ValNtl	NAS NMS	VNCP	Valley National Corp
Valspr	American	VAL	The Valspar Corp
ValyB	NAS NMS	VYBN	Valley Bancorporation (Wisconsin)
ValyRs	American	VR	Valley Resources Inc
ValyWst	NAS NL	VWBN	Valley West Bancorp
VanDrn	New York	VDC	Van Dorn Co
VanGld	NAS NMS	VAGO	Vanderbilt Gold Corp
Vanzeti	NAS NMS	VANZ	Vanzetti Systems Inc
Varco	New York	VRC	Varco International Inc
Varian	New York	VAR	Varian Associates Inc
VariCre	NAS NMS	VCRE	Vari-Care Inc
Varitrn	NAS NMS	VRSY	Varitronic Systems Inc
Varity	New York	VAT	Varity Corp
Varlen	NAS NMS	VRLN	Varlen Corp
Varo	New York	VRO	Varo Inc
Vaughn	NAS SL	VGHN	Vaughn's Inc
Veeco	New York	VEE	Veeco Instruments Inc
VegaBio	NAS SL	VEGA	Vega Biotechnologies Inc
Velcro	NAS NL	VELCF	Velcro Industries N.V.
VeloBd	NAS NMS	VBND	VeloBind Inc
Vendo	New York	VEN	The Vendo Co
Ventrex	NAS NMS	VTRX	Ventrex Laboratories Inc
Ventur	NAS NMS	VENT	Venturian Corp
Verdix	NAS SL	VRDX	Verdix Corp
Verit	American	VER	Verit Industries
Veronx	NAS NMS	VEOXF	Veronex Resources Ltd
Versa	NAS NMS	VRSA	Versa Technologies Inc
Versar	American	VSR	Versar Inc
VertexC	NAS NMS	VTEX	Vertex Communications Corp
Vertple	American	VRT	Vertipile Inc
Vestar	NAS NMS	VSTR	Vestar Inc
Vestrn	New York	VV	Vestron Inc
Vestro	NAS SL	VEST	Vestro Foods Inc
VestSe	New York	VES	Vestaur Securities Inc
VF Cp	New York	VFC	V.F. Corp
VgrdCl	NAS NMS	VCEL	Vanguard Cellular-Systems Inc
VHC	NAS NL	VHCL	VHC Ltd

NEWSPAPER ABBREV.	MARKET LISTING	TRADING SYMBOL	COMPANY NAME
VHT	American	VHT	VMS Hotel Investment Fund
Viacm	American	VIA	Viacom Inc
Viatch	American	VTK	Viatech Inc
Vicon	American	VII	Vicon Industries Inc
ViconF	NAS NMS	VFOX	Vicon Fiber Optics Corp
Vicorp	NAS NMS	VRES	VICORP Restaurants Inc
VictBn	NAS NMS	VICT	Victoria Bankshares Inc
VictCr	NAS NMS	VITC	Victoria Creations Inc
VictFn	NAS SL	VICF	Victoria Financial Corp
VidDsp	NAS NMS	VIDE	Video Display Corp
Videplx	NAS SL	VPLXE	Videoplex Inc
VidJuke	NAS SL	JUKE	Video Jukebox Network Inc
Vie deFr	NAS NMS	VDEF	Vie de France Corp
ViewMs	NAS NMS	VMIG	View-Master Ideal Group Inc
Viking	NAS NMS	VIKG	Viking Freight Inc
Vikonic	NAS NMS	VKSI	Vikonics Inc
VilSpM	NAS NMS	LVGE	Village Super Market Inc
Viner	NAS NL	EAVK	E.A. Viner Holdings Ltd
Vintage	NAS NL	VINT	Vintage Group Inc
Vintge	American	VIN	Vintage Enterprises Inc
Vipont	NAS NMS	VLAB	Vipont Laboratories Inc
Viragen	NAS SL	VRGN	Viragen Inc
ViralRp	NAS SL	VRSI	Viral Response Systems Inc
Viratek	NAS NMS	VIRA	Viratek Inc
Virco	American	VIR	Virco Manufacturing Corp
VirgnG	NAS NMS	VGINY	Virgin Group plc
Viscnt	NAS SL	VISRF	Viscount Resources Ltd
Vishay	New York	VSH	Vishay Intertechnology Inc
VislG B	American	VGC.B	Visual Graphics Corp (Class B)
VislGA	American	VGC.A	Visual Graphisc Corp (Class A)
VistaC	New York	VC	Vista Chemical Co
VistaOr	NAS NMS	VISA	Vista Organization Ltd
VistaRs	NAS NL	VIST	Vista Resources Inc
VisualI	NAS NMS	VISC	Visual Industries Inc
Vitalnk	NAS NMS	VITA	Vitalink Communications Corp
VitelFb	NAS SL	VTEL	Vitel Fiber Optics Corp
Vitronic	NAS NMS	VITX	Vitronics Corp
Vivigen	NAS NMS	VIVI	Vivigen Inc
VKmp	New York	VMT	Van Kampen Merritt Municipal Income Trust
VlFdAla	NAS SL	VAFD	Valley Federal Savings Bank (Alabama)
VLSI	NAS NMS	VLSI	VLSI Technology Inc
VlyCap	NAS NMS	VCCN	Valley Capital Corp
VlyFed	NAS NL	VAFB	Valley Federal Savings Bank (Indiana)
VM Sft	NAS NMS	VMSI	VM Software Inc
VMX	NAS NMS	VMXI	VMX Inc
Voicml	NAS SL	VOIC	Voicemail International Inc
VoltInf	NAS NMS	VOLT	Volt Information Sciences Inc

NEWSPAPER ABBREV.	MARKET LISTING	TRADING SYMBOL	COMPANY NAME
VolunBc	NAS NL	VOLB	Volunteer Bancshares Inc
Volvo	NAS NMS	VOLVY	Volvo A.B.
Vons	New York	VON	The Vons Companies Inc
Voplex	American	VOT	Voplex Corp
Vornad	New York	VNO	Vornado Inc
Votrax	NAS SL	VOTX	Votrax Inc
VSE	NAS NMS	VSEC	VSE Corp
VsnSci	NAS SL	LENZ	Vision Sciences Inc
VsnTch	NAS SL	IOLS	Vision Technologies International Inc
VtAmC	American	VAC.A	Vermont American Corp (Class A)
VtFin	NAS NMS	VFSC	Vermont Financial Services Corp
VtRsh	American	VRE	Vermont Research Corp
VTX	American	VTX	VTX Electronics Corp
VulcCp	American	VUL	Vulcan Corp
VulcM	New York	VMC	Vulcan Materials Co
VulcP	NAS NMS	VIPLF	Vulcan Packaging Inc
VWR	NAS NMS	VWRX	VWR Corp
Vyqust	American	VY	Vyquest Inc
Wackht	New York	WAK	The Wackenhut Corp
Wacoal	NAS NL	WACLY	Wacoal Corp
Wainoc	New York	WOL	Wainoco Oil Corp
Walbro	NAS NMS	WALB	Walbro Corp
WalCSv	New York	WCS	Wallace Computer Services Inc
Walgrn	New York	WAG	Walgreen Co
WallSnd	NAS NMS	WTWS	Wall to Wall Sound & Video Inc
WalMt	New York	WMT	Wal-Mart Stores Inc
Walshr	NAS NMS	WALS	Walshire Assurance Co
WaltCp	NAS NMS	WLBK	Waltham Corp
WAmB	American	WAB	WESTAMERICA BANCORPORATION
Wamplr	NAS NL	WLRF	Wampler-Longacre-Rockingham Inc
WangB	American	WAN.B	Wang Laboratories Inc (Class B)
WangC	American	WAN.C	Wang Laboratories Inc (Class C)
WardWh	NAS NMS	WWGPY	Ward White Group PLC
WarnC	New York	WCI	Warner Communications Inc
WarnrL	New York	WLA	Warner-Lambert Co
Warntc	NAS SL	WTEC	Warrantech Corp
Warren	NAS NMS	WFCS	Warren Five Cents Savings Bank (Massachusetts)
Warwk	NAS NMS	WIMI	Warwick Insurance Managers Inc
WashEn	NAS NMS	WECO	Washington Energy Co
WashGs	New York	WGL	Washington Gas Light Co
WashTr	NAS NL	Wash	Washington Trust Bancorp Inc (Rhode Island)
Waste	New York	WMX	Waste Management Inc
WasteRc	NAS SL	WRII	Waste Recovery Inc
WasteTc	NAS SL	WTEK	Waste Technology Corp
WatkJn	New York	WJ	Watkins-Johnson Co

NEWSPAPER ABBREV.	MARKET LISTING	TRADING SYMBOL	COMPANY NAME
WatrfGl	NAS NMS	WATFY	Waterford Glass Group plc
Watrhse	NAS NMS	WHOO	Waterhouse Investor Services Inc
WatrIn	NAS NMS	WHRG	Waters Instruments Inc
Watsc A	American	WSO.A	Watsco Inc (Class A)
Watsc B	American	WSO.B	Watsco Inc (Class B)
WattsInd	NAS NMS	WATTA	Watts Industries Inc (Class A)
WausP	NAS NMS	WSAU	Wausau Paper Mills Co
Waver	NAS NMS	WAVR	Waverly Inc
Wavetch	NAS SL	WAVE	Wavetech Inc
Wavetk	NAS NMS	WVTK	Wavetek Corp
Waxmn	NAS NMS	WAXM	Waxman Industries Inc
WBcDC	NAS NMS	WWBC	Washington Bancorporation (Washington D.C.)
WbstCl	NAS NMS	WEBS	Webster Clothes Inc
WbstFn	NAS NMS	WBST	Webster Financial Corp
WCNA	New York	WSN	The Western Company of North America
WCRS	NAS NMS	WCRSY	The WCRS Group PLC
WD 40	NAS NMS	WDFC	WD-40 Co
WDeep	NAS NL	WDEPY	Western Deep Levels Ltd
WDigitl	American	WDC	Western Digital Corp
Wdstrm	American	WOD	Woodstream Corp
WeanU	New York	WID	Wean Inc
WebbD	New York	WBB	Del E. Webb Corp
WebInv	American	DWP.A	Del E. Webb Investment Properties Inc (Class A)
Weblt	NAS NMS	WELB	Welbilt Corp
Wedco	American	WED	Wedco Technology Inc
Wedgtn	New York	WDG	Wedgestone Financial Trust
WeigTr	NAS NMS	WGHT	Weigh-Tronix Inc
Weiman	American	WC	Weiman Company Inc
WeingR	New York	WRI	Weingarten Realty Inc
Weisfld	NAS NMS	WEIS	Weisfield's Inc
WeisM	New York	WMK	Weis Markets Inc
Weitek	NAS NL	WWTK	Weitek Corp
WekG	NAS NL	WLKMY	Welkom Gold Holdings Ltd
Weldtrn	American	WLD	Weldotron Corp
WelFM	New York	WFM	Wells Fargo Mortgage & Equity Trust
WelGrd	American	WGA	Wells-Gardner Electronics Corp
WellAm	American	WAC	Wells American Corp
Wellco	American	WLC	Wellco Enterprises Inc
Wellmn	New York	WLM	Wellman Inc
WellsF	New York	WFC	Wells Fargo & Co
Wendt	NAS NMS	WNDT	Wendt-Bristol Co
Wendys	New York	WEN	Wendy's International Inc
Werner	NAS NMS	WERN	Werner Enterprises Inc
Wesbnc	NAS NMS	WSBC	Wesbanco Inc
Wesco	American	WSC	Wesco Financial Corp
Wespcp	American	WP	Wespercorp

NEWSPAPER ABBREV.	MARKET LISTING	TRADING SYMBOL	COMPANY NAME
Wessex	NAS NMS	WSSX	Wessex Corp
West	New York	WST	The West Company Inc
Westar	NAS SL	WSTR	Westar Corp
Westcp	American	WCRP	Westcorp
Weston	NAS NMS	WSTNA	Roy F. Weston Inc (Class A)
WetrPr	NAS NL	WTPR	Wetterau Properties Inc
Wettra	NAS NMS	WETT	Wetterau Inc
Weyerh	New York	WY	Weyerhaeuser Co
Weynbg	NAS NMS	WEYS	Weyenberg Shoe Manufacturing Co
WFdPR	NAS NMS	WFPR	Western Federal Savings Bank (Puerto Rico)
WFSL	NAS NMS	WFSL	Washington Federal S&L Assn of Seattle
Wharf	NAS NMS	WFRAF	Wharf Resources Ltd
WhelLE	New York	WLE	The Wheeling & Lake Erie Railway Co
WhelTch	NAS NMS	WHTI	Wheelabrator Technologies Inc
Whitehl	New York	WHT	Whitehall Corp
Whitmn	NAS SL	WHIT	Whitman Medical Corp
WhitPt	NAS SL	WPCO	Whiting Petroleum Corp
Whittak	New York	WKR	Whittaker Corp
Whlclub	NAS NMS	WHLS	The Wholesale Club Inc
WhPit	New York	WHX	Wheeling-Pittsburgh Steel Corp
Whrlpl	New York	WHR	Whirlpool Corp
Wicat	NAS NMS	WCAT	WICAT Systems Inc
WichRv	American	WRO	Wichita River Corp
Wicke	New York	WIX	Wickes Companies Inc
WICOR	New York	WIC	WICOR Inc
Wiener	American	WPB	Wiener Enterprises Inc
Wiland	NAS NMS	WSVS	Wiland Services Inc
Wilfred	New York	WAE	Wilfred American Educational Corp
WillAL	NAS NMS	ALWC	The A.L. Williams Corp
Willamt	NAS NMS	WMTT	Willamette Industries Inc
WillcG	New York	WG	Willcox & Gibbs Inc
William	New York	WMB	The Williams Companies Inc
WillmI	NAS NMS	WMSI	Williams Industries Inc
WillW	NAS NMS	WWWM	W.W. Williams Co
WilmT	NAS NMS	WILM	Wilmington Trust Co
WilSFS	NAS NMS	WSFS	Wilmington Savings Fund Society FSB
WilshrO	New York	WOC	Wilshire Oil Company of Texas
WilsnF	NAS NMS	WILF	Wilson Foods Corp
Wiltek	NAS SL	WLTK	Wiltek Inc
Wilton	NAS NMS	WLTN	Wilton Enterprises Inc
WilyJ A	NAS NMS	WILLA	John Wiley & Sons Inc (Class A)
WilyJ B	NAS NL	WILLB	John Wiley & Sons Inc (Class B)
Winchl	New York	WDH	Winchell's Donut Houses L.P.
WinDix	New York	WIN	Winn-Dixie Stores Inc
Windmr	NAS NMS	WDMR	Windmere Corp
WINE	NAS SL	VINO	WINE Inc
WinFur	American	WF	Winston Furniture Company Inc

NEWSPAPER ABBREV.	MARKET LISTING	TRADING SYMBOL	COMPANY NAME
Winjak	New York	WJI	Winjak Inc
Winnbg	New York	WGO	Winnebago Industries Inc
Winner	New York	WNR	Winners Corp
WinRs	American	WRS	Winston Resources Inc
WintIn	American	WMI	Winthrop Insured Mortgage Investors II
WIRET	American	WIR	Western Investment Real Estate Trust
WiscRE	NAS NL	WREI	Wisconsin Real Estate Investment Trust
WiscTy	NAS NMS	WTOY	Wisconsin Toy Co
WisEn	New York	WEC	Wisconsin Energy Corp
WiserO	NAS NMS	WISE	The Wiser Oil Co
WisPS	New York	WPS	Wisconsin Public Service Corp
WisSGs	NAS NMS	WISC	Wisconsin Southern Gas Company Inc
Witco	New York	WIT	Witco Corp
Wkmen	NAS NMS	WCBK	Workingmens Corp (Massachusetts)
WldInc	American	WOI	World Income Fund Inc
WldwdCpt	NAS NL	WCSI	Worldwide Computer Services Inc
WlkrTel	NAS NMS	WTEL	Walker Telecommunications Corp
WlsnSp	American	WIL	Wilson Sporting Goods Co
Wlwth	New York	Z	F.W. Woolworth Co
WmCmc	NAS NMS	WCCC	Western Commercial Inc
WMicr	NAS NMS	WMIC	Western Microwave Inc
WMicTc	NAS NMS	WSTM	Western Micro Technology Inc
WmorC	NAS NMS	WMOR	Westmoreland Coal Co
WMS	New York	WMS	WMS Industries Inc
WMSB	NAS NMS	WAMU	Washington Mutual Savings Bank
WmsSon	NAS NMS	WSGC	Williams-Sonoma Inc
WNewtn	NAS NMS	WNSB	West Newton Savings Bank (Massachusetts)
WnFncl	NAS NMS	WSTF	Western Financial Corp
WNS	NAS NMS	WNSI	WNS Inc
WnWste	NAS NMS	WWIN	Western Waste Industries
WolfFn	NAS NL	WOFG	Wolf Financial Group Inc
WolfHB	American	HBW	Howard B. Wolf Inc
Wolohn	NAS NMS	WLHN	Wolohan Lumber Co
WolvEx	NAS NMS	WEXC	Wolverine Exploration Co
WolvrW	New York	WWW	Wolverine World Wide Inc
WolvTc	New York	WOV	Wolverine Technologies Inc
Woodhd	NAS NMS	WDHD	Woodhead Industries Inc
WorlcDt	NAS SL	WDSI	Worlco Data Systems Inc
Worthg	NAS NMS	WTHG	Worthington Industries Inc
Worthn	American	WOR	Worthen Banking Corp
WPL Hld	New York	WPL	WPL Holdings Inc
WPP Gp	NAS NMS	WPPGY	WPP Group plc
WrhseC	NAS NMS	WCLB	Warehouse Club Inc
Wrigly	New York	WWY	William Wrigley Jr. Co
WRIT	American	WRE	Washington Real Estate Investment Trust
Writer	NAS NMS	WRTC	The Writer Corp
WrldCn	NAS SL	WRLD	World Container Corp

NEWSPAPER ABBREV.	MARKET LISTING	TRADING SYMBOL	COMPANY NAME
WrldCp	New York	WOA	WorldCorp Inc
WrldVl	New York	VLU	Worldwide Value Fund Inc
WrnCpt	New York	WCP	Warner Computer Systems Inc
WshBcp	NAS NMS	WBNC	Washington Bancorp Inc (New Jersey)
WshFDC	NAS NMS	WFSB	Washington Federal Saving Bank (Washington D.C.)
WshFOr	NAS NMS	WFOR	Washington Federal Savings Bank (Oregon)
WshNat	New York	WNT	Washington National Corp
WshPst	American	WPO.B	The Washington Post Co (Class B)
WshSci	NAS NMS	WSCI	Washington Scientific Industries Inc
WshSvg	NAS NMS	WSBXV	Washington Savings Bank
WshWt	New York	WWP	The Washington Water Power Co
WSMP	NAS NMS	WSMP	WSMP Inc
WstAcp	NAS SL	WACP	Western Acceptance Corp
WstAut	NAS NMS	WASC	Western Auto Supply Co
WstBc	NAS NMS	WBAT	Westport Bancorp Inc
WstBell	NAS SL	WBEL	Western Bell Communications Inc
WstBrC	American	WBC	Westbridge Capital Corp
WstCap	NAS NMS	WECA	Western Capital Investment Corp
WstctE	New York	WE	Westcoast Energy Inc
WstFSL	NAS NMS	WFSA	Western Federal S&L Assn (California)
WstgE	New York	WX	Westinghouse Electric Corp
WstHlth	American	WHP	Western Health Plans Inc
Wstmrk	NAS NMS	WMRK	Westmark International Inc
WstnPb	NAS NMS	WPGI	Western Publishing Group Inc
WstnSL	New York	WSL	Western S&L Assn
Wstrbke	NAS NMS	WTBK	Westerbeke Corp
Wstvc	New York	W	Westvaco Corp
WstwO	NAS NMS	WONE	Westwood One Inc
WtBank	NAS NMS	WSBK	Western Bank (Oregon)
WtCaSv	NAS NL	WCAR	Western Carolina S&L Assn (North Carolina)
WTD	NAS NMS	WTDI	WTD Industries Inc
Wthfrd	American	WII	Weatherford International Inc
WtMass	NAS NMS	WMBS	West Massachusetts Bankshares Inc
WtMrcA	NAS NMS	WSMCA	WestMarc Communications Inc (Class A)
WtMrcB	NAS NL	WSMCB	WestMarc Communications Inc (Class B)
WtnAlen	NAS NL	WABEF	Western Allenbee Oil & Gas Company Ltd
WtPtP	New York	WPM	West Point-Pepperell Inc
WUnion	New York	WU	Western Union Corp
Wurltch	New York	WUR	WurlTech Industries Inc
WWTch	NAS SL	WOTK	World-Wide Technology Inc
WyleLb	New York	WYL	Wyle Laboratories
Wyman	NAS NMS	WYMN	Wyman-Gordon Co
WymngNt	NAS NMS	WYNB	Wyoming National Bancorporation
Wynns	New York	WN	Wynn's International Inc
Wyse	New York	WYS	Wyse Technology

NEWSPAPER ABBREV.	MARKET LISTING	TRADING SYMBOL	COMPANY NAME
X-Rite	NAS NMS	XRIT	X-Rite Inc
Xebec	NAS NMS	XEBC	Xebec
Xerox	New York	XRX	Xerox Corp
Xeta	NAS NL	XETA	Xeta Corp
Xicor	NAS NMS	XICO	Xicor Inc
XL Dt	NAS NMS	XLDC	XL/Datacomp Inc
XOMA	NAS NMS	XOMA	XOMA Corp
Xplor	NAS NMS	XPLR	Xplor Corp
Xscribe	NAS NMS	XSCR	Xscribe Corp
Xsirus	NAS SL	XSIR	Xsirus Scientific Inc
XTRA	New York	XTR	XTRA Corp
Xylogic	NAS NMS	XLGX	Xylogics Inc
Xytrn	NAS SL	XYYX	Xytronyx Inc
Xyvsn	NAS NMS	XYVI	Xyvision Inc
YankCo	American	YNK	The Yankee Companies Inc
YlowF	NAS NMS	YELL	Yellow Freight System Inc of Delaware
YorkIn	New York	YRK	York International Corp
YorkRs	NAS NMS	YORK	York Research Corp
YrkFn	NAS NMS	YFED	York Financial Corp
Yrkrdg	NAS NMS	YCSL	Yorkridge-Calvert S&L Assn (Maryland)
YUBAA	NAS SL	YUBAA	Yuba Natural Resources Inc (Class A)
YukonE	NAS SL	YUKN	Yukon Energy Corp
Z Sevn	NAS NMS	ZSEV	Z-Seven Fund Inc
Zapata	New York	ZOS	Zapata Corp
Zayre	New York	ZY	Zayre Corp
Zemex	New York	ZMX	Zemex Corp
ZenIn	New York	ZIF	Zenith Income Fund
ZenithE	New York	ZE	Zenith Electronics Corp
ZenLab	New York	ZEN	Zenith Laboratories Inc
ZenNtl	New York	ZNT	Zenith National Insurance Corp
Zentec	NAS NMS	ZENT	Zentec Corp
Zero	New York	ZRO	Zero Corp
Zetek	NAS SL	ZETK	Zetek Inc
Zeus	NAS NMS	ZEUS	Zeus Components Inc
Ziegler	NAS NMS	ZEGL	The Ziegler Company Inc
Zimer	American	ZIM	Zimmer Corp
ZionUt	NAS NMS	ZION	Zions Bancorporation (Utah)
Zitel	NAS NMS	ZITL	Zitel Corp
Zondvn	NAS NMS	ZOND	The Zondervan Corp
ZurnIn	New York	ZRN	Zurn Industries Inc
Zweig	New York	ZF	The Zweig Fund Inc
Zycad	NAS NMS	ZCAD	Zycad Corp
Zygo	NAS NMS	ZIGO	Zygo Corp
Zymos	NAS NMS	ZMOS	ZyMOS Corp
Zytec	NAS SL	ZSILF	Zytec Systems Inc

TRADING SYMBOL	MARKET LISTING	NEWSPAPER ABBREV.	COMPANY NAME
A	American	AMBld	American Medical Buildings Inc
AA	New York	Alcoa	Aluminum Company of America
AAA	New York	ASLFla	American S&L Assn of Florida
AAC	New York	Anacmp	Anacomp Inc
AAGIY	NAS NL	AngAG	Anglo American Gold Investment Company Ltd
AAHS	NAS NMS	AlcoHlt	Alco Health Services Corp
AAICA	NAS NMS	AlbnyIn	Albany International Corp (Class A)
AAL	New York	AlexAlx	Alexander & Alexander Services Inc
AAME	NAS NMS	AtlAm	Atlantic American Corp
AAPL	NAS NMS	AppleC	Apple Computer Inc
AARC	NAS SL	AAcft	American Aircraft Corp
AATI	NAS NMS	AnalyTc	Analysis & Technology Inc
AB	American	ABI	ABI American Businessphones Inc
ABBK	NAS NMS	AbingB	Abington Bancorp Inc (Massachusetts)
ABCC	NAS SL	ABsCpt	American Business Computers Corp
ABCV	NAS NMS	AflBcCp	Affiliated Banc Corp (Massachusetts)
ABD	American	Abimd	ABIOMED Inc
ABF	New York	AirbFrt	Airborne Freight Corp
ABG	New York	AShip	The American Ship Building Co
ABGA	NAS NMS	AlldBk	Allied Bankshares Inc (Georgia)
ABI	American	AmBrit	AmBrit Inc
ABIG	NAS NMS	ABnkr	American Bankers Insurance Group Inc
ABIO	NAS NMS	ApldBio	Applied Biosystems Inc
ABK	American	AlliBc	Alliance Bancorporation
ABKR	NAS NMS	AnchSv	Anchor Savings Bank FSB (New York)
ABL	American	AmBilt	American Biltrite Inc
ABM	New York	ABldM	American Building Maintenance Industries
ABNK	NAS NL	Amribc	Ameribanc Inc (Missouri)
ABP	New York	ABusPr	American Business Products Inc
ABQC	NAS NMS	ABQ	ABQ Corp
ABRI	NAS NMS	Abrams	Abrams Industries Inc
ABS	New York	Albtsn	Albertson's Inc
ABSB	NAS NMS	AlexBr	Alex. Brown Inc
ABSI	NAS NMS	ABS	ABS Industries Inc
ABT	New York	AbtLab	Abbott Laboratories
ABW	New York	Armada	Armada Corp
ABX	New York	ABrck	American Barrick Resources Corp

276

TRADING SYMBOL	MARKET LISTING	NEWSPAPER ABBREV.	COMPANY NAME
ABY	New York	Abitibi	Abitibi-Price Inc
ABZ	New York	ArkBst	Arkansas Best Corp
AC	New York	AlnCap	Alliance Capital Management LP
ACA	New York	ACMR	American Capital Management & Research Inc
ACAD	NAS NMS	Autodk	Autodesk Inc
ACB	New York	ACapBd	American Capital Bond Fund Inc
ACC	American	AmCap	American Capital Corp
ACCC	NAS NMS	ACC Cp	ACC Corp
ACCI	NAS NL	AmCnsl	American Consulting Corp
ACCMA	NAS NMS	AsCmA	Associated Communications Corp (Class A)
ACCMB	NAS NMS	AsCmB	Associated Communications Corp (Class B)
ACCOB	NAS NMS	Coors B	Adolph Coors Co (Class B)
ACCT	NAS SL	CardTl	Card-Tel
ACD	New York	ACapIn	American Capital Income Trust
ACE	New York	AcmeE	Acme Electric Corp
ACET	NAS NMS	Aceto	Aceto Corp
ACG	New York	ACMIn	ACM Government Income Fund Inc
ACGC	NAS SL	ACGld	American Consolidated Gold Corp
ACGI	NAS NMS	ACapac	American Capacity Group Inc
ACHV	NAS NMS	Archive	Archive Corp
ACI	New York	AshCoal	Ashland Coal Inc
ACIG	NAS NMS	AcadIn	Academy Insurance Group Inc
ACIX	NAS NMS	AmCarr	American Carriers Inc
ACK	New York	ArmWI	Armstrong World Industries Inc
ACLE	NAS NMS	Accel	Accel International Corp
ACLV	NAS NMS	Autoclv	Autoclave Engineers Inc
ACM.B	American	AtlsCM	Atlas Consolidated Mining & Development Corp (Class B)
ACME	NAS NMS	AcmeSt	Acme Steel Co
ACMS	NAS NMS	CMS E	CMS Enhancements Inc
ACMT	NAS NMS	ACMT	ACMAT Corp
ACOL	NAS NMS	AmColid	American Colloid Co
ACOM	NAS NMS	Astrcm	Astrocom Corp
ACP	New York	AREst	American Real Estate Partners LP
ACPI	NAS NMS	AConsu	American Consumer Products Inc
ACPT	NAS NMS	AceptIn	Acceptance Insurance Holdings Inc
ACR	New York	AnglRl	Angell Real Estate Company Inc
ACRL	NAS SL	AmCrse	American Cruise Lines Inc
ACS	New York	ACapCv	American Capital Convertible Securities Inc
ACSN	NAS NMS	Acusn	Acuson Corp
ACT	New York	ACentC	American Century Corp
ACTA	NAS NMS	ActAuSt	Action Auto Stores Inc
ACTM	NAS NMS	Actmd	Actmedia Inc
ACTP	NAS NMS	AdCpt	Advanced Computer Techniques Corp

TRADING SYMBOL	MARKET LISTING	NEWSPAPER ABBREV.	COMPANY NAME
ACTS	NAS SL	ActnStf	Action Staffing Inc
ACU	American	AcmeU	Acme United Corp
ACV	New York	Alberto	Alberto-Culver Co
ACV.A	New York	AlbCulA	Alberto-Culver Co (Class A)
ACX	American	Action	Action Industries Inc
ACXM	NAS NMS	Acxiom	Acxiom Corp
ACY	New York	ACyan	American Cyanamid Co
ADAC	NAS NMS	AdacLb	ADAC Laboratories
ADB	New York	Adobe	Adobe Resources Corp
ADBE	NAS NMS	AdobS	Adobe Systems Inc
ADCC	NAS NMS	ApldDt	Applied Data Communications Inc
ADCO	NAS NMS	Advant	Advantage Companies Inc
ADCT	NAS NMS	ADC	ADC Telecommunications Inc
ADD	New York	AmesDp	Ames Department Stores Inc
ADDR	NAS NMS	Adingtn	Addington Resources Inc
ADI	New York	Analog	Analog Devices Inc
ADIA	NAS NMS	AdiaSv	Adia Services Inc
ADIE	NAS NMS	Autodie	Autodie Corp
ADL	American	Andal	Andal Corp
ADLAC	NAS NL	Adelph	Adelphia Communications Corp
ADM	New York	ArchDn	Archer-Daniels-Midland Co
ADMG	NAS NMS	AdvMag	Advanced Magnetics Inc
ADMR	NAS SL	Admar	Admar Group Inc
ADMS	NAS NMS	AdMkSv	Advanced Marketing Services Inc
ADNA	NAS SL	Ap DNA	Applied DNA Systems Inc
ADNEA	NAS NL	Alden	Alden Electronics Inc (Class A)
ADO	American	Audiotr	Audiotronics Corp
ADP	New York	AlldPd	Allied Products Corp
ADPT	NAS NMS	Adapt	Adaptec Inc
ADTI	NAS SL	AdvDis	Advance Display Technologies Inc
ADTX	NAS NL	Advatex	Advatex Associates Inc
ADV	New York	Advest	The Advest Group Inc
ADVA	NAS SL	AdMdPd	Advanced Medical Products Inc
ADVC	NAS NMS	AdvCir	Advance Circuits Inc
ADVN	NAS NMS	Advanta	ADVANTA Corp
ADVO	NAS NMS	AdvoSy	Advo System Inc
ADX	New York	AdaEx	The Adams Express Co
AE	American	AdmRs	Adams Resources & Energy Inc
AEAGF	NAS NMS	Agnico	Agnico-Eagle Mines Ltd
AEE	New York	Aileen	Aileen Inc
AEGNY	NAS NMS	Aegon	AEGON N.V.
AEL	American	AngE	Anglo Energy Inc
AELNA	NAS NMS	AEL	AEL Industries Inc (Class A)
AEN	American	AMC	AMC Entertainment Inc
AEOK	NAS NL	AlexEn	Alexander Energy Corp
AEP	New York	AElPw	American Electric Power Company Inc
AEPI	NAS NMS	AEP	AEP Industries Inc
AERO	NAS NMS	AerSvc	Aero Services International Inc

TRADING SYMBOL	MARKET LISTING	NEWSPAPER ABBREV.	COMPANY NAME
AESC	NAS SL	Amrco	AmerEco Environmental Services Inc
AET	New York	AetnLf	Aetna Life & Casualty Co
AEX	American	AirExp	Air Express International Corp
AFBK	NAS NMS	AflBsh	Affiliated Bankshares of Colorado Inc
AFC.A	American	AFruc A	American Fructose Corp (Class A)
AFC.B	American	AFruc B	American Fructose Corp (Class B)
AFCO	NAS NMS	AmFrst	American First Corp
AFED	NAS NMS	AtlFSv	Atlantic Federal Savings Bank (Maryland)
AFG	New York	AFG	AFG Industries Inc
AFGI	NAS NMS	AmbFn	Ambassador Financial Group Inc
AFIL	NAS NMS	AFiltrn	American Filtrona Corp
AFL	New York	AFaml	American Family Corp
AFN	American	Alfin	Alfin Inc
AFP	New York	AfilPb	Affiliated Publications Inc
AFPC	NAS SL	AFP	AFP Imaging Corp
AFS	New York	NwASh	New American Shoe Corp
AFSL	NAS NMS	AmFedF	AmFed Financial Corp
AG	New York	AlgInt	Allegheny International Inc
AGA	New York	Airgas	Airgas Inc
AGC	New York	AGnCp	American General Corp
AGE	New York	Edward	A.G. Edwards Inc
AGF	New York	AmGvI	American Government Income Fund
AGH	American	Atlants	Atlantis Group Inc
AGI	American	AlpinGr	The Alpine Group Inc
AGII	NAS NMS	ArgoGp	Argonaut Group Inc
AGL	New York	Angelic	Angelica Corp
AGNC	NAS NMS	AgncyR	Agency Rent-A-Car Inc
AGO	American	ABM G	ABM Gold Corp
AGPH	NAS SL	Agourn	Agouron Pharmaceuticals Inc
AGREA	NAS NMS	AGreet	American Greetings Corp (Class A)
AGRP	NAS NL	AndwGp	Andrews Group Inc
AGS	New York	AGS	AGS Computers Inc
AGSI	NAS NMS	AdvGen	Advanced Genetic Sciences Inc
AH	New York	AllisC	Allis-Chalmers Corp
AHA	American	AlphaIn	Alpha Industries Inc
AHC	New York	AmHes	Amerada Hess Corp
AHCS	NAS SL	AltrHlt	Alternative Health Care Systems Inc
AHE	New York	AHltP	American Health Properties Inc
AHH	American	Amhlth	AmeriHealth Inc
AHI	American	AHlthM	American Healthcare Management Inc
AHL	New York	AHerit	American Heritage Life Investment Corp
AHM	New York	Ahmans	H.F. Ahmanson & Co
AHO	New York	AHoist	American Hoist & Derrick Co
AHP	New York	AHome	American Home Products Corp
AHR	New York	AmHotl	Americana Hotels & Realty Corp
AHSC	NAS NMS	AHSld	American Home Shield Corp
AHST	NAS NMS	AsdHst	Associated Hosts Inc

TRADING SYMBOL	MARKET LISTING	NEWSPAPER ABBREV.	COMPANY NAME
AHT	American	Aircoa	AIRCOA Hotel Partners LP
AI	American	ArrowA	Arrow Automotive Industries Inc
AIF	American	AIFS	AIFS Inc
AIFC	NAS NMS	AIndF	American Indemnity Financial Corp
AIG	New York	AIntGr	American International Group Inc
AII	American	Altex	Altex Industries Inc
AIIC	NAS NMS	AmIntg	American Integrity Corp
AIKI	NAS SL	ArdenIn	Arden International Kitchens Inc
AIL	New York	AMCA	AMCA International Ltd
AILP	NAS NMS	AutLng	Automated Language Processing Systems Inc
AIMG	NAS NMS	AlnImg	Alliance Imaging Inc
AIMT	NAS NMS	AIM Tel	AIM Telephones Inc
AINC	NAS NMS	AminLf	American Income Life Insurance Co
AIND	NAS NMS	Arnold	Arnold Industries Inc
AIP	American	AIsrael	American Israeli Paper Mills Ltd
AIPN	NAS SL	AmInPt	American International Petroleum Corp
AIR	New York	AAR	AAR Corp
AIRC	NAS NMS	AIRCOA	AIRCOA Hospitality Services Inc
AIRSY	NAS NMS	AirInd	Airship Industries Ltd
AIS.A	American	Ampal	Ampal-American Israel Corp (Class A)
AIT	New York	Amrtc	American Information Technologies Corp
AITX	NAS NMS	Autmtx	Automatix Inc
AIZ	New York	Amcast	Amcast Industrial Corp
AJG	New York	Gallagr	Arthur J. Gallagher & Co
AJRL	NAS SL	RossLog	A.J. Ross Logistics Inc
AKLM	NAS NL	Acclaim	Acclaim Entertainment Inc
AKRN	NAS NL	Akorn	Akorn Inc
AL	New York	Alcan	Alcan Aluminium Ltd
ALBM	NAS NMS	Alpha1	Alpha 1 Biomedicals Inc
ALCC	NAS NMS	ALC Cm	ALC Communications Corp
ALCD	NAS SL	Alcide	Alcide Corp
ALCI	NAS NMS	AllCity	AllCity Insurance Co
ALCO	NAS NMS	Alico	Alico Inc
ALD	New York	AldSgnl	Allied-Signal Inc
ALDC	NAS NMS	Aldus	Aldus Corp
ALET	NAS NMS	Aloette	Aloette Cosmetics Inc
ALEX	NAS NMS	AlexBld	Alexander & Baldwin Inc
ALFA	NAS NMS	AlfaCp	Alfa Corp
ALFB	NAS NMS	AbeLinc	Abraham Lincoln Federal Savings Bank (Pennsylvania)
ALFD	NAS NMS	AlaFdl	Alabama Federal S&L Assn
ALFE	NAS SL	AlfaInt	Alfa International Corp
ALFL	NAS NMS	AllFinl	Alliance Financial Corp
ALG	New York	Arkla	Arkla Inc
ALGH	NAS NMS	AlegW	Allegheny & Western Energy Corp
ALGI	NAS NMS	AmLck	American Locker Group Inc
ALGO	NAS NMS	Algorex	Algorex Corp

TRADING SYMBOL	MARKET LISTING	NEWSPAPER ABBREV.	COMPANY NAME
ALGR	NAS NMS	AlldGp	ALLIED Group Inc
ALK	New York	AlskAir	Alaska Air Group Inc
ALL	New York	AdamMl	Adams-Millis Corp
ALLC	NAS NMS	AlldCa	Allied Capital Corp
ALLT	NAS NL	AllATV	All American Television Inc
ALM	New York	AlstMu	Allstate Municipal Income Trust
ALMI	NAS NMS	AlpMic	Alpha Microsystems
ALN	New York	AllenG	The Allen Group Inc
ALNT	NAS NMS	Alliant	Alliant Computer Systems Corp
ALOG	NAS NMS	Anlogic	Analogic Corp
ALOT	NAS NMS	AstroM	Astro-Med Inc
ALOY	NAS NMS	AloyCpt	Alloy Computer Products Inc
ALRN	NAS NMS	Altron	Altron Inc
ALS	New York	AlgLud	Allegheny Ludlum Corp
ALT	New York	AlsMI	Allstate Municipal Income Trust II
ALTI	NAS NMS	Altai	Altai Inc
ALTO	NAS NMS	Altos	Altos Computer Systems
ALTR	NAS NMS	Altera	Altera Corp
ALTS	NAS NMS	Altus	Altus Bank, A Federal Savings Bank (Alabama)
ALWC	NAS NMS	WillAL	The A.L. Williams Corp
ALWS	NAS NMS	Allwast	Allwaste Inc
ALX	New York	Alexdr	Alexander's Inc
AM	New York	AM Intl	AM International Inc
AMA	New York	Amfac	Amfac Inc
AMAC	NAS SL	AMdAlt	American Medical Alert Corp
AMAT	NAS NMS	ApldMt	Applied Materials Inc
AMB	New York	AmBrnd	American Brands Inc
AMBI	NAS SL	ABionet	American Bionetics Inc
AMBJ	NAS NMS	AmCity	American City Business Journals Inc
AMCC	NAS NMS	AContl	American Continental Corp
AMCE	NAS SL	AClaim	American Claims Evaluation Inc
AMCO	NAS NMS	AMidl	American Midland Corp
AMD	New York	AMD	Advanced Micro Devices Inc
AME	New York	Ametk	AMETEK Inc
AMEA	NAS NMS	AME	A.M.E. Inc
AMED	NAS SL	AutMed	AutoMedix Sciences Inc
AMEI	NAS SL	AMdE	American Medical Electronics Inc
AMFI	NAS NMS	Amcor	AMCORE Financial Inc
AMFN	NAS SL	AFN	A F N Inc
AMGN	NAS NMS	Amgen	Amgen Inc
AMGR	NAS SL	AGtyF	American Guaranty Financial Corp
AMH	American	Amdahl	Amdahl Corp
AMI	New York	AMI	American Medical International Inc
AMJX	NAS NMS	AFSvDu	American Federal Savings Bank of Duval County (Florida)
AMK	American	ATechC	American Technical Ceramics Corp
AMKG	NAS NMS	AmskBk	Amoskeag Bank Shares Inc

TRADING SYMBOL	MARKET LISTING	NEWSPAPER ABBREV.	COMPANY NAME
AMLE	NAS NMS	Amcole	Amcole Energy Corp
AMM	New York	Amre	AMRE Inc
AMMG	NAS NMS	AMagnt	American Magnetics Corp
AMMT	NAS SL	AMdTc	American Medical Technology Inc
AMN	New York	Ameron	Ameron Inc
AMOS	NAS NMS	Amosk	Amoskeag Co
AMP	New York	AMP	AMP Inc
AMPH	NAS NMS	APhyG	American Physicians Service Group Inc
AMPI	NAS NMS	Amplcn	Amplicon Inc
AMR	New York	AMR	AMR Corp
AMRC	NAS NL	ARecr	American Recreation Centers Inc
AMRF	NAS SL	Amrfrd	Amerford International Corp
AMRI	NAS NMS	AmFtBk	AmeriFirst Bank FSB (Florida)
AMS	American	AmShrd	American Shared Hospital Services
AMSB	NAS NMS	ASvWA	American Savings Financial Corp (Washington)
AMSE	NAS SL	AmMobl	American Mobile Systems Inc
AMSKQ	NAS SL	ASolr	American Solar King Corp
AMSR	NAS NMS	Amserv	Amserv Inc
AMSWA	NAS NMS	ASoft	American Software Inc (Class A)
AMSY	NAS NMS	AMS	American Management Systems Inc
AMT	New York	AcmeC	Acme-Cleveland Corp
AMTA	NAS NMS	Amistar	Amistar Corp
AMTC	NAS NMS	NtrSun	Nature's Sunshine Products Inc
AMTR	NAS NMS	Amritr	AmeriTrust Corp
AMTTF	NAS SL	AmTlc	American Telecommunications Corp (British Columbia)
AMTY	NAS NMS	AmtyBc	Amity Bancorp Inc
AMV	New York	AmevSc	AMEV Securities Inc
AMVC	NAS SL	AmVisn	American Vision Centers Inc
AMW	American	Amwest	Amwest Insurance Group Inc
AMWD	NAS NMS	AWood	American Woodmark Corp
AMWI	NAS NMS	AirMd	Air Midwest Inc
AMWS	NAS SL	Amnws	Ameriwest Financial Corp
AMX	New York	Amax	AMAX Inc
AMZ	American	AmList	American List Corp
AN	New York	Amoco	Amoco Corp
ANAT	NAS NMS	ANtIns	American National Insurance Co
ANC	New York	AnchGl	Anchor Glass Container Corp
ANCN	NAS SL	An-Con	An-Con Genetics Inc
AND	American	Andrea	Andrea Radio Corp
ANDB	NAS NMS	AndvBc	Andover Bancorp Inc (Massachusetts)
ANDO	NAS NMS	Andovr	Andover Controls Corp
ANDR	NAS NMS	AndGr	Andersen Group Inc
ANDW	NAS NMS	Andrew	Andrew Corp
ANDY	NAS NMS	Andros	Andros Analyzers Inc
ANEN	NAS NMS	Anaren	Anaren Microwave Inc
ANF	American	AnglFn	Angeles Finance Partners

TRADING SYMBOL	MARKET LISTING	NEWSPAPER ABBREV.	COMPANY NAME
ANG	American	Angeles	Angeles Corp
ANGLY	NAS NL	AngSA	Anglo American Corporation of South Africa Ltd
ANLT	NAS SL	AnlySu	Analytical Surveys Inc
ANLY	NAS NMS	AnalyI	Analysts International Corp
ANM	American	AngMtg	Angeles Mortgage Partners Ltd
ANMR	NAS SL	AdNMR	Advanced NMR Systems Inc
ANNA	NAS SL	Anndle	Annandale Corp
ANNX	NAS SL	LrnAnx	Learning Annex Inc
ANPC	NAS NL	ANtPt	American National Petroleum Co
ANSL	NAS NMS	AncrNJ	Anchor S&L Assn (New Jersey)
ANSY	NAS NMS	AmNurs	American Nursery Products Inc
ANT	New York	Anthony	Anthony Industries Inc
ANTQ	NAS NL	AA Imp	A.A. Importing Company Inc
ANUC	NAS NMS	ANuclC	American Nuclear Corp
AOC	New York	Aon Cp	Aon Corp
AOF	New York	ACM	ACM Government Opportunity Fund
AOG	American	AmOil	American Oil & Gas Corp
AOI	American	AOI	AOI Coal Co
AORGB	NAS NMS	AlnOrg	Allen Organ Co (Class B)
AP	New York	Ampco	Ampco-Pittsburgh Corp
APA	New York	Apache	Apache Corp
APAGF	NAS NL	Apco	Apco Argentina Inc
APAS	NAS NMS	AmPsg	American Passage Marketing Corp
APAT	NAS SL	APAOp	APA Optics Inc
APB	New York	AsiaPc	The Asia Pacific Fund Inc
APBI	NAS NMS	ABiosci	Applied Bioscience International Inc
APC	New York	Anadrk	Anadarko Petroleum Corp
APCC	NAS NL	APwCnv	American Power Conversion Corp
APCI	NAS NMS	ApoloC	Apollo Computer Inc
APD	New York	AirPrd	Air Products & Chemicals Inc
APER	NAS NMS	AtlPrm	Atlantic Permanent Savings Bank FSB (Virginia)
APFC	NAS NMS	AmPac	American Pacific Corp
APGE	NAS SL	ApogRb	Apogee Robotics Inc
APGI	NAS NMS	Green	A.P. Green Industries Inc
API.A	American	AmPetf	American Petrofina Inc (Class A)
APIE	NAS SL	API	API Enterprises Inc
APIO	NAS NMS	AmPion	American Pioneer Savings Bank (Florida)
APLOF	NAS SL	AlskAp	Alaska Apollo Gold Mines Ltd
APLY	NAS SL	ApdMicr	Applied Microbiology Inc
APM	New York	ApplM	Applied Magnetics Corp
APOG	NAS NMS	ApogEn	Apogee Enterprises Inc
APOS	NAS NMS	AdvPoly	Advanced Polymer Systems Inc
APR	American	APrec	American Precision Industries Inc
APS	New York	APresd	American President Companies Ltd
APWRA	NAS NMS	ApldPw	Applied Power Inc (Class A)
AQM	New York	QMS	QMS Inc

TRADING SYMBOL	MARKET LISTING	NEWSPAPER ABBREV.	COMPANY NAME
AQNT	NAS SL	Aquant	Aquanautics Corp
AQSI	NAS SL	AquaSc	AquaSciences International Inc
AQTN	NAS NMS	Aequtrn	Aequitron Medical Inc
AR	New York	Asarco	ASARCO Inc
ARAI	NAS NMS	AlldRsh	Allied Research Associates Inc
ARB	New York	AmRlty	American Realty Trust
ARBC	NAS NL	ARepBc	American Republic Bancorp
ARBR	NAS NMS	Arbor	Arbor Drugs Inc
ARC	New York	AtlRich	Atlantic Richfield Co
ARCE	NAS NMS	AirCrg	Air Cargo Equipment Corp
ARDNA	NAS NMS	Arden	Arden Group Inc (Class A)
AREL	NAS NMS	Alpharl	Alpharel Inc
ARIB	NAS NMS	AspenR	Aspen Ribbons Inc
ARID	NAS NMS	Aritch	Aridtech Inc
ARIG	NAS NMS	ARelian	American Reliance Group Inc
ARK	New York	ApplBk	Apple Bank for Savings (New York)
ARM	New York	Armtek	Armtek Corp
ARMR	NAS NMS	Armor	Armor All Products Corp
ARNX	NAS SL	Arnox	Arnox Corp
ARON	NAS NMS	AarnRt	Aaron Rents Inc
AROS	NAS NMS	AdvRos	Advance Ross Corp
AROW	NAS NMS	ArowB	Arrow Bank Corp
ARS	New York	Aristec	Aristech Chemical Corp
ARSD	NAS NMS	ArabSh	Arabian Shield Development Co
ARSN	NAS SL	AirSen	Air Sensors Inc
ART	American	Armtrn	Armatron International Inc
ARTG	NAS NL	ArtistG	Artistic Greetings Inc
ARTK	NAS SL	Artech	Artech Revocery Systems Inc
ARTW	NAS NMS	ArtWay	Art's-Way Manufacturing Company Inc
ARV	New York	Arvin	Arvin Industries Inc
ARW	New York	ArowE	Arrow Electronics Inc
ARWS	NAS NMS	AirWisc	Air Wisconsin Services Inc
ARX	New York	ARX	ARX Inc
ARYTF	NAS NL	ArytOp	Aryt Optronics Industries Ltd
AS	New York	Armco	Armco Inc
ASA	New York	ASA	ASA Ltd
ASAA	NAS SL	ASA Int	ASA International Ltd
ASAI	NAS NMS	AtlSeAr	Atlantic Southeast Airlines Inc
ASAL	NAS NMS	BankAtl	BankAtlantic A Federal Savings Bank
ASBC	NAS NMS	AsdBnc	Associated Banc-Corp
ASBI	NAS NMS	Amrian	Ameriana Savings Bank FSB (Indiana)
ASBS	NAS NMS	Asbst	Asbestec Industries Inc
ASC	New York	AmStor	American Stores Co
ASCI	NAS NMS	AssdCo	Associated Companies Inc
ASCL	NAS SL	ASafty	American Safety Closure Corp
ASCO	NAS SL	AlphaSo	Alpha Solarco Inc
ASCY	NAS SL	AlldSec	Allied Security Inc
ASDR	NAS SL	ASDR	ASDAR Corp

TRADING SYMBOL	MARKET LISTING	NEWSPAPER ABBREV.	COMPANY NAME
ASE	American	ASciE	American Science & Engineering Inc
ASEAY	NAS NL	ASEA	ASEA AB
ASH	New York	AshOil	Ashland Oil Inc
ASHA	NAS SL	Asha	Asha Corp
ASI	American	Astrex	Astrex Inc
ASII	NAS NMS	AutoSy	Automated Systems Inc
ASKI	NAS NMS	ASK	ASK Computer Systems Inc
ASM	American	Asmr	Asamera Inc
ASMIF	NAS NMS	AdvSem	Advanced Semiconductor Materials International N.V.
ASML	NAS NL	AsdMat	Associated Materials Inc
ASN	New York	AlcoS	Alco Standard Corp
ASO	New York	AmSth	AmSouth Bancorporation
ASON	NAS SL	Aerosn	Aerosonic Corp
ASPN	NAS SL	AspenE	Aspen Exploration Corp
ASR	American	ASwM	American Southwest Mortgage Investments Corp
ASTA	NAS NMS	AST	AST Research Inc
ASTE	NAS NMS	Astec	Astec Industries Inc
ASTI	NAS SL	ApldSpc	Applied Spectrum Technologies Inc
ASTN	NAS SL	McDanl	McDaniel Austin Corp
ASTR	NAS NMS	Astrosy	Astrosystems Inc
ASTV	NAS SL	AmCom	American Communications & Television Inc
AT	New York	ALLTL	ALLTEL Corp
ATA	New York	Artra	ARTRA GROUP Inc
ATBC	NAS NMS	AtlnBc	Atlantic Bancorporation (New Jersey)
ATC	American	Atari	Atari Corp
ATCC	NAS NMS	Airtran	Airtran Corp
ATCMA	NAS NMS	ATvCm	American Television & Communications Corp (Class A)
ATCX	NAS SL	AToxxic	American Toxxic Control Inc
ATE	New York	AtlEnrg	Atlantic Energy Inc
ATEKF	NAS NMS	Amertk	Amertek Inc
ATEL	NAS NMS	AdvTel	Advanced Telecommunications Corp
ATF	American	ATT Fd	AT&T Stock Fund (also known as Equity Income Fund)
ATFC	NAS NMS	AticoF	Atico Financial Corp
ATG	New York	AtlGas	Atlanta Gas Light Co
ATH	New York	Athlone	Athlone Industries Inc
ATI	American	ATI	ATI Medical Inc
ATKM	NAS NMS	Atek	Atek Metals Center Inc
ATKN	NAS NMS	Atkinsn	Guy F. Atkinson Company of California
ATL	New York	AtalSos	Atalanta/Sosnoff Capital Corp
ATLF	NAS NMS	AtlFin	Atlantic Financial Federal
ATM	New York	Anthm	Anthem Electronics Inc
ATML	NAS SL	AutoSpa	AutoSpa AutoMalls Inc
ATN	American	Acton	Acton Corp

TRADING SYMBOL	MARKET LISTING	NEWSPAPER ABBREV.	COMPANY NAME
ATNG	NAS NMS	Alaten	AlaTenn Resources Inc
ATNN	NAS NMS	AmTelmd	American Telemedia Network Inc
ATOG	NAS NMS	AndvTg	Andover Togs Inc
ATPC	NAS NMS	Athey	Athey Products Corp
ATR.A	American	AlnTre	Alliance Tire & Rubber Company Ltd (Class A)
ATRO	NAS NMS	Astron	Astronics Corp
ATTC	NAS NMS	AutTrT	Auto-trol Technology Corp
ATV	American	ARC	ARC International Corp
ATVC	NAS NMS	AmTrav	American Travellers Corp
ATW	American	AT&E	A.T.&E. Corp
ATWD	NAS NMS	Attwood	Attwood Oceanics Inc
ATX.A	American	Cross	A.T. Cross Co (Class A)
AU	New York	AmxG	Amax Gold Inc
AUD	New York	AutoDt	Automatic Data Processing Inc
AUG	New York	Augat	Augat Inc
AULT	NAS SL	Ault	Ault Inc
AUS	New York	Ausimt	Ausimont Compo N.V.
AUTO	NAS NMS	AutoInf	AutoInfo Inc
AUTR	NAS NMS	AutoCp	Autotrol Corp
AVA	New York	AudVd	Audio/Video Affiliates Inc
AVAK	NAS NMS	Avntek	Avantek Inc
AVDL	NAS NMS	Avndle	Avondale Industries Inc
AVE	New York	AVMC	AVEMCO Corp
AVFC	NAS NMS	Amvst	AmVestors Financial Corp
AVGA	NAS NMS	AvntGr	Avant-Garde Computing Inc
AVL	New York	Avalon	Avalon Corp
AVMRF	NAS SL	Avino	Avino Mines & Resources Ltd
AVP	New York	Avon	Avon Products Inc
AVRY	NAS NMS	Avry	Avery Inc
AVT	New York	Avnet	Avnet Inc
AVTR	NAS NMS	Avatar	Avatar Holdings Inc
AVX	New York	AVX	AVX Corp
AVY	New York	Avery	Avery International Corp
AWAL	NAS NMS	AWAirl	America West Airlines Inc
AWCSA	NAS NMS	AW A	AW Computer Systems Inc (Class A)
AWK	New York	AmWtr	American Water Works Company Inc
AWS	American	AlbaW	Alba-Waldensian Inc
AWST	NAS NMS	AWstCp	American Western Corp
AXO	American	Alamco	Alamco Inc
AXP	New York	AExp	American Express Co
AXR	New York	Amrep	AMREP Corp
AXXN	NAS NMS	ActARt	Action Auto Rental Inc
AXXX	NAS NMS	Artel	Artel Communications Corp
AYD	New York	Aydin	Aydin Corp
AYP	New York	AllgPw	Allegheny Power System Inc
AZ	New York	AtlasCp	Atlas Corp
AZA	American	Alza	ALZA Corp

TRADING SYMBOL	MARKET LISTING	NEWSPAPER ABBREV.	COMPANY NAME
AZB	American	ArizCm	Arizona Commerce Bank
AZE.A	American	AMzeA	American Maize-Products Co (Class A)
AZE.B	American	AMzeB	American Maize-Products Co (Class B)
AZL.A	American	ArzLd	Arizona Land Income Corp (Class A)
AZTC	NAS NMS	AztcM	Aztec Manufacturing Co
B	New York	BarnGp	Barnes Group Inc
BA	New York	Boeing	The Boeing Co
BAB	New York	BritAir	British Airways Plc
BABY	NAS SL	FertGn	Fertility & Genetics Research Inc
BAC	New York	BnkAm	BankAmerica Corp
BAGS	NAS SL	Pacad	Pacad Inc
BAIB	NAS NL	Bailey	Bailey Corp
BAIR	NAS NL	Branif	Braniff Inc
BAKR	NAS SL	BakrCm	Baker Communications Inc
BAL	American	BaldwS	Baldwin Securities Corp
BAMI	NAS NMS	BasAm	Basic American Medical Inc
BAN	American	Banstr	Banister Continental Ltd
BANG	NAS NMS	BangH	Bangor Hydro-Electric Co
BANQ	NAS NMS	Burrit	Burritt InterFinancial Bancorporation
BAR	New York	BaryWr	Barry Wright Corp
BARC	NAS NMS	BaretR	Barrett Resources Corp
BARD	NAS NMS	Barden	Barden Corp
BART	NAS SL	Barton	Barton Industries Inc
BARY	NAS NMS	BaryJw	Barry's Jewelers Inc
BAS	New York	BASIX	BASIX Corp
BASEA	NAS NMS	BsTnA	Base Ten Systems Inc (Class A)
BASEB	NAS NL	BsTnB	Base Ten Systems Inc (Class B)
BAUK	NAS NL	BaukNo	Baukol-Noonan Inc
BAW	New York	BlueAr	Blue Arrow PLC
BAX	New York	Baxter	Baxter International Inc
BAY	New York	BayFin	Bay Financial Corp
BAYL	NAS NMS	Bayly	Bayly Corp
BAYU	NAS NL	Bayou	Bayou International Ltd
BB	American	BnkBld	Bank Building & Equipment Corporation of America
BBAHF	NAS NMS	BsRInt	Basic Resources International Ltd
BBB	New York	BaltBcp	Baltimore Bancorp (Maryland)
BBC.A	American	BergBr	Bergen Brunswig Corp (Class A)
BBE	American	BeldBlk	Belden & Blake Energy Co
BBEC	NAS NMS	BlckEn	Blockbuster Entertainment Corp
BBF	New York	Barnet	Barnett Banks of Florida Inc
BBGS	NAS NMS	Babage	Babbage's Inc
BBIF	NAS NMS	BB&T	BB&T Financial Corp
BBKS	NAS NL	BobBrk	Bobbie Brooks Inc
BBN	New York	BoltBr	Bolt Beranek & Newman Inc
BBNK	NAS NMS	BayBks	BayBanks Inc
BBPI	NAS NMS	Blau	Barry Blau & Partners Inc

TRADING SYMBOL	MARKET LISTING	NEWSPAPER ABBREV.	COMPANY NAME
BBR	American	BB REI	B-B Real Estate Investment Corp
BBRC	NAS NMS	BurrBr	Burr-Brown Corp
BBY	New York	BestBy	Best Buy Company Inc
BC	New York	Brnwk	Brunswick Corp
BCC	New York	BoiseC	Boise Cascade Corp
BCE	New York	BCE	BCE Inc
BCF	New York	BurlnCt	Burlington Coat Factory Warehouse Corp
BCKY	NAS NMS	BckyFn	Buckeye Financial Corp
BCL	New York	Biocft	Biocraft Laboratories Inc
BCM	New York	BncCtr	Banco Central S.A.
BCO	American	Blessg	Blessings Corp
BCP	New York	BordC	Borden Chemicals & Plastics LP
BCR	New York	Bard	C.R. Bard Inc
BCS	New York	Barclay	Barclays PLC
BCV	American	BanFd	Bancroft Convertible Fund Inc
BDC	New York	Burndy	Burndy Corp
BDEL	NAS NMS	BkDel	Bank of Delaware Corp
BDEP	NAS NMS	BnPnc	BanPonce Corp
BDG	New York	Bandag	Bandag Inc
BDGT	NAS NMS	Budget	Budget Rent a Car Corp
BDK	New York	BlackD	The Black & Decker Corp
BDM	American	BDM	BDM International Inc
BDRM	NAS SL	BoardB	Boardroom Business Products Inc
BDVFC	NAS NL	BrdvwS	Broadview Savings Bank
BDX	New York	BectDk	Becton Dickinson & Co
BE	New York	BengtB	Benguet Corp (Class B)
BEAM	NAS SL	SumitTc	Summit Technology Inc
BEBA	NAS NMS	Beebas	Beeba's Creations Inc
BEC	American	Beard	The Beard Co
BECO	NAS NL	Beaman	Beaman Corp
BECR	NAS NMS	Bercor	Bercor Inc
BEIH	NAS NMS	BEI	BEI Holdings Ltd
BEL	New York	BellAtl	Bell Atlantic Corp
BELF	NAS NMS	BelFuse	Bel Fuse Inc
BELW	NAS SL	Belwet	Bellwether Exploration Co
BEMC	NAS SL	Belmac	Belmac Corp
BEN	New York	FrnkR	Franklin Resources Inc
BENE	NAS SL	BenNuc	Benedict Nuclear Pharmaceuticals Inc
BENF	NAS SL	Benfuel	Benafuels Inc
BENH	NAS NMS	Bnkest	BankEast Corp
BENJ	NAS NMS	BenjSv	Benjamin Franklin S&L Assn (Oregon)
BEP	New York	BET	BET Public Limited Co
BER	New York	Bearing	Bearings Inc
BERK	NAS NMS	Berklne	The Berkline Corp
BERS	NAS SL	Beres	Beres Industries Inc
BES	New York	BestPd	Best Products Company Inc
BEST	NAS SL	Bestway	Bestway Rental Inc
BET	American	BethCp	The Bethlehem Corp

TRADING SYMBOL	MARKET LISTING	NEWSPAPER ABBREV.	COMPANY NAME
BETZ	NAS NMS	BetzLb	Betz Laboratories Inc
BEV	New York	Bevrly	Beverly Enterprises Inc
BEZ	New York	Baldor	Baldor Electric Co
BEZRY	NAS NMS	Beazer	C.H. Beazer Holdings PLC
BFBS	NAS NMS	Brkfld	Brookfield Bancshares Corp (Illinois)
BFC	American	BkatlFn	BankAtlantic Financial Corp
BFCP	NAS NMS	BdwyFn	Broadway Financial Corp
BFCS	NAS NMS	BstnFB	Boston Five Bancorp Inc
BFD.A	American	BrnFA	Brown-Forman Corp (Class A)
BFD.B	American	BrnFB	Brown-Forman Corp (Class B)
BFELY	NAS NL	Buffels	Buffelsfontein Gold Mining Company Ltd
BFEN	NAS NL	BF Ent	BF Enterprises Inc
BFI	New York	BrwnF	Browning-Ferris Industries Inc
BFO	American	Baruch	Baruch-Foster Corp
BFS	New York	SaulRE	B.F. Saul Real Estate Investment Trust
BFTV	NAS SL	Birdfdr	Birdfinder Corp
BFX	American	Buffton	Buffton Corp
BG	New York	BrwnGp	Brown Group Inc
BGAS	NAS NMS	BerkGs	The Berkshire Gas Co
BGBR	NAS NMS	BgBear	Big Bear Inc
BGC	New York	BayStG	Bay State Gas Co
BGE	New York	BaltGE	Baltimore Gas & Electric Co
BGENF	NAS NMS	Biogen	Biogen N.V.
BGG	New York	BrigSt	Briggs & Stratton Corp
BGSS	NAS NMS	BGS	BGS Systems Inc
BHA	American	BiscH	Biscayne Holdings Inc
BHAG	NAS NMS	BHA	BHA Group Inc
BHAMY	NAS NMS	Bechm	Becham Group plc
BHC	New York	Brock	Brock Hotel Corp
BHI	New York	BakrHu	Baker Hughes Inc
BHL	New York	BunkrH	Bunker Hill Income Securities Inc
BHNC	NAS NMS	BnkNH	Bank of New Hampshire Corp
BHO	American	B&H	B&H Ocean Carriers Ltd
BHP	New York	BHP	The Broken Hill Proprietary Company Ltd
BHY	New York	BeldnH	Belding Heminway Company Inc
BI	New York	BelIn	Bell Industries Inc
BIAC	NAS SL	BI Inc	BI Inc
BIC	American	BicCp	BIC Corp
BICO	NAS SL	Bioctrl	Biocontrol Technology Inc
BID	American	Sothby	Sotheby's Holdings Inc (Class A)
BIG	New York	Bond	Bond International Gold Inc
BIGB	NAS NMS	Big B	Big B Inc
BIGO	NAS NL	BigOTr	Big O Tires Inc
BILT	NAS NMS	MicBlt	Microbilt Corp
BIM	American	ICN Bio	ICN Biomedicals Inc
BIN	American	BinkMf	Binks Manufacturing Co
BINC	NAS NMS	Biosph	Biospherics Inc
BIND	NAS NMS	Bindly	Bindley Western Industries Inc

TRADING SYMBOL	MARKET LISTING	NEWSPAPER ABBREV.	COMPANY NAME
BING	NAS NMS	BingSv	Binghamton Savings Bank
BINL	NAS NL	Blindr	Blinder International Enterprises Inc
BIO.A	American	BioR A	Bio-Rad Laboratories Inc (Class A)
BIO.B	American	BioR B	Bio-Rad Laboratories Inc (Class B)
BIOD	NAS SL	BiotcDv	Biotechnology Development Corp
BIOP	NAS NMS	Bioplst	Bioplasty Inc
BIOS	NAS NL	Bioson	Biosonics Inc
BIOT	NAS NMS	BioTInt	BioTechnica International Inc
BIOW	NAS NMS	BkIowa	Banks of Iowa Inc
BIP	New York	BevIP	Beverly Investment Properties Inc
BIR	New York	BirmStl	Birmingham Steel Corp
BIRD	NAS NMS	BirdInc	Bird Inc
BIRI	NAS SL	Branrd	Brainerd International Inc
BIRT	NAS NMS	Birtchr	The Birtcher Corp
BIS	American	Baristr	Barrister Information Systems Corp
BISH	NAS NMS	BishGr	Bishop Inc
BJICA	NAS NMS	BenJer	Ben & Jerry's Homemade Inc (Class A)
BK	New York	BkNY	The Bank of New York Company Inc
BKB	New York	BkBost	Bank of Boston Corp
BKC	American	ABkCT	American Bank of Connecticut
BKFR	NAS NMS	BakrFn	Baker Fentress & Co
BKH	New York	BlkHC	Black Hills Corp
BKHT	NAS NMS	BerkHa	Berkshire Hathaway Inc
BKI	New York	Beker	Beker Industries Corp
BKLA	NAS NL	BKLA	BKLA Bancorp
BKLMY	NAS NL	BkLeu	Bank Leumi le-Israel B.M.
BKLY	NAS NMS	Berkley	W.R. Berkley Corp
BKMD	NAS NL	BkMd	Bank Maryland Corp
BKNG	NAS NMS	Bnknth	Banknorth Group Inc
BKNT	NAS NMS	BkrNte	Banker's Note Inc
BKP	New York	BKInv	Burger King Investors Master LP
BKR	American	Baker	Michael Baker Corp
BKRS	NAS SL	BrkrSc	Brokers Securities Inc
BKSC	NAS SL	BkSC	Bank of South Carolina
BKSO	NAS NMS	BkSou	Bank South Corp
BKST	NAS NMS	BkStfd	Bank of Stamford (California)
BKT	New York	Blkstn	Blackstone Income Trust Inc
BKVT	NAS NMS	Bankvt	BankVermont Corp
BKY	New York	Berkey	Berkey Inc
BLA	New York	BritLnd	British Land of America Inc
BLAK	NAS NMS	BlackI	Black Industries Inc
BLAS	NAS NMS	Blasius	Blasius Industries Inc
BLC	New York	BeloAH	A.H. Belo Corp
BLCC	NAS NMS	Balchm	Balchem Corp
BLD	American	Baldwin	Baldwin Technology Company Inc
BLI	New York	Businld	Businessland Inc
BLII	NAS NMS	BritLee	Britton Lee Inc
BLL	New York	Ball	Ball Corp

TRADING SYMBOL	MARKET LISTING	NEWSPAPER ABBREV.	COMPANY NAME
BLLW	NAS NMS	BellW	W. Bell & Company Inc
BLMP	NAS SL	AirInt	Airship International Ltd
BLOCA	NAS NMS	BlckD	Block Drug Co (Class A)
BLR	American	BlrPh	Bolar Pharmaceutical Company Inc
BLS	New York	BellSo	BellSouth Corp
BLSC	NAS NMS	BioLog	Bio-Logic Systems Corp
BLT.A	American	BlountA	Blount Inc (Class A)
BLT.B	American	BlountB	Blount Inc (Class B)
BLU	New York	BluChp	Blue Chip Value Fund Inc
BLUD	NAS NMS	Imucor	Immucor Inc
BLV	American	Belvdre	Belvedere Corp
BLVD	NAS NMS	BlvdBc	Boulevard Bancorp Inc
BLY	New York	BallyMf	Bally Manufacturing Corp
BLYH	NAS SL	Blyth	Blyth Holdings Inc
BLYVY	NAS NMS	Blyvoor	Blyvooruitzicht Gold Mining Company Ltd
BMAC	NAS NMS	BMA	BMA Corp
BMC	New York	BMC	BMC Industries Inc
BMCC	NAS NMS	BandoM	Bando McGlocklin Capital Corp
BMCS	NAS NL	BMC Sft	BMC Software Inc
BMD	American	AL Lab	A.L. Laboratories Inc
BMDC	NAS SL	BimdDy	Biomedical Dynamics Corp
BMDS	NAS NMS	BiMedc	Bio-Medicus Inc
BMED	NAS NMS	Balard	Ballard Medical Products Inc
BMEEF	NAS NL	Belmrl	Belmoral Mines Ltd
BMET	NAS NMS	Biomet	Biomet Inc
BMG	New York	BatlMt	Battle Mountain Gold Co
BMI	American	Badger	Badger Meter Inc
BMJF	NAS NMS	BMJ	BMJ Financial Corp
BMLS	NAS SL	Burke	Burke Mills Inc
BMP	American	BurnAm	Burnham American Properties Inc
BMPI	NAS SL	BioMed	Biosearch Medical Products Inc
BMRA	NAS NMS	Biomer	Biomerica Inc
BMRG	NAS NMS	BMR Fin	BMR Financial Group Inc
BMS	New York	Bemis	Bemis Company Inc
BMTCD	NAS NMS	BrynM	Bryn Mawr Bank Corp (Pennsylvania)
BMY	New York	BristM	Bristol-Myers Co
BN	New York	Borden	Borden Inc
BNBC	NAS NL	BroadNt	Broad National Bancorporation
BNBGA	NAS NMS	BulBear	Bull & Bear Group Inc (Class A)
BNC	New York	ReglFn	Regional Financial Shares Investment Fund Inc
BNDY	NAS NMS	BrndySv	Brandywine S&L Assn (Pennsylvania)
BNE	American	Bowne	Bowne & Company Inc
BNER	NAS NL	BrenerC	Brenner Companies Inc
BNGO	NAS NMS	BingKg	Bingo King Company Inc
BNHB	NAS NMS	BNH	BNH Bancshares Inc
BNHI	NAS NMS	BcpHw	Bancorp Hawaii Inc
BNHN	NAS NMS	Benhan	Benihana National Corp

TRADING SYMBOL	MARKET LISTING	NEWSPAPER ABBREV.	COMPANY NAME
BNHNA	NAS NL	BenhnA	Benihana National Corp (Class A)
BNI	New York	BrlNth	Burlington Northern Inc
BNKF	NAS NMS	BnkFst	Bankers First Corp
BNKS	NAS NMS	UnNMx	United New Mexico Financial Corp
BNL	New York	BenfCp	Beneficial Corp
BNP	American	Boddie	Boddie-Noell Restaurant Properties Inc
BNR	New York	Banner	Banner Industries Inc
BNRY	NAS NL	Bonray	Bonray Drilling Corp
BNS	New York	BwnSh	Brown & Sharpe Manufacturing Co
BNTA	NAS NMS	Banta	George Banta Company Inc
BNY	New York	Bundy	Bundy Corp
BOAT	NAS NMS	BoatBn	Boatmen's Bancshares Inc
BOBE	NAS NMS	BobEvn	Bob Evans Farms Inc
BOCB	NAS NMS	Buffet	Buffets Inc
BOF	American	BkSFr	Bank of San Francisco Holding Co
BOFR	NAS NL	BkRedl	Bank of Redlands (California)
BOGN	NAS SL	Bogen	Bogen Corp
BOGO	NAS NMS	Bogert	Bogert Oil Co
BOHM	NAS NMS	Bohema	Bohemia Inc
BOKC	NAS NMS	Bancokl	BancOklahoma Corp
BOL	New York	Bausch	Bausch & Lomb Inc
BOLT	NAS NMS	BoltTc	Bolt Technology Corp
BOM	American	Bowmr	Bowmar Instrument Corp
BOMA	NAS NMS	BkMAm	Banks of Mid-America Inc
BOMD	NAS SL	Bomed	Bomed Medical Manufacturing Ltd
BOMS	NAS NMS	BcMis	Bancorp. of Mississippi Inc
BONI	NAS NL	BldrDsg	Builders Design Inc
BOOL	NAS NMS	BooleB	Boole & Babbage Inc
BOON	NAS NMS	BoonEl	Boonton Electronics Corp
BOS	New York	BCelts	Boston Celtics LP
BOSA	NAS NMS	BostAc	Boston Acoustics Inc
BOST	NAS NMS	BstnDig	Boston Digital Corp
BOW	New York	Bowatr	Bowater Inc
BP	New York	BritPt	The British Petroleum Company plc
BPAO	NAS NMS	BaldPia	Baldwin Piano & Organ Co
BPCO	NAS NMS	BonvlP	Bonneville Pacific Corp
BPH	American	Biophm	Biopharmaceuticals Inc
BPI	American	BambP	Bamberger Polymers Inc
BPL	New York	Buckeye	Buckeye Partners LP
BPMI	NAS NMS	Badger	Badger Paper Mills Inc
BPOP	NAS NMS	BnPop	Banco Popular de Puerto Rico
BPP	American	BurnPP	Burnham Pacific Properties Inc
BPWRF	NAS NL	CoBolv	Compania Boliviana de Energia Electrica S.A.
BQC	New York	Qantel	Qantel Corp
BQR	New York	QkReily	The Quick & Reilly Group Inc
BR	New York	BrlRsc	Burlington Resources Inc
BRAE	NAS NMS	BraeCp	BRAE Corp

TRADING SYMBOL	MARKET LISTING	NEWSPAPER ABBREV.	COMPANY NAME
BRALF	NAS NL	Bralrn	Bralorne Resources Ltd
BRAN	NAS NMS	Brand	Brand Companies Inc
BRBK	NAS NL	BrentB	Brenton Banks Inc
BRCOA	NAS NMS	BradyW	W.H. Brady Co (Class A)
BRD	American	Ragan	Brad Ragan Inc
BRDL	NAS NMS	Brendle	Brendle's Inc
BRDN	NAS NMS	Brandn	Brandon Systems Corp
BRE	New York	BRE	BRE Properties Inc
BREN	NAS NMS	Brenco	Brenco Inc
BRF	New York	Bormns	Borman's Inc
BRG	New York	BritGas	British Gas plc
BRID	NAS NMS	BrdgFd	Bridgford Foods Corp
BRIK	NAS NMS	Brnkmn	Brinkmann Instruments Inc
BRILF	NAS SL	Brilund	Brilund Ltd
BRIX	NAS NMS	BR Intec	BRIntec Corp
BRJS	NAS NMS	Brajds	Brajdas Corp
BRL	American	BarrLb	Barr Laboratories Inc
BRLN	NAS NMS	BklynSv	The Brooklyn Savings Bank (Connecticut)
BRN	American	Barnwl	Barnwell Industries Inc
BRNO	NAS NMS	Brunos	Bruno's Inc
BRRS	NAS NMS	Barris	Barris Industries Inc
BRRYA	NAS NMS	BerryP	Berry Petroleum Co (Class A)
BRS.A	American	Brscn	Brascan Ltd (Class A)
BRST	NAS SL	BristG	Bristol Gaming Corp
BRT	New York	BRT	BRT Realty Trust
BRWD	NAS SL	Brntwd	Brentwood Instruments Inc
BRX	American	Biother	Biotherapeutics Inc
BS	New York	BethStl	Bethlehem Steel Corp
BSBC	NAS NMS	BrnfdSv	Branford Savings Bank (Connecticut)
BSBL	NAS SL	ScoreB	Score Board Inc
BSBX	NAS NMS	BellSv	Bell Savings Bank PsSA (Pennsylvania)
BSC	New York	BearSt	The Bear Stearns Companies Inc
BSD	American	BSD	BSD Bancorp Inc
BSDM	NAS SL	BSD	BSD Medical Corp
BSE	New York	BostEd	Boston Edison Co
BSET	NAS NMS	BsetF	Bassett Furniture Industries Inc
BSH	American	Bush	Bush Industries Inc
BSIM	NAS NMS	BurnpS	Burnup & Sims Inc
BSL	American	BermSt	Bermuda Star Lines Inc
BSN	American	BSN	BSN Corp
BT	New York	BankTr	Bankers Trust New York Corp
BTCI	NAS NMS	BwnTrn	Brown Transport Company Inc
BTEC	NAS NMS	Banctec	BancTec Inc
BTEK	NAS NMS	Baltek	Baltek Corp
BTFC	NAS NMS	BT Fin	BT Financial Corp
BTGC	NAS SL	BioTG	Bio-Technology General Corp
BTHL	NAS NMS	BethlBc	Bethel Bancorp (Maine)
BTI	American	BAT	B.A.T. Industries plc

TRADING SYMBOL	MARKET LISTING	NEWSPAPER ABBREV.	COMPANY NAME
BTLR	NAS NMS	ButlrMf	Butler Manufacturing Co
BTRI	NAS NMS	BTR	BTR Realty Inc
BTRL	NAS NMS	BiotcR	Biotech Research Laboratories Inc
BTSB	NAS NMS	Brantre	The Braintree Savings Bank (Massachusetts)
BTU	New York	Pyro	Pyro Energy Corp
BTX	New York	BanTx	BancTEXAS Group Inc
BTY	New York	BritTel	British Telecommunications plc
BU	New York	BklyUG	The Brooklyn Union Gas Co
BUCS	NAS SL	BusCrd	Business Cards of Tomorrow Inc
BUD	New York	Anheus	Anheuser-Busch Companies Inc
BUE	American	Buell	Buell Industries Inc
BUGS	NAS NMS	CooprD	Cooper Development Co
BUGX	NAS SL	BarrSc	Barrier Science & Technology Inc
BULKF	NAS NL	BH Bulk	B&H Bulk Carriers Ltd
BULL	NAS NMS	BullRGd	Bull Run Gold Mines Ltd
BULR	NAS NMS	Buehlr	Buehler International Inc
BURMY	NAS NL	Burmh	Burmah Oil Public Limited Co
BUTI	NAS NMS	BeutiC	BeutiControl Cosmetics Inc
BUTL	NAS NMS	ButlrNt	Butler National Corp
BVFS	NAS NMS	BayVw	Bay View Federal S&L Assn (California)
BVI	American	BowVal	Bow Valley Industries Ltd
BW	New York	BrshWl	Brush Wellman Inc
BWAY	NAS SL	BwyHld	Broadway Holdings Inc
BWINA	NAS NMS	BldLy	Baldwin & Lyons Inc (Class A)
BWINB	NAS NMS	BldLyB	Baldwin & Lyons Inc (Class B)
BWL.A	American	BowlA	Bowl America Inc (Class A)
BWRLF	NAS NMS	Brkwt	Breakwater Resources Ltd
BWTRY	NAS NL	Bwater	Bowater Industries plc
BYRS	NAS SL	Byers	Byers Inc
BYTE	NAS NMS	Cmpcm	Compucom Systems Inc
BZ	New York	Bairnco	Bairnco Corp
BZF	New York	Brazil	Brazil Fund Inc
C	New York	Chryslr	Chrysler Corp
CA	New York	CmpAs	Computer Associates International Inc
CAAN	NAS SL	CambAn	Cambridge Analytical Associates Inc
CAB	American	Casblan	CasaBlanca Inudstries Inc
CABK	NAS NMS	ColABn	Colonial American Bankshares Corp
CABL	NAS SL	CmCblNC	Communication Cable Inc
CABS	NAS SL	CblAdv	Cable Advertising Systems Inc
CAC	New York	Cstam	CoastAmerica Corp
CACCB	NAS NMS	ColLfAc	Colonial Life & Accident Insurance Co (Class B)
CACH	NAS NMS	Cache	Caché Inc
CACIA	NAS NMS	CACI	CACI Inc (Class A)
CACOA	NAS NMS	CatoCp	Cato Corp (Class A)
CADA	NAS SL	CAM Dt	CAM Data Systems Inc

TRADING SYMBOL	MARKET LISTING	NEWSPAPER ABBREV.	COMPANY NAME
CADBY	NAS NMS	CbrySc	Cadbury Schweppes PLC
CADE	NAS NMS	CadeIn	Cade Industries Inc
CADX	NAS NMS	Cadntx	Cadnetix Corp
CAF	New York	FurrsB	Furr's/Bishop's Cafeterias LP
CAFC	NAS NL	CaroFst	Carolina First Corp
CAFS	NAS NMS	CardFd	Cardinal Federal Savings Bank (Kentucky)
CAG	New York	ConAg	ConAgra Inc
CAII	NAS NMS	CapAsc	Capital Associates Inc
CAKE	NAS NMS	CharCh	Charlotte Charles Inc
CAL	New York	CalFed	CalFed Inc
CALI	NAS NMS	Calumt	Calumet Industries Inc
CAMBY	NAS NMS	CambIn	The Cambridge Instrument Company plc
CAMD	NAS NMS	CalMD	California Micro Devices Corp
CAME	NAS NMS	Carme	Carme Inc
CAMI	NAS SL	CareAm	CareAmerica Inc
CAMP	NAS NMS	CalAmp	California Amplifier Inc
CAN	New York	CanonG	The Cannon Group Inc
CANNY	NAS NMS	CanonI	Canon Inc
CANO	NAS NMS	Canonie	Canonie Environmental Services Corp
CANX	NAS NL	CannEx	Cannon Express Inc
CAO	New York	CaroFt	Carolina Freight Corp
CAP	American	CapHo	Capital Housing & Mortgage Partners
CAPB	NAS NMS	CapBcp	Capitol Bancorporation
CAR	New York	CartWl	Carter-Wallace Inc
CARL	NAS NMS	Karcher	Carl Karcher Enterprises Inc
CARN	NAS NMS	Caringtn	Carrington Laboratories Inc
CAS	American	CastlA	A.M. Castle & Co
CASB	NAS NL	Cabarus	Cabarrus Savings Bank (North Carolina)
CASC	NAS NMS	Cascde	Cascade Corp
CASY	NAS NMS	Caseys	Casey's General Stores Inc
CAT	New York	Caterp	Caterpillar Inc
CATA	NAS NMS	CapTr	Capitol Transamerica Corp
CATV	NAS NMS	CablTV	Cable TV Industries
CAUT	NAS NMS	CptAut	Computer Automation Inc
CAVR	NAS NMS	Carver	Carver Corp
CAW	New York	Caesar	Caesars World Inc
CAYB	NAS NMS	Cayuga	Cayuga Savings Bank (New York)
CB	New York	Chubb	The Chubb Corp
CBAG	NAS SL	CrstCp	Crested Corp
CBAM	NAS NMS	Cambrx	Cambrex Corp
CBC	New York	CartBc	Carteret Bancorp Inc
CBCF	NAS NMS	CtzBkg	Citizens Banking Corp (Michigan)
CBCT	NAS NMS	Cenvst	Cenvest Inc
CBCX	NAS NMS	CamBS	Cambridge BioScience Corp
CBE	New York	Cooper	Cooper Industries Inc
CBEN	NAS SL	CarolB	Carolyn Bean Publishing Ltd
CBH	New York	CBI In	CBI Industries Inc

TRADING SYMBOL	MARKET LISTING	NEWSPAPER ABBREV.	COMPANY NAME
CBI	American	Curtce	Curtice-Burns Foods Inc
CBIO	NAS NMS	CalBio	California Biotechnology Inc
CBKS	NAS NMS	CwltBn	Commonwealth Bancshares Corp
CBL	New York	CorBlk	Corroon & Black Corp
CBLX	NAS SL	CblExc	Cable Exchange Inc
CBM	NAS NMS	Lfecore	Lifecore Biomedical Inc
CBNB	NAS NL	CmceBc	CommerceBancorp (California)
CBNEV	NAS NMS	CnBNE	Constitution Bancorp of New England Inc
CBNH	NAS NMS	CmtyBn	Community Bankshares Inc (New Hampshire)
CBOCA	NAS NMS	CmBCol	Commercial Bancorp. of Colorado (Class A)
CBOT	NAS NMS	CabotM	Cabot Medical Corp
CBR	New York	CrysBd	Crystal Brands Inc
CBRL	NAS NMS	CrkBrl	Cracker Barrel Old Country Store Inc
CBRYA	NAS NMS	NorldCr	Northland Cranberries Inc (Class A)
CBS	New York	CBS	CBS Inc
CBSH	NAS NMS	CmBsh	Commerce Bancshares Inc (Missouri)
CBSI	NAS NMS	CmtyBS	Community Bank System Inc (New York)
CBSS	NAS NMS	CnBsh	Central Bancshares of the South Inc
CBT	New York	Cabot	Cabot Corp
CBTB	NAS NMS	CB T	CB&T Bancshares Inc
CBTF	NAS NMS	CB&T F	CB&T Financial Corp
CBU	New York	Comdre	Commodore International Ltd
CBWA	NAS NMS	CBcWa	Central Bancorporation (Washington)
CC	New York	CirCty	Circuit City Stores Inc
CCA	American	CosmCr	Cosmopolitan Care Corp
CCAB	NAS NMS	CmsCbl	Communications & Cable Inc
CCAI	NAS SL	CreatvC	Creative Computer Applications Inc
CCAM	NAS NMS	CCA	CCA Industries Inc
CCAX	NAS NMS	CorctCp	Corrections Corporation of America
CCB	New York	CapCits	Capital Cities/ABC Inc
CCBF	NAS NMS	CCB	CCB Financial Corp
CCBK	NAS SL	ConnCm	Connecticut Community Bank
CCBL	NAS NMS	C COR	C-COR Electronics Inc
CCBT	NAS NMS	CCBT	Cape Cod Bank & Trust Co
CCC	New York	CmcCrd	Commercial Credit Co
CCCI	NAS NMS	3CI	3 CI Inc
CCCR	NAS SL	CCR	CCR Video Corp
CCE	New York	CocCE	Coca-Cola Enterprises Inc
CCEM	NAS NMS	Cmpch	CompuChem Corp
CCH	New York	CmpR	Campbell Resources Inc
CCI	New York	Citicrp	Citicorp
CCIMF	NAS NMS	CityRs	City Resources Ltd
CCK	New York	CrwnCk	Crown Cork & Seal Company Inc
CCL	American	CarnCr	Carnival Cruise Lines Inc
CCLR	NAS NMS	CmClr	Commerce Clearing House Inc
CCM	American	Clarmt	Claremont Capital Corp

TRADING SYMBOL	MARKET LISTING	NEWSPAPER ABBREV.	COMPANY NAME
CCMC	NAS NMS	CmwMg	Commonwealth Mortgage Company Inc (Massachusetts)
CCMM	NAS SL	CptCom	Computer Communications Inc
CCMS	NAS SL	CMS Ad	CMS Advertising Inc
CCN	New York	ChrisCr	Chris-Craft Industries Inc
CCNC	NAS NMS	CCNB	CCNB Corp
CCOA	NAS NMS	Comcoa	COMCOA Inc
CCOM	NAS SL	ColCmc	Colonial Commercial Corp
CCON	NAS NMS	Circon	Circon Corp
CCOR	NAS NL	Centcre	Centercore Inc
CCP	American	Corcp	Corcap Inc
CCPI	NAS SL	ComcPh	Comcast Cablevision of Philadelphia Inc
CCPT	NAS NMS	CncptI	Concept Inc
CCR	New York	CntCrd	Countrywide Credit Industries Inc
CCRS	NAS SL	CpCapit	Corporate Capital Resources Inc
CCS	American	CmpCn	Computer Consoles Inc
CCSC	NAS SL	Cardiac	Cardiac Control Systems Inc
CCTC	NAS NMS	CCTC	Computer & Communications Technology Corp
CCTVY	NAS NMS	CarlCm	Carlton Communications PLC
CCU	American	ClearCh	Clear Channel Communications Inc
CCUR	NAS NMS	ConcCpt	Concurrent Computer Corp
CCX	New York	CCX	CCX Inc
CCXLA	NAS NMS	Cont1Cl	Contel Cellular Inc (Class A)
CDA	New York	CtData	Control Data Corp
CDBK	NAS SL	CndlBk	Candlewood Bank & Trust Co
CDC	American	CompD	CompuDyne Corp
CDCRA	NAS NMS	ChldDis	Childrens Discovery Center of America Inc (Class A)
CDE	American	Coeur	Coeur d'Alene Mines Corp
CDG.A	American	CWineA	Canandaigua Wine Company Inc
CDG.B	American	CWineB	Canandaigua Wine Company Inc
CDGI	NAS NMS	CourDis	Courier Dispatch Group Inc
CDI	American	CDI	CDI Corp
CDIC	NAS NMS	CrdnlD	Cardinal Distribution Inc
CDIN	NAS SL	Coradn	Coradian Corp
CDL	American	Citadel	Citadel Holding Corp
CDMA	NAS SL	Cadema	Cadema Corp
CDMS	NAS NMS	Cadmu	Cadmus Communications Corp
CDNC	NAS NMS	Cadence	Cadence Design Systems Inc
CDNI	NAS SL	CardIn	Cardinal Industries Inc
CDO	New York	Comdis	Comdisco Inc
CDS	American	Cardis	Cardis Corp
CDV.A	American	ChDevA	Chambers Development Company Inc (Class A)
CDV.B	American	ChDevB	Chambers Development Company Inc (Class B)
CE	New York	Catlyst	Catalyst Energy Corp

TRADING SYMBOL	MARKET LISTING	NEWSPAPER ABBREV.	COMPANY NAME
CEBK	NAS NMS	CtrCOp	Central Co-operative Bank (Massachusetts)
CEC	American	Cetec	Cetec Corp
CECX	NAS NMS	CstlEn	Castle Energy Corp
CEDR	NAS NL	CedarI	Cedar Income Federal 1 Ltd
CEE	New York	C 3 Inc	C3 Inc
CEF	American	CFCda	Central Fund of Canada Ltd
CEFT	NAS NMS	ConcCm	Concord Computing Corp
CELG	NAS NMS	Celgene	Celgene Corp
CELI	NAS NMS	CelSci	Cel-Sci Corp
CELL	NAS NL	CellTch	Cell Technology Inc
CELM	NAS SL	CellAm	Cellular America Inc
CELP	NAS SL	CelrPr	Cellular Products Inc
CELS	NAS SL	CelrIn	Cellular Inc
CELT	NAS SL	Celtr	Celltronics Inc
CEMC	NAS SL	CntyMd	Century Medicorp
CEMX	NAS NMS	CEM	CEM Corp
CEN	New York	CentrCp	Centronics Data Computer Corp
CENT	NAS NMS	Centuri	Centuri Inc
CEP	American	Convst	ConVest Energy Partners Ltd
CEQ	American	CentGp	The Centennial Group Inc
CER	New York	Cilcorp	CILCORP Inc
CERB	NAS NMS	Cerbco	CERBCO Inc
CERN	NAS NMS	Cerner	Cerner Corp
CES	New York	ComES	Commonwealth Energy System
CESC	NAS NMS	CES	Computer Entry Systems Corp
CET	American	CentSe	Central Securities Corp
CETH	NAS NMS	CatlThr	Catalyst Thermal Energy Corp
CEXX	NAS NMS	CirclEx	Circle Express Inc
CF	New York	ColFds	Collins Foods International Inc
CFA	New York	CmFct	The Computer Factory Inc
CFB	American	CitzFst	Citizens First Bancorp
CFBI	NAS NMS	CullnFr	Cullen/Frost Bankers Inc
CFBK	NAS NMS	CalFst	California First Bank
CFBS	NAS NMS	CFidBk	Central Fidelity Banks Inc
CFCM	NAS SL	ChfCon	Chief Consolidated Mining Co
CFCN	NAS NMS	CmcFdl	Commercial Federal Corp
CFED	NAS NMS	ChtFSB	Charter Federal Savings Bank
CFG	American	Copelc	Copelco Financial Services Group Inc
CFHC	NAS NMS	CalFncl	California Financial Holding Co
CFI	New York	CalFIP	Cal Fed Income Partners LP
CFIB	NAS NMS	ConFbr	Consolidated Fibres Inc
CFIN	NAS NMS	ConsFn	Consumers Financial Corp
CFIP	NAS NMS	CFI St	CF&I Steel Corp
CFIX	NAS NMS	Chemfx	Chemfix Technologies Inc
CFK	American	ComFd	Comfed Bancorp Inc
CFMI	NAS NMS	CnvFd	Convenient Food Mart Inc
CFNE	NAS NMS	CirclFA	Circle Fine Art Corp

TRADING SYMBOL	MARKET LISTING	NEWSPAPER ABBREV.	COMPANY NAME
CFNH	NAS NMS	Cheshre	Cheshire Financial Corp
CFQ	American	QuakFb	Quaker Fabric Corp
CFSC	NAS NMS	CFS	CFS Financial Corp
CFSF	NAS NMS	CoastF	Coast Federal S&L Assn (Florida)
CG	New York	ColGas	The Columbia Gas System Inc
CGAS	NAS NMS	ClintGs	Clinton Gas Systems Inc
CGC	New York	CascNG	Cascade Natural Gas Corp
CGCO	NAS SL	CmceG	Commerce Group Corp
CGE	New York	CargInd	Carriage Industries Inc
CGEN	NAS NMS	Colagen	Collagen Corp
CGES	NAS NMS	ClnGas	Colonial Gas Co
CGIC	NAS NMS	CtlGn	Continental General Insurance Co
CGL.A	American	CagleA	Cagle's Inc (Class A)
CGN	American	Cognitr	Cognitronics Corp
CGNE	NAS NMS	Calgene	Calgene Inc
CGO	American	ChsMed	Chase Medical Group Inc
CGP	New York	Coastal	The Coastal Corp
CGPS	NAS NMS	Stamfrd	Stamford Capital Group Inc
CGR	American	Chariot	The Chariot Group Inc
CGS	American	ConsOG	Consolidated Oil & Gas Inc
CH	American	ChmpPd	Champion Products Inc
CHA	New York	ChmpIn	Champion International Corp
CHANF	NAS NMS	ChanIns	Chandler Insurance Ltd
CHAR	NAS NMS	Chapral	Chaparral Resources Inc
CHB	American	ChmpEn	Champion Enterprises Inc
CHCO	NAS NMS	CtyHld	City Holding Co
CHCR	NAS NMS	ChncCp	Chancellor Corp
CHD	New York	Chelsea	Chelsea Industries Inc
CHE	New York	Chemed	Chemed Corp
CHEF	NAS NL	ChefInt	Chefs International Inc
CHEK	NAS NMS	ChkPt	Checkpoint Systems Inc
CHER	NAS NMS	ChryCp	The Cherry Corp
CHES	NAS SL	ChesInd	Chesapeake Industries Inc
CHEY	NAS NMS	CheySf	Cheyenne Software Inc
CHF	New York	ChkFull	Chock Full O'Nuts Corp
CHFC	NAS NMS	ChmFin	Chemical Financial Corp
CHFD	NAS NMS	ChrtFdl	Charter Federal S&L Assn (Virginia)
CHG	New York	ChiMlw	Chicago Milwaukee Corp
CHH	New York	CartH	Carter Hawley Hale Stores Inc
CHHC	NAS NMS	HeistC	C.H. Heist Corp
CHIK	NAS NMS	GldPoul	Golden Poultry Company Inc
CHIPA	NAS SL	Chpwch	Chipwich Inc (Class A)
CHIR	NAS NMS	Chiron	Chiron Corp
CHLI	NAS NMS	Chilis	Chili's Inc
CHKE	NAS NMS	Cheroke	The Cherokee Group
CHL	New York	ChmBk	Chemical Banking Corp
CHLN	NAS NMS	Chalone	Chalone Inc
CHM	New York	ChampSp	Champion Spark Plug Co

TRADING SYMBOL	MARKET LISTING	NEWSPAPER ABBREV.	COMPANY NAME
CHMX	NAS NMS	Chemex	Chemex Pharmaceuticals Inc
CHNE	NAS SL	Cherne	Cherne Enterprises Inc
CHOL	NAS NMS	CtrlHld	Central Holding Co
CHP	American	ChtPwr	Charter Power Systems Inc
CHPK	NAS NMS	ChesUtl	Chesapeake Utilities Corp
CHPN	NAS NMS	ChapEn	Chapman Energy Inc
CHPS	NAS NMS	ChipsTc	Chips & Technologies Inc
CHR	New York	ChartC	The Charter Co
CHRS	NAS NMS	ChrmS	Charming Shoppes Inc
CHRZ	NAS NMS	CmptH	Computer Horizons Corp
CHS	New York	Chaus	Bernard Chaus Inc
CHTB	NAS NMS	Cohaset	Cohasset Savings Bank (Massachusetts)
CHTL	NAS SL	Chantl	Chantal Pharmaceutical Corp
CHTT	NAS NMS	Chattm	Chattem Inc
CHU	New York	Churchs	Church's Fried Chicken Inc
CHV	New York	Chevrn	Chevron Corp
CHW	New York	ChWst	Chemical Waste Management Inc
CHX	New York	PilgPr	Pilgrim's Pride Corp
CHY	New York	Chyron	Chyron Corp
CHZC	NAS NMS	Stendig	Stendig Industries Inc
CI	New York	CIGNA	CIGNA Corp
CIBA	NAS NL	CitznBk	Citizens Bank (North Carolina)
CIC	New York	CntlCp	The Continental Corp
CID	American	ChfDv	Chieftain Development Company Ltd
CIDN	NAS NMS	CmpIdn	Computer Identics Corp
CIF	New York	ColIHI	Colonial Intermediate High Income Fund
CIFR	NAS NMS	Cipher	Cipher Data Products Inc
CIG	American	ContGr	Continental Graphics Corp
CIGCF	NAS SL	Citdl	Citadel Gold Mines Inc
CIH	New York	CtlIHld	Continental Illinois Holding Corp
CII	New York	CRI II	CRI Insured Mortgage Investments II Inc
CIL	New York	ContIll	Continental Illinois Corp
CIM	American	CIM	CIM High Yield Securities
CIMC	NAS NMS	Cimco	CIMCO Inc
CIMG	NAS SL	ConsIm	Consolidated Imaging Corp
CIN	New York	CinGE	The Cincinnati Gas & Electric Co
CINC	NAS SL	Cochmn	Coachman Inc
CINF	NAS NMS	CinnFn	Cincinnati Financial Corp
CINNA	NAS NMS	CtzIns	Citizens Insurance Company of America, Texas (Class A)
CINS	NAS NL	CircInc	Circle Income Shares Inc
CIP	New York	CnlIPS	Central Illinois Public Service Co
CIR	New York	Circus	Circus Circus Enterprises Inc
CIRI	NAS SL	Ciro	Ciro Inc
CIS	American	ConcdF	Concord Fabrics Inc
CISA	NAS NMS	CtzSNY	Citizens Savings Bank FSB (New York)
CISIF	NAS NMS	CIS Tch	C.I.S. Technologies Inc
CITI	NAS NMS	Citpst	Citipostal Inc

TRADING SYMBOL	MARKET LISTING	NEWSPAPER ABBREV.	COMPANY NAME
CITN	NAS NMS	CtzFG	Citizens Financial Group Inc
CITUA	NAS NMS	CtzU A	Citizens Utilities Co (Class A)
CITUB	NAS NMS	CtzU B	Citizens Utilities Co (Class B)
CIV	American	ColREI	Columbia Real Estate Investments Inc
CIW	New York	CamrnI	Cameron Iron Works Inc
CJ	American	CalJky	California Jockey Club
CJER	NAS NMS	CJerB	Central Jersey Bancorp
CJN	American	CaesNJ	Caesars New Jersey Inc
CJSB	NAS NMS	CJerSv	Central Jersey Savings Bank SLA
CKC	American	Cnchm	Conchemco Inc
CKCP	NAS NMS	Cybertk	CYBERTEK Corp
CKDN	NAS NMS	Circadn	Circadian Inc
CKE	New York	CastlCk	Castle & Cooke Inc
CKL	New York	ClarkE	Clark Equipment Co
CKP	New York	CircleK	The Circle K Corp
CKRB	NAS SL	ChkRobt	Check Robot Inc
CKSB	NAS NMS	CK FSv	CK Federal Savings Bank (North Carolina)
CKT	American	CtlCrc	Continental Circuits Corp
CL	New York	ColgPal	Colgate-Palmolive Co
CLBGA	NAS NMS	CBcgp A	Colonial BancGroup Inc (Class A)
CLBGB	NAS NMS	CBcgp B	Colonial BancGroup Inc (Class B)
CLC	New York	CLC	CLC of America Inc
CLCM	NAS SL	Cellcom	Cellcom Corp
CLCR	NAS SL	Celcor	Celcor Inc
CLD	New York	Cptlnd	Computerland Corp
CLDA	NAS NMS	ClinDt	Clinical Data Inc
CLDRV	NAS NMS	ClifDr	Cliffs Drilling Co
CLE	New York	ClairSt	Claire's Stores Inc
CLEA	NAS NMS	ChLea	Chemical Leaman Corp
CLEO	NAS SL	CleKoh	Cleopatra Kohlique Inc
CLF	New York	ClvClf	Cleveland-Cliffs Inc
CLFI	NAS NMS	CtryLk	Country Lake Foods Inc
CLG	New York	Clabir	Clabir Corp
CLGBB	NAS SL	ClabrB	Clabir Corp (Class B)
CLHB	NAS NMS	CleanH	Clean Harbors Inc
CLIC	NAS NMS	Clairsn	Clairson International Corp
CLIF	NAS SL	ClifEgl	Cliff Engle Ltd
CLIN	NAS SL	CliniTh	Clini-Therm Corp
CLIX	NAS NMS	CmprsL	Compression Labs Inc
CLK	American	ClarkC	Clark Consolidated Industries Inc
CLM	New York	ClmGlb	Clemente Global Growth Fund Inc
CLN	New York	Colemn	The Coleman Company Inc
CLNP	NAS SL	Callon	Callon Petroleum Co
CLO	New York	Coleco	Coleco Industries Inc
CLR	American	ColorSy	Color Systems Technology Inc
CLRI	NAS NMS	CmpLR	Computer Language Research Inc
CLRK	NAS NMS	Clarcor	Clarcor Inc

TRADING SYMBOL	MARKET LISTING	NEWSPAPER ABBREV.	COMPANY NAME
CLRX	NAS SL	Colorcs	Colorocs Corp
CLSC	NAS NMS	ClinSci	Clinical Sciences Inc
CLSM	NAS NL	ClaySlv	Clayton Silver Mines Inc
CLSR	NAS SL	CtLasr	Control Laser International Corp
CLT	American	Cominc	Cominco Ltd
CLTH	NAS SL	CR Clt	C&R Clothiers Inc
CLX	New York	Clorox	The Clorox Co
CLZR	NAS SL	Candla	Candela Laser Corp
CMAFC	NAS NMS	Camp	Campeau Corp
CMB	New York	Chase	The Chase Manhattan Corp
CMBK	NAS NMS	CumbrFd	The Cumberland Federal Savings Bank (Kentucky)
CMC	New York	CmMtl	Commercial Metals Co
CMCA	NAS NMS	Cmeric	Comerica Inc
CMCL	NAS NMS	Chmclr	ChemClear Inc
CMCO	NAS NMS	CVN	CVN Companies Inc
CMCSA	NAS NMS	Comcst	Comcast Corp (Class A)
CMCSK	NAS NMS	Cmcs sp	Comcast Corp (special Class A)
CMD.A	American	ChtMdA	Charter Medical Corp (Class A)
CMD.B	American	ChtMdB	Charter Medical Corp (Class B)
CMDL	NAS NMS	Cmdial	Comdial Corp
CMDT	NAS SL	CmdtHd	Comdata Holdings Corp
CMED	NAS SL	Cybmed	Cybermedic Inc
CMFB	NAS NMS	ChFab	Chemical Fabrics Corp
CMGI	NAS NL	ComGrp	Communications Group Inc
CMH	New York	ClayHm	Clayton Homes Inc
CMHC	NAS SL	CaroMt	Carolina Mountain Holding Co
CMI	New York	ClubMd	Club Med Inc
CMIC	NAS NMS	CalMic	California Microwave Inc
CMIKA	NAS NMS	Carmik	Carmike Cinemas Inc (Class A)
CMIL	NAS SL	CamilSM	Camille St. Moritz Inc
CMIN	NAS NMS	CmptM	Computer Memories Inc
CML	New York	CML	CML Group Inc
CMLE	NAS NMS	CaslMle	The Casual Male Corp
CMN	New York	Callhn	Callahan Mining Corp
CMNT	NAS SL	CptNwk	Computer Network Technology Corp
CMO	New York	CareerC	CareerCom Corp
CMP	New York	CmpCre	Comprehensive Care Corp
CMPL	NAS SL	CamPl	Camera Platforms International Inc
CMR	American	Comtrn	Commtron Corp
CMRE	NAS SL	CmstkR	Comstock Resources Inc
CMRO	NAS NMS	Cmrco	COMARCO Inc
CMS	New York	CMS En	CMS Energy Corp
CMTC	NAS SL	CambM	Cambridge Medical Technology Corp
CMTL	NAS SL	Comtch	Comtech Telecommunications Corp
CMTX	NAS SL	Comtex	Comtex Scientific Corp
CMU	New York	ColMu	Colonial Municipal Income Trust
CMUC	NAS NMS	CmpU	Comp-U-Check Inc

TRADING SYMBOL	MARKET LISTING	NEWSPAPER ABBREV.	COMPANY NAME
CMW	American	CMarc	Canadian Marconi Co
CMX	American	CMI Cp	CMI Corp
CMY	New York	CPsyc	Community Psychiatric Centers
CMZ	New York	CinMil	Cincinnati Milacron Inc
CN	New York	Calton	Calton Inc
CNA	New York	CNA Fn	CNA Financial Corp
CNBE	NAS NMS	CNB	CNB Bancshares Inc
CNBK	NAS NMS	CntyBc	Century Bancorp Inc
CNBT	NAS NMS	CNBNY	Community National Bancorp Inc (New York)
CNC	New York	Consec	Conseco inc
CNCAA	NAS NMS	CentelCb	Centel Cable Television Co (Class A)
CNCD	NAS NMS	ConcCC	Concord Career Colleges Inc
CNCL	NAS NMS	Cmcl Nt	Commercial National Corp
CNCR	NAS NMS	Cencor	CenCor Inc
CNDN	NAS NMS	Chitnd	Chittenden Corp
CNE	New York	ConnE	Connecticut Energy Corp
CNET	NAS NMS	Comnet	COMNET Corp
CNF	New York	CnsFrt	Consolidated Freightways Inc
CNG	New York	ConsNG	Consolidated Natural Gas Co
CNH	New York	CenHud	Central Hudson Gas & Electric Corp
CNK	New York	CrmpK	Crompton & Knowles Corp
CNL	New York	CnLaEl	Central Louisiana Electric Company Inc
CNLF	NAS NMS	CNL Fn	C N L Financial Corp
CNMD	NAS NMS	Conmed	CONMED Corp
CNMW	NAS NMS	CinMic	Cincinnati Microwave Inc
CNN	New York	CNAI	CNA Income Shares Inc
CNNR	NAS NMS	ConrPr	Conner Peripherals Inc
CNO	American	Caspn	Caspen Oil Inc
CNP.A	American	CrnCP	Crown Central Petroleum Corp (Class A)
CNP.B	American	CrCPB	Crown Central Petroleum Corp (Class B)
CNRD	NAS NMS	Canrad	Canrad Inc
CNS	New York	CnStor	Consolidated Stores Corp
CNSL	NAS NMS	Consul	Consul Restaurant Corp
CNSP	NAS NMS	CnSprn	Central Sprinkler Corp
CNT	New York	Centel	Centel Corp
CNTO	NAS NMS	Centcor	Centocor Inc
CNTX	NAS NMS	Centex	Centex Telemanagement Inc
CNV	New York	ConvHld	Convertible Holdings Inc
CNVX	NAS NMS	Convex	Convex Computer Corp
CNW	New York	CNW	CNW Corp
CNY	New York	CntlInfo	Continental Information Systems Corp
COA	New York	Coachm	Coachmen Industries Inc
COAS	NAS NMS	ColFst	Columbia First Federal S&L Assn (Washington D.C.)
COBA	NAS NMS	ComBc	Commerce Bancorp Inc (New Jersey)
COBB	NAS NMS	CobRsc	Cobb Resources Corp
COBE	NAS NMS	CobeLb	Cobe Laboratories Inc

TRADING SYMBOL	MARKET LISTING	NEWSPAPER ABBREV.	COMPANY NAME
COBK	NAS NMS	CoOpBk	Co-Operative Bancorp (Massachusetts)
COCA	NAS NMS	CoCaM	CoCa Mines Inc
CODA	NAS NMS	StepSvr	Step-Saver Data Systems Inc
CODL	NAS NL	CodeAl	Code-Alarm Inc
CODN	NAS NMS	Codenol	Codenoll Technology Corp
CODS	NAS SL	CorpDt	Corporate Data Sciences Inc
COES	NAS NMS	ComdE	Commodore Environmental Services Inc
COFD	NAS NMS	ColFdl	Collective Federal Savings Bank (New Jersey)
COFI	NAS NMS	ChtOne	Charter One Financial Inc
COGNF	NAS NMS	Cognos	Cognos Inc
COGRA	NAS NMS	ColnGp	The Colonial Group Inc (Class A)
COH	American	Cohu	Cohu Inc
COHR	NAS NMS	Cohernt	Coherent Inc
COHY	NAS NL	CnsHyd	Consolidated Hydro Inc
COKE	NAS NMS	CocaBtl	Coca-Cola Bottling Company Consolidated
COLC	NAS NMS	ColoNt	Colorado National Bankshares Inc
COLD	NAS NL	TexAEn	Texas American Energy Corp
COM	American	CrowlM	Crowley Milner & Co
COMD	NAS NMS	CmdAir	Command Airways Inc
COMI	NAS NL	CmpMc	Computer Microfilm Corp
COMM	NAS NMS	CellCm	Cellular Communications Inc
COMR	NAS NMS	Comair	Comair Inc
COMS	NAS NMS	3Com	3Com Corp
COMW	NAS NMS	CmwSv	Commonwealth S&L Assn FA (Florida)
COMX	NAS NMS	Comtrx	Comtrex Systems Corp
CON	American	Connly	Connelly Containers Inc
CONH	NAS NMS	CtlHme	Continental Homes Holding Corp
CONS	NAS NL	ConsSv	Conservative Savings Bank
CONT	NAS NMS	CtlMed	Continental Medical Systems Inc
CONW	NAS NMS	ConWat	Consumers Water Co
COO	New York	CoopCo	The Cooper Companies Inc
COP	American	Copley	Copley Properties Inc
COPI	NAS NMS	ConsPd	Consolidated Products Inc
COPY	NAS NMS	Copytle	Copytele Inc
COR	American	CrystO	Crystal Oil Co
CORC	NAS NMS	Corcom	Corcom Inc
CORD	NAS NMS	Cordis	Cordis Corp
CORK	NAS SL	Corken	Corken International Corp
COS	New York	Copwld	Copperweld Corp
COSF	NAS NMS	CosmFr	Cosmetic & Fragrance Concepts Inc
COST	NAS NMS	Costco	Costco Wholesale Corp
COTG	NAS NMS	CotgSv	Cottage Savings Assn FA (Ohio)
COU	American	Courtld	Courtaulds PLC
COUS	NAS NMS	CousP	Cousins Properties Inc
COVIV	NAS SL	CtlVen	Continental Ventures Inc
COVT	NAS NMS	Covngt	Covington Development Group Inc
COW	New York	UnStck	United Stockyards Corp

TRADING SYMBOL	MARKET LISTING	NEWSPAPER ABBREV.	COMPANY NAME
CP	New York	CdnPac	Canadian Pacific Ltd
CPA	New York	ChiPac	Chicago Pacific Corp
CPAK	NAS NL	CPAC	CPAC Inc
CPAP	NAS NMS	CntryP	Century Papers Inc
CPB	New York	CamSp	Campbell Soup Co
CPBI	NAS NMS	CPB	CPB Inc
CPC	New York	CPC	CPC International Inc
CPCI	NAS NMS	Ciprico	Ciprico Inc
CPE	American	ColPr	Colorado Prime Corp
CPER	NAS NMS	CnsPap	Consolidated Papers Inc
CPF	New York	Comstk	Comstock Partners Strategy Fund Inc
CPH	New York	CapHld	Capital Holding Corp
CPIC	NAS NMS	CPI	CPI Corp
CPL	New York	CarPw	Carolina Power & Light Co
CPLS	NAS NMS	CarePl	Care Plus Inc
CPMNY	NAS NL	CPcMn	Central Pacific Minerals NL
CPN	New York	CP Ntl	CP National Corp
CPP	American	Calprop	Calprop Corp
CPPC	NAS SL	CntyPk	Century Park Pictures Corp
CPQ	New York	Compaq	COMPAQ Computer Corp
CPRC	NAS SL	CptrCm	Computer Components Corp
CPRD	NAS NMS	CmpPr	Computer Products Inc
CPS	American	CnsEP	Consolidated Energy Partners LP
CPSA	NAS NMS	CPaFin	Central Pennsylvania Financial Corp
CPSIA	NAS SL	CPS Cp	CPS Corporate Planning Services (Class A)
CPSL	NAS NMS	CSC Ind	CSC Industries Inc
CPST	NAS NMS	CPC	CPC Rexcel Inc
CPSX	NAS NL	CeramPr	Ceramics Process Systems Corp
CPTC	NAS NMS	CPT	CPT Corp
CPTD	NAS NMS	CmpDt	Computer Data Systems Inc
CPTLA	NAS SL	CmpTel	Computer Telephone Corp (Class 1)
CPUI	NAS NL	CmclPr	Commercial Programming Unlimited Inc
CPWR	NAS NL	CptPwr	Computer Power Inc
CPX	New York	CineOd	Cineplex Odeon Corp
CQ	New York	Comsat	Communications Satellite Corp
CQX	American	Conqst	Conquest Exploration Co
CR	New York	Crane	Crane Co
CRA	New York	Craig	Craig Corp
CRAB	NAS NMS	CapCrb	Capt. Crab Inc
CRAN	NAS NMS	CrwnAn	Crown Anderson Inc
CRAW	NAS NMS	CrwfCo	Crawford & Co
CRBI	NAS NMS	CalRep	Cal Rep Bancorp Inc
CRBN	NAS NMS	Calgon	Calgon Carbon Corp
CRC	New York	CarolP	Carolco Pictures Inc
CRCC	NAS NMS	Crftmtc	Craftmatic/Contour Industries Inc
CRCD	NAS SL	Codercd	Codercard Inc
CRCH	NAS NMS	ChrDwt	Church & Dwight Company Inc

TRADING SYMBOL	MARKET LISTING	NEWSPAPER ABBREV.	COMPANY NAME
CRCTC	NAS NMS	Crescot	Crescott Inc
CRDN	NAS NMS	Cerdyn	Ceradyne Inc
CRDO	NAS NL	ColEngy	Colorado Energy Corp
CRE.A	American	CareE A	Care Enterprises Inc (Class A)
CRE.B	American	CareE B	Care Enterprises Inc (Class B)
CREB	NAS NMS	ChmpPr	Champion Parts Inc
CRED	NAS SL	CredoPt	Credo Petroleum Corp
CRES	NAS NMS	CrstFdl	Crestmont Federal S&L Assn (New Jersey)
CRFC	NAS NMS	Crestar	Crestar Financial Corp
CRFT	NAS SL	CptCft	ComputerCraft Inc
CRI	New York	CoreIn	Core Industries Inc
CRIC	NAS NMS	ColabR	Collaborative Research Inc
CRIG	NAS NL	CumbR	Cumberland Gold Group Inc
CRII	NAS SL	CmpRs	Computer Resources Inc
CRITA	NAS NMS	CritGp	Criterion Group Inc (Class A)
CRIX	NAS NMS	CtrlRs	Control Resource Industries Inc
CRL	New York	CrosldS	Crossland Savings (New York)
CRLC	NAS NMS	CRsLf	Central Reserve Life Corp
CRLNF	NAS NMS	Carolin	Carolin Mines Ltd (Class A)
CRM	New York	CRIIM	CRI Insured Mortgage Investments LP
CRMK	NAS NMS	Cermtk	Cermetek Microelectronics Inc
CRN	New York	CarsP	Carson Pirie Scott & Co
CRNA	NAS NL	CrwnA	CrownAmerica Inc
CRNR	NAS NMS	Chronr	Chronar Corp
CRNS	NAS NMS	Cronus	Cronus Industries Inc
CRON	NAS SL	CrwnBd	Crown Brands Inc
CROP	NAS NMS	CropG	Crop Genetics International Corp
CRPB	NAS SL	Cerprb	CerProbe Corp
CRR	New York	Conrail	Consolidated Rail Corp
CRRC	NAS NMS	Courer	Courier Corp
CRRS	NAS SL	CwnRs	Crown Resource Corp
CRS	New York	CarTec	Carpenter Technology Corp
CRTN	NAS SL	Certron	Certron Corp
CRTR	NAS NMS	ChtCrl	Charter-Crellin Inc
CRTV	NAS SL	CreatTc	Creative Technologies Corp
CRV	American	CoastR	Coast R.V. Inc
CRVS	NAS NMS	Corvus	Corvus Systems Inc
CRW	American	CwnCr	Crown Crafts Inc
CRWN	NAS NMS	CwnBk	Crown Books Corp
CRYD	NAS SL	CryoDy	CryoDynamics Inc
CRZY	NAS NMS	CrzEd	Crazy Eddie Inc
CSA	New York	CoastSL	Coast S&L Assn (California)
CSAI	NAS SL	CogntSy	Cognitive Systems Inc
CSAR	NAS NMS	Calstar	Calstar Inc
CSBA	NAS NMS	CountyS	County Savings Bank (California)
CSBC	NAS NL	CtrlSou	Central & Southern Holding Co
CSBF	NAS NMS	CtzSMd	Citizens Savings Bank FSB (Maryland)
CSBM	NAS NMS	CitySv	City Savings Bank of Meriden

TRADING	MARKET	NEWSPAPER	COMPANY
SYMBOL	LISTING	ABBREV.	NAME

CSC	New York	CompSc	Computer Sciences Corp
CSCN	NAS NMS	Compus	CompuScan Inc
CSEL	NAS SL	CaribSl	Caribbean Select Inc
CSESF	NAS NMD	Connght	Connaught Biosciences Inc
CSFCA	NAS NMS	CitzSF	Citizens Savings Financial Corp (Florida)
CSFN	NAS NMS	CoreSt	CoreStates Financial Corp
CSGI	NAS NL	CtzSec	Citizens Security Group Inc
CSII	NAS NMS	ComSy	Communications Systems Inc
CSIT	NAS NMS	PrecTrg	Precision Target Marketing Inc
CSK	New York	Chspk	Chesapeake Corp
CSKKY	NAS NL	CSK	CSK Corp
CSL	New York	Carlisle	Carlisle Companies Inc
CSLH	NAS NMS	CtnSLf	Cotton States Life & Health Insurance Co
CSM	New York	ChpStl	Chaparral Steel Co
CSMO	NAS NMS	Cosmo	Cosmo Communications Corp
CSN	New York	CinBel	Cincinnati Bell Inc
CSOF	NAS NMS	CorpSft	Corporate Software Inc
CSOL	NAS SL	CnvSol	Convergent Solutions Inc
CSOU	NAS NMS	CtzSoCp	Citizens & Southern Corp
CSP	New York	CmbEn	Combustion Engineering Inc
CSPI	NAS NMS	CSP	CSP Inc
CSR	New York	CenSoW	Central & South West Corp
CSRE	NAS NMS	Comshr	COMSHARE Inc
CSS	American	CSS	CSS Industries Inc
CST	New York	Christn	The Christiana Companies Inc
CSTIF	NAS NMS	ChalInt	Challenger International Ltd
CSTK	NAS NMS	Comstk	Comstock Group Inc
CSTL	NAS NMS	CnstlBc	Constellation Bancorp
CSTN	NAS NMS	CrnrFn	CornerStone Financial Corp
CSTP	NAS NMS	ConStP	Congress Street Properties Inc
CSTR	NAS NMS	Costar	Costar Corp
CSV	New York	ColumS	Columbia S&L Assn
CSWC	NAS NMS	CapSw	Capital Southwest Corp
CSX	New York	CSX	CSX Corp
CSYI	NAS SL	CircSy	Circuit Systems Inc
CSYS	NAS NL	CnBSys	Central Banking System Inc
CT	New York	CalRE	California Real Estate Investment Trust
CTA	American	CnPacC	Central Pacific Corp
CTAS	NAS NMS	Cintas	Cintas Corp
CTB	New York	CoprTr	Cooper Tire & Rubber Co
CTBC	NAS NMS	CntrBc	Centerre Bancorporation
CTBX	NAS NMS	Centrbk	Centerbank (Connecticut)
CTC	New York	Contel	Contel Corp
CTCO	NAS NMS	CrosTr	Cross & Trecker Corp
CTCQ	NAS NMS	ChkTch	Check Technology Corp
CTEC	NAS NMS	CmpoT	Component Technology Corp

TRADING SYMBOL	MARKET LISTING	NEWSPAPER ABBREV.	COMPANY NAME
CTEK	NAS NMS	CmlTek	Commercial Intertech
CTEX	NAS NMS	CTEC	C-TEC Corp
CTEXB	NAS NL	CTEC B	C-TEC Corp (Class B)
CTF	New York	CTF	Counsellors Tandem Securities Fund Inc
CTG	New York	ConnNG	Connecticut Natural Gas Corp
CTH	New York	CRI III	CRI Insured Mortgage Investments III LP
CTHL	NAS NMS	CtlHlth	Continental Health Affiliates Inc
CTIA	NAS NMS	ComTrn	Communications Transmission Inc
CTK	American	Comptek	Comptek Research Inc
CTL	New York	CntryTl	Century Telephone Enterprises Inc
CTLC	NAS NMS	CnsTom	Consolidated-Tomoka Land Co
CTM	American	ComSy	COM Systems Inc
CTME	NAS NMS	Cloth	The Clothestime Inc
CTO	American	CmceT	Commerce Total Return Fund Inc
CTP	New York	CeMPw	Central Maine Power Co
CTR	New York	Constr	Constar International Inc
CTRL	NAS SL	CntrlCp	Central Corp (Georgia)
CTRN	NAS SL	Cortrnc	Cortronic Corp
CTS	New York	CTS	CTS Corp
CTUC	NAS NMS	Contin	The Continuum Company Inc
CTUS	NAS NMS	Cetus	Cetus Corp
CTWL	NAS NMS	Chrtwl	Chartwell Group Ltd
CTWS	NAS NMS	ConnWt	Connecticut Water Service Inc
CTX	New York	Centex	Centex Corp
CTY.A	American	CtyCom	Century Communications Corp (Class A)
CTYF	NAS NMS	CityFed	CityFed Financial Corp
CTYN	NAS NMS	CtyNC	City National Corp
CUB	American	Cubic	Cubic Corp
CUC	New York	Culbro	Culbro Corp
CUCD	NAS NMS	CUC Int	CUC International Inc
CUCO	NAS SL	Cucos	Cucos Inc
CUE	New York	Quantm	Quantum Chemical Corp
CUL	New York	Culinet	Cullinet Software Inc
CULL	NAS NMS	Culum	Cullum Companies Inc
CULP	NAS NMS	Culp	Culp Inc
CUM	New York	CumEn	Cummins Engine Company Inc
CUO	American	ContMtl	Continental Materials Corp
CUR	New York	CurInc	Current Income Shares Inc
CURY	NAS NMS	Bombay	Bombay Palace Restaurants Inc
CUS	American	Custmd	Customedix Corp
CUSIF	NAS SL	Cusac	Cusac Industries Ltd
CUTC	NAS NL	Cutco	CutCo Industries Inc
CUZZ	NAS NL	CousH	Cousins Home Furnishings Inc
CV	New York	CVtPS	Central Vermont Public Service Corp
CVBF	NAS NMS	CVBFn	CVB Financial Corp
CVC	American	Cablvsn	Cablevision Systems Corp
CVCO	NAS NL	Cavco	Cavco Industries Inc
CVF	American	CasFd	Castle Convertible Fund Inc

TRADING SYMBOL	MARKET LISTING	NEWSPAPER ABBREV.	COMPANY NAME
CVGT	NAS NMS	Convgt	Convergent Inc
CVI	New York	Cenvill	Cenvill Investors Inc
CVL	American	CenvD	Cenvill Development Corp
CVR	American	ChiRV	Chicago Rivet & Machine Co
CVSNF	NAS NMS	Convsn	Conversion Industries Inc
CVT	New York	TCW	TCW Convertible Securities Fund Inc
CW	New York	CurtW	Curtiss-Wright Corp
CWDI	NAS SL	CrftWld	Craft World International Inc
CWE	New York	CmwE	Commonwealth Edison Co
CWKTF	NAS NL	CamNt	Cam-Net Communications Network Inc
CWLD	NAS NMS	ChldWld	Child World Inc
CWM	New York	CntrMt	Countrywide Mortgage Investments Inc
CWTR	NAS NMS	CalWtr	California Water Service Co
CWTS	NAS NMS	CWTrns	Country Wide Transport Services Inc
CX	New York	CentEn	Centerior Energy Corp
CXC	American	CMX Cp	CMX Corp
CXI	American	Cuplex	Cuplex Inc
CXIM	NAS NMS	Criticre	Criticare Systems Inc
CXR	American	CXR	CXR Telecom Corp
CXV	American	CavalH	Cavalier Homes Inc
CXY	American	CdnOc	Canadian Occidental Petroleum Ltd
CYAN	NAS SL	Cyntch	Cyanotech Corp
CYBE	NAS SL	CybrOpt	CyberOptics Corp
CYNR	NAS SL	CanyRs	Canyon Resources Corp
CYPM	NAS NMS	Cyprus	Cyprus Minerals Co
CYPR	NAS NMS	CypSem	Cypress Semiconductor Corp
CYR	New York	CrayRs	Cray Research Inc
CYS	New York	Cycare	CyCare Systems Inc
CYT	New York	CityBcp	Citytrust Bancorp
CYTO	NAS NMS	Cytogn	Cytogen Corp
CYTR	NAS NMS	CytRx	CytRx Corp
CZM	New York	Calmat	CalMat Co
D	New York	DomRs	Dominion Resources Inc
DA	New York	CRSS	CRS Sirrine Inc
DAHL	NAS NMS	Dahlbrg	Dahlberg Inc
DAIEY	NAS NL	DaiEi	The Daiei Inc (Japan)
DAIO	NAS NMS	Dta IO	Data I/O Corp
DAL	New York	DeltaAr	Delta Air Lines Inc
DALT	NAS SL	Dalton	Dalton Communications Inc
DAM	American	Damson	Damson Oil Corporation
DAN	New York	Daniel	Daniel Industries Inc
DAPN	NAS NMS	Dauphn	Dauphin Deposit Corp
DARTA	NAS NMS	DartGp	Dart Group Corp (Class A)
DASA	NAS SL	DasaCp	Dasa Corp
DASW	NAS NMS	DtSwtch	Data Switch Corp
DATM	NAS NMS	Datum	Datum Inc
DATX	NAS NMS	DtaTrn	Data Translation Inc

TRADING SYMBOL	MARKET LISTING	NEWSPAPER ABBREV.	COMPANY NAME
DAVX	NAS NMS	Davox	Davox Corp
DAZY	NAS NMS	DaisySy	Daisy Systems Corp
DBAS	NAS NMS	DBA	DBA Systems Inc
DBD	New York	Diebold	Diebold Inc
DBF	New York	DrexB	Drexel Bond-Debenture Trading Fund
DBHI	NAS NMS	Hickam	Dow B. Hickam Inc
DBIO	NAS NMS	DmnBio	Damon Biotech Inc
DBRL	NAS NMS	Dibrel	Dibrell Brothers Inc
DBRN	NAS NMS	DresB	The Dress Barn Inc
DBRSY	NAS NL	DBeer	De Beers Consolidated Mines Ltd
DC	American	Datamet	Datametrics Corp
DCA	New York	DigtlCm	Digital Communications Associates Inc
DCI	New York	Donald	Donaldson Company Inc
DCN	New York	DanaCp	Dana Corp
DCO	American	Ducom	Ducommun Inc
DCOR	NAS NMS	Decor	Decor Corp
DCPI	NAS NMS	DClark	dick clark productions inc
DCSN	NAS NL	DecisSy	Decision Systems Inc
DCY	New York	DCNY	DCNY Corp
DD	New York	duPont	E.I. du Pont de Nemours & Co
DDAT	NAS NL	DiagDt	Diagonal Data Corp
DDDI	NAS NMS	DwnyDs	Downey Designs International Inc
DDIX	NAS NMS	DDI	DDI Pharmaceuticals Inc
DDL	New York	DtaDsg	Data-Design Laboratories Inc
DDRG	NAS SL	DartDg	Dart Drug Stores Inc
DDS.A	American	Dillard	Dillard Department Stores Inc (Class A)
DDSC	NAS SL	DeltaDt	Delta Data Systems Corp
DDTTF	NAS NL	DavTis	Davison Tisdale Mines Ltd
DE	New York	Deere	Deere & Co
DEAL	NAS NMS	Dial Re	Dial REIT Inc
DEBS	NAS NMS	DebSh	Deb Shops Inc
DEC	New York	Digital	Digital Equipment Corp
DEE	New York	DeeCp	Dee Corp PLC
DEER	NAS NMS	DeerfSv	Deerfield Federal S&L Assn (Illinois)
DEFI	NAS NMS	DefnPr	Defiance Precision Products Inc
DEG	American	DeLau	De Laurentiis Entertainment Group Inc
DEI	New York	DEI	Diversified Energies Inc
DELA	NAS SL	DlPaint	Del Paint Corp
DELE	NAS SL	DelEl	Del Electronics Corp
DELL	NAS NMS	DellCpt	Dell Computer Corp
DEMP	NAS NMS	DrgEm	Drug Emporium Inc
DEP.A	American	DamEA	Damson Energy Company LP (Class A)
DEP.B	American	DamEB	Damson Energy Company LP (Class B)
DEPC	NAS NMS	DEP	DEP Corp
DEPS	NAS NMS	DepGty	Deposit Guaranty Corp
DERM	NAS SL	DermaL	Derma-Lock Medical Corp
DESB	NAS NMS	DelSvg	Delaware Savings Bank FSB
DEST	NAS NMS	Dest	DEST Corp

TRADING SYMBOL	MARKET LISTING	NEWSPAPER ABBREV.	COMPANY NAME
DESI	NAS NL	DsgInc	Designs Inc
DETC	NAS NMS	DetSy	Detection Systems Inc
DEVC	NAS NMS	Devcon	Devcon International Corp
DEVN	NAS NMS	Devon	Devon Group Inc
DEW	New York	DelmP	Delmarva Power & Light Co
DEWY	NAS NMS	Dewey	Dewey Electronics Corp
DEX	New York	Dexter	The Dexter Corp
DEXO	NAS SL	Dexon	Dexon Inc
DF	New York	DeanFd	Dean Foods Co
DFED	NAS NMS	DmnFdl	Dominion Federal S&L Assn (Virginia)
DFI	American	DtyFr	Duty Free International Inc
DFLX	NAS NMS	Datflx	Dataflex Corp
DFP	American	DLauF	De Laurentiis Film Partners LP
DGAS	NAS NMS	DeltNG	Delta Natural Gas Company Inc
DGN	New York	DataGn	Data General Corp
DGSI	NAS SL	Digtl Sol	Digital Solutions Inc
DGTC	NAS NMS	Digtch	Digitech Inc
DH	New York	DaytHd	Dayton Hudson Corp
DHIN	NAS SL	Desgnh	Designhouse International Inc
DHR	New York	Danhr	Danaher Corp
DHTK	NAS NMS	DH Tch	DH Technology Inc
DI	New York	Dresr	Dresser Industries Inc
DIA	American	Diasonc	Diasonics Inc
DIBK	NAS NMS	DimeCT	The Dime Savings Bank of Wallingford (Connecticut)
DICN	NAS NMS	Diceon	Diceon Electronics Inc
DIDII	NAS SL	DisDet	Disease Detection International Inc
DIFSD	NAS NMS	DvFood	Diversified Foods Corp
DIG	New York	DiGior	Di Giorgio Corp
DIGI	NAS NMS	DSC	DSC Communications Corp
DIGT	NAS SL	Digitxt	Digitext Inc
DII	American	Decorat	Decorator Industries Inc
DILO	NAS NMS	Diglog	Digilog Inc
DING	NAS NMS	DivInvt	Diversified Investment Group Inc
DIO	American	Diodes	Diodes Inc
DION	NAS NMS	Dionic	Dionics Inc
DIPC	NAS SL	DigPd	Digital Products Corp
DIS	New York	Disney	The Walt Disney Co
DISC	NAS SL	Discus	Discus Corp
DISK	NAS SL	ImagEn	Image Entertainment Inc
DIV	American	PCL	PCL Diversifund
DIVY	NAS SL	DisAsc	Discovery Associates Inc
DIX	American	Dixilne	Dixieline Products Inc
DJ	New York	DowJns	Dow Jones & Company Inc
DJCO	NAS NMS	DlyJour	Daily Journal Co
DJI	American	DesgnI	Designcraft Industries Inc
DKEY	NAS NL	Datkey	Datakey Inc
DKLBB	NAS NMS	Dekalb	DEKALB Corp (Class B)

TRADING SYMBOL	MARKET LISTING	NEWSPAPER ABBREV.	COMPANY NAME
DLCFF	NAS NL	Develcn	Develcon Electronics Ltd
DLCH	NAS NMS	Delchm	Delchamps Inc
DLI	American	DelLab	Del Laboratories Inc
DLOG	NAS NMS	DistLog	Distributed Logic Corp
DLP	American	Centrst	CenTrust Savings Bank
DLPH	DelpInf	DelpInf	Delphi Information Systems Inc
DLS	New York	Dallas	Dallas Corp
DLT	New York	Deltona	The Deltona Corp
DLTA	NAS NMS	Deltaus	DeltaUS Corp
DLTK	NAS NMS	Deltak	Deltak Corp
DLTX	NAS SL	Daltex	Daltex Medical Sciences Inc
DLWD	NAS NMS	DltWod	Delta Woodside Industries Inc
DLX	New York	Deluxe	Deluxe Corp
DMAG	NAS SL	Dtamg	Datamag Inc
DMAR	NAS NMS	Datmar	Datamarine International Inc
DMBK	NAS NMS	DomBk	Dominion Bankshares Corp
DMC	New York	DivrsIn	Diversified Industries Inc
DMCB	NAS NMS	DtMea	Data Measurement Corp
DMCS	NAS SL	DatMC	Data Med Clinical Support Services Inc
DMCVA	NAS NMS	DairyA	Dairy Mart Convenience Stores Inc (Class A)
DMCVB	NAS NMS	DairyB	Dairy Mart Convenience Stores Inc (Class B)
DMD	American	Delmed	Delmed Inc
DME	New York	DimeNY	Dime Savings Bank of New York FSB
DMED	NAS SL	DimenMd	Dimensional Medicine Inc
DMGIF	NAS NMS	Dumag	Dumagami Mines Ltd
DMIC	NAS NMS	DigMic	Digital Microwave Corp
DMIF	NAS NL	DMI	DMI Furniture Inc
DMK	American	DirActn	Direct Action Marketing Inc
DML.A	American	DckMA	Dickenson Mines Ltd (Class A)
DML.B	American	DckMB	Dickenson Mines Ltd (Class B)
DMN	New York	DamnC	Damon Corp
DNA	New York	DianaCp	The Diana Corp
DNAP	NAS NMS	DNA Pl	DNA Plant Technology Corp
DNB	New York	DunBd	The Dun & Bradstreet Corp
DNEX	NAS NMS	Dionex	Dionex Corp
DNFC	NAS NMS	D&N Fn	D&N Financial Corp
DNI	American	DamCr	Damon Creations Inc
DNLC	NAS NL	DixieNt	Dixie National Corp
DNNY	NAS NMS	FranDn	The Frances Denney Companies Inc
DNP	New York	DuffPh	Duff & Phelps Selected Utilities
DNPC	NAS SL	Denpac	Denpac Corp
DNY	New York	Donley	R.R. Donnelley & Sons Co
DOBQ	NAS NL	Dghtie	Doughtie's Foods Inc
DOCC	NAS SL	Digtl0p	Digital Optronics Corp
DOCO	NAS NMS	DOC	D.O.C. Optics Corp
DOCP	NAS NMS	DelaOts	Delaware Otsego Corp

TRADING SYMBOL	MARKET LISTING	NEWSPAPER ABBREV.	COMPANY NAME
DOCX	NAS SL	Docgph	Docugraphix Inc
DOLR	NAS NMS	DlrGnl	Dollar General Corp
DOMN	NAS NMS	DomnT	Domain Technology Inc
DOMZ	NAS NMS	Domng	Dominguez Water Corp
DON	American	DonlyC	Donnelly Corp
DONEF	NAS NMS	Donegal	Donegal Resources Ltd
DOSE	NAS SL	ChcDrg	Choice Drug Systems Inc
DOSK	NAS NMS	Doskcl	Doskocil Companies Inc
DOTX	NAS NMS	Dotrnix	Dotronix Inc
DOUG	NAS NMS	DglLom	Douglas & Lomason Co
DOV	New York	Dover	Dover Corp
DOW	New York	DowCh	The Dow Chemical Co
DP	New York	DiagPr	Diagnostic Products Corp
DPC	American	DataPd	Dataproducts Corp
DPHZ	NAS NMS	Datphz	DATAPHAZ Inc
DPL	New York	DPL	DPL Inc
DPRX	NAS SL	DctPhr	Direct Pharmaceutical Corp
DPT	New York	Datapt	Datapoint Corp
DPX	American	Duplex	Duplex Products Inc
DQU	New York	DuqLt	Duquesne Light Co
DRAM	NAS NMS	MicrTc	Micron Technology Inc
DRAN	NAS NMS	Drantz	Dranetz Technologies Inc
DRCO	NAS NMS	DynRs	Dynamics Research Corp
DRE	New York	DukeRIn	Duke Realty Investments Inc
DRES	NAS NMS	Dreshr	Dresher Inc
DREW	NAS SL	Drewry	Drewry Photocolor Corp
DRFNY	NAS NL	DriefC	Driefontein Consolidated Ltd
DRH	American	DrivHar	Driver-Harris Co
DRI	American	DeRose	De Rose Industries Inc
DRKN	NAS NMS	Durkn	Durakon Industries Inc
DRL	American	DI Ind	DI Industries Inc
DRM	New York	DShRM	Diamond Shamrock R&M Inc
DRMD	NAS NMS	Duramd	Duramed Pharmaceuticals Inc
DRS.A	American	Diag A	Diagnostic/Retrieval Systems Inc (Class A)
DRS.B	American	Diag B	Diagnostic/Retrieval Systems Inc (Class B)
DRSDY	NAS NL	DresBk	Dresdner Bank AG
DRTK	NAS NMS	Duratek	Duratek Corp
DRV	New York	Dravo	Dravo Corp
DRWI	NAS NMS	DrewIn	Drew Industries Inc
DRXR	NAS NMS	Drexlr	Drexler Technology Corp
DRY	New York	Dreyfus	The Dreyfus Corp
DRYR	NAS NMS	DreyGr	Dreyer's Grand Ice Cream Inc
DSBC	NAS NMS	DS Bnc	DS Bancor Inc (Connecticut)
DSBE	NAS SL	Dasibi	Dasibi Environmental Corp
DSCC	NAS NMS	Dtasth	Datasouth Computer Corp
DSCP	NAS NMS	Datscp	Datascope Corp

TRADING SYMBOL	MARKET LISTING	NEWSPAPER ABBREV.	COMPANY NAME
DSG	American	Dsgntrn	Designatronics Inc
DSI	New York	DryStGn	Dreyfus Strategic Government Income Fund
DSIC	NAS SL	DiagSc	Diagnostic Sciences Inc
DSII	NAS NMS	Decom	Decom Systems Inc
DSL	New York	Downey	Downey S&L Assn
DSMI	NAS NMS	DalSem	Dallas Semiconductor Corp
DSO	New York	DeSoto	DeSoto Inc
DSN	New York	DensMf	Dennison Manufacturing Co
DSP	New York	DiaSO	Diamond Shamrock Offshore Partners LP
DSTS	NAS NMS	DST	DST Systems Inc
DTC	New York	Domtr	Domtar Inc
DTE	New York	DetEd	The Detroit Edison Co
DTINA	NAS SL	DigTrA	Digital Transmission Inc (Class A)
DTLN	NAS SL	DtTrNw	Data Transmission Network
DTM	American	Datarm	Dataram Corp
DTMD	NAS NMS	DentMd	Dento-Med Industries Inc
DTOM	NAS NMS	DTomas	De Tomaso Industries Inc
DTRH	NAS SL	DRX	DRX Inc
DTRX	NAS NMS	DetrxC	Detrex Corp
DTSI	NAS NMS	Datron	Datron Systems Inc
DTUN	NAS NL	DetCan	Detroit & Canada Tunnel Corp
DUCO	NAS NMS	Durhm	Durham Corp
DUFM	NAS NMS	DurFil	Durr-Fillauer Medical Inc
DUK	New York	DukeP	Duke Power Co
DUNK	NAS NMS	DunkDn	Dunkin' Donuts Inc
DUQN	NAS NMS	DuqSys	Duquesne Systems Inc
DURI	NAS NMS	Duriron	The Duriron Company Inc
DUSTF	NAS SL	DustMc	Dusty Mac Mines Ltd
DVH	American	DiviHtl	Divi Hotels NV
DVIC	NAS SL	DVI Fn	DVI Financial Corp
DVIS	NAS NMS	Datvsn	Datavision Inc
DVL	New York	DelVal	Del-Val Financial Corp
DVRFS	NAS NL	DovrReg	Dover Regional Financial Shares
DVRS	NAS NMS	Divrsc	Diversco Inc
DVTI	NAS SL	DivTch	Diversified Technology Inc
DWG	American	DWG	DWG Corp
DWIC	NAS SL	DWI	DWI Corp
DWP.A	American	WebInv	Del E. Webb Investment Properties Inc (Class A)
DWSN	NAS NMS	Dawson	Dawson Geophysical Co
DWW	New York	DavWtr	Davis Water & Waste Industries Inc
DXN	New York	DixnGp	Dixons Group plc
DXR	American	Daxor	Daxor Corp
DXT	American	DixnTi	Dixon Ticonderoga Co
DXTK	NAS NMS	Diagnst	Diagnostek Inc
DXYN	NAS NMS	DixieYr	Dixie Yarns Inc
DYA	New York	DynAm	Dynamics Corporation of America

TRADING SYMBOL	MARKET LISTING	NEWSPAPER ABBREV.	COMPANY NAME
DYAN	NAS NMS	Dyansn	Dyansen Corp
DYCO	NAS NMS	Dycom	Dycom Industries Inc
DYN	New York	Dyncrp	DynCorp
DYNA	NAS NMS	Dynsc	Dynascan Corp
DYNC	NAS SL	DynCls	Dynamic Classics Ltd
DYNS	NAS SL	DynmcSc	Dynamic Sciences International Inc
DYNT	NAS SL	DyntrL	Dynatronics Laser Corp
DYTC	NAS NMS	DytchC	Dynatech Corp
DYTR	NAS NMS	Dyatrn	Dyatron Corp
E	New York	Transco	Transco Energy Co
EA	New York	ElecAs	Electronic Associates Inc
EAC	American	EAC	EAC Industries Inc
EACO	NAS NMS	EA Eng	EA Engineering Science & Technology Inc
EAF	New York	EmryA	Emery Air Freight Corp
EAFC	NAS NMS	EastFn	Eastland Financial Corp
EAGL	American	EaglFn	Eagle Financial Corp
EAIC	NAS SL	EnAset	Energy Assets International Corp
EAST	NAS NMS	EngnSu	Engineered Support Systems Inc
EATN	NAS SL	BkEtTn	Bank of East Tennessee
EATO	NAS NMS	EatnFn	Eaton Financial Corp
EAVK	NAS NL	Viner	E.A. Viner Holdings Ltd
EAVN	NAS NMS	EatVan	Eaton Vance Corp
EB	American	EhrBbr	Ehrlich Bober Financial Corp
EBCI	NAS NMS	EglBnc	Eagle Bancorp Inc
EBF	New York	EnisBu	Ennis Business Forms Inc
EBKC	NAS NMS	EliotSv	Eliot Savings Bank (Massachusetts)
EBMI	NAS NMS	EB Mar	E&B Marine Inc
EBNC	NAS NMS	EqtBcp	Equitable Bancorporation (Maryland)
EBS	New York	EdisBr	Edison Brothers Stores Inc
EBSI	NAS NMS	EaglBn	Eagle Bancshares Inc
EC	New York	EnglC	Engelhard Corp
ECC	New York	ECC	ECC International Corp
ECDC	NAS SL	EnCap	Energy Capital Development Corp
ECF	American	Elswth	Ellsworth Convertible Growth & Income Fund Inc
ECGC	NAS NL	EsexCty	Essex County Gas Co
ECGI	NAS NMS	EnvCtl	Environmental Control Group Inc
ECH	New York	Echlin	Echlin Inc
ECILF	NAS NMS	ECI Tel	ECI Telecom Ltd
ECIN	NAS SL	ElctMis	Electronics Missiles & Communications Inc
ECL	New York	Ecolab	Ecolab Inc
ECLAY	NAS NMS	EngChn	English China Clays PLC
ECN	American	Ecogn	Ecogen Inc
ECO	American	EchoB	Echo Bay Mines Ltd
ECOA	NAS SL	EqAm	Equipment Company of America
ECOL	NAS NMS	AmEcol	American Ecology Corp

TRADING SYMBOL	MARKET LISTING	NEWSPAPER ABBREV.	COMPANY NAME
ECOW	American	MetRlt	Metropolitan Realty Corp
ECRC	NAS NL	EmpCas	Employers Casualty Co
ECTH	NAS NMS	ElCath	Electro-Catheter Corp
ECTL	NAS NMS	Elcotel	Elcotel Inc
ED	New York	ConsEd	Consolidated Edison Company of New York Inc
EDAC	NAS NL	Edac	Edac Technologies Corp
EDAT	NAS NL	ElcDta	Electronic Data Technologies
EDCO	NAS NMS	EdisCtr	Edison Control Corp
EDE	New York	EmpDs	The Empire District Electric Co
EDGC	NAS NMS	Edgcmb	Edgcomb Corp
EDIT	NAS SL	EnvDia	Environmental Diagnostics Inc
EDMC	NAS SL	EldrM	ElDorado Motor Corp
EDO	New York	EDO	EDO Corp
EDP	American	EnDvl	Energy Development Partners Ltd
EDSE	NAS NMS	EdSault	Edison Sault Electric Co
EE	American	EsqRd	Esquire Radio & Electronics Inc
EEC	American	EECO	EECO Inc
EEE	New York	Ensrce	Ensource Inc
EEI.A	American	EcolEn	Ecology & Environment Inc (Class A)
EESI	NAS NMS	EstnEn	Eastern Environmental Services Inc
EFG	New York	Equitec	Equitec Financial Group Inc
EFH	New York	HuttEF	The E.F. Hutton Group Inc
EFIC	NAS SL	EFIEle	EFI Electronics Corp
EFSB	NAS NMS	ElmwdFd	Elmwood Federal Savings Bank (Pennsylvania)
EFU	New York	EastGF	Eastern Gas & Fuel Associates
EFX	New York	Equifax	Equifax Inc
EGA	New York	EQK G	EQK Green Acres LP
EGAS	NAS NMS	Enrgas	Energas Co
EGCSC	NAS SL	EmpGs	Empire Gas Corp
EGG	New York	EGG	EG&G Inc
EGGS	NAS NL	Egghead	Egghead Inc
EGL	American	EaglCl	Eagle Clothes Inc
EGLC	NAS NMS	EagTl	Eagle Telephonics Inc
EGN	New York	Energen	Energen Corp
EGP	American	Estgp	EastGroup Properties
EGPC	NAS SL	EngGrh	English Greenhouse Products Corp
EGX	American	Engex	Engex Inc
EHP	New York	Emrld	Emerald Homes LP
EI	American	Endvco	Endevco Inc
EILI	NAS NMS	EIL Inst	E.I.L. Instruments Inc
EIPM	NAS NMS	EIP	EIP Microwave Inc
EIS	New York	Excelsr	Excelsior Income Shares Inc
EJ.A	American	EvrJ A	Everest & Jennings International Ltd (Class A)
EJ.B	American	EvrJ B	Everest & Jennings International Ltd (Class B)

TRADING SYMBOL	MARKET LISTING	NEWSPAPER ABBREV.	COMPANY NAME
EK	New York	EKodk	Eastman Kodak Co
EKR	New York	EQK Rt	EQK Realty Investors I
ELANY	NAS NMS	Elan	Elan Corporation plc
ELB	American	Eldorad	Eldorado Bancorp
ELBTF	NAS NMS	Elbit	Elbit Computers Ltd
ELCH	NAS NMS	ElChic	El Chico Corp
ELCN	NAS NMS	Elco	Elco Industries Inc
ELCS	NAS SL	ElctCtr	Electronic Control Systems Inc
ELD	New York	Eldon	Eldon Industries Inc
ELDC	NAS NMS	Eldec	Eldec Corp
ELE	New York	EmpNa	Empress Nacional de Electricidad sa
ELEX	NAS NMS	Elexis	Elexis Corp
ELIS	NAS SL	EliSci	Eli Scientific Inc
ELK	New York	Elcor	Elcor Corp
ELMD	NAS SL	Elcmd	Electromedics Inc
ELMG	NAS NMS	Elctmg	Electromagnetic Sciences Inc
ELOPF	NAS SL	ElDe El	El-De-Electro-Optic Developments Ltd
ELPA	NAS NMS	ElPas	El Paso Electric Co
ELRC	NAS NMS	ElcRnt	Electro Rent Corp
ELRNF	NAS NMS	ElronEl	Elron Electronic Industries Ltd
ELS	American	Elsinor	Elsinore Corp
ELSE	NAS NMS	ElcSens	Electro-Sensors Inc
ELSI	NAS SL	Elctsrc	Electrosource Inc
ELSX	NAS NMS	ELXSI	ELXSI Corp
ELT	New York	Elscint	Elscint Ltd
ELUXY	NAS NMS	EluxAB	Electrolux AB (Class B)
EM	American	EntMkt	Entertainment Marketing Inc
EMC	New York	EMC	EMC Corp
EMCI	NAS NMS	EMC In	EMC Insurance Group Inc
EMCO	NAS NMS	EngMea	Engineering Measurements Co
EME	New York	EmRad	Emerson Radio Corp
EMF	American	TmplE	Templeton Emerging Markets Fund Inc
EMGVF	NAS NL	Estmaq	Eastmaque Gold Mines Ltd
EMH	New York	Emhrt	Emhart Corp
EMI	American	EncrM	Encore Marketing International Inc
EML	American	EstnCo	The Eastern Co
EMLX	NAS NMS	Emulex	Emulex Corp
EMP	American	EmCar	Empire of Carolina Inc
EMPI	NAS NMS	EMPI	EMPI Inc
EMPR	NAS NMS	EmpSB	Empire Savings Bank SLA (New Jersey)
EMR	New York	EmrsE	Emerson Electric Co
EMSIF	NAS SL	EMS Sy	EMS Systems Ltd
EN	New York	Entera	Enterra Corp
ENCC	NAS NMS	Encore	Encore Computer Corp
ENCRF	NAS NL	Enscor	Enscor Inc
ENE	New York	Enron	Enron Corp
ENER	NAS NMS	EngCnv	Energy Conversion Devices Inc
ENEX	NAS NMS	EnexR	ENEX Resources Corp

TRADING SYMBOL	MARKET LISTING	NEWSPAPER ABBREV.	COMPANY NAME
ENG	New York	EnrOG	Enron Oil & Gas Co
ENGH	NAS NMS	Engrph	Engraph Inc
ENNI	NAS NMS	Engnth	EnergyNorth Inc
ENS	New York	Ensrch	ENSERCH Corp
ENTC	NAS NMS	Entrnc	Entronics Corp
ENTW	NAS SL	Entwist	Entwistle Co
ENUC	NAS NMS	EleNucl	Electro-Nucleonics Inc
ENV	American	Envrpct	Enviropact Inc
ENVI	NAS NMS	Envirsf	Envirosafe Services Inc
ENVR	NAS NMS	Envrd	Envirodyne Industries Inc
ENVS	NAS SL	Envrsur	Envirosure Management Corp
ENVT	NAS NMS	EnvrTc	Environmental Tectonics Corp
ENW	New York	Elgin	Elgin National Industries Inc
ENX	American	ENSR	ENSR Corp
ENZ	American	EnzoBi	Enzo Biochem Inc
ENZN	NAS NMS	Enzon	Enzon Inc
EOA	American	EmpirA	Empire of America Federal Savings Bank
EOBK	NAS NL	EastBk	Eastover Bank for Savings (Mississippi)
EORR	NAS NMS	EmpOrr	Empire-Orr Inc
EP	New York	EnsExp	Enserch Exploration Partners Ltd
EPAI	NAS NMS	ElPollo	El Pollo Asado Inc
EPI	New York	EagleP	Eagle-Picher Industries Inc
EPIC	NAS SL	EpicHlt	Epic Health Group Inc
EPSC	NAS NMS	Epsco	EPSCO Inc
EPSI	NAS NMS	Epsiln	Epsilon Data Management Inc
EPTO	NAS SL	Epitope	Epitope Inc
EPUB	NAS NMS	EntPub	Entertainment Publications Inc
EQBK	NAS SL	EqtyBk	Equity Bank (Connecticut)
EQICA	NAS NL	EqtIA	Equitable of Iowa Companies (Class A)
EQICB	NAS NMS	EqtIB	Equitable of Iowa Companies (Class B)
EQK	New York	Equimk	Equimark Corp
EQM	New York	EqtRl	Equitable Real Estate Shopping Centers LP
EQT	New York	EqtRes	Equitable Resources Inc
EQTX	NAS NMS	Equitex	Equitex Inc
EQTY	NAS NMS	EqtOil	Equity Oil Co
EQUI	NAS NMS	Equion	The Equion Corp
ERB	New York	Erbmnt	Erbamont NV
ERC	New York	ERC	ERC International Inc
ERICY	NAS NMS	EricTl	LM Ericsson Telephone Co
ERLY	NAS NMS	ErlyInd	Erly Industries Inc
ERO	American	Ero	Ero Industries Inc
ESB	New York	EssBus	Esselte Business Systems Inc
ESBK	NAS SL	ElmrSv	Elmira Savings Bank FSB
ESC	New York	EnvSys	Environmental Systems Co
ESCA	NAS NMS	Escalde	Escalade Inc
ESCC	NAS NMS	EvnSut	Evans & Sutherland Computer Corp
ESD	American	ESD	Engineered Systems & Development Corp

TRADING SYMBOL	MARKET LISTING	NEWSPAPER ABBREV.	COMPANY NAME
ESEX	NAS NMS	Essex	Essex Corp
ESG	American	ElecSd	ElectroSound Group Inc
ESH	American	Scheib	Earl Scheib Inc
ESI.A	American	ESI	ESI Industries Inc (Class A)
ESIO	NAS NMS	ElcSci	Electro Scientific Industries Inc
ESL	New York	Estrlne	Esterline Corp
ESN	American	Escagn	Escagenitics Corp
ESP	American	Espey	Espey Manufacturing & Electronics Corp
ESSF	NAS NMS	ESSEF	ESSEF Corp
ESTO	NAS SL	Eastco	Eastco Industrial Safety Corp
ESV	American	ENSCO	Energy Service Company Inc
ESX	New York	EsexCh	Essex Chemical Corp
ESY	New York	E Syst	E-Systems Inc
ETCIA	NAS NMS	ElecTel	Electronic Tele-Communications Inc (Class A)
ETCO	NAS NMS	EarthT	The Earth Technology Corp
ETEX	NAS NMS	Eastex	Eastex Energy Inc
ETI	American	Esprit	Esprit Systems Inc
ETN	New York	Eaton	Eaton Corp
ETRC	NAS NMS	EntreCp	Entree Corp
ETRE	NAS NMS	EntrCpt	Entré Computer Centers Inc
ETSL	NAS NL	EastTx	East Texas S&L Assn of Tyler Texas
ETT	New York	EnvTrt	Environmental Treatment & Technologies Corp
ETZ	American	EtzLav	Etz Lavud Ltd
EUA	New York	EastUtl	Eastern Utilities Associates
EURO	NAS SL	Eurocap	Eurocapital Corp
EVAN	NAS NMS	Evans	Envans Inc
EVER	NAS NMS	Evrgrn	Evergreen Resources Inc
EVGD	NAS NMS	Evrgd	Evergood Products Inc
EVRX	NAS NMS	Everex	Everex Systems Inc
EVSB	NAS NMS	EvnsFS	Evansville Federal Savings Bank
EWAT	NAS NMS	ETown	E'town Corp
EWSB	NAS NMS	EastWy	East Weymouth Savings Bank (Massachusetts)
EWSCA	NAS NMS	Scripps	E.W. Scripps Co (Class A)
EXAR	NAS NMS	Exar	Exar Corp
EXC	American	Excel	Excel Industries Inc
EXCG	NAS NMS	ExchBc	Exchange Bancorp Inc
EXLN	NAS NMS	Exceln	Excelan Inc
EXP	New York	TranEx	Transco Exploration Partners Ltd
EXPD	NAS NMS	ExpIn	Expeditors International of Washington Inc
EXPO	NAS NMS	Exposc	Exposaic Industries Inc
EY	New York	Ethyl	Ethyl Corp
EYES	NAS SL	Sal Oph	Salvatori Opthalmics Inc
EZEM	NAS NMS	EZEM	E-Z-Em Inc

TRADING SYMBOL	MARKET LISTING	NEWSPAPER ABBREV.	COMPANY NAME
F	New York	FordM	Ford Motor Co
FABC	NAS NMS	FAlaBk	First Alabama Bancshares Inc
FABK	NAS NMS	FstAm	First of America Bank Corp (Michigan)
FACT	NAS NMS	FAlban	First Albany Companies Inc
FAHC	NAS SL	FAmHlt	First American Health Concepts Inc
FAHS	NAS NMS	FrmHm	Farm & Home Savings Assn (Missouri)
FAL	American	FalCbl	Falcon Cable Systems Company LP
FALB	NAS NL	Falstaff	Fallstaff Brewing Corp
FALCF	NAS NL	FalcLt	Falconbridge Ltd
FAMA	NAS NMS	FtAmar	First Amarillo Bancorporation Inc
FAMB	NAS NMS	FtABcp	1st American Bancorp (Massachusetts)
FAME	NAS NMS	Flamstr	Flamemaster Corp
FAMF	NAS NMS	FtAFd	First AmFed Corp
FAMI	NAS SL	Famigl	Famiglia Brands Inc
FAMR	NAS NMS	FtAFn	The First American Financial Corp
FAMS	NAS NMS	FamRst	Famous Restaurants Inc
FARA	NAS NMS	FaradE	Faradyne Electronics Corp
FARC	NAS NMS	Farr	Farr Co
FARF	NAS NMS	FairNbl	Fairfield-Noble Corp
FARK	NAS NMS	FFArk	First Federal Savings of Arkansas FA
FARM	NAS NMS	FarmBr	Farmer Brothers Co
FARR	NAS NMS	Fargut	Farragut Mortgage Co
FASB	NAS NMS	FACant	First American Savings Bank FSB (Ohio)
FAST	NAS NMS	Fastenl	Fastenal Co
FATN	NAS NMS	FtATn	First American Corp (Tennessee)
FATV	NAS SL	FtAmCb	First American Cable Corp
FAU	New York	FMGC	Freeport-McMoRan Gold Co
FAX	American	FAusPr	First Australia Prime Income Fund
FAY	New York	FayDrg	Fay's Drug Company Inc
FBAC	NAS NMS	FNtGa	First National Bancorp (Georgia)
FBAN	NAS NL	FNB Cp	F.N.B. Corp
FBC	New York	FBostn	First Boston Inc
FBD	American	Fibrbd	Fibreboard Corp
FBF	New York	FBosIF	First Boston Income Fund Inc
FBGIA	NAS NL	FnBenA	Financial Benefit Group Inc (Class A)
FBH	New York	HallFB	Frank B. Hall & Company Inc
FBI	New York	FBosSt	First Boston Strategic Income Fund Inc
FBIC	NAS NMS	FstbkIll	Firstbank of Illinois Co
FBKP	NAS SL	FBkPhl	First Bank of Philadelphia
FBNC	NAS NMS	FtBNC	First Bancorp (North Carolina)
FBO	New York	FedlPB	Federal Paper Board Company Inc
FBOH	NAS NMS	FBOh	First Bancorporation of Ohio
FBRC	NAS NMS	Fabric	Fabricland Inc
FBRX	NAS NMS	Fibronc	Fibronics International Inc
FBS	New York	FtBkSy	First Bank System Inc
FBSI	NAS NMS	FtBnSc	First Banc Securities Inc
FBT	New York	FtBTex	First City Bankcorporation of Texas Inc
FBTC	NAS NL	FB&T	FB&T Corp

TRADING SYMBOL	MARKET LISTING	NEWSPAPER ABBREV.	COMPANY NAME
FBTR	NAS NL	ForBetr	For Better Living Inc
FBUS	NAS SL	FishBu	Fisher Business Systems Inc
FBXC	NAS NMS	FBX	FBX Corp
FC	American	FordCn	Ford Motor Company of Canada Ltd
FCA	New York	FabCtr	Fabri-Centers of America Inc
FCAP	NAS NMS	FtCapt	First Capital Corp
FCAR	NAS NL	FtCarIn	First Carolina Investors Inc
FCB	New York	FooteC	Foote Cone & Belding Communications Inc
FCBI	NAS NL	FComrB	First Commerce Bancshares Inc (Nebraska)
FCBN	NAS NMS	Flurocb	The Fluorocarbon Co
FCC	American	FtCntrl	First Central Financial Corp
FCDA	NAS NMS	FFdCD	First Federal S&L Assn of Coeur D'Alene
FCE.A	American	ForstC A	Forest City Enterprises Inc (Class A)
FCE.B	American	ForstC B	Forest City Enterprises Inc (Class B)
FCFI	NAS NMS	FCapFn	First Capitol Financial Corp (Colorado)
FCH	New York	FCapHd	First Capital Holdings Corp
FCHT	NAS NMS	FFdChat	First Federal S&L Assn of Chattanooga
FCI	New York	Fairfd	Fairfield Communities Inc
FCLCA	NAS SL	FCentn	First Centennial Corp (Class A)
FCLR	NAS NMS	FCmcl	First Commercial Corp (Arkansas)
FCNCA	NAS NMS	FCtzBA	First Citizens Bancshares Inc (Class A)
FCNCB	NAS NMS	FCtzBB	First Citizens Bancshares Inc (Class B)
FCO	American	FtConn	The First Connecticut Small Business Investment Co
FCOA	NAS NMS	ForAm	Foremost Corporation of America
FCOB	NAS NMS	FComB	First Commercial Bancorp (California)
FCOLA	NAS NMS	FColB	First Colonial Bankshares Corp (Class A) (Illinois)
FCOM	NAS NMS	FComC	First Commerce Corp (Louisiana)
FCR.A	American	Fstcrp	Firstcorp Inc (Class A)
FCSI	NAS SL	FCS	FCS Labs Inc
FCTN	NAS NL	FFColTn	First Federal S&L Assn (Tennessee)
FCTR	NAS NMS	FChart	First Charter Corp
FCX	New York	FMCC	Freeport-McMoRan Copper Co
FCY	New York	FtCity	First City Industries Inc
FDBK	NAS NL	FndrBk	Founders Bank (Connecticut)
FDLNA	NAS NMS	FLioA	Food Lion Inc (Class A)
FDLNB	NAS NMS	FLioB	Food Lion Inc (Class B)
FDO	New York	FamDlr	Family Dollar Stores Inc
FDOS	NAS NMS	FrkCpt	Franklin Computer Corp
FDPC	NAS NMS	FDP	FDP Corp
FDRC	NAS SL	FdlRsc	Federal Resources Corp
FDX	New York	FedExp	Federal Express Corp
FE	American	FriesEn	Fries Entertainment Inc
FEBC	NAS NMS	FtEstn	First Eastern Corp (Pennsylvania)
FED	New York	FstFed	FirstFed Financial Corp
FEDF	NAS NMS	FFnSL	Federated Financial S&L Assn (Wisc.)

TRADING SYMBOL	MARKET LISTING	NEWSPAPER ABBREV.	COMPANY NAME
FEI	American	FreqEl	Frequency Electronics Inc
FELE	NAS NMS	FrnkEl	Franklin Electric Company Inc
FEN	New York	Fairchd	Fairchild Industries Inc
FERO	NAS NMS	Feroflu	Ferrofluidics Corp
FES	American	FEmp	First Empire State Corp
FESX	NAS NMS	FtEsex	First Essex Bancorp Inc
FEXC	NAS NMS	FtExec	First Executive Corp
FF	New York	FFinFd	First Financial Fund Inc
FFA	American	FstFd	FirstFed America Inc
FFAL	NAS NMS	FtFAla	First Federal of Alabama FSB
FFAM	NAS NMS	FtFaml	First Family Group Inc
FFB	New York	FFB	First Fidelity Bancorporation (New Jersey)
FFBC	NAS NMS	FFncl	First Financial Bancorp (Ohio)
FFBK	NAS NMS	FtFlBk	First Florida Banks Inc
FFC	New York	FireFd	Fireman's Fund Corp
FFCA	NAS NMS	CaroBcp	Carolina Bancorp Inc
FFCH	NAS NMS	FtFnHd	First Financial Holdings Inc (West Virginia)
FFCS	NAS NMS	FtColFn	First Colorado Financial Corp
FFCT	NAS NMS	FFB Cp	FFB Corp
FFES	NAS NMS	FFdEH	First Federal S&L Assn of East Hartford
FFFC	NAS NMS	FrnkFst	Franklin First Financial Corp
FFGT	NAS NL	FFGtwn	First Federal S&L Assn of Georgetown
FFHC	NAS NMS	FtFnCp	First Financial Corp (Wisconsin)
FFHP	NAS NMS	FFdHar	First Federal S&L Assn of Harrisburg
FFHS	NAS NMS	FtFrnk	First Franklin Corp
FFKT	NAS NL	FrmCB	Farmers Capital Bank Corp
FFKY	NAS NMS	FFdElz	First Federal Savings Bank of Elizabethtown (Kentucky)
FFKZ	NAS NMS	FtFKal	First Federal S&L of Kalamazoo
FFMA	NAS NMS	FFdIndi	Fidelity Federal Savings Bank (Indiana)
FFMC	NAS NMS	FtFnMg	First Financial Management Corp
FFMY	NAS NMS	FFFtM	First Federal S&L Assn of Fort Myers
FFNS	NAS NMS	FtFnSv	First Financial Savings Assn FA (Ohio)
FFOD	NAS NMS	FFDTn	First Federal Savings Bank (Tennessee)
FFOM	NAS NMS	FFMic	First Federal of Michigan
FFP	American	FFP	FFP Partners LP
FFPC	NAS NMS	FlaFst	Florida First Federal Savings Bank
FFPR	NAS NMS	FFdPR	First Federal Savings Bank of Puerto Rico
FFS	American	FFBcp	First Federal Bancorp Inc (Michigan)
FFSD	NAS NMS	FFdAla	First Federal Savings Bank (Alabama)
FFSH	NAS NMS	FarmF	Farm Fresh Inc
FFSL	NAS NMS	FultFS	Fulton Federal S&L Assn of Atlanta
FFSM	NAS NMS	FFMon	First Federal Savings Bank of Montana
FFSW	NAS NMS	FFWoos	First Federal S&L Assn of Wooster (Ohio)

TRADING SYMBOL	MARKET LISTING	NEWSPAPER ABBREV.	COMPANY NAME
FFTN	NAS NMS	FidFTn	Fidelity Federal S&L Assn of Tennessee
FFWP	NAS NMS	FFWPa	First Federal of Western Pennsylvania
FFWS	NAS NMS	FFwst	First Farwest Corp
FFWV	NAS NMS	FFidWV	First Fidelity Bancorp Inc (West Virginia)
FG	New York	USFG	USF&G Corp
FGBC	NAS NMS	FtGoldn	First Golden Bancorporation
FGC	New York	FGIC	FGIC Corp
FGE	American	FitcGE	Fitchburg Gas & Electric Light Co
FGI	New York	FthillG	The Foothill Group Inc
FGL	New York	FMC G	FMC Gold Co
FGN	New York	FlwGen	Flow General Inc
FGRP	NAS NMS	FarGp	Farmers Group Inc
FGSV	NAS NMS	FtGaHd	First Georgia Holding Corp
FHFC	NAS NMS	FarHou	Farm House Foods Corp
FHO	American	FrdHly	Frederick's of Hollywood Inc
FHP	New York	FtHowd	Fort Howard Paper Co
FHPC	NAS NMS	FHP	FHP International Corp
FHR	New York	FishFd	Fisher Foods Inc
FHWN	NAS NMS	FtHaw	First Hawaiian Inc
FIAMA	NAS NMS	FABk A	First American Bank & Trust of Palm Beach County (Class A) (Florida)
FIAMB	NAS NL	FABk B	First American Bank & Trust of Palm Beach County (Class B) (Florida)
FIBR	NAS SL	AFibOp	American Fiber Optics Corp
FICI	NAS NMS	FairIsc	Fair, Isaac & Company Inc
FICO	NAS SL	Franch	Franchiseit Corp
FID	American	Fidata	Fidata Corp
FIF	New York	FinNws	Financial News Composite Fund Inc
FIFC	NAS NL	FFncrp	First Fincorp Inc
FIGIA	NAS NMS	FiggieA	Figgie International Holdings Inc (Class A)
FIGIB	NAS NMS	FiggieB	Figgie International Holdings Inc (Class B)
FIIA	NAS NMS	FInIowa	First Interstate of Iowa Inc
FIIF	NAS SL	Florafx	Florafax International Inc
FILE	NAS NMS	FileNet	FileNet Corp
FIN	New York	FinCpA	Financial Corporation of America
FINH	NAS NMS	FNHB	First NH Banks Inc
FINX	NAS NMS	Fingmx	Fingermatrix Inc
FIRF	NAS NMS	FFncPa	First Financial Savings Assn (Pennsylvania)
FIRO	NAS NMS	FOhBn	First Ohio Bancshares Inc
FIS	New York	Fischb	Fischbach Corp
FISB	NAS NMS	FtIndi	First Indiana Corp
FISNY	NAS NL	Fisons	Fisons plc
FISV	NAS NMS	Fiserv	FIserv Inc
FIT	American	FabInd	Fab Industries Inc

TRADING SYMBOL	MARKET LISTING	NEWSPAPER ABBREV.	COMPANY NAME
FITB	NAS NMS	FifthT	Fifth Third Bancorp (Ohio)
FITC	NAS NMS	FnTrst	Financial Trust Corp
FIWI	NAS NMS	FInsWi	First Interstate Corporation of Wisconsin
FJQ	New York	Feders	Fedders Corp
FKCM	NAS SL	FrkCon	Franklin Consolidated Mining Company Inc
FKFD	NAS NMS	Frnkfd	The Frankford Corp
FKL	American	Frnkln	The Franklin Corp
FKM	American	Fluke	John Fluke Manufacturing Company Inc
FLA	New York	FlaEC	Florida East Coast Industries Inc
FLAEF	NAS NMS	FlaEIns	Florida Employers Insurance Co
FLAG	NAS NMS	FFdLaG	First Federal S&L Assn of LaGrange
FLAR	NAS SL	Flare	Flare Inc
FLCO	NAS SL	Finalco	Finalco Group Inc
FLCP	NAS SL	FalcnPr	Falcon Products Inc
FLD	New York	Fldcrst	Fieldcrest Cannon Inc
FLE	New York	FleetEn	Fleetwood Enterprises Inc
FLEX	NAS NMS	Flextrn	Flextronics Inc
FLFC	NAS NMS	FtLbty	First Liberty Financial Corp
FLFE	NAS NMS	FlaFdl	Florida Federal S&L Assn
FLGLA	NAS NMS	Flagler	Flagler Bank Corp (Class A)
FLIC	NAS NL	FstLI	First of Long Island Corp
FLM	New York	Flemng	Fleming Companies Inc
FLO	New York	Flower	Flowers Industries Inc
FLOG	NAS NMS	FalcoOil	FalcoOil & Gas Company Inc
FLOW	NAS NMS	FlowSy	Flow Systems Inc
FLP	New York	FloatPt	Floating Point Systems Inc
FLR	New York	Fluor	Fluor Corp
FLS	New York	FlaStl	Florida Steel Corp
FLT	New York	FltNors	Fleet Norstar Financial Corp
FLTI	NAS NMS	FlghtIn	The Flight International Group Inc
FLXS	NAS NMS	Flexstl	Flexsteel Industries Inc
FLY	New York	Airlease	Airlease Ltd
FLYT	NAS SL	FlgtDy	Flight Dynamics Inc
FMBC	NAS NMS	FtMich	First Michigan Bank Corp
FMBI	NAS NMS	FMidB	First Midwest Bancorp Inc
FMC	New York	FMC	FMC Corp
FMDB	NAS NMS	FMdB	First Maryland Bancorp
FMDC	NAS SL	FtMed	First Medical Devices Corp
FMFS	NAS NMS	F&M	F&M Financial Services Corp
FMLY	NAS NMS	FamBc	Family Bancorp
FMNT	NAS NMS	FM Nt	F&M National Corp
FMO	New York	FdMog	Federal-Mogul Corp
FMP	New York	FMEP	Freeport-McMoRan Energy Partners Ltd
FMR	New York	FMOG	Freeport-McMoRan Oil & Gas Royalty Trust
FMSB	NAS NMS	FMWA	First Mutual Savings Bank (Washington)

TRADING SYMBOL	MARKET LISTING	NEWSPAPER ABBREV.	COMPANY NAME
FMSI	NAS SL	FidlMd	Fidelity Medical Inc
FN	American	FNtCal	First National Corp (California)
FNAC	NAS NMS	FNCinn	First National Cincinnati Corp
FNB	New York	FstChic	First Chicago Corp
FNBF	NAS NMS	FlaNBF	Florida National Banks of Florida Inc
FNBR	NAS NMS	FNBRo	F N B Rochester Corp
FNF	American	FidlFn	Fidelity National Financial Inc
FNGB	NAS NMS	FNthSL	First Northern S&L Assn (Wisconsin)
FNIN	NAS NL	FinlInd	Financial Industries Corp
FNL	New York	Fanstel	Fansteel Inc
FNM	New York	FedNM	Federal National Mortgage Assn
FNNG	NAS NMS	Finigan	Finnigan Corp
FNNI	NAS NMS	FinNws	Financial News Network Inc
FNPC	NAS NMS	FtNtlPa	First National Pennsylvania Corp
FNRCB	NAS NL	FedNtl	Federated Natural Resources Corp (Class B)
FNWB	NAS NMS	FNW	FNW Bancorp Inc
FOAM	NAS SL	Texstyr	Texstyrene Corp
FOBBA	NAS NMS	FtOak	First Oak Brook Bancshares Inc (Class A)
FOE	New York	Ferro	Ferro Corp
FOIL	NAS NMS	ForestO	Forest Oil Corp
FONE	NAS SL	FarmTel	Farmstead Telephone Group Inc
FONR	NAS NMS	Fonar	FONAR Corp
FOR	New York	Formc	Formica Corp
FORF	NAS NMS	FortnF	Fortune Financial Group Inc
FORL	NAS SL	Forelnd	Foreland Corp
FORM	NAS NL	FrmRe	Forum Re Group Inc
FORTA	NAS SL	Frtne44	Fortune 44 Co (Class A)
FOUR	NAS NMS	Forum	Forum Group Inc
FOX	New York	Foxbro	The Foxboro Co
FOXI	NAS SL	Foxmor	Foxmor International Films Ltd
FP	American	FischP	Fischer & Porter Co
FPA	New York	FstPa	First Pennsylvania Corp
FPBT	NAS NMS	FountPw	Fountain Powerboat Industries Inc
FPC	New York	FlaPrg	Florida Progress Corp
FPL	New York	FPL Gp	FPL Group Inc
FPNJ	NAS NMS	FPeoFn	First Peoples Financial Corp
FPO	American	FPA	FPA Corp
FPRY	NAS NL	FtFdPry	First Federal Savings Bank of Perry
FPUT	NAS NMS	FlaPU	Florida Public Utilities Co
FQA	New York	Fuqua	Fuqua Industries Inc
FRA	New York	Farah	Farah Manufacturing Company Inc
FRBK	NAS SL	FairFst	Fairfield 1st Bank & Trust Co
FRC	American	FtRpBc	First Republic Bancorp Inc (California)
FRCM	NAS SL	Firecm	Firecom Inc
FRD	American	Friedm	Friedman Industries Inc
FRFD	NAS NMS	FCmB	First Community Bancorp Inc (Illinois)

TRADING SYMBOL	MARKET LISTING	NEWSPAPER ABBREV.	COMPANY NAME
FRK	American	FlaRck	Florida Rock Industries Inc
FRKT	NAS NMS	FlaRck	Florida Rock & Tank Lines Inc
FRM	New York	FtMiss	First Mississippi Corp
FRMG	NAS NMS	FtMiss	FirstMiss Gold Inc
FRML	NAS NMS	Freym	Freymiller Trucking Inc
FRMT	NAS NMS	Fremnt	Fremont General Corp
FRN	New York	Franc	The France Fund Inc
FRP	New York	FMRP	Freeport-McMoRan Resource Patners LP
FRS	American	Frischs	Frisch's Restaurants Inc
FRSH	NAS SL	FrJuce	Fresh Juice Company Inc
FRST	NAS NMS	Firster	FirsTier Inc
FRT	New York	FedRlty	Federal Realty Investment Trust
FRTH	NAS NMS	FrthFn	Fourth Financial Corp
FRTL	NAS SL	Fertil	Fertil-A-Chron Inc
FRTR	NAS NMS	FrtrIns	Frontier Insurance Group Inc
FRTX	NAS SL	FrntTx	Frontier Texas Corp
FRV	American	FurVlt	The Fur Vault Inc
FRX	American	ForstL	Forest Laboratories Inc
FSAK	NAS NL	FrnkSv	Franklin Savings Assn (Kansas)
FSAM	NAS NMS	FtAmSv	First American Savings FA (Pennsylvania)
FSATE	NAS SL	FutrSt	Futuresat Industries Inc
FSB	New York	FnSBar	Financial Corporation of Santa Barbara
FSBC	NAS NMS	FSNM	First Savings Bank FSB (New Mexico)
FSBG	NAS NMS	FFdGa	First Federal Savings Bank of Georgia
FSBK	NAS NMS	FtSvBk	First Service Bank for Savings (Massachusetts)
FSBX	NAS NMS	FramSv	Framingham Savings Bank (Massachusetts)
FSCB	NAS NMS	FCmBc	First Commercial Bancshares (Alabama)
FSCC	NAS NMS	FFdChl	First Federal Savings Bank of Charlotte County (Florida)
FSCNY	NAS NL	FreSCn	Free State Consolidated Gold Mines Ltd
FSCO	NAS NMS	FSecC	First Security Corp (Utah)
FSCR	NAS NMS	FdScrw	Federal Screw Works
FSEB	NAS NMS	FHomF	First Home Federal S&L Assn (Florida)
FSFC	NAS NMS	FSecF	First Security Financial Corp (North Carolina)
FSFI	NAS NMS	FtStFin	First State Financial Services Inc
FSHG	NAS NMS	FishSci	Fisher Scientific Group Inc
FSI	New York	FlghtSf	FlightSafety International Inc
FSKY	NAS NMS	FtScKy	First Security Corporation of Kentucky
FSLA	NAS NMS	FrnkSL	Franklin S&L Assn (Michigan)
FSM	American	Foodrm	Foodarama Supermarkets Inc
FSNR	NAS NMS	Forsch	The Forschner Group Inc
FSPG	NAS NMS	FtHmSv	First Home Savings Bank SLA (New Jersey)
FSS	New York	FdSgnl	Federal Signal Corp
FST	American	Frstm	Forstmann & Company Inc

TRADING SYMBOL	MARKET LISTING	NEWSPAPER ABBREV.	COMPANY NAME
FSTRA	NAS NMS	Foster	L.B. Foster Co (Class A)
FSVA	NAS NL	FidSvA	Fidelity Savings Assn
FSVP	NAS SL	Fnd SVP	Find SVP Inc
FTCO	NAS SL	FrnkTl	Franklin Telecommunications Corp
FTD	New York	FtDear	Fort Dearborn Income Securities Inc
FTEN	NAS NMS	FTenn	First Tennessee National Corp
FTIL	NAS NMS	FtIllCp	First Illinois Corp
FTK	New York	Filtrk	The Filtertek Companies
FTL	American	FruitL	Fruit of the Loom Inc
FTNC	NAS NMS	FNDela	First National Corp (Ohio)
FTR.B	New York	FruhfB	Fruehauf Corp (Class B)
FTSB	NAS NL	FtFdTn	First Federal Savings Bank of Tennessee
FTSC	NAS NMS	FtFdSC	First Federal S&L Assn of South Carolina
FTSI	NAS NMS	FishTrn	Fisher Transportation Services Inc
FTSP	NAS SL	FtTeam	First Team Sports Inc
FTTR	NAS NMS	Fretter	Fretter Inc
FTU	New York	FstUC	First Union Corp
FTX	New York	FrptMc	Freeport-McMoRan Inc
FUDD	NAS NMS	Fudrck	Fuddruckers Inc
FUEL	NAS NL	Grifith	Griffith Consumers Co
FUJIY	NAS NL	FujiPh	Fuji Photo Film Company Ltd
FULL	NAS NMS	FulrHB	H.B. Fuller Co
FULT	NAS NMS	Fulton	Fulton Financial Corp (Pennsylvania)
FUN	New York	CedrF	Cedar Fair LP
FUR	New York	FUnRl	First Union Real Estate Equity & Mortgage Investments
FURSA	NAS NMS	Antonv	Antonovich Inc (Class A)
FUTR	NAS SL	JckCarl	Jack Carl/312-Futures Inc
FVB	New York	FtVaBk	First Virginia Banks Inc
FVF	New York	Finvst	Finevest Foods Inc
FW	New York	FtWach	First Wachovia Corp
FWAT	NAS SL	Flexwat	Flexwatt Corp
FWB	New York	FtWisc	First Wisconsin Corp
FWC	New York	FostWh	Foster Wheeler Corp
FWCH	NAS NL	FtWrld	First World Cheese Inc
FWES	NAS NMS	FtWFn	First Western Financial Corp
FWF	New York	FarWst	Far West Financial Corp
FWNC	NAS NMS	FtWyne	Fort Wayne National Corp
FWNY	NAS NMS	FtWomn	The First Women's Bank (New York)
FWO	American	FWymB	First Wyoming Bancorporation
FYBR	NAS NL	CritclIn	Critical Industries Inc
G	New York	Greyh	The Greyhound Corp
GA	American	GnAuto	General Automation Inc
GAB	New York	Gabeli	The Gabelli Equity Trust Inc
GACC	NAS NMS	GAmCm	Great American Communications Co
GACO	NAS NMS	GardA	Garden America Corp

TRADING SYMBOL	MARKET LISTING	NEWSPAPER ABBREV.	COMPANY NAME
GAEO	NAS NMS	Galileo	Galileo Electro-Optics Corp
GAF	New York	GAF	GAF Corp
GAI	American	GrndAu	Grand Auto Inc
GAL	New York	Galoob	Lewis Galoob Toys Inc
GALAF	NAS SL	Galgph	Galagraph Ltd
GALCF	NAS NMS	Galac	Galactic Resources Ltd
GALX	NAS SL	GlxyCh	Galaxy Cheese Co
GAM	New York	GAInv	General American Investors Company Inc
GAMA	NAS NMS	GamaB	Gamma Biologicals Inc
GAMBY	NAS NL	Gambro	Gambro AB
GAMI	NAS NL	GtAMg	Great American Management & Investment Inc
GAN	American	Garan	Garan Inc
GANDF	NAS NMS	Gandlf	Gandalf Technologies Inc
GAP	New York	GtAtPc	The Great Atlantic & Pacific Tea Company Inc
GARD	NAS SL	Denning	Denning Mobile Robotics Inc
GARN	NAS NL	Garnet	Garnet Resources Corp
GAS	New York	NICOR	NICOR Inc
GATI	NAS NMS	GamT	Gaming & Technology Inc
GATS	NAS NMS	GlfApld	Gulf Applied Technologies Inc
GATW	NAS NMS	GatwyFd	Gateway Federal S&L Assn (Ohio)
GB	American	GrdnB	Guardian Bancorp
GBAN	NAS NMS	GtwBcp	Gateway Bancorp Inc (New York)
GBBS	NAS NMS	GrtBay	Great Bay Bankshares Inc
GBCB	NAS NMS	GBC Bc	GBC Bancorp
GBE	New York	GrubEl	Grubb & Ellis Co
GBFH	NAS NMS	GaBnd	Georgia Bonded Fibers Inc
GBII	NAS SL	GBI	GBI International Industries Inc
GBLD	NAS NMS	GBldPr	General Building Products Corp
GBLNF	NAS SL	Gldnbel	Goldenbell Resources Inc
GBNC	NAS NL	GuarBn	Guaranty Bancshares Corp
GBND	NAS NMS	GnBnd	General Binding Corp
GCA	New York	GCA	GCA Corp
GCBK	NAS NMS	GCtryB	Great Country Bank (Connecticut)
GCCC	NAS NMS	GnCpt	General Computer Corp
GCER	NAS NMS	GenCer	General Ceramics Inc
GCGC	NAS SL	GldCycl	Golden Cycle Gold Corp
GCI	New York	Gannett	Gannett Company Inc
GCN	New York	GCinm	General Cinema Corp
GCO	New York	Gensco	Genesco Inc
GCOR	NAS NMS	Gencor	Gencor Industries Inc
GCR	American	GaylC	Gaylord Container Corp
GCRA	NAS NMS	GldCorr	Golden Corral Realty Corp
GD	New York	GnDyn	General Dynamics Corp
GDC	New York	GdData	General DataComm Industries Inc
GDEX	NAS SL	GoldEx	Gold Express Corp
GDIC	NAS SL	GnDvcs	General Devices Inc

TRADING SYMBOL	MARKET LISTING	NEWSPAPER ABBREV.	COMPANY NAME
GDM	New York	Gldme	Goldome
GDMK	NAS NMS	Goodmk	GoodMark Foods Inc
GDS.B	American	Glnmr	Glenmore Distilleries Co (Class B)
GDV	New York	GenDev	General Development Corp
GDW	New York	GldWF	Golden West Financial Corp
GDX	American	GenvD	Genovese Drug Stores Inc
GDYN	NAS NMS	Geodyn	Geodynamics Corp
GE	New York	GenEl	General Electric Co
GEB	New York	GerbPd	Gerber Products Co
GEC	New York	GEICO	GEICO Corp
GECM	NAS NMS	Genicm	Genicom Corp
GED	New York	GnEngy	General Energy Development Ltd
GEF	New York	NichApl	Nicholas-Applegate Growth Equity Fund Inc
GEMC	NAS NMS	GeriMd	Geriatric & Medical Centers Inc
GEMS	NAS SL	ElctSpc	Electronic Specialty Products Inc
GEN	New York	GnRad	GenRad Inc
GENBB	NAS NL	GenesCp	Genesee Corp (Class B)
GENI	NAS NMS	GenetIn	Genetics Institute Inc
GENZ	NAS NMS	Genzym	Genzyme Corp
GEO	American	GeoRes	Geothermal Resources International Inc
GEOD	NAS NMS	GeodRs	Geodyne Resources Inc
GEOX	NAS NMS	Geonex	Geonex Corp
GER	New York	GerFd	The Germany Fund Inc
GES	American	Genisco	Genisco Technology Corp
GEST	NAS NMS	GuestS	Guest Supply Inc
GF	American	AmFGr	America First Guaranteed Income Fund
GFB	New York	GF Cp	GF Corp
GFC	New York	GibrFn	Gibraltar Financial Corp
GFCT	NAS NMS	GrnwcFn	Greenwich Financial Corp
GFD	New York	Gulfrd	Guilford Mills Inc
GFGC	NAS NMS	GtFalls	Great Falls Gas Co
GFI	American	GrhmFld	Graham Field Health Products Inc
GFS.A	American	GiantF	Giant Foods Inc (Class A)
GGC	New York	GaGulf	Georgia Gulf Corp
GGF	New York	GGInc	Global Growth & Income Fund Inc
GGG	New York	Graco	Graco Inc
GGUY	NAS NMS	GoodGy	The Good Guys Inc
GH	New York	GnHost	General Host Corp
GHM	American	Graham	Graham Corp
GHO	New York	GnHme	General Homes Corp
GHW	New York	GnHous	General Housewares Corp
GHX	New York	GalHou	Galveston-Houston Co
GIBG	NAS NMS	GibsnG	Gibson Greetings Inc
GIBS	American	GibCR	C.R. Gibson Co
GIDE	NAS SL	SprtGde	Sportsmans Guide Inc
GIGA	NAS NMS	GigaTr	Giga-tronics Inc
GII	American	Greiner	Greiner Engineering Inc

TRADING SYMBOL	MARKET LISTING	NEWSPAPER ABBREV.	COMPANY NAME
GILBA	NAS NMS	GilbtA	Gilbert Associates Inc (Class A)
GIS	New York	GnMills	General Mills Inc
GISH	NAS NMS	GishBi	Gish Biomedical Inc
GKCI	NAS SL	GoldK	Gold King Consolidated Inc
GKIE	NAS NL	GnKinet	General Kinetics Inc
GKRVF	NAS NL	GldKngt	Golden Knight Resources Inc
GKSRA	NAS NMS	G&K Sv	G&K Services Inc (Class A)
GLBC	NAS NMS	GtLkBc	Great Lakes Bancorp FSB (Michigan)
GLCN	NAS SL	GldCoin	Gold Coin Mining Inc
GLD	New York	Gould	Gould Inc
GLDC	NAS NMS	GoldEn	Golden Enterprises Inc
GLDFY	NAS NL	GoldFd	Gold Fields of South Africa Ltd
GLDR	NAS SL	GoldRs	Gold Reserve Corp
GLE	New York	GleasC	Gleason Corp
GLGVF	NAS NMS	Glamis	Glamis Gold Ltd
GLI	New York	GIncPl	Global Income Plus Fund Inc
GLK	New York	GrtLkC	Great Lakes Chemical Corp
GLM	New York	GlbM	Global Marine Inc
GLN	New York	Glenfed	GLENFED Inc
GLP	American	GuldLP	Gould Investors LP
GLT	American	Glatflt	P.H. Glatfelter Co
GLVBF	NAS SL	GalvRs	Galveston Resources Ltd
GLW	New York	CornGl	Corning Glass Works
GLX	New York	Glaxo	Glaxo Holdings plc
GLXIF	NAS NMS	Glenex	Glenex Industries Inc
GLYT	NAS NMS	Genlyte	Genlyte Group Inc
GM	New York	GMot	General Motors Corp
GMC	American	Gruen	Gruen Marketing Corp
GMCC	NAS NMS	GnMag	General Magnaplate Corp
GME	New York	GM E	General Motors Class E Common Stock
GMED	NAS NMS	GMI	The GMI Group Inc
GMFD	NAS NMS	GermF	Germania Bank FSB (Illinois)
GMGW	NAS NMS	Geraght	Geraghty & Miller Inc
GMH	New York	GM H	General Motors Class H Common Stock
GMHC	NAS SL	GrMonk	Grease Monkey Holding Corp
GMN	American	Grenm	Greenman Brothers Inc
GMP	New York	GMP	Green Mountain Power Corp
GMT	New York	GATX	GATX Corp
GMTIF	NAS SL	GemTc	Gemini Technology Inc
GMW	American	GnMicr	General Microwave Corp
GNA	American	Gainsco	Gainsco Inc
GNC	New York	GNC	General Nutrition Inc
GNDR	NAS NMS	Gander	Gander Mountain Inc
GNE	New York	Genetch	Genentech Inc
GNEX	NAS NMS	Genex	Genex Corp
GNG	New York	GldNug	Golden Nugget Inc
GNI	New York	GNIrn	Great Northern Iron Ore Properties
GNIC	NAS NMS	GuarNt	Guaranty National Corp

TRADING SYMBOL	MARKET LISTING	NEWSPAPER ABBREV.	COMPANY NAME
GNL	American	Gemco	GEMCO NATIONAL INC
GNN	New York	GtNNk	Great Northern Nekoosa Corp
GNOXF	NAS SL	GldNth	Golden North Resource Corp
GNR	American	GlobNR	Global Natural Resources Inc
GNT	New York	GrenTr	Green Tree Acceptance Inc
GNTE	NAS NMS	GranC	Granite Co-Operative Bank
GNTX	NAS NMS	Gentex	Gentex Corp
GO	American	Collins	Collins Industries Inc
GOC	American	GCda	Gulf Canada Corp
GOEDF	NAS NL	Geodme	Geodome Resources Ltd
GOI	New York	Gearht	Gearhart Industries Inc
GOOD	NAS NMS	Goody	Goody Products Inc
GOP	American	GrahMc	Graham-McCormick Oil & Gas Partnership
GOR	New York	GordnJ	Gordon Jewelry Corp
GOSHA	NAS NMS	OshA	Oshkosh B'Gosh Inc (Class A)
GOSHB	NAS NMS	OshB	Oshkosh B'Gosh Inc (Class B)
GOT	New York	Gotchk	Gottschalks Inc
GOTLF	NAS NMS	Gotaas	Gotaas-Larsen Shipping Corp
GOV	New York	GlbGvt	The Global Government Plus Fund Inc
GOVO	NAS SL	GoVide	Go Video Inc
GP	New York	GaPac	Georgia-Pacific Corp
GPAK	NAS NMS	GphPck	Graphic Packaging Corp
GPAR	NAS NMS	GnPara	General Parametrics Corp
GPAX	NAS SL	GrowVn	Grow Ventures Corp
GPC	New York	GenuP	Genuine Parts Co
GPI	New York	GrdPrd	Guardsman Products Inc
GPO	New York	GIANT	GIANT GROUP LTD
GPPXF	NAS NMS	GtBay	Giant Bay Resources Ltd
GPRO	NAS NMS	GenPrb	Gen-Probe Inc
GPS	New York	Gap	The Gap Inc
GPU	New York	GPU	General Public Utilities Corp
GQ	New York	Grumn	Grumman Corp
GR	New York	Gdrich	The B.F. Goodrich Co
GRA	New York	Grace	W.R. Grace & Co
GRAIN	NAS NMS	BkGrn	Bank of Granite Corp (North Carolina)
GRAR	NAS NMS	GtAmR	Great American Recreation Inc
GRB	New York	GerbSc	Gerber Scientific Inc
GRBC	NAS NMS	GtSoFd	Great Southern Federal Savings Bank
GRC	American	GorRup	The Gorman-Rupp Co
GRCO	NAS NMS	Gradco	Gradco Systems Inc
GRE	New York	GulfRs	Gulf Resources & Chemical Corp
GREY	NAS NMS	GreyAd	Grey Advertising Inc
GRFS	NAS NL	GrncsSv	Greencastle Federal Savings Bank
GRGI	NAS NMS	GrnRhb	Greenery Rehabilitation Group Inc
GRIF	NAS NMS	GrifTch	Griffin Technology Inc
GRIT	NAS NMS	GrubER	Grubb & Ellis Realty Income Trust
GRL	New York	GnInst	General Instrument Corp
GRN	New York	GenRe	General Re Corp

TRADING SYMBOL	MARKET LISTING	NEWSPAPER ABBREV.	COMPANY NAME
GRO	New York	GrowGp	Grow Group Inc
GROF	NAS NMS	Groff	Groff Industries Inc
GROS	NAS NMS	Grosmn	Grossman's Inc
GROV	NAS NMS	GroveB	GroveBank for Savings
GRPH	NAS NMS	GrphI	Graphic Industries Inc
GRPI	NAS NMS	GrnwPh	Greenwich Pharmaceuticals Inc
GRR	American	GRI	G·R·I Corp
GRST	NAS NMS	Grist	Grist Mill Co
GRT	American	GrTch	Graphic Technology Inc
GRTR	NAS NMS	GtNYSv	Greater New York Savings Bank
GRX	New York	GnRefr	General Refractories Co
GS	New York	Gillete	The Gillette Co
GSBI	NAS NMS	GrantSt	Granite State Bankshares Inc (New Hampshire)
GSBK	NAS NMS	GrmSv	Germantown Savings Bank (Pennsylvania)
GSC	American	GelmS	Gelman Sciences Inc
GSCC	NAS NMS	GrphSc	Graphic Scanning Corp
GSCX	NAS NL	GnSci	General Sciences Corp
GSF	New York	ACMSc	ACM Government Securities Fund Inc
GSO	New York	GthStk	Growth Stock Outlook Trust Inc
GSOF	NAS NMS	Group1	Group 1 Software Inc
GSSC	NAS NMS	GrndSu	Grenada Sunburst System Corp
GSTD	NAS SL	GldStd	Gold Standard Inc
GSU	New York	GlfStUt	Gulf States Utilities Co
GSX	New York	GnSignl	General Signal Corp
GT	New York	Goodyr	The Goodyear Tire & Rubber Co
GTA	New York	GtAFst	Great American Fist Savings Bank
GTAM	NAS NMS	GtAmCp	Great American Corp
GTCH	NAS NMS	Gtech	GTECH Corp
GTE	New York	GTE	GTE Corp
GTI	American	GTI	GTI Corp
GTOS	NAS NMS	Gantos	Gantos Inc
GTRO	NAS SL	GoldT	Golden Triangle Royalty & Oil Inc
GTSC	NAS NMS	GTS	GTS Corp
GTSW	NAS SL	GrntrSft	Greentree Software Inc
GTV	American	GalxCbl	Galaxy Cablevision LP
GTWY	NAS NMS	GatwB	Gateway Bank (Connecticut)
GTY	New York	Getty	Getty Petroleum Corp
GULD	NAS NMS	GouldP	Goulds Pumps Inc
GULL	NAS NL	GullLb	Gull Laboratories Inc
GUN	American	Gundle	Gundle Environmental Systems Inc
GV	American	GldFld	The Goldfield Corp
GVMF	NAS NMS	GldnVly	Golden Valley Microwave Foods Inc
GVMI	NAS NMS	GV Med	GV Medical Inc
GVT	New York	DWGI	Dean Witter Government Income Trust
GW	New York	GlfWst	Gulf + Western Inc
GWAY	NAS NMS	Gatway	Gateway Communications Inc
GWCC	NAS NMS	GWC	GWC Corp

TRADING SYMBOL	MARKET LISTING	NEWSPAPER ABBREV.	COMPANY NAME
GWF	New York	GtWFn	Great Western Financial Corp
GWI	American	GtWash	Greater Washington Investors Inc
GWOX	NAS SL	Goodht	Goodheart Willcox Inc
GWSH	NAS NMS	GeoWsh	George Washington Corp
GWT	American	GW Ut	GW Utilities Ltd
GWTI	NAS NMS	Grdwtr	Groundwater Technology Inc
GWW	New York	Graingr	W.W. Grainger Inc
GX	New York	GEO	GEO International Corp
GXL	American	Grang	Granges Exploration Ltd
GXMNF	NAS SL	Gordex	Gordex Minerals Ltd
GXY	American	GalaxC	Galaxy Carpet Mills Inc
GY	New York	GnCrp	GenCorp Inc
GYK	American	GntYl	Giant Yellowknife Mines Ltd
GYMS	NAS SL	Cnc 90	Concept 90 Marketing Inc
GYRO	NAS SL	Gyrody	Gyrodyne Company of America Inc
H	American	HelmR	HelmResources Inc
HA	American	HAL	HAL Inc
HABE	NAS NMS	Haber	Haber Inc
HACH	NAS NMS	Hach	Hach Co
HAD	New York	Hadson	Hadson Corp
HADR	NAS SL	Halsey	Halsey Drug Co
HAI	American	HamptI	Hampton Industries Inc
HAKO	NAS NMS	Hako	Hako Minuteman Inc
HAL	New York	Halbtn	Halliburton Co
HALL	NAS NMS	HallFn	Hall Financial Group Inc
HAML	NAS NMS	HamOil	Hamilton Oil Corp
HAMS	NAS NMS	Smthfld	The Smithfield Companies Inc
HAN	New York	Hanson	Hanson Trust PLC
HANA	NAS NMS	HanaBi	Hana Biologics Inc
HAR	New York	Harman	Harman International Industries Inc
HARC	NAS SL	Harcor	HarCor Energy Co
HARG	NAS NMS	HarpG	The Harper Group Inc
HARL	NAS NMS	HarlySv	Harleysville Savings Assn (Pennsylvania)
HART	NAS SL	Cardpul	Cardiopulmonary Technologies Inc
HARVY	NAS NMS	HrvdSc	Harvard Securities Group PLC
HAS	American	Hasbr	Hasbro Inc
HASR	NAS NMS	Hauser	Hauserman Inc
HAT	New York	HattSe	Hatteras Income Securities Inc
HATH	NAS NMS	Hathw	Hathaway Corp
HAVA	NAS NMS	HarvIn	Harvard Industries Inc
HAVT	NAS NMS	Havrty	Haverty Furniture Companies Inc
HAVTA	NAS NMS	HavFuA	Haverty Furniture Companies Inc (Class A)
HB	New York	Hillnbd	Hillenbrand Industries Inc
HBAN	NAS NMS	HuntgB	Huntington Bancshares Inc
HBE	American	Honybe	Honeybee Inc

TRADING SYMBOL	MARKET LISTING	NEWSPAPER ABBREV.	COMPANY NAME
HBENB	NAS NMS	HmBen	Home Beneficial Corp (Class B)
HBJ	New York	HarBrJ	Harcourt Brace Jovanovich Inc
HBOC	NAS NMS	HBO	HBO & Co
HBOL	NAS NMS	HrtfdS	Hartford Steam Boiler Inspection & Insurance Co
HBSI	NAS NMS	HampBn	Hamptons Bancshares Inc
HBW	American	WolfHB	Howard B. Wolf Inc
HC	New York	HelneC	Helene Curtis Industries Inc
HCA	New York	HCA	Hospital Care Corporation of America
HCCC	NAS NMS	HlthCo	HealthCare COMPARE Corp
HCCI	NAS NMS	HCC	HCC Industries Inc
HCH	American	HlthCh	Health-Chem Corp
HCN	American	HlthCr	Health Care REIT Inc
HCO	American	HUBCO	HUBCO Inc
HCP	New York	HlthCP	Health Care Property Investors Inc
HCSB	NAS NMS	HmeCty	Home & City Savings Bank (New York)
HCSG	NAS NMS	HlthCS	Healthcare Services Group Inc
HD	New York	HmeD	The Home Depot Inc
HDCO	NAS NMS	Hadco	HADCO Corp
HDGH	NAS SL	Hodgsn	Hodgson Houses Inc
HDI	New York	Harley	Harley-Davidson Inc
HDL	New York	Handlm	Handleman Co
HDR	American	Heldor	Heldor Industries Inc
HDRN	NAS SL	Hadron	Hadron Inc
HDRP	NAS NMS	HDR	HDR Power Systems Inc
HDS	New York	HillDp	Hills Department Stores Inc
HDYN	NAS NMS	Hlthdyn	Healthdyne Inc
HE	New York	HawEl	Hawaiian Electric Industries Inc
HEAL	NAS SL	Hlthwc	Healthwatch Inc
HECHA	NAS NMS	HchgA	Hechinger Co (Class A)
HECHB	NAS NMS	HchgB	Hechinger Co (Class B)
HEI	American	Heico	HEICO Corp
HEIC	NAS NMS	HEI Tx	HEI Corp (Texas)
HEII	NAS NMS	HEI Mn	HEI Inc (Minnesota)
HEKN	NAS NMS	Heekin	Heekin Can Inc
HELE	NAS NMS	HelenT	Helen of Troy Corp
HELX	NAS NMS	Helix	Helix Technology Corp
HEMA	NAS SL	HemaC	HemaCare Corp
HEMO	NAS NMS	Hemtec	HemoTec Inc
HENG	NAS NMS	Henley	The Henley Group Inc
HERB	NAS NL	Herblfe	Herbalife International Inc
HERS	NAS NMS	HrtFSv	Heritage Financial Services Inc
HESI	NAS NL	HuntEn	Hunter Environmental Services Inc
HEVN	NAS SL	HE Ven	HE Ventures Inc
HEX	New York	Hecks	Heck's Inc
HF	New York	HouFab	House of Fabrics Inc
HFD	New York	HmFSD	Home Federal S&L Assn (California)
HFED	NAS NMS	HeartF	Heart Federal S&L Assn (California)

TRADING SYMBOL	MARKET LISTING	NEWSPAPER ABBREV.	COMPANY NAME
HFET	NAS NMS	HmFTn	Home Federal S&L Assn of Upper East Tennessee
HFF	New York	HollyFa	Holly Farms Corp
HFGA	NAS NMS	HFdGa	Home Federal Savings Bank of Georgia
HFHC	NAS NL	HeritFn	Heritage Financial Corp
HFI	American	HudFd	Hudson Foods Inc
HFIN	NAS NMS	HrznFn	Horizon Financial Services Inc
HFL	New York	HmstF	Homestead Financial Corp
HFL.B	New York	HmFB	Homestead Financial Corp (Class B)
HFLM	NAS SL	HydFlm	Hydro Flame Corp
HFMD	NAS NMS	HFMd	Home Federal Corp (Maryland)
HFNO	NAS NMS	HmFNO	Home Federal Savings Bank, Northern Ohio
HFOX	NAS NMS	HmFXn	Home Federal Savings Bank (Ohio)
HFSA	NAS NL	HFdNC	Home Federal Savings Bank (North Carolina)
HFSB	NAS NL	HmFChr	Home Federal Savings Bank (South Carolina)
HFSF	NAS NMS	HmFSF	Home Federal S&L Assn of San Francisco
HGC	American	HudGn	Hudson General Corp
HGCD	NAS SL	MagnCd	MagnaCard Inc
HGIC	NAS NMS	Harleys	Harleysville Group Inc
HH	American	HoopHl	Hooper Homes Inc
HHBX	NAS NMS	HHB Sy	HHB Systems Inc
HHC	New York	HrzHlt	Horizon Healthcare Corp
HHGP	NAS NMS	HarisHa	Harris & Harris Group Inc
HHH	American	HeritEn	Heritage Entertainment Inc
HHI	American	HampH	Hampton Healthcare Inc
HHOT	NAS NMS	HHOilT	H&H Oil Tool Company Inc
HI	New York	HousInt	Household International Inc
HIA	New York	Holidy	Holiday Corp
HIBCA	NAS NMS	Hiber	Hibernia Corp (Class A)
HIGB	NAS NMS	Higbys	J. Higby's Inc
HIGH	NAS NMS	HighSu	Highland Superstores Inc
HII.A	American	HlI	Healthcare International Inc (Class A)
HIMG	NAS NMS	HltImg	Health Images Inc
HINE	NAS NL	HneLu	Edward Hines Lumber Co
HIP	American	Hiptron	Hipotronics Inc
HIPC	NAS NL	HiPlain	High Plains Corp
HIPT	NAS NMS	Hi-Prt	Hi-Port Industries Inc
HIRE	NAS SL	DivHum	Diversified Human Resources Group Inc
HIRS	NAS SL	HghRes	High Resolution Sciences Inc
HIT	New York	Hitachi	Hitachi Ltd
HITK	NAS NMS	HITK	HITK Corp
HIVT	NAS NMS	HlthIns	Health Insurance of Vermont Inc
HIWDF	NAS NMS	Highwd	Highwood Resources Ltd
HKF	New York	HanFb	Hancock Fabrics Inc
HKME	NAS SL	KeithGp	The Keith Group of Companies Inc

TRADING SYMBOL	MARKET LISTING	NEWSPAPER ABBREV.	COMPANY NAME
HL	New York	HeclaM	Hecla Mining Co
HLCO	NAS NMS	Hlthco	Healthco International Inc
HLME	NAS NMS	HolmD	D.H. Holmes Company Ltd
HLT	New York	Hilton	Hilton Hotels Corp
HM	New York	Hmstke	Homestake Mining Co
HMA	American	HlthMn	Health Management Associates Inc
HMC	New York	Honda	Honda Motor Company Ltd
HMDY	NAS SL	Hemody	Hemodynamics Inc
HME	New York	HmeGp	The Home Group Inc
HMF	American	Hasting	Hastings Manufacturing Co
HMG	American	HMG	HMG Property Investors Inc
HMI	American	HelthM	Health-Mor Inc
HMOA	NAS NMS	HMO	HMO American Inc
HMSB	NAS NMS	HmeSav	The Home Savings Bank (New York)
HMSD	NAS NMS	HmstdS	Homestead Savings Assn (Pennsylvania)
HMSS	NAS NMS	HMSS	H.M.S.S. Inc
HMT	New York	Himont	HIMONT Inc
HMX	New York	Hartmx	Hartmarx Corp
HMY	New York	Heilig	Heilig-Meyers Co
HNBC	NAS NMS	HarlyNt	Harleysville National Corp
HNCO	NAS NMS	HenlMf	Henley Manufacturing Corp
HNCP	NAS NL	HmNtl	Home National Corp
HND	American	Hindrl	Hinderliter Industries Inc
HNGI	NAS NL	HospNw	Hospital Newspapers Group Inc
HNIS	NAS NMS	HrtgBc	Heritage Bancorp Inc (Massachusetts)
HNM	New York	Hanna	M.A. Hanna Co
HNH	New York	HandH	Handy & Harman
HNW	American	HeinWr	Hein-Werner Corp
HNZ	New York	Heinz	H.J. Heinz Co
HO	American	HouOT	Houston Oil Trust
HOBC	NAS NMS	HwrdB	Howard Bancorp
HOC	American	HollyCp	Holly Corp
HOF	American	Hofman	Hofmann Industries Inc
HOGI	NAS NMS	Harken	Harken Oil & Gas Inc
HOGN	NAS NMS	Hogan	Hogan Systems Inc
HOL.A	American	Holco	Holco Mortgage Acceptance Corp.-1 (Class A)
HOME	NAS NMS	IntAm	International American Homes Inc
HOMF	NAS NMS	HFdInd	Home Federal Savings Bank (Indiana)
HOMG	NAS NL	HmowG	Homeowners Group Inc
HON	New York	Honwell	Honeywell Inc
HONI	NAS NMS	HonInd	HON INDUSTRIES Inc
HOR	American	HrnHar	The Horn & Hardart Co
HORL	NAS NMS	HORL	Home Office Reference Laboratory Inc
HOSP	NAS NMS	Hospos	Hosposable Products Inc
HOSS	NAS SL	Hornbk	Hornbeck Offshore Services Inc
HOST	NAS SL	AmerPr	Amerihost Properties Inc
HOT	New York	HotlInv	Hotel Investors Trust/Corporation

TRADING SYMBOL	MARKET LISTING	NEWSPAPER ABBREV.	COMPANY NAME
HOU	New York	HouInd	Houston Industries Inc
HOV	American	HovnE	Hovnanian Enterprises Inc
HOW	American	HowlIn	Howell Industries Inc
HP	New York	HelmP	Helmerich & Payne Inc
HPBC	NAS NMS	HmPrt	Home Port Bancorp Inc
HPC	New York	Herculs	Hercules Inc
HPH	New York	Harnish	Harnischfeger Industries Inc
HPSC	NAS NMS	HPSC	HPSC Inc
HQH	New York	HQ Hlt	H&Q Healthcare Investors
HRA	American	Harvey	The Harvey Group Inc
HRB	New York	BlkHR	H&R Block Inc
HRCLY	NAS NMS	HntgnIn	Huntingdon International Holdings plc
HRD	New York	Hanfrd	Hannaford Brothers Co
HRDG	NAS NMS	HrdgAs	Harding Associates Inc
HRE	New York	HRE	HRE Properties
HRHC	NAS NMS	HilbRg	Hilb Rogal & Hamilton Co
HRI	American	HoweRh	Howe Richardson Inc
HRIGV	NAS NMS	HRI Gp	HRI Group Inc
HRIZ	NAS SL	HrzGld	Horizon Gold Shares Inc
HRK	American	HrdRk	Hard Rock Cafe plc
HRL	American	Hormel	George A. Hormel & Co
HRLD	NAS NMS	Harold	Harold's Stores Inc
HRLN	NAS NMS	Harlyn	Harlyn Products Inc
HRLY	NAS NMS	Herley	Herley Microwave Systems Inc
HRMN	NAS NMS	Harmon	Harmon Industries Inc
HRMR	NAS NMS	HuntMl	Hunter-Melnor Inc
HROK	NAS NMS	HmFRk	Home Federal S&L Assn of the Rockies
HRP	New York	HltRhb	Health & Rehabilitation Properties Trust
HRS	New York	Harris	Harris Corp
HRTI	NAS SL	HartInd	Hart Industries Inc
HRZB	NAS NMS	HrzBk	Horizon Bank, A Savings Bank (Washington)
HRZN	NAS NMS	HorzInd	Horizon Industries Inc
HS	New York	HoprSol	Hopper Soliday Corp
HSAI	NAS NMS	HltcrS	Healthcare Services of America Inc
HSBK	NAS NMS	HiberSv	The Hibernia Savings Bank (Massachusetts)
HSC	New York	Harsco	Harsco Corp
HSDMF	NAS SL	HemDv	Hemisphere Development Ltd
HSI	New York	HiShear	Hi-Shear Industries Inc
HSLD	NAS NMS	HomeSL	Home S&L Assn Inc (North Carolina)
HSN	American	HomeSh	Home Shopping Network Inc
HSO	American	HershO	Hershey Oil Corp
HSPA	NAS NMS	HmSvPa	Home Savings Assn of Pennsylvania
HSRC	NAS NMS	HltsthR	HEALTHSOUTH Rehabilitation Corp
HSSI	NAS NMS	HospSt	Hospital Staffing Services Inc
HSVLY	NAS NL	Highvld	Highveld Steel & Vanadium Corp Ltd

TRADING SYMBOL	MARKET LISTING	NEWSPAPER ABBREV.	COMPANY NAME
HSY	New York	Hrshey	Hershey Foods Corp
HTCH	NAS NMS	HutchT	Hutchinson Technology Inc
HTEK	NAS NMS	HytekM	Hytek Microsystems Inc
HTG.A	American	HtgMd	Heritage Media Corp (Class A)
HTK	American	Howtk	Howtek Inc
HTLD	NAS NMS	Hrtlnd	Heartland Express Inc
HTN	New York	HougM	Houghton Mifflin Co
HTRFZ	NAS NL	HlwdPk	Hollywood Park Realty Enterprises Inc
HTWN	NAS SL	HmtwBc	Hometown Bancorporation
HU	American	HmpU	Hampton Utilities Trust
HUB.A	American	HubelA	Hubbell Inc (Class A)
HUB.B	American	HubelB	Hubbell Inc (Class B)
HUF	New York	Huffy	Huffy Corp
HUFK	NAS NMS	HufKoo	Huffman Koos Inc
HUG	New York	HughSp	Hughes Supply Inc
HUHO	NAS NMS	HghHm	Hughes Homes Inc
HUM	New York	Human	Humana Inc
HUN	New York	HuntM	Hunt Manufacturing Co
HURC	NAS NMS	Hurco	Hurco Companies Inc
HUSB	NAS NMS	HUSB	Home Unity S&L Assn (Pennsylvania)
HVDK	NAS NMS	HarvKn	Harvard Knitwear Inc
HVT	American	Hltvst	HealthVest
HWCD	NAS NMS	HWC	HWC Distribution Corp
HWG	New York	Halwood	The Hallwood Group Inc
HWKB	NAS NMS	HawkB	Hawkeye Bancorporation (Class B)
HWKC	NAS NMS	HawkC	Hawkeye Bancorporation (Class C)
HWL	New York	HowlCp	Howell Corp
HWNC	NAS NL	HaywdS	Haywood S&L Assn
HWP	New York	HewlPk	Hewlett-Packard Co
HWRD	NAS NMS	HBNJ	The Howard Savings Bank (New Jersey)
HX	American	Halifax	Halifax Engineering Inc
HXL	New York	Hexcel	Hexcel Corp
HYBD	NAS SL	Hycor	Hycor Biomedical Inc
HYDE	NAS NMS	HydeAt	Hyde Athletic Industries Inc
HYI	New York	HiYld	The High Yield Income Fund Inc
HYP	New York	HiYldPl	High Yield Plus Fund Inc
HYPX	NAS NMS	Hyponx	Hyponex Corp
HZN	New York	Horizon	Horizon Corp
I	New York	FIntste	First Interstate Bancorp
IACI	NAS NMS	InAcous	Industrial Acoustics Company Inc
IAD	New York	InldStl	Inland Steel Industries Inc
IAF	American	FtAust	The First Australia Fund Inc
IAIR	NAS SL	IndepAir	Independent Air Holdings Inc
IAL	New York	IntAlu	International Aluminum Corp
IBAN	NAS NMS	ImprBc	Imperial Bancorp
IBC	New York	IntBkr	Interstate Bakeries Corp
IBCA	NAS NMS	InBcst	International Broadcasting Corp

TRADING SYMBOL	MARKET LISTING	NEWSPAPER ABBREV.	COMPANY NAME
IBCC	NAS SL	IntlBus	Intelligent Business Communications Corp
IBCP	NAS NMS	IndBkMi	Independent Bank Corp (Michigan)
IBF	American	FtIber	First Iberian Fund
IBGI	NAS NL	IndBkgp	Independent BankGroup Inc
IBISA	NAS NMS	IBI	IBI Security Service Inc (Class A)
IBK	American	IntBknt	International Banknote Company Inc
IBL	American	IroqBrd	Iroquois Brands Ltd
IBM	New York	IBM	International Business Machines Corp
IBP	New York	IBP	IBP inc
IBSI	NAS NMS	IndBnc	Independent Bancshares Inc (Texas)
IBSTF	NAS SL	IBS	IBS Technologies Ltd
ICA	New York	ICA	Imperial Corporation of America
ICAR	NAS NL	Intcar	Intercargo Corp
ICB	New York	ItcpSe	InterCapital Income Securities Inc
ICBI	NAS SL	IntCon	International Consumer Brands Inc
ICCC	NAS SL	Imucel	Immucell Corp
ICE	American	AAlska	Arctic Alaska Fisheries Corp
ICEYF	NAS NMS	InCapE	International Capital Equipment Ltd
ICG	American	IntCty	Inter-City Gas Corp
ICGI	NAS NL	IntgCpt	Integrated Computer Graphics Inc
ICGN	NAS SL	IntCogn	International Congeneration Corp
ICH	American	ICH	I.C.H. Corp
ICI	New York	ImpCh	Imperial Chemical Industries PLC
ICM	New York	ICM	ICM Property Investors Inc
ICN	New York	ICN Ph	ICN Pharmaceuticals Inc
ICNT	NAS SL	INCMNT	INCOMNET Inc
ICOT	NAS NMS	Icot	ICOT Corp
ICPYY	NAS NMS	ICP	The Institute of Clinical Pharmacology PLC
ICSI	NAS NMS	IntCnt	International Container Systems Inc
ICTI	NAS SL	IntrCel	Interstate Cellular Telecommunications Inc
ICTM	NAS NMS	ItgCirc	Integrated Circuits Inc
ICX	New York	IC Ind	IC Industries Inc
ICY	American	ICEE	ICEE-USA
IDA	New York	IdahoP	Idaho Power Co
IDBBY	NAS NL	IDB	IDB Bankholding Corporation Ltd
IDBX	NAS NMS	IDB Cm	IDB Communications Group Inc
IDCC	NAS SL	Intek	Intek Diversified Corp
IDEA	NAS NMS	InvtDsg	Invention Design Engineering Associates Inc
IDGI	NAS SL	IntDsg	International Design Group Inc
IDL	New York	IdealB	Ideal Basic Industries Inc
IDTI	NAS NMS	IntgDv	Integrated Device Technology Inc
IDXX	NAS SL	Identx	Identix Inc
IEC	American	PEC Isr	PEC Israel Economic Corp
IECE	NAS NMS	IEC	IEC Electronics Corp

TRADING SYMBOL	MARKET LISTING	NEWSPAPER ABBREV.	COMPANY NAME
IEHC	NAS NMS	IndEl	Industrial Electronic Hardware Corp
IEI	New York	IndiEn	Indiana Energy Inc
IEIB	NAS SL	IntlEl	International Electronics Inc
IEL	New York	IE Ind	IE Industries Inc
IFED	NAS NMS	IntrFd	InterFederal Savings Bank (Tennessee)
IFEI	NAS SL	ImgFlm	Imagine Films Entertainment Inc
IFF	New York	IntFlav	International Flavors & Fragrances Inc
IFG	New York	IntRFn	Inter-Regional Financial Group Inc
IFGN	NAS SL	InFGne	InFerGene Co
IFII	NAS NMS	IndnaF	Indiana Financial Investors Inc
IFL	New York	IMC F	IMC Fertilizer Group Inc
IFMX	NAS NMS	Infrmx	Informix Corp
IFND	NAS SL	Intrfd	Interfund Corp
IFRA	NAS SL	Infrsnc	Infrasonics Inc
IFRS	NAS NMS	IFR	IFR Systems Inc
IFSB	NAS NMS	IndFdl	Independence Federal Savings Bank (Washington D.C.)
IFSC	NAS SL	Interfrn	Interferon Sciences Inc
IFSIA	NAS NMS	IntrfcI	Interface Inc (Class A)
IFSL	NAS NMS	IndiFdl	Indiana Federal S&L Assn
IG	American	IGI	IGI Inc
IGAM	NAS NMS	IGame	International Game Technology
IGC	American	IGC	Interstate General Company LP
IGEI	NAS NMS	IntGen	International Genetic Engineering Inc
IGF	New York	India	India Growth Fund
IGII	NAS SL	IntmkG	Intermark Gaming International Inc
IGL	New York	IntMin	International Minerals & Chemical Corp
IGLSF	NAS NMS	Instgp	Insituform Group Ltd
IGNE	NAS SL	IGENE	IGENE Biotechnology Inc
IGSI	NAS NMS	InsitGlf	Insituform Gulf South Inc
IHBI	NAS NMS	IndHBk	Indian Head Banks Inc (New Hampshire)
IHEIF	NAS NMS	Inthm	Interhome Energy Inc
IHKSV	NAS NMS	ImpHly	Imperial Holly Corp
IHS	New York	IpcoCp	IPCO Corp
IICR	NAS NL	IsrlInv	Israel Investors Corp
III	American	Insteel	Insteel Industries Inc
IINT	NAS NMS	InfoIntl	Information International Inc
IIP	American	IIP	International Income Property Inc
IIS	New York	INAIn	INA Investment Securities Inc
IISLF	NAS NMS	IIS	I.I.S. Intelligent Information Systems Ltd
IIVI	NAS NMS	II-VI	II-VI Inc
IK	New York	Intrlke	Interlake Corp
ILCO	NAS NL	IntLfe	Intercontinental Life Corp
ILCT	NAS NMS	ILC	ILC Technology Inc
ILFC	NAS NMS	IntLse	International Lease Finance Corp
IMAG	NAS SL	ImagRtl	Image Retailing Group Inc
IMAR	NAS NL	Imark	Imark Industries Inc

TRADING SYMBOL	MARKET LISTING	NEWSPAPER ABBREV.	COMPANY NAME
IMAT	NAS NMS	Imatrn	Imatron Inc
IMC	New York	IntMult	International Multifoods Corp
IMD	New York	ImoDv	Imo Delaval Inc
IMDC	NAS SL	Inamed	Inamed Corp
IMET	NAS NMS	Intrmtr	Intermetrics Inc
IMI	American	Intrmk	Intermark Inc
IMIT	NAS SL	IMT	IMT Inc
IMKTA	NAS NMS	InglMkt	Ingles Markets Inc (Class A)
IMMC	NAS NMS	InMobil	International Mobile Machines Corp
IMMU	NAS NMS	Imunmd	Immunomedics Inc
IMNO	NAS SL	ImTher	Imuno Therapeutic Inc
IMNX	NAS NMS	Imunex	Immunex Corp
IMO.A	American	ImpOil	Imperial Oil Ltd (Class A)
IMPX	NAS NMS	IMP	International Microelectronics Products Inc
IMRC	NAS SL	IntMgR	International Management & Research Corp
IMRE	NAS SL	Imre	Imre Corp
IMRGA	NAS NMS	Imreg	Imreg Inc (Class A)
IMSF	NAS SL	InMcSf	International Microcomputer Software Inc
INAC	NAS NMS	Inacmp	Inacomp Computer Centers Inc
INAI	NAS NMS	Intelli	Intellicorp
INAT	NAS NMS	IndiNt	Indiana National Corp
INBA	NAS NL	InBanc	InBancshares
INBC	NAS NMS	IndBc	Independence Bancorp Inc (Pennsylvania)
INBK	NAS NL	IndiBn	Indiana Bancshares Inc
INBS	NAS NMS	IowaNtl	Iowa National Bankshares Corp
INCL	NAS NMS	Intelcal	Intellicall Inc
INCRF	NAS NMS	IncaRs	Inca Resources Inc
INDB	NAS NMS	IndBC	Independent Bank Corp (Massachusetts)
INDHK	NAS NMS	IndInsr	Independent Insurance Group Inc
INDI	NAS SL	Indepth	Indepth Data Inc
INDQA	NAS NMS	InDairA	International Dairy Queen Inc (Class A)
INDQB	NAS NMS	InDairB	International Dairy Queen Inc (Class B)
INDR	NAS NMS	IndRes	Industrial Resources Inc
INDX	NAS NMS	IndxTc	Index Technology Corp
INEC	NAS SL	Indtch	Indtech Corp
INEI	NAS NMS	InsitE	Insituform East Inc
INEL	NAS NMS	IntelEl	Intelligent Electronics Inc
INET	NAS NL	InstCp	Instinet Corp
INFD	NAS NMS	Infodat	Infodata System Inc
INFG	NAS NL	InfGrph	Infinite Graphics Inc
INFN	NAS NMS	Inftrn	Infotron Systems Corp
INGC	NAS SL	IntNtr	International Nutrition & Genetics Corp
INGN	NAS NMS	IntgGen	Integrated Genetics Inc
INGR	NAS NMS	Intgph	Intergraph Corp
INLF	NAS SL	InvLfKy	Investors Heritage Life Insurance of Ky

TRADING SYMBOL	MARKET LISTING	NEWSPAPER ABBREV.	COMPANY NAME
INMA	NAS NMS	Intrmgn	Intermagnetics General Corp
INMC	NAS NMS	Inmac	Inmac Corp
INMT	NAS NMS	IntmetC	Intermet Corp
INNS	NAS SL	Krisch	Krisch American Inns Inc
INP	American	IntlgSy	Intelligent Systems Master LP
INPH	NAS NMS	Intphse	Interphase Corp
INR	New York	Insilco	Insilco Corp
INRD	NAS NMS	Inrad	INRAD Inc
INS	American	IntSeaw	International Seaway Trading Corp
INSH	NAS NMS	IntShip	International Shipholding Corp
INSI	NAS NMS	InfoSc	Information Science Inc
INSMA	NAS NMS	InsitMd	Insituform Mid-America Inc (Class A)
INSP	NAS NMS	Inspch	InSpeech Inc
INSUA	NAS NMS	Instfr	Insituform of North America Inc (Class A)
INSY	NAS NMS	IntrmSy	Interim Systems Corp
INT	American	IntRec	International Recovery Corp
INTC	NAS NMS	Intel	Intel Corp
INTE	NAS NMS	Intech	Intech Inc
INTF	NAS NMS	Interfc	Interface Systems Inc
INTG	NAS NMS	Intgrp	Intergroup Corp
INTLA	NAS NMS	IntrTel	Inter-Tel Inc (Class A)
INTO	NAS NMS	Initio	Initio Inc
INTR	NAS NMS	Intmec	INTERMEC Corp
INTV	NAS NL	Intvce	InterVoice Inc
INTX	NAS NMS	US Intc	U.S. Intec Inc
INVG	NAS NMS	INVG	INVG Mortgage Securities Corp
INVN	NAS NMS	Invtrn	Invitron Corp
INVS	NAS NMS	InvSav	Investors Savings Corp (Minnesota)
INVX	NAS NMS	Innovex	Innovex Inc
IOLS	NAS SL	VsnTch	Vision Technologies International Inc
IOMG	NAS NMS	Iomega	Iomega Corp
IOMT	NAS NL	Isomet	Isomet Corp
ION	American	Ionics	Ionics Inc
IOR	New York	IowaRs	Iowa Resources Inc
IP	New York	IntPap	International Paper Co
IPC	New York	IllPowr	Illinois Power Co
IPG	New York	IntpbG	The Interpublic Group of Companies Inc
IPL	New York	Ipalco	IPALCO Enterprises Inc
IPLLF	NAS NL	Intphrm	InterPharm Laboratories Ltd
IPLSA	NAS NMS	IPL Sy	IPL Systems Inc (Class A)
IPM	American	IPM	IPM Technology Inc
IPS	American	AmIPrp	American Income Properties LP
IPT	New York	IPTim	IP Timberlands Ltd
IPW	New York	InstPw	Interstate Power Co
IR	New York	IngerR	Ingersoll-Rand Co
IRAFV	NAS NL	CoronaA	Corona Corp (Class A)
IRBFV	NAS NL	CoronaB	Corona Corp (Class B)

TRADING SYMBOL	MARKET LISTING	NEWSPAPER ABBREV.	COMPANY NAME
IRC	New York	InspRs	Inspiration Resources Corp
IRDV	NAS NMS	IntResh	International Research & Development Corp
IRE	New York	IntgRsc	Integrated Resources Inc
IRF	New York	IntRect	International Rectifier Corp
IRIC	NAS NMS	InfoRs	Information Resources Inc
IRIS	NAS NMS	IRIS	International Remote Imaging Systems Inc
IRON	NAS SL	Ironstn	Ironstone Group Inc
IRSN	NAS SL	Irvine	Irvine Sensors
IRT	New York	IRT	IRT Property Co
IRTR	NAS SL	IRT Rlt	IRT Realty Services Inc
IRWN	NAS NMS	IrwnMg	Irwin Magnetic Systems Inc
IS	New York	IntSec	Interstate Securities Inc
ISBJ	NAS NMS	IntrFn	Interchange Financial Services Corp (New Jersey)
ISCS	NAS NMS	ISC	ISC Systems Corp
ISEC	NAS NMS	InstfrS	Insituform Southeast Corp
ISI	American	ISS	ISS-International Service Systems Inc
ISIS	NAS NL	IndSqS	Independence Square Income Securities Inc
ISKO	NAS NMS	Isco	Isco Inc
ISLA	NAS NMS	InvstSL	Investors Savings Bank (Virginia)
ISLH	NAS NMS	IntHld	International Holding Capital Corp
ISMX	NAS NMS	Isomdx	Isomedix Inc
ISN	American	Instron	Instron Corp
ISPC	NAS NMS	Intspec	Interspec Inc
ISR	American	Incstar	Incstar Corp
ISRL	NAS SL	Isramc	Isramco Inc
ISS	New York	Interco	INTERCO INCORPORATED
ISTC	NAS SL	Instvsn	Instructivision Inc
ISTEF	NAS SL	IstecIn	Istec Industry & Technology Ltd
ISY	American	InstSy	Instrument Systems Corp
IT	New York	Intlog	Interlogic Trace Inc
ITA	New York	Italy	The Italy Fund Inc
ITAN	NAS NMS	Inttan	InterTAN Inc
ITB	American	IntThr	International Thoroughbred Breeders Inc
ITC	New York	IngrTec	Ingredient Technology Corp
ITCC	NAS NMS	IndTrn	Industrial Training Corp
ITCH	NAS NMS	Infotch	Infotechnology Inc
ITCM	NAS SL	Intrcim	Intercim Corp
ITELO	NAS NMS	Itel	Itel Corp
ITERF	NAS SL	Instat	Interstrat Resources Inc
ITGN	NAS NMS	Integon	Integon Corp
ITI	American	IntTch	International Telecharge Inc
ITIC	NAS NMS	InvTitl	Investors Title Co
ITIN	NAS SL	InvTr	Investors Trust Inc
ITM	New York	Intmed	Intermedics Inc

TRADING SYMBOL	MARKET LISTING	NEWSPAPER ABBREV.	COMPANY NAME
ITRN	NAS NMS	Intrtrn	Intertrans Corp
ITSI	NAS NMS	IntTotlz	International Totalizator Systems Inc
ITT	New York	ITT Cp	ITT Corp
ITW	New York	ITW	Illinois Tool Works Inc
ITX	New York	IT Crp	International Technology Corp
ITXI	NAS NMS	InactTc	Interactive Technologies Inc
IU	New York	IU Int	IU International Corp
IUCO	NAS SL	IrwnUn	Irwin Union Corp
IUTL	NAS NMS	IowaSo	Iowa Southern Utilities Co
IVCR	NAS NMS	Invcr	Invacare Corp
IVES	NAS SL	InvTech	Investment Technologies Inc
IVT.A	American	Iverson	Iverson Technology Corp (Class A)
IVX	American	IvaxCp	IVAX Corp
IWCR	NAS NMS	IWC	IWC Resources Corp
IWG	New York	IowIlG	Iowa-Illinois Gas & Electric Co
IX	American	IRT Cp	IRT Corp
IYCOY	NAS NMS	ItoYokd	Ito-Yokado Company Ltd
JAC	American	JohnAm	Johnstown American Co
JACK	New York	Jackpot	Jackpot Enterprises Inc
JACO	NAS NMS	JacoEl	Jaco Electronics Inc
JAGRY	NAS NMS	Jaguar	Jaguar plc
JAIL	NAS NMS	Adtec	Adtec Inc
JALC	NAS NMS	JAdams	John Adams Life Corp
JAPNY	NAS SL	JapnAir	Japan Air Lines Company Ltd
JASN	NAS NMS	Jason	Jason Inc
JAYA	NAS SL	Jayark	Jayark Corp
JAYT	NAS NMS	JayJacb	Jay Jacobs Inc
JBAK	NAS NMS	BakrJ	J. Baker Inc
JBBB	NAS NMS	JBRst	JB's Restaurants Inc
JBHT	NAS NMS	HuntJB	J.B. Hunt Transportation Services Inc
JBM	American	JanBel	Jan Bell Marketing Inc
JBNC	NAS NL	JeffBcp	Jefferson Bancorp Inc (Florida)
JBNK	NAS NMS	JefBsh	Jefferson Bankshares Inc (Virginia)
JC	New York	Jwlcr	Jewelcor Inc
JCBS	NAS NMS	Jacbsn	Jacobson Stores Inc
JCI	New York	JhnCn	Johnson Controls Inc
JCOR	NAS NMS	Jacor	Jacor Communications Inc
JCP	New York	Penney	J.C. Penney Company Inc
JCT	New York	JhnCRt	Johnstown/Consolidated Realty Trust
JEAN	NAS SL	PhilpJ	Jean Philippe Fragrances Inc
JEC	American	Jacobs	Jacobs Engineering Group Inc
JEFG	NAS NMS	JeffrGp	Jefferies Group Inc
JEM	American	Jwlmst	Jewelmasters Inc
JENN	NAS SL	JenfCv	Jennifer Convertibles Inc
JEP	New York	Jepson	Jepson Corp
JERR	NAS NMS	Jerico	Jerrico Inc
JET	American	Jetron	Jetronic Industries Inc

TRADING SYMBOL	MARKET LISTING	NEWSPAPER ABBREV.	COMPANY NAME
JETS	NAS NMS	Jetbrne	Jetborne International Inc
JFFN	NAS NL	JeffBk	Jefferson Bank (Pennsylvania)
JGIN	NAS NMS	JG Ind	JG Industries Inc
JGRP	NAS NMS	Jesup	Jesup Group Inc
JH	New York	Harlnd	The John H. Harland Co
JHI	New York	HanJI	John Hancock Investors Trust
JHS	New York	HanJS	John Hancock Income Securities Trust
JHSL	NAS NMS	JHansn	John Hanson Savings Bank FSB
JHSN	NAS NMS	JhnsnE	Johnson Electronics Inc
JIB	New York	Foodmk	Foodmaker Inc
JII	New York	JohnInd	Johnston Industries Inc
JJS	American	JumpJk	Jumping-Jack Shoes Inc
JJSC	NAS NMS	JefSmf	Jefferson Smurfit Corp
JJSF	NAS NMS	J&J Sn	J&J Snack Foods Corp
JKHY	NAS NMS	HnryJk	Jack Henry & Associates Inc
JKPT	NAS SL	MillsJn	Mills-Jennings Co
JLGI	NAS NMS	JLG	JLG Industries Inc
JLN	American	Jaclyn	Jaclyn Inc
JLUB	NAS NMS	JifyLub	Jiffy Lube International Inc
JMED	NAS NMS	JneMed	Jones Medical Industries Inc
JML	American	JMadsn	James Madison Ltd
JMP	American	Peters	J.M. Peters Company Inc
JMY	New York	Jamsw	Jamesway Corp
JNBK	NAS NMS	JeffNt	Jefferson National Bank (New York)
JNJ	New York	JohnJn	Johnson & Johnson
JOB	American	GnEmp	General Employment Enterprises Inc
JOIN	NAS NMS	JonIcbl	Jones Intercable Inc
JOINA	NAS NMS	JoneI A	Jones Intercable Inc (Class A)
JOL	American	Joule	Joulé Inc
JOR	New York	Jorgen	Earle M. Jorgensen Co
JOS	New York	Josten	Jostens Inc
JOSL	NAS NMS	Joslyn	Joslyn Corp
JP	New York	JeffPl	Jefferson-Pilot Corp
JPC	American	JohnPd	Johnson Products Company Inc
JPI	New York	JP Ind	J.P. Industries Inc
JPM	New York	Morgan	J.P. Morgan & Company Inc
JPMI	NAS NL	JPM	JPM Industries Inc
JR	New York	JRiver	James River Corporation of Virginia
JRMX	NAS NMS	JRM	JRM Holdings Inc
JSBK	NAS NMS	JohnsSv	Johnstown Savings Bank (Pennsylvania)
JSTN	NAS NMS	Justin	Justin Industries Inc
JTC	American	JetCa	Jet Capital Corp
JTMC	NAS SL	Moran	JT Moran Financial Corp
JTWO	NAS SL	J2 Com	J2 Communications
JUDGW	NAS SL	Judicte	Judicate Inc
JUDY	NAS NMS	Judys	Judy's Inc
JUKE	NAS SL	VidJuke	Video Jukebox Network Inc
JUNO	NAS NMS	Juno	Juno Lighting Inc

TRADING SYMBOL	MARKET LISTING	NEWSPAPER ABBREV.	COMPANY NAME
JWAIA	NAS NMS	JWA	Johnson Worldwide Associates Inc (Class A)
JWP	New York	JWP	JWP Inc
K	New York	Kellogg	Kellogg Co
KAB	New York	Kaneb	Kaneb Services Inc
KAMNA	NAS NMS	Kaman	Kaman Corp (Class A)
KAN	New York	KanPL	The Kansas Power & Light Co
KAPL	NAS NL	Kaplan	Kaplan Industries Inc
KASL	NAS NMS	Kasler	Kasler Corp
KAY	American	KayCp	Kay Corp
KB	New York	KaufB	Kaufman & Broad Inc
KBA	New York	KBAust	Kleinwort Benson Australian Income Fund Inc
KBALB	NAS NMS	Kimbal	Kimball International Inc (Class B)
KBH	New York	KaufBH	Kaufman & Broad Home Corp
KC.A	American	KeyCoA	The Key Co (Class A)
KC.B	American	KeyCoB	The Key Co (Class B)
KCFB	NAS NL	KingCty	King City Federal Savings Bank
KCH	American	Ketchm	Ketchum & Company Inc
KCLI	NAS NL	KnCtyL	Kansas City Life Insurance Co
KCOP	NAS NMS	Kencop	KenCope Energy Companies
KCRT	NAS SL	KCR	KCR Technology Inc
KCS	American	Constn	Conston Corp
KCSG	NAS NMS	KCS Gp	KCS Group Inc
KDI	New York	KDI	KDI Corp
KDNY	NAS NMS	HmInt	Home Intensive Care Inc
KDON	NAS NMS	Kaydon	Kaydon Corp
KDSI	NAS SL	Knwldg	Knowledge Data Systems Inc
KE	American	KogrEq	Koger Equity Inc
KEAN	NAS NMS	Keane	Keane Inc
KEC	American	KentEl	Kent Electronics Corp
KEI	American	Keithly	Keithly Instruments Inc
KELYA	NAS NMS	KlyS A	Kelly Services Inc (Class A)
KELYB	NAS NMS	KlyS B	Kelly Services Inc (Class B)
KEMC	NAS NMS	Kemp	Kemper Corp
KENCA	NAS NMS	KyCnL	Kentucky Central Life Insurance Co (Class A)
KENS	NAS NMS	Kenlwt	Kenilworth Systems Corp
KEP	New York	KanbEn	Kaneb Energy Partners Ltd
KEQU	NAS NMS	KewnSc	Kewaunee Scientific Corp
KES	New York	KeysCo	Keystone Consolidated Industries Inc
KEVN	NAS NMS	KimEn	Kimmins Environmental Service Corp
KEX	American	Kirby	Kirby Exploration Company Inc
KEY	New York	Keycp	KeyCorp
KEYC	NAS NMS	KeyCen	Key Centurion Bancshares Inc
KF	New York	Korea	The Korea Fund Inc
KFV	New York	QstVl	Quest For Value Dual Purpose Fund Inc

TRADING SYMBOL	MARKET LISTING	NEWSPAPER ABBREV.	COMPANY NAME
KGE	New York	KanGE	Kansas Gas & Electric Co
KGM	New York	KerrGl	Kerr Glass Manufacturing Corp
KHGI	NAS NMS	KeysHrt	Keystone Heritage Group Inc
KHI	New York	KmpHi	Kemper High Income Trust
KHLR	NAS NMS	Kahler	Kahler Corp
KII	New York	KeyInt	Keystone International Inc
KIMB	NAS NMS	Kimbrk	Kimbark Oil & Gas Co
KIN	American	Kinark	Kinark Corp
KIND	NAS NMS	Kinder	Kinder-Care Learning Centers Inc
KINV	NAS NL	KyInvst	Kentucky Investors Inc
KISC	NAS NMS	Kimin	Kimmins Corp
KIT	American	Kit Mfg	Kit Manufacturing Co
KITS	NAS NMS	MrdDia	Meridian Diagnostic Inc
KIX	American	Kerkhf	Kerkhoff Industries Inc
KJI	New York	KayJw	Kay Jewelers Inc
KLAC	NAS NMS	KLA	KLA Instruments Corp
KLIC	NAS NMS	Kulcke	Kulicke & Soffa Industries Inc
KLLM	NAS NMS	KLLM	KLLM Transport Services Inc
KLM	New York	KLM	KLM Royal Dutch Airlines
KLOFY	NAS NL	KloofG	Kloof Gold Mining Company Ltd
KLRT	NAS NL	Kleinrt	Kleinert's Inc
KLT	New York	KCtyPL	Kansas City Power & Light Co
KLU	New York	Kaisrtc	Kaisertech Ltd
KLY	American	KlyOG	Kelley Oil & Gas Partners Ltd
KM	New York	K mrt	K mart Corp
KMAG	NAS NMS	Komag	Komag Inc
KMB	New York	KimbC	Kimberly-Clark Corp
KMDC	NAS NMS	Kirschn	Kirschner Medical Corp
KMEC	NAS SL	KeyMed	Keystone Medical Corp
KMG	New York	KerrMc	Kerr-McGee Corp
KML	American	Carmel	Carmel Container Systems Ltd
KMSI	NAS NMS	KMS	KMS Industries Inc
KMT	New York	Kenmt	Kennametal Inc
KMW	American	KMW	KMW Systems Corp
KNAP	NAS NMS	KnapeV	Knape & Vogt Manufacturing Co
KNBW	NAS SL	KirinBr	Kirin Brewery Ltd
KNCI	NAS NMS	Kinetic	Kinetic Concepts Inc
KNE	New York	KN Eng	KN Energy Inc
KNMC	NAS NMS	Knutsn	Knutson Mortgage Corp
KNO	New York	Knogo	Knogo Corp
KNY	American	KearNt	Kearney-National Inc
KO	New York	CocaCl	The Coca-Cola Co
KOG	New York	Koger	Koger Properties Inc
KOL	New York	Kolmor	Kollmorgen Corp
KOOL	NAS SL	InstaCl	Insta Cool Inc. of North America
KOP	New York	Kopers	Koppers Company Inc
KORP	NAS SL	CpMgt	Corporate Management Group Inc
KOSS	NAS NMS	Koss	Koss Corp

TRADING SYMBOL	MARKET LISTING	NEWSPAPER ABBREV.	COMPANY NAME
KPA	American	Kappa	Kappa Networks Inc
KPE	New York	ColPict	Columbia Pictures Entertainment Inc
KPI	American	Kilern	Killearn Properties Inc
KPRO	NAS NMS	Kaypro	Kaypro Corp
KPT	New York	KPToy	Kenner Parker Toys Inc
KPTL	NAS NMS	Keptel	Keptel Inc
KR	New York	Kroger	The Kroger Co
KRA	New York	Kraft	Kraft Inc
KREN	NAS NMS	KingsRd	Kings Road Entertainment Inc
KRI	New York	KnghtR	Knight-Ridder Inc
KRLZ	NAS NL	Krelitz	Krelitz Industries Inc
KRMC	NAS SL	KRM	K.R.M. Petroleum Corp
KRSL	NAS SL	Kreislr	Kreisler Manufacturing Corp
KRUE	NAS NMS	Kruger	W.A. Krueger Co
KRUG	NAS NMS	Krug	KRUG International Corp
KSF	New York	QuakSC	Quaker State Corp
KSS	American	Keslr	Kessler Products Ltd
KSTN	NAS NMS	KeyFnc	Keystone Financial Inc
KSU	New York	KCSou	Kansas City Southern Industries Inc
KT	New York	KatyIn	Katy Industries Inc
KTCC	NAS NMS	KeyTrn	Key Tronic Corp
KTCO	NAS NMS	Kenan	Kenan Transport Co
KTII	NAS NMS	KTron	K-Tron International Inc
KU	New York	KyUtil	Kentucky Utilities Co
KUB	New York	Kubota	Kubota Ltd
KUH	New York	Kuhlm	Kuhlman Corp
KURM	NAS NL	KurzM	Kurzweil Music Systems Inc
KUST	NAS NMS	KustEl	Kustom Electronics Inc
KV	American	KV Ph	KV Pharmaceutical Co
KVLM	NAS NMS	Kevlin	Kevlin Microwave Corp
KVU	American	KleerV	Kleer-Vu Industries Inc
KWD	New York	Kellwd	Kellwood Co
KWN	American	Kenwin	Kenwin Shops Inc
KWP	New York	KngWld	King World Productions Inc
KYC	American	KeyCa	Keystone Camera Products Corp
KYLE	NAS SL	KyleTc	Kyle Technology Corp
KYMDA	NAS SL	KyMd	Kentucky Medical Insurance Co
KYO	New York	Kyocer	Kyocera Corp
KZ	New York	Kysor	Kysor Industrial Corp
LAB	American	NichIn	Nichols Institute
LABB	NAS NMS	BeautL	Beauty Labs Inc
LABL	NAS NMS	MultClr	Multi-Color Corp
LABORF	NAS SL	LaTeko	La Teko Resources Ltd
LAC	New York	LAC	LAC Minerals Ltd
LADF	NAS NMS	LaddFr	LADD Furniture Inc
LAF	New York	Lafarge	Lafarge Corp
LAFC	NAS NMS	LoanA	Loan America Financial Corp

TRADING SYMBOL	MARKET LISTING	NEWSPAPER ABBREV.	COMPANY NAME
LAGR	NAS NMS	LA Gear	L.A. Gear Inc
LAKE	NAS NMS	Lakelnd	Lakeland Industries Inc
LAN	American	Lancer	Lancer Corp
LANC	NAS NMS	Lancst	Lancaster Colony Corp
LARL	NAS NL	LaurlSv	Laurel Savings Assn
LARY	NAS SL	LaryIce	Larrys Ice Cream Inc
LAS	American	Laser	Laser Industries Ltd
LASR	NAS NMS	LaserPr	Laser Precision Corp
LASX	NAS SL	Lasrtch	Lasertechnics Inc
LAT	American	Latshw	Latshaw Enterprises Inc
LAUR	NAS NMS	LaurelE	Laurel Entertainment Inc
LAW	New York	LawtInt	Lawter International Inc
LAWS	NAS NMS	Lawsn	Lawson Products Inc
LAZR	NAS SL	LaserP	Laser Photonics Inc
LB	American	LaBarg	LaBarge Inc
LBC	New York	LndBnc	Landbank Bancshares Corp
LBSC	NAS NL	LSB SC	LSB Bancshares Inc. of South Carolina
LC	New York	LibtyCp	The Liberty Corp
LCBIV	NAS NMS	LdmCB	Landmark/Community Bancorp Inc
LCCC	NAS SL	LfeCare	Life Care Communities Corp
LCE	New York	LnStar	Lone Star Industries Inc
LCIC	NAS NMS	LeisCn	Leisure Concepts Inc
LCII	NAS SL	LasrMst	Laser Master International Inc
LCLD	NAS NMS	LacldSt	Laclede Steel Co
LCNB	NAS NMS	LincBc	Lincoln Bancorp
LCOR	NAS NMS	Langly	Langly Corp
LCSI	NAS NMS	LCS	LCS Industries Inc
LDBCD	NAS NMS	LDB	LDB Corp
LDG	New York	LongDr	Longs Drug Stores Corp
LDGX	NAS NMS	Lodgstx	Lodgistix Inc
LDIC	NAS NMS	LDI Cp	LDI Corp
LDL	American	Lydal	Lydall Inc
LDMFA	NAS NMS	LdlT A	Laidlaw Transportation Ltd (Class A)
LDMFB	NAS NMS	LdlT B	Laidlaw Transportation Ltd (Class B)
LDMK	NAS NMS	LdmkB	Landmark Bank for Savings (Massachusetts)
LDMM	NAS SL	LeadMn	Leadville Mining & Milling Corp
LE	New York	LndEd	Lands' End Inc
LEAD	NAS SL	Leadvle	Leadville Corp
LEAF	NAS NMS	Intrleaf	Interleaf Inc
LECO	NAS SL	Leeco	Leeco Diagnostics Inc
LECT	NAS NL	Lectec	LecTec Corp
LEDA	NAS NMS	LeeDta	Lee Data Corp
LEE	New York	LeeEnt	Lee Enterprises Inc
LEG	New York	LegPlat	Leggett & Platt Inc
LEIX	NAS NMS	Lowranc	Lowrance Electronics Inc
LEM	New York	Lehmn	The Lehman Corp
LEN	New York	Lennar	Lennar Corp

TRADING SYMBOL	MARKET LISTING	NEWSPAPER ABBREV.	COMPANY NAME
LENS	NAS NMS	CcdCam	Concord Camera Corp
LENZ	NAS SL	VsnSci	Vision Sciences Inc
LEO	New York	DryStr	Dreyfus Strategic Municipals Inc
LES	New York	LeslFay	The Leslie Fay Companies Inc
LEXB	NAS NMS	LexingS	Lexington Savings Bank (Massachusetts)
LEXI	NAS NMS	Lexicn	Lexicon Corp
LFA	American	Litfld	Littlefield Adams & Co
LFBR	NAS NMS	LongF	Longview Fibre Co
LFIN	NAS NMS	LincFn	Lincoln Financial Corp
LFSA	NAS NMS	FFdLen	First Federal S&L Assn of Lenawee County
LFT	American	Lfetime	Lifetime Corp
LG	New York	LaclGs	Laclede Gas Co
LGL	American	LynchC	Lynch Corp
LGN	New York	Logicon	Logicon Inc
LGS	New York	LaGenl	Louisiana General Services Inc
LGTK	NAS SL	Logitek	Logitek Inc
LHC	New York	LN Ho	L&N Housing Corp
LIBHA	NAS NMS	LbtyH A	Liberty Homes Inc (Class A)
LIBHB	NAS NMS	LbtyH B	Liberty Homes Inc (Class B)
LICF	NAS NMS	LICFn	The Long Island City Financial Corp
LICIA	NAS NMS	Lilly A	Lilly Industrial Coatings Inc (Class A)
LICO	NAS SL	Lifesur	Lifesurance Corp
LIFE	NAS NMS	Lfelne	Lifeline Systems Inc
LIG	New York	Ligget	Liggett Group Inc
LII	American	Larizz	Larizza Industries Inc
LIL	New York	LILCo	Long Island Lighting Co
LINB	NAS NMS	LinBrd	LIN Broadcasting Corp
LIND	NAS NMS	Lindbrg	Lindberg Corp
LINN	NAS NMS	LincFd	Lincoln Foodservice Products Inc
LINR	NAS SL	LinearI	Linear Instruments Corp
LIO	American	Lionel	The Lionel Corp
LIPO	NAS NMS	Liposm	Liposome Company Inc
LIQB	NAS NMS	LiqBox	Liqui-Box Corp
LIT	New York	Litton	Litton Industries Inc
LIZC	NAS NMS	LizCla	Liz Claiborne Inc
LJC	American	Lajolla	La Jolla Bancorp
LJSI	NAS SL	LJ Sim	L.J. Simone Inc
LK	New York	Lockhd	Lockheed Corp
LKI	American	LazKap	Lazare Kaplan International Inc
LLB	American	Cmptrc	CompuTrac Inc
LLEC	NAS NMS	LongLke	Long Lake Energy Corp
LLIC	NAS SL	Lamar	Lamar Life Corp
LLOG	NAS NMS	LincLg	Lincoln Logs Ltd
LLSI	NAS NMS	LSI Lg	LSI Logic Corp
LLSL	NAS NMS	LakldS	Lakeland Savings Bank SLA
LLTC	NAS NMS	LinearT	Linear Technology Corp
LLX	New York	LaLand	The Louisiana Land & Exploration Co

TRADING SYMBOL	MARKET LISTING	NEWSPAPER ABBREV.	COMPANY NAME
LLY	New York	Lilly	Eli Lilly & Co
LM	New York	LegMas	Legg Mason Inc
LMAC	NAS NMS	LdkAm	Landmark American Corp
LMAN	NAS NMS	Liebr	Lieberman Enterprises Inc
LMC	New York	LomasM	Lomas Mortgage Corp
LMED	NAS NMS	Lypho	LyphoMed Inc
LMG.A	American	Lawsn	Lawsen Mardon Group Ltd (Class A)
LML	American	Lndmk	Landmark Land Company Inc
LMS	New York	LamSes	The Lamson & Sessions Co
LNBC	NAS NMS	LibtNB	Liberty National Bancorp Inc
LNC	New York	LincNtl	Lincoln National Corp
LNCE	NAS NMS	Lance	Lance Inc
LND	New York	LincPl	Lincoln National Direct Placement Fund Inc
LNDL	NAS NMS	LindH	Lindal Cedar Homes Inc
LNF	New York	LomFn	Lomas & Nettleton Financial Corp
LNSB	NAS NMS	LincSB	Lincoln Savings Bank (Pennsylvania)
LNV	New York	LncNtC	Lincoln National Convertible Securities Inc
LOC	New York	Loctite	Loctite Corp
LOCL	NAS NMS	LocalF	Local Federal S&L Assn (Oklahoma)
LOG	New York	Rayonr	Rayonier Timberlands LP
LOJN	NAS SL	LoJack	Lo-Jack Corp
LOLS	NAS NMS	LdLnSL	Land of Lincoln S&L
LOM	New York	LomMt	Lomas & Nettleton Mortgage Investors
LOND	NAS NMS	LondnH	London House Inc
LONG	NAS SL	Longwd	Longwood Group Ltd
LOR	New York	Loral	Loral Corp
LOTS	NAS NMS	Lotus	Lotus Development Corp
LOU	New York	LouvGs	Louisville Gas & Electric Co
LOW	New York	Lowes	Lowe's Companies Inc
LOYC	NAS NMS	Loyola	Loyola Capital Corp
LPAI	NAS NMS	LaPete	La Petite Academy Inc
LPEP	NAS SL	LePeep	Le Peep Restaurants Inc
LPF	American	LndPc	Landsing Pacific Fund
LPG	New York	PtPar	Petrolane Partners LP
LPH	American	LeePhr	Lee Pharmaceuticals
LPI	American	LaPnt	La Pointe Industries Inc
LPLIA	NAS NMS	LPL	LPL Investment Group Inc (Class A)
LPO	American	LinPro	Linpro Specific Properties
LPP	American	LearPP	Lear Petroleum Partners LP
LPT	New York	LearPt	Lear Petroleum Corp
LPX	New York	LaPac	Louisiana-Pacific Corp
LQ	American	Lauren	Laurentian Capital Corp
LQM	New York	LQuint	La Quinta Motor Inns Inc
LQP	New York	LQuMt	La Quinta Motor Inns LP
LRC	American	LoriCp	The Lori Corp
LRCX	NAS NMS	LamRs	Lam Research Corp

TRADING SYMBOL	MARKET LISTING	NEWSPAPER ABBREV.	COMPANY NAME
LREXF	NAS SL	L Rex	L Rex International Corp
LRF	American	LncNC	Lincoln N.C. Realty Fund
LRI	New York	Learnl	LeaRonal Inc
LRT	New York	LLE Ry	LL&E Royalty Trust
LSA	American	LdmkSv	Landmark Savings Assn (Pennsylvania)
LSB	American	LSB Ind	LSB Industries Inc
LSC	American	Shopco	Shopco Laurel Centre LP
LSCO	NAS NMS	Lesco	LESCO Inc
LSER	NAS NMS	LaserCp	Laser Corp
LSMIF	NAS SL	Loadmst	Loadmaster Systems Inc
LSNB	NAS NMS	LkeShre	Lake Shore Bancorp Inc (Illinois)
LSSB	NAS NMS	LkSun	Lake Sunapee Savings Bank FSB (New Hampshire)
LSST	NAS NMS	LoneStr	Lone Star Technologies Inc
LSTIF	NAS SL	LkwdFr	Lakewood Forest Products Ltd
LT	American	LorTel	Lorimar-Telepictures Corp
LTD	New York	Limited	The Limited Inc
LTEC	NAS NMS	LincTl	Lincoln Telecommunications Co
LTEK	NAS NMS	LfeTch	Life Technologies Inc
LTG	American	CataLt	Catalina Lighting Inc
LTIZ	NAS NMS	LTI	Liposome Technology Inc
LTR	New York	Loews	Loews Corp
LTV	New York	LTV	The LTV Corp
LTXX	NAS NMS	LTX	LTX Corp
LUB	New York	Lubys	Luby's Cafeterias Inc
LUBE	NAS NMS	Autospa	AutoSpa Corp
LUC	New York	Lukens	Lukens Inc
LUK	New York	LeucNt	Leucadia National Corp
LUM	American	Lumex	Lumex Inc
LUND	NAS NMS	LundEnt	Lund Enterprises Inc
LUNG	NAS SL	CA Blk	CA Blockers Inc
LUR	American	Luria	L. Luria & Son Inc
LUSK	NAS NMS	Luskin	Luskin's Inc
LUTH	NAS SL	LuthMd	Luther Medical Products Inc
LUV	New York	SwAirl	Southwest Airlines Co
LUX	New York	LeisurT	Leisure & Technology Inc
LUXT	NAS SL	Luxtec	Luxtec Corp
LVC	American	LilVer	Lillian Vernon Corp
LVI	New York	LVI Gp	The LVI Group Inc
LVMH	NAS NMS	LVMH	LVMH Moet Hennessy Louis Vuitton
LVNVF	NAS SL	Levon	Levon Resources Ltd
LVT	American	Levitt	Levitt Corp
LWR	American	LawrG	Lawrence Insurance Group Inc
LXBK	NAS NMS	LSB NC	LSB Bancshares Inc (North Carolina)
LYDPY	NAS NL	Lydnbg	Lydenburg Platinum Ltd
LYTS	NAS NMS	LSI Lt	LSI Lighting Systems Inc
LZ	New York	Lubrzl	The Lubrizol Corp
LZB	New York	LaZ By	La-Z-Boy Chair Co

TRADING SYMBOL	MARKET LISTING	NEWSPAPER ABBREV.	COMPANY NAME
M	New York	MCorp	MCorp
MA	New York	MayDS	The May Department Stores Co
MAAR	NAS NL	Marcor	MarCor Development Company Inc
MABC	NAS NMS	MidABc	Mid-America Bancorp (Kentucky)
MABS	NAS NMS	MonAnt	Monoclonal Antibodies Inc
MACD	NAS NMS	MDmd	MacDermid Inc
MACK	NAS NMS	MackTr	Mack Trucks Inc
MAGAF	NAS NMS	MagnaI	Magna International Inc
MAGI	NAS NMS	MagGp	Magna Group Inc
MAHI	NAS NMS	MonAvl	Monarch Avalon Inc
MAI	New York	MACOM	M/A-Com Inc
MAIL	NAS NMS	MailBx	Mail Boxes Etc
MAIR	NAS NMS	MetAir	Metro Airlines Inc
MAJL	NAS NMS	MichAnt	Michael Anthony Jewelers Inc
MAJR	NAS NMS	MajRt	Major Realty Corp
MAJV	NAS NMS	MajVid	Major Video Corp
MAKL	NAS NMS	Markel	Markel Corp
MALC	NAS NMS	Mallard	Mallard Coach Company Inc
MALN	NAS SL	Malon	Mallon Minerals Corp
MALR	NAS NMS	Malrite	Malrite Communications Group Inc
MALRA	NAS NMS	MalritA	Malrite Communications Group Inc (Class A)
MAM	American	MidAm	Mid-America Industries Inc
MAN	New York	Manvl	Manville Corp
MANA	NAS NMS	Mantrn	Manatron Inc
MANT	NAS NMS	Manitw	The Manitowoc Company Inc
MAO	American	MrthOf	Marathon Office Supply Inc
MAP	American	MePS	Maine Public Service Co
MAR	New York	Marcde	The Marcade Group Inc
MARC	NAS NMS	MARC	M/A/R/C Inc
MARK	NAS SL	Markstr	MarkitStar Inc
MARS	NAS NMS	MrshSu	Marsh Supermarkets Inc
MAS	New York	Masco	Masco Corp
MASB	NAS NMS	Massbk	MASSBANK Corp (Massachusetts)
MASX	NAS NMS	MscoI	Masco Industries Inc
MAT	New York	Mattel	Mattel Inc
MAVR	NAS NMS	Mavrck	Maverick Restaurant Corp
MAX	American	Matrix	Matrix Corp
MAXC	NAS NMS	Maxco	Maxco Inc
MAXE	NAS NMS	MaxEr	Max & Ermas Restaurants Inc
MAXI	NAS NMS	Maxcre	Maxicare Health Plans Inc
MAYF	NAS NMS	MayfrIn	Mayfair Industries Inc
MAYS	NAS NMS	MaysJ	J.W. Mays Inc
MBAN	NAS SL	MtlBnc	MetalBanc Corp
MBC	New York	Micklby	Mickelberry Corp
MBCC	NAS NL	MailBCs	Mail Boxes Coast To Coast Inc
MBF	New York	MAIBF	MAI Basic Four Inc
MBI	New York	MBIA	MBIA Inc

TRADING SYMBOL	MARKET LISTING	NEWSPAPER ABBREV.	COMPANY NAME
MBIO	NAS SL	Moleculn	Moleculon Inc
MBLA	NAS NMS	NtMerc	National Mercantile Bancorp
MBLE	NAS NMS	MobGs	Mobile Gas Service Corp
MBLS	NAS NL	Micrbio	Microbiological Sciences Inc
MBMI	NAS SL	MicrBi	Micro Bio-Medics Inc
MBN	American	Metrbk	Metrobank NA (California)
MBNC	NAS SL	MoblNt	Mobile National Corp
MBNY	NAS NMS	MerNY	Merchants Bank of New York
MBSX	NAS NMS	MBS	MBS Textbook Exchange Inc
MBVT	NAS NMS	MrcBnc	Merchants Bancshares Inc (Vermont)
MBY	American	Midlby	Middleby Corp
MC	New York	Matsu	Matsushita Electric Industrial Company Ltd
MCA	New York	MCA	MCA Inc
MCAWA	NAS NMS	McCaw	McCaw Cellular Communications Inc (Class A)
MCBKA	NAS NMS	MrCaA	Merchants Capital Corp (Class A)
MCBKB	NAS NMS	MrCaB	Merchants Capital Corp (Class B)
MCC	New York	Mestek	Mestek Inc
MCCAA	NAS NMS	MoblC A	Mobile Communications Corporation of America (Class A)
MCCAB	NAS NMS	MoblC B	Mobile Communications Corporation of America (Class B)
MCCL	NAS NMS	McClain	McClain Industries Inc
MCCRK	NAS NMS	McCrm	McCormick & Company Inc
MCCS	NAS NMS	MedcC	Medco Containment Services Inc
MCD	New York	McDld	McDonald's Corp
MCDY	NAS NMS	Micrdy	Microdyne Corp
MCEG	NAS SL	MgtCo	Management Company Entertainment Group Inc
MCFE	NAS NMS	McFarl	McFarland Energy Inc
MCG	New York	MchER	Michigan Energy Resources Co
MCH	American	Medch	MedChem Products Inc
MCHM	NAS SL	MacrCh	MacroChem Corp
MCHN	NAS NMS	MrchNt	Merchants National Corp
MCI	New York	MasCp	MassMutual Corporate Investors
MCIC	NAS NMS	MCI	MCI Communications Corp
MCK	New York	McKes	McKesson Corp
MCL	New York	Moore	Moore Corporation Ltd
MCMC	NAS NL	MCM Cp	McM Corp
MCO	American	MCO Hd	MCO Holdings Inc
MCOM	NAS NMS	MdwCm	Midwest Communications Corp
MCON	NAS NMS	EMCON	EMCON Associates
MCOR	NAS NMS	MarIll	Marine Corp (Illinois)
MCR	American	MCO Rs	MCO Resources Inc
MCRD	NAS NMS	MicrD	Micro D Inc
MCRE	NAS SL	MicrEn	MicroEnergy Inc
MCRO	NAS NMS	MicrMk	Micro Mask Inc

TRADING SYMBOL	MARKET LISTING	NEWSPAPER ABBREV.	COMPANY NAME
MCRS	NAS NMS	Micros	MICROS Systems Inc
MCRY	NAS SL	MercEn	Mercury Entertainment Corp
MD	New York	McDnD	McDonnell Douglas Corp
MDA	New York	MAPCO	MAPCO Inc
MDC	New York	MDC	M.D.C. Holdings Inc
MDCI	NAS NMS	MedAct	Medical Action Industries Inc
MDD	New York	McDnl	McDonald & Company Investments Inc
MDEV	NAS NL	MedDv	Medical Devices Inc
MDEX	NAS NMS	Medex	Medex Inc
MDIN	NAS NMS	Medalst	Medalist Industries Inc
MDK	American	Mdcore	Medicore Inc
MDNT	NAS NMS	MNC	MNC Financial Inc
MDP	New York	Merdth	Meredith Corp
MDPI	NAS SL	MediaP	Media Products Inc
MDR	New York	McDerI	McDermott International Inc
MDSI	NAS NL	MicrDis	Micro Display Systems Inc
MDSN	NAS NMS	MadGE	Madison Gas & Electric Co
MDST	NAS NMS	Medstat	Medstat Systems Inc
MDT	New York	Medtrn	Medtronic Inc
MDTC	NAS NMS	MDT Cp	MDT Corp
MDU	New York	MDU	MDU Resources Group Inc
MDW	New York	MdwAir	Midway Airlines Inc
MDXR	NAS NMS	Medar	Medar Inc
MEA	New York	Mead	The Mead Corp
MED	American	Mediq	MEDIQ Inc
MEDC	NAS NMS	MedCre	Medical Care International Inc
MEDM	NAS SL	MedMbl	Med Mobile Inc
MEDR	NAS SL	MedcR	Medco Research Inc
MEG.A	American	Media	Media General Inc (Class A)
MEI	New York	MEI	MEI Diversified Inc
MEL	New York	Mellon	Mellon Bank Corp
MEM	American	Mem	MEM Company Inc
MEMB	NAS SL	MicMemb	Micro Membranes Inc
MEMX	NAS SL	MemryS	Memory Sciences Corp
MENT	NAS NMS	MentrG	Mentor Graphics Corp
MER	New York	MerLyn	Merril Lynch & Company Inc
MERY	NAS NMS	MeryLd	Merry Land & Investment Company Inc
MES	New York	Melvill	Melville Corp
MESL	NAS NMS	MesaAr	Mesa Airlines Inc
METB	NAS NMS	MetBcp	Metropolitan Bancorp Inc
METHA	NAS NMS	MethdA	Methode Electronics Inc (Class A)
METHB	NAS NMS	MthdB	Methode Electronics Inc (Class B)
METK	NAS SL	Memtek	Memtek Inc
METS	NAS NMS	MetCoil	Met-Coil Systems Corp
MEYER	NAS NMS	MeyerF	Fred Meyer Inc
MF	New York	Malaysa	The Malaysia Fund Inc
MFAC	NAS NMS	MktFct	Market Facts Inc
MFBZ	NAS NL	MtlFdl	Mutual Savings Bank A Stock Corp (Ohio)

TRADING SYMBOL	MARKET LISTING	NEWSPAPER ABBREV.	COMPANY NAME
MFC	New York	MetrFn	Metropolitan Financial Corp (North Dakota)
MFCO	NAS NMS	MicrFlt	Microwave Filter Company Inc
MFD	New York	Munfrd	Munford Inc
MFED	NAS NMS	Maury	Maury Federal Savings Bank (Tennessee)
MFFC	NAS NMS	MayflF	Mayflower Financial Corp
MFGC	NAS NMS	MdwFn	Midwest Financial Group Inc
MFGI	NAS NMS	MoorF	Moore Financial Group Inc
MFGR	NAS NMS	Mrsmr	Morsemere Financial Group Inc
MFLR	NAS NMS	MayflCo	Mayflower Co-operative Bank (Massachusetts)
MFM	New York	MFM	MFS Municipal Income Trust
MFO	New York	MFO	MFS Income & Opportunity Trust
MFSB	NAS NMS	MidFed	MidFed Savings Bank
MFSL	NAS NMS	MdFSL	Maryland Federal S&L Assn
MFT	New York	MFT	MFS Multimarket Total Return Trust
MFTN	NAS NMS	MetrF	Metropolitan Federal S&L Assn (Tennessee)
MGC	New York	MorgG	Morgan Grenfell SMALLCap Fund Inc
MGCC	NAS NMS	MedGr	Medical Graphics Corp
MGCO	NAS NMS	MediGl	Medicare-Glaser Corp
MGCP	NAS NMS	MagmC	Magma Copper Co
MGDVF	NAS SL	Murgold	Murgold Resources Inc
MGI	New York	MGI Prp	MGI Properties
MGLL	NAS NMS	McGill	McGill Manufacturing Company Inc
MGM	New York	MGMUA	MGM/UA Communications Co
MGMA	NAS NMS	MagmP	Magma Power Co
MGMG	NAS NL	MGM Gr	MGM Grand Inc
MGN	New York	MorgnP	Morgan Products Ltd
MGNC	NAS NMS	Medign	MEDIAGENIC
MGNTF	NAS SL	Migent	Migent Software Corp
MGP	American	MrchGp	Merchants Group Inc
MGRC	NAS NMS	McGrth	McGrath RentCorp
MGRE	NAS NMS	MeryG	Merry-Go-Round Enterprises Inc
MGS	American	MacGrg	MacGregor Sporting Goods Inc
MHBK	NAS NMS	MdHud	Mid-Hudson Savings Bank FSB (New York)
MHC	New York	MfrHan	Manufacturers Hanover Corp
MHCIV	NAS NMS	Maione	Maione-Hirschberg Companies Inc
MHCO	NAS NMS	MoreHd	Moore-Handley Inc
MHG	American	Malart	Malartic Hygrade Gold Mines Ltd (Canada)
MHP	New York	McGrH	McGraw-Hill Inc
MHS	New York	Marriot	Marriott Corp
MI	New York	MrshIn	Marshall Industries
MIAM	NAS NMS	MidAm	Mid-Am Inc
MICA	NAS NMS	Micrage	MicroAge Inc
MICH	NAS NL	MichJ	J. Michaels Inc
MICS	NAS NMS	Micom	Micom Systems Inc

TRADING SYMBOL	MARKET LISTING	NEWSPAPER ABBREV.	COMPANY NAME
MIDC	NAS NMS	MdConn	MidConn Bank (Connecticut)
MIDL	NAS NMS	MidlCp	Midlantic Corp
MIF	American	MunIn	MuniInsured Fund Inc
MIGI	NAS NMS	MerdIns	Meridian Insurance Group Inc
MIHO	NAS NMS	MI Hom	M/I Schottenstein Homes Inc
MII	New York	McLe	McLean Industries Inc
MIKA	NAS SL	MedImg	Medical Imaging Centers of America Inc
MIKL	NAS NMS	MichlFd	Michael Foods Inc
MIKR	NAS SL	Mikron	Mikron Instrument Company Inc
MIL	New York	Millipre	Millipore Corp
MILL	NAS NMS	Millicm	Millicom Inc
MILT	NAS NMS	Miltope	Miltope Group Inc
MILW	NAS NMS	MilwIns	Milwaukee Insurance Group Inc
MIN	New York	MIN	MFS Intermediate Income Trust
MIND	NAS NMS	Mindscp	Mindscape Inc
MINL	NAS NMS	Minetk	Minnetonka Corp
MINY	NAS NMS	Miniscr	MiniScribe Corp
MIP	American	MtgPl	Mortgage Investments Plus Inc
MIR	New York	MDCA	M.D.C. Asset Investors Inc
MISI	NAS SL	MicImg	Micro Imaging Systems Inc
MITK	NAS SL	MitekS	Mitek Systems Inc
MITSY	NAS NMS	Mitsui	Mitsui & Company Ltd
MIV	New York	MasInc	MassMutual Income Investors Inc
MKAI	NAS SL	Molokai	Molokai Ranch Ltd
MKC	New York	Marion	Marion Laboratories Inc
MKCO	NAS NMS	Kamnst	M. Kamenstein Inc
MKE	American	MichStr	Michaels Stores Inc
MKEY	NAS SL	Mast	Mast Keystone Inc
MKNLA	NAS NL	MultnA	Multnomah Kennel Club (Class A)
MKOR	NAS NL	McCrmC	McCormick Capital Inc
MKTAY	NAS NMS	Makita	Makita Electric Works Ltd
ML	New York	MartM	Martin Marrietta Corp
MLA	American	Midlnd	The Midland Co
MLAB	NAS NMS	MoniTc	Monitor Technologies Inc
MLC	New York	ManhNt	Manhattan National Corp
MLHR	NAS NMS	MillrHr	Herman Miller Inc
MLIS	NAS NMS	Microp	Micropolis Corp
MLL	New York	Macmil	Macmillan Inc
MLLE	NAS NMS	MartnL	Martin Lawrence Limited Editions Inc
MLMC	NAS NMS	MltLocl	Multi-Local Media Corp
MLP	New York	MesaLP	Mesa Limited Partnership
MLT	New York	Mitel	Mitel Corp
MLTF	NAS NMS	Multbk	Multibank Financial Corp
MLXX	NAS NMS	MLX	MLX Corp
MMA	American	MdMgt	Medical Management of America Inc
MMBLF	NAS NMS	MB	MacMillan Bloedel Ltd
MMC	New York	MrshMc	Marsh & McLennan Companies Inc
MMCT	NAS NMS	MetrMbl	Metro Mobile CTS Inc

TRADING SYMBOL	MARKET LISTING	NEWSPAPER ABBREV.	COMPANY NAME
MMD	American	MMed	Moore Medical Corp
MMEDC	NAS NMS	Multm	Multimedia Inc
MMII	NAS SL	MtrxM	Matrix Medica Inc
MMIM	NAS NMS	MMI	MMI Medical Inc
MMM	New York	MMM	Minnesota Mining & Manufacturing Co
MMO	New York	Monrch	The Monarch Machine Tool Co
MMPI	NAS NMS	Marqst	Marquest Medical Products Inc
MMRH	NAS NMS	MMR	MMR Holding Corp
MMSB	NAS NMS	MdMaine	Mid Maine Savings Bank FSB
MMST	NAS NMS	MedMst	Medmaster Systems Inc
MMT	New York	MMT	MFS Multimarket Income Trust
MNBC	NAS NMS	MinrNtl	Miners National Bancorp Inc
MNCO	NAS NMS	MichNt	Michigan National Corp
MND	American	MtchlE	Mitchell Energy & Development Corp
MNES	NAS NMS	MineSf	Mine Safety Appliances Co
MNH	American	ManfHo	Manufactured Homes Inc
MNI	American	McCla	McClatchy Newspapers Inc
MNPI	NAS NMS	Micrcm	Microcom Inc
MNR	New York	ManrCr	Manor Care Inc
MNRCY	NAS NL	Minorc	Minorco SA
MNS	American	MacNSc	The MacNeal-Schwendler Corp
MNST	NAS NMS	Minstar	Minstar Inc
MNT	New York	Monted	Montedison S.p.A
MNTL	NAS NMS	MfrsNt	Manufacturers National Corp
MNTR	NAS NMS	Mentor	Mentor Corp
MNTX	NAS NMS	Minntc	Minntech Corp
MNXI	NAS NMS	MNX	MNX Inc
MO	New York	PhilMr	Philip Morris Companies Inc
MOAI	NAS NMS	Morin	Morino Associates Inc
MOB	New York	Mobil	Mobil Corp
MOCO	NAS NMS	MOCON	Modern Controls Inc
MODI	NAS NMS	Modine	Modine Manufacturing Co
MOG.A	American	MoogA	Moog Inc (Class A)
MOG.B	American	MoogB	Moog Inc (Class B)
MOGN	NAS NMS	Moleclr	Molecular Genetics Inc
MOH	New York	Mohsc	Mohasco Corp
MOIL	NAS NMS	MaynOl	Maynard Oil Co
MOKG	NAS NMS	MOKG	Morgan Olmstead Kennedy & Gardner Capital Corp
MOLE	NAS NL	Flwmle	Flow Mole Corp
MOLX	NAS NMS	Molex	Molex Inc
MON	New York	MonCa	Monarch Capital Corp
MONY	NAS NMS	MetrCn	Metropolitan Consolidated Industries Inc
MOOD	NAS SL	Moodus	Moodus Savings Bank
MOR	New York	MorKeg	Morgan Keegan Inc
MORF	NAS NMS	MorFlo	Mor-Flo Industries Inc
MORP	NAS NMS	MooreP	Moore Products Co

TRADING SYMBOL	MARKET LISTING	NEWSPAPER ABBREV.	COMPANY NAME
MORR	NAS NMS	Morsn	Morrison Inc
MOS	New York	MesaOf	Mesa Offshore Trust
MOSI	NAS NMS	Mosine	Mosinee Paper Corp
MOT	New York	Motorla	Motorola Inc
MOTR	NAS NMS	MotClb	Motor Club of America
MOTTO	NAS NL	MotoPh	Moto Photo Inc
MOVE	NAS SL	Pergrn	Peregrine Entertainment Ltd
MP	New York	McInt	McIntyre Mines Ltd
MPAC	NAS NMS	ImpctSy	Impact Systems Inc
MPC	NAS NL	MagelPt	Magellan Petroleum Corp
MPHO	NAS SL	Medphn	Medphone Corp
MPL	New York	MinnPL	Minnesota Power & Light Co
MPP	American	MedPr	Medical Properties Inc
MPR	American	MetPro	Met-Pro Corp
MPRO	NAS NMS	Micrpro	MicroPro International Corp
MPSG	NAS NMS	MPSI	MPSI System Inc
MPSI	NAS NL	MeyrPk	Meyers Parking System Inc
MR	American	MorgnF	Morgan's Foods Inc
MRBK	NAS NMS	MercBk	Mercantile Bankshares Corp (Maryland)
MRBL	NAS NMS	MarbFn	Marble Financial Corp
MRC	New York	MiltnR	Milton Roy Co
MRCCV	NAS NMS	MarkCtl	Mark Controls Corp
MRCI	NAS NL	Marci	Marci International Imports Inc
MRCO	NAS SL	MrdnNt	Meridian National Corp
MRCS	NAS NMS	Marcus	The Marcus Corp
MRCY	NAS NMS	MercGn	Mercury General Corp
MRDN	NAS NMS	MrdnBc	Meridian Bancorp Inc
MRET	NAS NMS	Meret	Meret Inc
MRGC	NAS NMS	MGask	Mr. Gasket Co
MRGO	NAS NMS	Margo	Margo Nursery Farms Inc
MRGX	NAS NMS	Margux	Margaux Inc
MRI.A	American	McRae A	McRae Industries Inc (Class A)
MRI.B	American	McRae B	McRae Industries Inc (Class B)
MRIS	NAS NMS	Marshl	Marshall & Ilsley Corp
MRK	New York	Merck	Merck & Company Inc
MRLL	NAS NMS	MerilCp	Merrill Corp
MRM	American	Mermc	Merrimac Industries Inc
MRMK	NAS NMS	Mermck	Merrimack Bancorp Inc
MRMT	NAS SL	MemMtl	Memory Metals Inc
MRN	New York	MorKnd	Morrison Knudsen Corp
MRNCZ	NAS NL	MarnL	Marine Limited Partnership
MRP	American	MsmRs	Mission Resource Partners LP
MRT	New York	MtgRty	Mortgage & Realty Trust
MRTA	NAS NMS	Mariet	Marietta Corp
MRTN	NAS NMS	Marten	Marten Transport Ltd
MS	New York	MorgSt	Morgan Stanley Group Inc
MSAI	NAS NMS	MgtSci	Management Science America Inc
MSAM	NAS NMS	Marsm	Marsam Pharmaceuticals Inc

TRADING SYMBOL	MARKET LISTING	NEWSPAPER ABBREV.	COMPANY NAME
MSB	New York	Mesab	Mesabi Trust
MSBI	NAS NMS	MontSv	Montclair Savings Bank (New Jersey)
MSC	American	MatSci	Material Sciences Corp
MSCA	NAS NMS	MSCar	M.S. Carriers Inc
MSCC	NAS NMS	MicSem	Microsemi Corp
MSCM	NAS NL	Moscom	MOSCOM Corp
MSCO	NAS NMS	Masstor	MASSTOR Systems Corp
MSCP	NAS NMS	Mascmp	Massachusetts Computer Corp
MSEX	NAS NMS	MdsxW	Middlesex Water Co
MSFT	NAS NMS	Micsft	Microsoft Corp
MSHK	NAS NMS	Megdta	Megadata Corp
MSHR	NAS NMS	Mischer	The Mischer Corp
MSI	American	MSI Dt	MSI Data Corp
MSIE	NAS NL	MSI El	MSI Electronics Inc
MSII	NAS NMS	MedSh	Medicine Shoppe International Inc
MSL	New York	MercSL	Mercury S&L Assn
MSLA	NAS NMS	MetroSv	Metropolitan Financial S&L Assn (Texas)
MSM	American	Motts	Mott's Super Markets Inc
MSR	American	MSR	MSR Exploration Ltd
MSRR	NAS NMS	MidSou	MidSouth Corp
MSSL	NAS NMS	MdStFd	Mid-State Federal S&L Assn
MSST	NAS SL	JAM	JAMCO Ltd
MST	New York	MercSt	Mercantile Stores Company Inc
MSTI	NAS NMS	MedclSt	Medical Sterilization Inc
MSU	New York	MidSUt	Middle South Utilities Inc
MSW	American	MissnW	Mission West Properties
MTALA	NAS SL	Metlrg	Metallurgical Industries Inc (Class A)
MTC	New York	Monsan	Monsanto Co
MTCC	NAS NL	MgtTc	Magnetic Technologies Corp
MTEC	NAS NMS	MachTc	Machine Technology Inc
MTEK	NAS SL	Monitek	Monitek Technologies Inc
MTI	New York	Morton	Morton Thiokol Inc
MTIK	NAS NMS	ModuTc	Modular Technology Inc
MTL	American	MatRsh	Materials Research Corp
MTLC	NAS SL	Metlcld	Metalclad Corp
MTLI	NAS NMS	MarinT	Marine Transport Lines Inc
MTIX	NAS NMS	MechTc	Mechanical Technology Inc
MTN	American	MtMed	Mountain Medical Equipment Inc
MTNR	NAS NMS	MtnrBk	Mountaineer Bankshares of West Virginia Inc
MTOR	NAS NMS	Meritr	Meritor Savings Bank
MTP	New York	MonPw	The Montana Power Co
MTR	New York	MesaR	Mesa Royalty Trust
MTRC	NAS NMS	MercBc	Mercantile Bancorporation Inc (Missouri)
MTRM	NAS NMS	Monitr	Moniterm Corp
MTRO	NAS NMS	MetrTl	Metro-Tel Corp
MTS	New York	MonSt	Montgomery Street Income Securities Inc

TRADING SYMBOL	MARKET LISTING	NEWSPAPER ABBREV.	COMPANY NAME
MTSC	NAS NMS	MTS	MTS Systems Corp
MTWN	NAS NMS	MTwan	Mark Twain Bancshares Inc
MTWO	NAS NMS	Melami	Melamine Chemicals Inc
MTX	American	Metex	Metex Corp
MTY	American	Marlton	Marlton Technologies Inc
MUEL	NAS NMS	Mueller	Paul Mueller Co
MUF	American	Munvst	Munivest Fund Inc
MUN	New York	Munsng	Munsingwear Inc
MUNI	NAS NMS	MuniDv	Municipal Development Corp
MUO	New York	MutOm	Mutual of Omaha Interest Shares Inc
MUR	New York	MurpO	Murphy Oil Corp
MUSE	NAS NL	MustR	Mustang Resources Corp
MUSMF	NAS NL	Muscoch	Muscocho Explorations Ltd
MUTU	NAS NMS	MuFSL	Mutual Federal S&L Assn (North Carolina)
MV	American	McFad	McFaddin Ventures Inc
MVST	NAS SL	Multvst	Multivest Corp
MW	American	MattW	Matthews & Wright Group Inc
MWAY	NAS NMS	MicrLb	Microwave Laboratories Inc
MWE	New York	MWE	Midwest Energy Co
MX	New York	Mesrx	Measurex Corp
MXC	American	Matec	MATEC Corp
MXF	New York	MexFd	The Mexico Fund Inc
MXIM	NAS NMS	Maxim	Maxim Integrated Products Inc
MXM	New York	Maxam	MAXXAM Group Inc
MXP	American	Maxphrm	MaxPharma Inc
MXS	New York	Maxus	Maxus Energy Corp
MXTR	NAS NMS	Maxtor	Maxtor Corp
MXWL	NAS NMS	Maxwell	Maxwell Laboratories Inc
MXXX	NAS NMS	MarsSt	Mars Stores Inc
MYCO	NAS NMS	Mycogn	Mycogen Corp
MYE	American	MyerI	Myers Industries Inc
MYFRA	NAS NMS	MaySu	Mayfair Super Markets Inc (Class A)
MYG	New York	Maytag	The Maytag Co
MYL	New York	Mylan	Mylan Laboratories Inc
MYLX	NAS SL	Mylex	Mylex Corp
MYM	New York	MONY	MONY Real Estate Investors
MYO	New York	MurryO	Murry Ohio Manufacturing Co
MYR	New York	MyerL	The L.E. Myers Company Group
N	New York	INCO	Inco Ltd
NAB	New York	NtAust	National Australia Bank Ltd
NAF	New York	NAFCO	NAFCO Financial Group Inc
NAFC	NAS NMS	NashF	Nash-Finch Co
NAFI	NAS NMS	NoAir	Northern Air Freight Inc
NAHL	NAS NMS	NAHld	North American Holding Corp
NAHLA	NAS NMS	MAHdA	North American Holding Corp (Class A)
NAIG	NAS NMS	NtlIns	National Insurance Group

TRADING SYMBOL	MARKET LISTING	NEWSPAPER ABBREV.	COMPANY NAME
NAMC	NAS NMS	NoANat	North American National Corp
NAME	NAS NL	MblAm	Mobile America Corp
NAMVF	NAS SL	NAMtl	North American Metals Corp
NAN	American	Nantck	Nantucket Industries Inc
NANO	NAS NMS	Nanomt	Nanometrics Inc
NAPE	NAS NMS	NtProp	National Properties Corp
NAS	American	Nasta	Nasta International Inc
NASA	NAS NL	NAmSv	North American Savings Assn (Missouri)
NATA	NAS SL	NatAltr	Natural Alternatives Inc
NATG	NAS NMS	NtGuard	The National Guardian Corp
NATL	NAS NMS	NAtIn	North Atlantic Industries Inc
NAV	New York	Navistr	Navistar International Corp
NAVG	NAS NMS	NavgGp	Navigators Group Inc
NAVI	NAS NMS	NAmV	North American Ventures Inc
NAWE	NAS SL	Naham	Nahama & Weagant Energy Co
NBAK	NAS NMS	NB Alsk	National Bancorp of Alaska Inc
NBB	New York	NwBedf	New Bedford Institution for Savings
NBCC	NAS NMS	NBkWV	National Banc of Commerce Co (West Virginia)
NBCT	NAS NMS	NBnTex	National Bancshares Corporation of Texas
NBD	New York	NBD	NBD Bancorp Inc
NBI	New York	NBI	NBI Inc
NBIC	NAS NMS	NstBcp	Northeast Bancorp Inc
NBIO	NAS NMS	NABio	North American Biologicals Inc
NBKC	NAS NL	NE Bcp	New England Bancorp Inc
NBL	New York	NoblAf	Noble Affiliates Inc
NBSC	NAS NMS	NBrunS	New Brunswick Scientific Co
NBSIF	NAS NMS	NBusSy	National Business Systems Inc
NBTY	NAS NMS	NatrBty	Nature's Bounty Inc
NC	New York	NACCO	NACCO Industries Inc
NCA	New York	NuvCal	Nuveen California Municipal Value Fund Inc
NCB	New York	NCNB	NCNB Corp
NCBC	NAS NMS	NtCBc	National Commerce Bancorporation
NCBM	NAS NMS	NCtyB	National City Bancorporation (Minnesota)
NCBR	NAS NMS	NCNJ	National Community Bank of New Jersey
NCCI	NAS SL	NutrCh	Nutri-Cheese Co
NCCO	NAS NMS	Enseco	Enseco Inc
NCD	American	NCdO	North Canadian Oils Ltd
NCH	New York	NCH	NCH Corp
NCL	American	Nichols	S.E. Nichols Inc
NCM	New York	NvCMI	Nuveen California Municipal Income Fund
NCNG	NAS NMS	NCarG	North Carolina Natural Gas Corp
NCR	New York	NCR	NCR Corp
NCS	New York	NtlCnv	National Convenience Stores Inc
NCTY	NAS NMS	NtlCity	National City Corp

TRADING SYMBOL	MARKET LISTING	NEWSPAPER ABBREV.	COMPANY NAME
NDCO	NAS NMS	NbleDr	Noble Drilling Corp
NDI	American	NuclDt	Nuclear Data Inc
NDIC	NAS SL	NDtacpt	National Datacomputer Inc
NDLP	NAS SL	NDL	NDL Products Inc
NDSN	NAS NMS	Nordsn	Nordson Corp
NDTA	NAS NMS	NData	National Data Corp
NEB	New York	BkNE	Bank of New England Corp
NEBS	NAS NMS	NE Bus	New England Business Service Inc
NEC	New York	NatEdu	National Education Corp
NECC	NAS NMS	NECrit	New England Critical Care Inc
NECT	NAS SL	NEnvCt	National Environmental Controls Inc
NEEC	NAS NMS	NEECO	NEECO Inc
NEI	New York	NtEnt	National Enterprises Inc
NEIC	NAS SL	NE Ins	North East Insurance Co
NELL	NAS NMS	Nellcor	Nellcor Inc
NEM	New York	NwtM	Newmont Mining Corp
NENB	NAS NMS	NevNBc	Nevada National Bancorporation
NEOL	NAS Sl	Neolens	Neo-Lens Inc
NER	New York	Nerco	NERCO Inc
NERX	NAS NMS	Neorx	NeoRx Corp
NES	New York	NEngEl	New England Electric System
NESB	NAS NMS	NESB	NESB Corp
NEST	NAS NMS	Nestor	Nestor Inc
NET	New York	NEurO	North European Oil Royalty Trust
NETIF	NAS SL	NETI	NETI Technologies Inc
NETX	NAS NMS	NwkEq	Network Equipment Technologies Inc
NEW	American	Newcor	Newcor Inc
NEWE	NAS NMS	NewpEl	Newport Electronics Inc
NEWP	NAS NMS	Newpt	Newport Corp
NEWRZ	NAS NL	NEngRA	New England Realty Assn
NFBC	NAS NMS	NoFkB	North Fork Bancorporation
NFC	American	NCF	NCF Financial Corp
NFG	New York	NatFG	National Fuel Gas Co
NFSF	NAS NMS	NFS	NFS Financial Corp
NFSI	NAS NL	Ntl FSI	National FSI Inc
NFSL	NAS NMS	New SL	Newman Federal S&L Assn (Georgia)
NGC	New York	NwmtGd	Newmont Gold Co
NGE	New York	NYSEG	New York State Electric & Gas Corp
NGFCF	NAS NMS	NevGld	Nevada Goldfields Corp
NGNA	NAS NMS	Neutrg	Neutrogena Corp
NGS	New York	NiagSh	Niagara Share Corp
NGX	New York	Nthgat	Northgate Exploration Ltd
NHCI	NAS NMS	NtHltcr	National Healthcare Inc
NHDI	NAS NMS	NHD Str	NHD Stores Inc
NHES	NAS SL	NtHlthE	National Health Enhancement Systems Inc
NHI	American	NelsnH	Nelson Holdings International Ltd
NHIC	NAS NMS	NichHm	Nichols-Homeshield Inc
NHL	New York	Newhll	The Newhall Land & Farming Co

TRADING SYMBOL	MARKET LISTING	NEWSPAPER ABBREV.	COMPANY NAME
NHLI	NAS NMS	NHltLab	National Health Laboratories Inc
NHMO	NAS NMS	Nt HMO	National HMO Corp
NHR	New York	NtHert	National Heritage Inc
NHSB	NAS NMS	NHmB	New Hampshire Savings Bank Corp
NHY	New York	Norsk	Norsk Hydro a.s.
NI	New York	NIPSCO	NIPSCO Industries Inc
NIAM	NAS NL	NtImag	National Imaging Inc
NIBCA	NAS SL	NtInBc	National Industrial Bancorp Inc (Class A)
NIC	New York	Nicolet	Nicolet Instrument Corp
NICE	NAS SL	NtInst	National Institute of Careers Inc
NICLF	NAS NMS	NiCal	Ni-Cal Developments Ltd
NIEX	NAS NMS	NiagEx	Niagara Exchange Corp
NII	New York	NlI	National Intergroup Inc
NIKE	NAS NMS	NikeB	NIKE Inc (Class B)
NIMSY	NAS SL	Fairhvn	Fairhaven International Ltd
NIP	New York	Nwhall	Newhall Investment Properties
NIPNY	NAS NMS	NEC	NEC Corp
NIRAA	NAS SL	Niravce	Niravoice Inc (Class A)
NJR	New York	NJRsc	New Jersey Resources Corp
NJSB	NAS NMS	NJSvg	New Jersey Savings Bank
NJST	NAS NMS	NJ Stl	New Jersey Steel Corp
NKBK	NAS NL	CtBcp	Connecticut Bancorp Inc
NL	New York	NL Ind	NL Industries Inc
NLBK	NAS NMS	NtLoan	National Loan Bank (Texas)
NLC	New York	Nalco	Nalco Chemical Co
NLCS	NAS NMS	NtCptr	National Computer Systems Inc
NLG	American	NtGsO	National Gas & Oil Co
NLI	American	NewLew	Newmark & Lewis Inc
NLMC	NAS NL	NthLily	North Lily Mining Co
NLN	American	NewLine	New Line Cinema Corp
NLP	American	NtRty	National Realty LP
NLPI	NAS SL	NLamp	National Lampoon Inc
NLSI	NAS SL	NtwdLg	Nationwide Legal Services Inc
NLSL	NAS NL	NthldSv	Northland S&L Assn
NM	American	NeMtge	NorthEastern Mortgage Company Inc
NMBC	NAS NMS	MercBCt	The Merchants Bancorp Inc (Connecticut)
NMC	American	Numac	Numac Oil & Gas Ltd
NMCOC	NAS SL	NtMedia	National Media Corp
NMDY	NAS NMS	NrmOG	Normandy Oil & Gas Co
NME	New York	NMedE	National Medical Enterprises Inc
NMG	New York	NeimM	The Neiman-Marcus Group Inc
NMI	New York	NvMuI	Nuveen Municipal Income Fund
NMIC	NAS NMS	NMicrn	National Micronetics Inc
NMK	New York	NiaMP	Niagara Mohawk Power Corp
NMRC	NAS NMS	AHltSv	American Health Services Corp
NMRR	NAS SL	NMR	NMR of America Inc
NMS	New York	NMineS	National Mine Service Co

TRADING SYMBOL	MARKET LISTING	NEWSPAPER ABBREV.	COMPANY NAME
NMSB	NAS NMS	NM1Bc	NewMil Bancorp Inc
NMTX	NAS NMS	Novmtx	Novametrix Medical Systems Inc
NNET	NAS SL	NostN	Nostalgia Network Inc
NNM	American	NvNYM	Nuveen N.Y. Municipal Income Fund
NNSL	NAS NMS	NwprtN	Newport News Savings Bank (Virginia)
NNY	New York	NuvNY	Nuveen New York Municipal Value Fund Inc
NOAB	NAS NL	NABcp	North American Bancorporation Inc
NOAX	NAS NMS	NEOAX	NEOAX Inc
NOB	New York	Norwst	Northwest Corp
NOBE	NAS NMS	Nordst	Nordstrom Inc
NOBH	NAS SL	NobiltyH	Nobility Homes Inc
NOBLF	NAS NMS	Nobel	Nobel Insurance Ltd
NOC	New York	Nortrp	Northrop Corp
NOHL	NAS NMS	NthHill	North Hills Electronics Inc
NOL	American	NoelInd	Noel Industries Inc
NOLD	NAS NMS	Noland	Noland Co
NORKZ	NAS NMS	NorskB	Norsk-Data A.S. (Class B)
NOVL	NAS NMS	Novell	Novell Inc
NOVO	NAS NMS	NovoCp	Novo Corp
NOVR	NAS NMS	Novar	Novar Electronics Corp
NOVX	NAS NMS	NovaPh	Nova Pharmaceutical Corp
NOWT	NAS NMS	NWstT	North-West Telecommunications Inc
NOXLB	NAS NMS	Noxell	Noxell Corp (Class B)
NOZ	American	NProc	New Process Co
NPBC	NAS NMS	NtPenn	National Penn Bancshares Inc
NPCO	NAS NMS	Napco	Napco International Inc
NPD	American	NtPatnt	National Patent Development Corp
NPHIF	NAS NL	Nalcap	Nalcap Holdings Inc
NPI	New York	NuvPI	Nuveen Premium Income Municipal Fund Inc
NPK	New York	NtPrest	National Presto Industries Inc
NPR	New York	NPlnRl	New Plan Realty Trust
NPSI	NAS SL	NetwkPc	Networked Picture Systems Inc
NPT	American	NECO	NECO Enterprises Inc
NQRLF	NAS SL	NorQst	Nor-Quest Resources Ltd
NR	New York	NwhlRs	Newhall Resources
NRD	New York	NordRs	Nord Resources Corp
NREC	NAS NMS	NAC RE	NAC Re Corp
NRES	NAS NMS	NichRs	Nichols Research Corp
NRG	American	CalEgy	California Energy Co
NRM	American	NRM	NRM Energy Company LP
NROM	NAS SL	NobleR	Noble Romans Inc
NRRD	NAS NMS	Norstan	Norstan Inc
NRT	New York	Norton	Norton Co
NRTI	NAS NL	Nooney	Nooney Realty Trust Inc
NRTN	NAS NMS	NortnE	Norton Enterprises Inc
NSANY	NAS NL	Nissan	Nissan Motor Company Ltd

TRADING SYMBOL	MARKET LISTING	NEWSPAPER ABBREV.	COMPANY NAME
NSB	New York	NestSv	Northeast Savings FA
NSBA	NAS NMS	NtlSav	National Savings Bank of Albany
NSBK	NAS NMS	NoSdeSv	North Side Savings Bank (New York)
NSC	New York	NflkSo	Norfolk Southern Corp
NSCB	NAS NMS	NBSC	NBSC Corp
NSCO	NAS NMS	NtwkSy	Network Systems Corp
NSD	New York	NStand	National-Standard Co
NSH	New York	Nashua	Nashua Corp
NSI	New York	NtSvIn	National Service Industries Inc
NSIC	NAS NMS	NSecIns	National Security Insurance Co
NSKY	NAS SL	NewSky	New Sky Communications Inc
NSM	New York	NtSemi	National Semiconductor Corp
NSP	New York	NoStPw	Northern States Power Co
NSRU	NAS NMS	NStarU	North Star Universal Inc
NSS	American	NS Gp	NS Group Inc
NSSB	NAS NMS	NorwFn	Norwich Financial Corp
NSSI	NAS NMS	NuclSpt	Nuclear Support Services Inc
NSSX	NAS NMS	NtSanit	National Sanitary Supply Co
NSTS	NAS NL	NwPrC	Northwestern States Portland Cement Co
NSW	New York	NwStW	Northwestern Steel & Wire Co
NT	New York	NorTel	Northern Telecom Ltd
NTAR	NAS SL	NetAir	NetAir International Corp
NTK	New York	Nortek	Nortek Inc
NTLB	NAS NMS	NtLumb	National Lumber & Supply Inc
NTNI	NAS SL	NtTran	National Transaction Network Inc
NTRS	NAS NMS	NorTrst	Northern Trust Corp
NTSC	NAS NMS	NTech	National Technical Systems
NU	New York	NoestUt	Northeast Utilities
NUCM	NAS NMS	NucMet	Nuclear Metals Inc
NUCO	NAS NMS	NucrpE	Nucorp Energy Inc
NUCP	NAS NMS	NwVisn	New Visions Entertainment Corp
NUDYE	NAS SL	ND Rsc	ND Resources Inc
NUE	New York	Nucor	Nucor Corp
NUH	American	HuHrz	Nu Horizons Electronics Corp
NUI	New York	NUI	NUI Corp
NUME	NAS NMS	Numrc	Numerica Financial Corp
NUMR	NAS NMS	Numerex	Numerex Corp
NUMS	NAS NMS	NuMed	Nu-Med Inc
NURO	NAS SL	Neurtch	Neurotech Corp
NUT	New York	MauLoa	Mauna Loa Macadamia Partners LP
NUTM	NAS NMS	Nutmeg	Nutmeg Industries Inc
NUV	New York	NuvMu	Nuveen Municipal Value Fund Inc
NUVI	NAS NMS	NuVisn	NuVision Inc
NVA	New York	Nova	Nova Corp
NVBC	NAS NMS	NapaVl	Napa Valley Bancorp
NVCO	NAS NMS	Nodway	Nodaway Valley Co
NVIS	NAS NMS	NVideo	National Video Inc
NVLS	NAS NL	Novelus	Novellus Systems Inc

TRADING SYMBOL	MARKET LISTING	NEWSPAPER ABBREV.	COMPANY NAME
NVO	New York	Novo	Novo Industri A/S
NVP	New York	NesPw	Nevada Power Co
NVR	American	NVRyn	NVRyan LP
NVSI	NAS SL	NVision	National Vision Services Inc
NW	New York	NtWst	National Westminster Bank PLC
NWA	New York	NWA	NWA Inc
NWE	American	NWldE	New World Entertainment Ltd
NWELF	NAS NL	Nowsc	Nowsco Well Service Ltd
NWEN	NAS NMS	NwEng	Northwest Engineering Co
NWGI	NAS NMS	NW Grp	N-W Group Inc
NWIB	NAS NMS	NwstIll	Northwest Illinois Bancorp Inc
NWL	New York	Newell	Newell Co
NWLIA	NAS NMS	NtWnLf	National Western Life Insurance Co (Class A)
NWNG	NAS NMS	NwNG	Northwest Natural Gas Co
NWNL	NAS NMS	NwNLf	Northwestern National Life Insurance Co
NWOR	NAS NMS	NwldBk	Neworld Bancorp Inc (Massachusetts)
NWPH	NAS NMS	NwpPh	Newport Pharmaceuticals International Inc
NWPS	NAS NMS	NWPS	Northwestern Public Service Co
NWRK	NAS NMS	NtwkEl	Network Electronics Corp
NWS	New York	NewsCp	The News Corporation Ltd
NWTL	NAS NMS	NTelpd	Northwest Teleproductions Inc
NX	New York	Quanex	Quanex Corp
NYB	New York	NwAm	New American High Income Fund
NYBC	NAS NMS	NY Bcp	New York Bancorp Inc
NYCO	NAS NMS	NYCOR	NYCOR Inc
NYMG	NAS NMS	NY Mir	New York Marine & General Insurance Co
NYN	New York	Nynex	NYNEX Corp
NYT.A	American	NY Time	The New York Times Co (Class A)
NYTL	NAS SL	NYTst	New York Testing Laboratories Inc
NYTS	NAS SL	Nytest	Nytest Environmental Inc
NZ	American	NMxAr	New Mexico & Arizona Land Co
NZYM	NAS SL	Synthe	Synthetech Inc
O.A	American	OdetA	Odetics Inc (Class A)
O.B	American	OdetB	Odetics Inc (Class B)
OAK	New York	OakInd	Oak Industries Inc
OAR	American	OhArt	The Ohio Art Co
OAT	New York	QuakO	The Quaker Oats Co
OBCCC	NAS SL	OlyBdc	Olympic Broadcasting Corp
OBGI	NAS SL	OrionBd	Orion Broadcast Group Inc
OBPI	NAS SL	Otisvlle	Otisville BioPharm Inc
OBS	American	OBrien	O'Brien Energy Systems Inc
OC	New York	OrionC	Orion Capital Corp
OCAS	NAS NMS	OhioCas	Ohio Casualty Corp
OCENY	NAS NL	Oce-NY	Oce-Van Der Grinten NV
OCER	NAS NMS	Oceaner	Oceaneering International Inc

TRADING SYMBOL	MARKET LISTING	NEWSPAPER ABBREV.	COMPANY NAME
OCF	New York	OwenC	Owens-Corning Fiberglas Corp
OCGT	NAS NMS	OCG Tc	OCG Technology Inc
OCIL	NAS NMS	Ocilla	Ocilla Industries Inc
OCLI	NAS NMS	OpticC	Optical Coating Laboratory Inc
OCOMA	NAS NMS	OutletC	Outlet Communications Inc (Class A)
OCQ	New York	Oneida	Oneida Ltd
OCR	New York	Omncre	Omnicare Inc
OCTL	NAS NMS	Octel	Octel Communications Corp
ODEP	NAS NL	OfceDpt	Office Depot Inc
ODR	New York	ODECO	Ocean Drilling & Exploration Co
ODSI	NAS NMS	OldDom	Old Dominion Systems Inc
ODYY	NAS SL	Odysey	Odyssey Entertainment Ltd
OEA	American	OEA	OEA Inc
OEC	New York	OhioEd	Ohio Edison Co
OEH	New York	Orient	Orient Express Hotels Inc
OEN	American	OxfEgy	The Oxford Energy Co
OFFI	NAS NMS	OldFsh	Old Fashion Foods Inc
OFLDF	NAS NL	Oficeld	Officeland Inc
OFSB	NAS NMS	OrntFd	Orient Federal Savings Bank (Puerto Rico)
OFSLY	NAS NL	OrangF	Orange Free State Investments Ltd
OG	New York	Ogden	Ogden Corp
OGE	New York	OklaGE	Oklahoma Gas & Electric Co
OGIL	NAS NMS	OgilGp	The Ogilvy Group Inc
OGLE	NAS NMS	Oglbay	Oglebay Norton Co
OH	New York	Oakwd	Oakwood Homes Corp
OHBC	NAS NMS	OhioBc	Ohio Bancorp
OHC.A	American	OriolH A	Oriole Homes Corp (Class A)
OHC.B	American	OriolH B	Oriole Homes Corp (Class B)
OHSC	NAS NMS	OakHill	Oak Hill Sportswear Corp
OICO	NAS SL	OICorp	O.I. Corp
OIL	New York	TritEng	Triton Energy Corp
OILC	NAS NMS	OilDri	Oil-Dri Corporation of America
OJ	New York	OrngCo	Orange-co Inc
OKE	New York	ONEOK	ONEOK Inc
OKEN	NAS NMS	OldKnt	Old Kent Financial Corp
OKP	American	OOkiep	O'okiep Copper Company Ltd
OKT	New York	OakiteP	Oakite Products Inc
OLDR	NAS NMS	OldRep	Old Republic International Corp
OLGR	NAS NMS	Oilgear	Oilgear Co
OLN	New York	Olin	Olin Corp
OLOGP	NAS NMS	OffsLog	Offshore Logistics Inc
OLP	American	OneLibt	One Liberty Properties Inc
OLS	American	Olsten	The Olsten Corp
OLSN	NAS NMS	OlsonI	Olson Industries Inc
OM	New York	OutbdM	Outboard Marine Corp
OMCA	NAS SL	OccuMd	Occupational Medical Corporation of America Inc

TRADING SYMBOL	MARKET LISTING	NEWSPAPER ABBREV.	COMPANY NAME
OMCM	NAS NMS	Omnicm	Omnicom Group Inc
OMCO	NAS NL	Overmy	Overmyer Corp
OMD	American	Ormand	Ormand Industries Inc
OMET	NAS NMS	Orthmt	Orthomet Inc
OMI	New York	OwenM	Owens & Minor Inc
OMIC	NAS NMS	OMI Cp	OMI Corp
OMNX	NAS SL	OmniEx	Omni Exploration Inc
OMS	New York	OpnMl	Oppenheimer Multi-Sector Income Trust
OMT	New York	OhMatr	The Ohio Mattress Co
ONA	American	Oneita	Oneita Industries Inc
ONCS	NAS NMS	Oncogn	Oncogene Science Inc
ONCR	NAS SL	Oncor	Oncor Inc
ONE	New York	BncOne	Banc One Corp
ONPR	NAS NMS	OnePr	One Price Clothing Stores Inc
OPC	New York	OrionP	Orion Pictures Corp
OPER	NAS SL	CoinPhn	Coin Phones Inc
OPP	American	Oppenh	Oppenheimer Industries Inc
OPTC	NAS SL	Optlcm	Optelecom Inc
OPTO	NAS NMS	Opto	Opto Mechanik Inc
OPTX	NAS NMS	Optek	Optek Technology Inc
ORBT	NAS NMS	Orbit	Orbit Instrument Corp
ORCL	NAS NMS	Oracle	Oracle Systems Corp
ORCO	NAS NMS	OpticR	Optical Radiation Corp
OREM	NAS NMS	OregMt	Oregon Metallurgical Corp
ORFA	NAS NMS	Orfa	ORFA Corporation of America
ORG	American	Orgngn	Organogensis Inc
ORIG	NAS SL	OrigItl	Original Italian Pasta Products Company Inc
ORIR	NAS NMS	OrionRs	Orion Research Inc
ORU	New York	OranRk	Orange & Rockland Utilities Inc
OS	American	OregSt	Oregon Steel Mills Inc
OSBK	NAS SL	OrngSv	Orange Savings Bank
OSBN	NAS NL	Osborn	Osborn Communications Corp
OSBW	NAS NL	OlymSv	Olympic Savings Bank
OSG	New York	OvShip	Overseas Shipholding Group Inc
OSHM	NAS NMS	Oshmn	Oshman's Sporting Goods Inc
OSI	New York	OnLne	On-Line Software International Inc
OSIC	NAS NMS	Osicom	Osicom Technologies Inc
OSIX	NAS NMS	OpticlS	Optical Specialties Inc
OSL	American	OSulvn	O'Sullivan Corp
OSMO	NAS NMS	Osmnc	Osmonics Inc
OSTN	NAS NMS	OldStn	Old Stone Corp
OSWI	NAS NMS	OldSpag	Old Spagetti Warehouse Inc
OTRKB	NAS NMS	OshkT B	Oshkosh Truck Corp (Class B)
OTTR	NAS NMS	OttrTP	Otter Tail Power Co
OUCH	NAS NMS	OcuUrg	Occupational-Urgent Care Health Systems Inc
OUTB	NAS SL	OutbOM	Outback Oil & Mineral Exploration Corp

TRADING SYMBOL	MARKET LISTING	NEWSPAPER ABBREV.	COMPANY NAME
OVEX	NAS SL	Ovex	Ovex Fertility Corp
OVON	NAS NL	Ovonic	Ovonic Imaging Systems Inc
OVWV	NAS NMS	OneVl	One Valley Bancorp of West Virginia Inc
OXID	NAS NMS	Oxidyn	The Oxidyne Group Inc
OXM	New York	Oxford	Oxford Industries Inc
OXY	New York	OcciPet	Occidental Petroleum Corp
P	New York	PhilPet	Phillips Petroleum Co
PA	New York	Primca	Primerica Corp
PABC	NAS NL	PacBcp	Pacific Bancorporation
PAC	New York	PacTel	Pacific Telesis Group
PACC	NAS NMS	PrvLfe	Provident Life & Accident Insurance Co
PACN	NAS NMS	PacNuc	Pacific Nuclear Systems Inc
PAE	American	PionrSy	Pioneer Systems Inc
PAHC	NAS NMS	PionAm	Pioneer American Holding Co
PAI	New York	PacAS	Pacific American Income Shares Inc
PAIN	NAS SL	PainSu	Pain Suppresion Labs Inc
PAIR	NAS SL	PresAr	Presidential Airways Inc
PALM	NAS NMS	Palfed	PALFED Inc
PAMC	NAS NMS	ProvAm	Provident American Corp
PAMX	NAS NMS	PancMx	Pancho's Mexican Buffet Inc
PANT	NAS NMS	Pantera	Pantera's Corp
PAR	American	PrecsA	Precision Aerotech Inc
PARC	NAS NMS	ParkCm	Park Communications Inc
PASB	NAS NMS	PerpS	Perpetual Savings Bank FSB (Virginia)
PASI	NAS NMS	PacSlv	Pacific Silver Corp
PAT	New York	Patten	Patten Corp
PATI	NAS SL	PhnxAd	Phoenix Advanced Technology Inc
PATK	NAS NMS	PatrkI	Patrick Industries Inc
PAXTA	NAS NMS	Paxton	Frank Paxton Co (Class A)
PAYC	NAS NMS	Payco	Payco American Corp
PAYN	NAS NMS	PayNSv	Pay'n Save Inc
PAYX	NAS NMS	Paychx	Paychex Inc
PBCT	NAS NMS	PeopCT	People's Bank (Connecticut)
PBEN	NAS NMS	PuritB	Puritan-Bennett Corp
PBFI	NAS NMS	ParisBu	Paris Business Forms Inc
PBGI	NAS NMS	PiedB	Piedmont Bankgroup Inc
PBI	New York	PitnyB	Pitney Bowes Inc
PBKB	NAS NMS	PSBBrc	People's Savings Bank of Brockton (Massachusetts)
PBKC	NAS NMS	PrmBnc	Premier Bancshares Corp
PBKS	NAS NMS	PrvBksh	Provident Bankshares Corp
PBNB	NAS NMS	PeoSvCt	The Peoples Savings Bank of New Britain (Connecticut)
PBNC	NAS NMS	PeopBc	Peoples Bancorporation (North Carolina)
PBS	New York	PilgRg	Pilgrim Regional Bank Shares Inc
PBT	New York	Prmian	Permian Basin Royalty Trust
PBY	New York	PepBy	The Pep Boys-Manny Moe & Jack

TRADING SYMBOL	MARKET LISTING	NEWSPAPER ABBREV.	COMPANY NAME
PC	New York	PenCn	The Penn Central Corp
PCAI	NAS NMS	PCA Int	PCA International Inc
PCAR	NAS NMS	Pacar	PACCAR Inc
PCE	American	ProfCre	Professional Care Inc
PCEP	NAS NMS	PercTc	Perception Technology Corp
PCF	New York	PutnHi	Putnam High Income Convertible & Bond Fund
PCG	New York	PacGE	Pacific Gas & Electric Co
PCH	New York	Potltch	Potlatch Corp
PCI	New York	PayCsh	Payless Cashways Inc
PCLB	NAS NMS	PriceCo	The Price Co
PCMC	NAS SL	PsycCp	Psychemedics Corp
PCO	New York	Pittstn	The Pittston Co
PCOR	NAS NMS	Psicor	PSICOR Inc
PCPI	NAS SL	PerCpt	Personal Computer Products Inc
PCQT	NAS SL	PC Qut	P C Quote Inc
PCR	American	PeriniC	Perini Corp
PCRE	NAS SL	ProCre	ProCare Industries Inc
PCSI	NAS NMS	PCS	PCS Inc
PCSN	NAS NL	PrcStd	Precision Standard Inc
PCST	NAS NMS	PrecCst	Precision Castparts Corp
PCT	American	PropCT	Property Capital Trust
PCTL	NAS SL	PicTel	PictureTel Corp
PD	New York	PhelpD	Phelps Dodge Corp
PDA	American	PrnDia	Princeton Diagnostic Laboratories of America
PDAS	NAS NMS	PDA	PDA Engineering
PDEX	NAS SL	ProDex	Pro-Dex Inc
PDG	New York	PlcrD	Placer Dome Inc
PDL.A	American	PresR A	Presidential Realty Corp (Class A)
PDL.B	American	PresR B	Presidential Realty Corp (Class B)
PDLPY	NAS NMS	PacDunl	Pacific Dunlop Ltd
PDM	American	PitDsm	Pitt-DesMoines Inc
PDN	New York	Pardyn	Paradyne Corp
PDQ	New York	PrimeM	Prime Motor Inns Inc
PDS	New York	PeryDr	Perry Drug Stores Inc
PE	New York	PhilaEl	Philadelphia Electric Co
PEAL	NAS SL	Petro	Petro Global Inc
PEBW	NAS NMS	PBcWor	Peoples Bancorp of Worcester Inc (Massachusetts)
PECN	NAS NMS	PublEq	Publishers Equipment Corp
PEG	New York	PSEG	Public Service Enterprise Group Inc
PEI	American	PenRE	Pennsylvania Real Estate Investment Trust
PEL	New York	PanEC	Panhandle Eastern Corp
PELRY	NAS SL	Pelsart	Pelsart Resources NL

TRADING SYMBOL	MARKET LISTING	NEWSPAPER ABBREV.	COMPANY NAME
PEN	American	Pentron	Pentron Industries Inc
PENG	NAS NL	Prima	Prima Energy Corp
PENT	NAS NMS	PenaEn	Pennsylvania Enterprises Inc
PENW	NAS NMS	Penwt	PENWEST LTD
PEO	New York	PetRs	Petroleum & Resources Corp
PEP	New York	PepsiCo	PepsiCo Inc
PEPI	NAS NL	Piezo	Piezo Electric Products Inc
PER	American	PopeE	Pope, Evans & Robbins Inc
PERC	NAS NMS	Percpt	Perceptronics Inc
PERS	NAS SL	PerDia	Personal Diagnostics Inc
PEST	NAS SL	ReutrLb	Reuter Laboratories Inc
PET	New York	PacEnt	Pacific Enterprises Ltd
PETD	NAS NMS	PetDv	Petroleum Development Corp
PFBS	NAS NMS	PoncF	Ponce Federal Bank FSB (Puerto Rico)
PFDC	NAS NL	PeoFdDe	Peoples Federal Savings Bank of DeKalb County
PFDR	NAS NMS	PfdRsk	Preferred Risk Life Insurance Co
PFE	New York	Pfizer	Pfizer Inc
PFFS	NAS NMS	PacFst	Pacific First Financial Corp
PFINA	NAS NMS	P F	P&F Industries Inc (Class A)
PFLY	NAS NMS	PolifyFn	Polifly Financial Corp
PFNC	NAS NMS	ProgFn	Progress Financial Corp
PFP	American	PrmFn	Prime Financial Partners LP
PFR	New York	PerkF	Perkins Family Restaurants LP
PFSB	NAS NMS	PiedSB	Piedmont Federal Savings Bank (Virginia)
PFSI	NAS NMS	PionF	Pioneer Financial Services Inc (Illinois)
PFSL	NAS NMS	PrudFn	Prudential Financial Services Corp
PFTS	NAS NMS	ProfitS	Profit Systems Inc
PG	New York	ProctG	The Procter & Gamble Co
PGA	American	PuntaG	Punta Gorda Isles Inc
PGEN	NAS NMS	PlntGen	Plant Genetics Inc
PGI	American	PlyGem	Ply*Gem Industries Inc
PGL	New York	PeopEn	Peoples Energy Corp
PGN	New York	PortGC	Portland General Corp
PGR	New York	ProgCp	The Progressive Corp (Ohio)
PGU	American	PegGld	Pegasus Gold Ltd
PGY	New York	GlobYld	The Global Yield Fund Inc
PH	New York	ParkHn	Parker Hannifin Corp
PHABY	NAS NMS	Phrmci	Pharmacia AB
PHAR	NAS NMS	Phrmct	PharmaControl Corp
PHC	American	PratHt	Pratt Hotel Corp
PHEL	NAS NL	PtHel	Petroleum Helicopters Inc (voting)
PHELK	NAS NL	PtHel	Petroleum Helicopters Inc (non-voting)
PHG	New York	PhilGl	Philips NV
PHH	New York	PHH	PHH Group Inc
PHI	American	PhlLD	Philadelphia Long Distance Telephone Co

TRADING SYMBOL	MARKET LISTING	NEWSPAPER ABBREV.	COMPANY NAME
PHL	New York	PhilpIn	Philips Industries Inc
PHM	New York	PHM	PHM Corp
PHMT	NAS NMS	PhnMte	Phone-Mate Inc
PHNX	NAS NMS	PhnxMd	Phoenix Medical Technology Inc
PHOC	NAS NMS	PhotoC	Photo Control Corp
PHON	NAS SL	Photon	Photon Technology International Inc
PHP.B	American	PtHeat	Petroleum Heat & Power Company Inc (Class B)
PHPH	NAS NMS	PHP	PHP Healthcare Corp
PHR	American	PhnxR	Phoenix Realty Investors Inc
PHRS	NAS NMS	PaulH	Paul Harris Stores Inc
PHSY	NAS NMS	PacifCr	PacifiCare Health Systems Inc
PHTC	NAS SL	Phrmtc	Pharmatec Inc
PHX	New York	Phlcrp	PHLCORP Inc
PHXA	NAS NMS	PhnxAm	Phoenix American Inc
PHYB	NAS NMS	PionHi	Pioneer Hi-Bred International Inc
PHYP	NAS SL	PhysPh	Physicians Pharmaceutical Services Inc
PIBC	NAS NL	PacInld	Pacific Inland Bancorp
PICC	NAS NMS	PicCafe	Piccadilly Cafeterias Inc
PICI	NAS NMS	Polymr	Polymer International Corp
PICN	NAS NMS	PicSav	Pic'N' Save Corp
PICOA	NAS NMS	PhysIn	Physicians Insurance Company of Ohio (Class A)
PIED	NAS SL	PiedMn	Piedmont Mining Company Inc
PIF	New York	PruInt	Prudential Intermediate Income Fund Inc
PIFI	NAS NL	Piemnt	Piemonte Foods Inc
PII	New York	Pueblo	Pueblo International Inc
PIIBK	NAS NMS	PeopHrt	Peoples Heritage Financial Group Inc (Maine)
PIL	New York	PtrInv	Petroleum Investments Ltd
PIM	New York	PutMI	Putnam Master Intermediate Income Trust
PIN	New York	PSI	PSI Holdings Inc
PIO	New York	PionrEl	Pioneer Electronic Corp
PIOG	NAS NMS	PionGp	The Pioneer Group Inc
PION	NAS NMS	PionFn	Pioneer Financial Corp (Virginia)
PIOS	NAS NMS	PionSt	Pioneer-Standard Electronics Inc
PIP	American	PostlPr	Postal Instant Press
PIPR	NAS NMS	PiprJaf	Piper Jaffray Inc
PIR	New York	Pier 1	Pier 1 Imports Inc
PISC	NAS NMS	PacIntl	Pacific International Services Corp
PIX	American	SchoolP	School Pictures Inc
PIZA	NAS NMS	NtlPza	National Pizza Co
PKC	New York	Panill	Pannill Knitting Company Inc
PKD	New York	ParkDrl	Parker Drilling Co
PKE	New York	ParkEl	Park Electrochemical Corp
PKLB	NAS NMS	Phrmk	PharmaKinetics Laboratories Inc
PKN	New York	PerkEl	The Perkin-Elmer Cor
PKOH	NAS NMS	ParkOh	Park-Ohio Industries Inc

TRADING SYMBOL	MARKET LISTING	NEWSPAPER ABBREV.	COMPANY NAME
PKPS	NAS NMS	PoughSv	Poughkeepsie Savings Bank FSB
PKVL	NAS NL	Pikevle	Pikeville National Corp
PKWY	NAS NMS	Parkwy	Parkway Co
PLA	New York	Playboy	Playboy Enterprises Inc
PLAB	NAS NMS	PhtrLb	Photronic Labs Inc
PLEN	NAS NMS	Plenum	Plenum Publishing Corp
PLFC	NAS NMS	PulaskF	Pulaski Furniture Corp
PLFE	NAS NMS	PresLf	Presidential Life Corp
PLI	American	Leiner	P. Leiner Nutritional Products Corp
PLIT	NAS NMS	Petrlte	Petrolite Corp
PLL	American	PallCp	Pall Corp
PLNS	NAS NMS	PlainsR	Plains Resources Inc
PLP	New York	PlainsP	Plains Petroleum Co
PLR.A	American	PlyR A	Plymouth Rubber Company Inc (Class A)
PLR.B	American	PlyR B	Plymouth Rubber Company Inc (Class B)
PLS	American	PeerTu	Peerless Tube Co
PLTZC	NAS NMS	PultzPb	Pulitzer Publishing Co
PLUG	NAS SL	Cmpgrd	ComponetGuard Inc
PLUSF	NAS SL	PlexusR	Plexus Resources Corp
PLX	New York	Plantrn	Plantronics Inc
PLXS	NAS NMS	PlexusC	Plexus Corp
PLY	New York	Plesey	The Plessey Company plc
PLZA	NAS NMS	PlzCBc	Plaza Commerce Bancorp
PM	American	PratLm	Pratt & Lambert Inc
PMAN	NAS NMS	PiedMg	Piedmont Management Company Inc
PMBK	NAS NMS	PrmeBk	PRIMEBANK FSB (Michigan)
PMC	American	ProMed	Pro-Med Capital Inc
PMCP	NAS SL	PhotoMk	Photo Marker Corp
PMCX	NAS SL	PlrMol	Polar Molecular Corp
PMFG	NAS NMS	PeerMf	Peerless Manufacturing Co
PMI	New York	Premrk	Premark International Inc
PMK	New York	Primrk	Primark Corp
PMN	New York	Pullmn	Pullman Co
PMP	New York	PrMLt	Prime Motor Inns LP
PMR	American	Micron	Micron Products Inc
PMSC	NAS NMS	PlcyMg	Policy Management Systems Corp
PMSI	NAS NMS	PrmeMd	Prime Medical Services Inc
PMT	New York	PutMas	Putnam Master Income Trust
PMWI	NAS NMS	PACE	PACE Membership Warehouse Inc
PN	New York	PanAm	Pan Am Corp
PNBA	NAS NMS	Penbcp	Pennbancorp
PNBT	NAS NMS	PlantCp	The Planters Corp
PNC	New York	PNC	PNC Financial Corp
PNCR	NAS SL	Pancret	Pancretec Inc
PNET	NAS NMS	Pronet	ProNet Inc
PNF	American	PenTr	Penn Traffic Co
PNGR	NAS SL	Penguin	Penguin Group Inc
PNH	New York	PSNH	Public Service Company of New Hampshire

TRADING SYMBOL	MARKET LISTING	NEWSPAPER ABBREV.	COMPANY NAME
PNL	American	Penril	Penril Corp
PNM	New York	PSvNM	Public Service Company of New Mexico
PNN	American	PenEM	Penn Engineering & Manufacturing Corp
PNRE	NAS NMS	PanAtl	Pan Atlantic Re Inc
PNS	New York	Pansph	Pansophic Systems Inc
PNT	American	Pantast	Pantasote Inc
PNTA	NAS NMS	Pentair	Pentair Inc
PNTC	NAS NMS	Pantch	Panatech Research & Development Corp
PNTK	NAS SL	Pentch	Pentech International Inc
PNTL	NAS SL	Phonetl	Phonetel Technologies
PNU	American	PneuSc	Pneumatic Scale Corp
PNV	American	PeriniI	Perini Investment Properties Inc
PNW	New York	PinWst	Pinnacle West Capital Corp
PNY	New York	PiedNG	Piedmont Natural Gas Company Inc
POBS	NAS NMS	PortBk	Portsmouth Bank Shares Inc
POCI	NAS NMS	PortsCl	Ports of Call Inc
POEA	NAS NL	PoeAsc	Poe & Associates Inc
POLK	NAS NMS	PolkAu	Polk Audio Inc
POLXF	NAS SL	Polydex	Polydex Pharmaceuticals Ltd
POLY	NAS NMS	PolyTch	Poly-Tech Inc
POM	New York	PotmE	Potomec Electric Power Co
POOL	NAS NMS	PosdnP	Poseidon Pools of America Inc
POP	New York	PopTal	Pope & Talbot Inc
POPX	NAS SL	PopRad	Pop Radio Corp
POR	New York	Portec	Portec Inc
POSS	NAS NMS	Possis	Possis Corp
POW	American	PSE	PSE Inc
POWL	NAS NMS	Powell	Powell Industries Inc
POWR	NAS NMS	EnvPwr	Environmental Power Corp
POY	American	PraireO	Prairie Oil Royalties Company Ltd
PP	American	PaulPt	Pauley Petroleum Inc
PPAC	NAS SL	PennPc	Penn Pacific Corp
PPC	New York	PatPtr	Patrick Petroleum Co
PPD	American	PrpdLg	Pre-Paid Legal Services Inc
PPG	New York	PPG	PPG Industries Inc
PPI	American	PicoPd	Pico Products Inc
PPL	New York	PaPL	Pennsylvania Power & Light Co
PPP	New York	PogoPd	Pogo Producing Co
PPPI	NAS SL	PrivPay	Private Pay Phones Inc
PPRO	NAS SL	PatnPr	Pattern Processing Technologies Inc
PPSA	NAS NMS	PspctPk	Prospect Park Financial Corp (New Jersey)
PPT	New York	PutPr	Putnam Premier Income Trust
PPW	New York	Pacifcp	PacifiCorp
PQB	American	Quebc	Quebecor Inc
PR	American	PrcCm	Price Communications Corp
PRAB	NAS SL	PrabRbt	Prab Robots Inc
PRBC	NAS NMS	PrmrBc	Premier Bancorp Inc (Louisiana)

TRADING SYMBOL	MARKET LISTING	NEWSPAPER ABBREV.	COMPANY NAME
PRBK	NAS NL	ProvBc	Provident Bancorp Inc
PRC	New York	PrdRs	Products Research & Chemical Corp
PRCO	NAS NL	Pricor	Pricor Inc
PRD	New York	Polard	Polaroid Corp
PRE	New York	Premr	Premier Industrial Corp
PREM	NAS NL	PremFn	Premier Financial Services Inc
PRES	NAS SL	PrecRs	Precision Resources Inc
PREV	NAS NMS	ReverF	Revere Fund Inc
PRFT	NAS NMS	Proffitt	Proffitt's Inc
PRGR	NAS NMS	Progrp	ProGroup Inc
PRI	New York	PacRes	Pacific Resources Inc
PRIA	NAS NMS	Priam	Priam Corp
PRIM	NAS SL	Primge	Primages Inc
PRLX	NAS NMS	Parlex	Parlex Corp
PRM	New York	PrimeC	Prime Computer Inc
PRME	NAS NMS	PrmCap	Prime Capital Corp
PRN	New York	PR Cem	Puerto Rican Cement Company Inc
PRO	American	IntProt	International Proteins Corp
PROF	NAS NMS	ProfInv	Professional Investors Insurance Group Inc
PROP	NAS NMS	ProdOp	Production Operators Corp
PROSZ	NAS NMS	ProsGp	The Prospect Group Inc
PROT	NAS NMS	ProtLfe	Protective Life Corp
PRR	American	Perigo	Perrigo Co
PRS.A	American	Presd A	Presidio Oil Co (Class A)
PRS.B	American	Presd B	Presidio Oil Co (Class B)
PRTE	NAS NL	PrftTc	Profit Technology Inc
PRTK	NAS NL	PrestoT	Presto-Tek Corp
PRX	New York	ParPh	Par Pharmaceutical Inc
PRXS	NAS NMS	PraxBio	Praxis Biologics Inc
PRY	American	Pittway	Pittway Corp
PRZ	American	Prism	Prism Entertainment Corp
PS	New York	Proler	Proler International Corp
PSBF	NAS NMS	PionSB	Pioneer Savings Bank (Florida)
PSBK	NAS NMS	ProgBk	Progressive Bank Inc (New York)
PSBN	NAS NMS	PionSv	Pioneer Savings Bank Inc (North Carolina)
PSBX	NAS NMS	PeSvMch	Peoples Savings Bank FSB (Michigan)
PSC	New York	PhilSub	Philadelphia Suburban Corp
PSCX	NAS SL	PhotSci	Photographic Science Corp
PSD	New York	PugetP	Puget Sound Power & Light Co
PSF	New York	PruStr	Prudential Strategic Income Fund
PSG	New York	PS Grp	PS Group Inc
PSI	American	PortSys	Porta Systems Corp
PSIX	NAS SL	Periphl	Peripheral Systems Inc
PSLA	NAS NMS	PfdSav	Preferred Savings Bank Inc (North Carolina)
PSLI	NAS SL	Penta	Penta Systems International Inc

TRADING SYMBOL	MARKET LISTING	NEWSPAPER ABBREV.	COMPANY NAME
PSM	New York	Penwlt	Pennwalt Corp
PSNB	NAS NMS	PgSdBc	Puget Sound Bancorp
PSNC	NAS NMS	PbSNC	Public Service Company of North Carolina Inc
PSO	American	Penob	Penobscot Shoe Co
PSPA	NAS NMS	Penvw	Pennview Savings Assn (Pennsylvania)
PSR	New York	PSvCol	Public Service Company of Colorado
PSSP	NAS NMS	PSS Pub	Price/Stern/Sloan Publishers Inc
PST	New York	Petrie	Petrie Stores Corp
PSX	New York	PacSci	Pacific Scientific Co
PSY	New York	Pilsbry	The Pillsbury Co
PSYS	NAS NMS	ProgSys	Programming & Systems Inc
PTAC	NAS NMS	PenTrt	Penn Treaty American Corp
PTC	New York	ParTch	PAR Technology Corp
PTCH	NAS SL	PacTec	Pacer Technology Inc
PTCM	NAS NMS	PTelcm	Pacific Telecom Inc
PTCO	NAS NMS	PETCO	Petroleum Equipment Tools Co
PTEC	NAS NL	PhnxTc	Phoenix Technologies Ltd
PTG	American	Portage	Portage Industries Corp
PTI	American	PatTch	Patient Technology Inc
PTIS	NAS SL	PlasmT	Plasma-Therm Corp
PTLX	NAS NMS	Patlex	Patlex Corp
PTNM	NAS NL	PutnTr	Putnam Trust Co
PTNX	NAS NMS	Prtronx	Printronix Inc
PTRK	NAS NMS	PrstnCp	Preston Corp
PTRL	NAS NMS	PetInd	Petrol Industries Inc
PTRO	NAS NMS	Petrmn	Petrominerals Corp
PTSI	NAS NMS	PAM	P.A.M. Transportation Services Inc
PUBO	NAS NMS	PubcoC	Pubco Corp
PUL	New York	Publick	Publicker Industries Inc
PULP	NAS SL	KingstS	Kingston Systems Inc
PULS	NAS NMS	PulwS	Pulawski S&L Assn (New Jersey)
PVDC	NAS NMS	Prinvl	Princeville Corp
PVH	New York	PhlVH	Phillips-Van Heusen Corp
PVIR	NAS NMS	PenV	Penn Virginia Corp
PVNA	NAS NMS	Prvena	Provena Foods Inc
PVSA	NAS NMS	PrkvlSv	Parkvale Savings Assn (Pennsylvania)
PVY	American	ProvEn	Providence Energy Corp
PW	American	PitWVa	Pittsburgh & West Virginia Railroad
PWA	NAS NMS	PacWst	Pacific Western Airlines Corp
PWJ	New York	PainWb	PaineWebber Group Inc
PWN	American	CshAm	Cash America Investments Inc
PWR	American	IntPwr	International Power Machines Corp
PWRR	NAS NL	PrvWor	Providence & Worcester Railroad Co
PWSB	NAS NMS	PeoWst	Peoples Westchester Savings Bank (New York)
PXR	American	Paxar	PAXAR Corp
PXRE	NAS NMS	PhnxRe	Phoenix Re Corp

TRADING SYMBOL	MARKET LISTING	NEWSPAPER ABBREV.	COMPANY NAME
PY	American	PfdHlt	Preferred Health Care Ltd
PYE	New York	PrgInc	Progressive Income Equity Fund Inc
PYF	American	PayFon	Pay-Fone System Inc
PYOL	NAS NL	PyrmO	Pyramid Oil Co
PYRD	NAS NMS	PyrmT	Pyramid Technology Corp
PZL	New York	Pennzol	Pennzoil Co
QBDL	American	Flanign	Flanigan's Enterprises Inc
QBIO	NAS SL	QuestBi	Quest Biotechnology Inc
QBIX	NAS SL	Qubix	Qubix Graphic Systems Inc
QCHM	NAS NMS	QuakCh	Quaker Chemical Corp
QDRX	NAS SL	Qdrax	Quadrax Corp
QEDX	NAS NMS	QED	QED Exploration Inc
QEKG	NAS NMS	QMed	Q-MED Inc
QFCI	NAS NMS	QuFood	Quality Food Centers Inc
QILT	NAS SL	Pathe	Pathe Computer Control Systems Corp
QMAX	NAS NMS	Qmax	QMax Technology Group Inc
QMED	NAS NMS	QuestM	Quest Medical Inc
QMH	New York	MHI Gp	MHI Group Inc
QNTL	NAS NMS	ArizInst	Arizona Instrument Corp
QNTM	NAS NMS	Quantm	Quantum Corp
QPON	NAS NMS	SvOak	Seven Oaks International Inc
QRXL	NAS NMS	Quarex	Quarex Industries Inc
QSII	NAS NMS	QualSy	Quality Systems Inc
QSRTF	NAS NL	QuebcSt	Quebec Sturgeon River Mines Ltd
QTEC	NAS NMS	Questch	QuesTech Inc
QTMCC	NAS SL	QuanD	Quantum Diagnostics Ltd
QUAD	NAS NMS	Quadrx	Quadrex Corp
QUAN	NAS NMS	Qntrnx	Quantronix Corp
QUIK	NAS NMS	Quikslv	Quicksilver Inc
QUIP	NAS NMS	Quipp	Quipp Inc
QUIX	NAS NMS	Quixte	Quixote Corp
QUME	NAS NMS	Qume	Qume Corp
QURZ	NAS SL	QuartzI	Quartz Inc
QVCN	NAS NMS	QVC	QVC Network Inc
QZMGF	NAS NMS	QrtzMt	Quartz Mountain Gold Corp
R	New York	Rothch	L.F. Rothschild Unterberg Towbin Holdings Inc
RABT	NAS NMS	RabbitS	Rabbit Software Corp
RAC	American	RAI	RAI Research Corp
RACM	NAS SL	Raycom	Raycomm Transworld Industries Inc
RACO	NAS NL	RealAm	RealAmerica Co
RAD	New York	RiteAid	Rite Aid Corp
RADIF	NAS NL	RadaEl	Rada Electronic Industries Ltd
RADS	NAS NMS	RadSys	Radiation Systems Inc
RADX	NAS NMS	Radion	Radionics Inc
RAFI	NAS NL	Ravnwd	Ravenswood Financial Corp

TRADING SYMBOL	MARKET LISTING	NEWSPAPER ABBREV.	COMPANY NAME
RAGN	NAS NMS	Ragen	Ragen Corp
RAGS	NAS NMS	CoatSl	Coated Sales Inc
RAH	New York	Robins	A.H. Robins Company Inc
RAIL	NAS NL	RailSvg	Railroad S&L Assn (Kansas)
RAL	New York	RalsPur	Ralston Purina Co
RAM	New York	Ramad	Ramada Inc
RAND	NAS NL	RandCa	Rand Capital Corp
RANG	NAS NMS	Rangar	Rangaire Corp
RANKY	NAS NL	RankO	The Rank Organization Plc
RARB	NAS NMS	RartnBc	Raritan Bancorp Inc
RATNY	NAS NMS	Ratner	Ratners Group plc
RAUT	NAS NMS	RpAuto	Republic Automotive Parts Inc
RAV	American	Raven	Raven Industries Inc
RAWC	NAS NMS	RepAm	Republic American Corp
RAXR	NAS NMS	RAX	Rax Restaurants Inc
RAY	New York	Raytch	Raytech Corp
RAYM	NAS NMS	Raymd	The Raymond Corp
RB	New York	ReadBt	Reading & Bates Corp
RBC	American	RegalB	Regal-Beloit Corp
RBCO	NAS NMS	RyanBck	Ryan Beck & Co
RBD	New York	Rubmd	Rubbermaid Inc
RBG	American	Ransbg	Ransburg Corp
RBI	New York	RBInd	RB Industries Inc
RBK	New York	Rebok	Reebok International Ltd
RBNC	NAS NL	RepBcp	Republic Bancorp Inc
RBNH	NAS NMS	RckBcp	Rockingham Bancorp (New Hampshire)
RBPAA	NAS NL	RyBkPA	Royal Bank of Pennsylvania (Class A)
RBSN	NAS NMS	Robesn	Robeson Industries Corp
RBW	American	RBW	RB&W Corp
RCBI	NAS NMS	BrwnRb	Robert C. Brown & Company Inc
RCC	American	ReCap	Re Capital Corp
RCDC	NAS NMS	RossCs	Ross Cosmetics Distribution Centers Inc
RCE	New York	Reece	The Reece Corp
RCHFA	NAS NMS	Richfd	Richfood Holdings Inc (Class A)
RCHI	NAS NL	Rauch	Rauch Industries Inc
RCM	New York	ArcoCh	ARCO Chemical Co
RCMT	NAS SL	RCM	RCM Technologies Inc
RCOA	NAS NMS	Retail	Retailing Corporation of America
RCOT	NAS NMS	Recotn	Recoton Corp
RCP	New York	RckCtr	Rockefeller Center Properties Inc
RCSB	NAS NMS	RochCS	The Rochester Community Savings Bank
RCT	New York	REIT	Real Estate Investment Trust of California
RD	New York	RoylD	Royal Dutch Petroleum Co
RDC	New York	Rowan	Rowan Companies Inc
RDGC	NAS NMS	Readg	Reading Co
RDIS	NAS SL	RadtnDs	Radiation Disposal Systems Inc
RDK	American	Rudick	Ruddick Corp

TRADING SYMBOL	MARKET LISTING	NEWSPAPER ABBREV.	COMPANY NAME
RDKN	NAS NMS	RedknL	Redken Laboratories Inc
RDL	American	Redlw	Redlaw Industries Inc
RDON	NAS SL	Radon	Radon Testing Corporation of America Inc
RDR	New York	Ryder	Ryder System Inc
RDVA	NAS SL	Radva	Radva Corp
RDWI	NAS NMS	RdwayM	Roadway Motor Plazas Inc
RE	New York	Redmn	Redman Industries Inc
READ	NAS NL	AmLrn	American Learning Corp
REAL	NAS NMS	Reliab	Reliability Inc
REC	New York	RecnEq	Recognition Equipment Inc
RED	American	RedLn	Red Lion Inns LP
REDI	NAS NMS	RediCr	Readicare Inc
REDX	NAS SL	RedEagl	Red Eagle Resources Corp
REED	NAS NMS	ReedJwl	Reeds Jewelers Inc
REFC	NAS NMS	Refac	REFAC Technology Development Corp
REFR	NAS SL	RschFt	Research Frontiers Inc
REGB	NAS NMS	ReglBc	Regional Bancorp Inc
REGI	NAS NMS	Regina	Regina Company Inc
REIC	NAS NMS	RshInd	Research Industries Corp
REL	New York	RelGrp	Reliance Group Holdings Inc
RELL	NAS NMS	RichEl	Richardson Electronics Ltd
RELY	NAS NMS	RelTch	Relational Technology Inc
REN	New York	RolinE	Rollins Environmental Services Inc
RENX	NAS SL	RenGRX	Renaissance GRX Inc
REOGF	NAS SL	ReaGld	Rea Gold Corp
REPB	NAS SL	RepRs	Republic Resources Corp
REPR	NAS SL	ReprMd	Repro-Med Systems Inc
RES	New York	RPC	RPC Energy Services Inc
RESC	NAS NMS	RoanEl	Roanoke Electric Steel Corp
RESM	NAS NMS	RestMg	Restaurant Management Services Inc
RESP	NAS NMS	Respir	Respironics Inc
RESR	NAS NMS	ReshInc	Research Inc
REUT	NAS NMS	ReuterI	Reuter Inc
REXI	NAS NMS	RscEx	Resource Exploration Inc
REXN	NAS NMS	Rexon	Rexon Inc
REXW	NAS NMS	Rexwks	Rexworks Inc
REYNA	NAS NMS	ReyRy	The Reynolds & Reynolds Co
RFBC	NAS NMS	RivFor	River Forest Bancorp
RFBI	NAS NL	RegFdl	Regional Federal Bancorp Inc
RFBK	NAS NMS	RalghFS	Raleigh Federal Savings Bank (North Carolina)
RFED	NAS NMS	RsvltFd	Roosevelt Bank FSB (Missouri)
RFPCK	NAS NL	RF&P	RF&P Corp-Non-voting Dividend Obligation Common Stock
RFSB	NAS NMS	ReistFS	Reistertown Federal Savings Bank (Maryland)
RFTN	NAS NMS	Reflctn	Reflectone Inc

TRADING SYMBOL	MARKET LISTING	NEWSPAPER ABBREV.	COMPANY NAME
RGB	American	BaryRG	R.G. Barry Corp
RGC	New York	RepGyp	Republic Gypsum Co
RGCY	NAS NMS	RgcyEl	Regency Electronics Inc
RGEN	NAS NMS	Replgn	Repligen Corp
RGEQ	NAS NMS	RgcyEq	Regency Equities Corp
RGIS	NAS NMS	Regis	Regis Corp
RGL	New York	Regal	Regal International Inc
RGLD	NAS NMS	RoyGld	Royal Gold Inc
RGO	New York	RangrO	Ranger Oil Ltd
RGS	New York	RochG	Rochester Gas & Electric Corp
RHCC	NAS SL	RockgH	Rocking Horse Child Care Centers of America Inc
RHD	New York	Rhodes	Rhodes Inc
RHEM	NAS NMS	Rheomt	Rheometrics Inc
RHH	New York	Robtsn	H.H. Robertson Co
RHI	American	Halmi	Robert Halmi Inc
RHII	NAS NMS	RbtHlf	Robert Half Inc
RHNB	NAS NL	RHNB	RHNB Corp
RHPOY	NAS NMS	RhonPl	Rhone-Poulenc SA
RHR	New York	Rohr	Rohr Industries Inc
RI	New York	Radice	Radice Corp
RIBI	NAS NMS	RibiIm	Ribi ImmunoChem Research Inc
RICE	NAS NL	AmRice	American Rice Inc
RICH	NAS NMS	RchmHl	Richmond Hills Savings Bank
RIDE	NAS SL	PeoRide	People Ridesharing Systems Inc
RIE	American	Riedel	Riedel Environmental Technologies Inc
RIF	American	RESec	Real Estate Securities Income Fund Inc
RIGS	NAS NMS	RiggsNt	Riggs National Corp
RIHL	NAS NMS	Richton	Richton International Corp
RIO	New York	RoyInt	Royal International Optical Corp
RIPY	NAS NL	Ripley	Ripley Company Inc
RITZ	NAS NMS	Ritzys	G.D. Ritzy's Inc
RIV	American	Rivbnd	Riverbend International Corp
RJF	New York	RJamFn	Raymond James Financial Inc
RJR	New York	RJR Nb	RJR Nabisco Inc
RK	American	ArkRst	Ark Restaurants Corp
RKWD	NAS NMS	RckwdH	Rockwood Holding Co
RKY	New York	Rckwy	Rockaway Corp
RLAB	NAS SL	RoyceL	Royce Labs Inc
RLC	New York	RLC	RLC Corp
RLI	New York	RLI Cp	RLI Corp
RLIF	NAS NL	RelbLfe	Reliable Life Insurance Co
RLM	New York	ReyMt	Reynolds Metals Co
RLST	NAS SL	Realist	Realist Inc
RMC	American	ARestr	American Restaurant Partners LP
RMCF	NAS SL	RkMtCh	Rocky Mountain Chocolate Factory Inc
RMCI	NAS NMS	RghtMg	Right Management Consultants Inc
RMI	American	RestMg	Residential Mortgage Investments Inc

TRADING SYMBOL	MARKET LISTING	NEWSPAPER ABBREV.	COMPANY NAME
RMK.A	American	RobMk	Robert-Mark Inc (Class A)
RML	New York	Russell	Russell Corp
RMPO	NAS NMS	RamFin	Ramapo Financial Corp
RMR	American	RAC	RAC Mortgage Investment Corp
RMS	American	RMS Int	RMS International Inc
RMUC	NAS NMS	RMUnd	Rocky Mount Undergarment Company Inc
RNB	New York	RepNY	Republic New York Corp
RNBO	NAS NL	RainbwTc	Rainbow Technologies Inc
RNC	NAS NL	RckwdN	Rockwood National Corp
RNIC	NAS NMS	RobNug	Robinson Nugent Inc
RNRC	NAS NMS	RivrNtl	Riverside National Bank (California)
RNT	American	Reco	RECO International Inc
ROAD	NAS NMS	RoadSv	Roadway Services Inc
ROBN	NAS NMS	RobMyr	Robbins & Myers Inc
ROBO	NAS SL	Robtool	Robotool Ltd
ROBV	NAS NMS	RobVsn	Robotic Vision Systems Inc
RODMY	NAS NL	Rodime	Rodime PLC
ROE	American	Roeblg	Roebling Property Investors Inc
ROG	American	Rogers	Rogers Corp
ROH	New York	RoHaas	Rohm & Haas Co
ROI	New York	RvrOak	River Oaks Industries Inc
ROK	New York	Rockwl	Rockwell International Corp
ROL	New York	Rollins	Rollins Inc
ROM	American	RioAl	Rio Algom Ltd
RONC	NAS NMS	Ronson	Ronson Corp
ROPK	NAS NMS	Ropak	Ropak Corp
ROR	New York	Rorer	Rorer Group Inc
ROST	NAS NMS	RossStr	Ross Stores Inc
ROSX	NAS SL	RossInd	Ross Industries Inc
ROTC	NAS NMS	RoTech	RoTech Medical Corp
ROTO	NAS NMS	RotoRtr	Roto-Rooter Inc
ROUS	NAS NMS	Rouse	The Rouse Co
ROWE	NAS NMS	RoweF	Rowe Furniture Corp
ROYG	NAS NMS	RoylBu	Royal Business Group Inc
ROYL	NAS NMS	Roylpr	Royalpar Industries Inc
RPAL	NAS NMS	RoyPlm	Royal Palm Savings Assn (Florida)
RPAPF	NAS NMS	Repap	Repap Enterprises Corp Inc
RPCH	NAS NMS	Rosptch	Rospatch Corp
RPCO	NAS NMS	Repco	Repco Inc
RPICA	NAS NMS	RpPicA	Republic Pictures Corp (Class A)
RPICB	NAS NL	RpPicB	Republic Pictures Corp (Class B)
RPOW	NAS NMS	RPM	RPM Inc
RPSY	NAS SL	Rapitec	Rapitech Systems Inc
RR	New York	RodRen	Rodman & Renshaw Capital Group Inc
RRF	New York	RltRef	Realty ReFund Trust
RRR	American	ResRs	Residential Resources Mortgages Investments Corp
RSDL	NAS NMS	Resdel	Resdel Industries

TRADING SYMBOL	MARKET LISTING	NEWSPAPER ABBREV.	COMPANY NAME
RSFC	NAS NMS	RepSav	Republic Savings Financial Corp (Florida)
RSGI	NAS NMS	RvrsG	Riverside Group Inc
RSI	American	RltSou	Realty South Investors Inc
RSIC	NAS NMS	RSI	RSI Corp
RSLA	NAS NMS	RepCap	Republic Capital Group Inc
RSR	American	Riser	Riser Foods Inc (Class A)
RSTAF	NAS NL	Sunrst	Sunresorts Ltd NV (Class A)
RSTO	NAS NMS	RoseStr	Rose's Stores Inc
RSTOB	NAS NMS	RoseB	Rose's Stores Inc (Class B)
RT.A	American	Resrt A	Resorts International Inc (Class A)
RTC	New York	RochTl	Rochester Telephone Corp
RTE	New York	RTE	RTE Corp
RTEK	NAS SL	RiseTc	Rise Technology Inc
RTH	New York	HouOR	Houston Oil Royalty Trust
RTII	NAS NMS	RTI	RTI Inc
RTN	New York	Raythn	Raytheon Co
RTP	New York	ReichT	Reich & Tang LP
RTRSY	NAS NMS	ReutrH	Reuters Holdings plc
RTS	New York	RusTg	Russ Togs Inc
RUDY	NAS NMS	Rudys	Rudy's Restaurant Group Inc
RULE	NAS NMS	RuleInd	Rule Industries Inc
RUS	New York	RussBr	Russ Berrie & Company Inc
RVCC	NAS NMS	Reeves	Reeves Communications Corp
RVEE	NAS NL	HldyRV	Holiday RV Superstores Inc
RVR	American	AmLnd	American Land Cruisers Inc
RVT	New York	Royce	Royce Value Trust Inc
RWPI	NAS NMS	RdgwdP	Ridgewood Properties Inc
RXH	New York	Rexhm	Rexham Corp
RXN	New York	Rxene	Rexene Corp
RXSC	NAS SL	Rexcm	Rexcom Systems Corp
RYAN	NAS NMS	RyanF	Ryan's Family Steak Houses Inc
RYC	New York	Raycm	Raychem Corp
RYFL	NAS NMS	FamSt	Family Steak Houses of Florida Inc
RYK	New York	Rykoff	Rykoff-Sexton Inc
RYL	New York	Ryland	The Ryland Group Inc
RYR	New York	Rymer	The Rymer Company
S	New York	Sears	Sears Roebuck & Co
SA	American	Stage	Stage II Apparel Corp
SAA	New York	Saatchi	Saatchi & Saatchi Company PLC
SAB	New York	Sabine	Sabine Corp
SAF	New York	ScdNA	Scudder New Asia Fund Inc
SAFC	NAS NMS	Safeco	SAFECO Corp
SAFE	NAS NMS	SecAF	Security American Financial Enterprises Inc
SAFM	NAS NMS	SandFm	Sanderson Farms Inc
SAG	American	Sage	Sage Energy Co

TRADING SYMBOL	MARKET LISTING	NEWSPAPER ABBREV.	COMPANY NAME
SAGB	NAS SL	SageBd	Sage Broadcasting Corp
SAH	New York	SahCas	Sahara Casino Partners LP
SAI	American	Allstr	Allstar Inns LP
SAII	NAS SL	SageAn	Sage Analytics International Inc
SAJ	New York	StJoLP	St. Joesph Light & Power Co
SALN	NAS NMS	Sahlen	Sahlen & Associates Inc
SAM	American	Samson	Samson Energy Company LP
SAN	American	SCarlo	San Carlos Milling Company Inc
SAND	NAS NL	Sandata	Sandata Inc
SANF	NAS NMS	Sanfrd	Sanford Corp
SANT	NAS NL	StMonB	Santa Monica Bank
SANYY	NAS NL	Sanyo	Sanyo Electric Company Ltd
SAR	New York	SAnitRt	Santa Anita Realty Enterprises Inc
SASOY	NAS NL	Sasol	Sasol Ltd
SAT	New York	Schfr	Schafer Value Trust Inc
SATI	NAS SL	SatlInf	Satellite Information Systems Co
SAX	American	SaxnO	Saxon Oil Development Partners LP
SAXO	NAS NMS	SaxonO	Saxon Oil Co
SAYI	NAS NMS	SAY Ind	S.A.Y. Industries Inc
SAZZ	NAS SL	Saztec	SAZTEC International Inc
SB	New York	Salomn	Salomon Inc
SBA	American	Sbarro	Sbarro Inc
SBC	New York	SwBell	Southwestern Bell Corp
SBCFA	NAS NMS	SeaBnk	Seacost Banking Corporation of Florida (Class A)
SBEI	NAS SL	SBE	SBE Inc
SBIG	NAS NMS	Seibel	The Seibels Bruce Group Inc
SBIO	NAS NMS	Synbio	Synbiotics Corp
SBIZ	NAS SL	HawkEn	Hawkeye Entertainment Inc
SBK	New York	Signet	Signet Banking Corp
SBKSA	NAS NL	SuburB	Suburban Bankshares Inc (Class A)
SBL	New York	SyblTc	Symbol Technologies Inc
SBM	American	SpedOP	Speed-O-Print Business Machines Corp
SBN	American	SunbNu	Sunbelt Nursery Group Inc
SBO	New York	Shwbt	Showboat Inc
SBOS	NAS NMS	BostBc	Boston Bancorp
SBP	New York	StBPnt	Standard Brands Paint Co
SBR	New York	SabnR	Sabine Royalty Trust
SBRG	NAS SL	Seebrg	Seeberg Corp
SBRU	NAS NMS	Subaru	Subaru of America Inc
SBS	American	Salem	Salem Corp
SBTC	NAS NMS	SBT Cp	SBT Corp
SC	New York	ShellT	The Shell Transport & Trading Company plc
SCA	American	Servo	Servo Corporation of America
SCAF	NAS NMS	SurgAf	Surgical Care Affiliates Inc
SCAPY	NAS NMS	SvenCel	Svenska Cellulosa AB
SCAT	NAS SL	Scat	Scat Hovercraft Inc

TRADING SYMBOL	MARKET LISTING	NEWSPAPER ABBREV.	COMPANY NAME
SCC	American	SecCap	Security Capital Corp
SCOM	NAS NMS	SCS	SCS/Compute Inc
SCP	American	Scope	Scope Industries
SCE	New York	SCalEd	Southern California Edison Co
SCF	American	ScandF	The Scandinavia Fund Inc
SCFB	NAS NMS	SoCarF	South Carolina Federal Corp
SCFM	NAS NMS	Scnfrm	Scanforms Inc
SCG	New York	SCANA	SCANA Corp
SCGI	NAS SL	Starst	Starstream Communications Group Inc
SCH	New York	Schwb	The Charles Schwab Corp
SCHC	NAS NMS	Scherer	R.P. Scherer Corp
SCHR	NAS NL	SchrHlt	Scherer Healthcare Inc
SCIE	NAS NMS	Scicom	Scicom Data Services Ltd
SCIS	NAS NMS	SCI Sy	SCI Systems Inc
SCIXF	NAS NMS	Scitex	Scitex Corporation Ltd
SCL	American	Stepan	Stepan Co
SCLS	NAS SL	StarCls	Star Classics Inc
SCMS	NAS SL	SciMeas	Scientific Measurement Systems Inc
SCNC	NAS NMS	SCarNt	South Carolina National Corp
SCNG	NAS SL	ScanGp	Scan Graphics Inc
SCOR	NAS NMS	Syncor	Syncor International Corp
SCOT	NAS NMS	ScotSt	Scott & Stringfellow Financial Inc
SCPNA	NAS SL	Scorpn	Scorpion Technologies Inc (Class A)
SCPT	NAS SL	ScrptSy	Script Systems Inc
SCR	New York	SeaCnt	Sea Containers Ltd
SCRP	NAS NMS	ScripH	Scripps Howard Broadcasting Co
SCTC	NAS NMS	SystCpt	Systems & Computer Technology Corp
SCTI	NAS SL	ScotInst	Scott Instruments Corp
SCX	New York	Starrett	The L.S. Starrett Co
SDNB	NAS NMS	SDNB	SDNB Financial Corp
SDO	New York	SDieGs	San Diego Gas & Electric Co
SDP	New York	SunDis	Sun Distributors LP
SDRC	NAS NMS	StrucDy	Structural Dynamics Research Corp
SDW	New York	Soudwn	Southdown Inc
SDY	American	Sandy	Sandy Corp
SDYN	NAS NMS	Staodyn	Staodynamics Inc
SE	New York	SunEl	Sun Electric Corp
SEAB	NAS NMS	SbdSav	Seaboard S&L Assn (Virginia)
SEAF	NAS SL	Seafds	Seafoods From Alaska Inc
SEAG	NAS NMS	SeaFal	Sea Galley Stores Inc
SEAK	NAS NL	Seahk	Seahawk Oil International Inc
SEB	American	SbdCp	Seaboard Corp
SEC	American	SterlEl	Sterling Electronics Corp
SECB	NAS NMS	SecBcp	Security Bancorp Inc
SECM	NAS SL	Secom	Secom General Corp
SEE	New York	SealAir	Sealed Air Corp
SEEQ	NAS NMS	SEEQ	Seeq Technology Inc
SEFD	NAS SL	Seafood	Seafood Inc

TRADING SYMBOL	MARKET LISTING	NEWSPAPER ABBREV.	COMPANY NAME
SEIC	NAS NMS	SEI	SEI Corp
SEIS	NAS SL	Seitel	Seitel Inc
SELE	NAS SL	SelTrn	SelecTronics Inc
SEM	American	SystEn	Systems Engineering & Manufacturing Corp
SEMI	NAS SL	AllAm	All American Semiconductor Inc
SENE	NAS NMS	Seneca	Seneca Foods Corp
SENR	NAS SL	SenrSv	Senior Service Corp
SEO	American	Seaport	Seaport Corp
SEQ	New York	StorEq	Storage Equities Inc
SEQL	NAS SL	Sequel	Sequel Corp
SEQP	NAS NMS	SuprEq	Supreme Equipment & Systems Corp
SER	American	Siercn	Sierracin Corp
SERF	NAS NMS	SvcFrct	Service Fracturing Co
SESL	NAS NMS	SestSvL	Southeastern S&L Co (North Carolina)
SETC	NAS NMS	SierR 84	Sierra Real Estate Equity Trust '84
SETD	NAS NMS	SierCa	Sierra Capital Realty Trust IV Co
SEWY	NAS NMS	SeawFd	Seaway Food Town Inc
SF	New York	Stifel	Stifel Financial Corp
SFA	New York	SciAtl	Scientific-Atlanta Inc
SFB	New York	StFBk	Standard Federal Bank
SFBM	NAS NMS	SecFdl	Security Federal Savings Bank (Montana)
SFCD	NAS NMS	Safecd	SafeCard Services Inc
SFCP	NAS NMS	SuffFin	Suffield Financial Corp
SFDS	NAS NMS	SmthF	Smithfield Foods Inc
SFE	New York	SfgdSc	Safeguard Scientifics Inc
SFEM	NAS NMS	SFE	SFE Technologies
SFFD	NAS NMS	SFFed	SFFeD Corp (California)
SFGA	NAS NL	SoFdGa	Southern Federal Savings Bank (Georgia)
SFGD	NAS NMS	SafHlt	Safeguard Health Enterprises Inc
SFGI	NAS NMS	SFGI	Security Financial Group Inc (Minnesota)
SFIN	NAS NMS	SthdFn	Southland Financial Corp
SFM	American	SFM	SFM Corp
SFNCA	NAS NL	SimnFt	Simmons First National Corp (Class A)
SFNS	NAS NMS	SpearF	Spear Financial Services Inc
SFOK	NAS NMS	SonrFd	Sooner Federal S&L Assn
SFP	New York	SFeEP	Santa Fe Energy Partners LP
SFS	American	SuprFd	Super Food Services Inc
SFSI	NAS NMS	Sunwst	Sunwest Financial Services Inc
SFSL	NAS NL	SecFClv	Security Federal S&L Assn (Ohio)
SFX	New York	SFeSP	Santa Fe Southern Pacific Corp
SFY	American	SwftEng	Swift Energy Co
SG	American	SciLsg	Scientific Leasing Inc
SGAT	NAS NMS	Seagate	Seagate Technology
SGC	American	SuprSr	Superior Surgical Manufacturing Company Inc
SGDN	NAS SL	Surgidy	Surgidyne Inc

TRADING SYMBOL	MARKET LISTING	NEWSPAPER ABBREV.	COMPANY NAME
SGHB	NAS NMS	SagHbr	Sag Harbour Savings Bank (New York)
SGHI	NAS NL	SlkGrn	Silk Greenhouse Inc
SGI	New York	Slattery	Slattery Group Inc
SGIC	NAS NMS	SilcnGr	Silicon Graphics Inc
SGO	New York	Seagul	Seagull Energy Corp
SGOLY	NAS NL	StHlGd	St. Helena Gold Mines Ltd
SGP	New York	SchrPlg	Schering-Plough Corp
SGSI	NAS NMS	SageSft	Sage Software Inc
SH	American	Spartc	Spartech Corp
SHB	New York	Scottys	Scotty's Inc
SHC	New York	Shaklee	Shaklee Corp
SHCI	NAS NMS	Salick	Salick Health Care Inc
SHCO	NAS NMS	Schult	Schult Homes Corp
SHD	American	ShwdG	The Sherwood Group Inc
SHE	New York	ShLeh	Shearson Lehman Brothers Holdings Inc
SHEF	NAS NMS	SandChf	Sandwich Chef Inc
SHEL	NAS NMS	Sheldl	Sheldahl Inc
SHIP	NAS NMS	RgcyCr	Regency Cruises Inc
SHKIF	NAS NMS	SHL Sy	SHL Systemhouse Inc
SHLB	NAS NMS	ShelbyF	Shelby Federal Savings Bank (Indiana)
SHLM	NAS NMS	SchlmA	A. Schulman Inc
SHLY	NAS SL	ShlyAsc	Shelly Associates Inc
SHNA	NAS NMS	Shaw Nt	Shawmut National Corp
SHO	American	StarrtH	Starrett Housing Corp
SHON	NAS NMS	Shoney	Shoney's Inc
SHOP	NAS NMS	Shpsmt	Shopsmith Inc
SHOR	NAS NMS	Shrwd	Shorewood Packaging Corp
SHOW	NAS SL	Shwscn	Showscan Film Corp
SHRE	NAS NMS	Sahara	Sahara Resorts Inc
SHRP	NAS NMS	ShrpIm	Sharper Image Corp
SHS	American	ShaerS	Shaer Shoe Corp
SHV	American	StHavn	Standard Havens Inc
SHW	New York	Shrwin	The Sherwin-Williams Co
SHX	New York	ShawIn	Shaw Industries Inc
SI	New York	ACMSp	ACM Government Spectrum Fund
SIA	New York	SgnlApl	Signal Apparel Company Inc
SIAL	NAS NMS	SigmaAl	Sigma-Aldrich Corp
SIBR	NAS NMS	Sybra	Sybra Inc
SIDX	NAS NMS	SciDyn	Science Dynamics Corp
SIE	American	SierHS	Sierra Health Services Inc
SIF	American	Sifco	SIFCO Industries Inc
SIG	New York	SoIndGs	Southern Indiana Gas & Electric Co
SIGI	NAS NMS	SelctIns	Selective Insurance Group Inc
SIGM	NAS NMS	SigmaD	Sigma Designs Inc
SIGN	NAS NMS	PlastLn	Plasti-Line Inc
SIHS	NAS SL	SI Hand	SI Handling Systems Inc
SII	New York	SmithIn	Smith International Inc
SIL	New York	SiliconS	Silicon Systems Inc

TRADING SYMBOL	MARKET LISTING	NEWSPAPER ABBREV.	COMPANY NAME
SILI	NAS NMS	Silicnx	Siliconix Inc
SILN	NAS NMS	Silicon	Silicon General Inc
SILV	NAS NMS	SlvKing	Silver King Mines Inc
SIN	New York	SystInt	System Integrators Inc
SIRC	NAS NL	Sirco	Sirco International Corp
SISB	NAS NMS	SisCp	Sis Corp
SISC	NAS NMS	StwInf	Stewart Information Services Corp
SIVB	NAS NMS	SilcVly	Silicon Valley Bancshares (California)
SIX	New York	Motel	Motel 6 LP
SIZ	New York	Sizeler	Sizeler Property Investors Inc
SIZZ	NAS NMS	Sizler	Sizzler Restaurants International Inc
SJI	New York	SJerIn	South Jersey Industries Inc
SJM	New York	Smuckr	The J.M. Smucker Co
SJNB	NAS NL	SJNB	SJNB Financial Corp
SJR	New York	SJuanR	San Juan Racing Assn Inc
SJS	American	SunJr	Sunshine-Jr. Stores Inc
SJT	New York	SJuanB	San Juan Basin Royalty Trust
SJW	American	SJW	SJW Corp
SK	New York	SaftKln	Safety-Kleen Corp
SK.A	American	SikesA	Sikes Corp (Class A)
SKAN	NAS NMS	SkanSB	Skaneateles Savings Bank (New York)
SKB	New York	SmkB	SmithKline Beckman Corp
SKCH	NAS NL	SkyChili	Skyline Chili Inc
SKFB	NAS NMS	SK	S&K Famous Brands Inc
SKFRY	NAS NMS	SKR AB	SKF AB
SKII	NAS NMS	SKI	S-K-I Ltd
SKIP	NAS NMS	Skipper	Skippers Inc
SKN	American	Skolnk	Skolnicks Inc
SKY	New York	Skyline	Skyline Corp
SKYW	NAS NMS	SkyWst	SkyWest Inc
SL	New York	SL Ind	SL Industries Inc
SLAB	NAS SL	SageLb	Sage Labs Inc
SLAT	NAS SL	SlatrDv	Slater Development Corp
SLB	New York	Schlmb	Schlumberger Ltd
SLCR	NAS NMS	SalCpt	Salem Carpet Mills Inc
SLE	New York	SaraLee	Sara Lee Corp
SLFC	NAS NL	ShrlnFn	Shoreline Financial Corp
SLG	American	SeligAs	Seligman & Associates Inc
SLHC	NAS NMS	Sthlfe	Southlife Holding Co
SLIQ	NAS SL	ScotLiq	Scotts Liquid Gold Inc
SLM	New York	SallieM	Student Loan Marketing Assn
SLMAJ	NAS NMS	StudL	Student Loan Marketing Assn (voting)
SLP	New York	SunEng	Sun Energy Partners LP
SLS	American	Selas	Selas Corporation of America
SLT	New York	Salant	Salant Corp
SLTG	NAS NMS	SternL	Sterner Lighting Systems Inc
SLTM	NAS NMS	Select	SelecTerm Inc
SLV	American	Silvrcst	Silvercrest Corp

TRADING SYMBOL	MARKET LISTING	NEWSPAPER ABBREV.	COMPANY NAME
SLVC	NAS SL	Selvac	Selvac Corp
SLVRF	NAS SL	SlvMin	Silverado Mines Ltd
SM	New York	Soumrk	Southmark Corp
SMBX	NAS NMS	Symblic	Symbolics Inc
SMC.A	American	SmthA	A.O. Smith Corp (Class A)
SMC.B	American	SmthB	A.O. Smith Corp (Class B)
SMCH	NAS NMS	SvcMer	Service Merchandise Company Inc
SMCR	NAS NMS	Sumcrp	Summcorp
SMED	NAS NMS	ShrMed	Shared Medical Systems Corp
SMG	American	SciMgt	Science Management Corp
SMGS	NAS NMS	SMichG	Southeastern Michigan Gas Enterprises Inc
SMH	American	Semtch	Semtech Corp
SMI	New York	Spring	Springs Industries Inc
SMIN	NAS NMS	SoMinrl	Southern Mineral Corp
SMK	American	Sanmrk	Sanmark-Stardust Inc
SMLB	NAS NMS	SmithL	Smith Laboratories Inc
SMLS	NAS NMS	Scimed	SciMed Life Systems Inc
SMMT	NAS NMS	SumSav	Summit Savings Assn (Washington)
SMN	American	Seamn	Seamen's Corp
SMNA	NAS NMS	Samna	Samna Corp
SMNI	NAS NMS	SatlMus	Satellite Music Network Inc
SMP	New York	StMotr	Standard Motor Products Inc
SMPS	NAS NMS	SimpIn	Simpson Industries Inc
SMRT	NAS SL	Smrtcd	Smartcard International Inc
SMS	New York	StaMSe	State Mutual Securities Trust
SMSC	NAS NMS	StdMic	Standard Microsystems Corp
SMSI	NAS NMS	SciMic	Scientific Micro Systems Inc
SNA	New York	SnapOn	Snap-on Tools Corp
SNAT	NAS NMS	SthnNt	Southern National Corp
SNCO	NAS NMS	SensrCtl	Sensor Control Corp
SNDCF	NAS SL	SandTc	Sand Technology Systems Inc (Class A) (Canada)
SNDS	NAS NMS	SandReg	The Sands Regent
SNDT	NAS NMS	SunGrd	SunGard Data Systems Inc
SNE	New York	SonyCp	Sony Corp
SNEL	NAS NMS	SnelSnl	Snelling & Snelling Inc
SNF	New York	Spain	Spain Fund Inc
SNFS	NAS NMS	ScNtFd	Second National Federal Savings Bank (Maryland)
SNG	New York	SNETI	Southern New England Telecommunications Corp
SNI	American	SunCty	Sun City Industries Inc
SNIC	NAS SL	Sigmtrn	Sigmatron Nova Inc
SNKIV	NAS NL	Swank	Swank Inc
SNLFA	NAS NMS	SNL Fnc	S.N.L. Financial Corp (Class A)
SNLT	NAS NMS	Sunlite	Sunlite Inc
SNMD	NAS NMS	SunMed	Sunrise Medical Inc

TRADING SYMBOL	MARKET LISTING	NEWSPAPER .ABBREV.	COMPANY NAME
SNO	American	PolrIn	Polaris Industries Partners LP
SNPX	NAS NL	SynOpt	SynOptics Communications Inc
SNRU	NAS NMS	Sunair	Sunair Electronics Inc
SNS	New York	Sundstr	Sundstrand Corp
SNSR	NAS NMS	Sensor	Sensormatic Electronics Corp
SNSTA	NAS NMS	Sonesta	Sonesta International Hotels Corp (Class A)
SNT	New York	Sonat	Sonat Inc
SNTKY	NAS SL	Senetek	Senetek PLC
SO	New York	SouthCo	The Southern Co
SOBK	NAS NMS	SthnBsh	Southern Bankshares Inc
SOCI	NAS NMS	Society	Society Corp
SOCR	NAS NMS	ScanOp	Scan-Optics Inc
SOCS	NAS NMS	SoctySv	The Society for Savings Bancorp Inc (Connecticut)
SOD	New York	Solitron	Solitron Devices Inc
SODA	NAS NMS	A&W Bd	A&W Brands Inc
SOED	NAS NL	SouEdc	Southern Educators Life Insurance Co
SOFT	NAS NMS	Softech	SofTech Inc
SOI	New York	Snyder	Snyder Oil Partners LP
SOLI	NAS NMS	Solitec	Solitec Inc
SOLR	NAS NMS	ApldSlr	Applied Solar Energy Corp
SOLV	NAS SL	SolvEx	Solv-Ex Corp
SOMB	NAS NMS	SomerB	Somerset Bancorp Inc
SOME	NAS NMS	StMain	State-O-Maine Inc
SOMR	NAS NMS	SomrG	The Somerset Group Inc
SONNF	NAS NMS	Sonora	Sonora Gold Corp
SONO	NAS NMS	SonocP	Sonoco Products Co
SONX	NAS SL	Sonex	Sonex Research Inc
SOO	New York	SooLin	Soo Line Corp
SOON	NAS NMS	SoonDf	Sooner Defense of Florida Inc
SOR	New York	SourcC	Source Capital Inc
SOSA	NAS NMS	SomrSv	Somerset Savings Bank (Massachusetts)
SOTK	NAS SL	SonoTk	Sono Tek Corp
SOTR	NAS NMS	Soutrst	SouthTrust Corp
SOUT	NAS NMS	Sounet	SouthernNet Inc
SOV	New York	Sovran	Sovran Financial Corp
SP	American	Spellng	Aaron Spelling Productions Inc
SPA	New York	Sparton	Sparton Corp
SPAIB	NAS NMS	StratPl	Strategic Planning Associates Inc (Class B)
SPAN	NAS NMS	SpanAm	Span-America Medical Systems Inc
SPAR	NAS NMS	SprtMt	Spartan Motors Inc
SPBC	NAS NMS	StPaulB	St. Paul Bancorp Inc
SPBD	NAS NMS	Sprngbd	Springboard Software Inc
SPC	New York	SecPac	Security Pacific Corp
SPCL	NAS SL	SpctrCl	Spectrum Cellular Corp
SPCM	NAS NMS	SpecCm	Specialty Composites Corp

TRADING SYMBOL	MARKET LISTING	NEWSPAPER ABBREV.	COMPANY NAME
SPCO	NAS NMS	SftwPb	Software Publishing Corp
SPCT	NAS SL	SpcPhm	Spectra Pharmaceutical Services Inc
SPD	New York	StdPrd	The Standard Products Co
SPE	New York	SpcEq	Specialty Equipment Companies Inc
SPEC	NAS NMS	SpecCtl	Spectrum Control Inc
SPEDY	NAS SL	SirSpdy	Sir Speedy Printing Centres PLC
SPEK	NAS NMS	Specs	Spec's Music Inc
SPF	New York	StdPac	Standard-Pacific Corp
SPG	New York	Sprage	Sprague Technologies Inc
SPGLA	NAS NMS	Spiegel	Spiegel Inc (Class A)
SPI	American	SPI Ph	SPI Pharmaceuticals Inc
SPILF	NAS NMS	SPI Sus	S.P.I.-Suspension & Parts Industries Ltd
SPIR	NAS NMS	Spire	Spire Corp
SPLF	NAS SL	SprtLfe	The Sporting Life Inc
SPLKA	NAS NMS	JoneSpc	Jones Spacelink Ltd (Class A)
SPP	New York	ScottP	Scott Paper Co
SPPTY	NAS NL	SoPcPt	Southern Pacific Petroleum NL
SPR	American	StrlCap	Sterling Capital Corp
SPRH	NAS NMS	Spear	Spearhead Industries Inc
SPS	New York	SwtPS	Southwestern Public Service Co
SPTR	NAS NMS	Spctran	SpecTran Corp
SPW	New York	SPX Cp	SPX Corp
SQA.A	New York	SequaA	Sequa Corp (Class A)
SQA.B	New York	SequaB	Sequa Corp (Class B)
SQAI	NAS NMS	SquareI	Square Industries Inc
SQB	New York	Squibb	Squibb Corp
SQD	New York	SquarD	Square D Co
SQNT	NAS NMS	Sequent	Sequent Computer Systems Inc
SRB	American	ScurRn	Scurry-Rainbow Oil Ltd
SRC	New York	SvcRes	Service Resources Corp
SRCE	NAS NMS	1stSrc	1st Source Corp
SRCO	NAS NMS	Sealrgt	Sealright Company Inc
SRE	New York	StonRs	Stoneridge Resources Inc
SREG	NAS NMS	StdReg	The Standard Register Co
SRFI	NAS NMS	SupRte	Super Rite Foods Inc
SRG	American	SorgInc	Sorg Inc
SRL	American	Sceptre	Sceptre Resources Ltd
SRP	New York	SierPac	Sierra Pacific Resources
SRR	New York	StridRt	The Stride Rite Corp
SRSL	NAS NMS	SunrFd	Sunrise Federal S&L Assn (Kentucky)
SRV	New York	SvcCp	Service Corporation International
SRVI	NAS NMS	Servico	Servico Inc
SS	American	Schwab	Schwab Safe Company Inc
SSAL	NAS NMS	Sheltn	Shelton Savings Bank (Connecticut)
SSAX	NAS NMS	SySoftw	Systems Software Associates Inc
SSBA	NAS NMS	SeacstS	Seacoast Savings Bank (New Hampshire)
SSBB	NAS NMS	SthngS	Southington Savings Bank (Connecticut)

TRADING SYMBOL	MARKET LISTING	NEWSPAPER ABBREV.	COMPANY NAME
SSBG	NAS SL	SthStr	Southern Starr Broadcasting Group Inc
SSC	New York	SunMn	Sunshine Mining Holding Co
SSFT	NAS NMS	SciSft	Scientific Software-Intercomp Inc
SSIAA	NAS NMS	StockSy	Stockholder Systems Inc (Class A)
SSII	NAS SL	SpecSys	Specialized Systems Inc
SSLN	NAS NMS	SecSLn	Security Savings Bank SLA (New Jersey)
SSM	New York	SSMC	SSMC Inc
SSOA	NAS NMS	SoftSv	Software Services of America Inc
SSS	American	MSA	MSA Realty Corp
SSSL	NAS NMS	SunStSL	Sun State S&L Assn (Arizona)
SSSS	NAS NMS	Stew Stv	Stewart & Stevenson Services Inc
SSSV	NAS SL	SciSyst	Scientific Systems Services Inc
SST	American	ShltCm	Shelter Components Corp
SSW	American	SterlSft	Sterling Software Inc
SSYS	NAS SL	StrlMed	Sterling Medical Systems Inc
ST	New York	SPSTec	SPS Technologies Inc
STAAR	NAS NMS	StarSur	STAAR Surgical Co
STAF	NAS NMS	StafBld	Staff Builders Inc
STAG	NAS NMS	SecTag	Security Tag Systems Inc
STAM	NAS SL	CometEn	Comet Enterprises Inc
STAR	NAS NMS	Stars	Stars To Go Inc
STB	New York	SoestBk	Southeast Banking Corp
STBK	NAS NMS	StaStB	State Street Boston Corp
STBY	NAS NMS	Stansby	Stansbury Mining Corp
STD	New York	BnSant	Banco Santander
STEW	NAS SL	StewSn	Stewart Sandwiches Inc
STG	New York	Steego	Steego Corp
STGA	NAS NMS	SaratSt	Saratoga Standardbreds Inc
STGM	NAS NMS	StatGm	Status Game Corp
STH	New York	Stanhm	Stanhome Inc
STHF	NAS NMS	StnlyIn	Stanley Interiors Corp
STI	New York	SunTr	SunTrust Banks Inc
STII	NAS NMS	StanfTl	Stanford Telecommunications Inc
STJM	NAS NMS	StJude	St. Jude Medical Inc
STK	New York	StorTch	Storage Technology Corp
STKLF	NAS SL	StakeTc	Stake Technology Ltd
STKR	NAS NMS	StckYle	Stocker & Yale Inc
STKY	NAS NMS	Stokely	Stokely USA Inc
STL	New York	StrlBcp	Sterling Bancorp
STLTF	NAS NMS	Stolt	Stolt Tankers & Terminals SA
STM	New York	StratMt	Strategic Mortgage Investments Inc
STN	New York	StevnJ	J.P. Stevens & Company Inc
STO	New York	StoneC	Stone Container Corp
STOT	NAS NMS	Stotler	Stotler Group Inc
STOYD	NAS NL	Santos	Santos Ltd
STPL	NAS NMS	StPaul	The St. Paul Companies Inc
STPT	NAS NMS	StrptSv	Srarpointe Savings Bank (New Jersey)
STR	New York	Questar	Questar Corp

TRADING SYMBOL	MARKET LISTING	NEWSPAPER ABBREV.	COMPANY NAME
STRA	NAS NMS	Stratus	Stratus Computer Inc
STRB	NAS NMS	Strober	Strober Organization Inc
STRM	NAS NMS	StrmRg	Strum Ruger & Company Inc
STRN	NAS NMS	Sutron	Sutron Corp
STRR	NAS NMS	StarTc	Star Technologies Inc
STRS	NAS NMS	Sprouse	Sprouse-Reitz Stores Inc
STRU	NAS NL	Structfb	Structofab Inc
STRWA	NAS NMS	StrwbCl	Strawbridge & Clothier (Class A)
STRX	NAS NMS	Syntrex	Syntrex Inc
STRY	NAS NMS	Strykr	Stryker Corp
STTG	NAS NMS	StateG	The Statesman Group Inc
STTX	NAS NMS	SteelT	Steel Technologies Inc
STUH	NAS NMS	StuartH	Stuart Hall Company Inc
STUS	NAS NMS	StuDS	Stuarts Department Stores Inc
STVEA	NAS NL	SteveIC	Steve's Homemade Ice Cream Inc (Class A)
STVI	NAS NMS	STV	STV Engineers Inc
STW	New York	StdCom	Standard Commercial Corp
STWB	NAS NMS	StwBc	Statewide Bancorp
SUA	American	SumtTx	Summit Tax Exempt Bond Fund LP
SUBBA	NAS NMS	SubBcp	Suburban Bancorp Inc (Class A)
SUBK	NAS NMS	SuffBn	Suffolk Bancorp
SUBN	NAS NMS	SumitB	The Summit Bancorporation
SUDS	NAS NMS	Sudbry	Sudbury Holdings Inc
SUG	New York	SoUnCo	Southern Union Co
SUHC	NAS NMS	SumtH	Summit Holding Corp
SUMA	NAS NMS	Summa	Summa Medical Corp
SUMH	NAS NMS	SumtHl	Summit Health Ltd
SUMI	NAS NMS	Sumito	Sumitomo Bank of California
SUN	New York	SunCo	Sun Company Inc
SUND	NAS NMS	SoundA	Sound Advice Inc
SUNF	NAS NMS	SunstFd	Sunstar Foods Inc
SUNI	NAS NMS	SunCst	Sun Coast Plastics Inc
SUNR	NAS SL	SunPre	Sunrise Preschool Inc
SUNW	NAS NMS	SunMic	Sun Microsystems Inc
SUP	American	SupInd	Superior Industries International Inc
SUPD	NAS SL	Suprad	Supradur Companies Inc
SUPE	NAS NMS	SupEl	The Superior Electric Co
SUPX	NAS NMS	Suprtex	Supertex Inc
SUR	New York	SCOR U	SCOR US Corp
SURV	NAS NMS	SurvTc	Survival Technology Inc
SUSQ	NAS NMS	SusqBn	Susquehanna Bancshares Inc
SUW	American	StrutW	Struthers Wells Corp
SVAN	NAS NMS	SavnFd	Savannah Foods & Industries Inc
SVB	New York	Savin	Savin Corp
SVG	American	StvGph	Stevens Graphics Corp
SVGI	NAS NMS	SilcnVl	Silicon Valley Group Inc
SVM	New York	Svcmst	ServiceMaster LP

TRADING SYMBOL	MARKET LISTING	NEWSPAPER ABBREV.	COMPANY NAME
SVRL	NAS NMS	SilvLis	Silvar-Lisco
SVRN	NAS NMS	SovBcp	Sovereign Bancorp Inc
SVT	American	Servotr	Servotronics Inc
SVU	New York	SupValu	Super Value Stores Inc
SW	New York	StoneW	Stone & Webster Inc
SWABV	NAS NL	SchwtzB	Schwartz Brothers Inc (Class B)
SWAL	NAS SL	StwAir	Stateswest Airlines Inc
SWARA	NAS NMS	SchwtzA	Schwartz Brothers Inc (Class A)
SWB	American	SwBcp	Southwest Bancorp (California)
SWCB	NAS NMS	SandCop	The Sandwich Co-operative Bank (Massachusetts)
SWD	American	StdShr	Standard Shares Inc
SWEL	NAS NMS	SwElSv	Southwestern Electric Service Co
SWHI	NAS NMS	SoundW	Sound Warehouse Inc
SWIM	NAS SL	SanJuan	San Juan Fiberglass Pools Inc
SWIS	NAS NMS	StIves	St. Ives Laboratories Corp
SWK	New York	StanlWk	The Stanley Works
SWL	American	SwstRlt	Southwest Realty Ltd
SWMC	NAS NMS	StanWst	Stan West Mining Corp
SWN	New York	SwEnr	Southwestern Energy Co
SWPA	NAS NMS	SwstNt	Southwest National Corp
SWTR	NAS NMS	SCalWt	Southern California Water Co
SWTX	NAS NMS	Souwal	Southwall Technologies Inc
SWV	New York	SuavSh	Suave Shoe Corp
SWVA	NAS NMS	StlWVa	Steel of West Virginia Inc
SWWC	NAS NMS	SwWtr	Southwest Water Co
SWX	New York	SwtGas	Southwest Gas Corp
SWZ	New York	Helvet	The Helvetia Fund Inc
SXI	New York	Standex	Standex International Corp
SY	New York	Shelby	Shelby Williams Industries Inc
SYGN	NAS NMS	Synergn	Synergen Inc
SYM	New York	SymsCp	Syms Corp
SYMB	NAS NMS	Symbin	Symbion Inc
SYMK	NAS NMS	SymTk	Sym-Tek Systems Inc
SYN	New York	Syntex	Syntex Corp
SYNEP	NAS NMS	Syntech	Syntech International Inc
SYNG	NAS SL	Synget	Synergetics International Inc
SYNR	NAS NMS	Synrcm	Synercom Technology Inc
SYNT	NAS NMS	Syntro	Syntro Corp
SYO	American	Synaloy	Synalloy Corp
SYRA	NAS NMS	SyrSup	Syracuse Supply Co
SYS	American	ISI Sy	ISI Systems Inc
SYSM	NAS NMS	SystIn	System Industries Inc
SYST	NAS NMS	Systmt	Systematics Inc
SYX	American	Bayou	Bayou Steel Corporation of La Place
SYY	New York	Sysco	Sysco Corp
SZF	American	SierCap	Sierra Capital Realty Trust VI
SZG	American	SierCa7	Sierra Capital Realty Trust VII

TRADING SYMBOL	MARKET LISTING	NEWSPAPER ABBREV.	COMPANY NAME
T	New York	AT&T	American Telephone & Telegraph Co
TA	New York	Transm	Transamerica Corp
TAB	American	TandB	Tandy Brands Inc
TAC	New York	Tndycft	Tandycrafts Inc
TACT	NAS SL	Trnsact	Transact International Inc
TAI	New York	TranInc	Transamerica Income Shares Inc
TAL	New York	Talley	Talley Industries Inc
TAM	American	TubMex	Tubos de Acero de Mexico SA
TAN	New York	Tandy	Tandy Corp
TANT	NAS NMS	Tennant	Tennant Co
TAPP	NAS SL	TotlAst	Total Assets Protection Inc
TAROF	NAS NL	TaroVt	Taro Vit Industries Ltd
TATE	NAS NMS	Ashton	Ashton-Tate
TAVI	NAS NMS	ThrnAV	Thorn Apple Valley Inc
TAYS	NAS SL	TaylrS	S. Taylor Companies Inc
TBC	American	Tasty	Tasty Baking Co
TBCC	NAS NMS	TBC	TBC Corp
TBL	American	TmbCo	The Timberland Co
TBO	New York	TacBt	Tacoma Boatbuilding co
TBP	American	TabPrd	Tab Products Co
TBS.A	American	TurnB A	Turner Broadcasting System Inc (Class A)
TBS.B	American	TurnB B	Turner Broadcasting System Inc (Class B)
TC	New York	Telex	The Telex Corp
TCAT	NAS NMS	TCA	TCA Cable TV Inc
TCBC	NAS NMS	Trstco	The Trustcompany Bancorporation (New Jersey)
TCBY	NAS NMS	TCBY	TCBY Enterprises Inc
TCC	American	Telecon	TeleConcepts Corp
TCCO	NAS NMS	TchCom	Technical Communications Corp
TCDN	NAS NL	Tchdyn	Techdyne Inc
TCFC	NAS NMS	TCF	TCF Financial Corp (Minnesota)
TCGN	NAS NMS	Tecogen	Tecogen Inc
TCII	NAS NMS	TcCom	Technology for Communications International Inc
TCK	American	TEC	TEC Inc
TCL	New York	Transcn	Transcon Inc
TCOMA	NAS NMS	TlcmA	Tele-Communications Inc (Class A)
TCOMB	NAS NMS	TlcmB	Tele-Communications Inc (Class B)
TCOR	NAS NMS	Tandon	Tandon Corp
TCR	New York	Tramel	Trammell Crow Real Estate Investors
TCRD	NAS NMS	Telcrd	Telecredit Inc
TCSE	NAS NL	TCS Ent	TCS Enterprises Inc
TCSFY	NAS NMS	Thmsn	Thomson-CSF
TCST	NAS SL	Telecst	Telecast Inc
TCT	New York	Tricntr	Tricentrol PLC
TCTC	NAS NMS	Tompkn	Tompkins County Trust Co (New York)

TRADING	MARKET	NEWSPAPER	COMPANY
SYMBOL	LISTING	ABBREV.	NAME
TDAT	NAS NMS	Teradta	Teradata Corp
TDCX	NAS NL	TechDv	Technology Development Corp
TDD.A	American	ThrD A	Three D Departments Inc (Class A)
TDD.B	American	ThrD B	Three D Departments Inc (Class B)
TDI	New York	TwinDs	Twin Disc Inc
TDK	New York	TDK	TDK Corp
TDM	New York	Tandm	Tandem Computers Inc
TDRLF	NAS NMS	Tudor	Tudor Coporation Ltd
TDS	American	TelDta	Telephone & Data Systems Inc
TDW	New York	Tidwtr	Tidewater Inc
TDX	American	Tridex	Tridex Corp
TDY	New York	Teldyn	Teledyne Inc
TDYN	NAS SL	Thrmdy	Thermodynetics Inc
TE	New York	TECO	TECO Energy Inc
TECD	NAS NMS	TchDta	Tech Data Corp
TECN	NAS NMS	Tchnal	Technalysis Corp
TECU	NAS NMS	Tecum	Tecumseh Products Co
TEF	New York	Telef	Companie Telefonica Nacional de Espana SA
TEIR	NAS SL	ThEdIn	Thomas Edison Inns Inc
TEK	New York	Tektrnx	Tektronix Inc
TEL	New York	Telcom	TeleCom Corp
TELC	NAS NMS	Telco	Telco Systems Inc
TELE	NAS NMS	TPI En	TPI Enterprises Inc
TELQ	NAS NMS	TelQst	TeleQuest Inc
TELS	NAS SL	TEL El	TEL Electronics Inc
TELV	NAS NMS	Telvid	TeleVideo Systems Inc
TEMC	NAS NMS	Temco	Temco Home Health Care Products Inc
TEP	New York	TucsEP	Tucson Electric Power Co
TEQ	American	TrnEq	Turner Equity Investors Inc
TER	New York	Terdyn	Teradyne Inc
TERM	NAS NMS	TermDt	Terminal Data Corp
TESP	NAS SL	TelSpcl	Telephone Specialists Inc
TET	New York	TexEst	Texas Eastern Corp
TEV	American	ThrmE	Thermo Environmental Corp
TEVIY	NAS NMS	Teva	Teva Pharmaceutical Industries Ltd
TEX	American	TexAir	Texas Air Corp
TFC	New York	Trnscap	TransCapital Financial Corp
TFIT	NAS SL	TOFIT	TO FITNESS Inc
TFLX	NAS NMS	Termflx	Termiflex Corp
TFONY	NAS NL	TelMex	Telefonosa de Mexico SA
TFSB	NAS NMS	FdSvBk	The Federal Savings Bank (Connecticut)
TFTY	NAS NMS	ThftyRt	Thrifty Rent-A-Car System Inc
TFX	American	Teleflex	Teleflex Inc
TGCO	NAS NMS	Trnsdyn	Transidyne General Corp
TGI	New York	TGIF	TGI Friday's Inc
TGL	New York	TritnG	Triton Group Ltd
TGNXF	NAS SL	TourM	Tournigan Mining Explorations Ltd

TRADING SYMBOL	MARKET LISTING	NEWSPAPER ABBREV.	COMPANY NAME
TGR	New York	TigerIn	Tiger International Inc
TGT	New York	Tennco	Tenneco Inc
THC	New York	Hydral	The Hydraulic Co
THCO	NAS NMS	Hamnd	Hammond Co
THEI	NAS SL	TdyHm	Today Home Entertainment Inc
THEX	NAS SL	HitchE	Hitech Engineering Co
THFI	NAS NMS	PlyFve	Plymouth Five Cents Savings Bank (Massachusetts)
THFR	NAS NMS	Thetfd	Thetford Corp
THI	American	ThrIns	Thermo Instrument Systems Inc
THK	New York	Thack	Thackey Corp
THMP	NAS NL	ThrmIn	Thermal Industries Inc
THO	New York	ThorInd	Thor Industries Inc
THP	American	TriHme	Triangle Home Products Inc
THPR	NAS NMS	TherPr	Thermal Profiles Inc
THR	American	ThorEn	Thor Energy Resources Inc
THRX	NAS SL	Thrgen	Theragenics Corp
THT	New York	Thortec	Thortec International Inc
TI	American	TII	TII Industries Inc
TICI	NAS SL	TIC	TIC International Corp
TIE	American	TIE	TIE/communications Inc
TIER	NAS NMS	Tierco	The Tierco Group Inc
TIF	New York	Tiffny	Tiffany & Co
TII	New York	ThomIn	Thomas Industries Inc
TIM	New York	TmpGl	Templeton Global Income Fund
TIMM	NAS SL	TmbrM	Timberline Minerals Inc
TIN	New York	Templ	Temple-Inland Inc
TIC	New York	Travler	The Travelers Corp
TIRZC	NAS NL	TideR	Tidelands Royalty Trust "B"
TIS	New York	TIS	TIS Mortgage Investment Co
TJCK	NAS NL	Tmbrjk	Timberjack Corp
TJCO	NAS NMS	TrusJo	Trus Joist Corp
TJX	New York	TJX	The TJX Companies Inc
TKA	New York	Tonka	Tonka Corp
TKAI	NAS NMS	Teknwd	Teknowledge Inc
TKIOY	NAS NMS	TokioF	Tokio Marine & Fire Insurance Company Ltd
TKLC	NAS NMS	Tekelec	Tekelec
TKNA	NAS SL	Tekna	Tekna Tool Inc
TKR	New York	Timken	The Timken Co
TL	New York	Time	Time Inc
TLAB	NAS NMS	Telabs	Tellabs Inc
TLAM	NAS NMS	LamaT	Tony Lama Company Inc
TLARF	NAS SL	TeleArt	Tele Art Inc
TLCC	NAS SL	Telecalc	Telecalc Inc
TLCR	NAS NMS	Telcrft	Telecrafter Corp
TLEXF	NAS NL	TotlEr	Total Erickson Resources Ltd
TLHT	NAS NMS	TotlHlt	Total Health Systems Inc

TRADING SYMBOL	MARKET LISTING	NEWSPAPER ABBREV.	COMPANY NAME
TLII	NAS NMS	TrnLsg	Trans Leasing International Inc
TLMD	NAS NMS	Telmdo	Telemundo Group Inc
TLMN	NAS NMS	Talman	Talman Home Federal S&L Assn of Illinois
TLMT	NAS SL	Telmatn	Telemation Inc
TLOG	NAS SL	TrnfmL	Transform Logic Corp
TLOS	NAS NMS	Telos	Telos Corp
TLR	New York	Telrte	Telerate Inc
TLTM	NAS SL	Teletmr	Teletimer International Inc
TLX	American	TrnsLx	Trans-Lux Corp
TLXN	NAS NMS	Telxon	Telxon Corp
TM	New York	ThmMed	Thompson Medical Company Inc
TMA	New York	TMAM	Thomson McKinnon Asset Management LP
TMAX	NAS NMS	Telmatc	Telematrics International Inc
TMB	New York	Tambd	Tambrands Inc
TMBR	NAS NMS	BrTom	Tom Brown Inc
TMBS	NAS NMS	TimbSf	Timberline Software Corp
TMC	New York	TmMir	The Times Mirror Co
TMCI	NAS NMS	TM Com	TM Communications Inc
TMCO	NAS SL	TmeMgt	Time Management Corp
TMD	American	Thrmd	Thermedics Inc
TMED	NAS NMS	Trimed	Trimedyne Inc
TMEXF	NAS NL	TeraM	Terra Mines Ltd
TMG	New York	Muscld	The Musicland Group Inc
TMI	American	Team	Team Inc
TMK	New York	Trchmk	Torchmark Corp
TMNI	NAS SL	Trnmed	Transmedia Network Inc
TMO	New York	ThrmEl	Thermo Electron Corp
TMSTA	NAS NL	ThmMA	Thomaston Mills Inc (Class A)
TMSTB	NAS NL	ThmMB	Thomaston Mills Inc (Class B)
TMTX	NAS NMS	Temtex	Temtex Industries Inc
TNB	New York	ThmBet	Thomas & Betts Corp
TNC	American	TwCty	Town & Country Jewelry Manufacturing Corp
TND	American	Technd	Technodyne Inc
TNDS	NAS NMS	TS Ind	TS Industries Inc
TNEL	NAS NMS	NelsnT	Nelson Thomas Inc
TNELB	NAS SL	NelsnB	Nelson Thomas Inc (Class B)
TNET	NAS SL	Telenet	Telenetics Corp
TNI.A	American	TrnscoA	Transico Industries Inc (Class A)
TNI.B	American	TrnscoB	Transico Industries Inc (Class B)
TNII	NAS NMS	TelcN	Telecommunications Network Inc
TNL	American	Techtrl	Technitrol Inc
TNLS	NAS NMS	Trnsntl	Trans-National Leasing Inc
TNP	New York	TNP	TNP Enterprises Inc
TNSL	NAS NL	Tinsly	Tinsley Laboratories Inc
TNTO	NAS SL	Tintoret	Tintoretto Inc
TNV	New York	Trinov	Trinova Corp

TRADING SYMBOL	MARKET LISTING	NEWSPAPER ABBREV.	COMPANY NAME
TNY	American	Tenney	Tenney Engineering Inc
TNZ	American	Trnzn	The Tranzonic Companies
TOBK	NAS NMS	Tolland	Tolland Bank FSB (Connecticut)
TOC	American	TchOpS	Tech-Ops Sevcon Inc
TOD	New York	TodSh	Todd Shipyards Corp
TODD	NAS NMS	ToddAO	Todd-AO Corp
TOF	American	Tofutti	Tofutti Brands Inc
TOK	New York	Tokhem	Tokheim Corp
TOL	New York	TollBr	Toll Brothers Inc
TONE	NAS NMS	OneBc	The One Bancorp
TONS	NAS SL	TonToy	Tons of Toys Inc
TOOL	NAS NMS	Easco	Easco Hand Tools Inc
TOOT	NAS NMS	202 Dta	202 Data System Inc
TOPP	NAS NMS	Topps	Topps Company Inc
TOS	New York	Tosco	Tosco Corp
TOTE	NAS NMS	UnTote	United Tote Inc
TOTH	NAS NL	TothAl	Toth Aluminum Corp
TOTL	NAS SL	TotalRs	Total Research Corp
TOV	American	TchOpL	Tech/Ops Landauer Inc
TOWN	NAS NL	TownPl	Towne-Paulsen Inc
TOXY	NAS SL	TriCst	Tri Coast Environmental Corp
TOY	New York	ToyRU	Toys "R" Us Inc
TOYOY	NAS NL	Toyota	Toyota Motor Corp
TPI	American	ThrmP	Thermo Process Systems Inc
TPL	New York	TxPac	Texas Pacific Land Trust
TPLPZ	NAS NL	Teeco	Teeco Properties LP Co
TPN	American	TotlPt	Total Petroleum (North America) Ltd
TPO	American	Tempo	TEMPO Enterprises Inc
TPS	American	TPA Am	TPA of America Inc
TR	New York	TootR	Tootsie Roll Industries Inc
TRAD	NAS NMS	TradInd	Traditional Industries Inc
TRB	New York	Tribun	Tribune Co
TRC	American	TejnR	Tejon Ranch Co
TRCE	NAS SL	TracePd	Trace Products
TRCO	NAS NMS	TricoPd	Trico Products Corp
TRDY	NAS SL	Trudy	Trudy Corp
TREN	NAS NMS	Trnwck	Trenwick Group Inc
TREX	NAS NMS	Intrex	Intrex Financial Services Inc
TRFI	NAS NMS	TrnFnc	Trans Financial Bancorp Inc
TRG	American	TriaCp	The Triangle Corp
TRGL	NAS NMS	TorRoy	Toreador Royalty Corp
TRIAA	NAS NMS	TrianIn	Triangle Industries Inc (Class A)
TRIN	NAS NMS	TranIn	Trans-Industries Inc
TRKA	NAS NMS	TrakAu	Trak Auto Corp
TRLS	NAS NMS	ThouTr	Thousand Trails Inc
TRN	New York	Trinty	Trinity Industries Inc
TRNS	NAS NMS	Trnsmt	Transmation Inc
TRNT	NAS NMS	Trnsnt	TransNet Corp

TRADING SYMBOL	MARKET LISTING	NEWSPAPER ABBREV.	COMPANY NAME
TRON	NAS NMS	Trion	Trion Inc
TROU	NAS SL	Tround	Tround International Inc
TROW	NAS NMS	PrceTR	T. Rowe Price Associates Inc
TRP	New York	TrnCda	TransCanada PipeLines Ltd
TRR	American	TRC	TRC Companies Inc
TRS	American	TstAm	Trust America Service Corp
TRSC	NAS NMS	TriadSy	Triad Systems Corp
TRST	NAS NMS	TrNY	Trustco Bank Corp (New York)
TRTC	NAS SL	TrioTch	Trio-Tech International
TRTI	NAS NMS	Trntch	Transtech Industries Inc
TRUK	NAS NMS	BuildT	Builders Transport Inc
TRVL	NAS SL	Truvel	Truvel Corp
TRVMF	NAS NMS	TRV	TRV Minerals Corp
TRW	New York	TRW	TRW Inc
TSFC	NAS NL	TribSwb	Tribune/Swab-Fox Companies Inc
TSIC	NAS NMS	Trnsdcr	Transducer Systems Inc
TSII	NAS NMS	TSI	TSI Inc
TSK	New York	CmpTsk	Computer Task Group Inc
TSM	American	TriSM	Tri-State Motor Transit Company of Delaware
TSNG	NAS SL	Tseng	Tseng Labs Inc
TSO	New York	Tesoro	Tesoro Petroleum Corp
TSP	American	Telesph	Telesphere International Inc
TSQ	American	T2 Md	T2 Medical Inc
TSRI	NAS NMS	TSR	TSR Inc
TSTM	NAS SL	MediLg	Media Logistics Inc
TSTR	NAS SL	Telstar	Telstar Corp
TSY	New York	TchSym	Tech-Sym Corp
TSYS	NAS NMS	TotlSys	Total System Services Inc
TT	New York	TrnsTec	TransTechnology Corp
TTC	New York	Toro	The Toro Co
TTCO	NAS NMS	Trstcp	Trustcorp Inc
TTF	New York	Thai	Thai Fund
TTI	American	TechTp	Technical Tape Inc
TTII	NAS SL	TherTc	Therapeutic Technologies Inc
TTL	American	Tortel	Torotel Inc
TTME	NAS SL	TchTme	Tech Time Inc
TTN	New York	Titan	Titan Corp
TTOI	NAS NMS	TmpstTc	TEMPEST Technologies Inc
TTOR	NAS NMS	Trnstct	Transtector Systems Inc
TTOY	NAS NMS	TycoTy	Tyco Toys Inc
TTX	New York	Tultex	Tultex Corp
TUCK	NAS NMS	TuckDr	Tucker Drilling Co
TUES	NAS NMS	TuesM	Tuesday Morning Inc
TUG	New York	Maritrn	Maritrans Partners LP
TUHC	NAS NMS	TuckHd	Tucker Holding Co
TUNX	NAS SL	Tunex	Tunex International Inc
TUR	American	TurnrC	The Turner Corp

TRADING SYMBOL	MARKET LISTING	NEWSPAPER ABBREV.	COMPANY NAME
TURF	NAS NL	TurfPar	Turf Paradise Inc
TUSC	NAS NMS	TuscPl	Tuscarora Plastics Inc
TVIE	NAS SL	TVI Cp	TVI Corp
TVIV	NAS NMS	TacViv	Taco Viva Inc
TVLA	NAS NMS	TacVila	Taco Villa Inc
TVTK	NAS SL	TelevTc	Television Technology Corp
TVXG	NAS NMS	TVX	TVX Broadcast Group Inc
TW	New York	TW Svc	TW Services Inc
TWA	New York	TWA	Trans World Airlines Inc
TWBC	NAS NMS	TrwlBc	Transworld Bancorp
TWEN	NAS NMS	20thCnIn	20th Century Industries Inc
TWMC	NAS NMS	TrnMu	Trans World Music Corp
TWN	American	Taiwan	The Taiwan Fund Inc
TWP	American	TwPeso	Two Pesos Inc
TWST	NAS NMS	TwstTr	Twistee Treat Corp
TX	New York	Texaco	Texaco Inc
TXA	New York	TxABc	Texas American Bancshares Inc
TXC	American	TexCd	Texaco Canada Inc
TXCO	NAS SL	Explor	Exploration Co
TXELC	NAS SL	Texcel	Texcel International Inc
TXF	New York	Texfi	Texfi Industries Inc
TXHI	NAS SL	THT Lyd	THT Lloyds Inc
TXI	New York	TexInd	Texas Industries Inc
TXN	New York	TxInst	Texas Instruments Inc
TXNO	NAS SL	Tchgen	Technogenetics Inc
TXT	New York	Textrn	Textron Inc
TXU	New York	TexUtil	Texas Utilities Co
TY	New York	TriCon	Tri-Continental Corp
TYC	New York	TycoL	Tyco Laboratories Inc
TYGR	NAS NMS	Tigera	Tigera Group Inc
TYL	New York	Tyler	Tyler Corp
TYLN	NAS NMS	Tylan	Tylan Corp
TYRX	NAS SL	Tyrex	Tyrex Oil Co
TYSNA	NAS NMS	Tyson	Tyson Foods Inc (Class A)
U	New York	UsairG	USAir Group Inc
UAC	American	Unicorp	Unicorp American Corp
UACIA	NAS NMS	UACm	United Artists Communications Inc (Class A)
UAL	New York	UAL Cp	UAL Corp
UAM	New York	UAM	United Asset Management Corp
UASI	NAS SL	UAS	UAS Automation Systems Inc
UB	New York	UnBrnd	United Brands Co
UBCP	NAS NMS	Unibcp	Unibancorp Inc
UBKR	NAS NMS	UnBkrs	United Bankers Inc
UBKS	NAS NMS	UBCol	United Banks of Colorado Inc
UBMT	NAS NMS	USvBk	United Savings Bank FA (Montana)
UBN	American	UnvBk	University Bank NA

TRADING SYMBOL	MARKET LISTING	NEWSPAPER ABBREV.	COMPANY NAME
UBSC	NAS NMS	UnBldg	United Building Services Corporation of Delaware
UBSI	NAS NMS	UBWV	United Bankshares Inc (Virginia)
UCAM	NAS SL	CamEnt	Camera Enterprises Inc
UCAR	NAS NMS	UCaBk	United Carolina Bancshares Corp
UCC	New York	UCmp	Union Camp Corp
UCIT	NAS NMS	UCtyGs	United Cities Gas Co
UCL	New York	Unocal	Unocal Corp
UCO	New York	UnionC	The Union Corp
UCOA	NAS NMS	UnCoast	United Coasts Corp
UCT	New York	UCbTV	United Cable Television Corp
UCTC	NAS NL	UCount	United Counties Bancorporation
UCU	New York	UtiliCo	UtiliCorp United Inc
UDC	New York	UDC	UDC-Universal Development LP
UDRT	NAS NMS	UnDom	United Dominion Realty Trust Inc
UEP	New York	UnElec	Union Electric Co
UESS	NAS NMS	UnEdS	United Education & Software
UFBC	NAS NL	UnFncl	United Financial Banking Co
UFC	New York	UnvFds	Universal Foods Corp
UFCS	NAS NMS	UFireC	United Fire & Casualty Co
UFD.A	American	UFoodA	United Foods Inc (Class A)
UFD.B	American	UFoodB	United Foods Inc (Class B)
UFF	New York	UnfedF	UnionFed Financial Corp
UFGI	NAS NMS	UFnGrp	United Financial Group Inc
UFN	American	UniCre	UniCARE Financial Corp
UFRM	NAS NL	UFedS	United Federal S&L Assn (North Carolina)
UFSB	NAS NMS	UnvSvg	University Savings Bank (Washington)
UFST	NAS NMS	Unfast	Unifast Industries Inc
UFURF	NAS NMS	UnvFr	Universal Furniture Ltd
UGEN	NAS SL	UnvGen	University Genetics Co
UGI	New York	UGI	UGI Corp
UGNE	NAS NL	Unigene	Unigene Laboratories Inc
UH	New York	USHom	U.S. Home Corp
UHCO	NAS NMS	UnvHld	Universal Holding Corp
UHLI	NAS NMS	UtdHm	United Home Life Insurance Co
UHRNF	NAS SL	UnHrn	United Hearne Resources Ltd
UHSIB	NAS NMS	UnvHlt	Universal Health Services Inc (Class B)
UHT	New York	UnvHR	Universal Health Realty Income Trust
UI	New York	UnitInn	Inited Inns Inc
UIC	New York	UnitInd	United Industrial Corp
UICI	NAS NMS	UtdIns	United Insurance Companies Inc
UIF	New York	UslfeF	USLIFE Income Fund Inc
UIL	New York	UIllum	The United Illuminating Co
UIS	New York	Unisys	Unisys Corp
UJB	New York	UJerBk	United Jersey Banks
UK	New York	UCarb	Union Carbide Corp
UKM	New York	UKing	The United Kingdom Fund Inc

TRADING SYMBOL	MARKET LISTING	NEWSPAPER ABBREV.	COMPANY NAME
UL	New York	Unilvr	Unilever PLC
ULT	New York	Ultmte	The Ultimate Corp
ULTB	NAS NMS	UltrBc	Ultra Bancorporation
UM	American	UtMed	United Medical Corp
UMAP	NAS SL	Ultimap	ULTIMAP International Corp
UMB	New York	UnvMed	Universal Medical Buildings LP
UMED	NAS NMS	Unimed	Unimed Inc
UMG	New York	UMatch	Universal Matchbox Group Ltd
UMM	New York	UtdMM	United Merchants & Manufacturers Inc
UMR	American	Unimar	Unimar Co
UMSB	NAS NMS	UMoB	United Missouri Bancshares Inc
UN	New York	UnNV	Unilever NV
UNAM	NAS NMS	UnicoA	Unico American Corp
UNBC	NAS NMS	UnNatl	Union National Corp
UNBJ	NAS NL	UBkNJ	United National Bank (New Jersey)
UNC	New York	UNCIn	UNC Inc
UNCF	NAS NMS	UnCosF	United Companies Financial Corp
UNEWY	NAS NMS	UtdNwsp	United Newspapers Public Limited Co
UNF	New York	UniFrst	UniFirst Corp
UNFI	NAS NMS	Unifi	Unifi Inc
UNFR	NAS NMS	Unifrc	Uniforce Temporary Personnel Inc
UNIH	NAS NMS	UHltCr	United HealthCare Corp
UNIR	NAS NMS	UGrdn	United-Guardian Inc
UNIV	NAS SL	Univatn	Univation Inc
UNM	New York	UNUM	UNUM Corp
UNMAA	NAS NMS	UniMrt	Uni-Marts Inc (Class A)
UNNB	NAS NMS	UnivBT	University National Bank & Trust Co
UNO	American	UnoRt	UNO Restaurant Corp
UNP	New York	UnPac	Union Pacific Corp
UNRIQ	NAS NL	UNR	UNR Industries Inc
UNSA	NAS NMS	UFinSC	United Financial Corporation of South Carolina Inc
UNSI	NAS NMS	UnSvSc	United Service Source Inc
UNSL	NAS NMS	UnSvMo	United S&L Assn (Missouri)
UNSVA	NAS NMS	UnSvFl	United Savings Assn (Florida)
UNT	New York	Unit	Unit Corp
UNTD	NAS NMS	FtUtd	First United Bancshares Inc (Arkansas)
UNV	American	UnitelV	Unitel Video Inc
UPC	New York	USPCI	USPCI Inc
UPCM	NAS NMS	UnPlntr	Union Planters Corp
UPCO	NAS NMS	UPresd	United Presidential Corp
UPEN	NAS NMS	UPenP	Upper Peninsula Power Co
UPJ	New York	Upjohn	The Upjohn Co
UPK	New York	UPkMn	United Park City Mines Co
UPT	American	UnvPat	University Patents Inc
URT	American	USPRI	USP Real Estate Investment Trust
USA	New York	LbtyAS	Liberty All-Star Equity Fund
USAB	NAS NMS	USA Bc	USA Bancorp Inc

TRADING SYMBOL	MARKET LISTING	NEWSPAPER ABBREV.	COMPANY NAME
USAC	NAS NMS	US Ant	United States Antimony Corp
USBA	NAS NMS	USB Or	United Savings Bank (Oregon)
USBC	NAS NMS	US Bcp	U.S. Bancorp
USBI	NAS NMS	UtdSvrs	United Saver's Bancorp Inc
USBK	NAS NMS	USBkVa	United Savings Bank (Virginia)
USBP	NAS NMS	USBPa	USBANCORP (Pennsylvania)
USC	New York	USLICO	USLICO Corp
USDA	NAS SL	UtdShp	United Shoppers of America Inc
USEC	NAS NMS	UnvSec	Universal Security Instruments Inc
USEG	NAS NMS	US Enr	U.S. Energy Corp
USEN	NAS SL	Usenco	USENCO Inc
USF	New York	USACaf	USACafes LP
USG	New York	USG	USG Corp
USGL	NAS NMS	US Gold	U.S. Gold Corp
USH	New York	USLIFE	USLIFE Corp
USHC	NAS NMS	US HltC	U.S. Healthcare Inc
USHI	NAS NMS	USHltI	U.S. Health Inc
USM	American	US Cel	United States Cellular Corp
USMX	NAS NMS	USMX	US Minerals Exploration Co
USOL	NAS SL	US Oil	United States Oil Co
USPI	NAS SL	UnvSci	University Science Partners Inc
USPMF	NAS NMS	US Prc	U.S. Precious Metals Inc
USR	New York	USShoe	The United States Shoe Corp
USRE	NAS NMS	US Facl	US Facilities Corp
USRLZ	NAS NL	USRlty	US Realty Partners Ltd
USS	New York	US Surg	United States Surgical Corp
USSS	NAS NMS	US Shelt	U.S. Shelter Corp
UST	New York	UST	UST Inc
USTB	NAS NMS	UST Cp	UST Corp
USTC	NAS NMS	US Trst	U.S. Trust Corp
USTI	NAS SL	UnSyTc	United Systems Technology Inc
USTR	NAS NMS	UStatn	United Stationers Inc
USW	New York	USWest	U S WEST Inc
USWNA	NAS NMS	USWNV	U S WEST New Vector Group Inc (Class A)
UT	New York	UniTel	United Telecommunications Inc
UTDMK	NAS NMS	UtdInv	United Investors Management Co
UTH	New York	UnTex	Union Texas Petroleum Holdings Inc
UTL	American	Unitil	UNITIL Corp
UTLC	NAS NMS	UTL	UTL Corp
UTMD	NAS SL	UtahMd	Utah Medical Products Inc
UTP	New York	UtaPL	Utah Power & Light Co
UTR	New York	Unitrde	Unitrode Corp
UTRX	NAS NMS	Unitrnx	Unitronix Corp
UTVI	NAS NMS	UnTelev	United Television Inc
UTX	New York	UnTech	United Technologies Corp
UVC	American	UnValy	Union Valley Corp
UVOL	NAS NMS	UnVolt	Universal Voltronics Corp
UVTB	NAS NMS	UnVtBn	United Vermont Bancorporation

TRADING SYMBOL	MARKET LISTING	NEWSPAPER ABBREV.	COMPANY NAME
UVV	New York	UnvlCp	Universal Corp
UVX	New York	Univar	Univar Corp
UWR	New York	UWR	United Water Resources Inc
UXP	New York	UnExp	Union Exploration Partners Ltd
V	New York	IrvBnk	Irving Bank Corp
VAALY	NAS NL	VaalR	Vaal Reefs Exploration & Mining Company Ltd
VABF	NAS NMS	VaBch	Virginia Beach Savings Bank
VAC.A	American	VtAmC	Vermont American Corp (Class A)
VAFB	NAS NL	VlyFed	Valley Federal Savings Bank (Indiana)
VAFD	NAS SL	VlFdAla	Valley Federal Savings Bank (Alabama)
VAGO	NAS NMS	VanGld	Vanderbilt Gold Corp
VAL	American	Valspr	The Valspar Corp
VALM	NAS NMS	Valmnt	Valmont Industries Inc
VALN	NAS NMS	Vallen	Vallen Corp
VALU	NAS NMS	ValLn	Value Line Inc
VANZ	NAS NMS	Vanzeti	Vanzetti Systems Inc
VAR	New York	Varian	Varian Associates Inc
VAT	New York	Varity	Varity Corp
VBAN	NAS NMS	V Band	V-Band Systems Inc
VBND	NAS NMS	VeloBd	VeloBind Inc
VBVT	NAS SL	ValB VT	Valley Bank (Vermont)
VC	New York	VistaC	Vista Chemical Co
VCCN	NAS NMS	VlyCap	Valley Capital Corp
VCEL	NAS NMS	VgrdCl	Vanguard Cellular-Systems Inc
VCRE	NAS NMS	VariCre	Vari-Care Inc
VDC	New York	VanDrn	Van Dorn Co
VDEF	NAS NMS	Vie deFr	Vie de France Corp
VDR	American	Vader	Vader Group Inc
VDRY	NAS NL	VacDry	Vacu-dry
VEE	New York	Veeco	Veeco Instruments Inc
VEGA	NAS SL	VegaBio	Vega Biotechnologies Inc
VELCF	NAS NL	Velcro	Velcro Industries NV
VEN	New York	Vendo	The Vendo Co
VENT	NAS NMS	Ventur	Venturian Corp
VEOXF	NAS NMS	Veronx	Veronex Resources Ltd
VER	American	Verit	Verit Industries
VES	New York	VestSe	Vestaur Securities Inc
VEST	NAS SL	Vestro	Vestro Foods Inc
VETS	NAS NMS	Animed	Animed Inc
VF	American	ValFrg	Valley Forge Corp
VFBK	NAS NMS	EstnBc	Eastern Bancorp Inc
VFC	New York	VF Cp	V.F. Corp
VFED	NAS NMS	ValFSL	Valley Federal S&L Assn
VFOX	NAS NMS	ViconF	Vicon Fiber Optics Corp
VFSB	NAS NMS	VaFst	Virginia First Savings Bank FSB
VFSC	NAS NMS	VtFin	Vermont Financial Services Corp

TRADING SYMBOL	MARKET LISTING	NEWSPAPER ABBREV.	COMPANY NAME
VFSL	NAS NL	Valdost	Valdosta Federal S&L Assn
VGC.A	American	VislGA	Visual Graphics Corp (Class A)
VGC.B	American	VislG B	Visual Graphics Corp (Class B)
VGHN	NAS SL	Vaughn	Vaughn's Inc
VGINY	NAS NMS	VirgnG	Virgin Group plc
VHCL	NAS NL	VHC	VHC Ltd
VHI	New York	Valhi	Valhi Inc
VHT	American	VHT	VMS Hotel Investment Fund
VI	New York	ValeyIn	Valley Industries Inc
VIA	American	Viacm	Viacom Inc
VICF	NAS SL	VictFn	Victoria Financial Corp
VICT	NAS NMS	VictBn	Victoria Bankshares Inc
VIDE	NAS NMS	VidDsp	Video Display Corp
VII	American	Vicon	Vicon Industries Inc
VIKG	NAS NMS	Viking	Viking Freight Inc
VIN	American	Vintge	Vintage Enterprises Inc
VINO	NAS SL	WINE	WINE Inc
VINT	NAS NL	Vintage	Vintage Group Inc
VIPLF	NAS NMS	VulcP	Vulcan Packaging Inc
VIR	American	Virco	Virco Manufacturing Corp
VIRA	NAS NMS	Viratek	Viratek Inc
VISA	NAS NMS	VistaOr	Vista Organization Ltd
VISC	NAS NMS	VisualI	Visual Industries Inc
VISRF	NAS SL	Viscnt	Viscount Resources Ltd
VIST	NAS NL	VistaRs	Vista Resources Inc
VITA	NAS NMS	Vitalnk	Vitalink Communications Corp
VITC	NAS NMS	VictCr	Victoria Creations Inc
VITX	NAS NMS	Vitronic	Vitronics Corp
VIVI	NAS NMS	Vivigen	Vivigen Inc
VKSI	NAS NMS	Vikonic	Vikonics Inc
VLAB	NAS NMS	Vipont	Vipont Laboratories Inc
VLCM	NAS NMS	Valcom	ValCom Inc
VLGE	NAS NMS	VilSpM	Village Super Market Inc
VLID	NAS NMS	ValidLg	Valid Logic Systems Inc
VLO	New York	Valero	Valero Energy Corp
VLP	New York	ValNG	Valero Natural Gas Partners LP
VLSI	NAS NMS	VLSI	VLSI Technology Inc
VLU	New York	WrldVl	Worldwide Value Fund Inc
VMC	New York	VulcM	Vulcan Materials Co
VMIG	NAS NMS	ViewMs	View-Master Ideal Group Inc
VMSI	NAS NMS	VM Sft	VM Software Inc
VMT	New York	VKmp	Van Kampen Merritt Municipal Income Trust
VMXI	NAS NMS	VMX	VMX Inc
VNBP	NAS NMS	ValNBc	Valley National Bancorp (New Jersey)
VNCP	NAS NMS	ValNtl	Valley National Corp
VNO	New York	Vornad	Vornado Inc
VO	New York	Seargrm	The Seagram Company Ltd

TRADING SYMBOL	MARKET LISTING	NEWSPAPER ABBREV.	COMPANY NAME
VOIC	NAS SL	Voicml	Voicemail International Inc
VOLB	NAS NL	VolunBc	Volunteer Bancshares Inc
VOLT	NAS NMS	VoltInf	Volt Information Sciences Inc
VOLVY	NAS NMS	Volvo	Volvo AB
VON	New York	Vons	The Vons Companies Inc
VOT	American	Voplex	Voplex Corp
VOTX	NAS SL	Votrax	Votrax Inc
VOX	American	Audvx	Audiovox Corp
VPLXE	NAS SL	Videplx	Videoplex Inc
VR	American	ValyRs	Valley Resources Inc
VRC	New York	Varco	Varco International Inc
VRDX	NAS SL	Verdix	Verdix Corp
VRE	American	VtRsh	Vermont Research Corp
VRES	NAS NMS	Vicorp	VICORP Restaurants Inc
VRGN	NAS SL	Viragen	Viragen Inc
VRLN	NAS NMS	Varlen	Varlen Corp
VRO	New York	Varo	Varo Inc
VRSA	NAS NMS	Versa	Versa Technologies Inc
VRSI	NAS SL	ViralRp	Viral Response Systems Inc
VRSY	NAS NMS	Varitrn	Varitronic Systems Inc
VRT	American	Vertple	Vertipile Inc
VSEC	NAS NMS	VSE	VSE Corp
VSH	New York	Vishay	Vishay Intertechnology Inc
VSR	American	Versar	Versar Inc
VSTR	NAS NMS	Vestar	Vestar Inc
VTEL	NAS SL	VitelFb	Vitel Fiber Optics Corp
VTEX	NAS NMS	VertexC	Vertex Communications Corp
VTGO	NAS SL	VacTGo	Vacations To Go Inc
VTK	American	Viatch	Viatech Inc
VTRX	NAS NMS	Ventrex	Ventrex Laboratories Inc
VTX	American	VTX	VTX Electronics Corp
VUL	American	VulcCp	Vulcan Corp
VV	New York	Vestrn	Vestron Inc
VWBN	NAS NL	ValyWst	Valley West Bancorp
VWRX	NAS NMS	VWR	VWR Corp
VY	American	Vyqust	Vyquest Inc
VYBN	NAS NMS	ValyB	Valley Bancorporation (Wisconsin)
W	New York	Wstvc	Westvaco Corp
WAB	American	WAmB	WESTAMERICA BANCORPORATION
WABEF	NAS NL	WtnAlen	Western Allenbee Oil & Gas Company Ltd
WAC	American	WellAm	Wells American Corp
WACLY	NAS NL	Wacoal	Wacoal Corp
WACP	NAS SL	WstAcp	Western Acceptance Corp
WAE	New York	Wilfred	Wilfred American Educational Corp
WAG	New York	Walgrn	Walgreen Co
WAK	New York	Wackht	The Wackenhut Corp
WALB	NAS NMS	Walbro	Walbro Corp

TRADING SYMBOL	MARKET LISTING	NEWSPAPER ABBREV.	COMPANY NAME
WALS	NAS NMS	Walshr	Walshire Assurance Co
WAMU	NAS NMS	WMSB	Washington Mutual Savings Bank
WAN.B	American	WangB	Wang Laboratories Inc (Class B)
WAN.C	American	WangC	Wang Laboratories Inc (Class C)
WASC	NAS NMS	WstAut	Western Auto Supply Co
WASH	NAS NL	WashTr	Washington Trust Bancorporation (Rhode Island)
WATFY	NAS NMS	WatrfGl	Waterford Glass Group plc
WATTA	NAS NMS	WattsInd	Watts Industries Inc (Class A)
WAVE	NAS SL	Wavetch	Wavetech Inc
WAVR	NAS NMS	Waver	Waverly Inc
WAXM	NAS NMS	Waxmn	Waxman Industries Inc
WBAT	NAS NMS	WstBc	Westport Bancorp Inc
WBB	New York	WebbD	Del E. Webb Corp
WBC	American	WstBrC	Westbridge Capital Corp
WBED	NAS NMS	ClasicC	Classic Corp
WBEL	NAS SL	WstBell	Western Bell Communications Inc
WBNC	NAS NMS	WshBcp	Washington Bancorp Inc (New Jersey)
WBST	NAS NMS	WbstFn	Webster Financial Corp
WC	American	Weiman	Weiman Company Inc
WCAR	NAS NL	WtCaSv	Western Carolina S&L Assn (North Carolina)
WCAT	NAS NMS	Wicat	WICAT Systems Inc
WCBK	NAS NMS	Wkmen	Workingmens Corp (Massachusetts)
WCCC	NAS NMS	WmCmc	Western Commercial Inc
WCI	New York	WarnC	Warner Communications Inc
WCLB	NAS NMS	WrhseC	Warehouse Club Inc
WCP	New York	WrnCpt	Warner Computer Systems Inc
WCRP	American	Westcp	Westcorp
WCRSY	NAS NMS	WCRS	The WCRS Group PLC
WCS	New York	WalCSv	Wallace Computer Services Inc
WCSI	NAS NL	WldwdCpt	Worldwide Computer Services Inc
WCYS	NAS NMS	BkWorc	Bank Worcester Corp
WDC	American	WDigitl	Western Digital Corp
WDEPY	NAS NL	WDeep	Western Deep Levels Ltd
WDG	New York	Wedgtn	Wedgestone Financial Trust
WDFC	NAS NMS	WD 40	WD-40 Co
WDH	New York	Winchl	Winchell's Donut Houses LP
WDHD	NAS NMS	Woodhd	Woodhead Industries Inc
WDMR	NAS NMS	Windmr	Windmere Corp
WDSI	NAS NMS	WorlcDt	Worlco Data Systems Inc
WE	New York	WstctE	Westcoast Energy Inc
WEBS	NAS NMS	WbstCl	Webster Clothes Inc
WEC	New York	WisEn	Wisconsin Energy Corp
WECA	NAS NMS	WstCap	Western Capital Investment Corp
WECO	NAS NMS	WashEn	Washington Energy Co
WED	American	Wedco	Wedco Technology Inc
WEIS	NAS NMS	Weisfld	Weisfield's Inc

TRADING SYMBOL	MARKET LISTING	NEWSPAPER ABBREV.	COMPANY NAME
WELB	NAS NMS	Weblt	Welbilt Corp
WEN	New York	Wendys	Wendy's International Inc
WERN	NAS NMS	Werner	Werner Enterprises Inc
WETT	NAS NMS	Wettra	Wetterau Inc
WEXC	NAS NMS	WolvEx	Wolverine Exploration Co
WEYS	NAS NMS	Weynbg	Weyenberg Shoe Manufacturing Co
WF	American	WinFur	Winston Furniture Company Inc
WFC	New York	WellsF	Wells Fargo & Co
WFCS	NAS NMS	Warren	Warren Five Cents Savings Bank (Massachusetts)
WFM	New York	WelFM	Wells Fargo Mortgage & Equity Trust
WFOR	NAS NMS	WshFOr	Washington Federal Savings Bank (Oregon)
WFPR	NAS NMS	WFdPR	Western Federal Savings Bank (Puerto Rico)
WFRAF	NAS NMS	Wharf	Wharf Resources Ltd
WFSA	NAS NMS	WstFSL	Western Federal S&L Assn (California)
WFSB	NAS NMS	WshFDC	Washington Federal Savings Bank (Washington DC)
WFSL	NAS NMS	WFSL	Washington Federal S&L Assn of Seattle
WG	New York	WillcG	Willcox & Gibbs Inc
WGA	American	WelGrd	Wells-Gardner Electronics Corp
WGHT	NAS NMS	WeigTr	Weigh-Tronix Inc
WGL	New York	WashGs	Washington Gas Light Co
WGO	New York	Winnbg	Winnebago Industries Inc
WHEL	NAS SL	Roadmst	Roadmaster Industries Inc
WHIT	NAS SL	Whitmn	Whitman Medical Corp
WHLS	NAS NMS	Whlclub	The Wholesale Club Inc
WHOA	NAS SL	AEqune	American Equine Products Inc
WHOO	NAS NMS	Watrhse	Waterhouse Investor Services Inc
WHP	American	WstHlth	Western Health Plans Inc
WHR	New York	Whrlpl	Whirlpool Corp
WHRG	NAS NMS	WatrIn	Waters Instruments Inc
WHT	New York	Whitehl	Whitehall Corp
WHTI	NAS NMS	WhelTch	Wheelabrator Technologies Inc
WHX	New York	WhPit	Wheeling-Pittsburgh Steel Corp
WIC	New York	WICOR	WICOR Inc
WID	New York	WeanU	Wean Inc
WII	American	Wthfrd	Weatherford International Inc
WIL	American	WlsnSp	Wilson Sporting Goods Co
WILF	NAS NMS	WilsnF	Wilson Foods Corp
WILLA	NAS NMS	WilyJ A	John Wiley & Sons Inc (Class A)
WILLB	NAS NL	WilyJ B	John Wiley & Sons Inc (Class B)
WILM	NAS NMS	WilmT	Wilmington Trust Co
WIMI	NAS NMS	Warwk	Warwick Insurance Managers Inc
WIN	New York	WinDix	Winn-Dixie Stores Inc
WIR	American	WIRET	Western Investment Real Estate Trust
WISC	NAS NMS	WisSGs	Wisconsin Southern Gas Company Inc

TRADING SYMBOL	MARKET LISTING	NEWSPAPER ABBREV.	COMPANY NAME
WISE	NAS NMS	WiserO	The Wiser Oil Co
WIT	New York	Witco	Witco Corp
WIX	New York	Wickes	Wickes Companies Inc
WJ	New York	WatkJn	Watkins-Johnson Co
WJI	New York	Winjak	Winjak Inc
WJR	American	CyprFd	Cypress Fund Inc
WKR	New York	Whittak	Whittaker Corp
WLA	New York	WarnrL	Warner-Lambert Co
WLBK	NAS NMS	WaltCp	Waltham Corp
WLC	American	Wellco	Wellco Enterprises Inc
WLD	American	Weldtrn	Weldotron Corp
WLE	New York	WhelLE	The Wheeling & Lake Erie Railway Co
WLHN	NAS NMS	Wolohn	Wolohan Lumber Co
WLKMY	NAS NL	WekG	Welkom Gold Holdings Ltd
WLM	New York	Wellmn	Wellman Inc
WLRF	NAS NL	Wamplr	Wampler-Longacre-Rockingham Inc
WLTK	NAS SL	Wiltek	Wiltek Inc
WLTN	NAS NMS	Wilton	Wilton Enterprises Inc
WMB	New York	William	The Williams Companies Inc
WMBS	NAS NMS	WtMass	West Massachusetts Bankshares Inc
WMD	American	MarsG	Mars Graphic Services Inc
WMI	American	WintIn	Winthrop Insured Mortgage Investors II
WMIC	NAS NMS	WMicr	Western Microwave Inc
WMK	New York	WeisM	Weis Markets Inc
WMOR	NAS NMS	WmorC	Westmoreland Coal Co
WMRK	NAS NMS	Wstmrk	Westmark International Inc
WMS	New York	WMS	WMS Industries Inc
WMSI	NAS NMS	WillmI	Williams Industries Inc
WMT	New York	WalMt	Wal-Mart Stores Inc
WMTT	NAS NMS	Willamt	Willamette Industries Inc
WMX	New York	Waste	Waste Management Inc
WN	New York	Wynns	Wynn's International Inc
WNDT	NAS NMS	Wendt	Wendt-Bristol Co
WNR	New York	Winner	Winners Corp
WNSB	NAS NMS	WNewtn	West Newton Savings Bank (Massachusetts)
WNSI	NAS NMS	WNS	WNS Inc
WNT	New York	WshNat	Washington National Corp
WOA	New York	WrldCp	WorldCorp Inc
WOBS	NAS NMS	FWobrn	First Woburn Bancorp Inc
WOC	New York	WilshrO	Wilshire Oil Company of Texas
WOD	American	Wdstrm	Woodstream Corp
WOFG	NAS NL	WolfFn	Wolf Financial Group Inc
WOI	American	WldInc	World Income Fund Inc
WOL	New York	Wainoc	Wainoco Oil Corp
WONE	NAS NMS	WstwO	Westwood One Inc
WOR	American	Worthn	Worthen Banking Corp
WOTK	NAS SL	WWTch	World-Wide Technology Inc

TRADING SYMBOL	MARKET LISTING	NEWSPAPER ABBREV.	COMPANY NAME
WOV	New York	WolvTc	Wolverine Technologies Inc
WP	American	Wespcp	Wespercorp
WPB	American	Wiener	Wiener Enterprises Inc
WPCO	NAS SL	WhitPt	Whiting Petroleum Corp
WPGI	NAS NMS	WstnPb	Western Publishing Group Inc
WPL	New York	WPL Hld	WPL Holdings Inc
WPM	New York	WtPtP	West Point-Pepperell Inc
WPO.B	American	WshPst	The Washington Post Co (Class B)
WPPGY	NAS NMS	WPP Gp	WPP Group plc
WPS	New York	WisPS	Wisconsin Public Service Corp
WRE	American	WRIT	Washington Real Estate Investment Trust
WREI	NAS NL	WiscRE	Wisconsin Real Estate Investment Trust
WRI	New York	WeingR	Weingarten Realty Inc
WRII	NAS SL	WasteRc	Waste Recovery Inc
WRLD	NAS SL	WrldCn	World Container Corp
WRO	American	WichRv	Wichita River Corp
WRS	American	WinRs	Winston Resources Inc
WRTC	NAS NMS	Writer	The Writer Corp
WSAU	NAS NMS	WausP	Wausau Paper Mills Co
WSBC	NAS NMS	Wesbnc	Wesbanco Inc
WSBK	NAS NMS	WtBank	Western Bank (Oregon)
WSBXV	NAS NMS	WshSvg	Washington Savings Bank
WSC	American	Wesco	Wesco Financial Corp
WSCI	NAS NMS	WshSci	Washington Scientific Industries Inc
WSFS	NAS NMS	WilSFS	Wilmington Savings Fund Society FSB
WSGC	NAS NMS	WmsSon	Williams-Sonoma Inc
WSL	New York	WstnSL	Western S&L Assn
WSMCA	NAS NMS	WtMrcA	WestMarc Communications Inc (Class A)
WSMCB	NAS NL	WrMrcB	WestMarc Communications Inc (Class B)
WSMP	NAS NMS	WSMP	WSMP Inc
WSN	New York	WCNA	The Western Company of North America
WSO.A	American	Watsc A	Watsco Inc (Class A)
WSO.B	American	Watsc B	Watsco Inc (Class B)
WSSX	NAS NMS	Wessex	Wessex Corp
WST	New York	West	The West Company Inc
WSTF	NAS NMS	WnFncl	Western Financial Corp
WSTM	NAS NMS	WMicTc	Western Micro Technology Inc
WSTNA	NAS NMS	Weston	Roy F. Weston Inc (Class A)
WSTR	NAS SL	Westar	Westar Corp
WSVS	NAS NMS	Wiland	Wiland Services Inc
WTBK	NAS NMS	Wstrbke	Westerbeke Corp
WTDI	NAS NMS	WTD	WTD Industries Inc
WTEC	NAS SL	Warntc	Warrantech Corp
WTEK	NAS SL	WasteTc	Waste Technology Corp
WTEL	NAS NMS	WlkrTel	Walker Telecommunications Corp
WTHG	NAS NMS	Worthg	Worthington Industries Inc
WTOY	NAS NMS	WiscTy	Wisconsin Toy Co
WTPR	NAS NL	WetrPr	Wetterau Properties Inc

TRADING SYMBOL	MARKET LISTING	NEWSPAPER ABBREV.	COMPANY NAME
WTR	American	SierSpg	Sierra Spring Water Co
WTWS	NAS NMS	WallSnd	Wall to Wall Sound & Video Inc
WU	New York	WUnion	Western Union Corp
WUR	New York	Wurltch	WurlTech Industries Inc
WVTK	NAS NMS	Wavetk	Wavetek Corp
WWBC	NAS NMS	WBcDC	Washington Bancorporation (Washington DC)
WWGPY	NAS NMS	WardWh	Ward White Group PLC
WWIN	NAS NMS	WnWste	Western Waste Industries
WWP	New York	WshWt	The Washington Water Power Co
WWTK	NAS NL	Weitek	Weitek Corp
WWW	New York	WolvrW	Wolverine World Wide Inc
WWWM	NAS NMS	WillW	W.W. Williams Co
WWY	New York	Wrigly	William Wrigley Jr. Co
WX	New York	WstgE	Westinghouse Electric Corp
WY	New York	Weyerh	Weyerhaeuser Co
WYL	New York	WyleLb	Wyle Laboratories
WYMN	NAS NMS	Wyman	Wyman-Gordon Co
WYNB	NAS NMS	WymngNt	Wyoming National Bancorporation
WYS	New York	Wyse	Wyse Technology
X	New York	USX	USX Corp
XARTF	NAS SL	Artagph	Artagraph Reproduction Technology Inc
XCEL	NAS NMS	ExcelBc	Excel Bancorp Inc
XCOL	NAS NMS	ExpLa	The Exploration Company of Louisiana Inc
XEBC	NAS NMS	Xebec	Xebec
XETA	NAS NL	Xeta	Xeta Corp
XICO	NAS NMS	Xicor	Xicor Inc
XLDC	NAS NMS	XL Dt	XL/Datacomp Inc
XLGX	NAS NMS	Xylogic	Xylogics Inc
XOMA	NAS MNS	XOMA	XOMA Corp
XON	New York	Exxon	Exxon Corp
XOVR	NAS NMS	Exovir	Exovir Inc
XPLR	NAS NMS	Xplor	Xplor Corp
XRAY	NAS NMS	GENDX	GENDEX Corp
XRIT	NAS NMS	X-Rite	X-Rite Inc
XRX	New York	Xerox	Xerox Corp
XSCR	NAS NMS	Xscribe	Xscribe Corp
XSIR	NAS SL	Xsirus	Xsirus Scientific Inc
XTEL	NAS SL	ExecTl	Executive Telecommunications Inc
XTGX	NAS NMS	TGX	TGX Corp
XTON	NAS NMS	Exctne	Executone Information Systems Inc
XTR	New York	XTRA	XTRA Corp
XTX	American	NYTEI	The New York Tax-Exempt Income Fund Inc
XYVI	NAS NMS	Xyvsn	Xyvision Inc
XYYX	NAS SL	Xytrn	Xytronyx Inc

TRADING SYMBOL	MARKET LISTING	NEWSPAPER ABBREV.	COMPANY NAME
Y	New York	AllegCp	Alleghany Corp
YCSL	NAS NMS	Yrkrdg	Yorkridge-Calvert S&L Assn (Maryland)
YELL	NAS NMS	YlowF	Yellow Freight System Inc. of Delaware
YFED	NAS NMS	YrkFn	York Financial Corp
YLD	New York	HiInco	High Income Advantage Trust
YNK	American	YankCo	The Yankee Companies Inc
YOCM	NAS SL	IntYog	International Yogurt Co
YORK	NAS NMS	YorkRs	York Research Corp
YRK	New York	YorkIn	York International Corp
YUBAA	NAS SL	YUBAA	Yuba Natural Resources Inc (Class A)
YUKN	NAS SL	YukonE	Yukon Energy Corp
YUMY	NAS SL	Tofruz	Tofruzen Inc
Z	New York	Wlwth	F.W. Woolworth Co
ZAPSV	NAS NMS	CooprL	Cooper Life Sciences Inc
ZCAD	NAS NMS	Zycad	Zycad Corp
ZDC	American	Crosby	Philip Crosby Associates Inc
ZE	New York	ZenithE	Zenith Electronics Corp
ZEGL	NAS NMS	Ziegler	The Ziegler Company Inc
ZEN	New York	ZenLab	Zenith Laboratories Inc
ZENT	NAS NMS	Zentec	Zentec Corp
ZETK	NAS SL	Zetek	Zetek Inc
ZEUS	NAS NMS	Zeus	Zeus Components Inc
ZF	New York	Zweig	The Zweig Fund Inc
ZIF	New York	ZenIn	Zenith Income Fund
ZIGO	NAS NMS	Zygo	Zygo Corp
ZIM	American	Zimer	Zimmer Corp
ZION	NAS NMS	ZionUt	Zions Bancorporation (Utah)
ZIPP	NAS NL	NtlRef	National Reference Publishing Inc
ZITI	NAS SL	Sidari	Sidari Corp
ZITL	NAS NMS	Zitel	Zitel Corp
ZMOS	NAS NMS	Zymos	ZyMOS Corp
ZMX	New York	Zemex	Zemex Corp
ZNT	New York	ZenNtl	Zenith National Insurance Corp
ZOND	NAS NMS	Zondvn	The Zondervan Corp
ZOS	New York	Zapata	Zapata Corp
ZRN	New York	ZurnIn	Zurn Industries Inc
ZRO	New York	Zero	Zero Corp
ZSEV	NAS NMS	Z Sevn	Z-Seven Fund Inc
ZSILF	NAS SL	Zytec	Zytec Systems Inc
ZY	New York	Zayre	Zayre Corp